Research on Fuzzy Logic and Mathematics with Applications

Research on Fuzzy Logic and Mathematics with Applications

Guest Editor

Saeid Jafari

MDPI

Basel • Beijing • Wuhan • Barcelona • Belgrade • Novi Sad • Cluj • Manchester

Guest Editor
Saeid Jafari
Mathematical and Physical
Science Foundation
Slagelse
Denmark

Editorial Office
MDPI AG
Grosspeteranlage 5
4052 Basel, Switzerland

This is a reprint of the Special Issue, published open access by the journal *Symmetry* (ISSN 2073-8994), freely accessible at: www.mdpi.com/journal/symmetry/special_issues/Research_Fuzzy_Logic_Mathematics_Applications.

For citation purposes, cite each article independently as indicated on the article page online and using the guide below:

Lastname, A.A.; Lastname, B.B. Article Title. *Journal Name* **Year**, *Volume Number*, Page Range.

ISBN 978-3-7258-3094-7 (Hbk)
ISBN 978-3-7258-3093-0 (PDF)
https://doi.org/10.3390/books978-3-7258-3093-0

Contents

About the Editor

Saeid Jafari

Dr. Saeid Jafari received his Master's of Science in Mathematics and Philosophy in 1993 from Aalborg University and Copenhagen University in Denmark, respectively. He then studied relativity theory, statistical physics, and quantum physics at Aalborg university in 1994. He was also appointed to a teaching position in mathematics and philosophy at the College of Vestsjaelland South in Slagelse, Denmark, in 1994.

In 2004, he received a Dr. rer.nat. from Technische Üniversität Graz (Technical University of Graz) under the supervision of Prof. Dr. M. Ganster. Professor Jafari has been conducting research since 1993 in topology; fuzzy, neutrosophic, and digital topologies; neutrosophic operation research; functional analysis; differential geometry; and the mathematical aspects of particle physics. He has more than 30 years of teaching and research experience, has published more than 400 research papers, and is a member of the Editorial Board of several mathematical journals. He has completed review works for numerous journals and for Zentralblatt and Mathematical reviews. He is a member of Danish and European Mathematical Societies. He has been an external examiner of more than 70 Ph.D. students, mostly from India. He has been invited as a speaker/plenary speaker, resource person, and program chair to several international conferences and workshops in mathematics and its applications. Prof. Jafari is the head of the Neutrosophic Science International Association (NSIA) in Denmark.

As part of his research and collaboration, he has received several travel awards to, among others to the University of South Africa, Max Plank Institute in Bonn, and Graz university of Technology. He is the founder and director of the newly established research center for Mathematical and Physical Science Foundation in Slagelse, Denmark, which is his official address.

symmetry

Editorial

Research on Fuzzy Logic and Mathematics with Applications

Saeid Jafari

College of Vestsjaelland South & Mathematical and Physical Science Foundation, 4200 Slagelse, Denmark; saeidjafari@topositus.com

Preface

The notion of the fuzzy set was introduced by Lotfi A. Zadeh in 1965. He is also the founder of fuzzy logic. Since the advent of the notion of the fuzzy set, Zadeh and other researchers have used this important and interesting set and established a great deal of important and interesting research in fuzzy logic, fuzzy topology, fuzzy arithmetics, etc. This Special Issue deals with fuzzy logic and mathematics with applications in decision making, fuzzy control systems, and other engineering applications.

In this Issue, there are 12 research studies and in what follows we will provide a brief account of their results and findings.

In the first paper, "A New Representation of Semiopenness of L-fuzzy Sets in RL-fuzzy Bitopological Spaces", Ibtesam Alshammari, Omar H. Khalil, and A. Ghareeb present the notion of semiopenness in the context of RL-fuzzy bitopological spaces based on the concept of pseudo-complement. They also introduce and study the basic properties of pairwise RL-fuzzy semicontinuous and pairwise RL-fuzzy irresolute functions by utilizing (i,j)-RL-semiopen gradation.

In the second paper, "An Extension TOPSIS Method Based on the Decision Maker's Risk Attitude and the Adjusted Probabilistic Fuzzy Set", Donghai Liu, An Huang, Yuanyuan Liu, and Zaiming Liu present and study an extension of the Topsis method, which takes into account the decision maker's behavior tendencies. In this regard, they propose theories regarding the probabilistic linguistic q-rung orthopair set and the linguistic q-rung orthopair set. They also not only examine the validity of the extension TOPSIS method and the merits of the behavior decision method, but also present the sensitivity analysis results regarding the decision-maker's behavior.

In the third paper, "A Decision Analysis Model for the Brand Experience of Branded Apps Using Consistency Fuzzy Linguistic Preference Relations", the authors Tsuen-Ho Hsu, Chun-Hsien Chen, and Ya-Wun Yang focus on an investigation of the impact of branded apps on customers. To explore this impact, they construct a fuzzy multi-criteria decision-making analysis model that uses consistent fuzzy linguistic preference relations to establish a symmetric pairwise comparison matrix. Using this, the complexity and error rate of the calculations are significantly reduced. Moreover, they exhibit that, out of the brand experience facets of two retail chain branded apps, behavioral experience is the most favored, while affective experience is the least favored.

In the fourth paper, "Bipolar Picture Fuzzy Graphs with Application", Waheed Ahmad Khan, Babir Ali, and Abdelghani Taouti introduce and discuss the notion of bipolar picture fuzzy graphs, as well as some of their basic characteristics and applications. Further, they put forward the notion of complete bipolar picture fuzzy graphs and strong bipolar picture fuzzy graphs, and present their fundamental features. They also present the construction of a bipolar picture fuzzy acquaintanceship graph, which serves as an important tool to measure the symmetry or asymmetry of the acquaintanceship levels of social networks, computer networks, etc.

The authors Xiaofeng Wen, Xiaohong Zhang, and Tao Lei, in their fifth paper, "Intuitionistic Fuzzy (IF) Overlap Functions and IF-Rough Sets with Applications", not only

check for updates

Citation: Jafari, S. Research on Fuzzy Logic and Mathematics with Applications. *Symmetry* **2024**, *16*, 1684. https://doi.org/10.3390/sym16121684

Received: 12 December 2024
Accepted: 15 December 2024
Published: 19 December 2024

introduce the new concept of an IF-overlap function but also provide the generating method of the IF-overlap function. They introduce and investigate several new notions and improve the intuitive fuzzy TOPSIS method.

In the sixth paper, "Fuzzy Sawi Decomposition Method for Solving Nonlinear Partial Fuzzy Differential Equations", Atanaska Georgieva and Albena Pavlova come up with a new decomposition method to find solutions to nonlinear partial fuzzy differential equations by utilizing the fuzzy Sawi decomposition method, which is a combination of fuzzy Sawi transformation and the Adomian decomposition method. They also provide a numerical example to show the effectiveness of the proposed method.

In the seventh paper, "Applying the Dijkstra Algorithm to Solve a Linear Diophantine Fuzzy Environment", Mani Parimala, Saeid Jafari, Muhamad Riaz, and Muhammad Aslam, by introducing linear Diophantine fuzzy optimality constraints, constructed a solution technique for directed network graphs. Furthermore, they provided a calculation of the weights of distinct routes and further modified the conventional Dijkstra method in order to find the arc weights of the linear Diophantine fuzzy shortest path ((LDFSP) and coterminal LDFSP based on improved score functions and optimality requirements. Finally, they presented a small telecommunication network to validate the possible use of the proposed technique.

In the eighth paper, "Aggregation of Weak Fuzzy Norms", the authors Tatiana Pedraza, Jorge Ramos-Canós, and Jesús Rodríguez-López investigated and characterized the extended use of aggregation functions. In this way, they were able to drive a single weak fuzzy (quasi-)norm from an arbitrary family of weak fuzzy (quasi-)norms in two different senses: in the case where each weak fuzzy (quasi-)norm is defined on a possibly different vector space or when all of them are defined on the same vector space. They showed that weak fuzzy (quasi-)norm aggregation functions are equivalent to fuzzy (quasi-)metric aggregation functions. This is contrary to the crisp case.

In the ninth paper, "Experimental Analysis of a Fuzzy Scheme against a Robust Controller for a Proton Exchange Membrane Fuel Cell System", Cristian Napole, Mohamed Derbeli, and Oscar Barambones compared a robust controller with a fuzzy logic strategy (with symmetric membership functions). Both were implemented in commercial proton exchange membrane fuel cells using a dSPACE 1102 control board. Using an experimental test bench, both proposals were analysed. The authors used the outcomes to present the advantages and disadvantages of each scheme in terms of chattering reduction, accuracy, and convergence speed.

In the tenth paper, "Similarity Measures Based on T-Spherical Fuzzy Information with Applications to Pattern Recognition and Decision Making", the authors Muhammad Nabeel Abid, Miin-Shen Yang, Hanen Karamti, Kifayat Ullah, and Dragan Pamucar conducted an investigation into the possible defects and shortcomings of picture fuzzy similarity measures with the aim of introducing a new similarity measure in a T-spherical fuzzy environment. They also show that the newly improved similarity measure has the advantage of creating more ground to accommodate uncertain information with three degrees and is also responsible for the reduction in information loss.

In the eleventh paper, "Prime Cordial Labeling of Generalized Petersen Graph under Some Graph Operations", Weidong Zhao, Muhammad Naeem, and Irfan Ahmad study the prime cordial labeling of rotationally symmetric graphs, which is obtained from a generalized Petersen graph $p(n,k)$ using a duplication operation. They obtained two important and interesting results: the derived symmetric graphs are prime cordial and when a Petersen graph with some path graphs is glowed, the resulting graph is a prime cordial graph.

The authors Mohd Syafiq Bidin, Abd. Fatah Wahab, Mohammad Izat Emir Zulkifly and Rozaimi Zakaria, in their twelfth paper, entitled "Generalized Fuzzy Linguistic Bicubic *B*-Spline Surface Model for Uncertain Fuzzy Linguistic Data", state that the motivation behind their research is that since a fuzzy linguistic data set is uncertain, it is difficult to analyze and describe it as a smooth and continuous generic figure. This led them to investigate conduction in a new model of a *B*-spline surface by utilizing a different approach: a crisp and fuzzy linguistic point relation with three types of linguistic function. Then, they proposed an algorithm for the fuzzy linguistic bicubic *B*-spline surface model to convert fuzzy linguistic data into fuzzy linguistic control points. They also provided a numerical example of fuzzy linguistic data to visualize the suggested model.

Conflicts of Interest: The author declares no conflicts of interest.

List of Contributions

1. Alshammari, I.; Khalil, O.H.; Ghareeb, A. A New Representation of Semiopenness of L-fuzzy Sets in RL-fuzzy Bitopological Spaces. *Symmetry* **2021**, *13*, 611.
2. Liu, D.; Huang A.; Liu Y.; Liu, Z. An Extension TOPSIS Method Based on the Decision Maker's Risk Attitude and the Adjusted Probabilistic Fuzzy Set. *Symmetry* **2021**, *13*, 891.
3. Hsu, T.-H.; Chen, C.-H.; Yang, Y.-W. A Decision Analysis Model for the Brand Experience of Branded Apps Using Consistency Fuzzy Linguistic Preference Relations. *Symmetry* **2021**, *13*, 1151.
4. Khan, W.H.; Ali, B.; Taouti A. Bipolar Picture Fuzzy Graphs with Application. *Symmetry* **2021**, *13*, 1427.
5. Wen, X.; Zhang, X.; Lei, T. Intuitionistic Fuzzy (IF) Overlap Functions and IF-Rough Sets with Applications. *Symmetry* **2021**, *13*, 1494.
6. Georgieva, A.; Pavlova A. Fuzzy Sawi Decomposition Method for Solving Nonlinear Partial Fuzzy Differential Equations. *Symmetry* **2021**, *13*, 1580.
7. Parimala, M.; Jafari, S.; Riaz, M.; Aslam, M. Applying the Dijkstra Algorithm to Solve a Linear Diophantine Fuzzy Environment. *Symmetry* **2021**, *13*, 1616.
8. Pedraza, T.; Ramos-Canós, J.; Rodríguez-López, J. Aggregation of Weak Fuzzy Norms. *Symmetry* **2021**, *13*, 1908.
9. Napole, C.; Derbeli, M.; Barambones, O. Experimental Analysis of a Fuzzy Scheme against a Robust Controller for a Proton Exchange Membrane Fuel Cell System. *Symmetry* **2022**, *14*, 139.
10. Abid, M.N.; Yang, M.-S.; Karamti, H.; Ullah, K.; Pamucar, D. Similarity Measures Based on T-Spherical Fuzzy Information with Applications to Pattern Recognition and Decision Making. *Symmetry* **2022**, *14*, 410.
11. Zhao, W.; Naeem, M.; Ahmad, I. Prime Cordial Labeling of Generalized Petersen Graph under Some Graph Operations. *Symmetry* **2022**, *14*, 732.
12. Bidin, M.S.; Wahab, A.F.; Zulkifly, M.I.E.; Zakaria, R. Generalized Fuzzy Linguistic Bicubic B-Spline Surface Model for Uncertain Fuzzy Linguistic Data. *Symmetry* **2022**, *14*, 2267.

symmetry

Article

Generalized Fuzzy Linguistic Bicubic B-Spline Surface Model for Uncertain Fuzzy Linguistic Data

Mohd Syafiq Bidin [1], Abd. Fatah Wahab [1,*], Mohammad Izat Emir Zulkifly [2,*] and Rozaimi Zakaria [3]

[1] Faculty of Ocean Engineering Technology and Informatics, Universiti Malaysia Terengganu, Kuala Terengganu 21300, Malaysia
[2] Faculty of Science, Department of Mathematical Sciences, Universiti Teknologi Malaysia, Johor Bahru 81310, Malaysia
[3] Faculty of Science and Natural Resources, Universiti Malaysia Sabah, Kota Kinabalu 88450, Malaysia
* Correspondence: fatah@umt.edu.my (A.F.W.); izatemir@utm.my (M.I.E.Z.)

Abstract: A fuzzy linguistic data set that is uncertain is difficult to analyze and describe in the form of a smooth and continuous generic figure. Therefore, the study aims to develop a new model of a B-spline surface using a different approach of a crisp and fuzzy linguistic point relation with three types of linguistic function: low L, medium M_i and high H. These linguistic functions are defined first to introduce the fuzzy linguistic point relation. Then, a new algorithm of the fuzzy linguistic bicubic B-spline surface model is presented to convert fuzzy linguistic data into fuzzy linguistic control points. In addition, a numerical example of fuzzy linguistic data is considered at the end of this study to visualize the suggested model. Thus, the relation between the fuzzy linguistic data points can be analyzed to present another area of knowledge in which symmetry phenomena occur. The symmetry here plays an important role in solving the uncertain fuzzy linguistic data problem by using the suggested model.

Keywords: B-spline surface; fuzzy linguistic point relation; fuzzy linguistic data; fuzzy linguistic control point; fuzzy linguistic B-spline

check for updates

Citation: Bidin, M.S.; Wahab, A.F.; Zulkifly, M.I.E.; Zakaria, R. Generalized Fuzzy Linguistic Bicubic B-Spline Surface Model for Uncertain Fuzzy Linguistic Data. *Symmetry* **2022**, *14*, 2267. https://doi.org/10.3390/sym14112267

Academic Editor: Saeid Jafari

Received: 16 June 2022
Accepted: 2 September 2022
Published: 28 October 2022

1. Introduction

Real data from real phenomena and scenarios are difficult to describe and analyze using existing methods. There are even more problems when they involve linguistic terms that are uncertain by nature where they carry their own meaning depending on the individual's perception [1]. The use of linguistic terms in daily activities has various interpretations and assumptions. For example, the intonation of the use of sentences or words in conversation sometimes has a different meaning. Therefore, the relationship between linguistics and the uncertainty inherent in the concept of fuzzy sets is inseparable [2]. To deal with uncertain information, Zadeh [3] proposed the concept of the fuzzy set, which has been widely used in different fields. Then, it was followed by the concept of linguistic variables and its application, also proposed by Zadeh [4–6].

Language is one of the primary expressions of human intelligence. What makes language so difficult for artificial intelligence (AI) is its ambiguity, which refers to the possibility of interpreting linguistic units in different ways, and ubiquitous quality in natural language [7]. In the twenty-first century, the activities of human life have been revolutionized by the widespread application of the internet, and the capabilities of computing systems and intelligence that are driving a new era of AI. A variety of intelligent human behaviors such as memory, emotion, perception, judgment, reasoning, recognition, proof, communication, understanding, design, thinking, learning, creating and others, can be realized artificially by using machines or building systems and networks. However, these are built on certainty or precision and are very limited by their formal axiom systems, which cannot simulate the uncertainty of the human thought processes due to their precision [8].

The problems of linguistic terms can be translated into the form of linguistic data sets and need to be solved using appropriate models to produce clear visuals in the form of curves and surfaces. This method requires the acquisition of real data from the real world to be modeled with geometric modeling. Then, the data can be simulated and analyzed for the research conducted. However, the developed model will not lead to any change if the problem of data sets that are fuzzy and have uncertainty is not resolved first. Existing geometric functions in the field of geometric modeling cannot model a data set into curves and surfaces when there is an ambiguous property of the data set obtained. Geometric modeling can only be performed when the data set has full membership, while data sets that do not have full membership are ignored [9].

To solve this problem, a new model needs to be proposed using a fuzzy linguistic approach and combined with the spline function in geometric modeling. This research paper will define a fuzzy linguistic point relation where two sets of fuzzy linguistic data are connected to obtain the exact membership value, which can then form a clear and smooth surface. From the result of this surface, the process of evaluation and analysis can be carried out more easily and smoothly. Research in this field is still new, where the study of curves has only been conducted by Hussain et al. [1,2] and Wahab and Hussain [10]. Therefore, this paper presents another area of knowledge in which symmetry plays an important role in solving the problem of fuzzy linguistic data that have an uncertain nature. The process of developing a new model of the fuzzy linguistic bicubic B-spline surface will be discussed in the following sections.

2. Introduction to B-Spline Function

In 1946, Schoenberg [11] introduced the B-spline or basis spline for the uniform knot cases. Then, Boor [12] began using the B-spline function as a tool to present geometry curves and introduced a recursive assessment of the B-spline known as De Boor's algorithm in 1960. He became one of the most influential proponents of the B-spline in approximation theory. Dempski [13] and Farin [14] discussed that through the representations of curves and surfaces, a set of data can be modeled with B-spline functions. A curve approximates a set of control points without necessarily passing through any control points when polynomials are fitted to the path. Another method for geometric modeling is interpolation where a smooth curve is constructed through each data point, according to Salomon [15]. A B-spline surface can be obtained by taking a bidirectional net of control points, two knot vectors and the product of the univariate functions as follows (Piegl and Tiller [16])

$$Bs(u,v) = \sum_{i=0}^{n}\sum_{j=0}^{m} P_{i,j}N_{i,p}(u)N_{j,q}(v) \quad (1)$$

where $N_{i,p}(u)$ and $N_{j,q}(v)$ are the basic function of crisp B-splines with degree p and q in parameters u and v, respectively.

The B-spline surface is a tensor product basis function $N_{i,p}(u)N_{j,q}(v)$. The set of control points is often referred to as the control network, and the value of u and v is between 0 and 1. Both u and v are vectors that determine the intersection direction of the B-spline curve for the formation of the B-spline surface in the form of rows, i and columns, j. Hence, the B-spline surface maps a square unit to a surface patch, as shown in Figure 1.

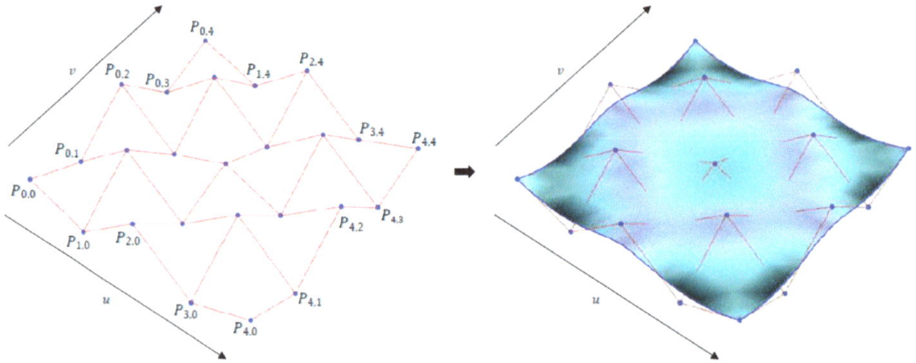

Figure 1. Formation of control network from crisp control points to B-spline surface.

3. Fuzzy Set Approach to B-Spline

Using fuzzy set theory (Zadeh, [3]), Wahab et al. [17,18] introduced a new approach of the fuzzy B-spline surface model using fuzzy control points, defined as

$$\widetilde{Bs}(s,t) = \sum_{i=0}^{n}\sum_{j=0}^{m} \widetilde{P}_{i,j} N_{i,p}(s) N_{j,q}(t) \quad (2)$$

where $N_{i,p}(s)$ and $N_{j,p}(t)$ are the B-spline basic functions with degree p and q, respectively, in parameters s and t, of which the value is between 0 and 1. Each knot vectors specified must qualify conditions $s = n + p + 1$ and $t = m + q + 1$. Therefore, the B-spline surface is a surface in the form of a tensor product. $\widetilde{P}_{i,j} = \left\langle \widetilde{P}^{\leftarrow}_{i,j}, P_{i,j}, \widetilde{P}^{\rightarrow}_{i,j} \right\rangle$ is the (i,j)th fuzzy control point in row i and column j that will form the fuzzy control network for surface patch formation.

Figure 2a shows an example of bicubic shape of the fuzzy B-spline surface model with fuzzy control points while without fuzzy control points in Figure 2b. The model is formed by 16 fuzzy control points that are also known as fuzzy data points. These fuzzy control points form the fuzzy control network that illustrate this surface model.

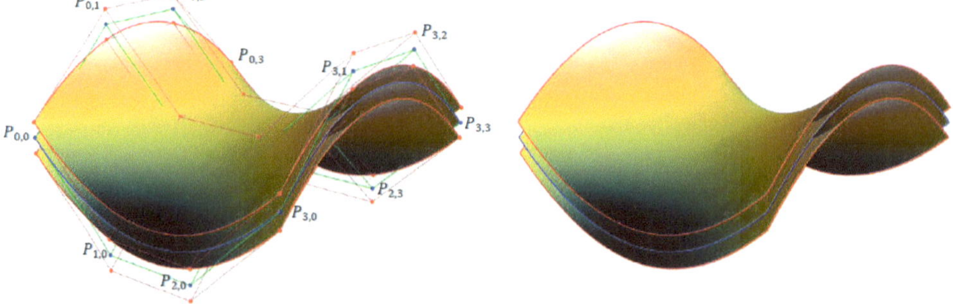

(a) (b)

Figure 2. Example of bicubic fuzzy B-spline surface models (**a**) with fuzzy control points and (**b**) without fuzzy control points.

The objective of this study is to introduce a new model of the fuzzy linguistic bicubic B-spline surface based on fuzzy set theory and the B-spline function in geometric modeling.

The use of fuzzy set theory can solve problems in modeling uncertainty data, while the model was developed geometrically through the production of curves and surfaces using the B-spline function corresponding to the study conducted to obtain clear and smooth visualization results. Thus, a new model was developed with a combination of all these concepts, which, subsequently, can be applied to linguistic data from the real world for the purpose of forecasting, data modeling and others.

This study is further structured as follows. Section 4 reviews the existing studies on fuzzy sets and linguistics. Then, Section 5 presents the introduction of fuzzy linguistic data processing and the definition of fuzzy set theory. Section 6 defines linguistic variables with an example of Body Mass Index (BMI) while Section 7 presents new definitions for fuzzy linguistic point relations. The fuzzy linguistic model with its algorithm is proposed in Section 8. Section 9 discusses a numerical example and visualization of the model. Lastly, conclusions and recommendations for further research are depicted in Section 10.

4. Literature Review

Linguistics is the scientific analysis of language, as opposed to the comprehensible but impressionistic analysis of language. Semantic studies examine how a meaning is managed in its journey from human thought to a word or sentence [19]. Kracht [20] said that language is a set of signs defined as a quadruple $(\pi, \mu, \lambda, \sigma)$, where π is its exponent (or phonological structure), μ its morphological structure, λ its syntactic structure and σ its meaning (or semantic structure). A text is certainly more than a sequence of sentences, and the study of discourse is indeed a very important one. Furthermore, sentences are so complicated that we need a long time to study them. In addition to that, Aikhenvald [21] discussed the properties of evidence systems that are related to discourse, and also the details of cross-linguistic study that will provide valuable insights into the nature of human cognition. Maynard [22] studied Japanese primarily from the perspective of discourse and conversation analysis by consistently analyzing real-life Japanese, part of contemporary Japanese culture, in a constant dynamic flow of being produced, consumed and interpreted. In particular, several studies have also been conducted to investigate concepts roughly corresponding to anger in languages such as Kovecses [23,24], Soriano [25], King [26] and Matsuki [27]. In normal situations, uncertain data are omitted from the data set regardless of their effect on any outcome. Therefore, the evaluation and analysis process of the visualized data will be incomplete. The data set should be filtered if there is an element of uncertainty so that it can be used to generate a model of a curve or surface to be studied.

To overcome this problem, linguistic fuzzy sets are used, which are a generalization of fuzzy set theory from Zadeh [3] and further extended in [4–6]. The concept of linguistic variables has been widely used and has become the main reference of researchers. The study discussed about linguistic variables characterized by a quintuple $(\mathcal{X}, T(\mathcal{X}), U, G, M)$, where $\mathcal{X}$ is the name of the variable, $T(\mathcal{X})$ is the term set of $\mathcal{X}$ (the collection of its linguistic values), U is a universe of discourse, G is a syntactic rule that generates the term in $T(\mathcal{X})$ and M is a semantic rule that associates with each linguistic value X and its meaning $M(X)$ where M denotes a fuzzy subset of U. Bonissone [28] proposed a solution for the problem of how to associate labels with unlabeled fuzzy sets based on semantic similarity (linguistic approximation) and also how to perform arithmetic operations with fuzzy numbers. In addition to that, Delgado et al. [29] defined an aggregation operation between linguistic labels based on their meaning that can be performed without any reference to this semantic representation. Therefore, it is very useful from a computational point of view because it can be implemented as a simple table or procedure. Bordogna and Pasi [30] introduced a solution to the problem of numerical query weights by defining an existing weighted Boolean retrieval model and a linguistic extension formalized in fuzzy set theory, where the numerical query weights are replaced by linguistic descriptors that determine the importance level of the terms, while Khoury et al. [31] proposed the use of a hybrid statistical fuzzy methodology to represent subject–verb–object triplets that calculates the membership of subject–verb pairs and verb–object pairs in various domains.

To deal with an unbalanced set of linguistic terms, Herrera et al. [32] presented a fuzzy linguistic methodology by developing a representation model for unbalanced linguistic information that uses the concept of linguistic hierarchy as the basis of representation. This methodology is built on the concept of linguistic hierarchy and on a 2-tuple fuzzy linguistic representation model that also consists of representation algorithms and computational approaches for unbalanced linguistic information. The linguistic application of fuzzy set theory to natural language analysis formulated a working definition of fuzziness that can be used in future research on fuzzy linguistics clarified by Ma [33]. Ramos-Soto and Pereira-Fariña [34] proposed a new understanding of interpretability in the context of the linguistic description of fuzzy data by approaching this concept from a natural language generation (NLG) perspective as opposed to focusing on the classical notions of interpretability for fuzzy systems and linguistic summaries or descriptions on data (LDD). In particular, many researchers have also used the fuzzy linguistic approach in multi-criteria decision making such as Tong and Bonissone [35], Herrera and Martinez [36], Rodriguez et al. [37,38], Wang et al. [39] and Nguyen et al. [40]. However, in order to evaluate and analyze a model, linguistic fuzzy data sets need to be visualized first as a curve or surface model.

The modeling of fuzzy linguistic data sets can be demonstrated through the construction of curves and surfaces using existing functions in computer-aided geometric design (CAGD). Geometric modeling is a process when a set of data is translated into a real 2-dimensional or 3-dimensional form to produce a smooth and clear visualization. Among the studies that have been conducted is that by Jaccas et al. [41,42] who discussed a fuzzy logic approach to curve and surface design in the context of CAGD. Gallo and Spagnuolo [43] and Gallo et al. [44] presented a new approach for modeling spatial data, which takes into account the uncertainty that may be associated with the original data set. The resulting model has explicitly embedded uncertainty properties that allow users to visualize and reason about the reconstructed model at different levels, as well as use different model layers according to the accuracy required by the specific analysis. In addition to that, Anile et al. [45] introduced an innovative approach to model fuzzy and sparse data by generalizing B-spline to fuzzy B-spline where its power depends on the possibility of being used as an approximation function for both fuzzy and crisp data. In addition, Wahab et al. [17,18] and Wahab and Ali [46] used fuzzy set theory and its properties through the concept of fuzzy numbers to introduce the fuzzy control point for fuzzy curve and fuzzy surface models, which can then solve the uncertainty problem in CAGD. This study was later continued by Zakaria et al. [47], Zakaria and Wahab [48,49], Karim et al. [50] and Bakar et al. [51].

Further studies in the field of fuzzy set theory and CAGD have been conducted, specifically by Zulkifly and Wahab [52,53] and Zulkifly et al. [54,55], by introducing a new concept of intuitionistic fuzzy sets with geometric modeling. Shah and Wahab [56] and Shah et al. [57] introduced fuzzy topological digital space concepts with their properties. Zakaria et al. [58,59], Wahab et al. [60] and Adesah et al. [61] extended the study of geometric modeling with fuzzy set theory to a type-2 fuzzy set. In the field of fuzzy linguistics, Hussain et al. [1,2] introduced fuzzy linguistic control points (FLCP), which can be used to generate spline models through linguistic terms. The FLCP theorem has been redefined using modifiers or linguistic hedges to solve the uncertainty problem of linguistic data in geometric modeling. The FLCP was blended with spline basis functions to produce several spline models characterized by fuzzy linguistics. Then, Wahab and Hussain [10] introduced new fuzzy spline models such as fuzzy linguistic Bézier and fuzzy linguistic B-spline by using the definition of fuzzy linguistic control points. The control points are redefined through the fuzzy linguistic approach to produce a new set of control points with linguistic terms. Bidin et al. [62] introduced a new approach for the fuzzy linguistic point relation that can generate a new model called as fuzzy linguistic cubic B-spline curve model. The presented method shows that the model can be generated using directive linguistic terms and functions.

However, previous studies on fuzzy linguistics blended with spline functions only involve a curve form, while a surface form has not yet been extensively studied. Therefore, this paper discusses and introduces a new model of fuzzy linguistic data visualized with spline functions in geometric modeling. There are three fuzzy linguistic variables, which are low L, medium M_i and high H, that are discussed in the section to define the fuzzy linguistic point relation. Then, a new algorithm is introduced to build a new model called the fuzzy linguistic bicubic B-spline surface model. Lastly, this new model is visualized using numerical examples of linguistic data sets with randomly selected membership values. From the results of visualization, the evaluation and analysis process is expected to be easier to perform and provide great benefits in various fields, especially the problem of ambiguity in the expression of human intelligence.

5. Preliminaries

Using a fuzzy linguistic set [63], we introduce the fuzzy linguistic control points using the fuzzy linguistic point relation. From any real phenomena or scenarios, we will obtain real data, but due to many factors, the data collected come with uncertainty. Therefore, a linguistic function is used to measure the real data into a linguistic data set. Then, the linguistic data set will visualize various curve (2-D) and surface (3-D) images as in the process described in Figure 3.

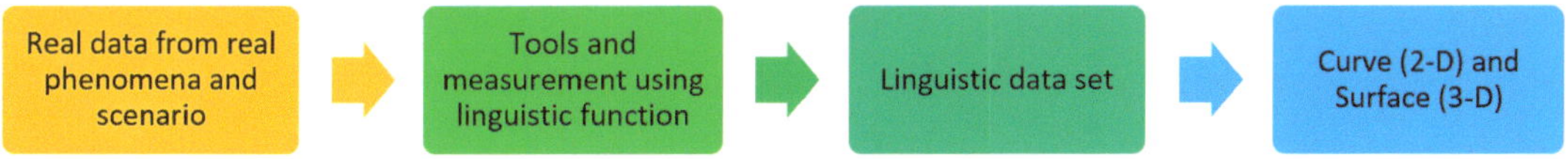

Figure 3. Fuzzy linguistic data process.

Several definitions related to the concepts of fuzzy sets, fuzzy numbers and fuzzy control points are briefly discussed as follows (Wahab and Husain [10]):

Definition 1. *Let X be a non-empty set. A fuzzy set A in X is characterized by a membership function $\mu_A : X \to [0,1]$ and $\mu_A(X)$ is called as the degree of membership of element x in A for $x \in X$ can be defined as*

$$\mu_A(X) = \begin{cases} 1 & if\ x \in A \\ c & if\ x \widetilde{\in} A \\ 0 & if\ x \notin A \end{cases} \tag{3}$$

where $\mu_A(x) = 1$ is a full membership function, $\mu_A(x) = c$ is a non-full membership function, $\mu_A(x) = 0$ is a non-membership function and c is the membership grade value between 0 and 1.

A fuzzy set can also be described as a set of ordered pairs and can be written as $\widetilde{A} = \{x, \mu_A(x)\}$. If $X = \{x_1, x_2, \ldots, x_n\}$ is a finite set and $\widetilde{A} \subseteq X$, then the fuzzy set A can be written as

$$\widetilde{A} = \{(x_1, \mu_A(x_1)), (x_2, \mu_A(x_2)), \ldots, (x_n, \mu_A(x_n))\} \subseteq X \tag{4}$$

Definition 2. *Let A be a fuzzy set in the universe of discourse X and μ_A be the membership of A. Then, the α-cut A_α of A in X is defined as*

$$A_\alpha = \{x_i \subseteq X | \mu_A(x_i) \geq \alpha\} \tag{5}$$

where $\alpha \subseteq (0,1)$.

Definition 3. *Let a fuzzy set A on the real line be the set of all normal, convex, continuous data, and the membership function in the closed interval and the support* $(A) = \{x|\mu_A(x)\rangle 0\}$ *is limited.*

A generalized fuzzy number $\widetilde{A}$ with the membership function $\mu_{\widetilde{A}}(x),\ x \in R$ can be defined as

$$\mu_{\widetilde{A}}(x) = \begin{cases} l_{\widetilde{A}}(x), & a \le x \le b \\ 1, & b \le x \le c \\ r_{\widetilde{A}}(x), & c \le x \le d \\ 0, & otherwise \end{cases} \tag{6}$$

where $l_{\widetilde{A}}(x)$ is the left membership function of the increasing function $[a,b]$ and $r_{\widetilde{A}}(x)$ is the right membership function of the decreasing function $[c,d]$ such that $l_{\widetilde{A}}(a) = r_{\widetilde{A}}(d) = 0$ and $l_{\widetilde{A}}(b) = r_{\widetilde{A}}(c) = 1$.

If $l_{\widetilde{A}}(x)$ and $r_{\widetilde{A}}(x)$ are linear, then $\widetilde{A} = (a,b,c,d)$ is a trapezoidal fuzzy number. If $b = c$, then the trapezoidal fuzzy number is defined as triangular fuzzy number written as $\widetilde{A} = (a,b,d)$ or $\widetilde{A} = (a,c,d)$.

Definition 4. *Fuzzy set* $\widetilde{P}$ *in space of S is said to be a set of fuzzy control points if, and only if, for every α-level set chosen, there exist pointed, which is* $P = \left\langle \widetilde{P}_i^{\leftarrow}, P_i, \widetilde{P}_i^{\rightarrow} \right\rangle$, *in S with every* P_i *is a crisp point and membership function* $\mu_P : S \to (0,1]$, *which is defined as* $\mu_P(P_i) = 1$.

$$\mu_P(P_i^{\leftarrow}) = \begin{cases} 0 & if\ P_i^{\leftarrow} \notin S \\ c \in (0,1) & if\ P_i^{\leftarrow} \widetilde{\in} S \\ 1 & if\ P_i^{\leftarrow} \in S \end{cases} \text{ and } \mu_P(P_i^{\rightarrow}) = \begin{cases} 0 & if\ P_i^{\rightarrow} \notin S \\ c \in (0,1) & if\ P_i^{\rightarrow} \widetilde{\in} S \\ 1 & if\ P_i^{\rightarrow} \in S \end{cases} \tag{7}$$

where $\mu_P(P_i^{\leftarrow})$ is the left membership grade value, $\mu_P(P_i^{\rightarrow})$ is the right membership grade value and c is the membership grade value between 0 and 1.

Fuzzy set $\widetilde{P}$ can generally be written as

$$\widetilde{P} = \left\{ \widetilde{P}_i : i = 0,1,2,\ldots,n \right\} \tag{8}$$

where with $P = \left\langle \widetilde{P}_i^{\leftarrow}, P_i, \widetilde{P}_i^{\rightarrow} \right\rangle$ and $\widetilde{P}_i^{\rightarrow}$ being the left fuzzy control point, crisp control point and right fuzzy control point, respectively.

6. Linguistic Variables

A linguistic variable is defined as a variable whose values are words or sentences in a natural or artificial language. According to Zadeh [4], a linguistic variable is characterized by a quintuple $(\mathcal{X}, T(\mathcal{X}), U, G, M)$, where $\mathcal{X}$ is the name of the variable, $T(\mathcal{X})$ is the term set of $\mathcal{X}$ (the collection of its linguistic values), U is a universe of discourse, G is a syntactic rule that generates the term in $T(\mathcal{X})$ and M is a semantic rule that associates each linguistic value X with its meaning $M(X)$ where M denotes a fuzzy subset of U.

As an example from weight categories based on body mass index (BMI), let $X = \{x_i | x_i \text{ BMI}\} \exists A_i \subset X$ subject to $A_i = \{A_1, A_2, A_3, A_4\}$, where A_1, A_2, A_3 and A_4 are underweight, normal, overweight, obesity and severe obesity, respectively, namely as a linguistic model of BMI shown in Figure 4.

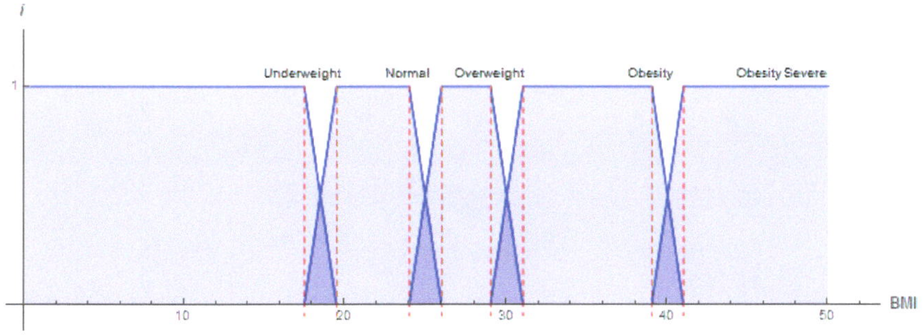

Figure 4. Linguistic model of BMI.

7. Fuzzy Linguistic Point Relation

There are three types of fuzzy linguistic functions: low L_i, medium M_i and high H_i, as shown in Figure 5.

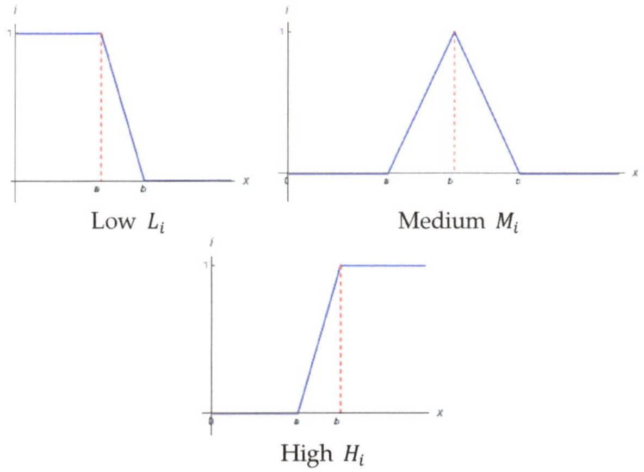

Figure 5. Three types of fuzzy linguistic function.

These fuzzy linguistic functions are also called linguistic behaviours where a, b and c are the elements of X that display the increase and decrease points for each function. Low L_i and high H_i have only one linguistic set, but there are probably more than one linguistic set for medium M_i, where linguistic set $LS = \{L, M_1, M_2, \ldots, M_n, H\}$ is shown in Figure 6. L is the one and only low linguistic set, M_1 is the first medium linguistic set, M_2 is the second medium linguistic set, M_n is the subsequent medium linguistic set and H is the one and only high linguistic set.

Referring to Figures 5 and 6, we can briefly state the definition for each linguistic function for low L_i, medium M_i and high H_i as follows (Bidin et al. [62]):

Definition 5. *Let low linguistic function L_i in domain $L \to [0,1]$ be defined by a linguistic set, then*

$$L_i(x) = \begin{cases} 1 & , 0 \le x \le a \\ \frac{b-x}{b-a} & , a \le x \le b \\ 0 & , x \ge b \end{cases} \tag{9}$$

where $L_i(x)$ is called the degree of membership of $x \in X$.

Definition 6. *Let medium linguistic function M_i in domain $M \to [0,1]$ be defined by a linguistic set, then*

$$M_i(x) = \begin{cases} 0 & , x \leq a \\ \frac{x-a}{b-a} & , a \leq x \leq b \\ \frac{c-x}{c-b} & , b \leq x \leq c \\ 0 & , x \geq c \end{cases} \tag{10}$$

where $M_i(x)$ is called the degree of membership of $x \in X$.

Definition 7. *Let high linguistic function H_i in domain $H \to [0,1]$ be defined by a linguistic set, then*

$$H_i(x) = \begin{cases} 0 & , x \leq a \\ \frac{x-a}{b-a} & , a \leq x \leq b \\ 1 & , x \geq b \end{cases} \tag{11}$$

where $H_i(x)$ is called the degree of membership of $x \in X$.

Definition 8. *Let X be a universal set of linguistics where $\forall x \in X$ and there exist linguistic functions $[L_i, M_i, H_i]$ such that there a set of ordered pairs $(x, L_i(x))$ or $(x, M_i(x))$ or $(x, H_i(x))$ when $L_i(x),\ M_i(x),\ H_i(x) \in [0,1]$*

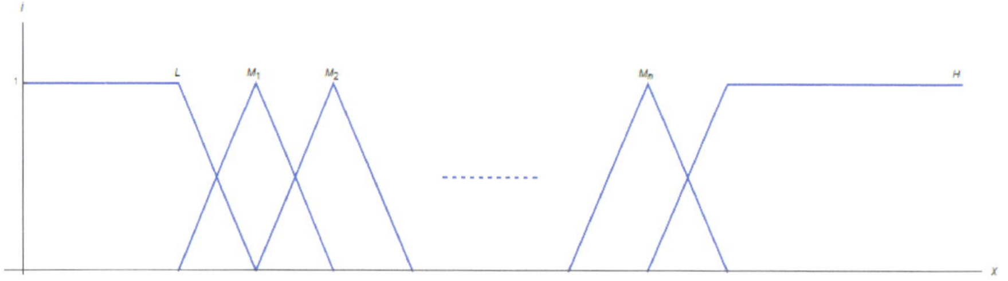

Figure 6. Fuzzy linguistic functions in the BMI linguistic model.

From Definition 5, the low linguistic function L_i in Figure 7 in accordance to (9) can be defined as $x_i \in X$ there $L_i(x_i) \in [0,1]$ exists such that $(x_i, L_i(x_i))$ where x_i is an element in X of the low linguistic function L_i.

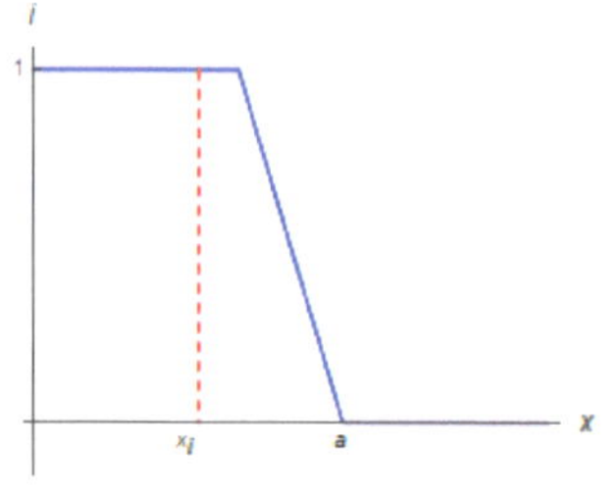

Figure 7. $x_i \in X$ of low linguistic function L_i.

Let X and Y be any collection of universal space, then $\widetilde{L_X} \times \widetilde{L_Y}$ is a fuzzy linguistic relation. Suppose that L_X and L_Y in Figure 8 are two low linguistic functions on $X = \{\ x_i\ : i = 0,1,2,\ldots,n\}$ and $Y = \{\ y_i\ : i = 0,1,2,\ldots,n\}$, respectively. Then

$$\widetilde{L_X} \times \widetilde{L_Y} = \left\{((x,y), \mu_{\widetilde{L_X} \times \widetilde{L_Y}}(x,y) \middle| \mu_{\widetilde{L_X} \times \widetilde{L_Y}}(x,y) \leq 1\right) \tag{12}$$

where $\mu_{\widetilde{L_X} \times \widetilde{L_Y}}(x,y)$ is the degree of membership of element $(x,y) \in X \times Y$.

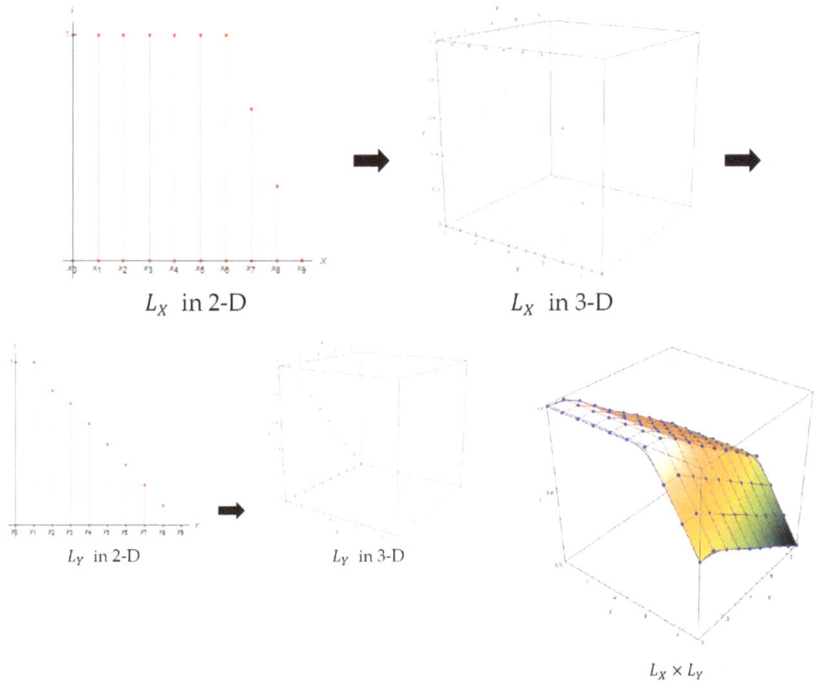

Figure 8. Fuzzy linguistic point relation of low linguistic functions L_X and L_Y.

From definition 6, the medium linguistic function M_i in Figure 9 in accordance to (10) can be defined as $x_i \in X$ and $M_i(x_i) \in [0,1]$ exists such that $(x_i, M_i(x_i))$ where x_i is an element in X of the medium linguistic function M_i.

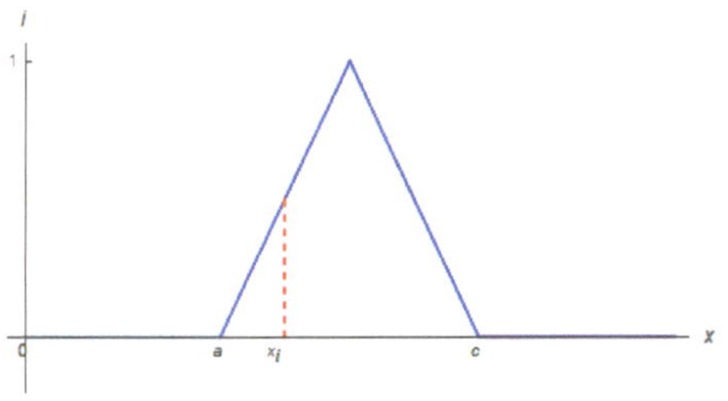

Figure 9. $x_i \in X$ of medium linguistic function M_i.

Let X and Y be any collection of universal spaces, then $\widetilde{M_X} \times \widetilde{M_Y}$ is a fuzzy linguistic relation. Suppose that M_X and M_Y in Figure 10 are two medium linguistic functions on $X = \{\, x_i \, : i = 0,1,2,\ldots,n\}$ and $Y = \{\, y_i \, : i = 0,1,2,\ldots,n\}$, respectively. Then

$$\begin{gathered} \widetilde{M_X} \times \widetilde{M_Y} = \{((x,y), \mu_{X\times Y}(x,y) | \mu_{X\times Y}(x,y) \leq 1\} \\ \widetilde{M_X} \times \widetilde{M_Y} = \left\{((x,y), \mu_{\widetilde{M_X}\times\widetilde{M_Y}}(x,y) \middle| \mu_{\widetilde{M_X}\times\widetilde{M_Y}}(x,y) \leq 1\right\} \end{gathered} \tag{13}$$

where $\mu_{\widetilde{M_X}\times\widetilde{M_Y}}(x,y)$ is the degree of membership of element $(x,y) \in X \times Y$.

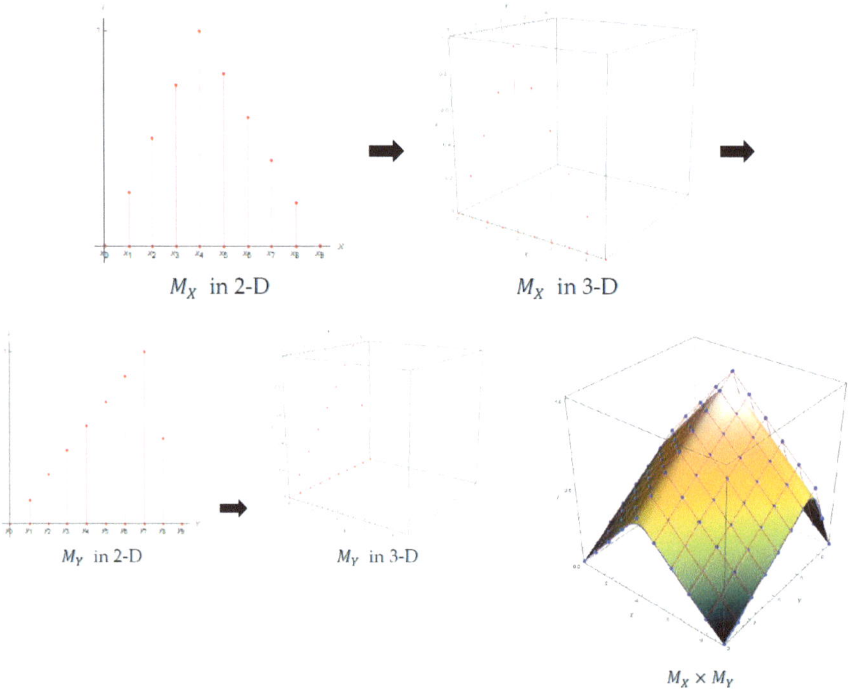

Figure 10. Fuzzy linguistic point relation of medium linguistic functions M_X and M_Y.

From Definition 7, the high linguistic function H_i in Figure 11 in accordance to (11) can be defined as $x_i \in X$ and $H_i(x_i) \in [0,1]$ exists such that $(x_i, H_i(x_i))$ where x_i is an element in X of the high linguistic function H_i.

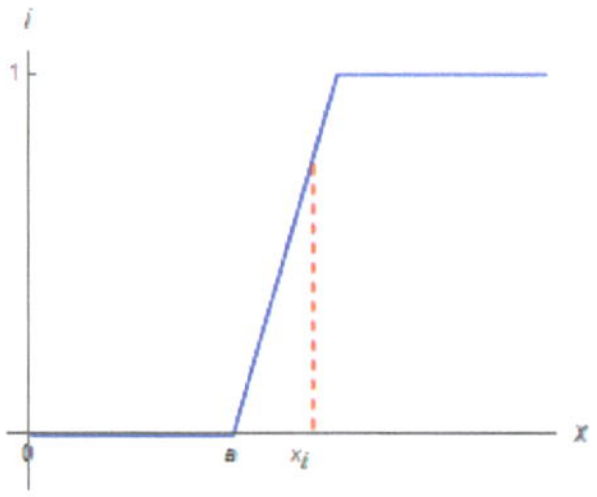

Figure 11. $x_i \in X$ of high linguistic function H_i.

Let X and Y be any collection of universal space, then $\widetilde{H_X} \times \widetilde{H_Y}$ is a fuzzy linguistic relation. Suppose that H_X and H_Y in Figure 12 are two high linguistic functions on $X = \{\, x_i \, : i = 0, 1, 2, \ldots, n\}$ and $Y = \{\, y_i \, : i = 0, 1, 2, \ldots, n\}$, respectively. Then

$$\widetilde{H_X} \times \widetilde{H_Y} = \left\{ ((x,y), \mu_{\widetilde{H_X} \times \widetilde{H_Y}}(x,y) \middle| \mu_{\widetilde{H_X} \times \widetilde{H_Y}}(x,y) \leq 1 \right\} \tag{14}$$

where $\mu_{\widetilde{H_X} \times \widetilde{H_Y}}(x,y)$ is the degree of membership of element $(x,y) \in X \times Y$.

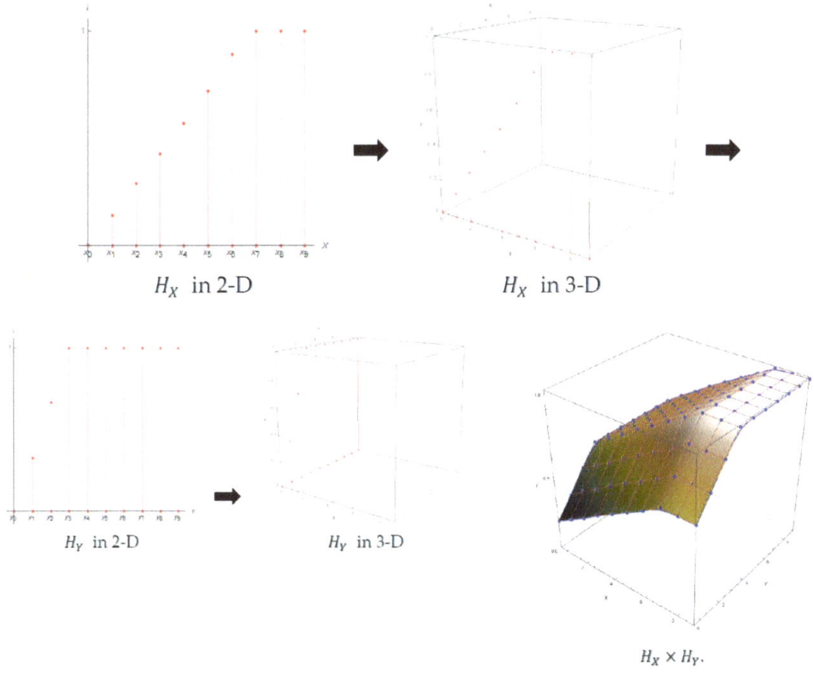

Figure 12. Fuzzy linguistic point relation of high linguistic functions H_X and H_Y.

Then, from Equations (12)–(14), the fuzzy linguistic point relations denoted as $L_i(x,y)$, $M_i(x,y)$ and $H_i(x,y)$, respectively, generate a fuzzy linguistic surface where

$$\forall(x,y) \in L_i \text{ or } (x,y) \in M_i \text{ or } (x,y) \in H_i \text{ and } L_i(x,y) \text{ or } M_i(x,y) \text{ or } H_i(x,y) \text{ exist in } [0,1]. \tag{15}$$

$\widetilde{L_X} \times \widetilde{L_Y}$, $\widetilde{M_X} \times \widetilde{M_Y}$ and $\widetilde{H_X} \times \widetilde{H_Y}$ are a fuzzy linguistic set in $X \times Y$ that can be defined as

$$\begin{aligned} \mu_{\widetilde{L_X}\times\widetilde{L_Y}}(x,y) &= \left\{\min\mu_{\widetilde{L_X}\times\widetilde{L_Y}}(x,y), max\mu_{\widetilde{L_X}\times\widetilde{L_Y}}(x,y)\right\} \\ \mu_{\widetilde{L_X}\times\widetilde{L_Y}}(x,y) &= \left\{\min\mu_{\widetilde{L_X}\times\widetilde{L_Y}}(x,y), max\mu_{\widetilde{L_X}\times\widetilde{L_Y}}(x,y)\right\} \\ \mu_{\widetilde{L_X}\times\widetilde{L_Y}}(x,y) &= \left\{\min\mu_{\widetilde{L_X}\times\widetilde{L_Y}}(x,y), max\mu_{\widetilde{L_X}\times\widetilde{L_Y}}(x,y)\right\} \end{aligned} \tag{16}$$

In the next section, a new model of the fuzzy linguistic bicubic B-spline surface is developed to generate a visualization through the fuzzy linguistic point relation and B-spline function.

8. Fuzzy Linguistic Bicubic B-Spline Surface Model

Based on the fuzzy linguistic point relation implemented with the B-spline basis function, a model of the fuzzy linguistic bicubic B-spline surface can be represented as $\widetilde{LBs}(s,t)$ and generated as follows

$$\widetilde{LBs}(s,t) = \sum_{i=0}^{n}\sum_{j=0}^{m} \widetilde{P}_{i,j} N_{i,p}(s) N_{j,q}(t) \tag{17}$$

where $\widetilde{P}_{i,j}$ is a fuzzy linguistic control point, $N_{i,p}(s)$ and $N_{j,p}(t)$ are the B-spline basic functions with degree p and q, respectively, in parameters $s,t \in [0,1]$, $s = n+p+1$ as well as $t = m+q+1$ and these are knot values for each vector, $i = 0,1,2,\ldots,n$ and $j = 0,1,2,\ldots,m$.

After all the definition processes in the previous section, the next processes represented by Algorithm 1 below are applied to obtain the result of the fuzzy linguistic bicubic B-spline surface model.

Algorithm 1 Fuzzy linguistic bicubic B-spline surface modeling

Step 1: Define all fuzzy data points. Let $\widetilde{P}_{i,j} = \left\{ \widetilde{P}_{(0,0)}, \widetilde{P}_{(1,0)}, \widetilde{P}_{(2,0)}, \ldots, \widetilde{P}_{n,m} \right\} \in X \times Y$ where $\widetilde{P}_0 = \{x_0, y_0, \widetilde{z}_0\}, \widetilde{P}_1 = \{x_1, y_1, \widetilde{z}_1\}, \widetilde{P}_2 = \{x_2, y_2, \widetilde{z}_2\}, \ldots, \widetilde{P}_n = \{x_n, y_n, \widetilde{z}_n\}$.

Step 2: Define all fuzzy point relations where
$\mu_L : L \to I = [0,1]$, $\mu_M : M \to I = [0,1]$ and $\mu_H : H \to I = [0,1]$.

Step 3: Define all fuzzy control points where

$$\widetilde{P}_{i,j} = \begin{bmatrix} (x_0, y_0), \mu_{\widetilde{P}_{(0,0)}}(x_0, y_0) & (x_0, y_1), \mu_{\widetilde{P}_{(1,0)}}(x_0, y_1) & \cdots & (x_0, y_m), \mu_{\widetilde{P}_{(0,m)}}(x_0, y_m) \\ (x_1, y_0), \mu_{\widetilde{P}_{(1,0)}}(x_1, y_0) & (x_1, y_1), \mu_{\widetilde{P}_{(1,1)}}(x_1, y_1) & \cdots & (x_1, y_m), \mu_{\widetilde{P}_{(1,m)}}(x_1, y_m) \\ \vdots & \vdots & \ddots & \vdots \\ (x_n, y_0), \mu_{\widetilde{P}_{(n.0)}}(x_n, y_0) & (x_n, y_1), \mu_{\widetilde{P}_{(n.1)}}(x_n, y_1) & \cdots & (x_n, y_m), \mu_{\widetilde{P}_{(n.m)}}(x_n, y_m) \end{bmatrix}$$

Step 4: Define all linguistic functions $[L_{i,}, M_i, H_i]$ to form fuzzy linguistic control points.

Step 5: Develop fuzzy linguistic bicubic B-spline surface model using fuzzy linguistic control points blended with B-spline basis function.

From the algorithm, the fuzzy linguistic bicubic B-spline surface model can be illustrated through each step. The visualization of the model can be seen in the next section.

9. Numerical Example and Visualization

In this section, we discuss a numerical example of the fuzzy linguistic bicubic B-spline surface model. B-spline surfaces are generated through linguistic commands appearing on the fuzzy linguistic point relation. Based on the algorithm from the previous section, let linguistic data $LD = \widetilde{P}_{i,j}$, then

$$LD = \begin{bmatrix} (x_0, y_0), \mu_{\widetilde{P}_{(0,0)}}(x_0, y_0) & (x_0, y_1), \mu_{\widetilde{P}_{(1,0)}}(x_0, y_1) & \cdots & (x_0, y_9), \mu_{\widetilde{P}_{(0,9)}}(x_0, y_9) \\ (x_1, y_0), \mu_{\widetilde{P}_{(1,0)}}(x_1, y_0) & (x_1, y_1), \mu_{\widetilde{P}_{(1,1)}}(x_1, y_1) & \cdots & (x_1, y_9), \mu_{\widetilde{P}_{(1,9)}}(x_1, y_9) \\ \vdots & \vdots & \ddots & \vdots \\ (x_n, y_0), \mu_{\widetilde{P}_{(9,0)}}(x_9, y_0) & (x_9, y_1), \mu_{\widetilde{P}_{(9,1)}}(x_9, y_1) & \cdots & (x_9, y_9), \mu_{\widetilde{P}_{(9,9)}}(x_9, y_9) \end{bmatrix} = \widetilde{P}_{i,j}$$

Table 1 is a numerical example of linguistic data with randomly selected membership values that generate the final result of the fuzzy linguistic bicubic B-spline surface model in Figure 13 through linguistic commands appearing on the fuzzy linguistic point relation introduced in this paper.

Table 1. Numerical example of linguistic data.

(x_n, y_n)	y_0	y_1	y_2	y_3	y_4	y_5	y_6	y_7	y_8	y_9
x_0	(0,0),1,00	(0,1),0.84	(0,2),0.84	(0,3),1.00	(0,4),1.00	(0,5),1.00	(0,6),1.00	(0,7),0.84	(0,8),0.84	(0,9),1.00
x_1	(1,0),1.00	(1,1),0.84	(1,2),0.84	(1,3),1.00	(1,4),1.00	(1,5),1.00	(1,6),1.00	(1,7),0.84	(1,8),0.84	(1,9),1.00
x_2	(2,0),0.84	(2,1),0.67	(2,2),0.67	(2,3),0.84	(2,4),0.84	(2,5),0.84	(2,6),0.84	(2,7),0.67	(2,8),0.67	(2,9),0.84
x_3	(3,0),0.84	(3,1),0.67	(3,2),0.67	(3,3),0.84	(3,4),0.84	(3,5),0.84	(3,6),0.84	(3,7),0.67	(3,8),0.67	(3,9),0.84
x_4	(4,0),1.00	(4,1),0.84	(4,2),0.84	(4,3),1.00	(4,4),1.00	(4,5),1.00	(4,6),1.00	(4,7),0.84	(4,8),0.84	(4,9),1.00
x_5	(5,0),1.00	(5,1),0.84	(5,2),0.84	(5,3),1.00	(5,4),1.00	(5,5),1.00	(5,6),1.00	(5,7),0.84	(5,8),0.84	(5,9),1.00
x_6	(6,0),0.84	(6,1),0.67	(6,2),0.67	(6,3),0.84	(6,4),0.84	(6,5),0.84	(6,6),0.84	(6,7),0.67	(6,8),0.67	(6,9),0.84
x_7	(7,0),0.84	(7,1),0.67	(7,2),0.67	(7,3),0.84	(7,4),0.84	(7,5),0.84	(7,6),0.84	(7,7),0.67	(7,8),0.67	(7,9),0.84
x_8	(8,0),1.00	(8,1),0.84	(8,2),0.84	(8,3),1.00	(8,4),1.00	(8,5),1.00	(8,6),1.00	(8,7),0.84	(8,8),0.84	(8,9),1.00
x_9	(9,0),1.00	(9,1),0.84	(9,2),0.84	(9,3),1.00	(9,4),1.00	(9,5),1.00	(9,6),1.00	(9,7),0.84	(9,8),0.84	(9,9),1.00

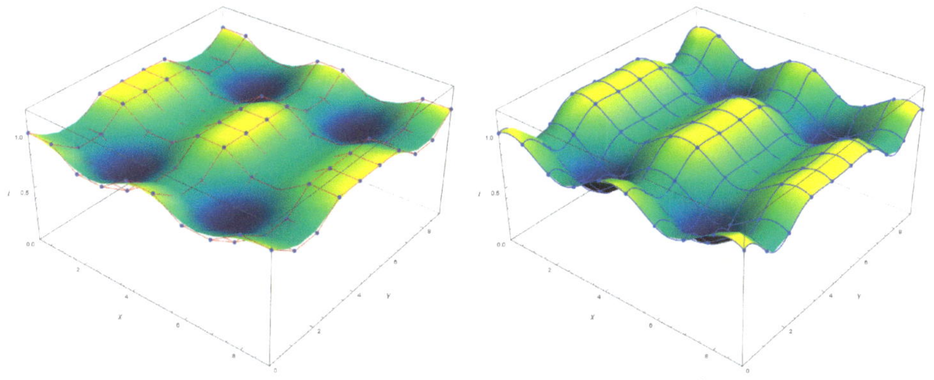

(a) (b)

Figure 13. Example of (**a**) fuzzy linguistic bicubic B-spline surface model and (**b**) fuzzy linguistic interpolation bicubic B-spline surface model.

Figure 13 show the final results of the fuzzy linguistic bicubic B-spline surface model from the numerical example of linguistic data that are generated through a linguistic command appearing on the fuzzy linguistic point relation introduced in this paper.

10. Conclusions

The main purpose of this study is to introduce a new model, namely, the fuzzy linguistic bicubic B-spline surface to model uncertain fuzzy linguistic data. This model is based on the fuzzy set theory approach and the B-spline in geometric modeling. Firstly, this study discusses a new approach to fuzzy linguistics by defining three types of fuzzy linguistic points: low L, medium M_i and high H. Then, based on these definitions, a new algorithm is developed. Finally, by using a random numerical example of linguistic data, a surface model of the B-spline is generated and can be used for analytical purposes for further studies.

This study only discusses in generalized form and shows the final results for the proposed model. Thus, more in-depth studies are needed with new definitions and theories to display the processes in more detail. Real data are required to apply this generalized model in order to produce the expected visualization and analyzation. The presented method shows that the model can be generated by directive linguistic terms and functions.

This model has limitations if the linguistic data used are fuzzy in nature, which leads to complexity. Therefore, advanced methods for the fuzzy set theory approach should be used to obtain more accurate results. The specific meaning of 'complex' in complex uncertain data is the uncertainty stack of two collected data point arguments. It is impossible to accurately model complex uncertain data using a suitable curve or surface such as a B-spline unless a new definition is formulated for a B-spline function with a complex uncertain meaning [59].

This study could also be extended to other spline models such as Bézier and NURBS (Non-Uniform Rational B-Spline), and also in future works, especially in the development of artificial intelligence (AI) technology for greater beneficial impact. The basic problem of computational linguistics is the modeling of basic linguistic processes such as language comprehension, production and learning. It includes the main problems of AI systems such as perception, communication, knowledge, planning, reasoning and learning. Each of these items has a linguistic function as discussed in this study. If this problem can be applied using the model introduced, it should be able to improve the weaknesses of the existing AI technology.

Author Contributions: Conceptualization, A.F.W. and M.S.B.; methodology, A.F.W., M.S.B. and M.I.E.Z.; formal analysis, M.S.B. and M.I.E.Z.; resources, M.S.B. and M.I.E.Z.; writing—original draft preparation, A.F.W. and M.S.B.; writing—review and editing, M.S.B., A.F.W. and M.I.E.Z.; visualization, M.S.B. and R.Z.; supervision, A.F.W. and M.I.E.Z.; funding acquisition, A.F.W. All authors have read and agreed to the published version of the manuscript.

Funding: This research was funded by the Ministry of Education Malaysia (MOE) grant number FRGS/1/2019/STG06/UMT/02/1.

Institutional Review Board Statement: Not applicable.

Informed Consent Statement: Not applicable.

Data Availability Statement: Not applicable.

Acknowledgments: The authors wish to thank the Ministry of Education Malaysia (MOE) as the sole funder and also the Centre for Research and Innovation Management (CRIM), Universiti Malaysia Terengganu (UMT) for providing facilities to conduct this study.

Conflicts of Interest: The authors declare no conflict of interest.

References

1. Husain, M.S.; Wahab, A.F.; Gobithaasan, R.U. Generalizations of fuzzy linguistic control points in geometric design. *AIP Conf. Proc.* **2014**, *1605*, 244.
2. Husain, M.S.; Wahab, A.F.; Gobithasaan, R.U. Fuzzy linguistic in geometric modeling. *Malays. J. Fundam. Appl. Sci.* **2015**, *11*, 36–41. [CrossRef]
3. Zadeh, L.A. Fuzzy sets. *Inf. Control* **1965**, *8*, 338–353. [CrossRef]
4. Zadeh, L.A. The concept of a linguistic variable and its application to approximate reasoning-I. *Inf. Sci.* **1975**, *8*, 199–249. [CrossRef]
5. Zadeh, L.A. The concept of a linguistic variable and its application to approximate reasoning-II. *Inf. Sci.* **1975**, *8*, 301–357. [CrossRef]
6. Zadeh, L.A. The concept of a linguistic variable and its application to approximate reasoning-III. *Inf. Sci.* **1975**, *9*, 43–80. [CrossRef]
7. McShane, M.; Nirenburg, S. *Linguistics for the Age of AI*; MIT Press: Cambridge, MA, USA, 2021.
8. Li, D.; Du, Y. *Artificial Intelligence with Uncertainty*; CRC Press: Boca Raton, FL, USA, 2017.
9. Zakaria, R. Pemodelan Interpolasi Splin-B Kabur Jenis-2 Teritlak Bagi Masalah Ketakpastian Kompleks. Ph.D. Thesis, Universiti Malaysia Terengganu, Terengganu, Malaysia, 2013.
10. Wahab, A.F.; Husain, M.S. A new types of spline modeling using fuzzy linguistic approach. *AIP Conf. Proc.* **2016**, *1750*, 020020.
11. Schoenberg, I.J. Contributions to the problem of approximation of equidistant data by analytic functions, Part B. On the problem of osculatory interpolation. A second class of analytic approximation formulae. *Q. Appl. Math.* **1946**, *4*, 112–141. [CrossRef]
12. De Boor, C. On calculating with B-splines. *J. Approx. Theory* **1972**, *6*, 50–62. [CrossRef]
13. Dempski, K. *Focus on Curves and Surfaces (Focus on Game Development)*; Course Technology Press: Boston, MA, USA, 2002.
14. Farin, G.E. *Curves and Surfaces for CAGD: A Practical Guide*; Morgan Kaufmann: Berkeley, CA, USA, 2002.
15. Salomon, D. *Curves and Surfaces for Computer Graphics*; Springer Science & Business Media: New York, NY, USA, 2007.
16. Piegl, L.; Tiller, W. *The NURBS Book*, 2nd ed.; Springer Science & Business Media: New York, NY, USA, 1997.
17. Wahab, A.F.; Ali, J.M.; Majid, A.A.; Tap, A.O.M. Fuzzy set in geometric modeling. In Proceedings of the International Conference on Computer Graphics, Imaging and Visualization, 2004 (CGIV 2004), Penang, Malaysia, 2 July 2004; pp. 227–232.
18. Wahab, A.F.; Ali, J.M.; Majid, A.A. Fuzzy geometric modeling. In Proceedings of the 2009 Sixth International Conference on Computer Graphics, Imaging and Visualization, Tianjin, China, 11–14 August 2009; pp. 276–280.
19. McWhorter, J.H. *Understanding Linguistic: The Science of Language*; The Teaching Company: Chantilly, VA, USA, 2008.
20. Kracht, M. *Introduction to Linguistics*; Hilgard Avenue: Los Angeles, LA, USA, 2007.
21. Aikhenvald, A. *Evidentiality: Problems and Challenges*; John Benjamins: Amsterdam, The Netherlands, 2004.
22. Maynard, S.K. *Linguistic Emotivity: Centrality of Place, the Topic-Comment Dynamic, and an Ideology of Pathos in Japanese Discourse*; John Benjamins Publishing: Amsterdam, The Netherlands, 2002; Volume 97.
23. Kövecses, Z. The "container" metaphor of anger in English, Chinese, Japanese and Hungarian. In *From a Metaphorical Point of View: A Multidisciplinary Approach to the Cognitive Content of Metaphor*; Walter de Gruyter: Berlin, Germany, 1995; pp. 117–145.
24. Kövecses, Z. Anger: Its language, conceptualization, and. *Lang. Cogn. Construal World* **1995**, *82*, 181.
25. Soriano, C. Some anger metaphors in Spanish and English. A contrastive review. *Int. J. Engl. Stud.* **2003**, *3*, 107–122.
26. King, B. *The Conceptual Structure of Emotional Experience in Chinese*; Lulu Press: Morrisville, NC, USA, 2005.
27. Matsuki, K. Metaphors of anger in Japanese. *Lang. Cogn. Construal World* **1995**, *82*, 137–151.
28. Bonissone, P.P. A fuzzy sets based linguistic approach: Theory and applications. In Proceedings of the 12th conference on Winter simulation, Orlando, FL, USA, 3–5 December 1980.

29. Delgado, M.; Verdegay, J.L.; Vila, M.A. On aggregation operations of linguistic labels. *Int. J. Intell. Syst.* **1993**, *8*, 351–370. [CrossRef]
30. Bordogna, G.; Pasi, G. A fuzzy linguistic approach generalizing Boolean Information Retrieval: A model and its evaluation. *J. Am. Soc. Inf. Sci.* **1993**, *44*, 70–82. [CrossRef]
31. Khoury, R.; Karray, F.; Sun, Y.; Kamel, M.; Basir, O. Semantic Understanding of General Linguistic Items by Means of Fuzzy Set Theory. *IEEE Trans. Fuzzy Syst.* **2007**, *15*, 757–771. [CrossRef]
32. Herrera, F.; Herrera-Viedma, E.; Martinez, L. A Fuzzy Linguistic Methodology to Deal With Unbalanced Linguistic Term Sets. *IEEE Trans. Fuzzy Syst.* **2008**, *16*, 354–370. [CrossRef]
33. Ma, L. Clarification on linguistic applications of fuzzy set theory to natural language analysis. In Proceedings of the 2011 Eighth International Conference on Fuzzy Systems and Knowledge Discovery (FSKD), Shanghai, China, 26–28 July 2011; pp. 811–815.
34. Ramos-Soto, A.; Pereira-Fariña, M. Reinterpreting interpretability for fuzzy linguistic descriptions of data. In Proceedings of the International Conference on Information Processing and Management of Uncertainty in Knowledge-Based Systems, Cádiz, Spain, 11–15 June 2018; Springer: Cham, Switzerland; pp. 40–51.
35. Tong, R.M.; Bonissone, P.P. A Linguistic Approach to Decisionmaking with Fuzzy Sets. *IEEE Trans. Syst. Man Cybern.* **1980**, *10*, 716–723. [CrossRef]
36. Herrera, F.; Martinez, L. An Approach for Combining Linguistic and Numerical Information Based on The 2-Tuple Fuzzy Linguistic Representation Model in Decision-Making. *Int. J. Uncertain. Fuzziness Knowl.-Based Syst.* **2000**, *8*, 539–562. [CrossRef]
37. Rodriguez, R.M.; Martinez, L.; Herrera, F. Hesitant Fuzzy Linguistic Term Sets for Decision Making. *IEEE Trans. Fuzzy Syst.* **2011**, *20*, 109–119. [CrossRef]
38. Rodríguez, R.M.; Martínez, L.; Herrera, F. A group decision making model dealing with comparative linguistic expressions based on hesitant fuzzy linguistic term sets. *Inf. Sci.* **2013**, *241*, 28–42. [CrossRef]
39. Wang, J.-Q.; Wu, J.-T.; Wang, J.; Zhang, H.-Y.; Chen, X.-H. Interval-valued hesitant fuzzy linguistic sets and their applications in multi-criteria decision-making problems. *Inf. Sci.* **2014**, *288*, 55–72. [CrossRef]
40. Nguyen, H.-T.; Dawal, S.Z.; Nukman, Y.; Aoyama, H.; Case, K. An Integrated Approach of Fuzzy Linguistic Preference Based AHP and Fuzzy COPRAS for Machine Tool Evaluation. *PLoS ONE* **2015**, *10*, e0133599. [CrossRef] [PubMed]
41. Jacas, J.; Monreal, A.; Recasens, J. A model for CAGD using fuzzy logic. *Int. J. Approx. Reason.* **1997**, *16*, 289–308. [CrossRef]
42. Jacas, J.; Monreal, A.; Recasens, J. Similarity Based Fuzzy Interpolation Applied to CAGD. In Proceedings of the IFSA-EUSFLAT 2009 Conference, Lisbon, Portugal, 20–24 July 2009; pp. 1696–1701.
43. Gallo, G.; Spagnuolo, M. Uncertainty coding and controlled data reduction using fuzzy-B-splines. In Proceedings of the Computer Graphics International 1998 Proceedings, Hannover, Germany, 26 June 1998; pp. 536–542.
44. Gallo, G.; Spagnuolo, M.; Spinello, S. Fuzzy B-splines: A surface model encapsulating uncertainty. *Graph. Models* **2000**, *62*, 40–55. [CrossRef]
45. Anile, A.; Falcidieno, B.; Gallo, G.; Spagnuolo, M.; Spinello, S. Modeling undertain data with fuzzy B-splines. *Fuzzy Sets Syst.* **2000**, *113*, 397–410. [CrossRef]
46. Wahab, A.F.; Ali, J.M. Penyelesaian Masalah Data Ketakpastian Menggunakan Splin-B Kabur. *Sains Malays.* **2010**, *39*, 661–670.
47. Zakaria, R.; Wahab, A.F.; Gobithaasan, U.R. Fuzzy B-Spline surface modeling. *J. Appl. Math.* **2014**, *2014*, 285045. [CrossRef]
48. Zakaria, R.; Wahab, A.F. Fuzzy B-spline modeling of uncertainty data. *Appl. Math. Sci.* **2012**, *6*, 6971–6991.
49. Zakaria, R.; Wahab, A.F. Pemodelan Titik Data Kabur Teritlak. *Sains Malays.* **2014**, *43*, 799–805.
50. Karim, N.A.A.; Wahab, A.F.; Gobithaasan, R.U.; Zakaria, R. Model of fuzzy B-spline interpolation for fuzzy data. *Far East J. Math. Sci.* **2013**, *72*, 269–280.
51. Bakar, N.A.; Yusoff, B.; Wahab, A.F.; Mamat, M. Modeling Fuzzy B-spline Interpolation Series using α-cut operation for spatial earth surface problem. *J. Phys. Conf. Ser.* **2021**, *1988*, 012011. [CrossRef]
52. Zulkifly, M.I.E.; Wahab, A.F. Intuitionistic fuzzy bicubic Bézier surface approximation. *AIP Conf. Proc.* **2018**, *1974*, 020064.
53. Zulkifly, M.I.E.; Wahab, A.F. 3-Tuple Bézier Surface Interpolation Model for Data Visualization. *IAENG Int. J. Appl. Math.* **2020**, *50*, 1–7.
54. Zulkifly, M.I.E.; Wahab, A.F.; Zakaria, R. B-Spline curve interpolation model by using intuitionistic fuzzy approach. *IAENG Int. J. Appl. Math.* **2020**, *50*, 6.
55. Zulkifly, M.I.E.; Wahab, A.F.; Bidin, M.S.; Embong, A.F.; Hoe, Y.S. Intuitionistic fuzzy piecewise Bézier curve modeling with C1 and G1 continuities for complex data. *Adv. Differ. Equ. Control. Process.* **2020**, *23*, 251–260. [CrossRef]
56. Shah, M.M.; Wahab, A.F. Fuzzy topological digital space and their properties of flat electroencephalography in epilepsy disease. *J. Phys. Conf. Ser.* **2017**, *890*, 12114. [CrossRef]
57. Shah, M.M.; Wahab, A.F.; Zulkifly, M.I.E. Fuzzy Cubic Bézier Curve Approximation in Fuzzy Topological Digital Space. *Malays. J. Math. Sci.* **2019**, *13*, 123–137.
58. Zakaria, R.; Wahab, A.F.; Gobithaasan, R.U. The Representative Curve of Type-2 Fuzzy Data Point Modeling. *Mod. Appl. Sci.* **2013**, *7*, 60. [CrossRef]
59. Zakaria, R.; Wahab, A.F.; Ismail, I.; Zulkifly, M.I.E. Complex uncertainty of surface data modeling via the type-2 fuzzy B-spline model. *Mathematics* **2021**, *9*, 1054. [CrossRef]
60. Wahab, A.F.; Yong, L.K.; Zulkifly, M.I.E. Type-2 Fuzzy Non-uniform Rational B-spline Model with Type-2 Fuzzy Data. *Malays. J. Math. Sci.* **2017**, *11*, 35–46.

61. Adesah, R.S.; Zakaria, R.; Wahab, A.F.; Talibe, A. Type-2 fuzzy curve model. *J. Phys. Conf. Ser.* **2017**, *890*, 012088. [CrossRef]
62. Bidin, M.S.; Wahab, A.F.; Zulkifly, M.I.E.; Zakaria, R. Generalized Fuzzy Linguistic Cubic B-Spline Curve Model for Uncertainty Fuzzy Linguistic Data. *Adv. Appl. Discret. Math.* **2020**, *25*, 285–302. [CrossRef]
63. Atanassov, K.T. Intuitionistic fuzzy sets. *Fuzzy Sets Syst.* **1986**, *20*, 87–96. [CrossRef]

symmetry

MDPI

Article

Prime Cordial Labeling of Generalized Petersen Graph under Some Graph Operations

Weidong Zhao [1,†], Muhammad Naeem [2,*,†] and Irfan Ahmad [2,†]

1 School of Computer Science, Chengdu University, Chengdu 610100, China; zwdbox@cdu.edu.cn
2 Department of Mathematics and Statistics, Institute of Southern Punjab, Multan 59300, Pakistan; irfanch784@gmail.com
* Correspondence: muhammadnaeem@isp.edu.pk or naeempkn@gmail.com
† These authors contributed equally to this work.

Abstract: A graph is a connection of objects. These objects are often known as vertices or nodes and the connection or relation in these nodes are called arcs or edges. There are certain rules to allocate values to these vertices and edges. This allocation of values to vertices or edges is called graph labeling. Labeling is prime cordial if vertices have allocated values from 1 to the order of graph and edges have allocated values 0 or 1 on a certain pattern. That is, an edge has an allocated value of 0 if the incident vertices have a greatest common divisor (gcd) greater than 1. An edge has an allocated value of 1 if the incident vertices have a greatest common divisor equal to 1. The number of edges labeled with 0 or 1 are equal in numbers or, at most, have a difference of 1. In this paper, our aim is to investigate the prime cordial labeling of rotationally symmetric graphs obtained from a generalized Petersen graph $P(n,k)$ under duplication operation, and we have proved that the resulting symmetric graphs are prime cordial. Moreover, we have also proved that when we glow a Petersen graph with some path graphs, then again, the resulting graph is a prime cordial graph.

Keywords: prime cordial labeling; duplication operations; glowing of graph; generalized Petersen graph

Citation: Zhao, W.; Naeem, M.; Ahmad, I. Prime Cordial Labeling of Generalized Petersen Graph under Some Graph Operations. *Symmetry* **2022**, *14*, 732. https://doi.org/10.3390/sym14040732

Academic Editor: Palle E.T. Jorgensen

Received: 19 February 2022
Accepted: 30 March 2022
Published: 3 April 2022

1. Introduction

Graph theory started with a solution for the Königsberg bridges problem in the 18th century by Leonhard Euler. In the beginning, it was considered a recreational subject. It took almost two centuries for its development as a mathematical subject, graph theory. Graph labelings started in the 19th century, when Arthur Cayley, the renouned British mathematician, showed that there are n^{n-2} different labeled trees of order n [1]. This subject attracted the attention of researchers in the previous century. Many conferences were organized for graph theory in 1950–1960. These conferences concluded that graph theory is an easy way for understanding mathematics, which attracts the interest of young students. These conferences were known as "Symposium on the Theory of Graphs and Its Applications", held in Smolenice (Czechoslovakia) in 1963 [2]. Graph theory conferences were held regularly in the 1970s. One member of the Rome conference was Alexander Rosa; a paper was presented by him [3]. This paper brought revolution in graph labeling. Four vertex labelings were mentioned by Rosa, described as α-valuations, β-valuations, σ-valuations and ρ-valuations. The β-valuation became graceful labeling in 1972 [4]. The main aim of graceful labeling was to minimize the values assigned to terminals. The number theory has an impact on graph labelings [5]. For many years, a lot of graph labelings have been introduced, which have an impact on many problems for their solution. The labeled graphs are working excellently in many mathematical models. For instance, radar codes and cyber security [6]. Prime cordial labeling is the assignment of values to vertices from 1 to order of graph and edge labeling induced from it where 0 and 1 valued to edges with respect to the greatest common divisor (gcd) of incident vertices. That is, incident vertices have a common divisor greater than 1 labeled with 0 and incident vertices have a common divisor equal to 1 labeled with 1. It was introduced by Sundaram et al. [7] and, in the same paper, they investigated several results on prime cordial. In this paper, we will investigate the generalized Petersen graph $P(n,k)$ under duplication operation and glowing of P_3 with $P(n,k)$ is prime cordial. All the graphs in this article are simple connected graphs and the notions and symbols are the same as those used by I. Ahmad in [8].

Definition 1. *Let $P_e(n,k)$ be a graph obtained by attaching a vertex to each edge of outer cycle of $P(n,k)$. Then, $P_e(n,k)$ has 3n vertices with vertex set $V(P_e(n,k)) = \{x_i, y_i, z_i : 0 \leqslant i \leqslant n-1\}$ and 5n edges has edge set $E(P_e(n,k)) = \{x_i x_{i+k}, x_i y_i, y_i y_{i+1}, y_i z_i, y_{i+1} z_i : 0 \leqslant i \leqslant n-1\}$. In Figure 1, we have depicted vertices and edges of this graph.*

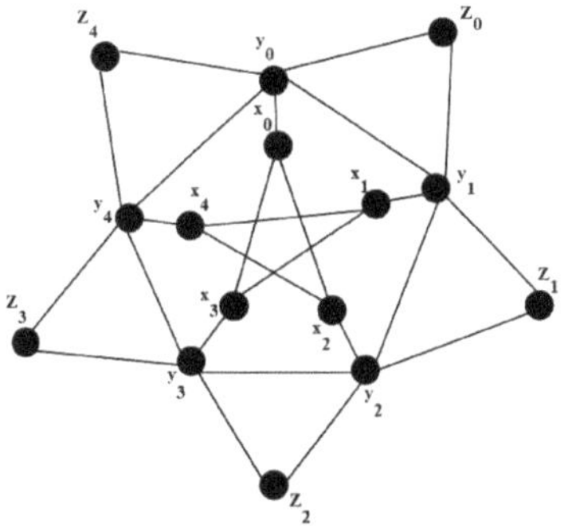

Figure 1. $P_e(5,k)$; duplication of edges by vertices.

Definition 2. *Let $P_v(n,k)_o$ be a graph obtained by duplicating outer cycle vertices $P(n,k)$ by an edge. Then, $P_v(n,k)_o$ has 4n vertices with vertex set $V(P_v(n,k)_o) = \{x_i, y_i : 0 \leqslant i \leqslant n-1$ and $z_i : 0 \leqslant i \leqslant 2n-1\}$ and 6n edges with edge set;*

$E(P_v(n,k)_o) = \{x_i x_{i+k}, x_i y_i, y_i y_{i+1}, y_i z_i, z_i z_{i+1}, y_i z_{i+1} : 0 \leqslant i \leqslant n-1\}$. *As shown in Figure 2.*

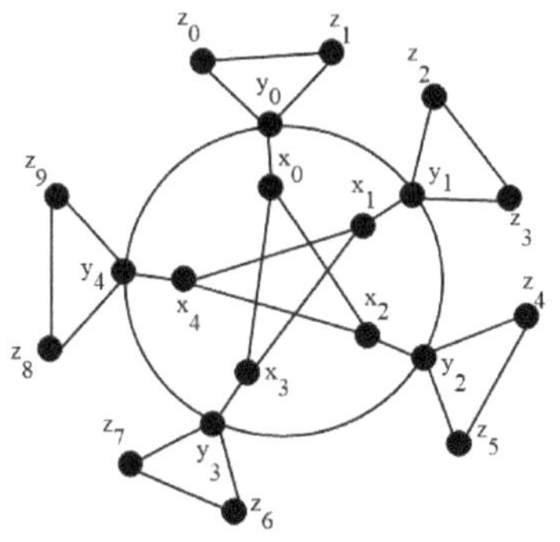

Figure 2. $P_v(5,k)_o$; outer cycle vertex duplication by an edge.

Definition 3. *Let $P_v(n,k)_i$ be a graph obtained by edge duplication of all the vertices on the inner cycle of $P(n,k)$, that is, the duplication of vertices such as x_i's of Figure 2 in $P(n,k)$. Then, the graph $P_v(n,k)_i$ has 4n vertices and 6n edges, having vertex set $V(P_v(n,k)_i) = \{x_i, z_i : 0 \leqslant i \leqslant n-1$ and $y_i : 0 \leqslant i \leqslant 2n-1\}$ and 6n edges with edge set;*

$E(P_v(n,k)_i) = \{x_i x_{i+k}, x_i y_i, x_i y_{i+1}, y_i y_{i+1}, x_i z_i, z_i z_{i+1}, : 0 \leqslant i \leqslant n-1, where\, 1 \leq k \leq \lfloor \frac{n}{2} \rfloor\}$. *As shown in Figure 3.*

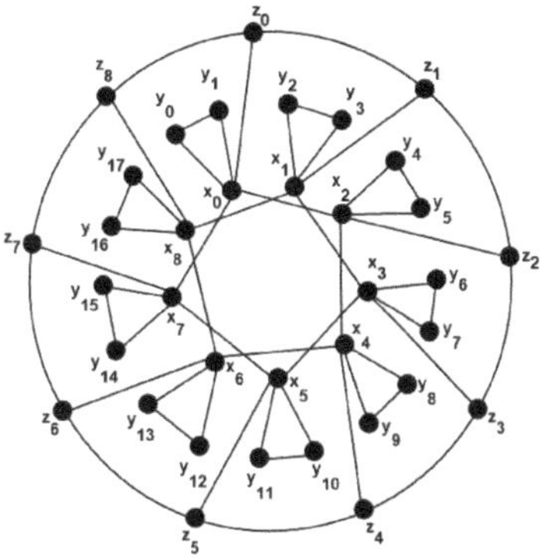

Figure 3. $P_v(9,2)_i$; inner vertex duplication by an edge.

Definition 4. *There is path graph* P_3 *and a generalized Petersen graph* $P(n,k)$*. In glowing operation, there is a subgraph denoted as* $(P_3, P(n,k))_{ev}$*. This graph has* $4n$ *vertices and* $5n$ *edges. These are* $V((P_3, P(n,k))_{ev}) = \{u_i, x_i, y_i, z_i; 0 \leq i \leq n-1\}$ *and* $E((P_3, P(n,k))_{ev}) = \{u_i u_{i+k}, u_i x_i, x_i x_{i+1}, x_i y_i, y_i z_i; 0 \leq i \leq n-1\}$*. Represented in Figure 4.*

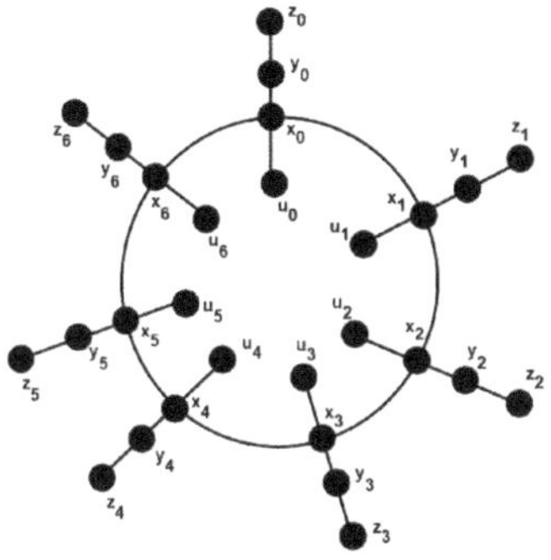

Figure 4. $(P_3, P(n,k))_{ev}$; end vertex glowing of P_3 with $P(n,k)$.

Definition 5. *Let* $(P_3, P(n,k))_{mv}$ *be a glowing of n copies of* P_3 *at its middle vertex common with* $P(n,k)$ *outer cycle. Glowing graph has* $4n$ *vertices and* $5n$ *edges. These are* $V((P_3, P(n,k))_{mv}) = \{x_i, y_i\,;\, 0 \leq i \leq n-1 \text{ and } z_i\,;\, 0 \leq i \leq 2n-1\}$ *and* $E((P_3, P(n,k))_{mv}) = \{x_i x_{i+k}, x_i y_i, y_i y_{i+1}, y_i z_i, y_i z_{i+1}; 0 \leq i \leq n-1\}$ *depicted in Figure 5.*

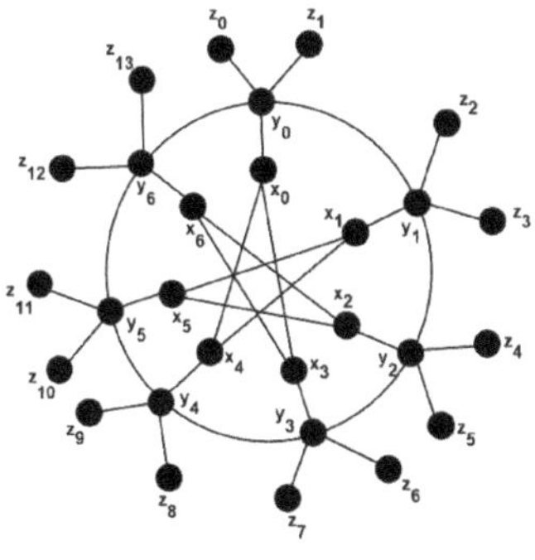

Figure 5. $(P_3, P(7,2))_{mv}$; middle vertex glowing of P_3 with $P(7,2)$.

Definition 6. *Let $V(P_v(n,k)_p$ be graph obtained by duplication of vertices by n pendant vertices in $P(n,k)$ outer cycle. There are $3n$ vertices and $4n$ edges with edge set $E(P_v(n,k)_p)$ shown in Figure 6,*

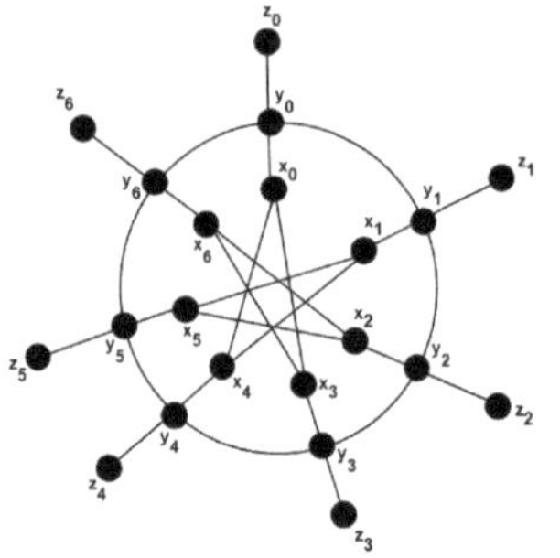

Figure 6. $P_v(7,3)_p$; Outer cycle vertices duplication by pendant vertices.

2. Main Results

In this section, we shall present the main results of the article.

Theorem 1. *The graph $P_e(n,k)$ is prime cordial for all $n \geqslant 3$ and $1 \leq k \leqslant \lfloor \frac{n}{2} \rfloor$.*

Proof. Let us assume $P(n,k)$ *where* $n \geqslant 3$ *and* $1 \leq k \leqslant \lfloor \frac{n}{2} \rfloor$ be generalized Petersen graph. On each outer edge, one vertex is added in such a way that duplicates edges in the outer cycle of the existing graph. There are $3n$ vertices and $5n$ edges having the vertex set $V(P_e(n,k)) = \{x_i, y_i, z_i : 0 \leqslant i \leqslant n-1\}$ and edge set $E(P_e(n,k)) = \{x_i x_{i+k}, x_i y_i, y_i y_{i+1}, y_i z_i, y_{i+1} z_i : 0 \leqslant i \leqslant n-1\}$. As we knew, in prime cordial labeling, we assign values to edges on the basis of the greatest common divisor of the incident vertices. In prime cordial labeling, assignment of values to vertices is a bijective function. Therefore, the values assigned to vertices are;

$$f(x_i) = \{3(i+1) \quad : 0 \leqslant i \leqslant n-1\}$$

$$f(y_i) = \begin{cases} 2+3i & : 0 \leqslant i \leqslant n-1 \text{ where } i \text{ is even;} \\ 4+3(i-1) & : 1 \leqslant i \leqslant n-1 \text{ where } i \text{ is odd.} \end{cases}$$

$$f(z_i) = \begin{cases} 1+3i & : 0 \leqslant i \leqslant n-1 \text{ where } i \text{ is even;} \\ 5+3(i-1) & : 1 \leqslant i \leqslant n-1 \text{ where } i \text{ is odd.} \end{cases}$$

There are five types of edges, incident to these vertices. The edge set of $P_e(n,k)$ is divided into five subsets that are mentioned below;

$$\begin{aligned} E_1 &= \{x_i x_{i+k} : 0 \leqslant i \leqslant n-1\}, \\ E_2 &= \{x_i y_i : 0 \leqslant i \leqslant n-1\}, \\ E_3 &= \{y_i y_{i+1} : 0 \leqslant i \leqslant n-1\}, \\ E_4 &= \{y_i z_i : 0 \leqslant i \leqslant n-1\}, \\ E_5 &= \{y_{i+1} z_i : 0 \leqslant i \leqslant n-1\}. \end{aligned}$$

In E_1 edge set, $gcd(f(x_i), f(x_{i+k})) > 1$. Therefore, n edges are labeled with 0.

There are two cases for labeling edge set E_2;

Case-I: For even n, there are $\frac{n}{2}$ edges incident vertices has $gcd(f(x_i), f(y_i)) > 1$. Therefore, labeled with 0 and $\frac{n}{2}$ edges incident vertices has $gcd(f(x_i), f(y_i)) = 1$. Therefore, labeled with 1.

Case-II: For odd n, there are $\frac{n-1}{2}$ edges incident vertices has $gcd(f(x_i), f(y_i)) > 1$, are labeled with 0 and $\frac{n+1}{2}$ edges incident vertices has $gcd(f(x_i), f(y_i)) > 1$ are labeled with 1.

In edge set E_3, n edges incident vertices has $gcd(f(y_i), f_(y_{i+1})) > 1$. Therefore, labeled with 0.

In edge set E_4, n edges incident vertices has $gcd(f(y_i), f(z_i)) = 1$. Therefore, labeled with 1.

In edge set E_5, n edges incident vertices has $gcd(f(y_{i+1}, f(z_i)) = 1$. Therefore, labeled with 1.

When n is even, there are $\frac{5n}{2}$ edges labeled with 0 and 1. In Figure 7, number of 0 and 1 are equal.

When n is odd, there are $\frac{5n-1}{2}$ edges valued 0 and $\frac{5n+1}{2}$ edges valued 1 , as shown in Figure 8.

Edges valued 0 and 1 are equal or supremum difference 1. Hence, the graph $P_e(n,k)$, and Petersen graph edges duplication is prime cordial. □

Example 1. *The graph $P_e(12,k)$ is prime cordial for $1 \le k \leqslant \lfloor \frac{n}{2} \rfloor$.*

In Figure 7, there are 36 vertices and 60 edges. Dark lines indicate that edges are labeled with 1 and dotted lines indicate that edges are labeled with 0. Here, 30 edges are valued 0 and 1, respectively. Therefore, it is prime cordial.

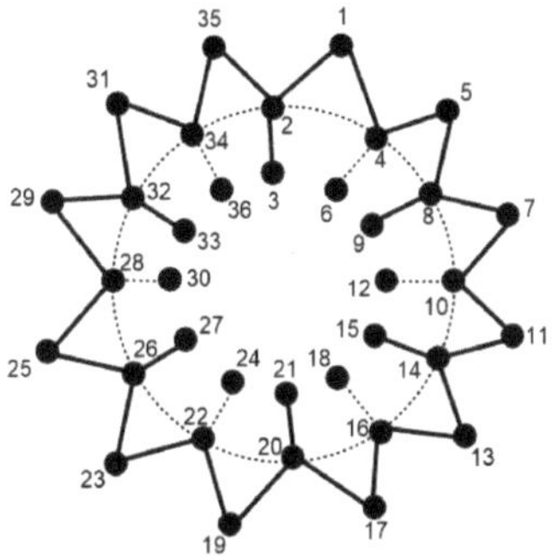

Figure 7. $P_e(12,k)$; duplication of edges by n vertices.

Example 2. *The graph $P_e(13,k)$ is prime cordial where $1 \le k \leqslant \lfloor \frac{n}{2} \rfloor$.*

In Figure 8, there are 39 vertices with 65 edges. Dark lines indicate that edges are labeled with 1 and dotted lines indicate that edges are labeled with 0. Here are 33 edges valued 1 and 32 edges valued 0. This $P_e(13,k)$ has supremum difference 1 in edge labeling. Therefore, it is prime cordial.

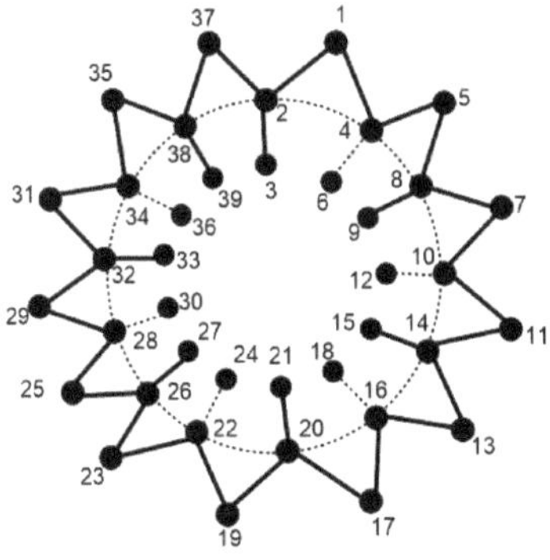

Figure 8. $P_e(13,k)$; duplication of edges by n vertices.

Theorem 2. *The graph $P_v(n,k)_o$ is prime cordial for all $n \geqslant 3$ and $1 \leq k \leqslant \lfloor \frac{n}{2} \rfloor$.*

Proof. Let us assume that $P(n,k)$ has n edges attached to each outer cycle vertex. Therefore, outer cycle vertices have duplication. There are $4n$ vertices with vertex set $V(P_v(n,k)_o) = \{x_i, y_i : 0 \leqslant i \leqslant n-1 \; and \; z_i : 0 \leqslant i \leqslant 2n-1\}$ and these vertices are labeled as

$$
\begin{aligned}
f(x_i) &= 4(i+1) : 0 \leqslant i \leqslant n-1; \\
f(y_i) &= 4i+2 : 0 \leqslant i \leqslant n-1; \\
f(z_i) &= 2i+1 : 0 \leqslant i \leqslant 2n-1.
\end{aligned}
$$

There are $6n$ edges, $E(P_v(n,k)_o) = \{x_i x_{i+k}, x_i y_i, y_i y_{i+1}, y_i z_i, z_i z_{i+1}, y_i z_{i+1} : 0 \leqslant i \leqslant n-1\}$.

These edges are further described as;

$$
\begin{aligned}
E_1 &= \{x_i x_{i+k} : 0 \leqslant i \leqslant n-1\}, \\
E_2 &= \{x_i y_i : 0 \leqslant i \leqslant n-1\}, \\
E_3 &= \{y_i y_{i+1} : 0 \leqslant i \leqslant n-1\}, \\
E_4 &= \{y_i z_i : 0 \leqslant i \leqslant n-1\}, \\
E_5 &= \{z_i z_{i+1} : 0 \leqslant i \leqslant n-1\}, \\
E_6 &= \{y_i z_{i+1} : 0 \leqslant i \leqslant n-1\}.
\end{aligned}
$$

In the E_1 edge set, there is $gcd(f(x_i), f(x_{i+k})) > 1$; therefore, n edges are labeled with 0. In the E_2 edge set, there is $gcd(f(x_i), f(y_i)) > 1$; therefore, n edges are labeled with 0. In the E_3 edge set, there is $gcd(f(y_i), f(y_{i+1})) > 1$; therefore, n edges are labeled with 0. In the E_4 edge set, there is $gcd(f(y_i), f(z_i)) = 1$; therefore, n edges are labeled with 1. In the E_5 edge set, there is $gcd(f(z_i), f(z_{i+1})) = 1$; therefore, n edges are labeled with 1. In the E_6 edge set, there is $gcd(f(y_i), f(z_{i+1})) = 1$; therefore, n edges are labeled with 1. Hence, $3n$ edges are valued 0 and 1 as depicted in Figures 9 and 10; thus, $P_v(n,k)_o$ is prime cordial. □

Example 3. *Figure 9 represents the prime cordial labeling of $P_v(12,k)_o$. The graph $P_v(12,k)_o$ has 48 vertices and 72 edges. Dark lines indicate that edges are labeled with 1 and dotted lines indicate that edges are labeled with 0. Here are 36 edges labeled with 1 and 36 edges labeled with 0. Hence, it is prime cordial.*

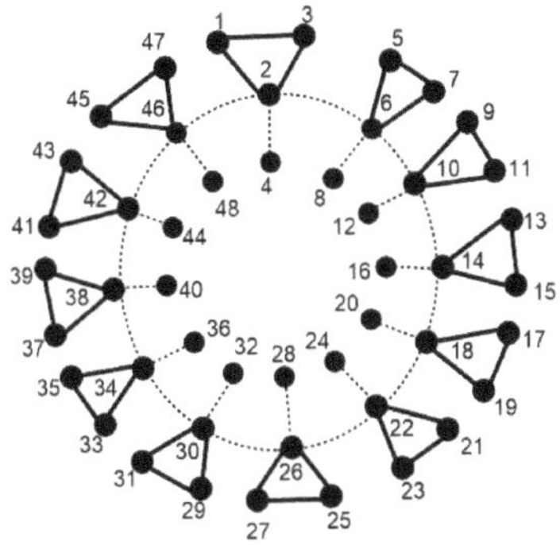

Figure 9. $P_v(12,k)_o$; duplication of outer cycle vertices by 12 edges is prime cordial.

Example 4. *Figure 10 represents the prime cordial labeling of* $P_v(13,k)_o$. *The graph* $P_v(13,k)_o$ *has 52 vertices and 78 edges. Dark lines indicate that edges are labeled with 1 and dotted lines indicate that edges are labeled with 0. Here are 39 edges labeled with 1 and 39 edges labeled with 0. Hence, it is prime cordial.*

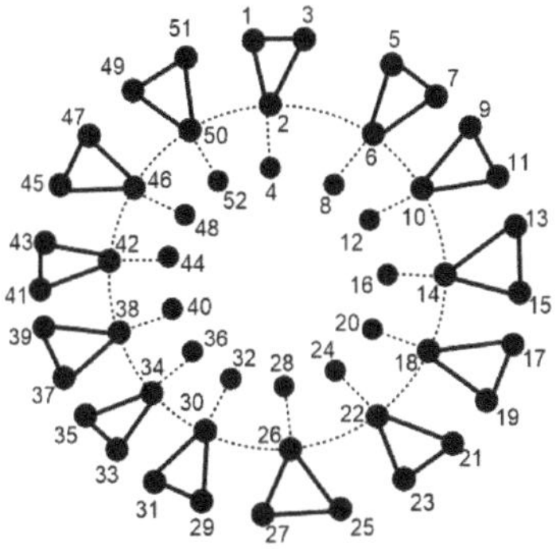

Figure 10. $P_v(13,k)_o$; duplication of outer cycle vertices is prime cordial.

Theorem 3. *The graph* $P_v(n,k)_i$ *is prime cordial for all* $n \geqslant 3$ *and* $1 \leq k \leqslant \lfloor \frac{n}{2} \rfloor$.

Proof. Let us assume $n - edges$ attached to generalized Petersen graph $P(n,k)$ inner cycle vertices. This graph is denoted as $P_v(n,k)_i$. This graph $P_v(n,k)_i$ has $4n$ vertices, $V(P_v(n,k)_i) = \{x_i, z_i : 0 \leqslant i \leqslant n-1 \; and \; y_i : 0 \leqslant i \leqslant 2n-1\}$ are labeled as;

$$\begin{aligned} f(x_i) &= \{4i+2 \quad : 0 \leqslant i \leqslant n-1\}; \\ f(y_i) &= \{2i+1 \quad : 0 \leqslant i \leqslant 2n-1\}; \\ f(z_i) &= \{4(i+1) \quad : 0 \leqslant i \leqslant n-1\}. \end{aligned}$$

The edges are $6n$, $E(P_v(n,k)_i) = \{x_i x_{i+k}, x_i y_i, x_i y_{i+1}, y_i y_{i+1}, x_i z_i, z_i z_{i+1}; 0 \leqslant i \leqslant n-1$ $and \; 1 \leq k \leqslant \lfloor \frac{n}{2} \rfloor\}$.

These edges are further described as;

$$
\begin{aligned}
E_1 &= \{x_i x_{i+k} \quad : 0 \leqslant i \leqslant n-1\}, \\
E_2 &= \{x_i y_i \quad : 0 \leqslant i \leqslant n-1\}, \\
E_3 &= \{x_i y_{i+1} \quad : 0 \leqslant i \leqslant n-1\}, \\
E_4 &= \{y_i y_{i+1} \quad : 0 \leqslant i \leqslant n-1\}, \\
E_5 &= \{x_i z_i \quad : 0 \leqslant i \leqslant n-1\}, \\
E_6 &= \{z_i z_{i+1} : 0 \leqslant i \leqslant n-1\}.
\end{aligned}
$$

In the E_1 edge set, we have $gcd(f(x_i), f(x_{i+k})) > 1$; therefore, n edges are labeled with 0. In the E_2 edge set, we have $gcd(f(x_i), f(y_i)) = 1$; therefore, n edges are labeled with 1. In the E_3 edge set, we have $gcd(f(x_i), f(y_i)) = 1$; therefore, n edges are labeled with 1. In the E_4 edge set, we have $gcd(f(y_i), f(y_{i+1})) = 1$; therefore, n edges are labeled with 1. In the E_5 edge set, we have $gcd(f(x_i), f(z_i)) > 1$; therefore, n edges are labeled with 0. In the E_6 edge set, we have $gcd(f(z_i), f(z_{i+1})) > 1$; therefore, n edges are labeled with 0. Hence, there are $3n$ edges labeled with 0 and 1, respectively, as shown in Figures 11 and 12; thus, $P_v(n,k)_i$ is prime cordial. □

Example 5. *The graph $P_v(8,k)_i$ is prime cordial for $1 \leq k \leqslant \lfloor \frac{n}{2} \rfloor$. The graph in Figure 11 has 32 vertices and 48 edges. Dark lines indicate that edges are labeled with 1 and dotted lines indicate that edges are labeled with 0. Here are 24 edges labeled with 1 and 24 edges labeled with 0. Hence, this is a prime cordial.*

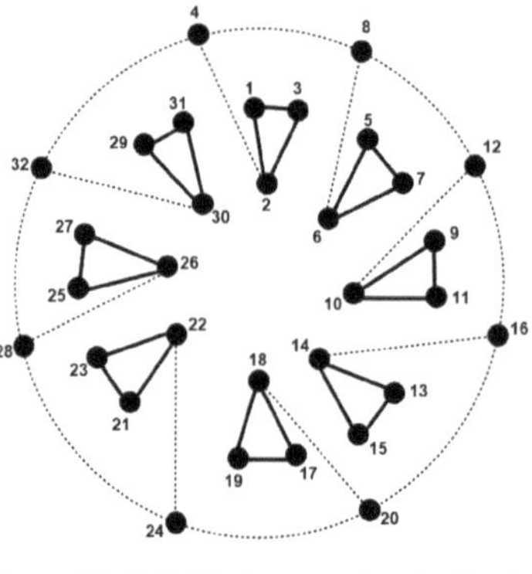

Figure 11. $P_v(8,k)_i$; inner vertex duplication by an edge.

Example 6. *The graph $P_v(9,k)_i$ is prime cordial for $1 \leq k \leqslant \lfloor \frac{n}{2} \rfloor$. The graph represented in Figure 12 has 36 vertices and 54 edges. Dark lines indicate edges are labeled with 1 and dotted lines indicate that edges are labeled with 0. Here are 27 edges labeled with 1 and 0, respectively. Hence, $P_v(9,k)_i$ is a prime cordial.*

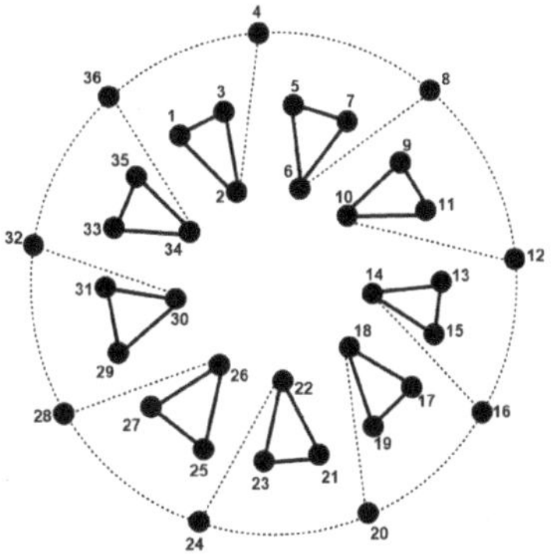

Figure 12. $P_v(9,k)_i$; inner vertex duplication by an edge.

Theorem 4. *The graph* $(P_3, P(n,k))_{ev}$ *is prime cordial for all* $n \geq 3$ *and* $1 \leq k \leq \lfloor \frac{n}{2} \rfloor$.

Proof. Let P_3 and $P(n,k)$ be two graphs. End vertex glowing of n copies of P_3 with outer cycle of $P(n,k)$, denoted as $(P_3, P(n,k))_{ev}$. The end vertex glowing graph $(P_3, P(n,k))_{ev}$ has $4n$ vertices and $5n$ edges. The vertices are $\{u_i, x_i, y_i, z_i; 0 \leq i \leq n-1\}$. The edges are,

$$
\begin{aligned}
E_1 &= \{u_i u_{i+k}\,;\ 0 \leq i \leq n-1 \; and \; 1 \leq k \leqslant \lfloor \frac{n}{2} \rfloor\}, \\
E_2 &= \{u_i x_i\,;\ 0 \leq i \leq n-1\}, \\
E_3 &= \{x_i x_{i+1}\,;\ 0 \leq i \leq n-1\}, \\
E_4 &= \{x_i y_i\,;\ 0 \leq i \leq n-1\}, \\
E_5 &= \{y_i z_i\,;\ 0 \leq i \leq n-1\}.
\end{aligned}
$$

Because we knew that values assignment to vertices is a bijective function. Therefore, we have,

<u>For all n greater or equal to 3</u>

$$f(u_i) = \{4(i+1)\,;\ 0 \leq i \leq n-1\}$$

Now, we will have different cases for assignment of values to the vertices x_i, y_i and z_i.

Case 1: for $n = 3$

$f(x_0) = 3, f(x_1) = 6, f(x_2) = 9$
$f(y_0) = 1, f(y_1) = 5, f(y_2) = 10$
$f(z_0) = 2, f(z_1) = 7, f(z_2) = 11$

Edge labeling is induced from vertex labeling; therefore, valuation of edges differs by 1. Depicted in Figure 13, dark lines indicate that edges are labeled with 1 and dotted lines indicate that edges are labeled with 0. Hence, it is prime cordial.

Case 2: for $n = 4$

$f(x_0) = 3, f(x_1) = 6, f(x_2) = 9, f(x_3) = 15$
$f(y_0) = 1, f(y_1) = 5, f(y_2) = 10, f(y_3) = 13$
$f(z_0) = 2, f(z_1) = 7, f(z_2) = 11, f(z_3) = 14$

Edge labeling is induced function; therefore, edges are equally labeled with 0 and 1. In Figure 13, dark lines indicate that edge is labeled with 1 and dotted line indicates that edge is labeled with 0. Hence, $(P_3, P(4,k))_{ev}$, $\forall\, 1 \leq k \leq \lfloor \frac{n}{2} \rfloor$ is prime cordial.

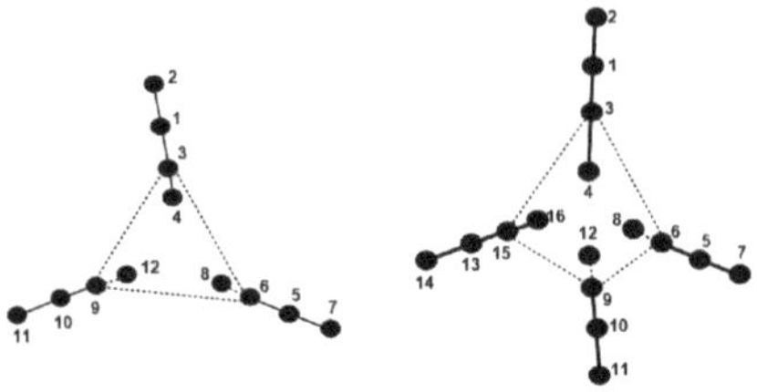

Figure 13. End vertex glowing of P_3 with $P(3,k)$ and $P(4,k)$ is prime cordial.

Case 3: for $n \equiv 0\ (mod\ 12)$

$$f(x_i) = \begin{cases} 2 & : i = 0; \\ 4i+3 & : 1 \leqslant i \leqslant \frac{n}{4}; \\ 4i+2 & : \frac{n}{4} < i \leq n-1. \end{cases}$$

$$f(y_i) = \{\ 4i+1 \quad : 0 \leq i \leq n-1.$$

$$f(z_i) = \begin{cases} 3 & : i = 0; \\ 4i+2 & : 1 \leqslant i \leqslant \frac{n}{4}; \\ 4i+3 & : \frac{n}{4} < i \leq n-1. \end{cases}$$

Edge labeling is induced function; therefore, $\frac{5n}{2}$ edges are equally valued 0 and 1. That is clear from Figure 14, where dark lines indicate that edges are labeled with 1 and dotted line indicate that edges are labeled with 0. This graph is prime cordial.

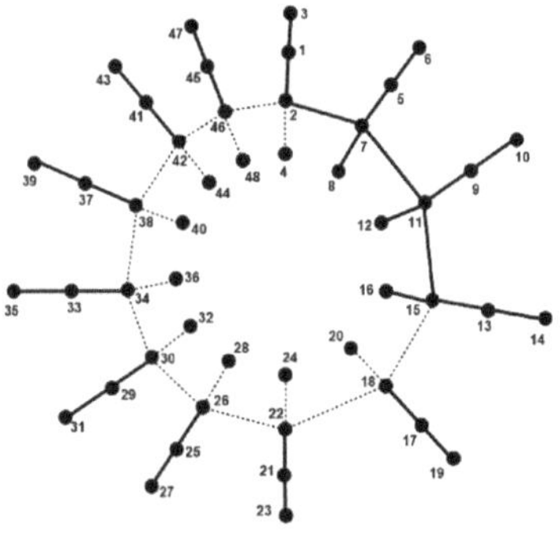

Figure 14. $(P_3, P(12,k))_{ev}$; end vertex glowing of P_3 with $P(12,k)$.

Case 4: for $n \equiv 4\ (mod\ 12)$

$$f(x_i) = \begin{cases} 1 & : i = 0; \\ 4i+3 & : 1 \leqslant i \leqslant [\frac{n}{4}] - 1; \\ 4i+2 & : [\frac{n}{4}] - 1 < i \leq n-1. \end{cases}$$

$$f(y_i) = \begin{cases} 2 & : i = 0; \\ 4i+1 & : 1 \leq i \leq n-1. \end{cases}$$

$$f(z_i) = \begin{cases} 3 & : i = 0; \\ 4i+2 & : 1 \leqslant i \leqslant \frac{n}{4} - 1; \\ 4i+3 & : \frac{n}{4} - 1 < i \leq n-1. \end{cases}$$

Since edge labeling is induced function, then $e_f(0) = \frac{5n}{2}$ and $e_f(1) = \frac{5n}{2}$. The valued edges are equal, depicted in Figure 15.

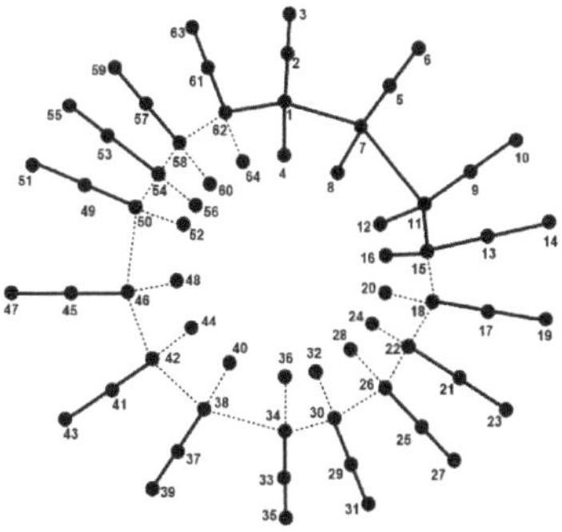

Figure 15. $(P_3, P(16,k))_{ev}$; end vertex P_3 glowing with $P(16,k)$ is prime cordial.

Case 5: for $n \equiv 6,7 \ (mod\ 12)$

$$f(x_i) = \begin{cases} 2 & : i = 0\,; \\ 4i+3 & : 1 \leqslant i \leqslant \lfloor \frac{n}{4} \rfloor\,; \\ 4i+2 & : \lfloor \frac{n}{4} \rfloor < i \leq n-1. \end{cases}$$

$$f(y_i) = \{\ 4i+1 \quad : 0 \leq i \leq n-1.$$

$$f(z_i) = \begin{cases} 3 & : i = 0\,; \\ 4i+2 & : 1 \leqslant i \leqslant \lfloor \frac{n}{4} \rfloor\,; \\ 4i+3 & : \lfloor \frac{n}{4} \rfloor < i \leq n-1. \end{cases}$$

Since edge labeling is induced function, then for even n, $e_f(0) = \frac{5n}{2}$ and $e_f(1) = \frac{5n}{2}$. In addition, for odd n, $e_f(0) = \frac{5n-1}{2}$ and $e_f(1) = \frac{5n+1}{2}$. That is prime cordial, depicted in Figure 16.

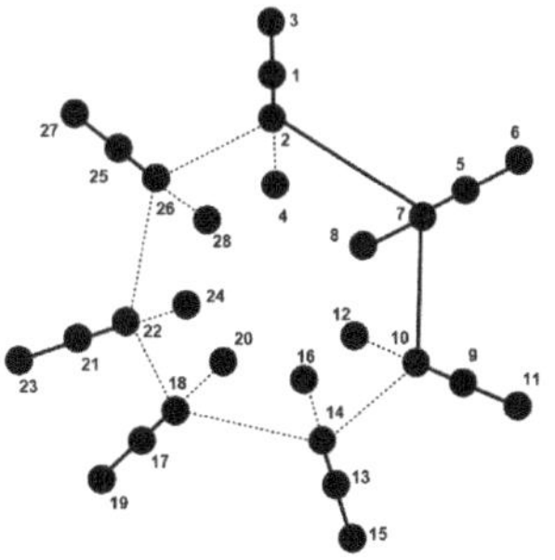

Figure 16. $(P_3, P(7,k))_{ev}$; end vertex P_3 glowing with $P(7,k)$ is prime cordial.

Case 6: for $n \equiv 1,2,3,5,9,10,11 \ (mod\ 12)$

$$f(x_i) = \begin{cases} 1 & : i = 0\,; \\ 4i+3 & : 1 \leqslant i \leqslant \lfloor \frac{n}{4} \rfloor - 1\,; \\ 4i+2 & : \lfloor \frac{n}{4} \rfloor - 1 < i \leq n-1. \end{cases}$$

$$f(y_i) = \begin{cases} 2 & : i = 0\,; \\ 4i+1 & : 1 \leq i \leq n-1. \end{cases}$$

$$f(z_i) = \begin{cases} 3 & : i = 0; \\ 4i+2 & : 1 \leqslant i \leqslant \lfloor \frac{n}{4} \rfloor - 1; \\ 4i+3 & : \lfloor \frac{n}{4} \rfloor - 1 < i \leq n-1. \end{cases}$$

Since edge labeling is induced function, then for even n, labeled edges have equal 0 and 1. In addition, for odd, labeled edges with 0 and 1 only have a difference of 1. Hence, the graph is prime cordial. There are Figures 17 and 18,

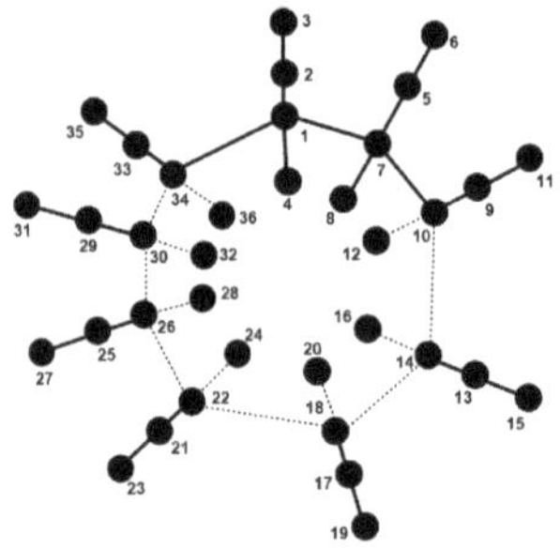

Figure 17. $(P_3, P(9,k))_{ev}$; end vertex P_3 glowing with $P(9,k)$ is prime cordial.

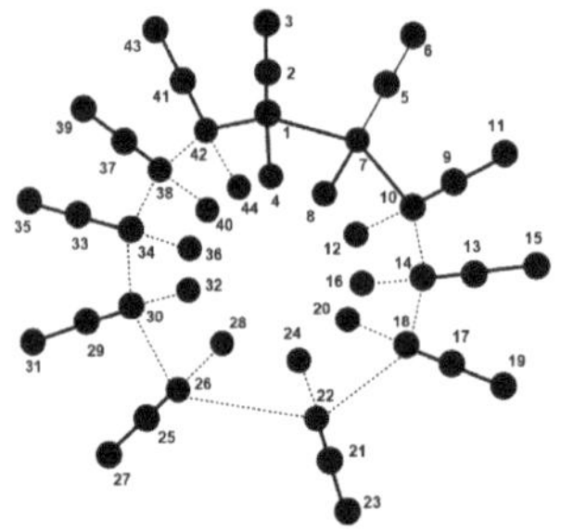

Figure 18. $(P_3, P(11,k))_{ev}$; end vertex P_3 glowing with $P(11,k)$ is prime cordial.

Case 7: for $n \equiv 8 \ (mod\ 12)$

$$f(x_i) = \begin{cases} 4i+3 & : 0 \leqslant i \leqslant \frac{n}{4}\,; \\ 4i+2 & : \frac{n}{4} < i \leq n-1. \end{cases}$$

$$f(y_i) = \{ \ 4i+1 \quad : 0 \leq i \leq n-1.$$

$$f(z_i) = \begin{cases} 4i+2 & : 0 \leqslant i \leqslant \frac{n}{4}; \\ 4i+3 & : \frac{n}{4} < i \leq n-1. \end{cases}$$

Since edge labeling is induced function, $\frac{5n}{2}$ edges are valued 0 and 1, respectively. That is clear from Figure 19, where dark lines indicate that edges are labeled with 1 and dotted line indicates that edges are labeled with 0. This graph is prime cordial.

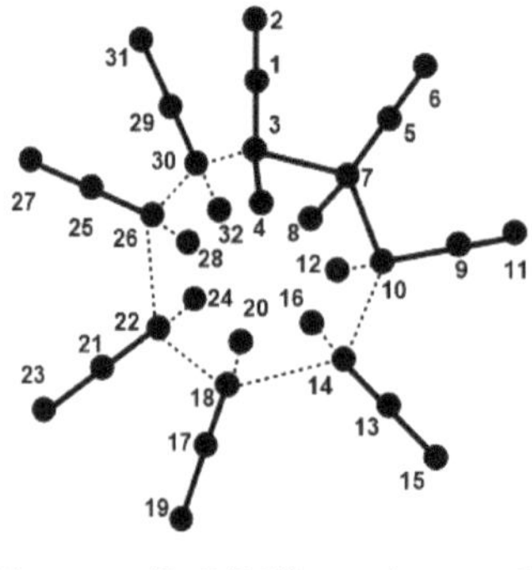

Figure 19. $(P_3, P(8,k))_{ev}$; end vertex glowing of P_3 with $P(8,k)$.

Hence, $(P_3, P(n,k))_{ev}$ *for* $n \geq 3$ *and* $1 \leq k \leq \lfloor \frac{n}{2} \rfloor$ is prime cordial. □

Theorem 5. *The graph* $(P_3, P(n,k))_{mv}$ *is prime cordial for all* $n \geq 3$ *and* $1 \leq k \leq \lfloor \frac{n}{2} \rfloor$.

Proof. Let us assume P_3 and $P(n,k)$ are path graph and generalized Petersen graph, respectively. P_3 has middle vertex glowing with $P(n,k)$ outer cycle n vertices, denoted as $(P_3, P(n,k))_{mv}$. The middle vertex glowing graph $(P_3, P(n,k))_{mv}$ has $4n$ vertices and $5n$ edges. The vertices are $\{x_i, y_i \,;\, 0 \leq i \leq n-1 \; and \; z_i \,;\, 0 \leq i \leq 2n-1\}$.

The edges are as following,

$$\begin{aligned} E_1 &= \{x_i x_{i+k};\; 0 \leq i \leq n-1 \; and \; 1 \leq k \leq \lfloor \frac{n}{2} \rfloor\}, \\ E_2 &= \{x_i y_i;\; 0 \leq i \leq n-1\}, \\ E_3 &= \{y_i y_{i+1};\; 0 \leq i \leq n-1\}, \\ E_4 &= \{y_i z_i;\; 0 \leq i \leq n-1\}, \\ E_5 &= \{y_i z_{i+1};\; 0 \leq i \leq n-1\}. \end{aligned}$$

For prime cordial labeling, we assign values to vertices from 1 to order of graph and edge labeling induced from it. Therefore, we assign values to vertices as given below;

$$f(x_i) = \{4(i+1);\; 0 \leq i \leq n-1\}$$

Now, we will have different cases for assignment of values to the vertices y_i and z_i.

Case 1: for $n = 3$

$f(y_0) = 3, f(y_1) = 6, f(y_2) = 9$

$f(z_0) = 1, f(z_1) = 2, f(z_2) = 5, f(z_3) = 7, f(z_4) = 10, f(z_5) = 11.$

Since edge labeling is induced function, valued edges have supremum difference 1, as shown in Figure 20. Hence, $(P_3, P(3,k))_{mv}\; \forall\, 1 \leq k \leq \lfloor \frac{n}{2} \rfloor$ is prime cordial.

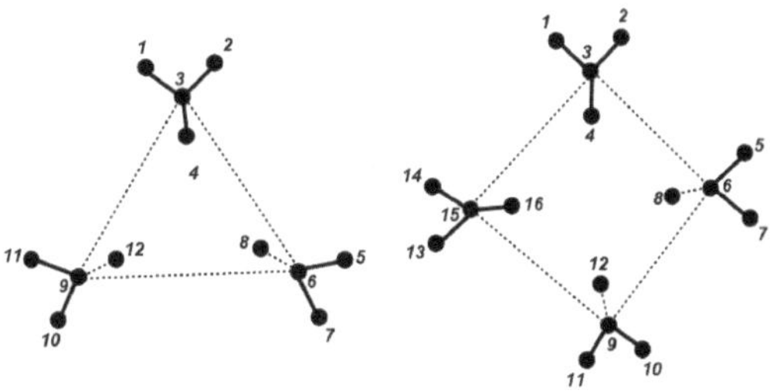

Figure 20. Middle vertex glowing of three copies of P_3 with $P(3,k)$ and $P(4,k)$ is prime cordial.

Case 2: for $n = 4$

$f(y_0) = 3, f(y_1) = 6, f(y_2) = 9, f(y_3) = 15$

$f(z_0) = 1, f(z_1) = 2, f(z_2) = 5, f(z_3) = 7, f(z_4) = 10, f(z_5) = 11, f(z_6) = 13, f(z_7) = 14.$

Since edge labeling is induced function, valued edges are equally labeled with 0 and 1. As shown in Figure 20, dark lines indicate that edges are labeled with 1 and dotted lines indicate that edges are labeled with 0. Hence, $(P_3, P(4,k))_{mv}\; \forall\, 1 \leq k \leq \lfloor \frac{n}{2} \rfloor$ is prime cordial.

Case 3: for $n \equiv 0 \; (mod\; 12)$

$$f(y_i) = \begin{cases} 2 & : i = 0\,; \\ 4i+3 & : 1 \leqslant i \leqslant \frac{n}{4}\,; \\ 4i+2 & : \frac{n}{4} < i \leq n-1. \end{cases}$$

$$f(z_i) = \begin{cases} 2i+1 & : 0 \leq i \leq 2n-1 \; and \; i \; is \; even \; ; \\ 3 & : i = 1; \\ 2i & : 3 \leqslant i \leqslant [\frac{n}{2}] + 1 \; and \; i \; is \; odd \; ; \\ 2i+1 & : [\frac{n}{2}] + 1 < i \leq 2n-1 \; and \; i \; is \; odd \, . \end{cases}$$

Since edge labeling is induced function, $\frac{5n}{2}$ edges are valued 0 and 1 equally as shown in Figure 21. The graph is prime cordial.

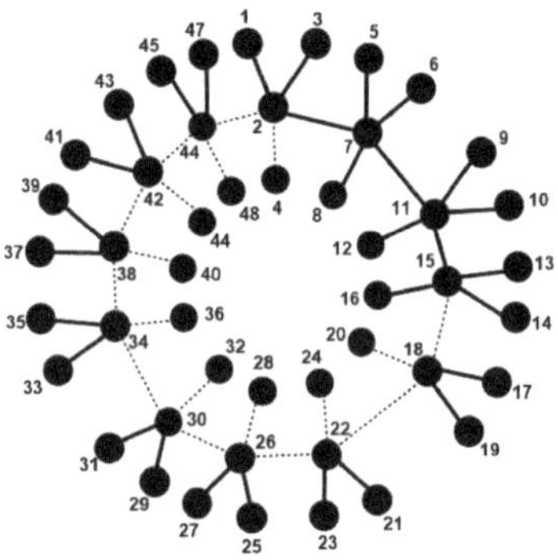

Figure 21. $(P_3, P(12,k))_{mv}$; middle vertex P_3 glowing with $P(12,k)$ is prime cordial.

Case 4: for $n \equiv 1 \; (mod \; 12)$

$$f(y_i) = \begin{cases} 1 & : i = 0; \\ 4i+3 & : 1 \leqslant i \leqslant \lfloor \frac{n}{4} \rfloor - 1; \\ 4i+2 & : \lfloor \frac{n}{4} \rfloor - 1 < i \leq n-1. \end{cases}$$

$$f(z_i) = \begin{cases} 2 & : i = 0; \\ 3 & : i = 1; \\ 2i+1 & : 2 \leq i \leq 2n-1 \; and \; i \; is \; even \; ; \\ 2i & : 3 \leqslant i \leqslant \lfloor \frac{n}{2} \rfloor \; and \; i \; is \; odd \; ; \\ 2i+1 & : \lfloor \frac{n}{2} \rfloor + 1 < i \leq 2n-1 \; and \; i \; is \; odd \, . \end{cases}$$

Since edge labeling is induced function, $\frac{5n-1}{2}$ edges are valued 0 and $\frac{5n+1}{2}$ edges are valued 1. The edges labeled with 0 and 1 have maximum difference of 1. The graph is prime cordial.

Case 5: for $n \equiv 2 \; (mod \; 12)$

$$f(y_i) = \begin{cases} 1 & : i = 0; \\ 4i+3 & : 1 \leqslant i \leqslant [\frac{n}{4}] - 1; \\ 4i+2 & : [\frac{n}{4}] - 1 < i \leq n-1. \end{cases}$$

$$f(z_i) = \begin{cases} 2 & : i = 0; \\ 3 & : i = 1; \\ 2i+1 & : 2 \leq i \leq 2n-1 \; and \; i \; is \; even \; ; \\ 2i & : 3 \leqslant i \leqslant [\frac{n}{2}] - 2 \; and \; i \; is \; odd \; ; \\ 2i+1 & : [\frac{n}{2}] - 2 < i \leq 2n-1 \; and \; i \; is \; odd \, . \end{cases}$$

From it, there are $\frac{5n}{2}$ edges labeled with 0 and 1 equally. The graph is prime cordial.

Case 6: for $n \equiv 3 \; (mod \; 12)$

$$f(y_i) = \begin{cases} 1 & : i = 0; \\ 4i+3 & : 1 \leqslant i \leqslant [\frac{n}{4}] - 1; \\ 4i+2 & : [\frac{n}{4}] - 1 < i \leq n-1. \end{cases}$$

$$f(z_i) = \begin{cases} 2 \quad : i = 0\,; \\ 3 \quad : i = 1\,; \\ 2i+1 \quad : 2 \leq i \leq 2n-1 \; and \;\; i \;\; is \;\; even \;\; ; \\ 2i \quad : 3 \leqslant i \leqslant \lfloor \frac{n}{2} \rfloor - 2 \; and \;\; i \;\; is \;\; odd \;\; ; \\ 2i+1 \quad : \lfloor \frac{n}{2} \rfloor - 2 < i \leq 2n-1 \; and \;\; i \;\; is \;\; odd\,. \end{cases}$$

Since edge labeling is induced function, $\frac{5n+1}{2}$ edges are valued 0 and $\frac{5n-1}{2}$ are valued 1 . Edges labeled with maximum 1 difference.

Case 7: for $n \equiv 4 \; (mod\; 12)$

$$f(y_i) = \begin{cases} 1 : i = 0\,; \\ 4i+3 : 1 \leqslant i \leqslant [\frac{n}{4}] - 1\,; \\ 4i+2 : [\frac{n}{4}] - 1 < i \leq n-1. \end{cases}$$

$$f(z_i) = \begin{cases} 2 \quad : i = 0\,; \\ 3 \quad : i = 1\,; \\ 2i+1 \quad : 2 \leq i \leq 2n-1 \; and \;\; i \;\; is \;\; even \;\; ; \\ 2i \quad : 3 \leqslant i \leqslant [\frac{n}{2}] - 1 \; and \;\; i \;\; is \;\; odd \;\; ; \\ 2i+1 \quad : [\frac{n}{2}] - 1 < i \leq 2n-1 \; and \;\; i \;\; is \;\; odd\,. \end{cases}$$

Since edge labeling is induced function, $\frac{5n}{2}$ edges are valued 0 and 1, respectively. The graph is prime cordial.

Case 8: for $n \equiv 5,9 \; (mod\; 12)$

$$f(y_i) = \begin{cases} 1 : i = 0\,; \\ 4i+3 : 1 \leqslant i \leqslant \lfloor \frac{n}{4} \rfloor - 1\,; \\ 4i+2 : \lfloor \frac{n}{4} \rfloor - 1 < i \leq n-1. \end{cases}$$

$$f(z_i) = \begin{cases} 2 \quad : i = 0\,; \\ 3 \quad : i = 1\,; \\ 2i+1 \quad : 2 \leq i \leq 2n-1 \; and \;\; i \;\; is \;\; even \;\; ; \\ 2i \quad : 3 \leqslant i \leqslant \lfloor \frac{n}{2} \rfloor - 1 \; and \;\; i \;\; is \;\; odd \;\; ; \\ 2i+1 \quad : \lfloor \frac{n}{2} \rfloor - 1 < i \leq 2n-1 \; and \;\; i \;\; is \;\; odd\,. \end{cases}$$

Since edge labeling is induced function, $\frac{5n-1}{2}$ labeled with 0 and $\frac{5n+1}{2}$ labeled with 1 . That is, $|e_f(0) - e_f(1)| = 1$. As shown in Figure 22, dark lines indicate that edges are labeled with 1 and dotted lines indicate that edges are labeled with 0. The graph is prime cordial.

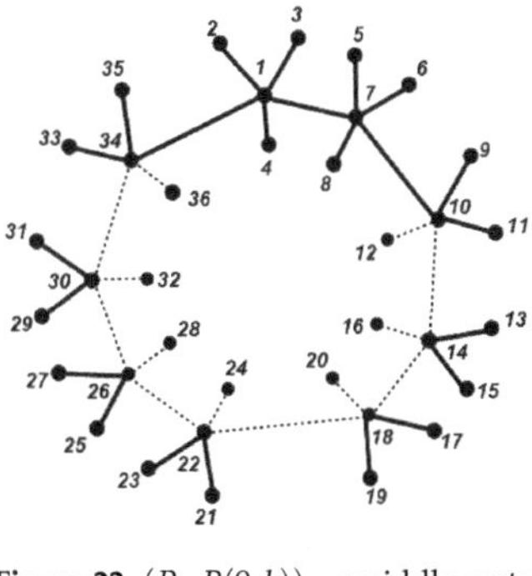

Figure 22. $(P_3, P(9,k))_{mv}$; middle vertex P_3 glowing with $P(9,k)$ is prime cordial.

Case 9: for $n \equiv 6,10 \; (mod\; 12)$

$$f(y_i) = \begin{cases} 1 \quad : i = 0\,; \\ 4i+3 \quad : 1 \leqslant i \leqslant \lfloor \frac{n}{4} \rfloor - 1\,; \\ 4i+2 \quad : \lfloor \frac{n}{4} \rfloor - 1 < i \leq n-1. \end{cases}$$

$$f(z_i) = \begin{cases} 2 & : i = 0\,; \\ 3 & : i = 1\,; \\ 2i+1 & : 2 \le i \le 2n-1 \text{ and } i \text{ is even }; \\ 2i & : 3 \leqslant i \leqslant \frac{n}{2} \text{ and } i \text{ is odd }; \\ 2i+1 & : \frac{n}{2} < i \le 2n-1 \text{ and } i \text{ is odd }. \end{cases}$$

Since edge labeling is induced function. Hence, $\frac{5n}{2}$ edges are labeled by 0 and 1 equally, as shown in Figure 23. The graph is prime cordial.

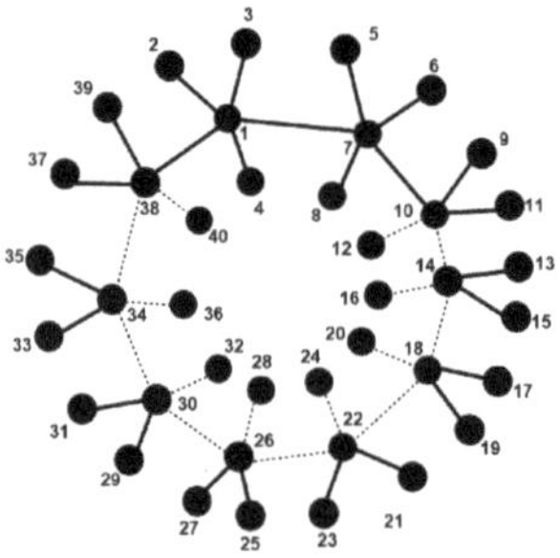

Figure 23. $(P_3, P(10,k))_{mv}$; middle vertex P_3 glowing with $P(10,k)$ is prime cordial.

Case 10: for $n \equiv 7\ (mod\ 12)$

$$f(y_i) = \begin{cases} 2 & : i = 0\,; \\ 4i+3 & : 1 \leqslant i \leqslant \lfloor \frac{n}{4} \rfloor\,; \\ 4i+2 & : \lfloor \frac{n}{4} \rfloor < i \le n-1. \end{cases}$$

$$f(z_i) = \begin{cases} 2i+1 & : 0 \le i \le 2n-1 \text{ where } i \text{ is even }; \\ 3 & : i = 1\,; \\ 2i & : 3 \leqslant i \leqslant \lfloor \frac{n}{2} \rfloor \text{ and } i \text{ is odd }; \\ 2i+1 & : \lfloor \frac{n}{2} \rfloor < i \le 2n-1 \text{ where } i \text{ is odd }. \end{cases}$$

Since edge labeling is induced function, then $e_f(0) = \frac{5n+1}{2}$ and $e_f(1) = \frac{5n-1}{2}$, represented in Figure 24. This is prime cordial.

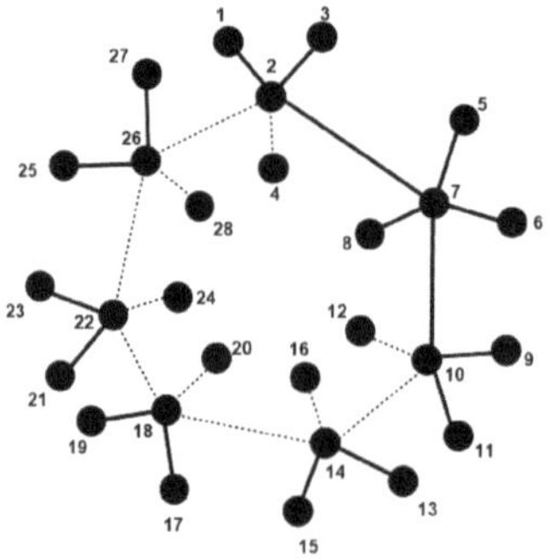

Figure 24. $(P_3, P(7,k))_{mv}$; middle vertex P_3 glowing with $P(7,k)$ is prime cordial.

Case 11: for $n \equiv 8\ (mod\ 12)$

$$f(y_i) = \begin{cases} 4i+3 & : 0 \leqslant i \leqslant \frac{n}{4}\,; \\ 4i+2 & : \frac{n}{4} < i \le n-1. \end{cases}$$

$$f(z_i) = \begin{cases} 2i+1 & : 0 \le i \le 2n-1 \text{ and } i \text{ is even }; \\ 2 & : i = 1; \\ 2i & : 3 \leqslant i \leqslant [\frac{n}{2}] - 1 \text{ and } i \text{ is odd }; \\ 2i+1 & : [\frac{n}{2}] - 1 < i \le 2n-1 \text{ and } i \text{ is odd }. \end{cases}$$

Since edge labeling is induced function, then $\frac{5n}{2}$ is equally valued with 0 and 1, as depicted in Figure 25. It is prime cordial.

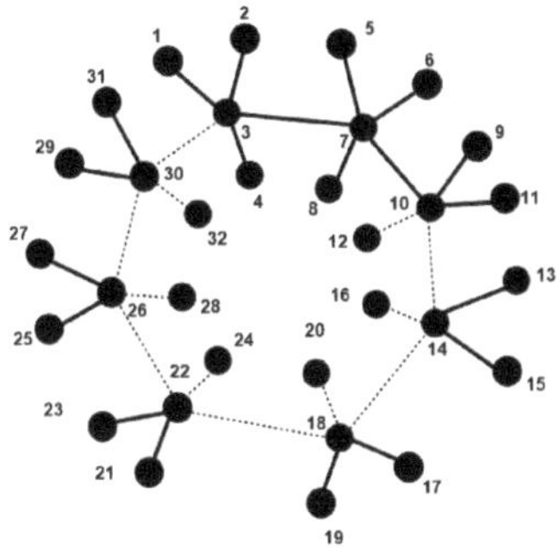

Figure 25. $(P_3, P(8,k))_{mv}$; middle vertex P_3 glowing with $P(8,k)$ is prime cordial.

Case 12: for $n \equiv 11 \ (mod \ 12)$

$$f(y_i) = \begin{cases} 2 & : i = 1; \\ 4i+3 & : 1 \leqslant i \leqslant \lfloor \frac{n}{4} \rfloor; \\ 4i+2 & : \lfloor \frac{n}{4} \rfloor < i \le n-1. \end{cases}$$

$$f(z_i) = \begin{cases} 1 & : i = 0; \\ 3 & : i = 1; \\ 2i+1 & : 2 \le i \le 2n-1 \text{ and } i \text{ is even }; \\ 2i & : 3 \leqslant i \leqslant \lfloor \frac{n}{2} \rfloor \text{ and } i \text{ is odd }; \\ 2i+1 & : \lfloor \frac{n}{2} \rfloor < i \le 2n-1 \text{ and } i \text{ is odd }. \end{cases}$$

Since edge labeling is induced function, the edges $\frac{5n+1}{2}$ are valued with 0 and $\frac{5n-1}{2}$ are valued with 1. There is maximum 1 difference in valued edges. As shown in Figure 26. The graph is prime cordial.

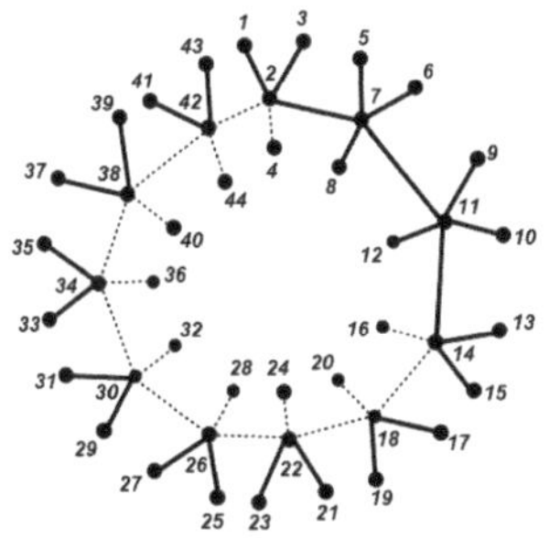

Figure 26. $(P_3, P(11,k))_{mv}$; middle vertex P_3 glowing with $P(11,k)$ is prime cordial.

Hence, $(P_3, P(n,k))_{mv}$ for all $n \ge 3$ *and* $1 \le k \le \lfloor \frac{n}{2} \rfloor$ is prime cordial. □

Theorem 6. *The graph* $P_v(n,k)_p$ *is prime cordial for all* $n \ge 3$ *and* $1 \le k \le \lfloor \frac{n}{2} \rfloor$.

Proof. Let $P(n,k)$ be a generalized Petersen graph. There are n copies of pendant vertices attached to outer cycle of $P(n,k)$.

There are $3n$ vertices and size $4n$. Described as,

$$V(P_v(n,k)_p) = \{x_i, y_i, z_i;\ 0 \le i \le n-1\},$$

$$E(P_v(n,k)_p) = \{x_i x_{i+k}, x_i y_i, y_i y_{i+1}, y_i z_i;\ 0 \le i \le n-1\ and\ 1 \le k \le \lfloor \frac{n}{2} \rfloor\}.$$

In prime cordial labeling, values assigned to vertices is a bijective function from 1 to order of graph and edge labeling induce from it. Therefore, values are assigned to vertices as;

$$f(x_i) = \{3i+3;\ 0 \le i \le n-1\}$$

For $f(y_i)$ and $f(z_i)$, we have following cases:

Case 1: for $n = 3$

$f(y_0) = 1, f(y_1) = 4, f(y_2) = 8$
$f(z_0) = 5, f(z_1) = 2, f(z_2) = 7$

Since edge labeling is induced function, edges are equally labeled with 0 and 1. As shown in Figure 27, $P_v(3,k)_p$ is prime cordial.

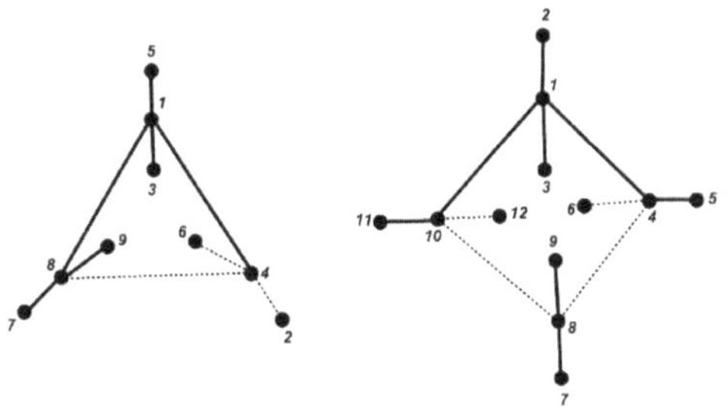

Figure 27. Outer cycle vertices duplication by pendant vertices in $P(3,k)$ and $P(4,k)$ is prime cordial.

Case 2: for $n = 4$

$f(y_0) = 1, f(y_1) = 4, f(y_2) = 8, f(y_3) = 10$
$f(z_0) = 2, f(z_1) = 5, f(z_2) = 7, f(z_3) = 11.$

Since edge labeling is induced function, 0 and 1 are equally assigned to edges. As shown in Figure 27, $P_v(4,k)_p$ is prime cordial.

Case 3: for $n \equiv 0\ (mod\ 6)$

$$f(y_i) = \begin{cases} 2 & : i = 0; \\ 3i+2 & : 1 \leqslant i \leqslant \frac{n-3}{3}\ when\ i\ is\ odd\ ; \\ 3i+1 & : 2 \leqslant i \leqslant \frac{n-3}{3}\ when\ i\ is\ even\ ; \\ 3i+2 & : \frac{n-3}{3} < i \leqslant n-1\ when\ i\ is\ even\ ; \\ 3i+1 & : \frac{n-3}{3} < i \leqslant n-1\ when\ i\ is\ odd\ . \end{cases}$$

$$f(z_i) = \begin{cases} 1 & : i = 0; \\ 3i+1 & : 1 \leqslant i \leqslant \frac{n-3}{3}\ when\ i\ is\ odd\ ; \\ 3i+2 & : 2 \leqslant i \leqslant \frac{n-3}{3}\ when\ i\ is\ even\ ; \\ 3i+1 & : \frac{n-3}{3} < i \leqslant n-1\ when\ i\ is\ even\ ; \\ 3i+2 & : \frac{n-3}{3} < i \leqslant n-1\ when\ i\ is\ odd\ . \end{cases}$$

This labeling is explained in Figure 28.

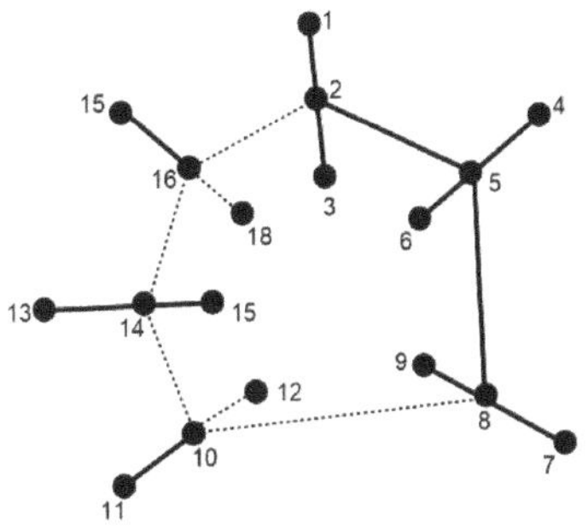

Figure 28. $P_v(6,k)_p$; outer vertex $P(6,k)$ duplication by pendant vertices is prime cordial.

Case 4: for $n \equiv 1\ (mod\ 6)$

$$f(y_i)=\begin{cases} 2 & : i=0; \\ 3i+2 & : 1 \leqslant i \leqslant \frac{n-4}{3} \text{ when } i \text{ is odd}; \\ 3i+1 & : 2 \leqslant i \leqslant \frac{n-4}{3} \text{ when } i \text{ is even}; \\ 3i+2 & : \frac{n-4}{3} < i \leqslant n-1 \text{ and when } i \text{ is even}; \\ 3i+1 & : \frac{n-4}{3} < i \leqslant n-1 \text{ and when } i \text{ is odd}. \end{cases}$$

$$f(z_i)=\begin{cases} 1 & : i=0; \\ 3i+1 & : 1 \leqslant i \leqslant \frac{n-4}{3} \text{ when } i \text{ is odd}; \\ 3i+2 & : 2 \leqslant i \leqslant \frac{n-4}{3} \text{ when } i \text{ is even}; \\ 3i+1 & : \frac{n-4}{3} < i \leqslant n-1 \text{ when } i \text{ is even}; \\ 3i+2 & : \frac{n-4}{3} < i \leqslant n-1 \text{ when } i \text{ is odd}. \end{cases}$$

This labeling is explained in Figure 29.

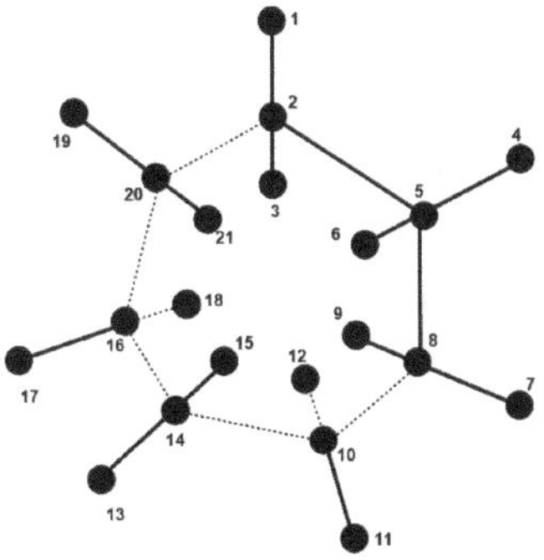

Figure 29. $P_v(7,k)_p$; outer vertex $P(7,k)$ duplication by pendant vertices is prime cordial.

Case 5: for $n \equiv 2\ (mod\ 6)$

$$f(y_i)=\begin{cases} 1 & : i=0; \\ 3i+2 & : 1 \leqslant i \leqslant \frac{n-5}{3} \text{ where } i \text{ is odd }; \\ 3i+1 & : 2 \leqslant i \leqslant \frac{n-5}{3} \text{ where } i \text{ is even }; \\ 3i+2 & : \frac{n-5}{3} < i \leqslant n-1 \text{ where } i \text{ is even }; \\ 3i+1 & : \frac{n-5}{3} < i \leqslant n-1 \text{ where } i \text{ is odd }. \end{cases}$$

$$f(z_i) = \begin{cases} 2 & : i = 0 ; \\ 3i+1 & : 1 \leqslant i \leqslant \frac{n-5}{3} \text{ where } i \text{ is odd} ; \\ 3i+2 & : 2 \leqslant i \leqslant \frac{n-5}{3} \text{ where } i \text{ is even} ; \\ 3i+1 & : \frac{n-5}{3} < i \leqslant n-1 \text{ where } i \text{ is even} ; \\ 3i+2 & : \frac{n-5}{3} < i \leqslant n-1 \text{ where } i \text{ is odd} . \end{cases}$$

This labeling is explained in Figure 30.

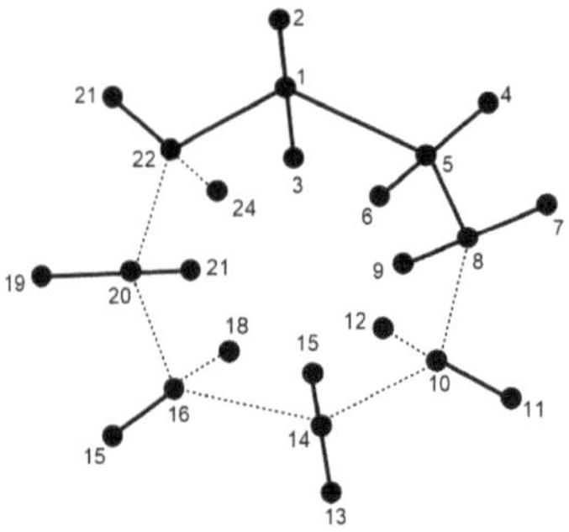

Figure 30. $P_v(8,k)_p$; outer vertex $P(8,k)$ duplication by pendant vertices is prime cordial.

Case 6: for $n \equiv 3 \ (mod\ 6)$

$$f(y_i) = \begin{cases} 1 & : i = 0 ; \\ 3i+2 & : 1 \leqslant i \leqslant \frac{n-6}{3} \text{ when } i \text{ is odd} ; \\ 3i+1 & : 2 \leqslant i \leqslant \frac{n-6}{3} \text{ when } i \text{ is even} ; \\ 3i+2 & : \frac{n-6}{3} < i \leqslant n-1 \text{ and when is even} ; \\ 3i+1 & : \frac{n-6}{3} < i \leqslant n-1 \text{ when } i \text{ is odd} . \end{cases}$$

$$f(z_i) = \begin{cases} 2 & : i = 0 ; \\ 3i+1 & : 1 \leqslant i \leqslant \frac{n-6}{3} \text{ when } i \text{ is odd} ; \\ 3i+2 & : 2 \leqslant i \leqslant \frac{n-6}{3} \text{ when } i \text{ is even} ; \\ 3i+1 & : \frac{n-6}{3} < i \leqslant n-1 \text{ when } i \text{ is even} ; \\ 3i+2 & : \frac{n-6}{3} < i \leqslant n-1 \text{ when } i \text{ is odd} . \end{cases}$$

This labeling is explained in Figure 31.

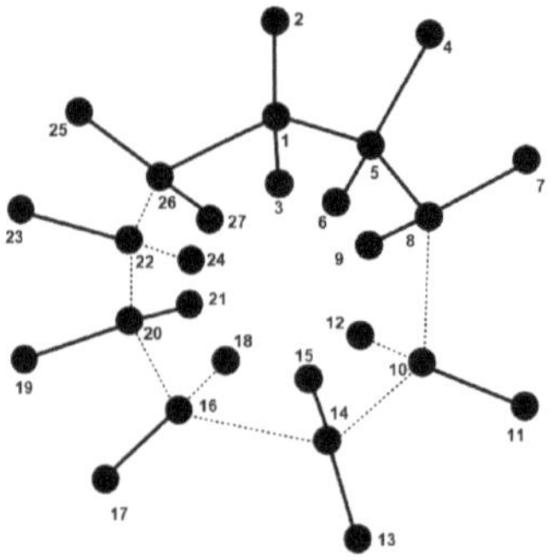

Figure 31. $P_v(9,k)_p$; outer vertex $P(9,k)$ duplication by pendant vertices is prime cordial.

Case 7: for $n \equiv 4 \ (mod\ 6)$

$$f(y_i) = \begin{cases} 1 & : i = 0\,; \\ 3i+2 & : 1 \leqslant i \leqslant \frac{n-4}{3} \text{ when } i \text{ is odd }; \\ 3i+1 & : 2 \leqslant i \leqslant \frac{n-4}{3} \text{ when } i \text{ is even }; \\ 3i+2 & : \frac{n-4}{3} < i \leqslant n-1 \text{ when } i \text{ is even }; \\ 3i+1 & : \frac{n-4}{3} < i \leqslant n-1 \text{ when } i \text{ is odd }. \end{cases}$$

$$f(z_i) = \begin{cases} 2 & : i = 0\,; \\ 3i+1 & : 1 \leqslant i \leqslant \frac{n-4}{3} \text{ when } i \text{ is odd }; \\ 3i+2 & : 2 \leqslant i \leqslant \frac{n-4}{3} \text{ when } i \text{ is even }; \\ 3i+1 & : \frac{n-4}{3} < i \leqslant n-1 \text{ when } i \text{ is even }; \\ 3i+2 & : \frac{n-4}{3} < i \leqslant n-1 \text{ when } i \text{ is odd }. \end{cases}$$

This labeling is explained in Figure 32.

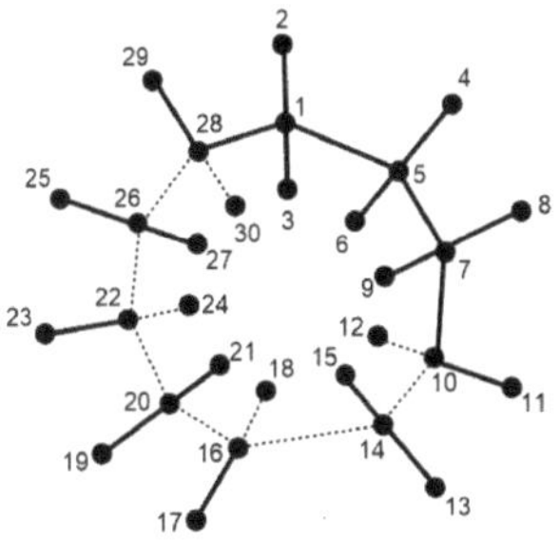

Figure 32. $P_v(10,k)_p$; outer vertex $P(10,k)$ duplication by pendant vertices is prime cordial.

Case 8: for $n \equiv 5\ (mod\ 6)$

$$f(y_i) = \begin{cases} 1 & : i = 0\,; \\ 3i+2 & : 1 \leqslant i \leqslant \frac{n-5}{3} \text{ when } i \text{ is odd }; \\ 3i+1 & : 2 \leqslant i \leqslant \frac{n-5}{3} \text{ when } i \text{ is even }; \\ 3i+2 & : \frac{n-5}{3} < i \leqslant n-1 \text{ when } i \text{ is even }; \\ 3i+1 & : \frac{n-5}{3} < i \leqslant n-1 \text{ when } i \text{ is odd }. \end{cases}$$

$$f(z_i) = \begin{cases} 2 & : i = 0\,; \\ 3i+1 & : 1 \leqslant i \leqslant \frac{n-5}{3} \text{ when } i \text{ is odd }; \\ 3i+2 & : 2 \leqslant i \leqslant \frac{n-5}{3} \text{ when } i \text{ is even }; \\ 3i+1 & : \frac{n-5}{3} < i \leqslant n-1 \text{ when } i \text{ is even }; \\ 3i+2 & : \frac{n-5}{3} < i \leqslant n-1 \text{ when } i \text{ is odd }. \end{cases}$$

This labeling is explained in Figure 33.

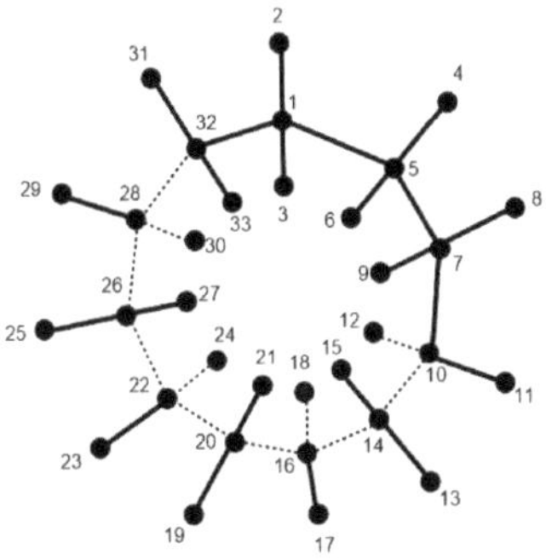

Figure 33. $P_v(11,k)_p$; outer vertex $P(11,k)$ duplication by pendant vertices is prime cordial.

Hence, the graph $P_v(n,k)_p$ is prime cordial for all $n \geq 3$ and $1 \leq k \leq \lfloor \frac{n}{2} \rfloor$. $\square$

3. Conclusions

In this article, we have studied the prime cordial labeling of a generalized Petersen graph under duplication operation, and we have proved that it is a prime cordial graph after duplication. We have also proved that glowing of path graph P_3 to $P(n,k)$ at a common vertex is prime cordial. These graphs invite the interest of researchers for their application in communication. Binary digits belong to Boolean Algebra, and in our results, edges are labeled with 0 and 1. These binary digits assignment to edges attracts the attention of computer programmers for data communication. Therefore, these results are fruitful for switching and data communication.

Author Contributions: Writing—original draft preparation, W.Z., M.N. and I.A.; writing—review and editing, W.Z., M.N. and I.A. All authors have read and agreed to the published version of the manuscript.

Funding: We thank the reviewers for their constructive comments in improving the quality of this paper. This work was supported by the National Key Research and Development Program under Grant 2018YFB0904205.

Institutional Review Board Statement: This research was conducted by Mr. Irfan Ahmad (Reg. No.: MPMT-023R19-24) in his M.Phil thesis under the supervision of Muhammad Naeem and funded by Weidong Zhao in the Department of Mathematics and Statistics, Institute of Southern Punjab, Multan.

Informed Consent Statement: Not applicable.

Data Availability Statement: Not applicable.

Conflicts of Interest: The authors declare no conflict of interest

References

1. Wilson, R.J. *History Graph Theory From: Handbook Graph Theory*; CRC Press: Boca Raton, FL, USA, 2013.
2. Chartrand, G.; Egan, C.; Zhang, P. *How to Label a Graph*; Springer Briefs in Mathematics: New York, NY, USA, 2019; pp. 19–23.
3. Rosa, A. *On Certain Valuations of the Vertices of a Graph, Theory of Graphs*; Gordon and Breach: New York, NY, USA, 1967; pp. 349–355.
4. Golomb, S.W. *How to Number a Graph, Graph Theory and Computing*; Academic Press: New York, NY, USA, 1972; pp. 23–37.
5. Beineke, L.W.; Hegde, S.M. Strongly Multiplicative Graphs. *Discuss. Math. Graph Theory* **2001**, *21*, 63–75. [CrossRef]
6. Liang, Z.H.; Bai, Z.L. On the odd harmonious graphs with applications. *J. App. Math. Comput.* **2008**, *29*, 105–116. [CrossRef]
7. Sundaram, M.; Ponraj, R.; Somasundram, S. Prime Cordial Labeling of Graphs. *J. Ind. Acad. Math.* **2005**, *27*, 373–390.
8. Ahmad, I. Muhammad Naeem, Prime Cordial Labeling of Generalized Petersen Graph under Some Graph Operations. MPhil Thesis, Institute of Southern Punjab, Multan, Pakistan, 2021.

symmetry MDPI

Article

Similarity Measures Based on T-Spherical Fuzzy Information with Applications to Pattern Recognition and Decision Making

Muhammad Nabeel Abid [1], Miin-Shen Yang [2,*], Hanen Karamti [3], Kifayat Ullah [1] and Dragan Pamucar [4]

1 Department of Mathematics, Riphah Institute of Computing & Applied Sciences (RICAS), Riphah International University (Lahore Campus), Lahore 54000, Pakistan; majormnabeelabid@gmail.com or 21830@students.riu.edu.pk (M.N.A.); kifayat.ullah@riphah.edu.pk or kifayat.khan.dr@gmail.com (K.U.)
2 Department of Applied Mathematics, Chung Yuan Christian University, Chung-Li, Taoyuan 32023, Taiwan
3 Department of Computer Sciences, College of Computer and Information Sciences, Princess Nourah bint Abdulrahman University, P.O. Box 84428, Riyadh 11671, Saudi Arabia; hmkaramti@pnu.edu.sa
4 Department of Logistics, Military Academy, University of Defense in Belgrade, 11000 Belgrade, Serbia; dragan.pamucar@va.mod.gov.rs
* Correspondence: msyang@math.cycu.edu.tw

Abstract: T-spherical fuzzy set (TSFS) is a fuzzy layout aiming to provide a larger room for the processing of uncertain information-based data where four aspects of unpredictable information are studied. The frame of picture fuzzy sets (PFSs) and intuitionistic fuzzy sets (IFSs) provide limited room for processing such kinds of information. On a scale of zero to one, similarity measures (SMs) are a tool for evaluating the degrees of resemblance between various items or phenomena. The goal of this paper is to investigate the shortcomings of picture fuzzy (PF) SMs in order to introduce a new SM in a T-spherical fuzzy (TSF) environment. The newly improved SM has a larger ground for accommodating the uncertain information with three degrees and is also responsible for the reduction of information loss. The proposed SM's validity is demonstrated mathematically and by examples. To examine the application of the suggested SM two real-life issues are discussed, including the concerns of medical diagnosis and pattern recognition. A comparison of the suggested SMs with current SMs is also made to assess the proposed work's reliability. Since symmetric triangular fuzzy numbers are quite useful in database acquisition, we will consider the proposed SM for symmetric T-spherical triangular fuzzy numbers in the near future.

Keywords: decision making; pattern recognition; similarity measures (SMs); fuzzy sets; picture fuzzy sets (PFSs); T-spherical fuzzy sets (TSFSs)

Citation: Abid, M.N.; Yang, M.-S.; Karamti, H.; Ullah, K.; Pamucar, D. Similarity Measures Based on T-Spherical Fuzzy Information with Applications to Pattern Recognition and Decision Making. *Symmetry* **2022**, *14*, 410. https://doi.org/10.3390/sym14020410

Academic Editor: Saeid Jafari

Received: 26 January 2022
Accepted: 16 February 2022
Published: 18 February 2022

1. Introduction

Zadeh [1] conceived the concept of fuzzy sets (FSs) in 1965. In FSs, a function of memberships on a scale of $\{0,1\}$ was used to show the degree of membership (DM) of an element in a set with the degree of non-membership (DNM) calculated by subtracting DM from 1, i.e., $DNM = 1 - DM$. Later, Atanassov [2] refined the concept from FSs to intuitionistic fuzzy sets (IFSs) which define DM and DNM separately, but have their full scope in the range of $\{0,\ 1\}$, i.e., $DM + DNM \in [0,\ 1]$. Atanassov's model of IFSs also has significant limitations, as the sum of DM and DNM might sometimes surpass the range of $\{0,\ 1\}$. As a result, Yager [3] developed Pythagorean FSs (PyFSs) by expanding the space of IFSs with a flexible constraint, i.e., $DM^2 + DNM^2 \in [0,\ 1]$. Yager [4] also introduced the concept of q-Rung Orthopair FSs (q-ROFSs). In q-ROFSs, the sum of qth power of DM and qth power of DNM is equal to or less than 1, i.e., $DM^q + DNM^q \in [0,\ 1]$.

Although Atanassov's IFSs model revealed Zadeh's notion of FSs, there exist some scenarios where there are more than two options including the degree of abstinence (DA) and degree of refusal (DR). In this case, IFSs failed to comment on these uncertainties. By considering all these shortcomings of IFSs, Cuong [5] devised picture FSs (PFSs) which have three membership functions represented by DM, DA, and DNM with a restriction that their total should lie in the range of $\{0, 1\}$, i.e., $DM + DA + DNM \in [0, 1]$. The term $(1 - (DM + DA + DNM))$ was referred to as the DR of an element of a PFS. Some recent studies on PFSs can be found in [6,7]. PFSs broadened the scope of FSs and IFSs, but there are still constraints, and we cannot assign DM, DA, and DNM independently. Mahmood et al. [8] proposed the idea of spherical fuzzy sets (SFSs) as a modification of PFSs by enhancing the range of PFSs by realizing the structures of FSs, IFSs, and PFSs. Similarly, the sum of DM, DA, and DNM may be more than the unit interval in the structure of SFSs, and their squares must fall within the unit interval which is defined as $DM^2 + DA^2 + DNM^2 \in [0, 1]$. SFSs have a wider range than PFSs due to their new restriction. However, even squaring is not enough as the squared sum of DM, DA, and DNM exceeds the unit interval, i.e., $DM^2 + DA^2 + DNM^2 > 1$. To deal with this kind of situation, Mahmood et al. [8] also presented a modification of SFSs which was known as T-spherical FSs (TSFSs). TSFSs have the condition that $DM^n + DA^n + DNM^n \in [0, 1]$ where $n \in \mathbb{Z}^+$. We see that TSFSs are a more generic version of IFSs, PFSs, and SFSs. Some recent work on SFSs and TSFSs can be found in [9–11].

Similarity measures (SMs) are used to assess the degree of similarity between different items or phenomena on a scale of zero to one. SMs had been discussed on FSs since Zadeh [1] introduced FSs. For example, Chen et al. [12] proposed the comparison of SMs of fuzzy values in which they use fuzzy values to compare the attributes of several SMs. Yang et al. [13] considered similarity measures between fuzzy numbers and then applied them to database acquisition. Since Atanassov [2] proposed IFSs as a generalization of FSs, despite the introduction of many SMs for FSs, they were unable to solve problems when placed in an IFS environment. As a result, Dengfeng and Chuntian [14] proposed new SMs on IFSs that can cope with the problems given in the environment of IFSs. Liang and Shi [15] presented a new SM on IFSs based on the fact that the previously defined SMs are not useful in some situations. Li et al. [16] evaluated and summarized known SMs between IFSs and intuitionistic vague sets (IVSs). The benefits of each SM are explored as well as the circumstances in which they may or may not operate as intended. For IFSs induced by the Jaccard index, Hwang et al. [17] developed a novel SM. They demonstrate that the recommended SMs are more logical than the alternatives using numerical examples. By expanding the space of IFSs with a flexible constraint, Yager [3] established PyFSs. To cope with the data given in the PyFSs environment, SMs for PyFSs were also introduced. Wei and Wei [18] presented 10 SMs between PyFSs based on the cosine function with applications to medical diagnosis. Zeng et al. [19] proposed distance and SMs of PyFSs and used them in multiple criteria group decision making. Peng and Garg [20] proposed multiparametric SMs between PyFSs and they were put to the test by applying them to pattern recognition problems. Based on the Hausdorff metric, Hussain and Yang [21] presented distances and SMs of PyFSs and then gave a fuzzy TOPSIS. Concerning SMs for q-ROFSs, PFSs, and SFSs, Wang et al. [22] gave the SMs of q-ROFSs based on cosine functions.

Wei [23] considered SMs for PFSs and then used them to recognize construction materials and mineral fields. SMs for SFS based cosine function were proposed by Mahmood et al. [24] with applications in pattern recognition and medical diagnosis. Rafiq et al. [25] proposed the cosine SM of SFSs and offered a number of numerical decision-making applications to test the proposed SM's correctness. After Mahmood et al. [8] presented the concept of TSFSs, which is the extension of FSs, IFSs, PFSs, and SFSs, Ullah et al. [26] proposed SMs for TSFSs with pattern recognition applications. Ye [27] proposed SMs based on the modified distance of neutrosophic Z-number sets and a multi-attribute decision-making technique. For pattern recognition and medical diagnostics, Mahmood et al. [28] suggested hybrid vector similarity metrics based on complex hesitant fuzzy sets. Power aggregation techniques and SMs based on improved intuitionistic hesitant fuzzy sets were suggested by Mahmood et al. [29], as well as their applicability to multiple attribute decision making. Chinram et al. [30] suggested and used a series of novel cosine SMs based on hesitant complex fuzzy sets. Mahmood et al. [31] introduced

Jaccard and dice SMs and their applications based on complicated dual hesitant fuzzy sets that are one-of-a-kind.

Although Ullah et al. [26] had proposed SMs for TSFSs, we shall establish a new SM for TSFSs in this paper so that it can be a generalized form of PFSs as done in the previously proposed SMs by Luo and Zhang [32]. We begin by reviewing previously defined SMs for PFSs and observe their limitations when it comes to their applicability. The main reason to develop a new SM was the fact that TSFSs provide a flexible and larger range for data representation under uncertain circumstances. To check the effectiveness of the proposed SMs we provide an example of a pattern recognition system with its application for decision-making. It can also be determined which example is more suitable and effective by having a comparative study of both examples with the previously defined SMs. The followings are the major contributions of this paper:

1. To view/observe the limitations of the previous SMs because of their applicability.
2. To propose a new SM with flexibility in the environment of TSFSs.
3. To check the validity of the proposed SM using some results.
4. To apply the proposed SM in pattern recognition and decision making.
5. To compare the proposed work with previous works by a comparative analysis where the efficacy of the suggested SM is discussed.

The rest of the paper is organized as follows. In Section 2, we go over some key TSFS concepts. A new SM for TSFSs is proposed in Section 3. In Section 4, the suggested SM is used to recognize patterns in a pattern recognition system as well as to make decisions. In Section 5, we come to a conclusion.

2. Preliminaries

Some SFSs and TSFSs definitions are outlined in this section. Throughout the work, X denotes a universal set.

Definition 1 [8]. *A SFS* S *on* X *is written as:*

$$S = \left\{ \mu(x), \eta(x), v(x) : 0 \le \mu^2(x) + \eta^2(x) + v^2(x) \le 1 \right\}$$

such that μ, η, *and* v *ranging from* 0 *to* 1 *denote the DM, DA, and DNM of* $x \in X$, *respectively, and* $r(x) = \sqrt{1 - \mathrm{sum}(\mu^2, \eta^2, v^2)}$, *with* $\mathrm{sum}(\mu^2, \eta^2, v^2) = \mu^2 + \eta^2 + v^2$, *is the DR of* x *in* S, *where* (μ, η, v) *is considered as a spherical fuzzy number (SFN) for* S.

Definition 2 [8]. *A TSFS* S *on* X *is written as*:

$$S = \{ \mu(x), \eta(x), v(x) : 0 \le \mu^n(x) + \eta^n(x) + v^n(x) \le 1 \}$$

such that μ, η, *and* v *ranging from* 0 *to* 1 *denote the DM, DA, and DNM of* $x \in X$, *respectively, for* $n \in \mathbb{Z}^+$, *and* $r(x) = \sqrt[n]{1 - \mathrm{sum}(\mu^n, \eta^n, v^n)}$ *is the DR of* x *in* S. (μ, η, v) *is considered as a T-spherical fuzzy number (TSFN).*

Now, some notions of SMs are comparatively examined. The definitions described in this section provided a base for this work.

Definition 3 [2]. *For two IFNs* $\acute{A} = \left(\mu_{\acute{A}}, v_{\acute{A}}\right)$ *and* $B = (\mu_B, v_B)$, *an SM is written as*:

$$\acute{S}\left(\acute{A}, B\right) = \frac{1}{m} \sum_{\mathrm{i}=1}^{m} \frac{\mu_{\acute{A}_{x_{\mathrm{i}}}} \mu_{B_{x_{\mathrm{i}}}} + v_{\acute{A}_{x_{\mathrm{i}}}} v_{B_{x_{\mathrm{i}}}}}{\sqrt{\mu^2_{\acute{A}_{x_{\mathrm{i}}}} + v^2_{\acute{A}}(x_{\mathrm{i}})} \sqrt{\mu^2_{B_{x_{\mathrm{i}}}} + v^2_{B_{x_{\mathrm{i}}}}}}$$

Definition 4 [5]. *For two PFNs* $\acute{A} = (\mu_{\acute{A}}, \eta_{\acute{A}}, v_{\acute{A}})$ *and* $B = (\mu_B, \eta_B, v_B)$, *an SM is written as:*

$$\acute{S}\left(\acute{A}, B\right) = \frac{1}{3}\left(\begin{array}{c} 2\sqrt{\mu_{\acute{A}}\mu_B} + 2\sqrt{\eta_{\acute{A}}\eta_B} + 2\sqrt{v_{\acute{A}}v_B} + \sqrt{(1-\eta_{\acute{A}}-v_{\acute{A}})(1-\eta_B-v_B)} + \\ \sqrt{(1-\mu_{\acute{A}}-v_{\acute{A}})(1-\mu_B-v_B)} + \sqrt{(1-\mu_{\acute{A}}-\eta_{\acute{A}})(1-\mu_B-\eta_B)} \end{array}\right)$$

Definition 5. *Let* $\acute{A} = (\mu_{\acute{A}}, \eta_{\acute{A}}, v_{\acute{A}})$ *and* $B = (\mu_B, \eta_B, v_B)$ *be two TSFNs. Then*

1. $\acute{A} \subseteq B$ iff $\mu_{\acute{A}} \preccurlyeq \mu_B, \eta_{\acute{A}} \succcurlyeq \eta_B, v_{\acute{A}} \succcurlyeq v_B$
2. $\acute{A} = B$ iff $\acute{A} \subseteq B$ and $B \subseteq \acute{A}$

Comparison rules are always crucial in FS theory, especially when it comes to decision-making and other challenges. The comparison criteria enable us to discriminate between two FNs or, in some situations, to assess the strength of a pair connection, i.e., how tightly two variables are linked.

Definition 6 [26]. *A SM between two TSFNs* $\acute{A} = (\mu_{\acute{A}}, \eta_{\acute{A}}, v_{\acute{A}})$ *and* $B = (\mu_B, \eta_B, v_B)$ *is a mapping* $\acute{S}(\acute{A}, B) : \text{TSFNs} \times \text{TSFNs} \rightarrow [0, 1]$ *satisfying the axioms:*

(S1) $\acute{S}(\acute{A}, B) \in [0, 1]$;
(S2) $\acute{S}(\acute{A}, B) = \acute{S}(B, \acute{A})$;
(S3) $\acute{S}(\acute{A}, B) = 1$ iff $\acute{A} = B$;
(S4) *Let* Ç *be any TSFN(X), if* $\acute{A} \subseteq B \subseteq Ç$, *then* $\acute{S}(\acute{A}, Ç) \leq \acute{S}(\acute{A}, B)$ *and* $\acute{S}(\acute{A}, Ç) \leq \acute{S}(B, Ç)$.

3. A New Similarity Measure between T-Spherical Fuzzy Sets

The proposed SM for TSFSs takes DM, DA, and DNM into account in which the DM is represented by μ, the DA is represented by η, and the DNM is represented by v. Furthermore, the RD is represented by r in this section. Let $\acute{A} = (\mu_{\acute{A}}, \eta_{\acute{A}}, v_{\acute{A}})$ be a T spherical fuzzy number (TSFN) where $\mu_{\acute{A}}, \eta_{\acute{A}}, v_{\acute{A}} \in [0, 1]$ with $\mu^n_{\acute{A}} + \eta^n_{\acute{A}} + v^n_{\acute{A}} \leq 1$.

Proposition 1. *Let* $\acute{A} = (\mu_{\acute{A}}, \eta_{\acute{A}}, v_{\acute{A}})$ *and* $B = (\mu_B, \eta_B, v_B)$ *be two TSFNs. Then, a mapping* $\acute{S}(\acute{A}, B) : \text{TSFNs} \times \text{TSFNs} \rightarrow [0, 1]$ *is defined as*

$$\acute{S}\left(\acute{A}, B\right) = \frac{1}{3}\left(\begin{array}{c} 2\sqrt{\mu^n_{\acute{A}}\mu^n_B} + 2\sqrt{\eta^n_{\acute{A}}\eta^n_B} + 2\sqrt{v^n_{\acute{A}}v^n_B} + \sqrt{\left(1-\eta^n_{\acute{A}}-v^n_{\acute{A}}\right)(1-\eta^n_B-v^n_B)} + \\ \sqrt{\left(1-\mu^n_{\acute{A}}-v^n_{\acute{A}}\right)(1-\mu^n_B-v^n_B)} + \sqrt{\left(1-\mu^n_{\acute{A}}-\eta^n_{\acute{A}}\right)(1-\mu^n_B-\eta^n_B)} \end{array}\right) \quad (1)$$

is a SM for the TSFNs Á *and* B.

Remark 1 . *In Proposition 1, let* $\acute{A} = (\mu_{\acute{A}}, \eta_{\acute{A}}, v_{\acute{A}})$ *and* $B = (\mu_B, \eta_B, v_B)$ *be TSFNs. For the* TSFN Á, $\mu_{\acute{A}}$ *can be equal to an arbitrary value in* $[\mu_{\acute{A}}, \mu_{\acute{A}} + \rho_{\acute{A}}]$, $\eta_{\acute{A}}$ *can be equal to an arbitrary value in* $[\eta_{\acute{A}}, \eta_{\acute{A}} + \rho_{\acute{A}}]$, *and* $v_{\acute{A}}$ *can be equal to an arbitrary value in* $[v_{\acute{A}}, v_{\acute{A}} + \rho_{\acute{A}}]$, *where* $r_{\acute{A}} = \sqrt[n]{1-\mu^n_{\acute{A}}-\eta^n_{\acute{A}}-v^n_{\acute{A}}}$. *Similarly,* μ_B *can be equal to an arbitrary value in* $[\mu_B, \mu_B + \rho_B]$, η_B *can be equal to an arbitrary value in* $[\eta_B, \eta_B + \rho_B]$, *and* v_B *can be equal to an arbitrary value in* $[v_B, v_B + \rho_B]$, *where* $r_B = \sqrt[n]{1-\mu^n_B-\eta^n_B-v^n_B}$. *Hence in Equation (1),* $\sqrt{\mu^n_{\acute{A}}\mu^n_B}$, $\sqrt{\eta^n_{\acute{A}}\eta^n_B}$ *and* $\sqrt{v^n_{\acute{A}}v^n_B}$ *represent the operations on the left endpoint of the interval of* $\mu_{\acute{A}}$, μ_B *and* $\eta_{\acute{A}}$, η_B *and* $v_{\acute{A}}$, v_B, *respectively. Furthermore,* $\sqrt{\left(1-\mu^n_{\acute{A}}-v^n_{\acute{A}}\right)(1-\mu^n_B-v^n_B)}$, $\sqrt{\left(1-\mu^n_{\acute{A}}-\eta^n_{\acute{A}}\right)(1-\mu^n_B-\eta^n_B)}$

and $\sqrt{\left(1-\eta_{\acute{A}}^{n}-v_{\acute{A}}^{n}\right)\left(1-\eta_{B}^{n}-v_{B}^{n}\right)}$ *represent the operations on the right endpoint of the interval of* $\mu_{\acute{A}}$, μ_{B} *and* $\eta_{\acute{A}}$, η_{B} *and* $v_{\acute{A}}$, v_{B}, *respectively.*

Proof of Proposition 1. Let $\acute{A}=\{(\mu_{\acute{A}},\eta_{\acute{A}},v_{\acute{A}})\}$, $B=\{(\mu_{B},\eta_{B},v_{B})\}$, and $\c{C}=\{(\mu_{\c{C}},\eta_{\c{C}},v_{\c{C}})\}$ be three TSFNs.

(S1) $0\leq\sqrt{xy}\leq\frac{x+y}{2}$, for each $x,y\in[0,+\infty)$. We have

$$0\leq 2\sqrt{\mu_{\acute{A}}^{n}\mu_{B}^{n}}+2\sqrt{\eta_{\acute{A}}^{n}\eta_{B}^{n}}+2\sqrt{v_{\acute{A}}^{n}v_{B}^{n}}+\sqrt{\left(1-\eta_{\acute{A}}^{n}-v_{\acute{A}}^{n}\right)\left(1-\eta_{B}^{n}-v_{B}^{n}\right)}+$$
$$\sqrt{\left(1-\mu_{\acute{A}}^{n}-v_{\acute{A}}^{n}\right)\left(1-\mu_{B}^{n}-v_{B}^{n}\right)}+\sqrt{\left(1-\mu_{\acute{A}}^{n}-\eta_{\acute{A}}^{n}\right)\left(1-\mu_{B}^{n}-\eta_{B}^{n}\right)}\leq$$
$$2.\frac{\mu_{\acute{A}}^{n}+\mu_{B}^{n}}{2}+2.\frac{\eta_{\acute{A}}^{n}+\eta_{B}^{n}}{2}+2.\frac{v_{\acute{A}}^{n}+v_{B}^{n}}{2}+\frac{\left(1-\eta_{\acute{A}}^{n}-v_{\acute{A}}^{n}\right)+\left(1-\eta_{B}^{n}-v_{B}^{n}\right)}{2}+$$
$$\frac{\left(1-\mu_{\acute{A}}^{n}-v_{\acute{A}}^{n}\right)+\left(1-\mu_{B}^{n}-v_{B}^{n}\right)}{2}+\frac{\left(1-\mu_{\acute{A}}^{n}-\eta_{\acute{A}}^{n}\right)\left(1-\mu_{B}^{n}-\eta_{B}^{n}\right)}{2}=3$$

Thus, we obtain

$$0\leq\tfrac{1}{3}2\sqrt{\mu_{\acute{A}}^{n}\mu_{B}^{n}}+2\sqrt{\eta_{\acute{A}}^{n}\eta_{B}^{n}}+2\sqrt{v_{\acute{A}}^{n}v_{B}^{n}}+\sqrt{\left(1-\eta_{\acute{A}}^{n}-v_{\acute{A}}^{n}\right)\left(1-\eta_{B}^{n}-v_{B}^{n}\right)}+$$
$$\sqrt{\left(1-\mu_{\acute{A}}^{n}-v_{\acute{A}}^{n}\right)\left(1-\mu_{B}^{n}-v_{B}^{n}\right)}+\sqrt{\left(1-\mu_{\acute{A}}^{n}-\eta_{\acute{A}}^{n}\right)\left(1-\mu_{B}^{n}-\eta_{B}^{n}\right)}\leq 1$$

From the above analysis, we get $0\leq\acute{S}\left(\acute{A},B\right)\leq 1$.

(S2) $\acute{S}\left(\acute{A},B\right)=\acute{S}\left(B,\acute{A}\right)$ is obvious.

(S3) $\sqrt{xy}$ achieves $\frac{x+y}{2}$ if $x=y$. Then,

$$\acute{S}\left(\acute{A},B\right)=1.$$

$$\Leftrightarrow 2\sqrt{\mu_{\acute{A}}^{n}\mu_{B}^{n}}+2\sqrt{\eta_{\acute{A}}^{n}\eta_{B}^{n}}+2\sqrt{v_{\acute{A}}^{n}v_{B}^{n}}+\sqrt{\left(1-\eta_{\acute{A}}^{n}-v_{\acute{A}}^{n}\right)\left(1-\eta_{B}^{n}-v_{B}^{n}\right)}+$$
$$\sqrt{\left(1-\mu_{\acute{A}}^{n}-v_{\acute{A}}^{n}\right)\left(1-\mu_{B}^{n}-v_{B}^{n}\right)}+\sqrt{\left(1-\mu_{\acute{A}}^{n}-\eta_{\acute{A}}^{n}\right)\left(1-\mu_{B}^{n}-\eta_{B}^{n}\right)}=3$$
$$\Leftrightarrow\mu_{\acute{A}}^{n}=\mu_{B}^{n},\ \eta_{\acute{A}}^{n}=\eta_{B}^{n},\ v_{\acute{A}}^{n}=v_{B}^{n}$$
$$\left(1-\eta_{\acute{A}}^{n}-v_{\acute{A}}^{n}\right)=\left(1-\eta_{B}^{n}-v_{B}^{n}\right)$$
$$\left(1-\mu_{\acute{A}}^{n}-v_{\acute{A}}^{n}\right)=\left(1-\mu_{B}^{n}-v_{B}^{n}\right)$$
$$\left(1-\mu_{\acute{A}}^{n}-\eta_{\acute{A}}^{n}\right)=\left(1-\mu_{B}^{n}-\eta_{B}^{n}\right)$$
$$\Leftrightarrow\acute{A}=B$$

From the above analysis, we get $\acute{S}\left(\acute{A},B\right)=1$ iff $\acute{A}=B$.

(S4) Let Á, B, Ç be three TSFNs that fulfills the criteria Á ⊆ B ⊆ Ç. Therefore, we have $0 \le \mu_{Á} \le \mu_B \le \mu_{Ç} \le 1, 0 \le \eta_{Á} \le \eta_B \le \eta_{Ç} \le 1$, and $0 \le v_{Ç} \le v_B \le v_{Á} \le 1$. According to Equation (1), we obtain the SMs as follows:

$$Ś(B, Ç) = \tfrac{1}{3}(2\sqrt{\mu_B^n\mu_{Ç}^n} + 2\sqrt{\eta_B^n\eta_{Ç}^n} + 2\sqrt{v_B^n v_{Ç}^n} + \sqrt{(1-\eta_B^n - v_B^n)\left(1-\eta_{Ç}^n - v_{Ç}^n\right)} + \sqrt{\left(1-\mu_B^n - v_{Ç}^n\right)\left(1-\mu_{Ç}^n - v_{Ç}^n\right)} + \sqrt{(1-\mu_B^n - \eta_B^n)\left(1-\mu_{Ç}^n - \eta_{Ç}^n\right)})$$

$$Ś\left(Á, Ç\right) = \tfrac{1}{3}(2\sqrt{\mu_{Á}^n\mu_{Ç}^n} + 2\sqrt{\eta_{Á}^n\eta_{Ç}^n} + 2\sqrt{v_{Á}^n v_{Ç}^n} + \sqrt{\left(1-\eta_{Á}^n - v_{Á}^n\right)\left(1-\eta_{Ç}^n - v_{Ç}^n\right)} + \sqrt{\left(1-\mu_{Á}^n - v_{Á}^n\right)\left(1-\mu_{Ç}^n - v_{Ç}^n\right)} + \sqrt{\left(1-\mu_{Á}^n - \eta_{Á}^n\right)\left(1-\mu_{Ç}^n - \eta_{Ç}^n\right)})$$

$$Ś\left(Á, B\right) = \tfrac{1}{3}(2\sqrt{\mu_{Á}^n\mu_B^n} + 2\sqrt{\eta_{Á}^n\eta_B^n} + 2\sqrt{v_{Á}^n v_B^n} + \sqrt{\left(1-\eta_{Á}^n - v_{Á}^n\right)(1-\eta_B^n - v_B^n)} + \sqrt{\left(1-\mu_{Á}^n - v_{Á}^n\right)(1-\mu_B^n - v_B^n)} + \sqrt{\left(1-\mu_{Á}^n - \eta_{Á}^n\right)(1-\mu_B^n - \eta_B^n)})$$

For $ã, Ƅ, ç, \in [0, 1], ã + Ƅ + ç \le 1, x, y, ż \in [0, 1], x + y + ż \in [0, 1]$, then

$$f\left(x, y, ż\right) = 2\sqrt{ãx} + 2\sqrt{Ƅy} + 2\sqrt{çż} + \sqrt{\left(1-y-ż\right)(1-Ƅ-ç)} + \sqrt{(1-x-ż)(1-ã-ç)} + \sqrt{\left(1-x-y\right)(1-ã-Ƅ)}$$

We can obtain

$$\frac{\partial f}{\partial x} = \frac{\sqrt{ã}}{\sqrt{x}} - \frac{\sqrt{1-ã-ç}}{2\sqrt{1-x-ż}} - \frac{\sqrt{1-ã-Ƅ}}{2\sqrt{1-x-y}}$$

$$\frac{\partial f}{\partial x} = \frac{\sqrt{ã}}{2\sqrt{x}} - \frac{\sqrt{1-ã-ç}}{2\sqrt{1-x-ż}} + \frac{\sqrt{ã}}{2\sqrt{x}} - \frac{\sqrt{1-ã-Ƅ}}{2\sqrt{1-x-y}}$$

$$\frac{\partial f}{\partial x} = \frac{ã(1-ż)-x(1-ç)}{2\sqrt{x(1-x-ż)}\left(\sqrt{ã(1-x-ż)}+\sqrt{x(1-ã-ç)}\right)} + \frac{ã\left(1-y\right)-x(1-Ƅ)}{2\sqrt{x\left(1-x-y\right)}\left(\sqrt{ã(1-x-y)}+\sqrt{x(1-ã-Ƅ)}\right)}$$

$$\left|\frac{\partial f}{\partial x}\right|_{\substack{y = Ƅ \\ ż = ç}} = \frac{(ã-x)(1-ç)}{2\sqrt{x(1-x-ç)}\left(\sqrt{ã(1-x-ç)}+\sqrt{x(1-ã-ç)}\right)} + \frac{(ã-x)(1-Ƅ)}{2\sqrt{x(1-x-Ƅ)}\left(\sqrt{ã(1-x-Ƅ)}+\sqrt{x(1-ã-Ƅ)}\right)}$$

$$\frac{\partial f}{\partial y} = \frac{\sqrt{Ƅ}}{\sqrt{y}} - \frac{\sqrt{1-Ƅ-ç}}{2\sqrt{1-y-z}} - \frac{\sqrt{1-ã-Ƅ}}{2\sqrt{1-x-y}}$$

$$\frac{\partial f}{\partial y} = \frac{\sqrt{Ƅ}}{2\sqrt{y}} - \frac{\sqrt{1-Ƅ-ç}}{2\sqrt{1-y-z}} + \frac{\sqrt{Ƅ}}{2\sqrt{y}} - \frac{\sqrt{1-ã-Ƅ}}{2\sqrt{1-x-y}}$$

$$\frac{\partial f}{\partial y} = \frac{Ƅ(1-ż)-y(1-ç)}{2\sqrt{y\left(1-y-ż\right)}\left(\sqrt{Ƅ(1-y-ż)}+\sqrt{y(1-Ƅ-ç)}\right)} + \frac{Ƅ(1-x)-y(1-ã)}{2\sqrt{y\left(1-x-y\right)}\left(\sqrt{Ƅ(1-x-y)}+\sqrt{y(1-ã-Ƅ)}\right)}$$

$$\left|\frac{\partial f}{\partial y}\right|_{\substack{x = ã \\ ż = ç}} = \frac{\left(Ƅ-y\right)(1-ç)}{2\sqrt{y\left(1-y-ç\right)}\left(\sqrt{Ƅ(1-y-ç)}+\sqrt{y(1-Ƅ-ç)}\right)} + \frac{\left(Ƅ-y\right)(1-ã)}{2\sqrt{y\left(1-y-Ƅ\right)}\left(\sqrt{Ƅ(1-y-ã)}+\sqrt{y(1-ã-Ƅ)}\right)}$$

and

$$\frac{\partial f}{\partial \dot{z}} = \frac{\sqrt{ç}}{\sqrt{\dot{z}}} - \frac{\sqrt{1-Ь-ç}}{2\sqrt{1-y-\dot{z}}} - \frac{\sqrt{1-ã-ç}}{2\sqrt{1-x-\dot{z}}}$$

$$\frac{\partial f}{\partial \dot{z}} = \frac{\sqrt{ç}}{2\sqrt{\dot{z}}} - \frac{\sqrt{1-Ь-ç}}{2\sqrt{1-y-\dot{z}}} + \frac{\sqrt{ç}}{2\sqrt{\dot{z}}} - \frac{\sqrt{1-ã-ç}}{2\sqrt{1-x-\dot{z}}}$$

$$\frac{\partial f}{\partial \dot{z}} = \frac{ç\left(1-y\right)-\dot{z}(1-Ь)}{2\sqrt{z\left(1-y-\dot{z}\right)}\left(\sqrt{ç(1-y-\dot{z})}+\sqrt{\dot{z}(1-Ь-ç)}\right)} + \frac{ç(1-x)-z(1-ã)}{2\sqrt{z(1-x-\dot{z})}\left(\sqrt{ç(1-x-\dot{z})}+\sqrt{\dot{z}(1-ã-ç)}\right)}$$

$$\left|\frac{\partial f}{\partial \dot{z}}\right|_{\substack{x=ã \\ y=Ь}} = \frac{(ç-\dot{z})(1-Ь)}{2\sqrt{z(1-Ь-\dot{z})}\left(\sqrt{ç(1-\dot{z}-Ь)}+\sqrt{\dot{z}(1-Ь-ç)}\right)} + \frac{(ç-\dot{z})(1-ã)}{2\sqrt{\dot{z}(1-\dot{z}-ã)}\left(\sqrt{ç(1-\dot{z}-ã)}+\sqrt{\dot{z}(1-ã-ç)}\right)}$$

For $ã \le x \le 1$, we have $\partial f/\partial x \le 0$, which shows that f is a reducing function of x, when $y = Ь$, $\dot{z} = ç$, $x \ge ã$. For $0 \le x \le ã$, we have $\partial f/\partial x \ge 0$, which means that f is a growing function of x, when $y = Ь$, $\dot{z} = ç$, $x < ã$.

Similarly, we may get $\partial f/\partial y \le 0$ for $Ь \le y \le 1$. It indicates that f is a reducing function of y when $x = ã$, $\dot{z} = ç$, $y \ge Ь$. We have $\partial f/\partial y \ge 0$ for $0 \le y < Ь$ and it indicates that f is an increasing function of y when $x = ã$, $\dot{z} = ç$, $y < Ь$. Since $\partial f/\partial \dot{z} \le 0$ for $ç \le \dot{z} \le 1$, it indicates that f is a reducing function of $\dot{z}$ when $x = ã$, $y = Ь$, $\dot{z} \ge ç$. We have $\partial f/\partial \dot{z} \ge 0$ for $0 \le \dot{z} < ç$ which indicates that f is a growing function of $\dot{z}$ when $x = ã$, $y = Ь$, $\dot{z} < ç$.

Let $ã = \mu_{Á}$, $Ь = \eta_{Á}$, $ç = v_{Á}$, with two TSFNs (μ_B, η_B, v_B) and $(\mu_Ç, \eta_Ç, v_Ç)$, satisfying:

$$ã = \mu_{Á} \le \mu_B \le \mu_Ç$$
$$Ь = \eta_{Á} \le \eta_B \le \eta_Ç$$
$$ç = v_Ç \le v_B \le v_{Á}$$

we can obtain

$$f(\mu_Ç, Ь, ç) \le f(\mu_B, Ь, ç) \le f(ã, Ь, ç)$$
$$f(ã, \eta_Ç, ç) \le f(ã, \eta_B, ç) \le f(ã, Ь, ç)$$
$$f(ã, Ь, v_Ç) \le f(ã, Ь, v_B) \le f(ã, Ь, ç)$$

and then

$$f\left(\mu_Ç, \eta_Ç, v_Ç\right) \le f(\mu_B, \eta_B, v_B)$$

i.e.,

$$2\sqrt{\mu_B^n \mu_Ç^n} + 2\sqrt{\eta_B^n \eta_Ç^n} + 2\sqrt{v_B^n v_Ç^n} + \sqrt{\left(1-\eta_B^n - v_B^n\right)\left(1-\eta_Ç^n - v_Ç^n\right)} + \sqrt{\left(1-\mu_B^n - v_Ç^n\right)\left(1-\mu_Ç^n - v_Ç^n\right)} + \sqrt{\left(1-\mu_B^n - \eta_B^n\right)\left(1-\mu_Ç^n - \eta_Ç^n\right)}$$
$$\le 2\sqrt{\mu_{Á}^n \mu_B^n} + 2\sqrt{\eta_{Á}^n \eta_B^n} + 2\sqrt{v_{Á}^n v_B^n} + \sqrt{\left(1-\eta_{Á}^n - v_{Á}^n\right)\left(1-\eta_B^n - v_B^n\right)} + \sqrt{\left(1-\mu_{Á}^n - v_{Á}^n\right)\left(1-\mu_B^n - v_B^n\right)} + \sqrt{\left(1-\mu_{Á}^n - \eta_{Á}^n\right)\left(1-\mu_B^n - \eta_B^n\right)}$$

Thus, $Ś\left(Á, Ç\right) \le Ś\left(Á, B\right)$ according to the above analysis.

Similarly, if we suppose $ã = \mu_Ç$, $Ь = \eta_Ç$, $ç = v_Ç$, and the two TSFNs $\left(\mu_{Á}, \eta_{Á}, v_{Á}\right)$ and (μ_B, η_B, v_B) satisfy:

$$ã = \mu_{Á} \le \mu_B \le \mu_Ç Ь = \eta_{Á} \le \eta_B \le \eta_Ç c = v_Ç \le v_B \le v_{Á}$$

we can obtain

$$f(\mu_{Á}, Ƅ, ç) \leq f(\mu_B, Ƅ, ç) \leq f(a, Ƅ, ç)$$
$$f(ã, \eta_{Á}, ç) \leq f(ã, \eta_B, ç) \leq f(ã, Ƅ, ç)$$
$$f(ã, Ƅ, v_{Á}) \leq f(ã, Ƅ, v_B) \leq f(ã, Ƅ, ç)$$

and then

$$f(\mu_{Á}, \eta_{Á}, v_{Á}) \leq f(\mu_B, \eta_B, v_B)$$

i.e.,

$$2\sqrt{\mu_{Á}^n \mu_{Ç}^n} + 2\sqrt{\eta_{Á}^n \eta_{Ç}^n} + 2\sqrt{v_{Á}^n v_{Ç}^n} + \sqrt{\left(1 - \eta_{Á}^n - v_{Á}^n\right)\left(1 - \eta_{Ç}^n - v_{Ç}^n\right)} +$$
$$\sqrt{\left(1 - \mu_{Á}^n - v_{Á}^n\right)\left(1 - \mu_{Ç}^n - v_{Ç}^n\right)} + \sqrt{\left(1 - \mu_{Á}^n - \eta_{Á}^n\right)\left(1 - \mu_{Ç}^n - \eta_{Ç}^n\right)} \leq$$
$$2\sqrt{\mu_B^n \mu_{Ç}^n} + 2\sqrt{\eta_B^n \eta_{Ç}^n} + 2\sqrt{v_B^n v_{Ç}^n} + \sqrt{\left(1 - \eta_B^n - v_B^n\right)\left(1 - \eta_{Ç}^n - v_{Ç}^n\right)} +$$
$$\sqrt{\left(1 - \mu_B^n - v_{Ç}^n\right)\left(1 - \mu_{Ç}^n - v_{Ç}^n\right)} + \sqrt{\left(1 - \mu_B^n - \eta_B^n\right)\left(1 - \mu_{Ç}^n - \eta_{Ç}^n\right)}.$$

Thus, $Ś\left(Á, Ç\right) \leq Ś(B, Ç)$ based on the preceding analysis. The SM $Ś\left(Á, B\right)$ with Equation (1) satisfies Definition 6. □

Theorem 3. *Let* $Á = \left\{\left(\mu_{Á_{x_ï}}, \eta_{Á_{x_ï}}, v_{Á_{x_ï}}\right) | x_ï \in X\right\}$, $B = \{(\mu_{Bx_ï}, \eta_{Bx_ï}, v_{Bx_ï}) | x_ï \in X\}$ *be two TSFSs on* $X = \{x_1, x_2, \ldots, x_n\}$. *The mapping* $Ś\left(Á, B\right) : TSFS(X) \times TSFS(X) \to [0, 1]$ *is defined as follows:*

$$Ś\left(Á, B\right) = \frac{1}{3n}\sum_{ï=1}^{n}\left(\begin{array}{c} 2\sqrt{\mu_{Á_{x_ï}}^n \mu_{B_{x_ï}}^n} + 2\sqrt{\eta_{Á_{x_ï}}^n \eta_{B_{x_ï}}^n} + 2\sqrt{v_{Á_{x_ï}}^n v_{B_{x_ï}}^n} + \\ \sqrt{\left(1 - \eta_{Á_{x_ï}}^n - v_{Á_{x_ï}}^n\right)\left(1 - \eta_{B_{x_ï}}^n - v_{B_{x_ï}}^n\right)} + \\ \sqrt{\left(1 - \mu_{Á_{x_ï}}^n - v_{Á_{x_ï}}^n\right)\left(1 - \mu_{B_{x_ï}}^n - v_{B_{x_ï}}^n\right)} + \\ \sqrt{\left(1 - \mu_{Á_{x_ï}}^n - \eta_{Á_{x_ï}}^n\right)\left(1 - \mu_{B_{x_ï}}^n - \eta_{B_{x_ï}}^n\right)} \end{array}\right). \quad (2)$$

Then, $Ś\left(Á, B\right)$ is a SM for the TSFSs Á and B.

Proof of Theorem 3. Let $Á = \left\{\left(\mu_{Á_{x_ï}}, \eta_{Á_{x_ï}}, v_{Á_{x_ï}}\right) | x_ï \in X\right\}$, $B = \{(\mu_{Bx_ï}, \eta_{Bx_ï}, v_{Bx_ï}) | x_ï \in X\}$ and $Ç = \left\{\left(\mu_{Ç_{x_ï}}, \eta_{Ç_{x_ï}}, v_{Ç_{x_ï}}\right) | x_ï \in X\right\}$ be the three TSFSs on $X = \{x_1, x_2, \ldots, x_n\}$.

(S1) $0 \leq \sqrt{xy} \leq \frac{x+y}{2}$, for each $x, y \in [0, +\infty)$. We have

$$
\begin{aligned}
0 \leq\ & 2\sqrt{\mu^{n}_{\acute{A}_{x_{\bar{i}}}} \mu^{n}_{B_{x_{\bar{i}}}}} + 2\sqrt{\eta^{n}_{\acute{A}_{x_{\bar{i}}}} \eta^{n}_{B_{x_{\bar{i}}}}} + 2\sqrt{v^{n}_{\acute{A}_{x_{\bar{i}}}} v^{n}_{B_{x_{\bar{i}}}}} + \\
& \sqrt{\left(1 - \eta^{n}_{\acute{A}_{x_{\bar{i}}}} - v^{n}_{\acute{A}_{x_{\bar{i}}}}\right)\left(1 - \eta^{n}_{B_{x_{\bar{i}}}} - v^{n}_{B_{x_{\bar{i}}}}\right)} + \\
& \sqrt{\left(1 - \mu^{n}_{\acute{A}_{x_{\bar{i}}}} - v^{n}_{\acute{A}_{x_{\bar{i}}}}\right)\left(1 - \mu^{n}_{B_{x_{\bar{i}}}} - v^{n}_{B_{x_{\bar{i}}}}\right)} + \\
& \sqrt{\left(1 - \mu^{n}_{\acute{A}_{x_{\bar{i}}}} - \eta^{n}_{\acute{A}_{x_{\bar{i}}}}\right)\left(1 - \mu^{n}_{B_{x_{\bar{i}}}} - \eta^{n}_{B_{x_{\bar{i}}}}\right)} \leq \\
& 2.\frac{\mu^{n}_{\acute{A}_{x_{\bar{i}}}} + \mu^{n}_{B_{x_{\bar{i}}}}}{2} + 2.\frac{\eta^{n}_{\acute{A}_{x_{\bar{i}}}} + \eta^{n}_{B_{x_{\bar{i}}}}}{2} + 2.\frac{v^{n}_{\acute{A}_{x_{\bar{i}}}} + v^{n}_{B_{x_{\bar{i}}}}}{2} + \\
& \frac{\left(1-\mu^{n}_{\acute{A}_{x_{\bar{i}}}} - v^{n}_{\acute{A}_{x_{\bar{i}}}}\right) + \left(1-\mu^{n}_{B_{x_{\bar{i}}}} - v^{n}_{B_{x_{\bar{i}}}}\right)}{2} + \frac{\left(1-\mu^{n}_{\acute{A}_{x_{\bar{i}}}} - v^{n}_{\acute{A}_{x_{\bar{i}}}}\right) + \left(1-\mu^{n}_{B_{x_{\bar{i}}}} - v^{n}_{B_{x_{\bar{i}}}}\right)}{2} + \\
& \frac{\left(1-\mu^{n}_{\acute{A}_{x_{\bar{i}}}} - \eta^{n}_{\acute{A}_{x_{\bar{i}}}}\right) + \left(1-\mu^{n}_{B_{x_{\bar{i}}}} - \eta^{n}_{B_{x_{\bar{i}}}}\right)}{2} = 3
\end{aligned}
$$

Thus, we can obtain

$$
0 \leq \frac{1}{3n}\sum_{i=1}^{n}\left(
\begin{array}{c}
2\sqrt{\mu^{n}_{\acute{A}_{x_{\bar{i}}}} \mu^{n}_{B_{x_{\bar{i}}}}} + 2\sqrt{\eta^{n}_{\acute{A}_{x_{\bar{i}}}} \eta^{n}_{B_{x_{\bar{i}}}}} + 2\sqrt{v^{n}_{\acute{A}_{x_{\bar{i}}}} v^{n}_{B_{x_{\bar{i}}}}} + \\
\sqrt{\left(1 - \eta^{n}_{\acute{A}_{x_{\bar{i}}}} - v^{n}_{\acute{A}_{x_{\bar{i}}}}\right)\left(1 - \eta^{n}_{B_{x_{\bar{i}}}} - v^{n}_{B_{x_{\bar{i}}}}\right)} + \\
\sqrt{\left(1 - \mu^{n}_{\acute{A}_{x_{\bar{i}}}} - v^{n}_{\acute{A}_{x_{\bar{i}}}}\right)\left(1 - \mu^{n}_{B_{x_{\bar{i}}}} - v^{n}_{B_{x_{\bar{i}}}}\right)} + \\
\sqrt{\left(1 - \mu^{n}_{\acute{A}_{x_{\bar{i}}}} - \eta^{n}_{\acute{A}_{x_{\bar{i}}}}\right)\left(1 - \mu^{n}_{B_{x_{\bar{i}}}} - \eta^{n}_{B_{x_{\bar{i}}}}\right)}
\end{array}
\right) \leq 1.
$$

From the above analysis, we get $0 \leq \acute{S}\left(\acute{A}, B\right) \leq 1$.

(S2) $\acute{S}\left(\acute{A}, B\right) = \acute{S}\left(B, \acute{A}\right)$ is obvious.

(S3) $\sqrt{xy}$ achieves $\frac{x+y}{2}$ if $x = y$. Then

$$
\begin{aligned}
& \acute{S}\left(\acute{A}, B\right) = 1 \\
\Leftrightarrow\ & 2\sqrt{\mu^{n}_{\acute{A}_{x_{\bar{i}}}} \mu^{n}_{B_{x_{\bar{i}}}}} + 2\sqrt{\eta^{n}_{\acute{A}_{x_{\bar{i}}}} \eta^{n}_{B_{x_{\bar{i}}}}} + 2\sqrt{v^{n}_{\acute{A}_{x_{\bar{i}}}} v^{n}_{B_{x_{\bar{i}}}}} + \\
& \sqrt{\left(1 - \eta^{n}_{\acute{A}_{x_{\bar{i}}}} - v^{n}_{\acute{A}_{x_{\bar{i}}}}\right)\left(1 - \eta^{n}_{B_{x_{\bar{i}}}} - v^{n}_{B_{x_{\bar{i}}}}\right)} + \\
& \sqrt{\left(1 - \mu^{n}_{\acute{A}_{x_{\bar{i}}}} - v^{n}_{\acute{A}_{x_{\bar{i}}}}\right)\left(1 - \mu^{n}_{B_{x_{\bar{i}}}} - v^{n}_{B_{x_{\bar{i}}}}\right)} + \\
& \sqrt{\left(1 - \mu^{n}_{\acute{A}_{x_{\bar{i}}}} - \eta^{n}_{\acute{A}_{x_{\bar{i}}}}\right)\left(1 - \mu^{n}_{B_{x_{\bar{i}}}} - \eta^{n}_{B_{x_{\bar{i}}}}\right)} = 3 \\
\Leftrightarrow\ & \mu_{\acute{A}_{x_{\bar{i}}}} = \mu_{B_{x_{\bar{i}}}},\ \eta_{\acute{A}_{x_{\bar{i}}}} = \eta_{B_{x_{\bar{i}}}},\ v_{\acute{A}_{x_{\bar{i}}}} = v_{B_{x_{\bar{i}}}} \\
& \left(1 - \eta_{\acute{A}_{x_{\bar{i}}}} - v_{\acute{A}_{x_{\bar{i}}}}\right) = \left(1 - \eta_{B_{x_{\bar{i}}}} - v_{B_{x_{\bar{i}}}}\right) \\
& \left(1 - \mu_{\acute{A}_{x_{\bar{i}}}} - v_{\acute{A}_{x_{\bar{i}}}}\right) = \left(1 - \mu_{B_{x_{\bar{i}}}} - v_{B_{x_{\bar{i}}}}\right) \\
& \left(1 - \mu_{\acute{A}_{x_{\bar{i}}}} - \eta_{\acute{A}_{x_{\bar{i}}}}\right) = \left(1 - \mu_{B_{x_{\bar{i}}}} - \eta_{B_{x_{\bar{i}}}}\right) \\
\Leftrightarrow\ & \acute{A} = B.
\end{aligned}
$$

Therefore, $\acute{S}(\acute{A}, B) = 1$ iff $\acute{A} = B$.

$$\acute{S}(\acute{A}, B) = \frac{1}{3n}\sum_{\ddot{i}=1}^{n}\left(\frac{2\sqrt{\mu^n_{\acute{A}_{x_{\ddot{i}}}}\mu^n_{B_{x_{\ddot{i}}}}} + 2\sqrt{\eta^n_{\acute{A}_{x_{\ddot{i}}}}\eta^n_{B_{x_{\ddot{i}}}}} + 2\sqrt{v^n_{\acute{A}_{x_{\ddot{i}}}}v^n_{B_{x_{\ddot{i}}}}} + \sqrt{\left(1-\eta^n_{\acute{A}_{x_{\ddot{i}}}} - v^n_{\acute{A}_{x_{\ddot{i}}}}\right)\left(1-\eta^n_{B_{x_{\ddot{i}}}} - v^n_{B_{x_{\ddot{i}}}}\right)} +}{\sqrt{\left(1-\mu^n_{\acute{A}_{x_{\ddot{i}}}} - v^n_{\acute{A}_{x_{\ddot{i}}}}\right)\left(1-\mu^n_{B_{x_{\ddot{i}}}} - v^n_{B_{x_{\ddot{i}}}}\right)} + \sqrt{\left(1-\mu^n_{\acute{A}_{x_{\ddot{i}}}} - \eta^n_{\acute{A}_{x_{\ddot{i}}}}\right)\left(1-\mu^n_{B_{x_{\ddot{i}}}} - \eta^n_{B_{x_{\ddot{i}}}}\right)}}\right)$$

$$\acute{S}(B, \c{C}) = \frac{1}{3n}\sum_{\ddot{i}=1}^{n}\left(\frac{2\sqrt{\mu^n_{B_{x_{\ddot{i}}}}\mu^n_{\c{C}_{x_{\ddot{i}}}}} + 2\sqrt{\eta^n_{B_{x_{\ddot{i}}}}\eta^n_{\c{C}_{x_{\ddot{i}}}}} + 2\sqrt{v^n_{B_{x_{\ddot{i}}}}v^n_{\c{C}_{x_{\ddot{i}}}}} + \sqrt{\left(1-\eta^n_{B_{x_{\ddot{i}}}} - v^n_{B_{x_{\ddot{i}}}}\right)\left(1-\eta^n_{\c{C}_{x_{\ddot{i}}}} - v^n_{\c{C}_{x_{\ddot{i}}}}\right)}}{+\sqrt{\left(1-\mu^n_{B_{x_{\ddot{i}}}} - v^n_{B_{x_{\ddot{i}}}}\right)\left(1-\mu^n_{\c{C}_{x_{\ddot{i}}}} - v^n_{\c{C}_{x_{\ddot{i}}}}\right)} + \sqrt{\left(1-\mu^n_{B_{x_{\ddot{i}}}} - \eta^n_{B_{x_{\ddot{i}}}}\right)\left(1-\mu^n_{\c{C}_{x_{\ddot{i}}}} - \eta^n_{\c{C}_{x_{\ddot{i}}}}\right)}}\right)$$

$$\acute{S}(\acute{A}, \c{C}) = \frac{1}{3n}\Sigma_{\ddot{i}=1}^{n}\left(\frac{2\sqrt{\mu^n_{\acute{A}_{x_{\ddot{i}}}}\mu^n_{\c{C}_{x_{\ddot{i}}}}} + 2\sqrt{\eta^n_{\acute{A}_{x_{\ddot{i}}}}\eta^n_{\c{C}_{x_{\ddot{i}}}}} + 2\sqrt{v^n_{\acute{A}_{x_{\ddot{i}}}}v^n_{\c{C}_{x_{\ddot{i}}}}} + \sqrt{\left(1-\eta^n_{\acute{A}_{x_{\ddot{i}}}} - v^n_{\acute{A}_{x_{\ddot{i}}}}\right)\left(1-\eta^n_{\c{C}_{x_{\ddot{i}}}} - v^n_{\c{C}_{x_{\ddot{i}}}}\right)} +}{\sqrt{\left(1-\mu^n_{\acute{A}_{x_{\ddot{i}}}} - v^n_{\acute{A}_{x_{\ddot{i}}}}\right)\left(1-\mu^n_{\c{C}_{x_{\ddot{i}}}} - v^n_{\c{C}_{x_{\ddot{i}}}}\right)} + \sqrt{\left(1-\mu^n_{\acute{A}_{x_{\ddot{i}}}} - \eta^n_{\acute{A}_{x_{\ddot{i}}}}\right)\left(1-\mu^n_{\c{C}_{x_{\ddot{i}}}} - \eta^n_{\c{C}_{x_{\ddot{i}}}}\right)}}\right).$$

This proof is similar to Proposition 1. We can get $\acute{S}(\acute{A}, \c{C}) \leq \acute{S}(\acute{A}, B), \acute{S}(\acute{A}, \c{C}) \leq \acute{S}(B, \c{C})$ according to the above analysis, and thus, SM $\acute{S}(\acute{A}, B)$ with Equation (2) fulfills the criteria of Definition 6. □

4. Consequences of the Proposed Work

In the previous Section 3, we proposed a new SM for TSFNs $\acute{A} = (\mu_{\acute{A}}, \eta_{\acute{A}}, v_{\acute{A}})$ and $B = (\mu_B, \eta_B, v_B)$, and also another SM for TSFSs $\acute{A} = \left\{\left(\mu_{\acute{A}_{x_{\ddot{i}}}}, \eta_{\acute{A}_{x_{\ddot{i}}}}, v_{\acute{A}_{x_{\ddot{i}}}}\right) | x_{\ddot{i}} \in X\right\}$, and $B = \{(\mu_{Bx_{\ddot{i}}}, \eta_{Bx_{\ddot{i}}}, v_{Bx_{\ddot{i}}}) | x_{\ddot{i}} \in X\}$ on $X = \{x_1, x_2, \ldots, x_n\}$. Since the proposed SMs for TSFNs and TSFSs can be the generalizations of some SMs, we will present some consequences of the proposed SMs under some special cases in this section.

Recall that the proposed SM of Equation (1) for TSFNs $\acute{A} = (\mu_{\acute{A}}, \eta_{\acute{A}}, v_{\acute{A}})$ and $B = (\mu_B, \eta_B, v_B)$ is as follows:

$$\acute{S}(\acute{A}, B) = \frac{1}{3}\left(\frac{2\sqrt{\mu^n_{\acute{A}}\mu^n_B} + 2\sqrt{\eta^n_{\acute{A}}\eta^n_B} + 2\sqrt{v^n_{\acute{A}}v^n_B} + \sqrt{\left(1-\eta^n_{\acute{A}} - v^n_{\acute{A}}\right)(1-\eta^n_B - v^n_B)} +}{\sqrt{\left(1-\mu^n_{\acute{A}} - v^n_{\acute{A}}\right)(1-\mu^n_B - v^n_B)} + \sqrt{\left(1-\mu^n_{\acute{A}} - \eta^n_{\acute{A}}\right)(1-\mu^n_B - \eta^n_B)}}\right)$$

- If we replace $n = 2$ in the proposed SM, then SM for SFSs is obtained and given as:

$$\acute{S}(\acute{A}, B) = \frac{1}{3}\left(\frac{2\sqrt{\mu^2_{\acute{A}}\mu^2_B} + 2\sqrt{\eta^2_{\acute{A}}\eta^2_B} + 2\sqrt{v^2_{\acute{A}}v^2_B} + \sqrt{\left(1-\eta^2_{\acute{A}} - v^2_{\acute{A}}\right)(1-\eta^2_B - v^2_B)} +}{\sqrt{\left(1-\mu^2_{\acute{A}} - v^2_{\acute{A}}\right)(1-\mu^2_B - v^2_B)} + \sqrt{\left(1-\mu^2_{\acute{A}} - \eta^2_{\acute{A}}\right)(1-\mu^2_B - \eta^2_B)}}\right).$$

- If we replace $n = 1$ in the proposed SM, then the SM for PFSs is obtained and given as:

$$\acute{S}(\acute{A}, B) = \frac{1}{3}\left(\frac{2\sqrt{\mu_{\acute{A}}\mu_B} + 2\sqrt{\eta_{\acute{A}}\eta_B} + 2\sqrt{v_{\acute{A}}v_B} + \sqrt{(1-\eta_{\acute{A}} - v_{\acute{A}})(1-\eta_B - v_B)} +}{\sqrt{(1-\mu_{\acute{A}} - v_{\acute{A}})(1-\mu_B - v_B)} + \sqrt{(1-\mu_{\acute{A}} - \eta_{\acute{A}})(1-\mu_B - \eta_B)}}\right).$$

- If we neglect the DA in the proposed SM, then the SM for q-ROFSs is obtained and given as:

$$\acute{S}(\acute{A}, B) = \frac{1}{3}\left(\frac{2\sqrt{\mu^n_{\acute{A}}\mu^n_B} + 2\sqrt{v^n_{\acute{A}}v^n_B} + \sqrt{\left(1-v^n_{\acute{A}}\right)(1-v^n_B)} +}{\sqrt{\left(1-\mu^n_{\acute{A}} - v^n_{\acute{A}}\right)(1-\mu^n_B - v^n_B)} + \sqrt{\left(1-\mu^n_{\acute{A}}\right)(1-\mu^n_B)}}\right).$$

- If we replace $n = 2$ and neglect the DA in the proposed SM, then the SM for PyFSs is obtained and given as:

$$\acute{S}\left(\acute{A},\ B\right)=\frac{1}{3}\left(\begin{array}{c}2\sqrt{\mu_{\acute{A}}^{2}\mu_{B}^{2}}+2\sqrt{v_{\acute{A}}^{2}v_{B}^{2}}+\sqrt{\left(1-v_{\acute{A}}^{2}\right)\left(1-v_{B}^{2}\right)}+\\ \sqrt{\left(1-\mu_{\acute{A}}^{2}-v_{\acute{A}}^{2}\right)\left(1-\mu_{B}^{2}-v_{B}^{2}\right)}+\sqrt{\left(1-\mu_{\acute{A}}^{2}\right)\left(1-\mu_{B}^{2}\right)}\end{array}\right).$$

- If we replace $n = 1$ and neglect the DA in the proposed SM, then the SM for IFSs is obtained and given as:

$$\acute{S}\left(\acute{A},\ B\right)=\frac{1}{3}\left(\begin{array}{c}2\sqrt{\mu_{\acute{A}}\mu_{B}}+2\sqrt{v_{\acute{A}}v_{B}}+\sqrt{(1-v_{\acute{A}})(1-v_{B})}+\\ \sqrt{(1-\mu_{\acute{A}}-v_{\acute{A}})(1-\mu_{B}-v_{B})}+\sqrt{(1-\mu_{\acute{A}})(1-\mu_{B})}\end{array}\right).$$

Based on the preceding findings, we conclude that the proposed SMs can obtain some new SMs for IFSs, PyFSs, PFSs, and SFSs. The major goal of the SMs presented in this work is that they can solve problems when the data is provided in the TSF environment.

5. Applications and Algorithm

In this section, we create an algorithm for pattern recognition based on the proposed SMs to find out which pattern is the best to use. We also discuss the application of the proposed SMs in decision-making to sketch out which alternative is the finest for making a decision.

5.1. Algorithm for Pattern Recognition

Let $X = \{x_1, x_2, \ldots, x_n\}$, and let us have m patterns $P_j = \left\{\left(\mu_{P_j}(x_{\ddot{i}}),\ \eta_{P_j}(x_{\ddot{i}}), v_{P_j}(x_{\ddot{i}})\right)|x_{\ddot{i}} \in X\right\}$, $j = 1,2,3,\ldots,m$, and a test sample $P = \left\{\left(\mu_p(x_{\ddot{i}}),\ \eta_p(x_{\ddot{i}}), v_p(x_{\ddot{i}})\right)|x_{\ddot{i}} \in X\right\}$. To check which pattern of $P_j, j = 1,2,3,\ldots,m$ will mostly match the pattern P, we give the following recognition steps:

Step 1. We calculate the SMs $\acute{S}(P_j,\ P), j = 1,2,3,\ldots,m$ between P_j and P.

Step 2. We have to choose the maximum one $\acute{S}(P_{j0},\ P)$ from $\acute{S}(P_j,\ P), j = 1,2,3,\ldots,m$, i.e., $\acute{S}(P_{j0},\ P) = \max_{1\leq j\leq m}\left\{\acute{S}(P_j,\ P)\right\}$. Then, the sample P is classified to the pattern P_{j0} by the maximum principle of SMs.

Example 1. *We use the proposed SMs to solve the building material recognition challenge in Ullah et al.* [26]. *Consider TSFNs* $P_{\ddot{i}}(\ddot{i} = 1,2,3,4)$ *which represent four types of construction materials. Let us consider* $X = \{x_{\ddot{i}} : \ddot{i} = 1,2,3,\ldots,7\}$ *to be the attributes. We have another unknown material P. Using the proposed SMs for TSFNs and TSFSs, we use four materials to determine the class of an unknown material denoted by* $P_{\ddot{i}}(\ddot{i} = 1,2,3,4)$. *Now we have to evaluate class* $P_{\ddot{i}}$ to P.

Step 1. All the data are in the form of TSFNs given in Table 1. Assume that given values are TSFNs for $n = 4$; in Table 1, this indicates that when data is presented in the TSF environment, neither IFSs nor PFSs tools can resolve this issue.

Table 1. Data on building material.

		P_1			P_2			P_3			P_4			P	
x_1	0.56	0.47	0.22	0.81	0.3	0.37	0.43	0.43	0.55	0.57	0.51	0.39	0.34	0.56	0.78
x_2	0.11	0.11	0.11	0.59	0.66	0.66	0.91	0.34	0.68	0.56	0.76	0.31	0.47	0.38	0.84
x_3	0.35	0.45	0.61	0.42	0.56	0.71	0.81	0.41	0.35	0.27	0.59	0.72	0.55	0.44	0.65
x_4	0.33	0.54	0.31	0.59	0.45	0.9	0.44	0.55	0.77	0.46	0.46	0.45	0.76	0.46	0.85
x_5	0.35	0.2	0.64	0.16	0.33	0.42	0.55	0.44	0.77	0.57	0.66	0.91	0.13	0.35	0.57
x_6	0.47	0.37	0.68	0.68	0.46	0.88	0.47	0.66	0.75	0.41	0.73	0.41	0.24	0.54	0.45
x_7	0.78	0.55	0.03	0.49	0.54	0.39	0.58	0.34	0.23	0.21	0.43	0.13	0.82	0.46	0.69

Step 2. In this step, we apply Equation (1) on the information given in Table 1. The results using the SM for TSFNs are given in Table 2.

Table 2. Similarity Measure of $P_{ï}$ with P.

SM	(P_1, P)	(P_2, P)	(P_3, P)	(P_4, P)
Values	0.8872037	0.9014245	0.9010272	0.8464994

Step 3. Analyzing Table 2, we conclude that

$$(P_4, P) < (P_1, P) < (P_3, P) < (P_2, P)$$

As a result, the material P_2 is nearest to P because the SM of (P_2, P) is greater than all the other pairs. Consequently, it is concluded that the unidentified material P corresponds to the P_2 category of material. The results of Table 2 are also portrayed in Figure 1 where it shows that the unknown pattern P is closed to P_2. The results also show that the unknown pattern P is still sufficiently close to the pattern P_3 as well.

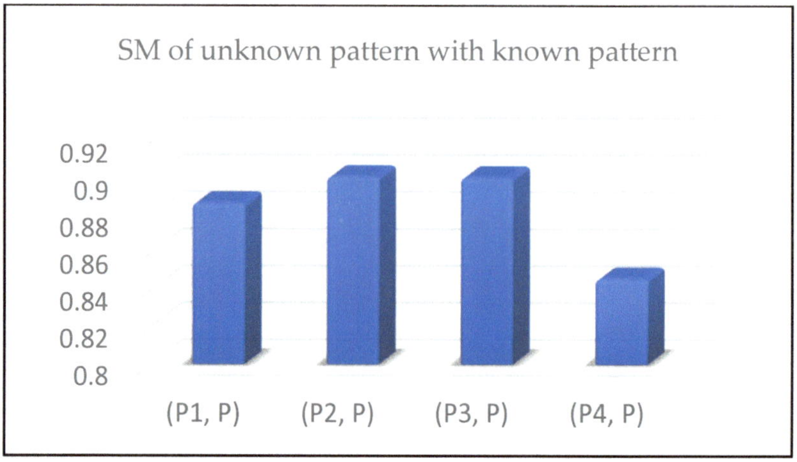

Figure 1. Results of SM of unknown pattern with known pattern.

5.2. Comparative Study

In this section, we make comparisons of the results using the proposed SM for TSFSs with the results using the SM for TSFSs proposed by Ullah et al. [26] and Wu et al. [33]. Table 3 summarizes the findings. We find that the results using the proposed SM for TSFSs are the same as the results using the SM for TSFSs proposed by Wu et al. [33]. Here, we also show the limited nature of IFSs and PFSs. A brief comparison of the current paper's aggregated results with those of other previous papers is provided in Table 3.

Table 3. Comparative Study.

SM	Environment	Results
The proposed SM for TSFSs	TSFSs	$(P_4,P) < (P_1,P) < (P_3,P) < (P_2,P)$
The SM for TSFSs by Ullah et al. [25]	TSFSs	$(P_4,P) < (P_3,P) < (P_1,P) < (P_2,P)$
The SM for TSFSs by Wu et al. [32]	TSFSs	$(P_4,P) < (P_1,P) < (P_3,P) < (P_2,P)$

5.3. Applications for Decision Making

Now we will discuss how the proposed SM can be used to make decisions. The bigger the SM, according to the SM principle, the more correct the decision.

Example 2. *We use the proposed SM to solve the decision-making challenge proposed in Ullah et al. [34]. Islamabad, Pakistan's capital, is regarded as one of the most beautiful cities in the world. There are various parks and picnic areas in Islamabad where a large number of people visit on a daily basis. The Metropolitan Corporation of Islamabad (MCI) is in charge of the city government. To maintain its appeal, the MCI decided to restore all of the parks and picnic areas. MCI will need to recruit some private contractors to do so. MCI chose four private firms for further consideration after some preliminary screening.* $Á_1$*: Arish Associates,* $Á_2$*: Nauman Estate and Builders,* $Á_3$*: Areva Engineering, Construction and Interiors, and* $Á_4$*: The Wow Architects, are among the four firms. MCI's specialists devised five point criteria for selecting the best corporation or company.* $Ç_1$*: Cost,* $Ç_2$*: Previous performance,* $Ç_3$*: Time constraint,* $Ç_4$*: Quality assurance, and* $Ç_5$*: Labor quantity, are the five criteria. The decision-making panel has given all the information in TSFNs which is given in Table 3. The followings are the designated steps for the decision-making algorithm:*

Step 1. Decision-makers' views are expressed in the form of TSFNs, as indicated in Table 4.

Table 4. Data on decision making.

		$Ç_1$			$Ç_2$			$Ç_3$			$Ç_4$			$Ç_5$	
$Á_1$	0.1	0.7	0.4	0.5	0.8	0.9	0.8	0.8	0.8	0.6	0.7	0.8	0.3	0.5	0.7
$Á_2$	0.2	0.7	0.6	0.6	0.7	0.8	0.3	0.7	0.7	0.1	0.7	0.9	0.4	0.6	0.8
$Á_3$	0.5	0.6	0.6	0.5	0.6	0.7	0.5	0.7	0.1	0.9	0.6	0.2	0.5	0.6	0.9
$Á_4$	0.5	0.6	0.8	0.8	0.7	0.4	0.8	0.7	0.3	0.6	0.6	0.1	0.8	0.4	0.4
$Ç$	1	0	0	1	0	0	1	0	0	1	0	0	1	0	0

Step 2. The SM of each TSFN given in Table 4 are evaluated with $Ç(1,0,0)$ based on Equation (1). Table 5 summarizes the findings.

Table 5. SM of $Á_ϒ$ with $Ç$.

SM	**$(Á_1, Ç)$**	**$(Á_2, Ç)$**	**$(Á_3, Ç)$**	**$(Á_4, Ç)$**
Values	0.5110507	0.3707117	0.5988922	0.7403513

Step 3. Analyzing Table 5, we obtain

$$Á_2 < Á_1 < Á_3 < Á_4.$$

Therefore, $Á_4$ is the best choice. The results of Table 5 are also shown in Figure 2 which indicates that, after applying the proposed SM, $Á_4$ should be the best choice.

The findings of the proposed SM for TSFSs are then compared to the results of the SMs for TSFSs proposed by Ullah et al. [34]. Table 6 summarizes the findings. We find that both methods give the same decision.

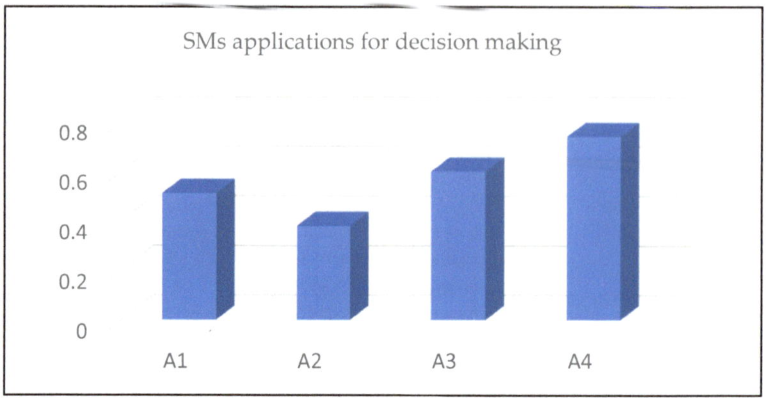

Figure 2. Results of SM for decision making.

Table 6. Comparative Study.

SM	Environment	Results
The proposed SM for TSFSs	TSFSs	$\acute{A}_2 < \acute{A}_1 < \acute{A}_3 < \acute{A}_4$
The SM for TSFSs by Ullah et al. [29]	TSFSs	$\acute{A}_2 < \acute{A}_1 < \acute{A}_3 < \acute{A}_4$

6. Conclusions

In this paper, a new SM was presented for TSFSs which is based on DM, DA, and DNM. We had shown that the proposed SM for TSFSs satisfies the axiom of SM. It was also observed that the proposed SM provides a flexible and larger range for data representation under uncertain circumstances in which it can be a generalized SM for IFSs, PyFSs, PFSs, or SFSs. By using numerical examples, it was shown that the presented SM is more efficient and can provide accurate results as the information under consideration was based on TSFNs where more than two aspects of uncertain information were discussed. In addition, we applied the proposed SM in pattern recognition and decision-making to observe its effectiveness. The comparative studies on pattern recognition and decision making indicate that the proposed SM is valid and can be used in some real-life problems, especially in decision making, pattern recognition, and clustering. In general, symmetric triangular fuzzy numbers can be well used in database acquisition and so our further work shall first consider the proposed SM for symmetric T-spherical triangular fuzzy numbers. In our future works, we will also extend the proposed SM for interval valued TSFSs and complex TSFSs. We shall further develop new distances for TSFSs and give more entropy measures for TSFSs and then apply them in clustering and medical diagnosis problems under TSFSs environment.

Author Contributions: Conceptualization, M.N.A., H.K. and K.U.; methodology, M.N.A., M.-S.Y. and D.P.; validation, M.N.A., M.-S.Y. and K.U.; formal analysis, K.U. and D.P.; investigation, M.-S.Y., H.K. and D.P.; resources, M.N.A. and H.K.; data curation, M.N.A. and K.U.; writing—original draft preparation, M.N.A. and H.K.; writing—review and editing, M.-S.Y. and K.U.; visualization, H.K. and M.-S.Y.; supervision, M.-S.Y. and D.P. All authors have read and agreed to the published version of the manuscript.

Funding: The Ministry of Science and Technology of Taiwan under Grant MOST-110-2118-M-033-003-. Princess Nourah bint Abdulrahman University Researchers Supporting Project number (PNURSP2022R192), Princess Nourah bint Abdulrahman University, Riyadh, Saudi Arabia.

Data Availability Statement: Not applicable.

Conflicts of Interest: The authors declare no conflict of interest.

References

1. Zadeh, L.A. Fuzzy sets. *Inf. Control* **1965**, *8*, 338–353. [CrossRef]
2. Atanassov, K.T. Intuitionistic fuzzy set. *Fuzzy Sets Syst.* **1986**, *20*, 87–96. [CrossRef]
3. Yager, R.R. Pythagorean fuzzy subsets. In Proceedings of the 2013 Joint IFSA World Congress and NAFIPS Annual Meeting (IFSA/NAFIPS), Edmonton, AB, Canada, 24–28 June 2013; pp. 57–61.
4. Yager, R.R. Generalized orthopair fuzzy sets. *IEEE Trans. Fuzzy Syst.* **2016**, *25*, 1222–1230. [CrossRef]
5. Cuong, B.C.; Kreinovich, V. Picture fuzzy sets-a new concept for computational intelligence problems. In Proceedings of the 2013 Third World Congress on Information and Communication Technologies (WICT 2013), Hanoi, Vietnam, 15–18 December 2013; pp. 1–6.
6. Ullah, K. Picture fuzzy maclaurin symmetric mean operators and their applications in solving multiattribute decision-making problems. *Math. Probl. Eng.* **2021**, *2021*, e1098631. [CrossRef]
7. Liu, P.; Munir, M.; Mahmood, T.; Ullah, K. Some similarity measures for interval-valued picture fuzzy sets and their applications in decision making. *Information* **2019**, *10*, 369. [CrossRef]
8. Mahmood, T.; Ullah, K.; Khan, Q.; Jan, N. An approach toward decision-making and medical diagnosis problems using the concept of spherical fuzzy sets. *Neural Comput. Appl.* **2019**, *31*, 7041–7053. [CrossRef]
9. Akram, M.; Ullah, K.; Pamucar, D. Performance evaluation of solar energy cells using the interval-valued T-spherical fuzzy Bonferroni mean operators. *Energies* **2022**, *15*, 292. [CrossRef]
10. Ullah, K.; Mahmood, T.; Garg, H. Evaluation of the performance of search and rescue robots using T-spherical fuzzy Hamacher aggregation operators. *Int. J. Fuzzy Syst.* **2020**, *22*, 570–582. [CrossRef]
11. Ali, Z.; Mahmood, T.; Yang, M.S. Complex T-spherical fuzzy aggregation operators with application to multi-attribute decision making. *Symmetry* **2020**, *12*, 1311. [CrossRef]
12. Chen, S.-M.; Yeh, M.-S.; Hsiao, P.-Y. A comparison of similarity measures of fuzzy values. *Fuzzy Sets Syst.* **1995**, *72*, 79–89. [CrossRef]
13. Yang, M.S.; Hung, W.L.; Chang-Chien, S.J. On a similarity measure between LR-type fuzzy numbers and its application to database acquisition. *Int. J. Intell. Syst.* **2005**, *20*, 1001–1016. [CrossRef]
14. Dengfeng, L.; Chuntian, C. New Similarity measures of intuitionistic fuzzy sets and application to pattern recognitions. *Pattern Recognit. Lett.* **2002**, *23*, 221–225. [CrossRef]
15. Liang, Z.; Shi, P. Similarity measures on intuitionistic fuzzy sets. *Pattern Recognit. Lett.* **2003**, *24*, 2687–2693. [CrossRef]
16. Li, Y.; Olson, D.L.; Qin, Z. Similarity measures between intuitionistic fuzzy (vague) sets: A comparative analysis. *Pattern Recognit. Lett.* **2007**, *28*, 278–285. [CrossRef]
17. Hwang, C.-M.; Yang, M.-S.; Hung, W.-L. New similarity measures of intuitionistic fuzzy sets based on the Jaccard index with its application to clustering. *Int. J. Intell. Syst.* **2018**, *33*, 1672–1688. [CrossRef]
18. Wei, G.; Wei, Y. Similarity measures of pythagorean fuzzy sets based on the cosine function and their applications. *Int. J. Intell. Syst.* **2018**, *33*, 634–652. [CrossRef]
19. Zeng, W.; Li, D.; Yin, Q. Distance and similarity measures of pythagorean fuzzy sets and their applications to multiple criteria group decision making. *Int. J. Intell. Syst.* **2018**, *33*, 2236–2254. [CrossRef]
20. Peng, X.; Garg, H. Multiparametric similarity measures on pythagorean fuzzy sets with applications to pattern recognition. *Appl. Intell.* **2019**, *49*, 4058–4096. [CrossRef]
21. Hussian, Z.; Yang, M.-S. Distance and similaritymeasures of pythagorean fuzzy sets based on the Hausdorff metric with application to fuzzy TOPSIS. *Int. J. Intell. Syst.* **2019**, *34*, 2633–2654. [CrossRef]
22. Wang, P.; Wang, J.; Wei, G.; Wei, C. Similarity measures of q-rung orthopair fuzzy sets based on cosine function and their applications. *Mathematics* **2019**, *7*, 340. [CrossRef]
23. Wei, G. Some similarity measures for picture fuzzy sets and their applications. *Iran. J. Fuzzy Syst.* **2018**, *15*, 77–89.
24. Mahmood, T.; Ilyas, M.; Ali, Z.; Gumaei, A. Spherical fuzzy sets-based cosine similarity and information measures for pattern recognition and medical diagnosis. *IEEE Access* **2021**, *9*, 25835–25842. [CrossRef]
25. Rafiq, M.; Ashraf, S.; Abdullah, S.; Mahmood, T.; Muhammad, S. The cosine similarity measures of spherical fuzzy sets and their applications in decision making. *J. Intell. Fuzzy Syst.* **2019**, *36*, 6059–6073. [CrossRef]
26. Ullah, K.; Mahmood, T.; Jan, N. Similarity measures for T-spherical fuzzy sets with applications in pattern recognition. *Symmetry* **2018**, *10*, 193. [CrossRef]
27. Ye, J. Similarity measures based on the generalized distance of neutrosophic z-number sets and their multi-attribute decision making method. *Soft Comput.* **2021**, *25*, 13975–13985. [CrossRef]
28. Mahmood, T.; Ur Rehman, U.; Ali, Z.; Mahmood, T. Hybrid vector similarity measures based on complex hesitant fuzzy sets and their applications to pattern recognition and medical diagnosis. *J. Intell. Fuzzy Syst.* **2021**, *40*, 625–646. [CrossRef]
29. Mahmood, T.; Ali, W.; Ali, Z.; Chinram, R. Power aggregation operators and similarity measures based on improved intuitionistic hesitant fuzzy sets and their applications to multiple attribute decision making. *Comput. Modeling Eng. Sci.* **2021**, *126*, 1165–1187. [CrossRef]
30. Chinram, R.; Mahmood, T.; Ur Rehman, U.; Ali, Z.; Iampan, A. Some novel cosine similarity measures based on complex hesitant fuzzy sets and their applications. *J. Math.* **2021**, *2021*, 6690728. [CrossRef]

31. Mahmood, T.; Ur Rehman, U.; Ali, Z.; Chinram, R. Jaccard and dice similarity measures based on novel complex dual hesitant fuzzy sets and their applications. *Math. Probl. Eng.* **2020**, *2020*, 5920432. [CrossRef]
32. Luo, M.; Zhang, Y. A New similarity measure between picture fuzzy sets and its application. *Eng. Appl. Artif. Intell.* **2020**, *96*, 103956. [CrossRef]
33. Wu, M.-Q.; Chen, T.-Y.; Fan, J.-P. Similarity measures of T-spherical fuzzy sets based on the cosine function and their applications in pattern recognition. *IEEE Access* **2020**, *8*, 98181–98192. [CrossRef]
34. Ullah, K.; Garg, H.; Mahmood, T.; Jan, N.; Ali, Z. Correlation coefficients for T-spherical fuzzy sets and their applications in clustering and multi-attribute decision making. *Soft Comput.* **2020**, *24*, 1647–1659. [CrossRef]

symmetry

MDPI

Article

Experimental Analysis of a Fuzzy Scheme against a Robust Controller for a Proton Exchange Membrane Fuel Cell System

Cristian Napole *, **Mohamed Derbeli** * and **Oscar Barambones** *

System Engineering and Automation Deparment, Faculty of Engineering of Vitoria-Gasteiz, Basque Country University (UPV/EHU), 01006 Vitoria-Gasteiz, Spain

* Correspondence: cristianmario.napole@ehu.eus (C.N.); mderbeli001@ikasle.ehu.es (M.D.); oscar.barambones@ehu.eus (O.B.)

Abstract: Proton exchange membrane fuel cells (PEMFC) are capable of transforming chemical energy into electrical energy with zero emissions. Therefore, these devices had been a point of attention for the scientific community as to provide another solution to renewable sources of energy. Since the PEMFC is commonly driven with a power converter, a controller has to be implemented to supply a convenient voltage. This is an important task as it allows the system to be driven at an operative point, which can be related to the maximum power or an user desired spot. Along this research article, a robust controller was compared against a fuzzy logic strategy (with symmetric membership functions) where both were implemented to a commercial PEMFC through a dSPACE 1102 control board. Both proposals were analysed in an experimental test bench. Outcomes showed the advantages and disadvantages of each scheme in chattering reduction, accuracy, and convergence speed.

Keywords: fuzzy logic; fuzzy control; fuzzy set; sliding mode control; PEMFC; renewable energies

Citation: Napole, C.; Derbeli, M.; Barambones, O. Experimental Analysis of a Fuzzy Scheme against a Robust Controller for a Proton Exchange Membrane Fuel Cell System. *Symmetry* **2022**, *14*, 139. https://doi.org/10.3390/sym14010139

Academic Editor: Saeid Jafari

Received: 14 December 2021
Accepted: 4 January 2022
Published: 12 January 2022

1. Introduction

Renewable energies are a trending topic nowadays due to the future of climate change. In this sense, current main technologies that could replace conventional sources are photovoltaic systems (conversion efficiency of ≈20%), wind turbines (conversion efficiency of ≈25%), and turbine generators (conversion efficiency of ≈30–40%) [1,2]. Nevertheless, fuel cells are emerging technological devices that stand out over conventional renewable energy options.

These devices have captured attention since they were discovered by William Grove in 1838 when he realised a constant current can be obtained when two platinum electrodes are immersed in a sulphuric acid solution and connected to sealed tubes with oxygen and hydrogen [3]. Thenceforth, the attractiveness of fuel cells is still a trend in research as it is expected that this technology could reach its maturity near 2030 [4]. Additionally, because of the groundbreaking innovation of fuel cell electric vehicles (FCEV) and large capacity stationary fuel cells (LCSFC), the interest has been growing exponentially since 2007 [5]. This is principally due to their emissions level that could reach up to 0% (depending on the type and fuel) and a high efficiency that yields up to 60% [6,7].

Despite the types of available fuel cells, Proton exchange membrane fuel cells (PEMFC) stand out as the production emissions are the lowest and it produces high energy densities with sufficient robustness [8,9]. Still, their performance can be improved through the usage of a power converter as its able to manipulate the output voltage which the end-user may require [10]. Furthermore, as the PEMFC output voltage can vary according to the load requirement, oxygen/hydrogen feeding, and temperature, it is highly endorsed to use a control algorithm to follow an appropriate path.

Linear approaches can be a suitable first option for a shallow control of PEMFC. For instance, Kodra and Zhong [11] produced a linear quadratic regulator (LQR) for a modelled PEMFC where they controlled the feeding air and H_2. Simulation outcomes showed suitable results in terms of settling time and overshoot reduction. A similar strategy also based on flow control has been achieved by authors of [12], where they used a linear parameter varying (LPV) model. In this case, the outcomes were gathered experimentally where capabilities of dynamic response control were achieved. Despite in real-time applications, the direct manipulation of gases for PEMFC can increase the risk of accidents because of the sensitivity of H_2 [13]. Additionally, accurate models of PEMFC are mainly non-linear due to the dependence on partial reactancts pressures and temperature [14]. On the other hand, linear strategies for converters tend to be useful in proximity of an equilibrium point along a slow response; this implies that there are numerous limitations for other operative setups [15]. For instance Belhaj et al. [10] showed in a simulated PEMFC with a power converter, suitable results can be achieved provided that an optimised PID ensures its work around an operative range. Therefore, non-linear strategies can be a reasonable approach for real PEMFC systems.

In this sense, several nonlinear techniques had been developed for PEMFC with a boost converter. Authors of [16], modelled a fuel cell where they used neural feedback linearization, which was compared with a neural and adaptive proportional-integral-derivative (PID) controllers. Simulated results showed that the proposed method had better stability and reliability. Nevertheless, feedback linearization is known for its lack of robustness at parameter uncertainties [17]. A well-known robust controller that can tackle this issue is a sliding mode controller (SMC), which is also notorious for its fast convergence [18]. Bjaoui et al. [19] analysed an SMC for maximum power point tracking (MPPT) of a fuel cell with a boost converter; in this case, they obtained the results through experiments where proper outcomes were reached in terms of performance and robustness. Another example has been developed by Valderrama-Blavi et al. [20]; in this case, a boost converter arrangement for a step-up DC-AC output was designed and a SMC controller was embedded for plant order reduction. Experiments showed an increment of efficiency of around 90%. However, major drawbacks of SMC are related to the chattering [21]. Even though a solution to these disadvantages is the usage of high-order SMC, this implies the employment of high order derivatives which induces an increment of noise in the feedback [22].

On the other hand, fuzzy logic control (FLC) is another strategy in which its main features reside in its simplicity of implementation and explicit configuration as it depends on expert knowledge rather than on an accurate mathematical model [23]. Usually, human knowledge is expressed through simple rules and membership functions, which can be symmetric or asymmetric [24,25]. This tool introduced by Zadeh in 1965 [26,27] has been an example of employment in decision making processes [28] and mathematical modelling [29,30]. Examples of experimental tests on a converter had been developed by Ramalu et al. [31]. In this case, they used a single ended primary-inductor converter (SEPIC) for MPPT and a FLC strategy was embedded. The gathered results showed an enhanced performance in terms of over-/undershoot reduction. Additionally, Harrag and Messalti made a study about the benefits of using FLC in a PEMFC for performance enhancement [32]. They were able to show that features like robustness improvement with reduction of response time and chattering in comparison to conventional techniques.

In this research, an FLC and a conventional SMC are contrasted in a real-time PEMFC system. The objective is the performance inspection of these structures in a constant current following when a disturbance appears. The constant value can be a variable under the requirements of an expert, which can be linked to an MPPT or a concerned efficient position. This latter effect was simulated with programmable resistance during a specific time range. Different phenomena were analysed, such as chattering, settling time, and robustness.

The arrangement of this article is as follows. Section 2 gives an overview of the used hardware like the PEMFC, boost converter, programmable load, and real-time controller board. Sections 2.2–2.4 are related to the controllers used with their details and tools used to gather suitable parameters. Section 3 shows the obtained outcomes from the experimental implementation of the mentioned schemes with detailed analysis. Finally, major lessons are summarised in Section 4.

2. Materials And Methods

2.1. Employed Hardware

A real-time platform was designed for the implementation of controllers and achievement of suitable performance of the system. Thus, a fuel cell Heliocentris PEMFC FC50 was used and supplied with high-purity hydrogen (99.999% vol) from a compressed reservoir at 1 Mpa. This device is able to produce above 40W with 5VCC output and a current rate of 8–10 A. Additionally, the manufacturer included a safety circuit to control the fuel supply also linked to the oxygen, inner humidity, and stack temperature.

On the other hand, the converter used in the platform is a TEP-192 boost type. This device possesses a direct control of the metal-oxide-semiconductor-field-effect transistor (MOSFET) for switching that originates from a pulse-width-modulation (PWM) signal. The maximum switching frequency is 20 kHz. This device is modelled in the electric circuit of Figure 1. The involved elements are an inductor (L), a switching device (S_1), a capacitor (C), a load (R, as the BK Precision 8500), and a diode (D).

The device in charge of acquisition and generation of the PWM signal was a dSPACE MicroLabBox DS1202, that is a common hardware used for mechatronics investigations because of its robustness and performance. The inner configuration is based on a programmable field-programmable gate array (FPGA), with a clock that can achieve up to 2 GHz. The manufacturer included the ability to use this device under analogue, digital, or PWM signals on 100 available channels. Furthermore, dSPACE included a Real-Time Interface (RTI), a tool that helps in the C code generation and allows further concentration on the process design.

To replicate a load in the circuit, a programmable resistance BK Precision 8500 was used. This device is capable of being configured in values between 0.1 and 1000 Ω. In addition, the operating voltage is in the range of 0–250 V and the current in 0–30 A. Further details in regards to the described hardware are enlisted in Table 1.

Table 1. Heliocentris PEMFC FC50.

Heliocentris PEMFC FC50	**Values**	**Units**
Operating voltage	2.5–9	VDC
Operating current	0–10	A
Rated output power	40	W
Open-circuit voltage	9	VDC
Boost converter TEP192		
Inductance	6	μH
Input capacitor	1500	μF
Output capacitor	3000	μF
Max. input voltage	60	V
Max. input current	30	A
Max. output voltage	250	V
Max. output current	30	A

In regards to the employed software, Simulink was employed to design the proposed control architectures, whereas MATLAB was used for data and signal processing. Additionally, ControlDesk (from dSPACE) was used in real-time to verify the involved variables for performance enhancement. A descriptive resume of the described hardware and software is provided in Figure 1.

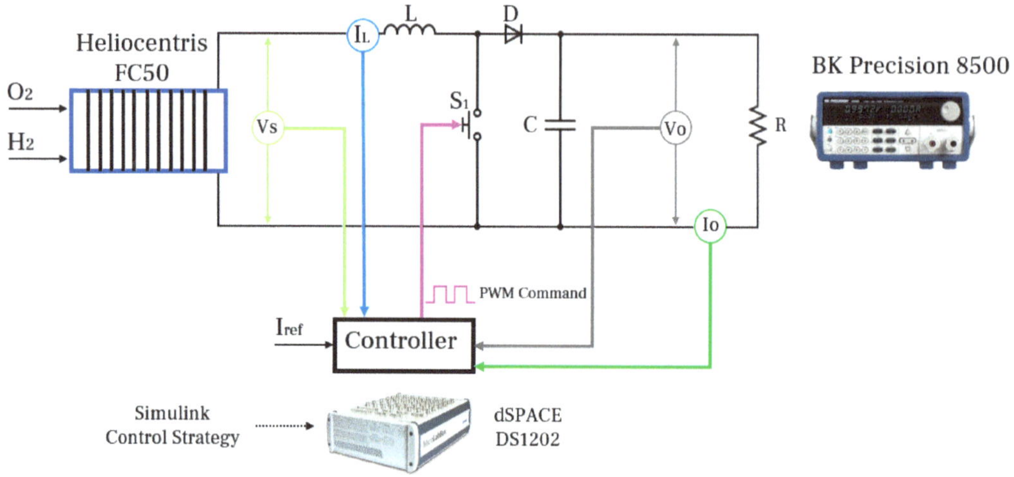

Figure 1. Hardware flow.

2.2. Control Design

The main objective of this work is to track a reference current I_{ref} which was carried out mainly with an FLC controller that has been contrasted with a conventional SMC. Main comparisons are aimed to test the robustness of both controllers, a well-known feature as it was previously described in background research. Hence, the error in terms of the reference current is defined as Equation (1):

$$e = I_{ref} - I_L. \quad (1)$$

The output (V_o) and stack voltages (V_s) are related to each other by means of the duty cycle d. This value is driven by the PWM signal generated by the dSPACE hardware. Thus, this implies that there are two different switching arrangements that are modelled by the following state-space of Equation (2). Further details about the derivation of this system can be found in the research made by the authors in [33].

$$\begin{cases} \begin{bmatrix} \frac{di_L}{dt} \\ \frac{dV_{out}}{dt} \end{bmatrix} = \begin{bmatrix} 0 & \frac{-(1-d)}{L} \\ \frac{(1-d)}{C} & -\frac{1}{RC} \end{bmatrix} \cdot \begin{bmatrix} i_L \\ V_o \end{bmatrix} + \begin{bmatrix} \frac{1}{L} \\ 0 \end{bmatrix} V_s \\ y = \begin{bmatrix} 0 & 1 \end{bmatrix} \cdot \begin{bmatrix} i_L \\ V_o \end{bmatrix} \end{cases} \quad (2)$$

Additionally, the main features of the PEMFC were useful for the following structures to be explained. In this sense, Figure 2 is the relation between stack voltage and current which was gathered experimentally. In this graph it can be seen that the fuel cell resistance (R_{PEMFC}) changes when the current is reduced and vice-versa. Moreover, this mentioned resistance is related to the BK Precision (R_{Out}) through the duty cycle of the expression from Equation (3) [34]:

$$R_{PEMFC} = (1-d)^2 \cdot R_{Out}. \quad (3)$$

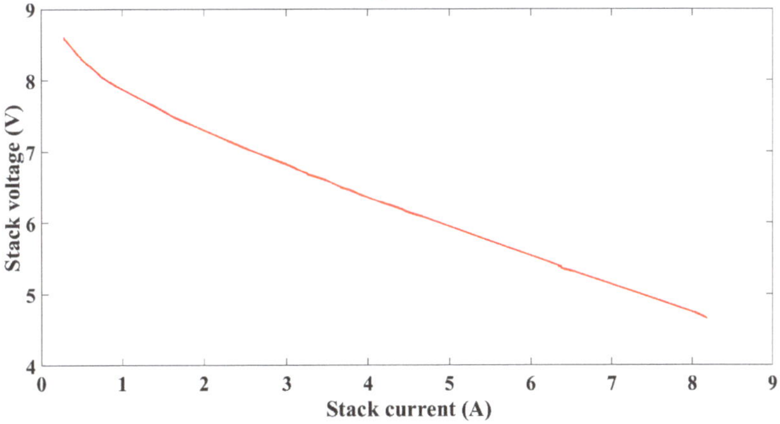

Figure 2. Characteristic dynamic curve of the fuel cell.

The proposed controllers have variables that had to be tuned. Thus, through ControlDesk it is possible to change desired gains in specific ranges that can be glided manually with the aim of achieving an objective. In regards to this goal, a real-time metric was calculated in order to figure out a suitable performance. The minimization of integral of the absolute error (*IAE*) was used in this case, and its mathematical expression is established in Equation (4). This definition has terms like the error (e_i), sampling time (Δt), and an established number of samples (N):

$$IAE = \sum_{i=1}^{N} |e_i| \Delta t. \tag{4}$$

2.3. Fuzzy Logic Control

This is a robust intelligent strategy as it has rules and constraints for mathematical calculation during the process [35]. FLC works on the principle of expertise knowledge about a system so that the parameters can be tuned based on previous experience [24]. In this case, a type-1 FLC was used (defined in Figure 3); this is a fuzzy set in which the input goes though a fuzzification process. This method refers to values that are transformed into fuzzy values in the range of $[-1, 1]$ through overlapped symmetric triangular membership functions which are exposed in Figure 4. Alternatives, like trapezoidal and Gaussian may require higher computational resources because of the parameters increments and analytical solutions, respectively [36].

These are also terms, such as negative big (NB), negative medium (NM), negative small (NS), zero (Z), positive small (PS), positive medium (PM), and positive big (PB) [36,37]. These previous mentioned relationships are resumed in the assymetric Table 2. Later, the evaluation of these values is conducted in the inference engine which is the point at where the expert applies and tunes linguistic rules [38]. In this case, these rules are settled conditioned variables in the form of IF-THEN structures [39,40]. The fuzzification set up had been through singleton in uniformly discretized constants within the range of $[-1, 1]$.

The structure presented in Figure 3, has the described blocks of FLC and gain like K_e, K_{Ed}, and K_o. These are normalisation factors, which are tuned over the real system so that the input and output ranges are in accordance to the previous specified values [41]. The suitable values of these gains were achieved through the minimisation of IAE as it was previously presented in Equation (4).

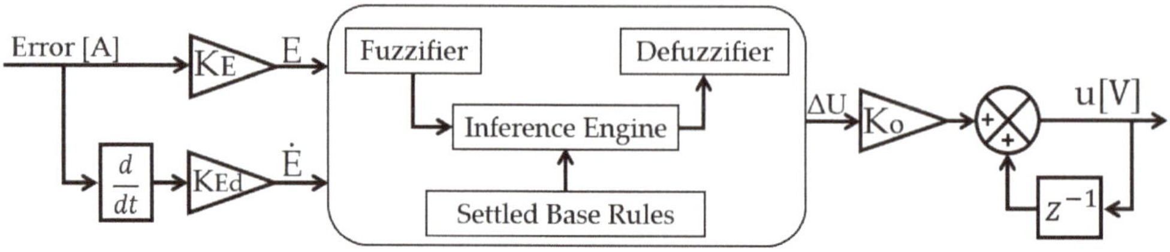

Figure 3. FLC Type-1 structure.

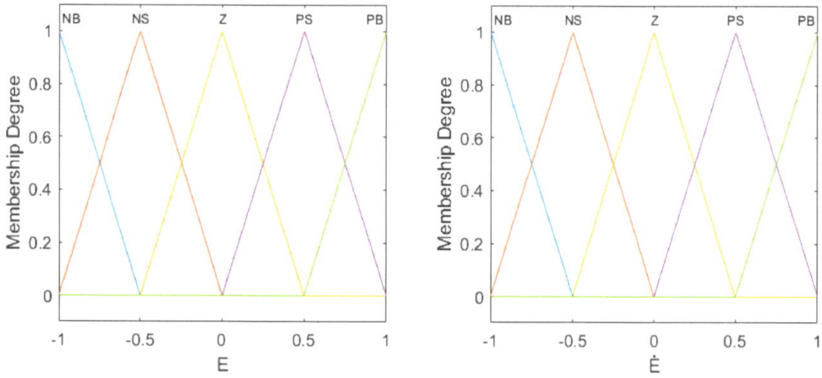

Figure 4. Membership functions.

Table 2. FLC linguistic rules.

E\\$\dot{E}$	**NB**	**NS**	**Z**	**PS**	**PB**
NB	NB	NM	NM	NS	Z
NS	NM	NM	NS	Z	Z
Z	NM	NS	Z	PS	PM
PS	Z	Z	PS	PM	PM
PB	Z	PS	PM	PM	PB

Based on Table 2, a stability proof is provided in order to show the logic of the chosen rules. Taking into account the Lyapunov stability proof establishes that a system is stable in a dynamic perspective provided that a definite positive function V exists such that $V(x) > 0$, $V(\infty) = \infty$, $V(0) = 0$ & $\dot{V}(x) < 0, \forall x \neq 0$. Thus, this function is defined in Equation (5) where E is a normalised error such that $E = I_{Nref} - I_N$ and its derivative is $\dot{E} = -\dot{I}_N$. Therefore, a Lyapunov function is defined and differentiated in Equations (5) and (6):

$$V = \frac{1}{2}E^2 \tag{5}$$

$$\dot{V} = E\dot{E} = -(I_{Nref} - I_N)\dot{I}_N. \tag{6}$$

Provided that Equation (6) is negative, thus, the system is asymptotically stable and the error tends to a null value. Since Table 2 is symmetric, the following reasoning is generated for one side of the table. Taking into account that the control action U is related to the duty cycle, the following cases are analysed.

- Case 1 (red cells from Table 2): $\Rightarrow U > 0$. In this situation, the duty cycle increment is positive. Equation (3) shows that an increment of d will decrease R_{PEMFC}. As $R_{PEMFC} = V_{stack}/I_{stack}$ and according to Figure 2, the resistance is reduced when the current increases. This means to move to the right of curve showed in the mentioned graph. Therefore, it can be concluded that $\dot{I}_N$ and E will have positive values. Thus, Equation (6) will be negative.
- Case 2 (green cell from Table 2): $\Rightarrow U > 0$. For this case, it is assumed that $\dot{E}$ is negative while E is positive. Nevertheless, a positive increment of the duty cycle will cause the same action as in Case 1 where $\dot{I}_N$ yields to a positive, which is the same sign as E. Consequently, $\dot{V} < 0$.
- Case 3 (orange cell from Table 2): $\Rightarrow U = 0$. In this instance, the control action is null which implies that there is no change. Thus, since the derivative of the normalised error is positive while the error is negative, it can be concluded that $\dot{V} < 0$. This reasoning can be used as well in the table diagonal since it will drive to the same conclusion.

2.4. Sliding Mode Control

Based on the established error of Equation (1), thus, an integral sliding surface is defined in Equation (7) where λ is a positive value:

$$s = e - \lambda \int e \cdot dt. \tag{7}$$

A control signal generated from a SMC approach is composed by an equivalent (u_{eq}) and a switching term (u_{sw}), that is expressed in Equation (8) [42]. The mechanics of this controller is as follows: u_{eq} aims to move the states to an equilibrium point by establishing the condition $\dot{s} = 0$, which is the origin of a phase plane [43]. As it is expected that the states will move through time, then the u_{sw} intention is to force the states to stay in the sliding surface [44,45]. The latter is defined in Equation (9) as a first-order discontinuous expression where K is a parameter to be tuned and high values can increase the response time in exchange for strong oscillations that may induce hardware damage [22]:

$$u = u_{eq} + u_{sw}. \tag{8}$$

$$u_{sw} = -\frac{K \cdot L}{V_o} \cdot sign(s) \tag{9}$$

The derivative of the sliding surface $\dot{s}$ can be calculated using Equations (1), (2), and (7):

$$\dot{s} = \dot{e} + \lambda e = \frac{1}{L}(V_s - V_o) + \lambda e + \frac{V_o}{L} u. \tag{10}$$

Based on the mentioned condition $\dot{s} = 0$ and the boost converter system from Equation (2), the equivalent term is expressed as the following Equation (11):

$$u_{eq} = 1 - \frac{V_s}{V_o} - \frac{\lambda \cdot e \cdot L}{V_o}. \tag{11}$$

To prove the stability of the SMC control signal which is obtained in (8), a positive definite cost function as given in Equation (12) is designed according to the Lyapunov second method criterion [46,47]:

$$V(s) = \frac{1}{2} s^2. \tag{12}$$

To ensure that the cost function V is converging to zero in finite-time, its derivative $\dot{V}$ must be negative definite. By using Equations (8)–(11), differentiating Equation (12) with respect to time yields to:

$$\begin{aligned} \dot{V} &= s \cdot \dot{s} \\ &= s\left(\frac{1}{L}(V_s - V_o) + \lambda \cdot e + \frac{V_o}{L}\left(-\frac{k \cdot L}{V_o} sign(s) + 1 - \frac{V_s}{V_o} - \frac{\lambda \cdot e \cdot L}{V_o}\right)\right) \\ &= -k \cdot s \cdot sign(s) \\ &= -k \cdot |s| \\ &\leq 0. \end{aligned} \quad (13)$$

Consequently, according to the Lyapunov theory, the asymptotic stability is ensured. Besides, by using Equations (12) and (13), the following demonstration can be obtained:

$$\begin{aligned} \frac{1}{2}\frac{d}{dt}s^2 &= -k \cdot |s| \\ \frac{1}{2} \cdot \int_{t_0}^{t_{reach}} \frac{d}{dt}|s|^2 \, dt &= -k \cdot \int_{t_0}^{t_{reach}} |s| \, dt \\ \frac{1}{2} \cdot \int_{t_0}^{t_{reach}} \frac{d}{dt}|s| \, dt &= -k \cdot \int_{t_0}^{t_{reach}} dt \\ |s(t_{reach})| - |s(t_0)| &= -2 \cdot k \cdot t \Big|_{t_0}^{t_{reach}} \\ t_{reach} &= \frac{|s(t_0)|}{2 \cdot k}. \end{aligned} \quad (14)$$

Therefore, the system converges to the sliding surface $s = e + \lambda \int e \cdot dt$ in the finite time $t = t_{reach}$, which implies that $\dot{s} = \dot{e} + \lambda e$ also converges to 0. From the previous equation, the tracking error (defined by $e = c \cdot e^{-\lambda t}$) tends asymptotically to 0.

3. Experimental Results

Both described control architectures were embedded and contrasted in the PEMFC system were the outcomes are explained as follows. Thus, the load was used to induce disturbances in the system, which occurred at 25 s and 45 s. During the first action, the load step jumped from 20 Ω to 50 Ω, which was steady until 45 s (where the resistance plummeted to the initial value). The controllers parameters were obtained by minimisation of the IAE. Therefore, the SMC parameters K and λ were, respectively, 0.01 and 0.1; for the FLC, the values of K_E, K_{Ed}, and K_o were 18, 0.2, and 0.001, respectively.

The first graph to be analysed is the acquired current, which was the variable to be followed. This is mainly because the controller objective is to keep the PEMFC current at a constant value (which is related to a desired operative point) even when external perturbations are presented. The whole experiment, which took 60 s, is split in three sub-graphs as shown in Figure 5b–d. The programmable resistance has uncertainty in terms of time response which can be appreciated in certain phase-delay in the results contrast. Nevertheless, the results could still be analysed in terms of robustness and response times.

In the first action of resistance increment of Figure 5b at around 25 s, the SMC induced an undershoot of 1.63 A whereas the FLC had a higher value of 1.79 A. This means that the FLC has a robustness 9.81% lower than the SMC. A similar analysis can be done in the settling time in which the FLC is 60% higher in contrast to the SMC.

The second action is depicted in Figure 5c where the SMC still carries the trend for the fastest response. Nevertheless, the robustness is different in this case since the overshoot value of the FLC is 3.76 A in comparison to the SMC, which is 3.03 A. This made a difference of 24% of better performance for the SMC.

During the constant following, the situation has a diverse demeanour in terms of absolute values. Figure 5 shows the current during the action of 50 Ω, which has an average of 4 A in both schemes but with different amplitudes. For instance, the SMC showed an amplitude of around 0.61 A whereas the FLC enhanced this value as it produced 0.25 A, which made a difference of 60% in contrast to the SMC. This implies that the chattering is fairly reduced with the FLC approach.

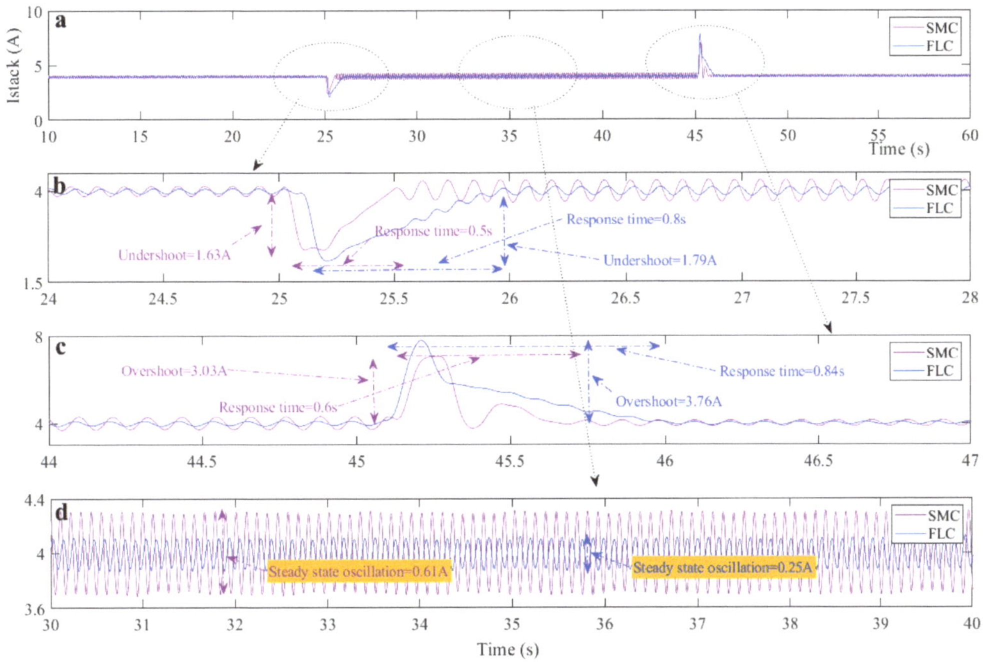

Figure 5. (**a**) Stack current signal; (**b**) influence of the first load variation; (**c**) influence of the second load variation; and (**d**) steady state.

In regards to the voltage, shown in Figure 6, the situation was similar as previously analysed in the current. The SMC showed higher chattering along the whole experiment but with slight better performance in the dynamic changes that were induced at 25 s and 45 s. The overshoot value of 1.06 V of the FLC against the 1V delivers a difference of 6%, whereas the undershoot presented a difference of 2.4%.

The generated power of the system was acquired as well, and is shown in Figure 7. At the first interruption of 25 s, the SMC behaved again better than the FLC as undershoot values differed in 20%. The same situation happened at 45 s during the resistance reduction where the overshoot was 17.5% higher with FLC in contrast to the SMC.

Finally, Figure 8 shows the boost converter duty cycle and output variables (current, voltage, and power). These real-time responses show the impact consequence of the load resistance at the previous analysed times. As previously, it can be seen that the major advantage of the FLC is its capability to reduce chattering during steady states, which allows an energy overspend. However, the SMC generates more robustness during dynamical changes.

Previous analysis results are summarized in Table 3 in terms of numbers. In this case, the overshoot, undershoot, response time and oscillation had been established as it had been the most important features to be highlighted.

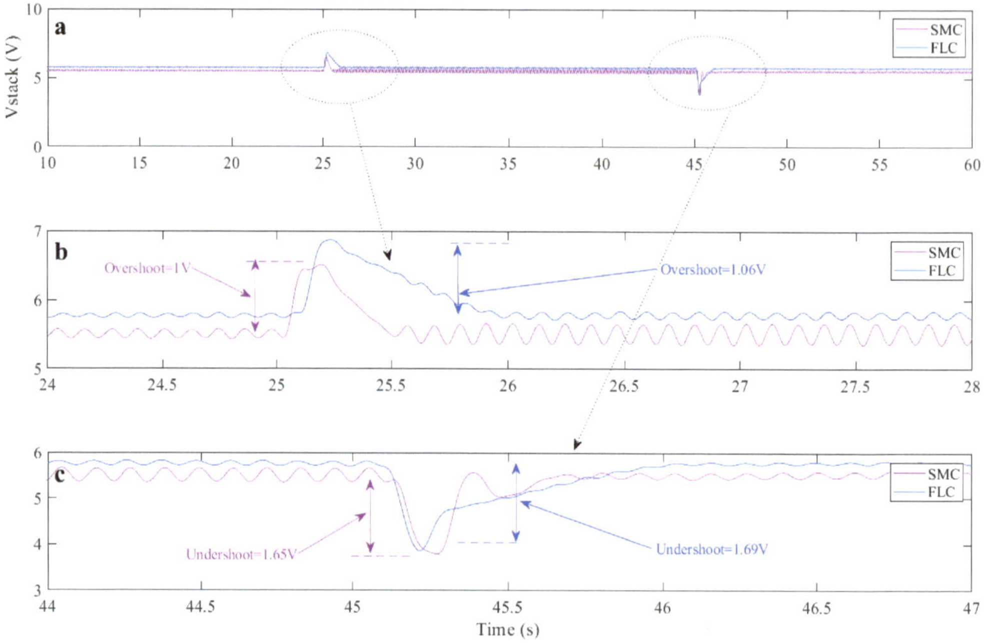

Figure 6. (**a**) Stack voltage signal; (**b**) influence of the first load variation and (**c**) influence of the second load variation.

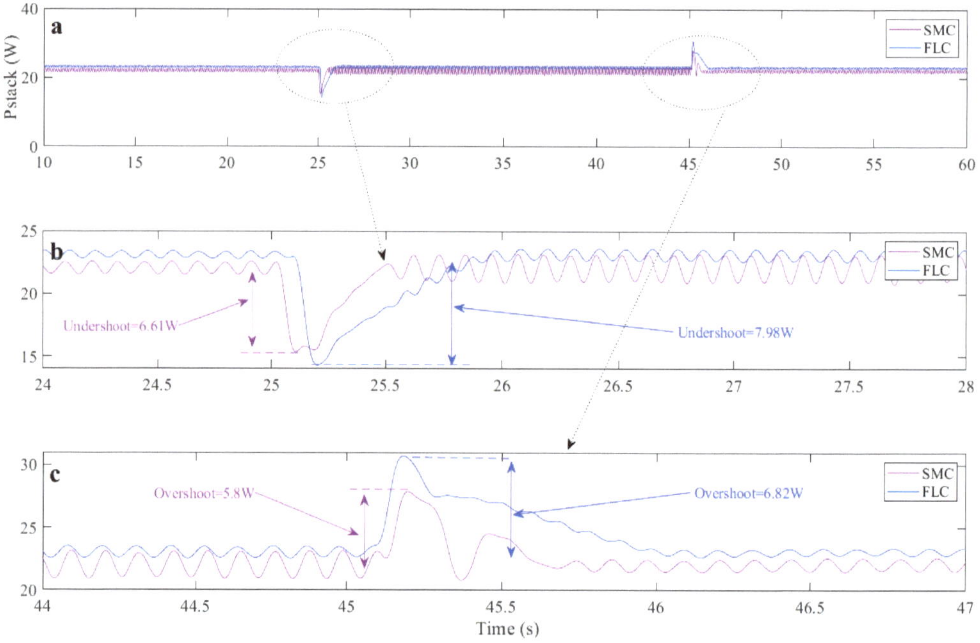

Figure 7. (**a**) Stack power signal; (**b**) influence of the first load variation and (**c**) influence of the second load variation.

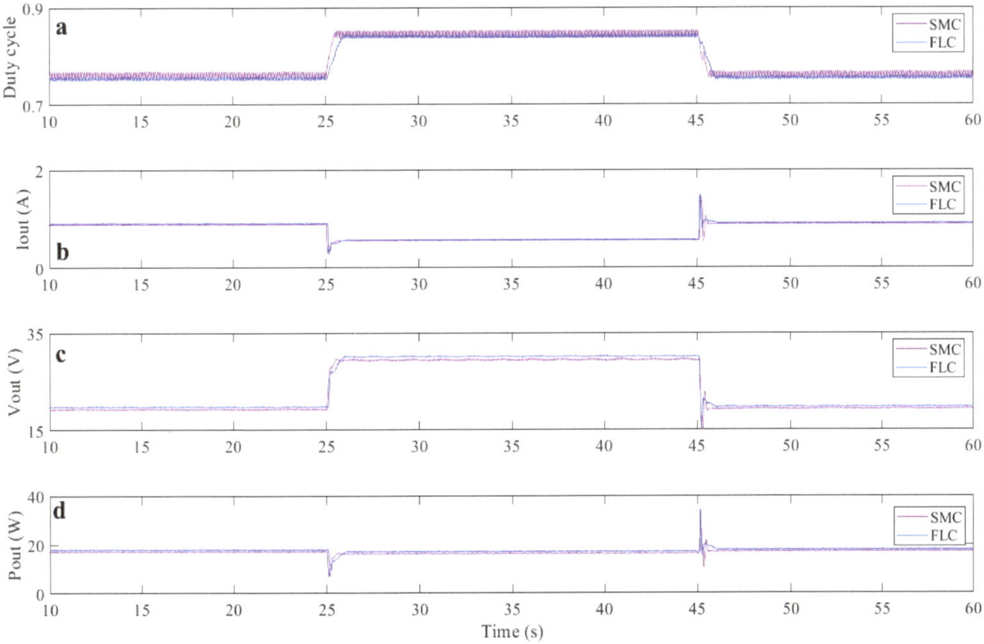

Figure 8. (**a**) Duty cycle signal; (**b**) boost converter output current; (**c**) boost converter output voltage; and (**d**) boost converter output power.

Table 3. Comparative results.

	Current (A)		**Voltage (V)**		**Power (W)**	
	SMC	**FLC**	**SMC**	**FLC**	**SMC**	**FLC**
Overshoot	3.03	3.76	1	1.06	5.8	6.82
Undershoot	1.63	1.79	1.65	1.69	6.61	7.98
Response Time	0.5	0.8	0.5	0.8	0.5	0.8
Oscillation	0.61	0.25	0.33	0.14	2.2	0.9

4. Conclusions

This research depicted a comparative analysis of two control algorithms aimed to enhance the performance of a PEMFC during a constant reference following disturbances. Additionally, the usage of a real system constraints theoretical ranges of power and duty cycle.

The objective was to maintain a constant current following that can be associated to a user-desired operative point or an MPPT. This target usually has inconveniences, such as external disturbances as analysed. SMC was chosen for its capabilities in robustness and fast response. FLC is known for its expertise involvement so that the tuning can be made from a personal perspective.

A programmable load was adopted to simulate an peripheral charge which affects the circuit. In addition, commercial hardware was used to generate a real environment where the proposed control structures were embedded with a dSPACE controller board in real-time. The latter mentioned device was also used for acquisition of signals and further processing with MATLAB.

Both control architectures were implemented where several interesting points were highlighted. For instance, it was shown that the SMC provided suitable capabilities in terms of robustness. In this sense, SMC had better robustness during dynamical changes, such as sudden load variations. Additionally, another suitable observed feature was the fast response. These aspects were noticed in variables such as current, voltage, and power.

Despite the dynamical changes, the SMC was superior in terms of performance, the FLC promoted an attractive efficacy during the constant following. In this case, for SMC, it was already known that its main disadvantage is related to the chattering generation, which was observed in the outcomes. Thus, FLC reduced this feature, not only providing better accuracy but also an energy reduction which could enhance system efficiency.

To conclude this research, future perspective lines are based on different branches of the analysed control structures. For instance, a study of a FLC Type-2 with different inference algorithms can be an interesting comparison. Additionally, the FLC used in this case had the aim to track a constant reference, thus it would be intriguing to implement the same algorithm for MPPT where the reference is a variable.

Author Contributions: Conceptualisation, O.B., M.D. and C.N.; methodology, M.D. and C.N.; software, C.N.; validation, M.D.; formal analysis, O.B., M.D. and C.N.; investigation, O.B. and C.N.; resources, O.B.; writing—original draft preparation, C.N.; writing—review and editing, O.B., C.N. and M.D.; supervision, O.B.; project administration, O.B. All authors have read and agreed to the published version of the manuscript.

Funding: This research was funded by the Basque Government through project EKOHEGAZ (ELKARTEK KK-2021/00092), by the Diputación Foral de Álava (DFA), through project CONAVANTER, and by the UPV/EHU, through project GIU20/063.

Institutional Review Board Statement: Not applicable.

Informed Consent Statement: Not applicable.

Acknowledgments: The authors wish to express their gratitude to the Basque Government, through project EKOHEGAZ (ELKARTEK KK-2021/00092), to the Diputación Foral de Álava (DFA), through project CONAVANTER, and to the UPV/EHU, through project GIU20/063, for supporting this work.

Conflicts of Interest: The authors declare no conflict of interest.

Abbreviations

The following abbreviations are used in this manuscript:

PEMFC	Proton exchange membrane fuel cells
FCEV	Fuel cell electric vehicles
LCSFC	Large capacity stationary fuel cells
LQR	Linear quadratic regulator
LPV	Linear parameter varying
PID	Proportional-integral-derivative
SMC	Sliding mode control
MPPT	Maximum power point tracking
FLC	Fuzzy logic control
SEPIC	Single ended primary-inductor converter
MOSFET	Metal-oxide-semiconductor-field-effect transistor
PWM	Pulse-width-modulation
FPGA	Field-programmable gate array
RTI	Real-time interface

References

1. Hasan, A.; McCormack, S.J.; Huang, M.J.; Norton, B. Energy and Cost Saving of a Photovoltaic-Phase Change Materials (PV-PCM) System through Temperature Regulation and Performance Enhancement of Photovoltaics. *Energies* **2014**, *7*, 1318–1331. [CrossRef]
2. Mahapatra, M.K.; Singh, P. Chapter 24-Fuel Cells: Energy Conversion Technology. In *Future Energy*, 2nd ed.; Letcher, T.M., Ed.; Elsevier: Boston, MA, USA, 2014; pp. 511–547. [CrossRef]
3. Andújar, J.; Segura, F. Fuel cells: History and updating. A walk along two centuries. *Renew. Sustain. Energy Rev.* **2009**, *13*, 2309–2322. [CrossRef]
4. Ho, J.; Saw, E.C.; Lu, L.; Liu, J. Technological barriers and research trends in fuel cell technologies: A citation network analysis. *Technol. Forecast. Soc. Chang.* **2014**, *82*, 66–79. [CrossRef]

5. Weidner, E.; Cebolla, R.O.; Davies, J. Global deployment of large capacity stationary fuel cells. In *JRC Technical Reports*; Joint Research Centre: Ispra, Italy, 2019. [CrossRef]
6. Yonoff, R.E.; Ochoa, G.V.; Cardenas-Escorcia, Y.; Silva-Ortega, J.I.; Meriño-Stand, L. Research trends in proton exchange membrane fuel cells during 2008–2018: A bibliometric analysis. *Heliyon* **2019**, *5*, e01724. [CrossRef] [PubMed]
7. Louzazni, M.; Al-Dahidi, S.; Mussetta, M. Fuel Cell Characteristic Curve Approximation Using the Bézier Curve Technique. *Sustainability* **2020**, *12*, 8127. [CrossRef]
8. Mayyas, A.; Mann, M. Emerging Manufacturing Technologies for Fuel Cells and Electrolyzers. *Procedia Manuf.* **2019**, *33*, 508–515. [CrossRef]
9. Abdelkareem, M.A.; Elsaid, K.; Wilberforce, T.; Kamil, M.; Sayed, E.T.; Olabi, A. Environmental aspects of fuel cells: A review. *Sci. Total Environ.* **2021**, *752*, 141803. [CrossRef] [PubMed]
10. Belhaj, F.Z.; El Fadil, H.; Idrissi, Z.E.; Koundi, M.; Gaouzi, K. Modeling, Analysis and Experimental Validation of the Fuel Cell Association with DC-DC Power Converters with Robust and Anti-Windup PID Controller Design. *Electronics* **2020**, *9*, 1889. [CrossRef]
11. Kodra, K.; Zhong, N. Singularly Perturbed Modeling and LQR Controller Design for a Fuel Cell System. *Energies* **2020**, *13*, 2735. [CrossRef]
12. Chen, F.X.; Jiao, J.R.; Liu, S.G.; Yu, Y.; Xu, S.C. Control-oriented LPV Modeling for the Air Supply System of Proton Exchange Membrane Fuel Cells. *Fuel Cells* **2018**, *18*, 433–440. [CrossRef]
13. Rosli, R.; Majlan, E.H.; Wan Daud, W.; Hamid, S. Hydrogen rate manipulation of proton exchange membrane fuel cell (PEMFC) stack using feedback control system. In Proceedings of the 2012 IEEE International Conference on Power and Energy (PECon), Kota Kinabalu, Malaysia, 2–5 December 2012; pp. 553–557. [CrossRef]
14. Cruz Rojas, A.; Lopez Lopez, G.; Gomez-Aguilar, J.F.; Alvarado, V.M.; Sandoval Torres, C.L. Control of the Air Supply Subsystem in a PEMFC with Balance of Plant Simulation. *Sustainability* **2017**, *9*, 73. [CrossRef]
15. Wang, M.; Tang, F.; Wu, X.; Niu, J.; Zhang, Y.; Wang, J. A Nonlinear Control Strategy for DC-DC Converter with Unknown Constant Power Load Using Damping and Interconnection Injecting. *Energies* **2021**, *14*, 3031. [CrossRef]
16. Awais, M.; Khan, L.; Ahmad, S.; Jamil, M. Feedback-Linearization-Based Fuel-Cell Adaptive-Control Paradigm in a Microgrid Using a Wavelet-Entrenched NeuroFuzzy Framework. *Energies* **2021**, *14*, 1850. [CrossRef]
17. Chen, Y.T.; Yu, C.S.; Chen, P.N. Feedback Linearization Based Robust Control for Linear Permanent Magnet Synchronous Motors. *Energies* **2020**, *13*, 5242. [CrossRef]
18. Li, T.; Liu, X. Model-Free Non-Cascade Integral Sliding Mode Control of Permanent Magnet Synchronous Motor Drive with a Fast Reaching Law. *Symmetry* **2021**, *13*, 1680. [CrossRef]
19. Bjaoui, M.; Khiari, B.; Benadli, R.; Memni, M.; Sellami, A. Practical Implementation of the Backstepping Sliding Mode Controller MPPT for a PV-Storage Application. *Energies* **2019**, *12*, 3539. [CrossRef]
20. Valderrama-Blavi, H.; Rodríguez-Ramos, E.; Olalla, C.; Genaro-Muñoz, X. Sliding-Mode Approaches to Control a Microinverter Based on a Quadratic Boost Converter. *Energies* **2019**, *12*, 3697. [CrossRef]
21. Wang, B.; Jahanshahi, H.; Volos, C.; Bekiros, S.; Yusuf, A.; Agarwal, P.; Aly, A.A. Control of a Symmetric Chaotic Supply Chain System Using a New Fixed-Time Super-Twisting Sliding Mode Technique Subject to Control Input Limitations. *Symmetry* **2021**, *13*, 1257. [CrossRef]
22. Napole, C.; Derbeli, M.; Barambones, O. A global integral terminal sliding mode control based on a novel reaching law for a proton exchange membrane fuel cell system. *Appl. Energy* **2021**, *301*, 117473. [CrossRef]
23. Muthugala, M.A.V.J.; Vega-Heredia, M.; Mohan, R.E.; Vishaal, S.R. Design and Control of a Wall Cleaning Robot with Adhesion-Awareness. *Symmetry* **2020**, *12*, 122. [CrossRef]
24. Khairuddin, S.H.; Hasan, M.H.; Hashmani, M.A.; Azam, M.H. Generating Clustering-Based Interval Fuzzy Type-2 Triangular and Trapezoidal Membership Functions: A Structured Literature Review. *Symmetry* **2021**, *13*, 239. [CrossRef]
25. Viswanathan, K.; Oruganti, R.; Srinivasan, D. Non-linear function controller: A simple alternative to fuzzy logic controller for a power electronic converter. In Proceedings of the 30th Annual Conference of IEEE Industrial Electronics Society, 2004, IECON 2004, Busan, Korea, 2–6 November 2004; Volume 3, pp. 2655–2660. [CrossRef]
26. Khan, W.A.; Ali, B.; Taouti, A. Bipolar Picture Fuzzy Graphs with Application. *Symmetry* **2021**, *13*, 1427. [CrossRef]
27. Parimala, M.; Jafari, S.; Riaz, M.; Aslam, M. Applying the Dijkstra Algorithm to Solve a Linear Diophantine Fuzzy Environment. *Symmetry* **2021**, *13*, 1616. [CrossRef]
28. Liu, D.; Huang, A.; Liu, Y.; Liu, Z. An Extension TOPSIS Method Based on the Decision Maker's Risk Attitude and the Adjusted Probabilistic Fuzzy Set. *Symmetry* **2021**, *13*, 891. [CrossRef]
29. Georgieva, A.; Pavlova, A. Fuzzy Sawi Decomposition Method for Solving Nonlinear Partial Fuzzy Differential Equations. *Symmetry* **2021**, *13*, 1580. [CrossRef]
30. Pedraza, T.; Ramos-Canós, J.; Rodríguez-López, J. Aggregation of Weak Fuzzy Norms. *Symmetry* **2021**, *13*, 1908. [CrossRef]
31. Ramalu, T.; Mohd Radzi, M.A.; Mohd Zainuri, M.A.A.; Abdul Wahab, N.I.; Abdul Rahman, R.Z. A Photovoltaic-Based SEPIC Converter with Dual-Fuzzy Maximum Power Point Tracking for Optimal Buck and Boost Operations. *Energies* **2016**, *9*, 604. [CrossRef]
32. Harrag, A.; Messalti, S. How fuzzy logic can improve PEM fuel cell MPPT performances? *Int. J. Hydrog. Energy* **2018**, *43*, 537–550. [CrossRef]

33. Derbeli, M.; Barambones, O.; Silaa, M.Y.; Napole, C. Real-Time Implementation of a New MPPT Control Method for a DC-DC Boost Converter Used in a PEM Fuel Cell Power System. *Actuators* **2020**, *9*, 105. [CrossRef]
34. Farhat, M.; Barambones, O.; Sbita, L. Efficiency optimization of a DSP-based standalone PV system using a stable single input fuzzy logic controller. *Renew. Sustain. Energy Rev.* **2015**, *49*, 907–920. [CrossRef]
35. Urrea, C.; Jara, D. Design, Analysis, and Comparison of Control Strategies for an Industrial Robotic Arm Driven by a Multi-Level Inverter. *Symmetry* **2021**, *13*, 86. [CrossRef]
36. Azam, M.H.; Hasan, M.H.; Hassan, S.; Abdulkadir, S.J. A Novel Approach to Generate Type-1 Fuzzy Triangular and Trapezoidal Membership Functions to Improve the Classification Accuracy. *Symmetry* **2021**, *13*, 1932. [CrossRef]
37. Napole, C.; Derbeli, M.; Barambones, O. Fuzzy Logic Approach for Maximum Power Point Tracking Implemented in a Real Time Photovoltaic System. *Appl. Sci.* **2021**, *11*, 5927. [CrossRef]
38. Sałabun, W.; Shekhovtsov, A.; Pamučar, D.; Wątróbski, J.; Kizielewicz, B.; Więckowski, J.; Bozanić, D.; Urbaniak, K.; Nyczaj, B. A Fuzzy Inference System for Players Evaluation in Multi-Player Sports: The Football Study Case. *Symmetry* **2020**, *12*, 2029. [CrossRef]
39. Sangeetha, V.; Krishankumar, R.; Ravichandran, K.S.; Cavallaro, F.; Kar, S.; Pamucar, D.; Mardani, A. A Fuzzy Gain-Based Dynamic Ant Colony Optimization for Path Planning in Dynamic Environments. *Symmetry* **2021**, *13*, 280. [CrossRef]
40. Wen, X.; Zhang, X.; Lei, T. Intuitionistic Fuzzy (IF) Overlap Functions and IF-Rough Sets with Applications. *Symmetry* **2021**, *13*, 1494. [CrossRef]
41. Napole, C.; Barambones, O.; Calvo, I.; Derbeli, M.; Silaa, M.Y.; Velasco, J. Advances in Tracking Control for Piezoelectric Actuators Using Fuzzy Logic and Hammerstein-Wiener Compensation. *Mathematics* **2020**, *8*, 2071. [CrossRef]
42. Hong, Q.; Shi, Y.; Chen, Z. Adaptive Sliding Mode Control Based on Disturbance Observer for Placement Pressure Control System. *Symmetry* **2020**, *12*, 1057. [CrossRef]
43. Zenteno-Torres, J.; Cieslak, J.; Dávila, J.; Henry, D. Sliding Mode Control with Application to Fault-Tolerant Control: Assessment and Open Problems. *Automation* **2021**, *2*, 1–30. [CrossRef]
44. Lin, C.H.; Hsiao, F.Y. Proportional-Integral Sliding Mode Control with an Application in the Balance Control of a Two-Wheel Vehicle System. *Appl. Sci.* **2020**, *10*, 5087. [CrossRef]
45. Munteanu, L.; Dumitriu, D.; Brisan, C.; Bara, M.; Chiroiu, V.; Nedelcu, N.; Rugina, C. Sliding Mode Control and Geometrization Conjecture in Seismic Response. *Symmetry* **2021**, *13*, 353. [CrossRef]
46. Kalman, R.E.; Bertram, J.E. Control system analysis and design via the "second method" of Lyapunov: I—Continuous-time systems. *J. Basic Eng.* **1960**, *82*, 371–393. [CrossRef]
47. LaSalle, J.; Lefschetz, S. *Stability by Lyapunov's Second Method with Applications*; Academic Press: New York, NY, USA, 1961; Volume 5, pp. 371–393.

symmetry MDPI

Article

Aggregation of Weak Fuzzy Norms

Tatiana Pedraza, Jorge Ramos-Canós and Jesús Rodríguez-López *

Instituto Universitario de Matemática Pura y Aplicada, Universitat Politècnica de València, Camino de Vera s/n, 46022 Valencia, Spain; tapedraz@mat.upv.es (T.P.); jramcan@posgrado.upv.es (J.R.-C.)
* Correspondence: jrlopez@mat.upv.es

Abstract: Aggregation is a mathematical process consisting in the fusion of a set of values into a unique one and representing them in some sense. Aggregation functions have demonstrated to be very important in many problems related to the fusion of information. This has resulted in the extended use of these functions not only to combine a family of numbers but also a family of certain mathematical structures such as metrics or norms, in the classical context, or indistinguishability operators or fuzzy metrics in the fuzzy context. In this paper, we study and characterize the functions through which we can obtain a single weak fuzzy (quasi-)norm from an arbitrary family of weak fuzzy (quasi-)norms in two different senses: when each weak fuzzy (quasi-)norm is defined on a possibly different vector space or when all of them are defined on the same vector space. We will show that, contrary to the crisp case, weak fuzzy (quasi-)norm aggregation functions are equivalent to fuzzy (quasi-)metric aggregation functions.

Keywords: weak fuzzy quasi-norms; aggregation function; asymmetric $*$-triangular triplet

MSC: 46B99; 46A99; 54E70

Citation: Pedraza, T.; Ramos-Canós, J.; Rodríguez-López, J. Aggregation of Weak Fuzzy Norms. *Symmetry* **2021**, *13*, 1908. https://doi.org/10.3390/sym13101908

Academic Editor: Saeid Jafari

Received: 17 September 2021
Accepted: 6 October 2021
Published: 11 October 2021

1. Introduction

In mathematics, an aggregation procedure amounts to a method for merging a family of structures of the same type into the only structure of this type. For example, the union or the intersection of subsets of a nonempty set X gave rise to another subset of X by aggregating the family of sets. On the other hand, given a finite family $\{d_i : i = 1, \ldots, n\}$ of metrics on X, then $\max\{d_1, \ldots, d_n\}$ is also a metric on X that is obtained by merging the original family of metrics. This metric can be constructed by means of the composition of the following functions:

- $\boldsymbol{d} : X \times X \to [0, +\infty)^n$ given by $\boldsymbol{d}(x, y) = (d_1(x, y), \ldots, d_n(x, y))$;
- $f : [0, +\infty)^n \to [0, +\infty)$ given by $f(x_1, \ldots, x_n) = \max\{x_1, \ldots, x_n\}$.

In the literature, we can find other schemes of merging mathematical structures. If $\{(X_n, d_n) : n \in \mathbb{N}\}$ is a countable collection of metric spaces then $d(\boldsymbol{x}, \boldsymbol{y}) = \sum_{n=1}^{\infty} \frac{\min\{d_n(x_n, y_n), 1\}}{2^n}$ is a metric on $\prod_{n\in\mathbb{N}} X_n$, which is compatible with product topology. In this case, the new metric on $\prod_{n\in\mathbb{N}} X_n$ can be obtained with the composition of the following functions:

- $\widetilde{\boldsymbol{d}} : \prod_{n\in\mathbb{N}} X_n \times \prod_{n\in\mathbb{N}} X_n \to [0, +\infty)^{\mathbb{N}}$ given by $\widetilde{\boldsymbol{d}}(\boldsymbol{x}, \boldsymbol{y}) = (d_n(x_n, y_n))_{n\in\mathbb{N}}$;
- $f : [0, +\infty)^{\mathbb{N}} \to [0, +\infty)$ defined as $f(\boldsymbol{x}) = \sum_{n=1}^{\infty} \frac{\min\{x_n, 1\}}{2^n}$.

In a similar manner, the sup norm $\|\cdot\|_\infty$ on $\mathbb{R}^n$ can be viewed as the aggregation of the absolute value norm on $\mathbb{R}$. This means that this norm is the composition of the following functions:

- $\widetilde{\boldsymbol{abs}} : \mathbb{R}^n \to [0, +\infty)^n$ given by $\widetilde{\boldsymbol{abs}}(x_1, \ldots, x_n) = (|x_1|, \ldots, |x_n|)$;
- $f : [0, +\infty)^n \to [0, +\infty)$ given by given by $f(x_1, \ldots, x_n) = \max\{x_1, \ldots, x_n\}$.

In all the above cases, a function f is involved in the aggregation process, so it is natural to study which functions allow making these kinds of aggregations. This research has already been carried out for some mathematical structures. Concretely, Borsík and Doboš [1,2] have analyzed when, given a function $f : [0,+\infty)^I \to [0,+\infty)$ and an arbitrary family $\{(X_i, d_i) : i \in I\}$ of metric spaces, the function $f \circ \widetilde{\boldsymbol{d}} : (\prod_{i\in I} X_i) \times (\prod_{i\in I} X_i) \to [0,+\infty)$ given by $f \circ \widetilde{\boldsymbol{d}}(x, y) = f((d_i(x_i, y_i))_{i\in I})$ is a metric on the cartesian product $\prod_{i\in I} X_i$. The corresponding study for quasi-metric spaces was made by Mayor and Valero [3]. Related results appear in the papers [4–6], where the authors characterize functions $f : [0,+\infty)^k \to [0,+\infty)$ that allow combining a finite collection of pseudometrics (with respect to metrics and quasi-metrics) $\{d_i : i = 1,\ldots,k\}$ defined over the same set X into a single one pseudometric (with respect to metric and quasi-metric) on X given by $f \circ \boldsymbol{d}(x, y) = f(d_1(x, y),\ldots, d_k(x, y))$ for all $x, y \in X$.

In addition to functions that merge metrics, some researchers have characterized functions that aggregate other mathematical structures, such as norms. Thus, Herburt and Moszyńska [7] studied the functions $f : [0,+\infty)^2 \to [0,+\infty)$ which produces the function $\|\cdot\|_f : V_1 \times V_2 \to [0,+\infty)$ given by $\|(v_1, v_2)\|_f = f(\|v_1\|_1, \|v_2\|_2)$ be a norm on $V_1 \times V_2$, where $(V_1, \|\cdot\|_1), (V_2, \|\cdot\|_2)$ are two normed vector spaces. A similar study for asymmetric norms was developed by Martín, Mayor and Valero [8]. Recently, Pedraza and Rodríguez-López [9] have addressed the problem of the aggregation of norms on the same set.

Until now, we have only mentioned crisp mathematical structures. Nevertheless, several authors have considered the aggregation of fuzzy structures. Saminger, Mesiar and Bodenhofer [10] characterized the aggregation functions that preserve $*$-transitive fuzzy binary relations, where $*$ is a t-norm. Later on, a related problem about the preservation of $*$-transitivity of fuzzy binary relations was studied by Drewniak and Dudziak [11] (see also [12,13]). Moreover, Mayor and Recasens [14] obtained a characterization of the functions through which we can fuse indistinguishability operators, which are a special kind of $*$-transitive fuzzy binary relations (see also [15,16]).

Recently, Valero, Pedraza and Rodríguez-López [17] have studied the functions that permit the generation of a unique fuzzy (quasi-)metric from a collection of fuzzy (quasi-)metrics. They proved that, compared to the classical case, the functions aggregating fuzzy metrics are exactly the same than compared to the functions that aggregate fuzzy quasi-metrics. They also proved some results about the aggregation of other fuzzy structures such as fuzzy preorders and indistinguishability operators.

In this article, we continue the study of functions that aggregate a particular fuzzy structure: weak fuzzy (quasi-)norms [18]. This fuzzy structure is a generalization of the concept of fuzzy norm considered by Goleţ [19], and it is useful when studying duality in the fuzzy context [18]. Here, we characterize the functions that can afford to obtain a weak fuzzy (quasi-)norm starting from an arbitrary family of fuzzy quasi-norms. We consider two types of aggregation: on sets and on products (see Definition 4). We are able to characterize these functions with two methods: on the one hand, using the properties of $*$-supmultiplicativity (see Definition 7) and isotonicity; on the other hand, using the property of conservation of asymmetric $*$-triangular triplets (see Definition 5). These results can be considered, in some sense, similar to those obtained in the crisp case. Surprisingly, and in contrast with the crisp case, functions that aggregate weak fuzzy (quasi-)norm are the same as the functions that aggregate fuzzy (quasi-)metrics (see Corollaries 1 and 2).

2. Aggregation of Metrics and Norms

In this section, we compile some results about the aggregation of metrics and norms that constitute a necessary antecedent of our study. We first establish some notations.

We will denote by I an arbitrary index set. The elements of the Cartesian product $[0,+\infty)^I$ will be written down in bold letters $\boldsymbol{a}$. Moreover, and for the sake of simplicity, given $\boldsymbol{a} \in [0,+\infty)^I$, its ith coordinate $\boldsymbol{a}(i)$ will be denoted by $\boldsymbol{a}_i$ for any $i \in I$.

We notice that we can endow the set $[0,+\infty)^I$ with a partial order $\preceq$ defined as $\boldsymbol{a} \preceq \boldsymbol{b}$ if $\boldsymbol{a}_i \leq \boldsymbol{b}_i$ for all $i \in I$. Furthermore, $\boldsymbol{0}$ represents the element of $[0,+\infty)^I$ such that $\boldsymbol{0}_i = 0$ for all $i \in I$.

As we have sketched, in the Introduction, that classical constructions of metrics in a Cartesian product are obtained by composing an appropriate function with a Cartesian product of metrics. The study of these functions, called *metric preserving functions*, has been mainly developed by Borsík and Doboš [1,2]. The corresponding study for quasi-metrics was made by Mayor and Valero [3], who characterized the so-called *quasi-metric aggregation functions*. In both cases, the underlying idea is to construct a (quasi-)metric in the Cartesian product of a family of (quasi-)metric spaces.

Another related problem was addressed by Pradera and Trillas [6], who studied how to merge a family of pseudometrics defined over the same set into a single one. This question for metrics has been also considered recently by Mayor and Valero [4]. Therefore, we have two different but related problems, which gave rise to two different families of functions that we next define using the terminology of [9,17,20].

Definition 1 ([1,3,4]). *A function $f : [0, +\infty)^I \to [0, +\infty)$ is called the following:*

- *A* (quasi-)metric aggregation function on products *if given an arbitrary family of (quasi-)metric spaces $\{(X_i, d_i) : i \in I\}$ then $f \circ \widetilde{\boldsymbol{d}}$ is a (quasi-)metric on $\prod_{i\in I} X_i$ where $\widetilde{\boldsymbol{d}} : (\prod_{i\in I} X_i) \times (\prod_{i\in I} X_i) \to [0, +\infty)^I$ is defined as*

$$(\widetilde{\boldsymbol{d}}(\boldsymbol{x}, \boldsymbol{y}))_i = d_i(x_i, y_i)$$

  for all $i \in I$, $\boldsymbol{x}, \boldsymbol{y} \in \prod_{i\in I} X_i$;
- *A* (quasi-)metric aggregation function on sets *if given a family of (quasi-)metrics $\{d_i : i \in I\}$ on an arbitrary nonempty set X, then $f \circ \boldsymbol{d}$ is a (quasi-)metric on X where $\boldsymbol{d} : X \times X \to [0, +\infty)^I$ is defined as follows:*

$$(\boldsymbol{d}(x, y))_i = d_i(x, y)$$

  for all $i \in I$, $x, y \in X$.

Recall that a triplet $(\boldsymbol{a}, \boldsymbol{b}, \boldsymbol{c}) \in ([0, +\infty)^I)^3$ is a *triangular triplet* if $\boldsymbol{a}_i \leq \boldsymbol{b}_i + \boldsymbol{c}_i$, $\boldsymbol{b}_i \leq \boldsymbol{a}_i + \boldsymbol{c}_i$ and $\boldsymbol{c}_i \leq \boldsymbol{a}_i + \boldsymbol{b}_i$ for all $i \in I$ (see [2]). As we next observe, this concept was introduced in [1] for characterizing metric aggregation functions on products. Moreover, if $(\boldsymbol{a}, \boldsymbol{b}, \boldsymbol{c})$ solely verifies that $\boldsymbol{a}_i \leq \boldsymbol{b}_i + \boldsymbol{c}_i$ for all $i \in I$, then it is called an *asymmetric triangular triplet* ([3]). A function $f : [0, +\infty)^I \to [0, +\infty)$ is said to preserve (asymmetric) triangular triplets if given an asymmetric triangular triplet $(\boldsymbol{a}, \boldsymbol{b}, \boldsymbol{c}) \in ([0, +\infty)^I)^3$, then $(f(\boldsymbol{a}), f(\boldsymbol{b}), f(\boldsymbol{c}))$ is an asymmetric triangular triplet.

Borsík and Doboš [1] characterized metric aggregation functions on products in the following manner.

Theorem 1 ([1]). *A function $f : [0, +\infty)^I \to [0, +\infty)$ is a metric aggregation function on products if and only if $f^{-1}(0) = \{\boldsymbol{0}\}$ and f preserves triangular triplets.*

On its part, Mayor and Valero [3] proved the next result which characterizes the functions merging quasi-metrics on products.

Theorem 2 ([3]). *Consider a function $f : [0, +\infty)^I \to [0, +\infty)$. Then, the following statements are equivalent:*

(1) f is a quasi-metric aggregation function on products;
(2) $f^{-1}(0) = \{\boldsymbol{0}\}$ and f preserves asymmetric triangular triplets;
(3) $f^{-1}(0) = \{\boldsymbol{0}\}$, f is subadditive and isotone.

The two previous theorems bring to light that every quasi-metric aggregation function on products is a metric aggregation function on products. However, the reciprocal implication does not hold in general [3] (Example 8).

On the other hand, if you consider (asymmetric) normed vector spaces rather than (quasi-)metric spaces, the concepts of (asymmetric) norm aggregation function on products and (asymmetric) norm aggregation function on sets can be considered in a natural manner. The former has been characterized in [7,8], while the latter has been studied in [9]. As the main objective of this paper is to study this problem in the fuzzy context, we recall the known results for crisp (asymmetric) norms. In the following, a function $f : [0, +\infty)^I \to [0, +\infty)$ is said to be positive homogeneous if $f(\lambda \cdot x) = \lambda f(x)$ for all $\lambda \geq 0, x \in [0, +\infty)^I$.

We first recall the following result showing that the family of asymmetric norm aggregation functions on products is equal to the family of norm aggregation functions on products.

Theorem 3 ([7–9]). *Given a function $f : [0, +\infty)^I \to [0, +\infty)$, the following statements are equivalent:*

(1) *f is an asymmetric norm aggregation function on products;*
(2) *f is a norm aggregation function on products;*
(3) *$((\mathbb{R}^2)^I, \|\cdot\|_f)$ is a normed space where $\|x\|_f = f((\|x_i\|)_{i\in I})$ and $\|\cdot\|$ is the Euclidean norm for all $x \in (\mathbb{R}^2)^I$;*
(4) *$f^{-1}(0) = \mathbf{0}$, f is positive homogeneous, and it preserves asymmetric triangular triplets;*
(5) *$f^{-1}(0) = \mathbf{0}$, f is positive homogeneous, and it preserves triangular triplets;*
(6) *$f^{-1}(0) = \mathbf{0}$, f is positive homogeneous, subadditive and isotone.*

From Theorems 1, 2 and 3, we have it that every (asymmetric) norm aggregation function on products is also a (quasi-)metric aggregation function on products. However, the reciprocal implication does not hold in general. We can provide an easy example.

Example 1. *Let $f : [0, +\infty) \to [0, +\infty)$ be given by $f(x) = \min\{x, 1\}$. It is straightforward to check that $f^{-1}(0) = 0$, and f is subadditive and isotone. Therefore, f is a (quasi-)metric aggregation function on sets. However, f is not positive homogeneous since, for example, $f\left(4 \cdot \frac{1}{2}\right) = 1 \neq 2 = 4f\left(\frac{1}{2}\right)$. Hence, f is not an asymmetric norm aggregation function on products.*

In the case of the aggregation on sets, norm aggregation functions and asymmetric norm aggregation functions are different classes of functions.

Theorem 4 ([9]). *Let $f : [0, +\infty)^I \to [0, +\infty)$ be a function and let g be the restriction of f to $(0, +\infty)^I \cup \{\mathbf{0}\}$. The following conditions are equivalent:*

(1) *f is a norm aggregation function on sets;*
(2) *For every family of norms $\{n_i : i \in I\}$ on $\mathbb{R}^2$, $(\mathbb{R}^2, f \circ \mathbf{n})$ is a normed space;*
(3) *$g^{-1}(0) = \mathbf{0}$, g is positive homogeneous, and it preserves asymmetric triangular triplets;*
(4) *$g^{-1}(0) = \mathbf{0}$, g is positive homogeneous, and it preserves triangular triplets;*
(5) *$g^{-1}(0) = \mathbf{0}$, g is positive homogeneous, subadditive and isotone.*

Theorem 5 ([9]). *Let $f : [0, +\infty)^I \to [0, +\infty)$ be a function. The following statements are equivalent*

(1) *f is an asymmetric norm aggregation function on sets;*
(2) *For every family of asymmetric norms $\{n_i : i \in I\}$ on $\mathbb{R}^2$, $(\mathbb{R}^2, f \circ \mathbf{n})$ is an asymmetric normed space;*
(3) *$f(\mathbf{0}) = 0$; if $\mathbf{a}, \mathbf{b} \in f^{-1}(0)$ then there exists $j \in I$ such that $\mathbf{a}_j = \mathbf{b}_j = 0$; f is positive homogeneous, and it preserves asymmetric triangular triplets;*
(4) *$f(\mathbf{0}) = 0$; if $\mathbf{a}, \mathbf{b} \in f^{-1}(0)$ then there exists $j \in I$ such that $\mathbf{a}_j = \mathbf{b}_j = 0$; f is positive homogeneous, and it preserves triangular triplets;*
(5) *$f(\mathbf{0}) = 0$; if $\mathbf{a}, \mathbf{b} \in f^{-1}(0)$ then there exists $j \in I$ such that $\mathbf{a}_j = \mathbf{b}_j = 0$; f is positive homogeneous, subadditive and isotone.*

3. Weak Fuzzy (Quasi-)Norms

As the goal of the paper is to study in the fuzzy context those functions that aggregate fuzzy norms in the spirit of the results of the previous section, in the following, we present the basic definitions about fuzzy norms and some examples. First, we remind the reader of the well-known notion of a triangular norm.

Definition 2 ([21]). *We say that a binary operation* $*: [0,1] \times [0,1] \to [0,1]$ *is a* triangular norm *or a* t-norm *if, for every* $a, b, c, d \in [0,1]$, *it satisfies the following properties:*

- $a * (b * c) = (a * b) * c$;
- $a * b = b * a$;
- $a * 1 = a$;
- $a * b \leq c * d$ *whenever* $a \leq c$ *and* $b \leq d$.

A t-norm $*$ *is said to be* continuous *if* $*$ *is a continuous function.*

Example 2 ([21]). *Some of the most renowned examples of triangular norms are the following:*

- $x \wedge y := \min\{x, y\}$; *(minimum t-norm)*
- $x *_P y := x \cdot y$; *(product t-norm)*
- $x *_D y := \begin{cases} x & \text{if } y = 1, \\ y & \text{if } x = 1, \\ 0 & \text{otherwise.} \end{cases}$ *(drastic t-norm)*

The origins of fuzzy normed spaces can be found in the concept of probabilistic normed space and Šerstnev space [22,23]. This notion was first adapted to the fuzzy context by Katsaras [24]. Later on, Cheng and Mordeson [25] introduced a new definition of a fuzzy norm, which induces a fuzzy metric in the sense of Kramosil and Michalek [26]. Bag and Samanta considered a more general concept of fuzzy norm [27] by removing the left-continuity condition (see next definition). In this paper, we use the concept of fuzzy norm as considered by Goleţ [19] as well as the terminology of [18,28] relative to (weak) fuzzy (quasi-)norms.

Definition 3 ([18,19,28]). *A* weak fuzzy quasi-norm *on a real vector space* V *is a pair* $(N, *)$ *such that* $*$ *is a continuous t-norm and* N *is a fuzzy set on* $V \times [0, +\infty)$ *such that, for any vectors* $x, y \in V$ *and for any parameters* $t, s > 0$, *it satisfies the following conditions:*

(FQN1) $N(x, 0) = 0$;
(FQN2) $N(x, t) = N(-x, t) = 1$ *for all* $t > 0$ *if and only if* $x = 0_V$;
(FQN3) $N(\lambda x, t) = N(x, \frac{t}{\lambda})$ *for all* $\lambda > 0$;
(FQN4) $N(x, t) * N(y, s) \leq N(x + y, t + s)$;
(FQN5) $N(x, \cdot) : [0, \infty) \to [0, 1]$ *is left-continuous.*

If N also satisfies the following:

(FQN6) $\lim_{t \to +\infty} N(x, t) = 1$

then $(N, *)$ *is called a* fuzzy quasi-norm.

A (weak) fuzzy norm on a real vector space V *is a (weak) fuzzy quasi-norm* $(N, *)$ *on* V *such that the following is the case.*

(FQN3') $N(\lambda x, t) = N\left(x, \frac{t}{|\lambda|}\right)$ *for all* $\lambda \in \mathbb{R} \setminus \{0\}$.

A (weak) fuzzy (quasi-)normed *space is a triple* $(V, N, *)$ *such that* V *is a real vector space and* $(N, *)$ *is a (weak) fuzzy (quasi-)norm on* V.

Remark 1. *Notice that the definition of fuzzy norm that we have considered is that of Goleţ. It differs slightly from that defined in [25] by Cheng and Mordeson since they considered a real or complex vector space* V. *They allow that the parameter* t *also takes negative values by considering* *that $N(x,t) = 0$ for every $t < 0$, and they only create the definition for the minimum t-norm. The above definition is equal to that given in [18,28].*

There are also other notions of a fuzzy norm that modify the previous conditions as the elimination of (FQN5) [27].

Remark 2. *The definition of a (weak) fuzzy (quasi-)normed space $(V, N, *)$ given above requires the continuity of the triangular norm $*$. This property is used for ensuring that $(N, *)$ endows the vector space V with a classical topology τ_N (see [18,28]) having as its base, $\{B_N(x,r,t) : x \in V, r \in]0,1[, t > 0\}$, where*

$$B_N(x,r,t) = \{y \in V : N(y - x, t) > 1 - r\}.$$

Despite this, since we do not need $(N, *)$ generating a topology, as we can suppose that $*$ is an arbitrary t-norm rather than a continuous one.

Remark 3. *If $(V, N, *)$ is a (weak) fuzzy (quasi-)normed space then $N(x, \cdot) : [0, +\infty) \to [0, +\infty)$ is an isotone function for every $x \in V$. In fact, given $x \in V$, if $t < s$ then, by (FQN2) and (FQN4), we have that $N(v,t) = N(v,t) * 1 = N(v,t) * N(0_V, s-t) \leq N(v + 0_V, t + s - t) = N(v,s)$. We will use this fact throughout the paper.*

Example 3 (cf. [28,29] [Example 1]). *Let (V, q) be a quasi-normed space. Let $k, m, n \in \mathbb{R}^+$ be fixed. Define $N : V \times [0, +\infty) \to [0,1]$ as the following.*

$$N(x,t) = \begin{cases} 0 & if\, t = 0 \\ \dfrac{kt^n}{kt^n + mq(x)} & if\, t > 0 \end{cases}$$

Then, $(V, N, *)$ is a fuzzy quasi-normed space for every continuous t-norm $*$. If $k = n = m = 1$ then $(N, *)$ is called the standard fuzzy quasi-norm, and it will be denoted by $(N_q, *)$.

Example 4. *Let $a \in [0,1[$ and consider $N_a : \mathbb{R} \times [0, +\infty) \to [0,1]$ defined as the following.*

$$N_a(x,t) = \begin{cases} 1 & if\, t > |x| \\ a & if\, 0 < t \leq |x| \\ 0 & if\, t = 0 \end{cases}.$$

We can easily prove that $(\mathbb{R}, N_a, *)$ is a fuzzy normed space for every continuous t-norm $*$.

The reason for having chosen the definition of weak fuzzy (quasi-)norm as considered in 3 instead of other definition of fuzzy norm is that every weak fuzzy (quasi-)norm $(N, *)$ on a vector space V induces a fuzzy (quasi-)metric $(M_N, *)$ on V (in the sense of the paper [26]) given as $M_N(x,y,t) = N(y - x, t)$ for all $x, y \in V$ and all $t \geq 0$ (see [18]). Since (quasi-)metric aggregation functions have been already characterized in [17] and we plan to characterize here the functions that aggregate fuzzy (quasi-)norms, it is natural to select a concept of fuzzy (quasi-)norm that allows constructing a fuzzy (quasi-)metric.

4. Aggregation of Weak Fuzzy (Quasi-)Norms

In Section 2 we have summarized the known results about the aggregation of (quasi-)metrics and asymmetric norms on products and on sets. On the other hand, in [17], the functions that aggregate fuzzy (quasi-)metrics on products and on sets were completely characterized. Nevertheless, to the best of our knowledge, the problem for fuzzy (quasi-)norms has not been already solved. The goal of this section is fill in this gap. We first set the definitions of the functions that we intend to characterize.

Definition 4. *A function $F : [0,1]^I \to [0,1]$ is said to be the following:*

- A weak fuzzy (quasi-)norm aggregation function on products *if given a t-norm $*$ and a collection of weak fuzzy (quasi-)normed spaces $\{(V_i, N_i, *) : i \in I\}$ then $(F \circ \widetilde{\mathbf{N}}, *)$ is a weak fuzzy (quasi-)norm on $\prod_{i\in I} V_i$ where $\widetilde{\mathbf{N}} : \prod_{i\in I} V_i \times [0, +\infty) \to [0, 1]^I$ is given by the following:*
$$(\widetilde{\mathbf{N}}(\boldsymbol{x}, t))_i = N_i(x_i, t)$$
for every $\boldsymbol{x} \in \prod_{i\in I} V_i$ and $t \geq 0$.
If the previous condition is only verified for a t-norm $*$, then F is called an $*$-weak fuzzy (quasi-)norm aggregation function on products.
- A weak fuzzy (quasi-)norm aggregation function on sets *if given a t-norm $*$ and a collection of weak fuzzy (quasi-)norms $\{(N_i, *) : i \in I\}$ defined on a real vector space V then $(F \circ \mathbf{N}, *)$ is a weak fuzzy (quasi-)norm on V where $\mathbf{N} : V \times [0, +\infty) \to [0, 1]^I$ is given by the following:*
$$(\mathbf{N}(x, t))_i = N_i(x, t)$$
for every $x \in V$ and $t \geq 0$.
If the previous condition is only verified for a t-norm $*$, then F is called a $*$-weak fuzzy (quasi-)norm aggregation function on sets.

Remark 4. *It can be easily proved that a weak fuzzy (quasi-)norm aggregation function on products $F : [0, 1]^I \to [0, 1]$ is also a weak fuzzy (quasi-)norm aggregation function on sets. Trivially, if the cardinality of I is one, then the two notions are equivalent. However, if the cardinality of I is greater than one, the two concepts are different in general as we next illustrate with an example.*

Example 5. *Consider I an index set and $j \in I$ is fixed. Denote by P_j the jth projection. It is obvious that P_j is a weak fuzzy (quasi-)norm aggregation function on sets since if $\{(N_i, *) : i \in I\}$ is a collection of weak fuzzy (quasi-)norms on a vector space V, then $(P_j \circ \mathbf{N}, *) = (N_j, *)$.*

Nevertheless, if $\{(V_i, N_i, *) : i \in I\}$ is a collection of nontrivial weak fuzzy (quasi-)normed spaces, consider $\boldsymbol{x} \in \prod_{i\in I} V_i$ such that $\boldsymbol{x}_j = 0_{V_j}$ and $\boldsymbol{x}_i \neq 0_{V_i}$ whenever $i \neq j$. Then $F \circ \widetilde{\mathbf{N}}(\boldsymbol{x}) = 0$, but $\boldsymbol{x} \neq 0_{\prod_{i\in I} V_i}$, so $(F \circ \widetilde{\mathbf{N}}, *)$ is not a weak fuzzy quasi-norm on $\prod_{i\in I} V_i$.

In the following, we will introduce several valuable concepts used in [17] for proving a characterization of fuzzy (quasi-)metric aggregation functions which will be also useful in our work. Actually, it will be shown that weak fuzzy (quasi-)norm aggregation functions are exactly the fuzzy (quasi-)metric aggregation functions. Notice that this is not true in the crisp context where norm aggregation functions are metric aggregation functions, but the reciprocal implication does not hold in general [2,3,8,9].

We begin by recalling the notion of (asymmetric) $*$-triangular triplet [14,17] in which we will use the operation $*^I$ on $[0, 1]^I$ defined as $(\boldsymbol{a} *^I \boldsymbol{b})_i = \boldsymbol{a}_i * \boldsymbol{b}_i$ for every $i \in I$ and every $\boldsymbol{a}, \boldsymbol{b} \in [0, 1]^I$.

Definition 5 ([14,17]). *Consider an index set I and a t-norm $*$. A triplet $(\boldsymbol{a}, \boldsymbol{b}, \boldsymbol{c}) \in ([0, 1]^I)^3$ is said to be the following:*

- $*$-triangular *if*
$$\boldsymbol{a} *^I \boldsymbol{b} \preceq \boldsymbol{c}, \quad \boldsymbol{a} *^I \boldsymbol{c} \preceq \boldsymbol{b} \quad \text{and} \quad \boldsymbol{b} *^I \boldsymbol{c} \preceq \boldsymbol{a},$$
in other words,
$$a_i * b_i \leq c_i, \quad a_i * c_i \leq b_i \quad \text{and} \quad b_i * c_i \leq a_i, \quad \text{for every } i \in I.$$
- Asymmetric $*$-triangular *if $\boldsymbol{a} *^I \boldsymbol{b} \preceq \boldsymbol{c}$.*

If $(\boldsymbol{a}, \boldsymbol{b}, \boldsymbol{c})$ is an asymmetric $*$-triangular triplet for every t-norm $*$, then $(\boldsymbol{a}, \boldsymbol{b}, \boldsymbol{c})$ is called a(n) (asymmetric) triangular triplet.

Example 6. *Consider a weak fuzzy (quasi-)normed space* $(V, N, *)$. *Then* $(N(x,t), N(y,s), N(x+y, t+s))$ *is an asymmetric* $*$*-triangular triplet for every vector* $x, y, z \in V$ *and every* $t, s > 0$.

Definition 6 ([17]). *Consider an index set* I *and a t-norm* $*$. *A function* $F : [0,1]^I \to [0,1]$ *is said to* preserve $*$-triangular (asymmetric $*$-triangular) triplets *if for every* $*$*-triangular (asymmetric* $*$*-triangular) triplet* $(\boldsymbol{a}, \boldsymbol{b}, \boldsymbol{c}) \in ([0,1]^I)^3$ *then* $(F(\boldsymbol{a}), F(\boldsymbol{b}), F(\boldsymbol{c}))$ *is a* $*$*-triangular (an asymmetric* $*$*-triangular) triplet.*

If F preserves $*$*-triangular (asymmetric* $*$*-triangular) triplets for every t-norm* $*$, *then F is said to* preserve triangular (asymmetric triangular) triplets.

We next provide a concept that is a particular case of the concept of domination as considered in [10]. Domination has been demonstrated to be useful in the study of the preservation by means of aggregation functions of some properties of certain fuzzy structures [10,17,30]. It has also been used for constructing other fuzzy structures such as m-polar $*$-orderings [31].

Definition 7 ([10,17]). *Given a triangular norm* $*$, *a function* $F : [0,1]^I \to [0,1]$ *is* $*$-supmultiplicative *if the following is the case.*

$$F(\boldsymbol{a}) * F(\boldsymbol{b}) \leq F(\boldsymbol{a} *^I \boldsymbol{b}), \quad \text{for every } \boldsymbol{a}, \boldsymbol{b} \in [0,1]^I.$$

We will say that F is supmultiplicative *if F is* $*$*-supmultiplicative for every t-norm* $*$.

$*$-supmultiplicative functions and functions preserving (asymmetric) $*$-triangular triplets can appear to be unrelated concepts. However, both have been used for characterizing, in different senses, the functions preserving the property of $*$-transitivity of fuzzy binary relations [10,14]. Its relationship has been disclosed in [17] in the following way.

Proposition 1 ([17] (Proposition 3.30)). *Let* $F : [0,1]^I \to [0,1]$ *be a function and* $*$ *be a t-norm. Each of the following statements implies its successor:*

(1) *F preserves asymmetric* $*$*-triangular triplets;*
(2) *F preserves* $*$*-triangular triplets;*
(3) *F is* $*$*-supmultiplicative.*

If F is isotone then all the above statements are equivalent.

We still need to recall two concepts that will be needed in our characterization.

Definition 8 ([32,33]). *A function* $F : [0,1]^I \to [0,1]$ *is called* sequentially left-continuous *if F is sequentially continuous when* $[0,1]^I$ *is endowed with the product topology of the upper limit topology, and* $[0,1]$ *carries the usual topology. Recall that the upper limit topology on* $[0,1]$ *has as base* $\{(a,b] : a, b \in [0,1], a \leq b\}$.

Remark 5. *Notice that if F is isotone then, for proving that F is sequentially left-continuous, it is enough to consider nondecreasing sequences on* $[0,1]^I$. *In fact, let* $\{\boldsymbol{t}_n\}_{n\in\mathbb{N}}$ *be a sequence in* $[0,1]^I$ *converging to* $\boldsymbol{t}$ *with respect to the product topology of the upper limit topology. For all* $n \in \mathbb{N}$, *define* $\boldsymbol{s}_n \in [0,1]^I$ *as* $(\boldsymbol{s}_n)_i = \inf_{k\geq n}(\boldsymbol{t}_k)_i$ *for all* $i \in I$. *It is obvious that* $\{\boldsymbol{s}_n\}_{n\in\mathbb{N}}$ *is a nondecreasing sequence and* $\boldsymbol{s}_n \preceq \boldsymbol{t}_n$ *for all* $n \in \mathbb{N}$. *Moreover,* $\bigvee_{n\in\mathbb{N}} \boldsymbol{t}_n = \bigvee_{n\in\mathbb{N}} \boldsymbol{s}_n = \boldsymbol{t}$. *Suppose that* $\{F(\boldsymbol{s}_n)\}_{n\in\mathbb{N}}$ *converges to* $F(\boldsymbol{t}) = F(\bigvee_{n\in\mathbb{N}} \boldsymbol{t}_n)$, *that is,* $\bigvee_{n\in\mathbb{N}} F(\boldsymbol{s}_n) = F(\bigvee_{n\in\mathbb{N}} \boldsymbol{t}_n)$. *Then, the following is the case:*

$$F(\bigvee_{n\in\mathbb{N}} \boldsymbol{t}_n) = \bigvee_{n\in\mathbb{N}} F(\boldsymbol{s}_n) \leq \bigvee_{n\in\mathbb{N}} F(\boldsymbol{t}_n) \leq F(\bigvee_{n\in\mathbb{N}} \boldsymbol{t}_n)$$

since F is isotone. Therefore, $\bigvee_{n\in\mathbb{N}} F(\boldsymbol{t}_n) = F(\bigvee_{n\in\mathbb{N}} \boldsymbol{t}_n) = F(\boldsymbol{t})$.

Recall (see Section 2) that the characterizations of an asymmetric norm aggregation function or a (quasi-)metric aggregation function f require the imposition of some conditions on the set $f^{-1}(0)$. These conditions will be substituted by certain properties of the core in the fuzzy framework.

Definition 9 ([17]). *Given a function* $F : [0,1]^I \to [0,1]$, *its* core *is the set* $F^{-1}(1)$.
We say the following:

- F *has a* trivial core *if* $F^{-1}(1) = \{\mathbf{1}\}$;
- *The* core of F is countably included in a unitary face *if given* $\{\boldsymbol{a}_n : n \in \mathbb{N}\} \subseteq F^{-1}(1)$ *there exists* $i \in I$ *such that* $(\boldsymbol{a}_n)_i = 1$ *for all* $n \in \mathbb{N}$.

The following result characterizes the weak fuzzy (quasi-)norm aggregation functions on products (compare with [17] (Theorem 4.15)).

Theorem 6. *Let* $F : [0,1]^I \to [0,1]$ *be a function and* $*$ *be a t-norm. The following statements are equivalent:*

(1) *F is a ($*$-)weak fuzzy quasi-norm aggregation function on products;*
(2) *F is a ($*$-)weak fuzzy norm aggregation function on products;*
(3) *$F(\mathbf{0}) = 0$, F is isotone, ($*$-)supmultiplicative, sequentially left-continuous and F has trivial core;*
(4) *$F(\mathbf{0}) = 0$, F is sequentially left-continuous with trivial core, and F preserves asymmetric ($*$-)triangular triplets.*

Proof. (1) $\Rightarrow$ (2) This implication can be easily observed. (2) $\Rightarrow$ (3) We begin showing that $F(\mathbf{0}) = 0$. Let $(V, N, *)$ be a weak fuzzy normed space and $x \in V$. Let $\{(V_i, N_i, *) : i \in I\}$ be the family of weak fuzzy normed spaces such that $(V_i, N_i, *) = (V, N, *)$ for all $i \in I$. By assumption, $(F \circ \widetilde{\mathbf{N}}, *)$ is a weak fuzzy norm on V^I so $0 = F \circ \widetilde{\mathbf{N}}(\boldsymbol{x}, 0) = F(\mathbf{0})$ where $\boldsymbol{x}_i = x$ for all $i \in I$.

Let us check that F has a trivial core. We first notice that if $t > 0$ then $F(\mathbf{1}) = F((N(0_V, t))_{i\in I}) = F \circ \widetilde{\mathbf{N}}(\mathbf{0}_{V^I}, t) = 1$ by (FQN2).

In order to obtain a contradiction, suppose that there exists $\boldsymbol{a} \in [0,1]^I$ verifying that $F(\boldsymbol{a}) = 1$ but $\boldsymbol{a} \neq \mathbf{1}$. Let $J = \{i \in I : \boldsymbol{a}_i \neq 1\}$, which is nonempty. Consider the family of weak fuzzy normed spaces $\{(\mathbb{R}, N_i, *) : i \in I\}$ where the following is the case.

- If $i \in J$, then $(N_i, *) = (N_{\boldsymbol{a}_i}, *)$ is the fuzzy norm of Example 4;
- If $i \notin J$, then $(N_i, *) = (N, *)$ is an arbitrary fixed weak fuzzy norm on $\mathbb{R}$.

By assumption, $(F \circ \widetilde{\mathbf{N}}, *)$ is a weak fuzzy norm on $\mathbb{R}^I$. Let $\boldsymbol{x} \in \mathbb{R}^I$ such that $\boldsymbol{x}_i = 1$ if $i \in J$ and $\boldsymbol{x}_i = 0$ otherwise. Then, given $t > 0$, we have the following:

$$F \circ \widetilde{\mathbf{N}}(\boldsymbol{x}, t) = F((N_i(\boldsymbol{x}_i, t))_{i\in I}) = \begin{cases} F(\mathbf{1}) = 1 & \text{if } t > 1 \\ F(\boldsymbol{a}) = 1 & \text{if } 0 < t \leq 1. \end{cases}.$$

which contradicts (FQN2). Hence, F has trivial core.

We next show the isotonicity of F. Consider two elements $\boldsymbol{a}, \boldsymbol{b}$ belonging to $[0,1]^I$ verifying $\boldsymbol{a} \preceq \boldsymbol{b}$. Let us consider the real vector space $\mathbb{R}$ and, for every index $i \in I$, we define $N_i : \mathbb{R} \times [0, +\infty) \to [0,1]$ as follows.

$$N_i(x,t) = \begin{cases} 0 & \text{if } 0 \leq t \leq |x|, \\ \boldsymbol{a}_i & \text{if } |x| < t \leq 2|x|, \\ \boldsymbol{b}_i & \text{if } 2|x| < t \leq 3|x|, \\ 1 & \text{if } t > 3|x|. \end{cases}$$

It is simple to show that $(\mathbb{R}, N_i, *)$ is a weak fuzzy normed space for every $i \in I$. Furthermore, $N_i(1,2) = \boldsymbol{a}_i$ and $N_i(1,3) = \boldsymbol{b}_i$ for every $i \in I$. Since $(F \circ \widetilde{\mathbf{N}}, *)$ is a weak fuzzy norm on $\mathbb{R}$, then $F \circ \widetilde{\mathbf{N}}(\mathbf{1}, \cdot)$ is increasing. Consequently, we have the following.

$$\begin{aligned} F \circ \widetilde{\mathbf{N}}(\mathbf{1}, 2) &\leq F \circ \widetilde{\mathbf{N}}(\mathbf{1}, 3) \\ F((N_i(1,2))_{i \in I}) &\leq F((N_i(1,3))_{i \in I}) \\ F((\boldsymbol{a}_i)_{i \in I}) &\leq F((\boldsymbol{b}_i)_{i \in I}) \\ F(\boldsymbol{a}) &\leq F(\boldsymbol{b}) \end{aligned}$$

Thus, F is isotone.

Now, we show the $*$-supmultiplicativity of F. Let $\boldsymbol{a}, \boldsymbol{b} \in [0,1]^I$. Define $L_1 = \{(x,y) \in \mathbb{R}^2 : x \neq 0, y = 0\}$, $L_2 = \{(x,y) \in \mathbb{R}^2 : x = 0, y \neq 0\}$ and $L_3 = \mathbb{R}^2 \backslash (L_1 \cup L_2 \cup \{(0,0)\})$. For each $i \in I$, define a function $N_i : \mathbb{R}^2 \times [0, +\infty) \to [0,1]$ as follows:

$$N_i(\boldsymbol{x}, t) = \begin{cases} 0 & \text{if } 0 \leq t \leq \|\boldsymbol{x}\|, \\ \boldsymbol{a}_i & \text{if } \boldsymbol{x} \in L_1 \text{ and } t > \|\boldsymbol{x}\|, \\ \boldsymbol{b}_i & \text{if } \boldsymbol{x} \in L_2 \text{ and } t > \|\boldsymbol{x}\|, \\ \boldsymbol{a}_i * \boldsymbol{b}_i & \text{if } \boldsymbol{x} \in L_3 \text{ and } t > \|\boldsymbol{x}\|, \\ 1 & \text{if } \boldsymbol{x} = \mathbf{0} \text{ and } t > 0, \end{cases}$$

where $\| \cdot \|$ is the Euclidean norm. Then $(N_i, *)$ is a weak fuzzy norm on $\mathbb{R}^2$ for all $i \in I$. We only verify that $(N_i, *)$ satisfies (FQN4). Let $\boldsymbol{x}, \boldsymbol{y} \in \mathbb{R}^2$ and $t, s > 0$. If $\boldsymbol{x} + \boldsymbol{y} = \mathbf{0}$, the inequality is trivially true. If $\boldsymbol{x} = \mathbf{0}$ or $\boldsymbol{y} = \mathbf{0}$, we also obtain the inequality since $N_i(\boldsymbol{z}, \cdot)$ is isotone for every $\boldsymbol{z} \in \mathbb{R}^2$. Thus, let us suppose that $\boldsymbol{x} + \boldsymbol{y} \neq \mathbf{0}$, $\boldsymbol{x} \neq \mathbf{0}$ and $\boldsymbol{y} \neq \mathbf{0}$. Let $j \in \{1,2,3\}$ such that $\boldsymbol{x} + \boldsymbol{y} \in L_j$. If $\boldsymbol{x} \in L_j$ or $\boldsymbol{y} \in L_j$, then it is clear that $N_i(\boldsymbol{x}, t) * N_i(\boldsymbol{y}, s) \leq N_i(\boldsymbol{x} + \boldsymbol{y}, t + s)$. If $\boldsymbol{x} \notin L_j$ and $\boldsymbol{y} \notin L_j$, we distinguish the following three cases:

- If $j = 3$, then $\boldsymbol{x} \in L_1$ and $\boldsymbol{y} \in L_2$ or viceversa. If $t \leq \|\boldsymbol{x}\|$ or $s \leq \|\boldsymbol{y}\|$, then $N_i(\boldsymbol{x}, t) = 0$ or $N_i(\boldsymbol{y}, s) = 0$. so the inequality holds. Otherwise $t > \|\boldsymbol{x}\|$ and $s > \|\boldsymbol{y}\|$, which implies that $t + s > \|\boldsymbol{x}\| + \|\boldsymbol{y}\| \geq \|\boldsymbol{x} + \boldsymbol{y}\|$. Hence, $N_i(\boldsymbol{x}, t) * N_i(\boldsymbol{y}, s) = \boldsymbol{a}_i * \boldsymbol{b}_i \leq N_i(\boldsymbol{x} + \boldsymbol{y}, t + s) = \boldsymbol{a}_i * \boldsymbol{b}_i$;
- If $j = 2$, then at least one of $\boldsymbol{x}, \boldsymbol{y}$ belongs to L_3. Without loss of generality, we can suppose that $\boldsymbol{x} \in L_3$. As above, if $t \leq \|\boldsymbol{x}\|$ or $s \leq \|\boldsymbol{y}\|$, then $N_i(\boldsymbol{x}, t) = 0$ or $N_i(\boldsymbol{y}, s) = 0$, so the inequality holds. Otherwise $t > \|\boldsymbol{x}\|$ and $s > \|\boldsymbol{y}\|$, which implies that $t + s > \|\boldsymbol{x}\| + \|\boldsymbol{y}\| \geq \|\boldsymbol{x} + \boldsymbol{y}\|$. Hence, $N_i(\boldsymbol{x}, t) * N_i(\boldsymbol{y}, s) = \boldsymbol{a}_i * \boldsymbol{b}_i * N_i(\boldsymbol{y}, s) \leq \boldsymbol{b}_i = N_i(\boldsymbol{x} + \boldsymbol{y}, t + s)$.
- If $j = 1$, we can reason as in the previous case.

Since $(F \circ \widetilde{\mathbf{N}}, *)$ is a weak fuzzy norm on $(\mathbb{R}^2)^I$, it verifies (FQN4). By defining $(\mathbf{1}, \mathbf{0}), (\mathbf{0}, \mathbf{1}), (\mathbf{1}, \mathbf{1}) \in (\mathbb{R}^2)^I$ such that $(\mathbf{1}, \mathbf{0})_i = (1,0)$, $(\mathbf{0}, \mathbf{1})_i = (0,1)$ and $(\mathbf{1}, \mathbf{1})_i = (1,1)$ for all $i \in I$, we have the following.

$$\begin{aligned} F \circ \widetilde{\mathbf{N}}((\mathbf{1}, \mathbf{0}), 2) * F \circ \widetilde{\mathbf{N}}((\mathbf{0}, \mathbf{1}), 2) &\leq F \circ \widetilde{\mathbf{N}}((\mathbf{1}, \mathbf{1}), 4) \\ F((\boldsymbol{a}_i)_{i \in I}) * F((\boldsymbol{b}_i)_{i \in I}) &\leq F((\boldsymbol{a}_i * \boldsymbol{b}_i)_{i \in I}) \end{aligned}$$

Thus, F is $*$-supmultiplicative.

Finally, we demonstrate that the function F is sequentially left-continuous. By Remark 5, let $\{\boldsymbol{s}_n\}_{n \in \mathbb{N}}$ be a nondecreasing sequence in $[0,1]^I$ having as limit $\boldsymbol{s} \in [0,1]^I$ in the product topology of the lower limit topology.

For each $i \in I$, define $N_i : \mathbb{R} \times [0, +\infty) \to [0,1]$ as the following.

$$N_i(x,t) = \begin{cases} 0 & \text{if } 0 \le t \le \frac{|x|}{2}, \\ (s_n)_i & \text{if } |x|\left(1 - \frac{1}{n+1}\right) < t \le |x|\left(1 - \frac{1}{n+2}\right),\ n \in \mathbb{N} \\ s_i & \text{if } 0 < |x| \le t, \\ 1 & \text{if } x = 0,\ t > 0. \end{cases}$$

Then, $(\mathbb{R}, N_i, *)$ is a weak fuzzy normed space for all $i \in I$. We only check (FQN4). Let $x, y \in \mathbb{R}$ and $t, s > 0$. If $N_i(x,t) = 0$ or $N_i(y,s) = 0$, then the conclusion is obvious, so we suppose that $N_i(x,t) \neq 0$ and $N_i(y,s) \neq 0$. We may also assume that $x \neq 0, y \neq 0$ and $x + y \neq 0$ (otherwise, the conclusion follows trivially). If $|x| \le t$ and $|y| \le s$ then $|x+y| \le |x| + |y| \le t + s$, so $N_i(x+y, t+s) = s_i \ge N_i(x,t) * N_i(y,s) = s_i * s_i$.

Now suppose that $|x| > t$ and $|y| \le s$. Since $N_i(x,t) \neq 0$ and $x \neq 0$, we also have it that $0 < \frac{|x|}{2} < t$. Then, there exists $n_x \in \mathbb{N}$ such that the following is the case.

$$|x|\left(1 - \frac{1}{n_x+1}\right) < t \le |x|\left(1 - \frac{1}{n_x+2}\right).$$

Therefore, the following obtains.

$$\begin{aligned} t + s &> |x|\left(1 - \frac{1}{n_x+1}\right) + |y| > |x|\left(1 - \frac{1}{n_x+1}\right) + |y|\left(1 - \frac{1}{n_x+1}\right) \\ &= (|x| + |y|)\left(1 - \frac{1}{n_x+1}\right) \ge |x+y|\left(1 - \frac{1}{n_x+1}\right). \end{aligned}$$

From this and since $\{(s_n)_i\}_{n \in \mathbb{N}}$ is nondecreasing, $N_i(x+y, t+s) \ge (s_{n_x})_i = N_i(x,t) \ge N_i(x,t) * N_i(y,s)$.

If $|x| \le t$ and $|y| > s$, we can reason as above.

Finally, let us suppose that $|x| > t$ and $|y| > s$. Then, we can find $n_x, n_y \in \mathbb{N}$ such that the following is the case.

$$|x|\left(1 - \frac{1}{n_x+1}\right) < t \le |x|\left(1 - \frac{1}{n_x+2}\right) \text{ and } |y|\left(1 - \frac{1}{n_y+1}\right) < s \le |y|\left(1 - \frac{1}{n_y+2}\right).$$

Then, we have the following.

$$\begin{aligned} |x+y|\left(1 - \frac{1}{(n_x \wedge n_y)+1}\right) &\le |x| + |y| - \frac{|x|}{(n_x \wedge n_y)+1} - \frac{|y|}{(n_x \wedge n_y)+1} \\ &\le |x| + |y| - \frac{|x|}{n_x+1} - \frac{|y|}{n_y+1} < t + s. \end{aligned}$$

Hence, the following is the case.

$$N_i(x+y, t+s) \ge (s_{n_x \wedge n_y})_i \ge (s_{n_x})_i * (s_{n_y})_i = N_i(x,t) * N_i(y,s).$$

Consequently, $(N_i, *)$ satisfies (FQN4).

Consider the collection of fuzzy normed spaces $\{(\mathbb{R}, N_i, *) : i \in I\}$. By assumption, $(F \circ \widetilde{\mathbf{N}}, *)$ is a weak fuzzy norm on $\mathbb{R}^I$. Then $F \circ \widetilde{\mathbf{N}}(\mathbf{1}, \cdot)$ is left-continuous so $\{F \circ \widetilde{\mathbf{N}}(\mathbf{1}, 1 - \frac{1}{n+2})\}_{n \in \mathbb{N}}$ converges to $F \circ \widetilde{\mathbf{N}}(\mathbf{1}, 1)$. We observe that the following is the case:

$$F \circ \widetilde{\mathbf{N}}\left(\mathbf{1}, 1 - \frac{1}{n+2}\right) = F\left(\left(N_i\left(1, 1 - \frac{1}{n+2}\right)\right)_{i \in I}\right) = F(((s_n)_i)_{i \in I}) = F(s_n)$$

for every $n \in \mathbb{N}$ and

$$F \circ \widetilde{\mathbf{N}}(\mathbf{1}, 1) = F((N_i(1,1))_{i \in I}) = F((s_i)_{i \in I}) = F(s).$$

Thus, F is sequentially left-continuous.

(3) $\Rightarrow$ (4) We are required to demonstrate that F preserves asymmetric ($*$-)triangular triplets. This was proved in [17] (Proposition 3.30), but we will reproduce it here. Let $(\boldsymbol{a}, \boldsymbol{b}, \boldsymbol{c}) \in ([0,1]^I)^3$ such that $\boldsymbol{a} *^I \boldsymbol{b} \preceq \boldsymbol{c}$. Since F is $*$-supmultiplicative and isotone, then the following is the case.

$$F(\boldsymbol{a}) * F(\boldsymbol{b}) \leq F(\boldsymbol{a} *^I \boldsymbol{b}) \leq F(\boldsymbol{c}).$$

Hence, $(F(\boldsymbol{a}), F(\boldsymbol{b}), F(\boldsymbol{c}))$ is an asymmetric $*$-triangular triplet.

(4) $\Rightarrow$ (1) Let $\{(V_i, N_i, *) : i \in I\}$ be a collection of weak fuzzy quasi-normed spaces. We need to prove that $(F \circ \widetilde{\mathbf{N}}, *)$ is a weak fuzzy quasi-norm on $\prod_{i \in I} V_i$.

Given $\boldsymbol{x} \in \prod_{i \in I} V_i$, then $F \circ \widetilde{\mathbf{N}}(\boldsymbol{x}, 0) = F((N_i(\boldsymbol{x}_i, 0))_{i \in I}) = F(\mathbf{0}) = 0$; thus, (FQN1) holds.

Now, suppose that $F \circ \widetilde{\mathbf{N}}(\boldsymbol{x}, t) = F \circ \widetilde{\mathbf{N}}(-\boldsymbol{x}, t) = 1$ for all $t > 0$. F has trivial core this is equivalent to $\widetilde{\mathbf{N}}(\boldsymbol{x}, t) = \widetilde{\mathbf{N}}(-\boldsymbol{x}, t) = \mathbf{1}$ for all $t > 0$, that is, $N_i(\boldsymbol{x}_i, t) = N_i(-\boldsymbol{x}_i, t) = 1$ for all $i \in I$ and all $t > 0$. Since $(N_i, *)$ is a weak fuzzy quasi-norm for all $i \in I$, then $\boldsymbol{x} = (0_{V_i})_{i \in I} = 0_{\prod_{i \in I} V_i}$; thus, $(FQN2)$ is true.

Obviously, $F \circ \widetilde{\mathbf{N}}$ verifies (FQN3) since given $\lambda, t > 0$ and $\boldsymbol{x} \in \prod_{i \in I} V_i$, we the following.

$$F \circ \widetilde{\mathbf{N}}(\lambda \boldsymbol{x}, t) = F((N_i(\lambda \boldsymbol{x}_i, t))_{i \in I}) = F\left(\left(N_i\left(\boldsymbol{x}_i, \frac{t}{\lambda}\right)\right)_{i \in I}\right) = F \circ \widetilde{\mathbf{N}}\left(\boldsymbol{x}, \frac{t}{\lambda}\right).$$

Now, we verify (FQN4). Let $\boldsymbol{x}, \boldsymbol{y} \in \prod_{i \in I} V_i$ and $t, s > 0$. Since $(N_i, *)$ is a weak fuzzy quasi-norm for all $i \in I$, it is clear that the triplet $((N_i(\boldsymbol{x}_i, t))_{i \in I}, (N_i(\boldsymbol{y}_i, s))_{i \in I}, (N_i(\boldsymbol{x}_i + \boldsymbol{y}_i, t + s))_{i \in I})$ is asymmetric $*$-triangular. By hypothesis, $(F((N_i(\boldsymbol{x}_i, t))_{i \in I}), F((N_i(\boldsymbol{y}_i, s))_{i \in I}),$ $F((N_i(\boldsymbol{x}_i + \boldsymbol{y}_i, t + s))_{i \in I}))$ is an asymmetric $*$-triangular triplet, so the following is the case:

$$F((N_i(\boldsymbol{x}_i, t))_{i \in I}) * F((N_i(\boldsymbol{y}_i, s))_{i \in I}) \leq F((N_i(\boldsymbol{x}_i + \boldsymbol{y}_i, t + s))_{i \in I})$$

which means that $F \circ \widetilde{\mathbf{N}}$ verifies (FQN4).

At last, we must prove (FQN5), that is, $F \circ \widetilde{N}(\boldsymbol{x}, \cdot)$ is sequentially left-continuous for every $\boldsymbol{x} \in \prod_{i \in I} V_i$. Let $\{t_n\}_{n \in \mathbb{N}}$ be a nondecreasing sequence on $[0,1]$ converging to t. It is clear that $\{\widetilde{\mathbf{N}}(\boldsymbol{x}, t_n)\}_{n \in \mathbb{N}}$ is a nondecreasing sequence on $[0,1]^I$ due to the fact that $N_i(\boldsymbol{x}_i, \cdot)$ is isotone for every $i \in I$. Furthermore, the sequence $\{N_i(\boldsymbol{x}_i, t_n)\}_{n \in \mathbb{N}}$ is convergent to $N_i(\boldsymbol{x}_i, t)$ for all $i \in I$. Thus, $\{\widetilde{\mathbf{N}}(\boldsymbol{x}, t_n)\}_{n \in \mathbb{N}}$ converges to $\widetilde{\mathbf{N}}(\boldsymbol{x}, t)$. Since F is sequentially left-continuous, the conclusion follows. □

Observe that, in the crisp context, the norm aggregation functions on products also coincide with the asymmetric norm aggregation functions on products [8,9]. Nevertheless, these functions are different from the (quasi-)metric aggregation functions on products [2,3]. Surprisingly, this does not occur in the fuzzy framework.

Corollary 1. *Let $F : [0,1]^I \rightarrow [0,1]$ be a function and $*$ be a t-norm. Then F is a ($*$-)weak fuzzy (quasi-)norm aggregation function on products if and only if F is a ($*$-)fuzzy (quasi-)metric aggregation function on products.*

Proof. This is a direct consequence of the previous theorem and [17] (Theorem 4.15) (notice that, in that paper, sequentially left-continuity is called simply left-continuity). □

Example 7.

- *Let $F : [0,1] \to [0,1]$ be an isotone and left-continuous function such that $F(0) = 0$ and $F^{-1}(1) = \{1\}$. Then, F is a $\wedge$-weak fuzzy (quasi-)norm aggregation function on products since it is a $\wedge$-supmultiplicative function;*
- *Let $F : [0,1]^n \to [0,1]$ be an isotone and left-continuous function such that $F(0) = 0$ and $F^{-1}(1) = \{\mathbf{1}\}$. Then, F is a $*_D$-weak fuzzy (quasi-)norm aggregation function on products where $*_D$ is the drastic t-norm since it is a $*_D$-supmultiplicative function;*
- *Given a continuous t-norm $*$ and $n \in \mathbb{N}$, the function $F_* : [0,1]^n \to [0,1]$ given by $F_*(a_1, \ldots, a_n) = a_1 * \ldots * a_n$ satisfies the conditions of Theorem 6. Therefore, F is a $*$-weak fuzzy (quasi-)norm aggregation function on products.*
- *Consider an index set I. Then, the function $\mathsf{Inf} : [0,1]^I \to [0,1]$ given by $\mathsf{Inf}(\mathbf{x}) = \inf_{i \in I} \mathbf{x}_i$ satisfies the conditions of Theorem 6. Therefore, it is a weak fuzzy (quasi-)norm aggregation function on products.*

The following theorem, which must be compared with [17] (Theorem 4.19), provides a characterization of the functions that aggregate weak fuzzy (quasi-)norm aggregation on sets.

Theorem 7. *Let $F : [0,1]^I \to [0,1]$ be a function and $*$ be a t-norm. The following statements are equivalent:*

(1) F is a ($*$-)weak fuzzy quasi-norm aggregation function on sets;
(2) F is a ($*$-)weak fuzzy norm aggregation function on sets;
(3) $F(\mathbf{0}) = 0$ and $F(\mathbf{1}) = 1$. The core of F is countably included in a unitary face, and F is isotone, ($*$-)supmultiplicative and sequentially left-continuous ;
(4) $F(\mathbf{0}) = 0$ and $F(\mathbf{1}) = 1$. The core of F is countably included in a unitary face, and F is sequentially left-continuous, and F preserves asymmetric ($*$-)triangular triplets.

Proof. (1) $\Rightarrow$ (2) This is trivial.

(2) $\Rightarrow$ (3) We first prove that $F(\mathbf{0}) = 0$. Let $(V, N, *)$ be an arbitrary weak fuzzy normed space, $v \in V$ and $t > 0$. Considering the collection of weak fuzzy normed spaces $\{(V, N_i, *) : i \in I\}$ where $N_i = N$ for all $i \in I$, we have that $(F \circ \mathbf{N}, *)$ is a weak fuzzy norm on V so $0 = F \circ \mathbf{N}(v, 0) = F((N(v,0))_{i \in I}) = F(\mathbf{0})$.

On the other hand, $F(\mathbf{1}) = F((N(0_V, t))_{i \in I}) = F \circ \mathbf{N}(0_V, t) = 1$ by (FQN2).

For proving that F is $*$-supmultiplicative, we can proceed as in the proof of this fact in the implication (2) $\Rightarrow$ (3) of Theorem 6.

Now, we check that the core of F is countably included in a unitary face.

Suppose, contrary to our claim, that we can find a sequence $\{\mathbf{a}_n : n \in \mathbb{N}\} \subseteq F^{-1}(1)$ such that for any $i \in I$ there exists $n_i \in \mathbb{N}$ verifying $(\mathbf{a}_{n_i})_i \neq 1$. Let us consider the vector space $\mathbb{R}$ and, for each $i \in I$, we define $N_i : \mathbb{R} \times [0, +\infty) \to [0,1]$ as the following.

$$N_i(x,t) = \begin{cases} 0 & \text{if } t = 0, \\ 1 & \text{if } x = 0,\ t > 0, \\ (\mathbf{a}_1)_i & \text{if } x \neq 0,\ t > |x|, \\ (\mathbf{a}_1)_i * \ldots * (\mathbf{a}_{n+1})_i & \text{if } x \neq 0,\ \frac{|x|}{n+1} < t \leq \frac{|x|}{n},\ n \in \mathbb{N}. \end{cases}$$

Notice that $(\mathbb{R}, N_i, *)$ is a weak fuzzy normed space for all $i \in I$. Let us verify this. It is obvious that (FQN1) is satisfied. On the other hand, let $x \in \mathbb{R}$ such that $N_i(x,t) = N_i(-x,t) = 1$ for all $t > 0$. By assumption, we can find $n_i \in \mathbb{N}$ such that $(\mathbf{a}_{n_i}) \neq 1$. Hence, if $x \neq 0$ then $N_i(x, \frac{|x|}{n_i}) = (\mathbf{a}_1)_i * \ldots * (\mathbf{a}_{n_i+1})_i \leq (\mathbf{a}_1)_i \wedge \ldots \wedge (\mathbf{a}_{n_i+1})_i < 1$, which is a contradiction. Therefore $x = 0$.

Furthermore, let $x \in \mathbb{R}$ and $\lambda \in \mathbb{R} \backslash \{0\}$. If $x = 0$, it is clear that $N_i(\lambda 0, t) = 1 = N_i\left(0, \frac{t}{|\lambda|}\right)$. If $x \neq 0$, the equality $N_i(\lambda x, t) = N_i\left(x, \frac{t}{|\lambda|}\right)$ follows from the equivalences of the inequalities $t > |\lambda x|$ and $\frac{|\lambda x|}{n+1} < t \leq \frac{|\lambda x|}{n}$ with $\frac{t}{|\lambda|} > x$ and $\frac{|x|}{n+1} < \frac{t}{|\lambda|} \leq \frac{|x|}{n}$, respectively, so (FQN3') is proved.

We next check (FQN4). Let $x, y \in \mathbb{R}$ and $t, s > 0$. If $x + y = 0$, it is obvious that $N_i(x,t) * N_i(y,s) \leq N_i(x+y, t+s) = 1$. Moreover, if $x + y \neq 0$ and $x = 0$ or $y = 0$, the inequality is also clear since if, for example, $y = 0$ then $N_i(x,t) * N_i(y,s) = N_i(x,t) = (\boldsymbol{a}_1)_i * \ldots * (\boldsymbol{a}_{n+1})_i$ for some $n \in \mathbb{N}$. Since $t < s + t$, the factors that appear in multiplication by the t-norm $*$ in the value of $N_i(x, t+s)$ are less or equal than the factors in $N_i(x,t)$, so $N_i(x,t) \leq N_i(x, t+s)$. Finally, suppose that $x + y \neq 0$ and $x \neq 0, y \neq 0$. If $t + s > |x + y|$, the inequality is clear since $N_i(x+y, t+s) = (\boldsymbol{a}_1)_i$. Otherwise, $t + s \leq |x+y| \leq |x| + |y|$. Then, $t \leq |x|$ or $s \leq |y|$. We distinguish some of the following cases:

- $t \leq |x|$ and $s > |y|$. Then, there exists $n_x \in \mathbb{N}$ such that $\frac{|x|}{n_x+1} < t \leq \frac{|x|}{n_x}$. Then, the following is the case.

$$t + s > \frac{|x|}{n_x + 1} + |y| > \frac{|x| + |y|}{n_x + 1} \geq \frac{|x+y|}{n_x+1}$$

  This means that the number of factors that appear in $N_i(x+y, t+s)$ is less than or equal to $n_x + 1$, which is the number of factors that appear in $N_i(x,t)$. Consequently, $N_i(x,t) * N_i(y,s) \leq N_i(x,t) \leq N_i(x+y, t+s)$.
- $t > |x|$ and $s \leq |y|$. In this case, we can reason as above.
- $t \leq |x|$ and $s \leq |y|$. Let $n_x, n_y \in \mathbb{N}$ such that the following is the case.

$$\frac{|x|}{n_x+1} < t \leq \frac{|x|}{n_x} \text{ and } \frac{|y|}{n_y+1} < s \leq \frac{|y|}{n_y}.$$

  Then, we have the following.

$$t + s > \frac{|x|}{n_x+1} + \frac{|y|}{n_y+1} \geq \frac{|x|+|y|}{\max\{n_x, n_y\}+1} \geq \frac{|x+y|}{\max\{n_x, n_y\}+1}.$$

  This means that the number of factors that appear in $N_i(x+y, t+s)$ is less than or equal to $\max\{n_x, n_y\} + 1$. By reasoning as above, we obtain the desired inequality.

What remains is proving that $N_i(x, \cdot)$ is left-continuous. If $x = 0$, it is obvious. Suppose now that $x \neq 0$ and let $t > 0$. By construction, if $\{t_n\}_{n \in \mathbb{N}}$ is a sequence in $(0, +\infty)$ for which its upper limit is t, we can find $n_0 \in \mathbb{N}$ such that $N(x, t_n)$ is constant for every $n \geq n_0$; thus, the conclusion follows. We conclude that $(N_i, *)$ is a weak fuzzy norm on $\mathbb{R}$ for all $i \in I$.

Notice that if $t > 1$, then $N_i(1,t) = (\boldsymbol{a}_1)_i$. Thus, we have the following.

$$F \circ \mathbf{N}(1,t) = F((N_i(1,t))_{i \in I}) = F(((\boldsymbol{a}_1)_i)_{i \in I}) = F(\boldsymbol{a}_1) = 1.$$

If $0 < t \leq 1$, then we can find $n \in \mathbb{N}$ such that $N_i(1,t) = (\boldsymbol{a}_1)_i * \ldots * (\boldsymbol{a}_{n+1})_i$ for all $i \in I$. Since F is $*$-supmultiplicative, then we have the following.

$$\begin{aligned} F \circ \mathbf{N}(1,t) &= F((N_i(1,t))_{i \in I}) = F(((\boldsymbol{a}_1)_i * \ldots * (\boldsymbol{a}_{n+1})_i)_{i \in I}) = F(\boldsymbol{a}_1 * \ldots * \boldsymbol{a}_{n+1}) \\ &\geq F(\boldsymbol{a}_1) * \ldots * F(\boldsymbol{a}_n) = 1. \end{aligned}$$

Therefore, $F \circ \mathbf{N}(1,t) = 1$ for all $t > 0$, which contradicts the fact that $(F \circ \mathbf{N}, *)$ is a weak fuzzy norm. Consequently, the core of F is countably included in a unitary face.

The proofs that F is isotone and the proof that F is sequentially left-continuous are similar to the same proofs in the implication (2)$\Rightarrow$ (3) of Theorem 6.

(3) $\Rightarrow$ (4) This is similar to the implication (3) $\Rightarrow$ (4) of Theorem 6.

(4) $\Rightarrow$ (1) Let $\{(V, N_i, *) : i \in I\}$ be a collection of weak fuzzy quasi-normed spaces. Let us check that $(F \circ \mathbf{N}, *)$ is a weak fuzzy quasi-norm on V.

Given $x \in V$, then $F \circ \mathbf{N}(x, 0) = F((N_i(x,0))_{i \in I}) = F(\mathbf{0}) = 0$; thus, (FQN1) holds.

Now, suppose that there exists $x \in V$ such that $F \circ \mathbf{N}(x,t) = F \circ \mathbf{N}(-x,t) = 1$ for all $t > 0$. Since $(N_i(x,t), N_i(-x,t), N_i(x_i,t) * N_i(-x,t))$ is an asymmetric $*$-triangular triplet for all $i \in I$, by assumption $(F((N_i(x,t))_{i\in I}), F((N_i(-x,t))_{i\in I}), F((N_i(x,t) * N_i(-x,t))_{i\in I}))$ is also an asymmetric $*$-triangular triplet. Thus, the following is the case.

$$1 = 1 * 1 = F((N_i(x,t))_{i\in I}) * F((N_i(-x,t))_{i\in I}) \leq F((N_i(x,t) * N_i(-x,t))_{i\in I}).$$

Hence, $F((N_i(x,t) * N_i(-x,t))_{i\in I}) = 1$ for all $t > 0$. Let us define $\boldsymbol{a}_n = (N_i(x, \frac{1}{n}) * N_i(-x, \frac{1}{n}))_{i\in I}$. Then, $\{\boldsymbol{a}_n : n \in \mathbb{N}\} \subseteq F^{-1}(1)$. Since the core of F is countably included in a unitary face, then $(\boldsymbol{a}_n)_j = 1$ for some $j \in I$ and for all $n \in \mathbb{N}$, that is, $N_j(x, \frac{1}{n}) * N_j(-x, \frac{1}{n}) = 1$ for all $n \in \mathbb{N}$. Consequently, $N_j(x, \frac{1}{n}) = N_j(-x, \frac{1}{n}) = 1$ for all $n \in \mathbb{N}$. Moreover, since $N_i(x, \cdot)$ and $N_i(-x, \cdot)$ are isotone, we immediately obtain that $N_j(x,t) = N_j(-x,t) = 1$ for all $t > 0$. Since $(N_i, *)$ is a weak fuzzy quasi-metric on V, then $x = 0_V$. Therefore, $F \circ \mathbf{N}$ satisfies (FQN2).

It is clear that $F \circ \mathbf{N}$ verifies (FQN3) since, given $\lambda, t > 0$ and $x \in V$, we have the following.

$$F \circ \mathbf{N}(\lambda x, t) = F((N_i(\lambda x, t))_{i\in I}) = F\left(\left(N_i\left(x, \frac{t}{\lambda}\right)\right)_{i\in I}\right) = F \circ \mathbf{N}\left(x, \frac{t}{\lambda}\right).$$

In order to prove (FQN4), let $x, y \in V$ and $t, s > 0$. Since $(N_i, *)$ is a weak fuzzy quasi-norm for all $i \in I$, it is obvious that $((N_i(x,t))_{i\in I}, (N_i(y,s))_{i\in I}, (N_i(x+y, t+s))_{i\in I})$ is an asymmetric $*$-triangular triplet. By hypothesis, $(F((N_i(x,t))_{i\in I}), F((N_i(y,s))_{i\in I}), F((N_i(x+y, t+s))_{i\in I}))$ is an asymmetric $*$-triangular triplet. Thus, the following is the case.

$$F((N_i(x,t))_{i\in I}) * F((N_i(y,s))_{i\in I}) \leq F((N_i(x+y, t+s))_{i\in I})$$

Thus, $F \circ \mathbf{N}$ verifies (FQN4).

To this end, (FQN5) follows in a similar manner as in the implication (4)$\Rightarrow$ (1) of Theorem 6. □

Corollary 2. *Let $F : [0,1]^I \to [0,1]$ be a function and $*$ be a t-norm. Then, F is a ($*$-)weak fuzzy (quasi-)norm aggregation function on sets if and only if F is a ($*$-)fuzzy (quasi-)metric aggregation function on sets.*

Proof. This is a direct consequence of the previous theorem and [17] (Theorem 4.19) (notice that in that, in the paper, sequentially left-continuity is called simply left-continuity). □

We provide an example of a $\wedge$-weak fuzzy (quasi-)norm aggregation function on sets that are not a $\wedge$-weak fuzzy (quasi-)norm aggregation function on products.

Example 8. *Let I be a subset of $[0,1]$ having minimum greater than 0 with cardinality greater than 1. Let $F : [0,1]^I \to [0,1]$, given by the following:*

$$F(\boldsymbol{x}) = \alpha \cdot \inf\{i \cdot \boldsymbol{x}_i : i \in I\}$$

for all $\boldsymbol{x} \in [0,1]^I$, where $\alpha = \frac{1}{\min I}$.

It is obvious that $F(\mathbf{1}) = 1$ and $F(\mathbf{0}) = 0$. Moreover, F is clearly isotone. We prove that F is $\wedge$-supmultiplicative. Let $\boldsymbol{x}, \boldsymbol{y} \in [0,1]^I$. Then, we have the following:

$$F(\boldsymbol{x}) \wedge F(\boldsymbol{y}) \leq (\alpha \cdot i \cdot \boldsymbol{x}_i) \wedge (\alpha \cdot i \cdot \boldsymbol{y}_i) = \alpha \cdot i \cdot (\boldsymbol{x}_i \wedge \boldsymbol{y}_i)$$

for all $i \in I$. Hence, $F(\boldsymbol{x}) \wedge F(\boldsymbol{y}) \leq \alpha \cdot \inf\{i \cdot (\boldsymbol{x}_i \wedge \boldsymbol{y}_i) : i \in I\} = F(\boldsymbol{x} \wedge^I \boldsymbol{y})$.

Furthermore, if $F(\boldsymbol{a}) = 1$, then $\boldsymbol{a}_{\min I} = 1$. Otherwise, $\min I \cdot \boldsymbol{a}_{\min I} < \min I$, which implies that $\inf\{i \cdot \boldsymbol{x}_i : i \in I\} \leq \min I \cdot \boldsymbol{a}_{\min I} < \min I$. Thus, $F(\boldsymbol{a}) < 1$ follows, which is a contradiction. Consequently, the core of F is countably included in a unitary face. Thus, F is a $\wedge$-weak fuzzy (quasi-)norm aggregation functions on sets.

However, the core of F is not trivial. In fact, given $j \in I\backslash\{\min I\}$, *then* $F(\boldsymbol{b}) = 1$ *where* $\boldsymbol{b} \in [0,1]^I$ *is given by* $\boldsymbol{b}_i = 1$ *whenever* $i \neq j$ *and* $\boldsymbol{b}_j = \frac{\min I}{j}$.

Author Contributions: Conceptualization, investigation,writing–original draft preparation, writing–review and editing, supervision, T.P., J.R.-C. and J.R.-L.; funding acquisition, J.R.-L. All authors have read and agreed to the published version of the manuscript.

Funding: J.R.-L. acknowledges financial support from the research project PGC2018-095709-B-C21 funded by MCIN/AEI/10.13039/501100011033 and FEDER "Una manera de hacer Europa".

Acknowledgments: The suggestions and corrections of the anonymous reviewers are gratefully acknowledged.

Conflicts of Interest: The authors declare no conflicts of interest.

References

1. Borsík, J.; Doboš, J. On a product of metric spaces. *Math. Slovaca* **1981**, *31*, 193–205.
2. Doboš, J. *Metric Preserving Functions*; Košice: Štroffek, Slovakia, 1998.
3. Mayor, G.; Valero, O. Aggregation of asymmetric distances in Computer Science. *Inf. Sci.* **2010**, *180*, 803–812. [CrossRef]
4. Mayor, G.; Valero, O. Metric aggregation functions revisited. *Eur. J. Combin.* **2019**, *80*, 390–400. [CrossRef]
5. Miñana, J.-J.; Valero, O. Characterizing quasi-metric aggregation functions. *Int. J. Gen. Syst.* **2019**, *48*, 890–909. [CrossRef]
6. Pradera, A.; Trillas, E. A note on pseudometrics aggregation. *Int. J. Gen. Syst.* **2002**, *31*, 41–51.
7. Herburt, I.; Moszyńska, M. On metric products. *Colloq. Math.* **1991**, *62*, 121–133. [CrossRef]
8. Martín, J.; Mayor, G.; Valero, O. On aggregation of normed structures. *Math. Comput. Model.* **2011**, *54*, 815–827. [CrossRef]
9. Pedraza, T.; Rodríguez-López, J. New results on the aggregation of norms. *Mathematics* **2021**, *9*, 2291. [CrossRef]
10. Saminger, S.; Mesiar, R.; Bodenhofer, U.Domination of aggregation operators and preservation of transitivity. *Internat. Uncertain. Fuzziness-Knowl.-Based Syst.* **2002**, *10*, 11–35. [CrossRef]
11. Drewniak, J.; Dudziak, U. Preservation of properties of fuzzy relations during aggregation processes. *Kybernetika* **2007**, *43*, 115–132.
12. Drewniak, J.; Dudziak, U. Aggregation in classes of fuzzy relations. *Stud. Math.* **2006**, *5*, 33–43.
13. Dudziak, U. Preservation of *t*-norm and *t*-conorm based properties of fuzzy relations during aggregation process. In Proceedings of the 8th Conference of the European Society for Fuzzy Logic and Technology (EUSFLAT 2013), Milan, Italy, 11–13 September 2013; pp. 376–383.
14. Mayor, G.; Recasens, J. Preserving T-Transitivity. In *Artificial Intelligence Reserach and Development*; IOS Press: Amsterdam, The Netherlands, 2016; Volume 288, pp. 79–87.
15. Pradera, A.; Trillas, E.; Castiñeira, E. Technologies for constructing intelligent systems. In *Ch. On the Aggregation of Some Classes of Fuzzy Relations*; Springer: Berlin/Heidelberg, Germany, 2002; pp. 125–147.
16. Recasens, J. Indistinguishability operators. In *Modelling Fuzzy Equalities and Fuzzy Equivalence Relations*; Springer: Berlin/Heidelberg, Germany, 2010.
17. Pedraza, T.; Rodríguez-López, J.; Valero, O. Aggregation of fuzzy quasi-metrics. *Inform. Sci.* **2021**, *581*, 362–389. [CrossRef]
18. Alegre, C.; Romaguera, S. The Hahn-Banach extension theorem for fuzzy normed spaces. *Abstr. Appl. Anal.* **2014**, *2014*, 151472. [CrossRef]
19. Goleţ, I. On fuzzy normed spaces. *Southeast Asian Bull. Math.* **2007**, *31*, 1–10.
20. Pedraza, T.; Rodríguez-López, J. Aggregation of *L*-probabilistic quasi-uniformities. *Mathematics* **2020**, *8*, 1980. [CrossRef]
21. Klement, E.P.; Mesiar, R.; Pap, E. Triangular Norms; Kluwer: Hongkong, China, 2000.
22. Lafuerza-Guillén, B.; Harikrishnan, P. *Probabilistic Normed Spaces*; World Scientific Publishing: Singapore, 2014.
23. Šerstnev, A.N. On the notion of a random normed space. *Dokl. Acad. Nauk. SSSR* **1963**, *49*, 280–285.
24. Katsaras, A. Fuzzy topological vector spaces. II. *Fuzzy Sets Syst.* **1984**, *12*, 143–154. [CrossRef]
25. Cheng, S.C.; Mordeson, J.N. Fuzzy linear operator and fuzzy normed linear spaces. *Bull. Calcutta Math. Soc.* **1994**, *86*, 429–436.
26. Kramosil, I.; Michalek, J. Fuzzy metric and statistical metric spaces. *Kybernetica* **1975**, *11*, 326–334.
27. Bag, T.; Samanta, S.K. Some fixed point theorems in fuzzy normed linear spaces. *Inform. Sci.* **2007**, *177*, 3271–3289. [CrossRef]
28. Alegre, C.; Romaguera, S. Characterizations of metrizable topological vector spaces and their asymmetric generalizations in terms of fuzzy (quasi-)norms. *Fuzzy Sets Syst.* **2010**, *161*, 2181–2192. [CrossRef]
29. Saadati, R.; Vaezpour, S.M. Some results on fuzzy Banach spaces. *J. Appl. Math. Comput.* **2005**, *17*, 475–484. [CrossRef]
30. Li, L.; Luo, Q. Sufficient conditions for triangular norms preserving $\otimes$-convexity. *Symmetry* **2018**, *10*, 729. [CrossRef]
31. Khameneh, A.Z.; Kilicman, A. *m*-polar generalization of fuzzy *T*-ordering relations: An approach to group decision making. *Symmetry* **2021**, *13*, 51. [CrossRef]
32. Grabisch, M.; Marichal, J.-L.; Mesiar, R.; Pap, E. Aggregation functions. In *Encyclopedia of Mathematics and its Applications*; Cambridge University Press: Cambridge, UK, 2009; Volume 127.
33. Mesiar, R.; Pap, E. Aggregation of infinite sequences. *Inform. Sci.* **2008**, *178*, 3557–3564. [CrossRef]

symmetry

MDPI

Article

Applying the Dijkstra Algorithm to Solve a Linear Diophantine Fuzzy Environment

Mani Parimala [1], Saeid Jafari [2,*], Muhamad Riaz [3] and Muhammad Aslam [4]

1 Department of Mathematics, Bannari Amman Institute of Technology, Sathyamangalam 638401, Tamil Nadu, India; parimalam@bitsathy.ac.in or rishwanthpari@gmail.com
2 College of Vestsjaelland South & Mathematical and Physical Science Foundation, 4200 Slagelse, Denmark
3 Department of Mathematics, University of the Punjab, Lahore 54590, Pakistan; mriaz.math@pu.edu.pk
4 Department of Mathematics, College of Sciences, King Khalid University, Abha 61413, Saudi Arabia; muamin@kku.edu.sa
* Correspondence: saeidjafari@topositus.com

Abstract: Linear Diophantine fuzzy set (LDFS) theory expands Intuitionistic fuzzy set (IFS) and Pythagorean fuzzy set (PyFS) theories, widening the space of vague and uncertain information via reference parameters owing to its magnificent feature of a broad depiction area for permissible doublets. We codify the shortest path (SP) problem for linear Diophantine fuzzy graphs. Linear Diophantine fuzzy numbers (LDFNs) are used to represent the weights associated with arcs. The main goal of the presented work is to create a solution technique for directed network graphs by introducing linear Diophantine fuzzy (LDF) optimality constraints. The weights of distinct routes are calculated using an improved score function (SF) with the arc values represented by LDFNs. The conventional Dijkstra method is further modified to find the arc weights of the linear Diophantine fuzzy shortest path (LDFSP) and coterminal LDFSP based on these enhanced score functions and optimality requirements. A comparative analysis was carried out with the current approaches demonstrating the benefits of the new algorithm. Finally, to validate the possible use of the proposed technique, a small-sized telecommunication network is presented.

Keywords: linear Diophantine fuzzy graphs; Dijkstra's algorithm; linear Diophantine fuzzy numbers; score function; shortest path problem

check for updates

Citation: Parimala, M.; Jafari, S.; Riaz, M.; Aslam, M. Applying the Dijkstra Algorithm to Solve a Linear Diophantine Fuzzy Environment. *Symmetry* **2021**, *13*, 1616. https://doi.org/10.3390/sym13091616

Academic Editor: José Carlos R. Alcantud

Received: 28 June 2021
Accepted: 10 August 2021
Published: 2 September 2021

1. Introduction

At the heart of a network's flow is the shortest path problem (SPP). The main challenge of an extensive range of real-life network issues is to transfer any products between two defined nodes efficiently and inexpensively. Therefore, the shortest path (SP) should then be used to formulate such real applications as discovering a route with respect to the length with the lowest cost, time, or distance from the start node (SN) to the terminal node (TN). Traditionally, it was believed that the costs traversing of edges can be represented as crisp numbers (CNs). However, since prices fluctuate with traffic patterns and weather, these values are usually imprecise or ambiguous in nature. The fuzzy set (FS) concept was introduced by Zadeh [1] to address such ambiguity. Economics, medical science research, and many other areas struggle daily with unclear, imprecise, and sometimes inadequate knowledge in ambiguous data modeling. There have been proposals for non-classical and higher-order fuzzy sets for various specialized purposes after the proposal of fuzzy set theory. Zadeh's [1] FS theory is a valuable method for dealing with imprecise knowledge in SPPs. As a result, researchers have made numerous attempts to solve various forms of SPPs in the fuzzy domain.

Okada [2] suggested an algorithm to solve the fuzzy SPP, hinging on the possibility principle, to decide the degree of chance for each arc. Based on the fuzzy SPP, Keshavarz and Khorram [3] generalized the fuzzy SPP to a bi-level programming problem and suggested an appropriate algorithm. A constant quantity is a predicament in SPs in solving the resulting issue. With ambiguous multicriteria decision-making (MCDM) approaches focused on similarity tests, Dou et al. [4] tackled the fuzzy SP issue in a multiple constraint network. Deng et al. [5] used the ranked mean integration definition of fuzzy numbers to extend the Dijkstra algorithm to solve fuzzy SPPs. Furthermore, a few experts [6,7] have spotlighted solving the SPP in a network using heterogeneous forms of heuristic algorithm-based fuzzy arc values.

Nevertheless, FS only takes a satisfaction grade and does not convey a dissatisfaction grade. The dissatisfaction grade here is the counterpart of the satisfaction grade. The intuitionistic FS (IFS) is a generalization of FS theory, and it was introduced by Atanassov [8], who incorporated the dissatisfaction grade during the analysis. Here, the sum of the satisfaction grade and the dissatisfaction grade is less than or equal to one. In the IFS environment, some researchers are working on solving the SPP with IFS arc values. Mukherjee [9] found the SP in an IFS theory world. To address the IFS theory SPP, an alternative algorithm for the shortest path length protocol and a similarity metric for the intuitionistic fuzzy sets were proposed by Geetharamani and Jayagowri [10]. Biswas et al. [11] established a protocol for finding an intuitionist fuzzy set theory SPP between the start node (SN) and the terminal node (TN). An algorithm was developed by Kumar et al. [12] to identify the SP and the shortest distance (SD) in a network using arc weights under an interval-valued intuitionistic fuzzy set. Sujatha and Hyacinta [13] contemplated two distinct methods to solve the issue of the SP in an IFS setting. With an additional limitation under the intuitionist fuzzy setting, Motameni and Ebrahimnejad [14] focused on solving the SPP.

IFSs have attracted much attention and are seen in many different aspects of real life. In IFSs, the constraint sum of membership μ and nonmembership ν does not exceed one, which restricts the option to the satisfaction and dissatisfaction classes. To avoid this, Yager [15–17] proposed the Pythagorean fuzzy set (PyFS), which is represented by a satisfaction grade (μ) and a dissatisfaction grade (ν) with the constraint that the sum of squares of μ and ν does not exceed one. The principle of the Pythagorean fuzzy number (PyFN) was introduced by Zhang and Xu [18] to interpret the dual aspect of an element: the expert gives the details about an option with a satisfaction score of 0.9 and a dissatisfaction grade of 0.3 in a decision-making environment; the IFN struggles to resolve this case, as $0.9 + 0.3 > 1$; however, $(0.9)^2 + (0.3)^2 \leq 1$. Akram et al. [19,20] recently implemented several new Pythagorean fuzzy graph (PyFG) operations, such as exclusion, symmetric disparity, residue product, and maximal product. To extend fuzzy sets, several researchers [21–28] implemented and examined different forms of the SP algorithm.

IFSs and PyFSs have diverse applications in multiple real-life environments, but both concepts have their own limitations in the satisfaction and dissatisfaction grades. Riaz and Hashmi et al. in [29,30] presented the approach of the linear Diophantine fuzzy set (LDFS) with the inclusion of comparison parameters in order to eliminate these constraints. LDFSs are more flexible and efficient compared to the other concepts as a result of the adoption of reference parameters, which have seen a boom in recent times [31–35]. Recently, in 2021, Riaz et al. [30] extended their study to linear Diophantine fuzzy graph (LDFG) theory.

The SPP is the most prominent graph theory problem. For basically any fuzzy structure, it has been extensively tested (see [2,36–38]) with an algorithm that is relatively straightforward and gives us the best-predicted performance, as in [7], at that time. Some common methods for solving SPPs were proposed by Warshall [39], Dijkstra [40], Bellman [41], and Floyd [42]. One of the classical and best methods among them is Dijkstra's algorithm (DA). Dijkstra's dynamic programming (DDP) [5,43] approach may be used to solve fuzzy shortest path problems (FSPPs) by treating the weights of the edges of a network as uncertain or fuzzy. LDFSs and LDFGs are more efficient, flexible, and compatible than the existing fuzzy concepts as they have reference parameters. The research gap between these two concepts motivated us to introduce the linear Diophantine fuzzy shortest path via Dijkstra's algorithm. This work expands the traditional Dijkstra algorithm in accordance with the aforementioned fruitful investigations, allowing us to compute the linear Diophantine fuzzy SPP's lowest cost (LDFSPP). The LDFSPP attempts to give decision-makers the length of the LDFSP and the shortest path in a network with the linear Diophantine fuzzy arc lengths. LDFNs are assumed to be the cost parameters of the arcs. A pseudocode for this problem is provided based on Dijkstra's techniques. Several operational requirements are described, as well as the expected LDFN values and the similarity measure LDFNs using the score and accuracy functions. Finally, a numerical example is provided to clarify the technique and demonstrate its utility and efficiency. Furthermore, our findings are compared to the current research.

The objectives of this manuscript are as follows:

1. Linear Diophantine fuzzy set (LDFS) theory is superior to intuitionistic fuzzy set (IFS), Pythagorean fuzzy set (PyFS), and q-rung orthopair fuzzy set (q-ROFS) theories, with a wide space of vague and uncertain information via reference parameters owing to its magnificent feature of a broad depiction area for permissible doublets;
2. In decision analysis, the membership and nonmembership grades are not enough to analyze objects in the universe. The addition of reference parameters provides freedom to the decision-makers in selecting the membership and nonmembership grades. The LDFS with the associated reference parameters provides a robust approach for modeling uncertainties;
3. We codify the shortest path (SP) problem for linear Diophantine fuzzy graphs;
4. Linear Diophantine fuzzy numbers are used to represent the weights associated with arcs (LDFNs);
5. The main goal of the presented work is to create a solution technique for directed network graphs by introducing linear Diophantine fuzzy (LDF) optimality constraints;
6. The weights of distinct routes are then calculated using an improved score function (SF) with the arc values represented by LDFNs;
7. The conventional Dijkstra method is further modified to find the arc weights of linear Diophantine fuzzy shortest path (LDFSP) and coterminal LDFSP based on these enhanced score functions and 11 optimality requirements;
8. A comparative analysis is carried out with the current approaches demonstrating the benefits of the new algorithm. Finally, to validate the possible use of the proposed technique, a small-sized telecommunication network is presented;
9. The suggested approach's efficiency, rationality, and superiority are examined using a numerical example to describe the communications network; the symmetry of the optimal decision and the ranking of possible alternatives are then compared.
10. The suggested approach's efficiency, rationality, and superiority are examined using a numerical example to describe the communications network;
11. A comparative analysis follows the symmetry of the best decision and the ranking of viable alternatives.

Therefore, this manuscript aims to suggest a technique for solving the SP problem in the LDFG context. To do so, the mathematical formulation on the SP issues is discussed first, where the traversal cost of arcs is expressed in terms of LDFNs. Then, we define the conditions of optimality in LDF networks for the solution algorithm's design. To do so, an enhanced score feature is used to compare the costs of various routes with LDFNs representing their arc costs. The cost of the LDFSP and the corresponding LDFSP are then calculated using the standard Dijkstra algorithm. A minimal telecommunication network in the LDF setting is used to explain the proposed algorithm. The rest of the paper is organized as follows: Section 2 covers some fundamental principles of linear Diophantine fuzzy sets, while Section 3 covers the statistical formulation of the SP problem in the context of an LDF network, the LDF shortest path optimality conditions and the expanded Dijkstra algorithm. Section 4 provides a numerical example that illustrates the proposed solution methodology. The article is finally concluded in Section 5.

2. Preliminaries

The definitions from [8,15–17,29,30] are used in the sequel.

Definition 1 ([8]). *An IFS $\mathfrak{I}$ on the universe $\mathfrak{Q}$ is defined by:*

$$\mathfrak{I} = \{\zeta, \mathfrak{m}(\zeta), \mathfrak{n}(\zeta) | \zeta \in \mathfrak{Q}\}$$

where $\mathfrak{m}, \mathfrak{n} : \mathfrak{Q} \to [0,1]$ are the satisfaction and dissatisfaction grades, respectively. The condition for an IFS is that $\mathfrak{m} + \mathfrak{n} \leq 1$. A doublet set $(\mathfrak{m}, \mathfrak{n})$ is said to be an intuitionistic fuzzy number (IFN). The graphical representation of the two-dimensional (2D) and three-dimensional (3D) plots of an IFS is given in Figure 1.

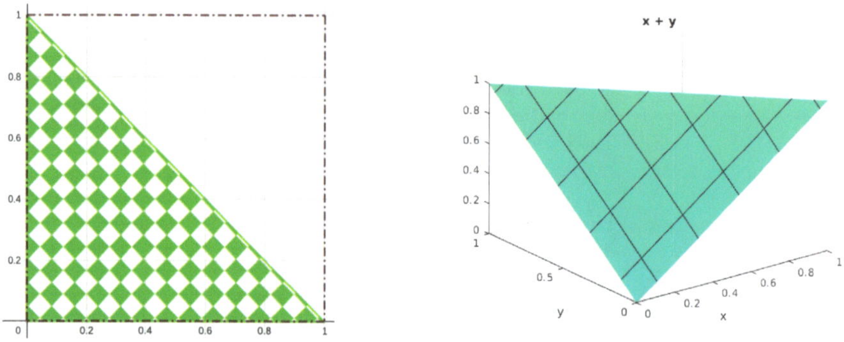

(**a**) 2D representation of an IFS (**b**) 3D representation of an IFS

Figure 1. Graphical representation of an IFS.

Definition 2 ([15–17]). *A PyFS $\mathfrak{P}$ on the universe $\mathfrak{U}$ is defined by:*

$$\mathfrak{P} = \{\zeta, \mathfrak{m}(\zeta), \mathfrak{n}(\zeta) | \zeta \in \mathfrak{P}\}$$

where $\mathfrak{m}, \mathfrak{n} : \mathfrak{P} \to [0,1]$ are the satisfaction and dissatisfaction grades, respectively. The condition for a PyFS is that $\mathfrak{m}^2 + \mathfrak{n}^2 \leq [0,1]$. A doublet set $(\mathfrak{m}, \mathfrak{n})$ is said to be a PyFN. The graphical representation of the 2D and 3D plots of a PyFS is given in Figure 2.

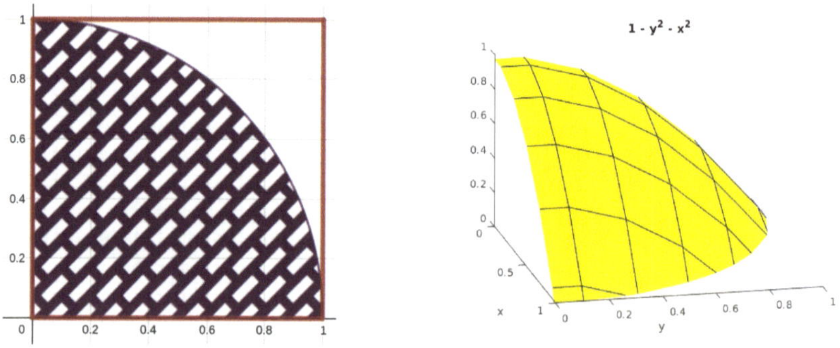

(**a**) 2D representation of a PyFS (**b**) 3D representation of a PyFS

Figure 2. Graphical representation of a PyFS.

Definition 3 ([29,30])**.** *An LDFS $\mathfrak{L}$ is an object on the nonempty reference set $\mathfrak{Q}$ of the form:*

$$\mathfrak{L}_{\mathfrak{D}} = \{(\zeta, \langle \mathfrak{m}_{\mathfrak{D}}(\zeta), \mathfrak{n}_{\mathfrak{D}}(\zeta)\rangle, \langle \alpha, \beta \rangle) : \zeta \in \mathfrak{Q}\}$$

where $\mathfrak{m}_{\mathfrak{D}}(\zeta), \mathfrak{n}_{\mathfrak{D}}(\zeta)$ are the satisfaction grade and dissatisfaction grade and $\alpha, \beta \in [0,1]$ are the reference parameters, respectively. These grades satisfy the constraint $0 \leq \alpha\mathfrak{m}_{\mathfrak{D}}(\zeta) + \beta\mathfrak{n}_{\mathfrak{D}}(\zeta) \leq 1$ for all $\zeta \in \mathfrak{Q}$ and with $0 \leq \alpha + \beta \leq 1$. In describing or classifying a specific system, these comparison parameters will help. By moving the physical meaning of these parameters, we can categorize the system. They expand the space used in LDFSs for grades and lift the limitations on them. The refusal grade is defined as $\gamma\pi_{\mathfrak{D}} = (\zeta) = 1 - (\alpha\mathfrak{m}_{\mathfrak{D}}(\zeta) + \beta\mathfrak{n}_{\mathfrak{D}}(\zeta))$, where γ is the refusal reference parameter. The linear Diophantine fuzzy number (LDFN) is defined as $\mathfrak{T}_{\mathfrak{D}} = (\langle \mathfrak{m}_{\mathfrak{D}}, \mathfrak{n}_{\mathfrak{D}} \rangle, \langle \alpha, \beta \rangle)$ with $0 \leq \alpha + \beta \leq 1$ and $0 \leq \alpha\mathfrak{m}_{\mathfrak{D}} + \beta\mathfrak{n}_{\mathfrak{D}} \leq 1$. The graphical representation of the 2D and 3D plots of an LDFS can be seen in Figure 3, and the comparison spaces of the IFS, PyFS, and LDFS are given in Figure 4.

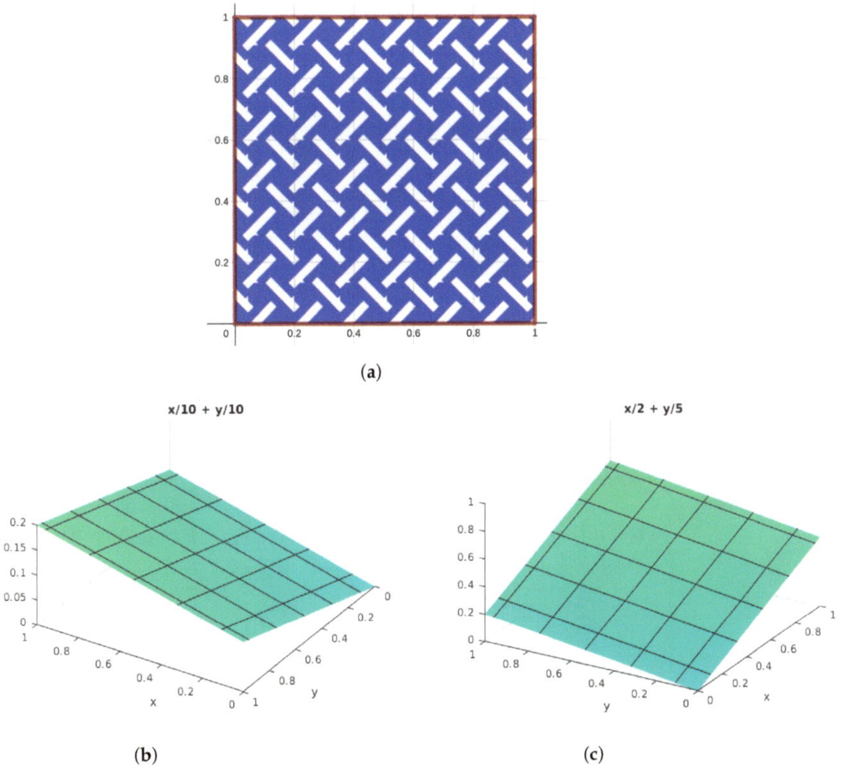

Figure 3. Graphical representation of an LDFS. (**a**) The 2D representation of an LDFS; (**b**) the 3D representation of an LDFS with $(\alpha, \beta) = (0.1, 0.1)$; (**c**) the 3D representation of an LDFS with $(\alpha, \beta) = (0.5, 0.2)$.

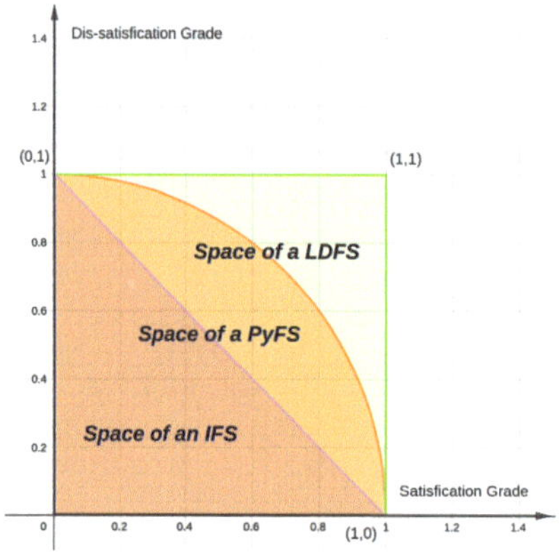

Figure 4. Spaces of the IFS, PyFS, and LDFS.

Example 1. *If* $\mathfrak{m}_{\mathfrak{D}} = 0.96$ *and* $\mathfrak{n}_{\mathfrak{D}} = 0.62$*, then* $0.96 + 0.62 = 1.58 \nleq 1$ *and* $(0.96)^2 + (0.62)^2 \nleq 1.306$*, but for an arbitrary choice of reference parameters* $(\alpha, \beta) \in [0, 1]$ *with* $0 \leq \alpha + \beta \leq 1$*, we have* $0 \leq \alpha\mathfrak{m}_{\mathfrak{D}} + \beta\mathfrak{n}_{\mathfrak{D}} \leq 1$*. As for* $(\alpha, \beta) = (0.46, 0.58)$*, we have* $(0.46)(0.96) + (0.58)(0.62) = 0.8012 < 1$*. As a result, we managed to establish a space that is bigger than the IFS and PyFS, and we have more options to assign values to* $\mathfrak{m}_{\mathfrak{D}}$ *and* $\mathfrak{n}_{\mathfrak{D}}$*, which is unachievable in the IFS and PyFS.*

Definition 4. *An LDFS on* $\mathfrak{Q}$ *is said to be:*

(i) *An absolute LDFS, if it is of the form* $\mathfrak{L}^{1}_{\mathfrak{D}} = \{\zeta, (\langle 1, 0 \rangle, \langle 1, 0 \rangle) : \zeta \in \mathfrak{Q}\}$*;*
(ii) *A null or empty LDFS, if it is of the form* $\mathfrak{L}^{0}_{\mathfrak{D}} = \{\zeta, (\langle 0, 1 \rangle, \langle 0, 1 \rangle) : \zeta \in \mathfrak{Q}\}$*.*

Definition 5. *Let* $\mathfrak{T}_{\mathfrak{D}} = (\langle \mathfrak{m}_{\mathfrak{D}}, \mathfrak{n}_{\mathfrak{D}} \rangle, \langle \alpha, \beta \rangle)$ *be an LDFN, then the score function (SF) is denoted by* $\mathfrak{S}_{(\mathfrak{T}_{\mathfrak{D}})}$ *and the accuracy function (AF) by* $\mathfrak{A}_{(\mathfrak{T}_{\mathfrak{D}})}$ *on* $\mathfrak{D}$ *and can be defined by the mapping* $\mathfrak{S} : \mathfrak{T}_{\mathfrak{D}}(\mathfrak{Q}) \longrightarrow [-1, 1]$ *and given by:*

1. $\mathfrak{S}_{(\mathfrak{T}_{\mathfrak{D}})} = \frac{1}{2}[(\mathfrak{m}_{\mathfrak{D}} - \mathfrak{n}_{\mathfrak{D}}) + (\alpha - \beta)]$
2. $\mathfrak{A}_{(\mathfrak{T}_{\mathfrak{D}})} = \frac{1}{2}[\frac{(\mathfrak{m}_{\mathfrak{D}} + \mathfrak{n}_{\mathfrak{D}})}{2} + (\alpha + \beta)]$

where $\mathfrak{T}_{\mathfrak{D}}(\mathfrak{Q})$ *is the assembling of all LDFNs on* $\mathfrak{Q}$*.*

Definition 6. *Let* $\mathfrak{T}_{\mathfrak{D}_i} = (\langle \mathfrak{m}_{\mathfrak{D}_i}, \mathfrak{n}_{\mathfrak{D}_i} \rangle, \langle \alpha_{D_i}, \beta_{D_i} \rangle)$ *for* $\mathrm{i} \in \Delta$ *be an assembling of LDFNs on* $\mathfrak{Q}$ *and* $\mathfrak{X} > 0$*, then:*

(i) $\mathfrak{T}^{c}_{\mathfrak{D}_1} = (\langle \mathfrak{n}_{\mathfrak{D}_1}, \mathfrak{m}_{\mathfrak{D}_1} \rangle, \langle \beta_{D_1}, \alpha_{D_1} \rangle)$;
(ii) $\mathfrak{T}_{\mathfrak{D}_1} = \mathfrak{T}_{\mathfrak{D}_2} \Leftrightarrow \mathfrak{m}_{\mathfrak{D}_1} = \mathfrak{m}_{\mathfrak{D}_2}, \mathfrak{n}_{\mathfrak{D}_1} = \mathfrak{n}_{\mathfrak{D}_2}, \alpha_{D_1} = \alpha_{D_2}, \beta_{D_1} = \beta_{D_2}$;
(iii) $\mathfrak{T}_{\mathfrak{D}_1} \subseteq \mathfrak{T}_{\mathfrak{D}_2} \Leftrightarrow \mathfrak{m}_{\mathfrak{D}_1} \leq \mathfrak{m}_{\mathfrak{D}_2}, \mathfrak{n}_{\mathfrak{D}_1} \geq \mathfrak{n}_{\mathfrak{D}_2}, \alpha_{D_1} \leq \alpha_{D_2}, \beta_{D_1} \geq \beta_{D_2}$;
(iv) $\mathfrak{T}_{\mathfrak{D}_1} \oplus \mathfrak{T}_{\mathfrak{D}_2} = (\langle \mathfrak{m}_{\mathfrak{D}_1} + \mathfrak{m}_{\mathfrak{D}_2} - \mathfrak{m}_{\mathfrak{D}_1}\mathfrak{m}_{\mathfrak{D}_2}, \mathfrak{n}_{\mathfrak{D}_1}\mathfrak{n}_{\mathfrak{D}_2} \rangle, \langle \alpha_{D_1} + \alpha_{D_2} - \alpha_{D_1}\alpha_{D_2}, \beta_{D_1}\beta_{D_2} \rangle)$;
(v) $\mathfrak{T}_{\mathfrak{D}_1} \otimes \mathfrak{T}_{\mathfrak{D}_2} = (\langle \mathfrak{m}_{\mathfrak{D}_1}\mathfrak{m}_{\mathfrak{D}_2}, \mathfrak{n}_{\mathfrak{D}_1} + \mathfrak{n}_{\mathfrak{D}_2} - \mathfrak{n}_{\mathfrak{D}_1}\mathfrak{n}_{\mathfrak{D}_2} \rangle, \langle \alpha_{D_1}\alpha_{D_2}, \beta_{D_1} + \beta_{D_2} - \beta_{D_1}\beta_{D_2} \rangle)$;
(vi) $\mathfrak{X}\mathfrak{T}_{\mathfrak{D}_1} = (\langle (1 - (1 - \mathfrak{m}_{\mathfrak{D}_1})^{\mathfrak{X}}), \mathfrak{n}^{\mathfrak{X}}_{\mathfrak{D}_1} \rangle, \langle (1 - (1 - \alpha_{\mathfrak{D}_1})^{\mathfrak{X}}), \beta^{\mathfrak{X}}_{\mathfrak{D}_1} \rangle)$;
(vii) $\mathfrak{T}^{\mathfrak{X}}_{\mathfrak{D}_1} = (\langle \mathfrak{m}^{\mathfrak{X}}_{\mathfrak{D}_1}, (1 - (1 - \mathfrak{n}_{\mathfrak{D}_1})^{\mathfrak{X}}) \rangle, \langle \alpha^{\mathfrak{X}}_{\mathfrak{D}_1}, (1 - (1 - \beta_{\mathfrak{D}_1})^{\mathfrak{X}}) \rangle)$;
(viii) $\mathfrak{T}_{\mathfrak{D}_1} \cup \mathfrak{T}_{\mathfrak{D}_2} = (\langle \mathfrak{m}_{\mathfrak{D}_1} \vee \mathfrak{m}_{\mathfrak{D}_2}, \mathfrak{n}_{\mathfrak{D}_1} \wedge \mathfrak{n}_{\mathfrak{D}_2} \rangle, \langle \alpha_{D_1} \vee \alpha_{D_2}, \beta_{D_1} \wedge \beta_{D_2} \rangle)$;
(ix) $\mathfrak{T}_{\mathfrak{D}_1} \cap \mathfrak{T}_{\mathfrak{D}_2} = (\langle \mathfrak{m}_{\mathfrak{D}_1} \wedge \mathfrak{m}_{\mathfrak{D}_2}, \mathfrak{n}_{\mathfrak{D}_1} \vee \mathfrak{n}_{\mathfrak{D}_2} \rangle, \langle \alpha_{D_1} \wedge \alpha_{D_2}, \beta_{D_1} \vee \beta_{D_2} \rangle)$.

Example 2. *Let* $\mathfrak{T}_{\mathfrak{D}_1} = (\langle 0.72, 0.37 \rangle, \langle 0.51, 0.41 \rangle)$ *and* $\mathfrak{T}_{\mathfrak{D}_2} = (\langle 0.93, 0.31 \rangle, \langle 0.66, 0.25 \rangle)$ *be two LDFNs, then:*

(i) $\mathfrak{T}^{c}_{\mathfrak{D}_1} = (\langle 0.37, 0.72 \rangle, \langle 0.41, 0.51 \rangle)$;
(ii) $\mathfrak{T}_{\mathfrak{D}_1} \subseteq \mathfrak{T}_{\mathfrak{D}_2}$ *by the Definition 6 (iii);*
(iii) $\mathfrak{T}_{\mathfrak{D}_1} \oplus \mathfrak{T}_{\mathfrak{D}_2} = (\langle 0.9804, 0.1147 \rangle, \langle 0.8334, 0.1025 \rangle)$;
(iv) $\mathfrak{T}_{\mathfrak{D}_1} \otimes \mathfrak{T}_{\mathfrak{D}_2} = (\langle 0.6696, 0.5653 \rangle, \langle 0.3366, 0.5575 \rangle)$;
(v) $\mathfrak{T}_{\mathfrak{D}_1} \cup \mathfrak{T}_{\mathfrak{D}_2} = (\langle 0.93, 0.31 \rangle, \langle 0.66, 0.25 \rangle) = \mathfrak{T}_{\mathfrak{D}_2}$;

(vi) $\mathfrak{T}_{\mathfrak{D}_1} \cap \mathfrak{T}_{\mathfrak{D}_2} = (\langle 0.72, 0.37\rangle, \langle 0.51, 0.41\rangle) = \mathfrak{T}_{\mathfrak{D}_1}$.
If $\mathfrak{X} = 0.2$, *then we have the following:*
(vii) $\mathfrak{X}\mathfrak{T}_{\mathfrak{D}_1} = (\langle 0.2248, 0.8197\rangle, \langle 0.1330, 0.8367\rangle)$;
(viii) $\mathfrak{T}_{\mathfrak{D}_1}^{\mathfrak{X}} = (\langle 0.9364, 0.0883\rangle, \langle 0.8740, 0.0214\rangle)$.

Definition 7. *Two LDFNs* $\mathfrak{T}_{\mathfrak{D}_1}$ *and* $\mathfrak{T}_{\mathfrak{D}_2}$ *can be comparable using the SF and the AF. This is defined as follows:*

(i) $\mathfrak{T}_{\mathfrak{D}_1} > \mathfrak{T}_{\mathfrak{D}_2}$ *if* $\mathfrak{S}(\mathfrak{T}_{\mathfrak{D}_1}) > \mathfrak{S}(\mathfrak{T}_{\mathfrak{D}_2})$;
(ii) $\mathfrak{T}_{\mathfrak{D}_1} < \mathfrak{T}_{\mathfrak{D}_2}$ *if* $\mathfrak{S}(\mathfrak{T}_{\mathfrak{D}_1}) < \mathfrak{S}(\mathfrak{T}_{\mathfrak{D}_2})$;
(iii) *If* $\mathfrak{S}(\mathfrak{T}_{\mathfrak{D}_1}) = \mathfrak{S}(\mathfrak{T}_{\mathfrak{D}_2})$, *then:*
  (a) $\mathfrak{T}_{\mathfrak{D}_1} > \mathfrak{T}_{\mathfrak{D}_2}$ *if* $\mathfrak{A}(\mathfrak{T}_{\mathfrak{D}_1}) > \mathfrak{A}(\mathfrak{T}_{\mathfrak{D}_2})$;
  (b) $\mathfrak{T}_{\mathfrak{D}_1} < \mathfrak{T}_{\mathfrak{D}_2}$ *if* $\mathfrak{A}(\mathfrak{T}_{\mathfrak{D}_1}) < \mathfrak{A}(\mathfrak{T}_{\mathfrak{D}_2})$;
  (c) $\mathfrak{T}_{\mathfrak{D}_1} = \mathfrak{T}_{\mathfrak{D}_2}$ *if* $\mathfrak{A}(\mathfrak{T}_{\mathfrak{D}_1}) = \mathfrak{A}(\mathfrak{T}_{\mathfrak{D}_2})$.

Definition 8. *A pair* $\mathfrak{G} = (\mathfrak{M}, \mathfrak{N})$ *is called an LDFG on an underlying set* $\mathfrak{V}$, *where* $\mathfrak{M}$ *is an LDFS in* $\mathfrak{V}$ *and* $\mathfrak{N}$ *is a linear Diophantine fuzzy relation on* $\mathfrak{V} \times \mathfrak{V}$ *such that:*

$$\mathfrak{m}_{\mathfrak{N}}(\mathfrak{ab}) \le min\{\mathfrak{m}_{\mathfrak{M}}(\mathfrak{a}), \mathfrak{m}_{\mathfrak{M}}(\mathfrak{b})\}, \alpha_{\mathfrak{M}}(\mathfrak{ab}) \le min\{\alpha_{\mathfrak{M}}(\mathfrak{a}), \alpha_{\mathfrak{M}}(\mathfrak{b})\}$$

$$\mathfrak{n}_{\mathfrak{N}}(\mathfrak{ab}) \le max\{\mathfrak{n}_{\mathfrak{M}}(\mathfrak{a}), \mathfrak{n}_{\mathfrak{M}}(\mathfrak{b})\}, \beta_{\mathfrak{N}}(\mathfrak{ab}) \le max\{\beta_{\mathfrak{M}}(\mathfrak{a}), \beta_{\mathfrak{M}}(\mathfrak{b})\}$$

where $\mathfrak{m}$ *is known as the satisfaction grade,* $\mathfrak{n}$ *is known as the dissatisfaction grade, and* α, β *are the reference parameters that fulfill the condition* $0 \le \alpha + \beta \le 1$ *and* $0 \le \alpha_{\mathfrak{N}}(\mathfrak{ab})\mathfrak{m}_{\mathfrak{N}}(\mathfrak{ab}) + \beta_{\mathfrak{N}}(\mathfrak{ab})\mathfrak{n}_{\mathfrak{N}}(\mathfrak{ab}) \le 1$ *for all* $\mathfrak{a}, \mathfrak{b} \in \mathfrak{V}$, *where* $\mathfrak{M}$ *is a linear Diophantine fuzzy vertex set and* $\mathfrak{N}$ *is a linear Diophantine fuzzy edge set of* $\mathfrak{G}$.

Definition 9. *A linear Diophantine fuzzy digraph or linear Diophantine fuzzy directed graph (LDFDG) with an underlying set* $\mathfrak{V}$ *is defined to be a pair* $\mathfrak{G} = (\mathfrak{L}_{\mathfrak{D}}; \mathfrak{L}_{\mathfrak{P}})$ *where* $\mathfrak{L}_{\mathfrak{D}}$ *is an LDF set on the vertex set* $\mathfrak{V}$ *and* $\mathfrak{L}_{\mathfrak{P}}$ *is an LDF set on the edge set* $\mathfrak{E} \subseteq \mathfrak{V} \times \mathfrak{V}$ *such that:*

$$\mathfrak{m}_{\mathfrak{P}}(\mathfrak{ab}) \le min\{\mathfrak{m}_{\mathfrak{D}}(\mathfrak{a}), \mathfrak{m}_{\mathfrak{D}}(\mathfrak{b})\}, \mathfrak{n}_{\mathfrak{P}}(\mathfrak{ab}) \le max\{\mathfrak{n}_{\mathfrak{D}}(\mathfrak{a}), \mathfrak{n}_{\mathfrak{D}}(\mathfrak{b})\}$$

$$\alpha_{\mathfrak{P}}(\mathfrak{ab}) \le min\{\alpha_{\mathfrak{D}}(\mathfrak{a}), \alpha_{\mathfrak{D}}(\mathfrak{b})\}, \beta_{\mathfrak{P}}(\mathfrak{ab}) \le max\{\beta_{\mathfrak{D}}(\mathfrak{a}), \beta_{\mathfrak{D}}(\mathfrak{b})\}$$

for all $\mathfrak{a}, \mathfrak{b} \in \mathfrak{V}$, *where* $\alpha_{\mathfrak{D}}(\mathfrak{a}), \alpha_{\mathfrak{D}}(\mathfrak{b})$ *are the reference parameters associated with the vertex* $\mathfrak{a}$, $\beta_{\mathfrak{D}}(\mathfrak{a}), \beta_{\mathfrak{D}}(\mathfrak{b})$ *are the reference parameters associated with the vertex* $\mathfrak{b}$, *and* $\alpha_{\mathfrak{P}}(\mathfrak{ab}), \beta_{\mathfrak{P}}(\mathfrak{ab})$ *are the reference parameters associated with the edge* $\mathfrak{ab}$.

Remark 1. *As the name implies, an LDFDG does not hold a symmetric relation on* $\mathfrak{V}$, *as an LDFG holds on* $\mathfrak{V}$.

Example 3. *Let* $\mathfrak{G} = (\mathfrak{V}; \mathfrak{E})$ *with the vertices* $\mathfrak{V} = \{\mathfrak{v}_1, \mathfrak{v}_2, \mathfrak{v}_3, \mathfrak{v}_4, \mathfrak{v}_5, \mathfrak{v}_6\}$ *where the LDFNs of each vertex in* $\mathfrak{V}$ *are* $\mathfrak{v}_1 = (\langle 0.98, 0.11\rangle, \langle 0.43, 0.10\rangle)$, $\mathfrak{v}_2 = (\langle 0.52, 0.23\rangle, \langle 0.25, 0.61\rangle)$, $\mathfrak{v}_3 = (\langle 0.69, 0.33\rangle, \langle 0.74, 0.12\rangle)$, $\mathfrak{v}_4 = (\langle 0.73, 0.61\rangle, \langle 0.63, 0.33\rangle)$, $\mathfrak{v}_5 = (\langle 0.95, 0.14\rangle, \langle 0.57, 0.31\rangle)$, *and* $\mathfrak{v}_6 = (\langle 0.85, 0.24\rangle, \langle 0.51, 0.29\rangle)$ *and the edge values are* $\mathfrak{v}_{12} = \mathfrak{e}_1 = (\langle 0.51, 0.23\rangle, \langle 0.25, 0.60\rangle)$, $\mathfrak{v}_{13} = \mathfrak{e}_2 = (\langle 0.69, 0.33\rangle, \langle 0.42, 0.61\rangle)$, $\mathfrak{v}_{23} = \mathfrak{e}_3 = (\langle 0.52, 0.32\rangle, \langle 0.25, 0.50\rangle)$, $\mathfrak{v}_{24} = \mathfrak{e}_4 = (\langle 0.45, 0.61\rangle, \langle 0.21, 0.59\rangle)$, $\mathfrak{v}_{25} = \mathfrak{e}_5 = (\langle 0.52, 0.14\rangle, \langle 0.23, 0.61\rangle)$, $\mathfrak{v}_{34} = \mathfrak{e}_6 = (\langle 0.65, 0.60\rangle, \langle 0.61, 0.12\rangle)$, $\mathfrak{v}_{36} = \mathfrak{e}_7 = (\langle 0.64, 0.21\rangle, \langle 0.43, 0.10\rangle)$, $\mathfrak{v}_{45} = \mathfrak{e}_8 = (\langle 0.71, 0.11\rangle, \langle 0.52, 0.29\rangle)$, $\mathfrak{v}_{46} = \mathfrak{e}_9 = (\langle 0.70, 0.22\rangle, \langle 0.49, 0.28\rangle)$, *and* $\mathfrak{v}_{56} = \mathfrak{e}_{10} = (\langle 0.81, 0.13\rangle, \langle 0.49, 0.25\rangle)$. *The LDFDG and its index matrix are shown below in Figure 5 and Table 1.*

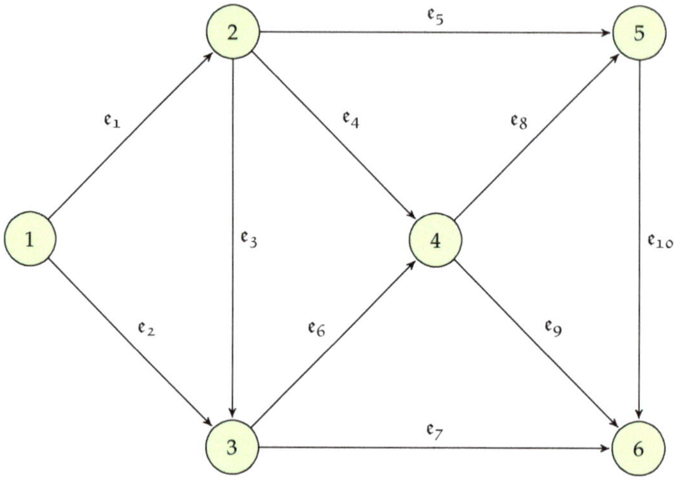

Figure 5. $\mathfrak{G}$: the linear Diophantine fuzzy digraph (LDFDG).

Table 1. Index matrix of the graph $\mathfrak{G}$.

Vertices	$\mathfrak{v}_1$	$\mathfrak{v}_2$	$\mathfrak{v}_3$	$\mathfrak{v}_4$	$\mathfrak{v}_5$	$\mathfrak{v}_6$
$\mathfrak{v}_1$	$\mathfrak{L}^o_{\mathfrak{D}}$	$\mathfrak{e}_1$	$\mathfrak{e}_2$	$\mathfrak{L}^o_{\mathfrak{D}}$	$\mathfrak{L}^o_{\mathfrak{D}}$	$\mathfrak{L}^o_{\mathfrak{D}}$
$\mathfrak{v}_2$	$\mathfrak{L}^o_{\mathfrak{D}}$	$\mathfrak{L}^o_{\mathfrak{D}}$	$\mathfrak{e}_3$	$\mathfrak{e}_4$	$\mathfrak{e}_5$	$\mathfrak{L}^o_{\mathfrak{D}}$
$\mathfrak{v}_3$	$\mathfrak{L}^o_{\mathfrak{D}}$	$\mathfrak{L}^o_{\mathfrak{D}}$	$\mathfrak{L}^o_{\mathfrak{D}}$	$\mathfrak{e}_6$	$\mathfrak{L}^o_{\mathfrak{D}}$	$\mathfrak{e}_7$
$\mathfrak{v}_4$	$\mathfrak{L}^o_{\mathfrak{D}}$	$\mathfrak{L}^o_{\mathfrak{D}}$	$\mathfrak{L}^o_{\mathfrak{D}}$	$\mathfrak{L}^o_{\mathfrak{D}}$	$\mathfrak{e}_8$	$\mathfrak{e}_9$
$\mathfrak{v}_5$	$\mathfrak{L}^o_{\mathfrak{D}}$	$\mathfrak{L}^o_{\mathfrak{D}}$	$\mathfrak{L}^o_{\mathfrak{D}}$	$\mathfrak{L}^o_{\mathfrak{D}}$	$\mathfrak{L}^o_{\mathfrak{D}}$	$\mathfrak{e}_{10}$
$\mathfrak{v}_6$	$\mathfrak{L}^o_{\mathfrak{D}}$	$\mathfrak{L}^o_{\mathfrak{D}}$	$\mathfrak{L}^o_{\mathfrak{D}}$	$\mathfrak{L}^o_{\mathfrak{D}}$	$\mathfrak{L}^o_{\mathfrak{D}}$	$\mathfrak{L}^o_{\mathfrak{D}}$

3. Dijkstra Algorithm for Finding the Shortest Path in a Network

The SPP is the most prominent graph theory problem. For basically any fuzzy structure, it has been extensively tested (see [2,36–38])) with an algorithm that is relatively straightforward and that gives us the best-predicted performance, as in [7], at that time.

The graph $\mathfrak{G} = (\mathfrak{V}, \mathfrak{E})$ is an LDF-directed graph, where $\mathfrak{V} = \{\mathfrak{s} = 1, 2, ..., \mathfrak{e} = m\}$ and $\mathfrak{V} \times \mathfrak{V} = \mathfrak{E} = \{(\mathrm{i}, \mathrm{j}) : \mathrm{i}, \mathrm{j} \in \mathfrak{V}, \mathrm{i} \neq \mathrm{j}\}$ represents the vertex and edge set, respectively. The ordered pair (i, j) denotes an edge of the graph that connects the two different vertices $\mathrm{i}, \mathrm{j} \in \mathfrak{V}$. It is considered a connected network with given arcs and nodes in which $\mathfrak{s}$ is the SN and $\mathfrak{e}$ is the TN. It is assumed that from the node i to the node j, there is only one directed arc. The route (path) $\mathfrak{p}_{\mathrm{ij}}$ from node i to node j is a series of arcs $\mathfrak{p}_{\mathrm{ij}} = \{(\mathrm{i}, \mathrm{i}_1), (\mathrm{i}_1, \mathrm{i}_2), ..., (\mathrm{i}_k, \mathrm{j})\}$ in which each arc's initial node is the same as the corresponding arc's terminal node in the sequence. The cost of the path that is directed is specified as the route costs the sum of the arc. The problem is to identify the SP between $\mathfrak{s}$ and $\mathfrak{e}$ for each arc-related parameter in terms of cost (or time, or space, etc.). In terms of LDFNs, this parameter is assumed to be $\mathfrak{C}_{\mathrm{i}}\mathrm{j} = \langle \alpha_{\mathfrak{M}}(\mathfrak{ab})\mathfrak{m}_{\mathfrak{N}}(\mathfrak{ab}), \beta_{\mathfrak{N}}(\mathfrak{ab})\mathfrak{n}_{\mathfrak{N}}(\mathfrak{ab})\rangle$, where $\mathfrak{m}_{\mathfrak{N}}(\mathfrak{ab})$ is the satisfaction grade, $\mathfrak{n}_{\mathfrak{N}}(\mathfrak{ab})$ is the dissatisfaction grade, and $\alpha_{\mathfrak{M}}(\mathfrak{ab})$, $\beta_{\mathfrak{M}}(\mathfrak{ab})$ are the reference parameters of the arc $\mathrm{i} - \mathrm{j}$. This is included in the shortest path with respect to the cost for traveling along the arc $\mathrm{i} - \mathrm{j}$.

The parameters associated with each arc i, j reflect the expense of the arc in consideration. The objective of the SPP is to find the path or route with the lowest cost, from starting node $\mathfrak{s}$ to destination node $\mathfrak{e}$. Certain and precise values for the arc are considered in conventional SP issues.As time and costs fluctuate regarding the payload, weather, and traffic conditions, various fuzzy set extensions may be used to reflect imprecise and ambiguous arc costs. LDFNs are used in this work to represent the ambiguous criteria of the issue of the SP under discussion. Therefore, the subsequent problem is referred to as the linear Diophantine fuzzy SP (LDFSP) problem. In an LDFSP problem with LDFNs for the arc length setting, there are two major topics that must be addressed:

1. To the linear Diophantine fuzzy arc prices, two edges are added;
2. Score functions are used to compare distance values between two distinct paths with edge lengths depicted by LDFNs.

The linear Diophantine fuzzy Dijkstra algorithm is a generalized form of the fuzzy Dijkstra's algorithm based on its predicted values. In our next subsection, we give the linear Diophantine fuzzy Dijkstra algorithm followed by an example.

3.1. The Dijkstra Algorithm: Our Extension via the LDFG

The algorithm assigns a state to each point, with the state of a node consisting of two specificities: the distance value and the status mark. A node's "distance value" is a measurement of its source distance, and the "status mark" is a function that decides when a node's distance value equals the shortest distance. If this is the case, the status label is permanent; otherwise, it is temporary. The algorithm incrementally preserves and updates the nodes. A single node is allocated as the current one at every stage. The pseudocode and the flowchart for the suggested process are introduced in the algorithm below and in Figure 6, respectively. Table 2 explains the set of notations used in Algorithm 1.

Algorithm 1: Pseudo-code for the proposed linear Diophantine fuzzy Dijkstra's algorithm (LDFDA).

1. **function** linear Diophantine fuzzy Dijkstra's $(\mathfrak{G}, \mathfrak{s})$
2. **for** each node $j \in \mathfrak{G}$ //initialization
3. status label $[j] \leftarrow (\infty, t)$; //an attribute specifying the distance value of node j
4. previous $[j] \leftarrow$ not defined; //former node in optimized path from the start node
5. **end for**
6. status label $[\mathfrak{s}] \leftarrow (0, p)$; // distance of the start node to itself
7. $\mathfrak{T} \leftarrow$ set of all possible nodes with temporary labels in $\mathfrak{G}$
8. **while** $\mathfrak{T}$ is nonvoid // the main loop
9. $i \leftarrow$ node in $\mathfrak{T}$ with the minimum distance value $\mathfrak{d}_i$;
10. **if** status label $[i] \leftarrow (\infty, p)$, **then**
11. stop; // all the other nodes are impenetrable form the start node
12. **end if**
13. delete i from $\mathfrak{T}$;
14. **for** every j such that there exists link (i, j)
15. $alt \leftarrow \mathfrak{d}_i + \mathfrak{c}_{ij}$; //defuzzification of the linear Diophantine fuzzy number
16. **if** $alt < \mathfrak{d}_i$, **then** // comparison of the distance values values to obtain the smallest distance value
17. $\mathfrak{d}_i \leftarrow alt$;
18. previous $[j] \leftarrow [i]$;
19. **end if**
20. status label $[j] \leftarrow (alt, p)$; //updated distance label
21. **end for**
22. **end while**
23. **return** status label [];
24. **end function**

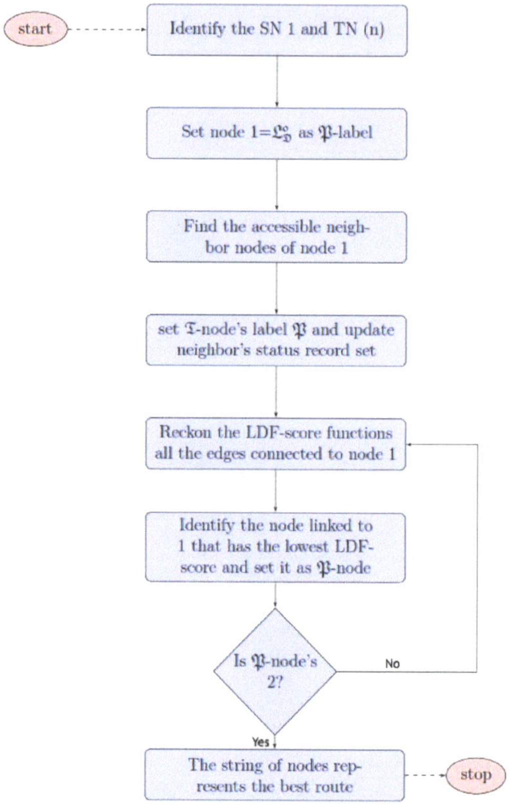

Figure 6. Flowchart for the proposed algorithm.

Table 2. Notations used in the proposed Algorithm 1.

$\mathfrak{T}$	{all temporary labeled nodes}
$\mathfrak{P}$	{all permanent labeled nodes}
i	the SD from the start node to a node
j	a variant
∂_j	renovated distance from the start node
c_{ij}	cost value between nodes i and j
alt	alternate variant

3.2. The Proposed Dijkstra Algorithm: A View

The methodology suggested in this article, in contrast to the available techniques, is more useful in finding the SP. The primary benefit of using FNs' predicted values is that they bring out only a single value. Without the method of rating FNs, decision-making can be achieved quickly. In an area of highly ambiguous parameters, this is computationally useful for addressing SPPs. The characteristics and a comparison analysis of the four types of systems that can be used in the evaluation of SPPs are summarized in Table 3.

We claim that there are benefits to linear Diophantine fuzzy sets over ordinary FSs and IFSs, as they have a more impartial perspective of the functional situation. Therefore, our approach deals with the SPP with a network with linear Diophantine fuzzy arc lengths from the SN to the TN.

The shortest path analysis of the linear Diophantine fuzzy set is as follows:

- First of all, our approach modifies the principle of the predicted values for LDFNs. For the predicted values of LDFNs, we obtain novel results;
- We use this method of implementation to solve a well-known shortest path algorithm, the so-called Dijkstra algorithm, under which the method of the defuzzification of LDFNs allocated to network arcs is performed by computing their predicted values;
- To calculate the SD value, a juxtaposition of the LDFNs is accomplished in terms of the score function, gleaned from the predicted LDFN values, leading directly to a crisp number.

Therefore, as compared to other fuzzy shortest path methods, our accomplishment is rationally more structured, sound, and simple to add.

Table 3. Comparison to crisp and other fuzzy models.

SPP under Models	Links or Edges	Satisfaction Grade	Dissatisfaction Grade	Parameterization
Crisp set	CN	-	-	-
FS	FN	✓	-	-
IFS	IFN	✓	✓	-
PyFS	PyFN	✓	✓	-
LDFS	LDFN	✓	✓	✓

4. Numerical Application

It is very important to save any victims anytime a disaster happens. The urgency of time is the most salient characteristic of time-sensitive decision-making. The rescue plan must be completed within a short period, and helping the rescuers immediately know the position of any trapped persons is the job of the decision-maker. The time required to reach the rescue location almost always directly affects the performance of the rescue mission; the primary objective function is therefore considered to be the soonest achievable arrival time. When the rescue team and the police have fixed arrival times, it is possible to simplify the shortest rescue time as the shortest path desired and further as the shortest transportation time. For other factors that may present obstacles, such as damage to a bridge, the accumulation of water on a road, and damaged roads, the grade values are defined by the amount of damage to the transport infrastructure, and the weight of the path is represented by the LDFNs. This combinatorial optimization dilemma is typical of SPPs. Dijkstra's algorithm is used to solve these types of problem. In real-time applications, a digital vector map is typically the descriptive model of an urban road network. The layout of the map related to the vertices and edges is abstracted to effectively analyze the SP. During the emergency, finding the SP to reach the destination/target is difficult. An effective deployment will boost the rescue team's rapid response capability and total command capacity. An algorithm for the SP is developed for the directed graph, and the weights of all the edges are represented by LDFNs. Because of the unrestricted choice of attribute grades and the parameterized classification of the LDFS, this model is superior to the others. As a result, this model provides the best option for selecting an appropriate action.

The rescue location and the location of each rescue team are denoted by the vertices of the graph. The $\mathfrak{N}$ emergency team sites, passing points, and rescue points comprise a disaster area. In directed graph $\mathfrak{G}(\mathfrak{V}, \mathfrak{E})$, $\mathfrak{V}$ denotes the location of the rescue team, the passing points, and the recovery location, and $\mathfrak{E}$ denotes the path between two rescue locations. The length of the path is important to find the minimum time to reach the rescue locations, the road conditions, etc. The edge weight is represented as an LDFN.

Node $\mathfrak{v}_1$, considering the geography, geographical location, the degree of the disaster's impact, and other factors, is the beginning point of the rescue, and the point of the rescue site is node $\mathfrak{v}_n$. A directed path from node $\mathfrak{v}_1$ to node $\mathfrak{v}_n$ can be represented in the form of $(\mathfrak{v}_1;\mathfrak{v}_2);(\mathfrak{v}_2;\mathfrak{v}_3);\ldots,(\mathfrak{v}_\mathfrak{k};\mathfrak{v}_n)$ as a series of directed edge sequences in a directed graph. Depending on the strength of the relations of a directed graph, the number of paths that connect node $\mathfrak{v}_1$ to node $\mathfrak{v}_n$ can differ.

4.1. Case Study

The coastal area of Wenling City, Zhejiang Province, was hit by the strong typhoon Lekima on 10 August 2019. The highest wind force was 16 levels (52 m/s), and a mean air pressure of 930 hPa was recorded at the center. Due to this strong typhoon, roads were blocked with floods, rocks, and trees, bridges were destroyed, etc. Because of this condition, it was impossible to traverse the road network based on the prior conditions. Given the road conditions, it was important to identify the safest way to the rescue point and provide the emergency rescue teams of the appropriate departments with decision-making support. During this time, the topological structure of the road network was as seen in Figure 7. We built the input data in the context of LDFSs, where the satisfaction and dissatisfaction grades informed us about the satisfaction and dissatisfaction with respect to the associated routes and their traffic signal parameters α, β, which symbolize "very less traffic" and "very heavy traffic". Table 4 indicates the side lengths considered. A rescue team in Fuzhou must start from Point (1) and proceed to Point (7) to rescue trapped people, so the shortest route from Point (1) to Point (7) must be identified; the sequence is illustrated below.

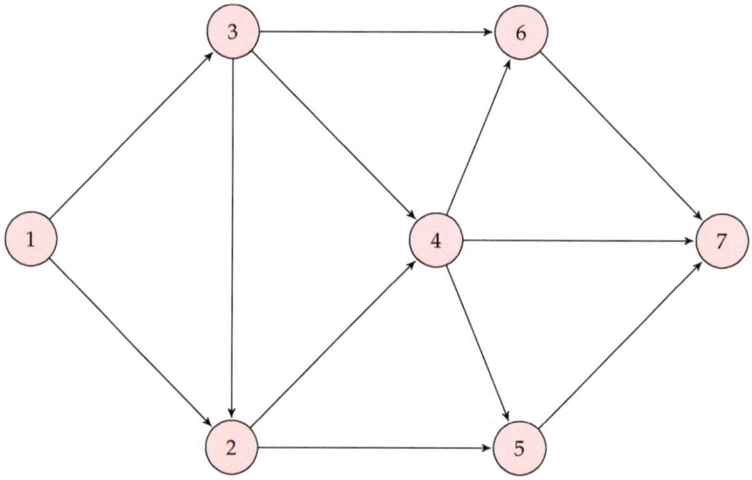

Figure 7. The graph of the road network with the linear Diophantine fuzzy distance.

Table 4. Details of the edge information in terms of the LDFN.

Edges	LDFN	Edges	LDFN
(1,2)	$(\langle 0.81, 0.37\rangle, \langle 0.51, 0.18\rangle)$	(3,6)	$(\langle 0.91, 0.73\rangle, \langle 0.46, 0.18\rangle)$
(1,3)	$(\langle 0.93, 0.68\rangle, \langle 0.53, 0.12\rangle)$	(4,5)	$(\langle 0.64, 0.29\rangle, \langle 0.37, 0.28\rangle)$
(2,4)	$(\langle 0.74, 0.47\rangle, \langle 0.43, 0.32\rangle)$	(4,6)	$(\langle 0.87, 0.39\rangle, \langle 0.25, 0.22\rangle)$
(2,5)	$(\langle 0.93, 0.63\rangle, \langle 0.46, 0.29\rangle)$	(4,7)	$(\langle 0.78, 0.57\rangle, \langle 0.45, 0.21\rangle)$
(3,2)	$(\langle 0.94, 0.58\rangle, \langle 0.58, 0.13\rangle)$	(5,7)	$(\langle 0.73, 0.68\rangle, \langle 0.41, 0.37\rangle)$
(3,4)	$(\langle 0.64, 0.21\rangle, \langle 0.37, 0.28\rangle)$	(6,7)	$(\langle 0.83, 0.43\rangle, \langle 0.51, 0.15\rangle)$

Let $\mathfrak{T} =$ {nodes labeled as temporary nodes}, and let $\mathfrak{P} =$ {nodes labeled as permanent nodes}. The start node (1) is moved from set $\mathfrak{T}$ to set $\mathfrak{P}$ at the initial point since the distance from (1) to (1) is zero, which is the shortest. The steps defined by Figure 7 to define the shortest path in the network and the SD value for all paths are defined as follows:
Let $\mathfrak{T}$ be the set of nodes labeled temporarily, and let $\mathfrak{P}$ be the set of nodes labeled permanently. The start node (1) is moved from set $\mathfrak{T}$ to set $\mathfrak{P}$ at the initial point since the distance from (1) to (1) is zero, which is the shortest:

- Iteration 0: Assign Node (1) = the permanent label = $[(\langle 0,1\rangle,\langle 0,1\rangle),-]$;
- Iteration 1: We calculated the distance from the start (last permanently marked) Node (1) to its accessible neighbor Nodes (2) and (3). Consequently, the lexicon (temporary and permanent) of tagged nodes is:

Nodes	Label	Status
1	$[(\langle 0,1\rangle,\langle 0,1\rangle),-]$	$\mathfrak{P}$
2	$[(\langle 0.81,0.37\rangle,\langle 0.51,0.18\rangle),1]$	$\mathfrak{T}$
3	$[(\langle 0.93,0.68\rangle,\langle 0.53,0.12\rangle),1]$	$\mathfrak{T}$

In order to compare $(\langle 0.81,0.37\rangle,\langle 0.51,0.18\rangle)$, $(\langle 0.93,0.68\rangle,\langle 0.53,0.12\rangle)$ and $(\langle 0.74,0.47\rangle,\langle 0.43,0.32\rangle)$, we used Definition 5 (1)
$\mathfrak{S}(\langle 0.81,0.37\rangle,\langle 0.51,0.18\rangle) = \frac{1}{2}[(0.81-0.37)+(0.51-0.18)] = 0.385$
$\mathfrak{S}(\langle 0.93,0.68\rangle,\langle 0.53,0.12\rangle) = \frac{1}{2}[(0.93-0.68)+(0.53-0.12)] = 0.33.$
Since the score value of $[(\langle 0.93,0.68\rangle,\langle 0.53,0.12\rangle),1]$ is less than the score value of $[(\langle 0.81,0.37\rangle,\langle 0.51,0.18\rangle),1]$, the status of Node (3) is changed to permanent;
- Iteration 2: Nodes (2), (4), and (6) can be accessed from the (last permanently marked) Node (3). Thus, the list (temporary and permanent) of labeled nodes becomes:

Nodes	Label	Status
1	$[(\langle 0,1\rangle,\langle 0,1\rangle),-]$	$\mathfrak{P}$
2	$[(\langle 0.81,0.37\rangle,\langle 0.51,0.18\rangle),1]$ (or) $[(\langle 0.9958,0.3944\rangle,\langle 0.8026,0.0156\rangle),3]$	$\mathfrak{T}$
3	$[(\langle 0.93,0.68\rangle,\langle 0.53,0.12\rangle),1]$	$\mathfrak{P}$
4	$[(\langle 0.95060.1739\rangle,\langle 0.72070.0576\rangle),2]$ (or) $[(\langle 0.9748,0.1428\rangle,\langle 0.7039,0.0336\rangle),3]$	$\mathfrak{T}$
6	$[(\langle 0.9937,0.4964\rangle,\langle 0.7462,0.0216\rangle),3]$ (or) $[(\langle 0.9935780.067821\rangle,\langle 0.7905250.012672\rangle),4]$	$\mathfrak{T}$

$\mathfrak{S}(\langle 0.81,0.37\rangle,\langle 0.51,0.18\rangle) = \frac{1}{2}[(0.81-0.37)+(0.51-0.18)] = 0.385$
$\mathfrak{S}(\langle 0.9958,0.3944\rangle,\langle 0.8026,0.0156\rangle) = 0.6942$
$\mathfrak{S}((\langle 0.95060.1739\rangle,\langle 0.72070.0576\rangle) = 0.7199$
$\mathfrak{S}(\langle 0.9748,0.1428\rangle,\langle 0.7039,0.0336\rangle) = 0.75115$
$\mathfrak{S}(\langle 0.9937,0.4964\rangle,\langle 0.7462,0.0216\rangle) = 0.61095$
$\mathfrak{S}(\langle 0.9935780.067821\rangle,\langle 0.7905250.012672\rangle) = 0.851805.$
Since the score value of $[(\langle 0.81,0.37\rangle,\langle 0.51,0.18\rangle),1]$ is less than the remaining nodes, the status of Node (2) is changed to permanent;
- Iteration 3: Nodes (4) and (5) can be accessed from the (last permanently marked) Node (2). Thus, the list (temporary and permanent) of labeled nodes becomes:

Nodes	Label	Status
1	$[(\langle 0,1\rangle,\langle 0,1\rangle),-]$	$\mathfrak{P}$
2	$[(\langle 0.81,0.37\rangle,\langle 0.51,0.18\rangle),1]$	$\mathfrak{P}$
3	$[(\langle 0.93,0.68\rangle,\langle 0.53,0.12\rangle),1]$	$\mathfrak{P}$
4	$[(\langle 0.95060.1739\rangle,\langle 0.72070.0576\rangle),2]$ (or) $[(\langle 0.9748,0.1428\rangle,\langle 0.7039,0.0336\rangle),3]$	$\mathfrak{T}$
5	$[(\langle 0.9867,0.2331\rangle,\langle 0.7354,0.0522\rangle),2]$ (or) $[(\langle 0.9822160.050431\rangle,\langle 0.824041,0.016128\rangle),4]$	$\mathfrak{T}$
6	$[(\langle 0.9937,0.4964\rangle,\langle 0.7462,0.0216\rangle),3]$ (or) $[(\langle 0.9935780.067821\rangle,\langle 0.7905250.012672\rangle),4]$	$\mathfrak{T}$

$\mathfrak{S}(\langle 0.9506,0.1739\rangle,\langle 0.7207,0.0576\rangle) = 0.7199$
$\mathfrak{S}(\langle 0.9748,0.1428\rangle,\langle 0.7039,0.0336\rangle) = 0.75115$
$\mathfrak{S}(\langle 0.9867,0.2331\rangle,\langle 0.7354,0.0522\rangle) = 0.7184$
$\mathfrak{S}(\langle 0.9822160.050431\rangle,\langle 0.8240410.016128\rangle) = 0.869849$
$\mathfrak{S}(\langle 0.9937,0.4964\rangle,\langle 0.7462,0.0216\rangle) = 0.61095$
$\mathfrak{S}(\langle 0.9935780.067821\rangle,\langle 0.7905250.012672\rangle) = 0.851805.$
Since the score value of $[(\langle 0.9937,0.4964\rangle,\langle 0.7462,0.0216\rangle),3]$ is less than the remaining nodes, the status of Node (6) is changed to permanent;

- Iteration 4: Node (7) can be accessed from the (last permanently marked) Node (6). Thus, the list (temporary and permanent) of labeled nodes becomes:

Nodes	Label	Status
1	$[(\langle 0,1\rangle,\langle 0,1\rangle),-]$	$\mathfrak{P}$
2	$[(\langle 0.81,0.37\rangle,\langle 0.51,0.18\rangle),1]$	$\mathfrak{P}$
3	$[(\langle 0.93,0.68\rangle,\langle 0.53,0.12\rangle),1]$	$\mathfrak{P}$
4	$[(\langle 0.9506,0.1739\rangle,\langle 0.7207,0.0576\rangle),2]$ (or) $[(\langle 0.9748,0.1428\rangle,\langle 0.7039,0.0336\rangle),3]$	$\mathfrak{T}$
5	$[(\langle 0.9867,0.2331\rangle,\langle 0.7354,0.0522\rangle),2]$ (or) $[(\langle 0.982216,0.050431\rangle,\langle 0.824041,0.016128\rangle),4]$	$\mathfrak{T}$
6	$[(\langle 0.9937,0.4964\rangle,\langle 0.7462,0.0216\rangle),3]$	$\mathfrak{P}$
7	$[(\langle 0.989132,0.099123\rangle,\langle 0.846385,0.012096\rangle),4]$ (or) $[(\langle 0.996409,0.158508\rangle,\langle 0.843886,0.019314\rangle),5]$ (or) $[(\langle 0.998929,0.213452\rangle,\langle 0.8756380.00324\rangle),6]$	$\mathfrak{P}$

$\mathfrak{S}(\langle 0.989132,0.099123\rangle,\langle 0.846385,0.012096\rangle) = 0.862149,$
$\mathfrak{S}(\langle 0.996409,0.158508\rangle,\langle 0.843886,0.019314\rangle) = 0.8312365,$
$\mathfrak{S}(\langle 0.998929,0.213452\rangle,\langle 0.8756380.00324\rangle) = 0.8289375.$
Since the score value of $[(\langle 0.998929,0.213452\rangle,\langle 0.8756380.00324\rangle),6]$ is less than the remaining nodes, the position of the seventh node is converted to permanent.
As the point TN 7 has the permanent label, we can stop the operations at this point, and to change the remaining points as the permanent label, we have
$\mathfrak{S}(\langle 0.9506,0.1739\rangle,\langle 0.7207,0.0576\rangle) = 0.7199$
$\mathfrak{S}(\langle 0.9748,0.1428\rangle,\langle 0.7039,0.0336\rangle) = 0.75115.$
Here, the score of $[(\langle 0.9506,0.1739\rangle,\langle 0.7207,0.0576\rangle),2]$ is less than the score $[(\langle 0.9748,0.1428\rangle,\langle 0.7039,0.0336\rangle),3]$
$\mathfrak{S}(\langle 0.9867,0.2331\rangle,\langle 0.7354,0.0522\rangle) = 0.7184$
$\mathfrak{S}(\langle 0.982216,0.050431\rangle,\langle 0.824041,0.016128\rangle) = 0.869849.$

Here, the score of $[(\langle 0.9867, 0.2331\rangle, \langle 0.7354, 0.0522\rangle), 2]$ is less than the score $[(\langle 0.982216, 0.050431\rangle, \langle 0.824041, 0.016128\rangle), 4]$:

Nodes	Label	Status
1	$[(\langle 0,1\rangle, \langle 0,1\rangle), -]$	$\mathfrak{P}$
2	$[(\langle 0.81, 0.37\rangle, \langle 0.51, 0.18\rangle), 1]$	$\mathfrak{P}$
3	$[(\langle 0.93, 0.68\rangle, \langle 0.53, 0.12\rangle), 1]$	$\mathfrak{P}$
4	$[(\langle 0.9506, 0.1739\rangle, \langle 0.7207, 0.0576\rangle), 2]$	$\mathfrak{P}$
5	$[(\langle 0.9867, 0.2331\rangle, \langle 0.7354, 0.0522\rangle), 2]$	$\mathfrak{P}$
6	$[(\langle 0.9937, 0.4964\rangle, \langle 0.7462, 0.0216\rangle), 3]$	$\mathfrak{P}$
7	$[(\langle 0.998929, 0.213452\rangle, \langle 0.8756380.00324\rangle), 6]$	$\mathfrak{P}$

Working backward from the terminal point "7", one can conveniently create the shortest path by moving to the predecessor from which the current node received its permanent name. Going backward, the shortest or least-expensive route becomes $1 \to 3 \to 6 \to 7$. Here, $L(7) = (\langle 0.998929, 0.213452\rangle, \langle 0.875638, 0.00324\rangle)$, the weighted aggregated LDFN of the minimum cost path or the shortest path in terms of the overall linear Diophantine fuzzy cost/time for going along the shortest path is as seen in Figure 8.

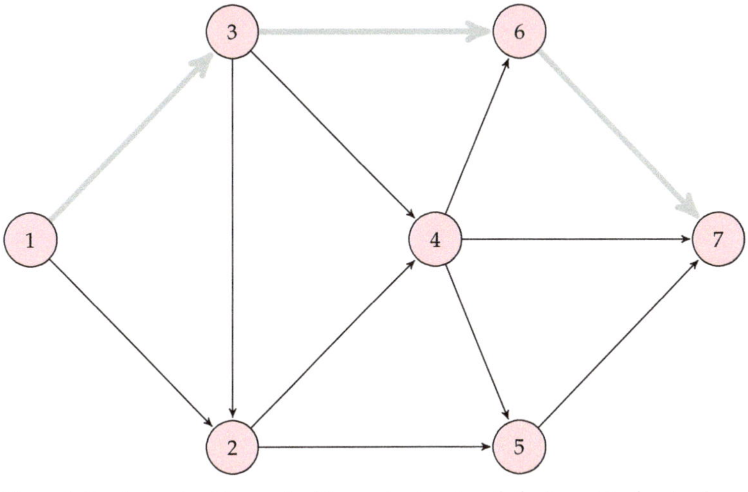

Figure 8. Shortest path of the graph of the road network with the linear Diophantine fuzzy distance.

The comparative analysis of the characteristics of Dijkstra's algorithms in the four types of systems that were used in the evaluation of SPPs are elaborated in the following Table 5.

Table 5. Comparison analysis of Dijkstra's algorithm under different environments.

Types of DAs	Advantages	Limitations
Classical DA [40]	It can be applied when precise arc weights are available	Its performance is degradedwhen arc weights are imprecise
Fuzzy DA [5]	It can be applied when arc weights are imprecise	It is degradedby the degree of rejection present in the arc weight
IF DA [9]	It deals with imprecise arc weights involving both the degree of acceptance and the degree of rejection	It does not work if the sum of the acceptance grade and the rejection grade of an arc weight exceeds 1
PyF DA [44]	It can handle imprecise arc weights even if the sum of the acceptance grade and the rejection grade exceeds 1 with some constraints	It does not work if a reference parameter is added to the arc weight
LDF DA (proposed method)	It can be applied in many real-time situations that ave the reference parameters	It cannot work if the indeterminacy grade is present in the arc weight

4.2. *Summary*

The SPP under an LDF environment is important when the reference parameter is added to the arc weight. People and their livelihoods are affected by natural disasters in many countries such as flood, high wind force, land slides, tsunamis, etc. We considered the disaster that occurred in Wenling City, Zhejiang. Dijkstra's algorithm was used under an LDF environment to make the right decision during an emergency. A novel Dijkstra's algorithm was introduced and developed under an LDF setting to find the SP with the aid of the SF. The classical, fuzzy, IF, and PyF theories have their own limitations in finding the shortest paths and fail to address the reference parameters, which are important to our problem. Therefore, the LDFSPP using Dijkstra's algorithm helped a rescue team reach the rescue destination in a short time. The proposed algorithm is more suitable for any network involving the satisfaction and dissatisfaction grades with the reference parameters.

5. Conclusions

The shortest path problem is a very important field of analysis, and it is used to solve a variety of real-world problems. In this article, a new and groundbreaking approach for solving SPPs in an unpredictable world was presented. In real-world settings, the exact cost, time, or distance values relative to the network arcs may not be possible to obtain. Fuzzy numbers can be used to describe imprecise parameters to account for this ambiguity. To reflect the unknown weights of going along each arc, the most generic kind of fuzzy numbers, LDFNs, were used. The decision-maker's hopeful and cynical views were represented by LDFNs. The suggested technique of LDFDA was developed successfully using the LDF operator and its score functions, which are essential areas of LDFSs. SPPs with the LDF edge weight/distance have never been addressed or solved in the literature before this work. This kind of real-world problem was successfully solved using the proposed LDFDA, which successfully applied the various existing theories of LDFSs. The benefits and objectives of the paper were that the LDF optimality restrictions in directed network graphs be established and a solution method created, and then, an improved SF was used to compute the weights of alternative pathways with edge weights represented by LDFNs. To find the LDFSP and coterminal LDFSP established on these enhanced scores, the score functions and the optimality constraints of the traditional Dijkstra method were modified. Finally, to confirm the potential usage of the suggested technique, a small-scale communications network was presented, as well as a comparison study with the present approaches, proving the value of the proposed algorithm. This is the paper's most significant contribution. Other methods for solving certain problems could be suggested in the future, and the outcomes could be compared. For large networks, computer programs may be designed to incorporate the suggested technique. In future work, we will apply the existing algorithm to solve large-scale real-time problems in a linear Diophantine fuzzy environment and compare the results with the existing algorithms with respect to the efficiency, time for computation, optimality, etc.

Author Contributions: All authors contributed equally to this paper. The individual responsibilities and contributions of all authors can be described as follows: the idea of this whole paper was put forward by M.P., M.R., S.J. and M.A. completed the preparatory work of the paper. M.R. and M.A. analyzed the existing work. The revision and submission of this paper were completed by S.J. and M.P. All authors read and agreed to the published version of the manuscript.

Funding: This research was funded by Deanship of Scientific Research at King Khalid University, Abha 61413, Saudi Arabia, grant number R.G. P-2/29/42.

Institutional Review Board Statement: Not applicable.

Informed Consent Statement: Not applicable.

Data Availability Statement: Not applicable.

Conflicts of Interest: The authors declare no conflict of interest.

Abbreviations

The following abbreviations are used in this manuscript:

FS	fuzzy set
IFS	intuitionistic fuzzy set
PyFS	Pythagorean fuzzy set
LDFS	linear Diophantine fuzzy set
CN	crisp number
DA	Dijkstra's algorithm
FN	fuzzy number
IFN	intuitionistic fuzzy number
PyFN	Pythagorean fuzzy number
LDFN	linear Diophantine fuzzy number
SN	start node
TN	terminal node
SP	shortest path
SF	score function
SPP	shortest path problem
2D plot	two-dimensional plot
3D plot	three-dimensional plot
SD	shortest distance
LDFSP	linear Diophantine fuzzy shortest path
MCDM	multicriteria decision-making

References

1. Zadeh, L.A. Fuzzy sets. *Inf. Control* **1965**, *8*, 338–353. [CrossRef]
2. Okada, S.; Soper, T. A shortest path problem on a network with fuzzy arc lengths. *Fuzzy Sets Syst.* **2000**, *109*, 129–140. [CrossRef]
3. Keshavarz, E.; Khorram, E. A fuzzy shortest path with the highest reliability. *J. Comput. Appl. Math.* **2009**, *230*, 204–212.
4. Dou, Y.; Zhu, L.; Wang, H.S. Solving the fuzzy shortest path problem using multi-criteria decision method based on vague similarity measure. *Appl. Soft Comput.* **2012**, *12*, 1621–1631. [CrossRef]
5. Deng, Y.; Chen, Y.; Zhang, Y.; Mahadevan, S. Fuzzy Dijkstra algorithm for shortest path problem under uncertain environment. *Appl. Soft Comput.* **2012**, *12*, 1231–1237. [CrossRef]
6. Ebrahimnejad, A.; Karimnejad, Z.; Alrezaamiri, H. Particle swarm optimisation algorithm for solving shortest path problems with mixed fuzzy arc weights. *Int. J. Appl. Decis. Sci.* **2015**, *8*, 203–222. [CrossRef]
7. Ebrahimnejad, A.; Tavana, M.; Alrezaamiri, H. A novel artificial bee colony algorithm for shortest path problems with fuzzy arc weights. *Measurement* **2016**, *93*, 48–56.
8. Atanassov, K.T. Intuitionistic fuzzy sets. In *Intuitionistic Fuzzy Sets*; Physica: Heidelberg, Germany, 1999; pp. 1–137.
9. Mukherjee, S. Dijkstra's algorithm for solving the shortest path problem on networks under intuitionistic fuzzy environment. *J. Math. Model. Algorithms* **2012**, *11*, 345–359. [CrossRef]

10. Geetharamani, G.; Jayagowri, P. Using similarity degree approach for shortest path in intuitionistic fuzzy network. In Proceedings of the 2012 International Conference on Computing, Communication and Applications, Dindigul, India, 22–24 February 2012; pp. 1–6.
11. Biswas, S.S.; Alam, B.; Doja, M.N. An algorithm for extracting intuitionistic fuzzy shortest path in a graph. *Appl. Comput. Intell. Soft Comput.* **2013**, *2013*, 970197. [CrossRef]
12. Kumar, G.; Bajaj, R.K.; Gandotra, N. Algorithm for shortest path problem in a network with interval-valued intuitionistic trapezoidal fuzzy number. *Procedia Comput. Sci.* **2015**, *70*, 123–129. [CrossRef]
13. Sujatha, L.; Hyacinta, J.D. The shortest path problem on networks with intuitionistic fuzzy edge weights. *Glob. J. Pure Appl. Math.* **2017**, *13*, 3285–3300.
14. Motameni, H.; Ebrahimnejad, A. Constraint shortest path problem in a network with intuitionistic fuzzy arc weights. In Proceedings of the International Conference on Information Processing and Management of Uncertainty in Knowledge-Based Systems, Cadiz, Spain, 11–15 June 2018; Springer: Cham, Switzerland, 2018; pp. 310–318.
15. Yager, R.R. Pythagorean fuzzy subsets. In Proceedings of the 2013 Joint IFSA World Congress and NAFIPS Annual Meeting (IFSA/NAFIPS), Edmonton, AB, Canada, 24–28 June 2013; pp. 57–61.
16. Yager, R.R.; Abbasov, A.M. Pythagorean membership grades, complex numbers, and decision-making. *Int. J. Intell. Syst.* **2013**, *28*, 436–452. [CrossRef]
17. Yager, R.R. Pythagorean membership grades in multicriteria decision-making. *IEEE Trans. Fuzzy Syst.* **2013**, *22*, 958–965. [CrossRef]
18. Zhang, X.; Xu, Z. Extension of TOPSIS to multiple criteria decision-making with Pythagorean fuzzy sets. *Int. J. Intell. Syst.* **2014**, *29*, 1061–1078. [CrossRef]
19. Akram, M.; Habib, A.; Ilyas, F.; Mohsan Dar, J. Specific types of Pythagorean fuzzy graphs and application to decision-making. *Math. Comput. Appl.* **2018**, *23*, 42. [CrossRef]
20. Akram, M.; Dar, J.M.; Naz, S. Certain graphs under Pythagorean fuzzy environment. *Complex Intell. Syst.* **2019**, *5*, 127–144. [CrossRef]
21. Karthikeyan, P.; Mani, P. Applying Dijkstra Algorithm for Solving Spherical fuzzy Shortest Path Problem. *Solid State Technol.* **2020**, *63*, 4239–4250.
22. Mani, P.; Vasudevan, B.; Sivaraman, M. Shortest path algorithm of a network via picture fuzzy digraphs and its application. *Mater. Today Proc.* **2021**, *45*, 3014–3018. [CrossRef]
23. Parimala, M.; Broumi, S.; Prakash, K.; Topal, S. Bellman-Ford algorithm for solving shortest path problem of a network under picture fuzzy environment. *Complex Intell. Syst.* **2021**. [CrossRef]
24. Broumi, S.; Talea, M.; Bakali, A.; Smarandache, F.; Nagarajan, D.; Lathamaheswari, M.; Parimala, M. Shortest path problem in fuzzy, intuitionistic fuzzy and neutrosophic environment: An overview. *Complex Intell. Syst.* **2019**, *5*, 371–378. [CrossRef]
25. Starczewski, J.T.; Goetzen, P.; Napoli, C. Triangular fuzzy-rough set based fuzzification of fuzzy rule-based systems. *J. Artif. Intell. Soft Comput. Res.* **2020**, *10*, 271–285. [CrossRef]
26. Napoli, C.; Pappalardo, G.; Tramontana, E. A mathematical model for file fragment diffusion and a neural predictor to manage priority queues over BitTorrent. *Int. J. Appl. Math. Comput. Sci.* **2016**, *26*, 147–160. [CrossRef]
27. Wróbel, M.; Starczewski, J.T.; Napoli, C. Grouping Handwritten Letter Strokes Using a Fuzzy Decision Tree. In Proceedings of the International Conference on Artificial Intelligence and Soft Computing, Zakopane, Poland, 12–14 October 2020; pp. 103–113.
28. Fornaia, A.; Napoli, C.; Tramontana, E. Cloud services for on-demand vehicles management. *Inf. Technol. Control* **2017**, *46*, 484–498. [CrossRef]
29. Riaz, M.; Hashmi, M.R. Linear Diophantine fuzzy set and its applications towards multi-attribute decision-making problems. *J. Intell. Fuzzy Syst.* **2019**, *37*, 5417–5439. [CrossRef]
30. Riaz, M.; Hashmi, M.R.; Kalsoom, H.; Pamucar, D.; Chu, Y.M. Linear Diophantine Fuzzy Soft Rough Sets for the Selection of Sustainable Material Handling Equipment. *Symmetry* **2020**, *12*, 1215. [CrossRef]
31. Ayub, S.; Shabir, M.; Riaz, M.; Aslam, M.; Chinram, R. Linear Diophantine Fuzzy Relations and Their Algebraic Properties with Decision Making. *Symmetry* **2021**, *13*, 945. [CrossRef]
32. Almagrabi, A.O.; Abdullah, S.; Shams, M.; Al-Otaibi, Y.D.; Ashraf, S. A new approach to q-linear Diophantine fuzzy emergency decision support system for COVID19. *J. Ambient. Intell. Humaniz. Comput.* **2021**. [CrossRef]
33. Kamacı, H. Linear Diophantine fuzzy algebraic structures. *J. Ambient. Intell. Humaniz. Comput.* **2021**. [CrossRef]
34. Iampan, A.; García, G.S.; Riaz, M.; Athar Farid, H.M.; Chinram, R. Linear Diophantine Fuzzy Einstein Aggregation Operators for Multi-Criteria Decision-Making Problems. *J. Math.* **2021**, *2021*, 5548033. [CrossRef]
35. Riaz, M.; Farid, H.M.A.; Aslam, M.; Pamucar, D.; Bozanic, D. Novel Approach for Third-Party Reverse Logistic Provider Selection Process under Linear Diophantine Fuzzy Prioritized Aggregation Operators. *Symmetry* **2021**, *13*, 1152. [CrossRef]
36. Chuang, T.N.; Kung, J.Y. A new algorithm for the discrete fuzzy shortest path problem in a network. *Appl. Math. Comput.* **2006**, *174*, 660–668. [CrossRef]
37. Gani, A.N.; Jabarulla, M.M. On searching intuitionistic fuzzy shortest path in a network. *Appl. Math. Sci.* **2010**, *4*, 3447–3454.
38. Hernandes, F.; Lamata, M.T.; Verdegay, J.L.; Yamakami, A. The shortest path problem on networks with fuzzy parameters. *Fuzzy Sets Syst.* **2007**, *158*, 1561–1570. [CrossRef]
39. Warshall, S. A theorem on boolean matrices. *J. ACM* **1962**, *9*, 11–12. [CrossRef]

40. Dijkstra, E.W. A note on two problems in connexion with graphs. *Numer. Math.* **1959**, *1*, 269–271. [CrossRef]
41. Bellman, R. On a routing problem. *Q. Appl. Math.* **1958**, *16*, 87–90. [CrossRef]
42. Floyd, R.W. Algorithm 97: Shortest path. *Commun. ACM* **1962**, *5*, 345. [CrossRef]
43. Makariye, N. Towards shortest path computation using Dijkstra algorithm. In Proceedings of the 2017 International Conference on IoT and Application (ICIOT), Nagapattinam, India, 19–20 May 2017; pp. 1–3.
44. Enayattabar, M.; Ebrahimnejad, A.; Motameni, H. Dijkstra algorithm for shortest path problem under interval-valued Pythagorean fuzzy environment. *Complex Intell. Syst.* **2019**, *5*, 93–100. [CrossRef]

symmetry

MDPI

Article

Fuzzy Sawi Decomposition Method for Solving Nonlinear Partial Fuzzy Differential Equations

Atanaska Georgieva [1,*] and Albena Pavlova [2]

[1] Department of Mathematical Analysis, University of Plovdiv Paisii Hilendarski, 24 Tzar Asen, 4003 Plovdiv, Bulgaria

[2] Department of MPC, Technical University-Sofia, Plovdiv Branch, 25 Tzanko Djustabanov Str., 4000 Plovdiv, Bulgaria; akosseva@gmail.com

* Correspondence:atanaska@uni-plovdiv.bg

Abstract: The main goal of this paper is to propose a new decomposition method for finding solutions to nonlinear partial fuzzy differential equations (NPFDE) through the fuzzy Sawi decomposition method (FSDM). This method is a combination of the fuzzy Sawi transformation and Adomian decomposition method. For this purpose, two new theorems for fuzzy Sawi transformation regarding fuzzy partial gH-derivatives are introduced. The use of convex symmetrical triangular fuzzy numbers creates symmetry between the lower and upper representations of the fuzzy solution. To demonstrate the effectiveness of the method, a numerical example is provided.

Keywords: fuzzy Sawi decomposition method; fuzzy partial gH-derivative; nonlinear partial fuzzy differential equations

Citation: Georgieva, A.; Pavlova, A. Fuzzy Sawi Decomposition Method for Solving Nonlinear Partial Fuzzy Differential Equations. *Symmetry* **2021**, *13*, 1580. https://doi.org/10.3390sym13091580

Academic Editors: Lorentz Jantschi and Saeid Jafari

Received: 22 July 2021
Accepted: 12 August 2021
Published: 27 August 2021

1. Introduction

A fundamental problem in the process of modeling phenomena is the immense quantity and quality of information that has to be included, such that it is as representative as possible of the real system. The process of the derivation of mathematical models is set to limitations, such as correct understanding, ambiguity in the accuracy and uncertainty of the data, and measurement errors that lead to uncertainties in the model. Fuzzy modeling is an effective method that enables researchers to express scientific issues.

The modeling of many physical phenomena, such as dynamical and magnetic systems, engineering, biological and environmental issues, and humanities phenomena, result in the use of differential equations. Partial differential equations are mathematical equations that appear in a number of fields, such as physics, engineering, chemistry and biology. Many authors have developed analytical and numerical methods for solving different kinds of partial differential equations; see [1–4].

In order to apply fuzzy differential equations as a modeling tool for dynamical systems, some authors have extended the concept of derivatives in the fuzzy context. This allows to define differential equation in the fuzzy context, which was studied by some authors, such as [5–8].

In some cases, partial differential equations are not the best option when dealing with real-life phenomena. To model dynamic systems, we need to collect information from a variety of sources. Such data sets are often uncertain. The modeling of these systems with uncertain data has promoted fuzzy partial differential equations to become one of the main topics of modern mathematical analysis, attracting the attention of many authors [9–14]. In [15], the reduced differential transformation method was successfully applied for solving fuzzy nonlinear partial differential equations under gH-differentiability.

Integral transformations are the first choice of researchers when finding solutions to critical problems. In [16], the Laplace transformation was applied on mathematical models of population growth and decay. Many scholars [17–20] applied different integral transforms (Mahgoub; Aboodh; Elzaki transforms) on important problems in mechanics, physical chemistry and life science for finding their exact solutions.

Mahgub [21] proposed the Sawi transformation and determined the primitives of constant coefficient ordinary linear differential equations. Aggarwal and Gupta [22] presented a relationship between Sawi and other fundamental transforms. Singh and Aggarwal [23] applied Sawi transformation in finding solutions to biological problems of growth and decay.

The fuzzy integral transforms are very useful in solving linear partial differential equations because they convert the original function into a function that is simpler to solve [24–26]. They do not function well in real applications and can only be used for solving fuzzy linear problems.

The objective of the present paper is to propose a stylish combination of the Adomian decomposition method [27,28] and fuzzy Sawi transformation that can solve nonlinear partial fuzzy differential equations. By using fuzzy Sawi transform, equations are reduced to an algebraic equation. Then, the method of Adomian is used to handle the nonlinear parts of the equation for obtaining the solution. The new decomposition method is then called the fuzzy Sawi decomposition method.

In this paper, we consider symmetric fuzzy triangular numbers. From their parametric form, we obtain the parametric form of the fuzzy functions and we establish symmetry between their upper and lower representations. We also observe symmetry in the parametric representation of fuzzy Sawi transform. The symmetry is also preserved in the application of the fuzzy Sawi transformation of the partial derivatives of the fuzzy functions. When applying the fuzzy Sawi decomposition method to solve the nonlinear partial equation, we obtain a symmetry between the lower and upper representations of of the fuzzy solution.

This paper is organized as follows: In Section 2, definitions on a fuzzy number, fuzzy-valued function and gH-Hukuhara differentiability are given. In Section 3, the definition of fuzzy Sawi transform is introduced. Fuzzy Sawi transformation for the fuzzy partial gH-derivative is proposed. In Section 4, the fuzzy Sawi decomposition method is applied to solve nonlinear partial fuzzy differential equations. Section 5 provides a numerical example to demonstrate the proposed method. Finally, Section 6 consists of conclusions.

2. Basic Concepts

In this section, we review some notions and results of fuzzy numbers, fuzzy-number-valued functions and strongly generalized Hukuhara differentiability.

Definition 1 ([29]). *A fuzzy number is a function $u : \mathbb{R} \to [0,1]$ that satisfies the following properties:*

(i) *u is upper semi-continuous on $\mathbb{R}$;*
(ii) *$u(x) = 0$ outside of some interval $[c,d]$;*
(iii) *there are a, $b \in \mathbb{R}$ with $c \leq a \leq b \leq d$ such that u is increasing on $[c,a]$, and decreasing on $[b,d]$ and $u(x) = 1$ for each $x \in [a,b]$;*
(iv) *$u(rx + (1-r)y) \geq \min\{u(x), u(y)\}$ for any $x, y \in \mathbb{R}$, $r \in [0,1]$.*

Denote E^1 the set of all fuzzy numbers. If $a \in \mathbb{R}$, then it can be interpreted as a fuzzy number; $\tilde{a} = \chi_{\{a\}}$ is characteristic function and therefore $\mathbb{R} \subset E^1$.

Definition 2 ([30]). *For $0 < r \leq 1$ and $u \in E^1$, the r-level set of u is the crisp set*

$$[u]^r = \{x \in \mathbb{R} : u(x) \geq r\}.$$

Then, any r-level set is a bounded and closed interval and denoted by $[\underline{u}(r), \overline{u}(r)]$ for all $0 \leq r \leq 1$, where $\underline{u}, \overline{u} : [0,1] \to \mathbb{R}$ are the lower and upper bounds of $[u]^r$, respectively.

Definition 3 ([30]). *A parametric form of fuzzy number u is an ordered pair $u = (\underline{u}(r), \overline{u}(r))$ of functions $\underline{u}(r)$ and $\overline{u}(r)$ for any $0 \leq r \leq 1$, which satisfies the following conditions:*

(i) *The function* $\underline{u}(r)$ *is a bounded left continuous monotonic increasing in* $[0,1]$;
(ii) *The function* $\overline{u}(r)$ *is a bounded left continuous monotonic decreasing in* $[0,1]$;
(iii) $\underline{u}(r) \leq \overline{u}(r)$.

For fuzzy number $u = (\underline{u}(r), \overline{u}(r)), v = (\underline{v}(r), \overline{v}(r))$ and $k \in \mathbb{R}$, the addition and the scalar multiplication are defined by the following:
$[u \oplus v]^r = [u]^r + [v]^r = [\underline{u}(r) + \underline{v}(r), \overline{u}(r) + \overline{v}(r)]$ and

$$[k \odot u]^r = k \cdot [u]^r = \begin{cases} [k\underline{u}(r), k\overline{u}(r)], & k \geq 0 \\ [k\overline{u}(r), k\underline{u}(r)], & k < 0. \end{cases}$$

The neutral element, with respect to $\oplus$ in E^1, is denoted by $\tilde{0} = \chi_{\{0\}}$. For basic algebraic properties of fuzzy numbers, please see ([29]).

We use the Hausdorff metric as a distance between fuzzy numbers.

Definition 4 ([29]). *For arbitrary fuzzy numbers* $u = (\underline{u}(r), \overline{u}(r))$ *and* $v = (\underline{v}(r), \overline{v}(r))$, *the quantity*

$$d(u,v) = \sup_{r \in [0,1]} \max\{|\underline{u}(r) - \underline{v}(r)|, |\overline{u}(r) - \overline{v}(r)|\}$$

is the distance between u and v.

Definition 5 ([31]). *A fuzzy number* $u \in E^1$ *is called to be positive if* $\underline{u}(1) \geq 0$, *strict positive if* $\underline{u}(1) > 0$, *negative if* $\overline{u}(1) \leq 0$ *and strict negative if* $\overline{u}(1) < 0$.

The set of positive (negative) fuzzy numbers is denoted by E^1_+ (E^1_-).

Theorem 1 ([32,33]). *Let u and v be positive fuzzy numbers, then* $w = u \odot v$ *defined by* $w(r) = [\underline{w}(r), \overline{w}(r)]$, *where the following holds:*

$$\underline{w}(r) = \underline{u}(r)\underline{v}(1) + \underline{u}(1)\underline{v}(r) - \underline{u}(1)\underline{v}(1)$$

and

$$\overline{w}(r) = \overline{u}(r)\overline{v}(1) + \overline{u}(1)\overline{v}(r) - \overline{u}(1)\overline{v}(1)$$

for every $r \in [0,1]$ *is a positive fuzzy number.*

Let the set D be domain of fuzzy-valued function w. Define the functions $\underline{w}(.,.,r), \overline{w}(.,.,r) : D \to \mathbb{R}$ for all $0 \leq r \leq 1$. These functions are said to be the left and right $r-$ level functions of the function w.

Definition 6 ([34]). *A fuzzy-valued function* $w : D \to E^1$ *is said to be continuous at* $(s_0, t_0) \in D$ *if for each* $\varepsilon > 0$ *there is* $\delta > 0$ *such that* $d(w(s,t), w(s_0,t_0)) < \varepsilon$ *whenever* $|s - s_0| + |t - t_0| < \delta$. *If w is continuous for each* $(s,t) \in D$, *then we say that w is continuous on D.*

Definition 7 ([35]). *Let* $x,\ y \in E^1$ *and exists* $z \in E^1$, *such that the following holds:*

(i) $x = y \oplus z$
or
(ii) $z = x \oplus (-1) \odot y$.

Then, z is said to be the generalized Hukuhara difference (gH- *difference*) *of fuzzy numbers x and y and is given by* $x \ominus_{gH} y$.

Now consider $x,\ y \in E^1$, then
$x \ominus_{gH} y = z \Leftrightarrow$

(i) $z = (\underline{x}(r) - \underline{y}(r), \overline{x}(r) - \overline{y}(r))$
or
(ii) $z = (\overline{x}(r) - \overline{y}(r), \underline{x}(r) - \underline{y}(r))$.

The following Lemma shows the connection between the gH-difference and the Hausdor distance.

Lemma 1 ([35]). *For all $u, v \in E^1$, we have the following:*

$$d(u,v) = \sup_{r\in[0,1]} \|[u]^r \ominus_{gH} [v]^r\|,$$

where, for an interval $[a,b]$, the norm is $\|[a,b]\| = \max\{|a|,|b|\}$.

Definition 8 ([36]). *Let $w : D \to E^1$ and $(x_0,t) \in D$. We say that w is strongly generalized Hukuhara differentiable on (x_0,t) (gH-differentiable for short) if there exists an element $\frac{\partial w(x_0,t)}{\partial x} \in E^1$ such that the following holds:*

(i) *For all $h > 0$ sufficiently small, the following gH-differences exist:*

$$w(x_0+h,t) \ominus_{gH} w(x_0,t), \;\; w(x_0,t) \ominus_{gH} w(x_0-h,t)$$

and the following limits hold (in the metric d):

$$\lim_{h\to 0} \frac{w(x_0+h,t)\ominus_{gH} w(x_0,t)}{h} = \lim_{h\to 0} \frac{w(x_0,t)\ominus_{gH} w(x_0-h,t)}{h} = \frac{\partial w(x_0,t)}{\partial x}$$

(ii) *For all $h > 0$ sufficiently small, the following gH-differences exist:*

$$w(x_0,t) \ominus_{gH} w(x_0+h,t), \;\; w(x_0-h,t) \ominus_{gH} w(x_0,t),$$

and the following limits hold (in the metric d):

$$\lim_{h\to 0} \frac{w(x_0,t)\ominus_{gH} w(x_0+h,t)}{-h} = \lim_{h\to 0} \frac{w(x_0-h,t)\ominus_{gH} w(x_0,t)}{-h} = \frac{\partial w(x_0,t)}{\partial x}$$

Lemma 2 ([37]). *Let $w : D \to E^1$ be a continuous fuzzy-valued function and $w(x,t) = (\underline{w}(x,t,r), \overline{w}(x,t,r))$ for all $r \in [0,1]$. Then, the following holds:*

(i) *If $w(x,t)$ is (i)-partial differentiable for x (i.e., w is partial differentiable for x under the meaning of Definition 8 (i)), then we have the following:*

$$\frac{\partial w(x,t)}{\partial x} = \left(\frac{\partial \underline{w}(x,t,r)}{\partial x}, \; \frac{\partial \overline{w}(x,t,r)}{\partial x}\right), \tag{1}$$

(ii) *If $w(x,t)$ is (ii)-partial differentiable for x (i.e., w is partial differentiable for x under the meaning of Definition 8 (ii)), then we have the following:*

$$\frac{\partial w(x,t)}{\partial x} = \left(\frac{\partial \overline{w}(x,t,r)}{\partial x}, \; \frac{\partial \underline{w}(x,t,r)}{\partial x}\right). \tag{2}$$

Theorem 2 ([38]). *Let $w : \mathbb{R}_+ \to E^1$ and for all $r \in [0;1]$.*

(i) *The functions $\underline{w}(t,r)$ and $\overline{w}(x,r)$ are Riemann-integrable on $[0,b]$ for every $b \geq 0$.*

(ii) *There are constants $\underline{M}(r) > 0$ and $\overline{M}(r) > 0$ such that the following holds:*

$$\int_0^b |\underline{w}(t,r)|dx \leq \underline{M}(r), \;\; \int_0^b |\overline{w}(t,r)|dx \leq \overline{M}(r),$$

for every $b \geq 0$.

Then, the function $w(t)$ is improper fuzzy Riemann-integrable on $[0,\infty)$ and the following holds:

$$(FR)\int_0^\infty w(t)dt = \left(\int_0^\infty \underline{w}(t,r)dt, \int_0^\infty \overline{w}(t,r)dt\right). \tag{3}$$

3. Fuzzy Sawi Transform

In this part, we give the fuzzy Sawi transform (FST) definition and its inverse. We introduce new results of FST for the fuzzy partial derivative.

Definition 9 ([21,39]). *Let $w : \mathbb{R}_+ \to E^1$ be a continuous fuzzy-valued function and for $\sigma > 0$, the function $\frac{1}{\sigma^2}e^{-\frac{t}{\sigma}} \odot w(t)$ is improper fuzzy Riemann-integrable on $[0,\infty)$. Then, we have the following:*

$$(FR)\int_0^\infty \frac{1}{\sigma^2}e^{-\frac{t}{\sigma}} \odot w(t)dt,$$

which is called FST and is denoted by the following:

$$W(\sigma) = S[w(t)] = (FR)\int_0^\infty \frac{1}{\sigma^2}e^{-\frac{t}{\sigma}} \odot w(t)dt, \tag{4}$$

where the variables σ are used to factor the variable t in the argument of the fuzzy-valued function.

The parametric form of FST is as follows:

$$S[w(t)] = (s[\underline{w}(t,r)], s[\overline{w}(t,r)]), \tag{5}$$

where

$$s[\underline{w}(t,r)] = \frac{1}{\sigma^2}\int_0^\infty e^{-\frac{t}{\sigma}}\underline{w}(t,r)dt, \tag{6}$$

$$s[\overline{w}(t,r)] = \frac{1}{\sigma^2}\int_0^\infty e^{-\frac{t}{\sigma}}\overline{w}(t,r)dt. \tag{7}$$

We can rewrite Equation (4) in the following form:

$$W(\sigma) = S[w(t)] = \frac{1}{\sigma}(FR)\int_0^\infty e^{-t} \odot w(\sigma t)dt. \tag{8}$$

Definition 10 ([21,39]). *The fuzzy inverse Sawi transform can be written as the following formula:*

$$S^{-1}[W(\sigma)] = w(t) = \left(s^{-1}[\underline{W}(\sigma,r)], s^{-1}[\overline{W}(\sigma,r)]\right), \tag{9}$$

where the following holds:

$$s^{-1}[\underline{W}(\sigma,r)] = \frac{1}{2\pi i}\int_{\gamma-i\infty}^{\gamma+i\infty} e^{\frac{t}{\sigma}}\underline{W}(\sigma,r)d\sigma,$$

$$s^{-1}[\overline{W}(\sigma,r)] = \frac{1}{2\pi i}\int_{\gamma-i\infty}^{\gamma+i\infty} e^{\frac{t}{\sigma}}\overline{W}(\sigma,r)d\sigma.$$

For all $r \in [0,1]$ the functions $\underline{W}(\sigma,r)$ and $\overline{W}(\sigma,r)$ must be analytic functions for all σ in the region defined by the inequalities $Re\sigma \geq \gamma$, where γ is the real constant to be chosen suitably.

In [39], classical Sawi transform is applied on some special functions. Some properties generated by Sawi transform are given.

(i) Let $g(t) = 1$ for $t > 0$, then $s[g(t)] = \frac{1}{\sigma}$.
(ii) Let $g(t) = t^n$, where n are positive integers; then, $s[g(t)] = (n!)\sigma^{n-1}$.

We introduce the results of FST for fuzzy partial gH-derivatives.

Theorem 3. *Let $w : \mathbb{R}_+ \times \mathbb{R}_+ \to E^1$ be a continuous fuzzy-valued function. Suppose the functions $\frac{1}{\sigma^2}e^{-\frac{t}{\sigma}} \odot w(x,t)$, $\frac{1}{\sigma^2}e^{-\frac{t}{\sigma}} \odot \frac{\partial^n w(x,t)}{\partial x^n}$ are improper fuzzy Riemann-integrable with respect to t on $[0,\infty)$. Then, we have the following:*

$$S\left[\frac{\partial^n w(x,t)}{\partial x^n}\right] = \frac{\partial^n}{\partial x^n} S[w(x,t)], \tag{10}$$

where $S[w(x,t)]$ denotes the FST of the function w and $n \in \mathbb{N}$.

Proof. Let the function $w(x,t)$ be (i)-differentiable. From (3) and the parametric form of FST (5), we have the following:

$$S\left[\frac{\partial^n w(x,t)}{\partial x^n}\right] = (FR)\int_0^\infty \frac{1}{\sigma^2}e^{-\frac{t}{\sigma}} \odot \frac{\partial^n w(x,t)}{\partial x^n}dt$$

$$= \left(\int_0^\infty \frac{1}{\sigma^2}e^{-\frac{t}{\sigma}}\frac{\partial^n \underline{w}(x,t,r)}{\partial x^n}dt, \int_0^\infty \frac{1}{\sigma^2}e^{-\frac{t}{\sigma}}\frac{\partial^n \overline{w}(x,t,r)}{\partial x^n}dt\right)$$

$$= \frac{\partial^n}{\partial x^n}\left(\int_0^\infty \frac{1}{\sigma^2}e^{-\frac{t}{\sigma}}\underline{w}(x,t,r)dt, \int_0^\infty \frac{1}{\sigma^2}e^{-\frac{t}{\sigma}}\overline{w}(x,t,r)dt\right) = \frac{\partial^n}{\partial x^n}S[w(x,t)].$$

□

Theorem 4. *Let $w : \mathbb{R}_+ \times \mathbb{R}_+ \to E^1$ be a fuzzy-valued function. The functions $\frac{1}{\sigma^2}e^{-\frac{t}{\sigma}} \odot w(x,t)$, $\frac{1}{\sigma^2}e^{-\frac{t}{\sigma}} \odot \frac{\partial^n w(x,t)}{\partial t^n}$ are improper fuzzy Riemann-integrable with respect to t on $[0,\infty)$. For all $t > 0$ and $n \in \mathbb{N}$, there exist continuous partial gH-derivatives to the $(n-1)-th$ order with respect to t, and there exists $\frac{\partial^n w(x,t)}{\partial t^n}$.*

1. If the function $w(x,t)$ is (i)-differentiable, then the following holds:

$$S\left[\frac{\partial^n w(x,t)}{\partial t^n}\right] = \left(s\left[\frac{\partial^n \underline{w}(x,t,r)}{\partial t^n}\right], s\left[\frac{\partial^n \overline{w}(x,t,r)}{\partial t^n}\right]\right),$$

where

$$s\left[\frac{\partial^n \underline{w}(x,t,r)}{\partial t^n}\right] = \frac{1}{\sigma^n}s[\underline{w}(x,t,r)] - \sum_{j=0}^{n-1}\frac{1}{\sigma^{n-j+1}}\frac{\partial^j \underline{w}(x,0,r)}{\partial t^j}, \tag{11}$$

$$s\left[\frac{\partial^n \overline{w}(x,t,r)}{\partial t^n}\right] = \frac{1}{\sigma^n}s[\overline{w}(x,t,r)] - \sum_{j=0}^{n-1}\frac{1}{\sigma^{n-j+1}}\frac{\partial^j \overline{w}(x,0,r)}{\partial t^j}. \tag{12}$$

2. If the function $w(x,t)$ is (ii)-differentiable then we have the following:

2.1 If $n = 2k - 1$, $k = 1, 2, \dots$

$$S\left[\frac{\partial^{2k-1}w(x,t)}{\partial t^{2k-1}}\right] = \left(s\left[\frac{\partial^{2k-1}\overline{w}(x,t,r)}{\partial t^{2k-1}}\right], s\left[\frac{\partial^{2k-1}\underline{w}(x,t,r)}{\partial t^{2k-1}}\right]\right),$$

where

$$\begin{aligned} s\left[\frac{\partial^{2k-1}\overline{w}(x,t,r)}{\partial t^{2k-1}}\right] &= \frac{1}{\sigma^{2k-1}}s[\underline{w}(x,t,r)] - \sum_{j=0}^{k-1}\frac{1}{\sigma^{2(k-j)}}\frac{\partial^{2j}\underline{w}(x,0,r)}{\partial t^{2j}} \\ &- \sum_{j=0}^{k-2}\frac{1}{\sigma^{2(k-j)-1}}\frac{\partial^{2j+1}\overline{w}(x,0,r)}{\partial t^{2j+1}}, \end{aligned} \quad (13)$$

$$\begin{aligned} s\left[\frac{\partial^{2k-1}\underline{w}(x,t,r)}{\partial t^{2k-1}}\right] &= \frac{1}{\sigma^{2k-1}}s[\overline{w}(x,t,r)] - \sum_{j=0}^{k-1}\frac{1}{\sigma^{2(k-j)}}\frac{\partial^{2j}\overline{w}(x,0,r)}{\partial t^{2j}} \\ &- \sum_{j=0}^{k-2}\frac{1}{\sigma^{2(k-j)-1}}\frac{\partial^{2j+1}\underline{w}(x,0,r)}{\partial t^{2j+1}}. \end{aligned} \quad (14)$$

2.2 If $n = 2k$, $k = 1, 2, \dots$

$$S\left[\frac{\partial^{2k}w(x,t)}{\partial t^{2k}}\right] = \left(s\left[\frac{\partial^{2k}\underline{w}(x,t,r)}{\partial t^{2k}}\right], s\left[\frac{\partial^{2k}\overline{w}(x,t,r)}{\partial t^{2k}}\right]\right),$$

where

$$\begin{aligned} s\left[\frac{\partial^{2k}\underline{w}(x,t,r)}{\partial t^{2k}}\right] &= \frac{1}{\sigma^{2k}}s[\underline{w}(x,t,r)] - \sum_{j=0}^{k-1}\frac{1}{\sigma^{2(k-j)+1}}\frac{\partial^{2j}\underline{w}(x,0,r)}{\partial t^{2j}} \\ &- \sum_{j=0}^{k-1}\frac{1}{\sigma^{2(k-j)}}\frac{\partial^{2j+1}\overline{w}(x,0,r)}{\partial t^{2j+1}}, \end{aligned} \quad (15)$$

$$\begin{aligned} s\left[\frac{\partial^{2k}\overline{w}(x,t,r)}{\partial t^{2k}}\right] &= \frac{1}{\sigma^{2k}}s[\overline{w}(x,t,r)] - \sum_{j=0}^{k-1}\frac{1}{\sigma^{2(k-j)+1}}\frac{\partial^{2j}\overline{w}(x,0,r)}{\partial t^{2j}} - \\ &- \sum_{j=0}^{k-1}\frac{1}{\sigma^{2(k-j)}}\frac{\partial^{2j+1}\underline{w}(x,0,r)}{\partial t^{2j+1}}. \end{aligned} \quad (16)$$

Proof. Let the function $w(x,t)$ be (i)-differentiable. By induction, we prove Equation (11). For $n = 1$, from condition (5), we have the following:

$$S[w'_t(x,t)] = (s[\underline{w}'_t(x,t,r)],\ s[\overline{w}'_t(x,t,r)]).$$

By using integration by parts on t, we obtain the following:

$$s[\underline{w}'_t(x,t,r)] = \int_0^\infty \frac{1}{\sigma^2}e^{-\frac{t}{\sigma}}\underline{w}'_t(x,t,r)dt = \frac{1}{\sigma}s[\underline{w}(x,t,r)] - \frac{1}{\sigma^2}\underline{w}(x,0,r).$$

Let for $n = k$ the Equation (11) holds. Hence, for $n = k+1$ we obtain the following:

$$\begin{aligned} s\left[\frac{\partial^{k+1}\underline{w}(x,t,r)}{\partial t^{k+1}}\right] &= \frac{1}{\sigma}s\left[\frac{\partial^{k}\underline{w}(x,t,r)}{\partial t^{k}}\right] - \frac{1}{\sigma^2}\frac{\partial^{k}\underline{w}(x,0,r)}{\partial t^{k}} \\ &= \frac{1}{\sigma^{k+1}}s[\underline{w}(x,t,r)] - \sum_{j=0}^{k-1}\left(\frac{1}{\sigma}\right)^{k-j+2}\frac{\partial^{j}\underline{w}(x,0,r)}{\partial t^{j}} - \frac{1}{\sigma^2}\frac{\partial^{k}\underline{w}(x,0,r)}{\partial t^{k}} \\ &= \frac{1}{\sigma^{k+1}}s[\underline{w}(x,t,r)] - \sum_{j=0}^{k}\left(\frac{1}{\sigma}\right)^{k-j+2}\frac{\partial^{j}\underline{w}(x,0,r)}{\partial t^{j}}. \end{aligned}$$

Let the function $w(x,t)$ be (ii)-differentiable and $n = 2k$. Then, for $n = 2$, we obtain the following:

$$S\left[\frac{\partial^2 w(x,t)}{\partial t^2}\right] = \left(s\left[\frac{\partial^2 \underline{w}(x,t,r)}{\partial t^2}\right], s\left[\frac{\partial^2 \overline{w}(x,t,r)}{\partial t^2}\right]\right).$$

By using integration by parts on t we obtain the following:

$$s\left[\frac{\partial^2 \underline{w}(x,t,r)}{\partial t^2}\right] = \frac{1}{\sigma^2}\int_0^\infty e^{-\frac{t}{\sigma}} \frac{\partial^2 \underline{w}(x,t,r)}{\partial t^2}dt$$
$$= -\frac{1}{\sigma^2}\frac{\partial \overline{w}(x,0,r)}{\partial t} + \frac{1}{\sigma^3}\int_0^\infty e^{-\frac{t}{\sigma}} \frac{\partial \overline{w}(x,t,r)}{\partial t}dt = -\frac{1}{\sigma^2}\frac{\partial \overline{w}(x,0,r)}{\partial t} + \frac{1}{\sigma^3}\int_0^\infty e^{-\frac{t}{\sigma}} d\underline{w}(x,t,r)$$
$$= -\frac{1}{\sigma^2}\frac{\partial \overline{w}(x,0,r)}{\partial t} - \frac{1}{\sigma^3}\underline{w}(x,0,r) + \frac{1}{\sigma^4}\int_0^\infty e^{-\frac{t}{\sigma}} \underline{w}(x,t,r)dt$$
$$= \frac{1}{\sigma^2}s[\underline{w}(x,t,r)] - \frac{1}{\sigma^3}\underline{w}(x,0,r) - \frac{1}{\sigma^2}\frac{\partial \overline{w}(x,0,r)}{\partial t}.$$

Let, for $n = 2k$, Equation (15) hold. Hence, for $n = 2k+2$ we have the following:

$$S\left[\frac{\partial^{2k+2} w(x,t)}{\partial t^{2k+2}}\right] = \left(s\left[\frac{\partial^{2k+2} \underline{w}(x,t,r)}{\partial t^{2k+2}}\right], s\left[\frac{\partial^{2k+2} \overline{w}(x,t,r)}{\partial t^{2k+2}}\right]\right).$$

By using integration by parts on t, we obtain the following:

$$s\left[\frac{\partial^{2k+2} \underline{w}(x,t,r)}{\partial t^{2k+2}}\right] = \frac{1}{\sigma^2}\int_0^\infty e^{-\frac{t}{\sigma}} \frac{\partial^{2k+2} \underline{w}(x,t,r)}{\partial t^{2k+2}}dt$$
$$= -\frac{1}{\sigma^2}\frac{\partial^{2k+1} \overline{w}(x,0,r)}{\partial t^{2k+1}} + \frac{1}{\sigma^3}\int_0^\infty e^{-\frac{t}{\sigma}} \frac{\partial^{2k+1} \overline{w}(x,t,r)}{\partial t^{2k+1}}dt$$
$$= -\frac{1}{\sigma^2}\frac{\partial^{2k+1} \overline{w}(x,0,r)}{\partial t^{2k+1}} - \frac{1}{\sigma^3}\frac{\partial^{2k} \underline{w}(x,0,r)}{\partial t^{2k}} + \frac{1}{\sigma^2}\frac{1}{\sigma^2}\int_0^\infty e^{-\frac{t}{\sigma}} \frac{\partial^{2k} \underline{w}(x,t,r)}{\partial t^{2k}}dt$$
$$= -\frac{1}{\sigma^2}\frac{\partial^{2k+1} \overline{w}(x,0,r)}{\partial t^{2k+1}} - \frac{1}{\sigma^3}\frac{\partial^{2k} \underline{w}(x,0,r)}{\partial t^{2k}} + \frac{1}{\sigma^2}s\left[\frac{\partial^{2k} \underline{w}(x,t,r)}{\partial t^{2k}}\right]$$
$$= \frac{1}{\sigma^{2k+2}}s[\underline{w}(x,t,r)] - \sum_{j=0}^{k} \frac{1}{\sigma^{2(k+1-j)+1}}\frac{\partial^{2j} \underline{w}(x,0,r)}{\partial t^{2j}} - \sum_{j=0}^{k} \frac{1}{\sigma^{2(k+1-j)}}\frac{\partial^{2j+1} \overline{w}(x,0,r)}{\partial t^{2j+1}}.$$

□

4. Sawi Decomposition Method for Solving NPFDE

In this section, we apply the combined form of FSM and the Adomian decomposition method for solving NPFDE. This equation is defined as follows:

$$\sum_{i=1}^{m} a_i \odot \frac{\partial^i w(x,t)}{\partial x^i} \oplus \sum_{j=0}^{l} b_j \odot \frac{\partial^j w(x,t)}{\partial t^j} \oplus \sum_{k=0}^{2}\sum_{p=k}^{2} c_{kp} \odot \frac{\partial^k w(x,t)}{\partial x^k} \odot \frac{\partial^p w(x,t)}{\partial x^p} = g(x,t), \quad (17)$$

with initial conditions

$$\frac{\partial^j w(x,0)}{\partial t^j} = \psi_j(x), \ \ j = 0,1,...,l-1, \quad (18)$$

where $g,\ w : [0,b] \times [0,d] \rightarrow E^1$, $\psi_j : [0,b] \rightarrow E^1$ are continuous fuzzy functions, and a_i, $i = 1,2,...,m$, b_j, $j = 1,2,...,l$, c_{kp}, $k = 0,1,2$, $p = 0,1,2$, are positive constants.

Applying the fuzzy Sawi transform to both sides of Equation (17) gives the following:

$$\sum_{i=1}^{m} a_i \odot S\left[\frac{\partial^i w(x,t)}{\partial x^i}\right] \oplus \sum_{j=0}^{l} b_j \odot S\left[\frac{\partial^j w(x,t)}{\partial t^j}\right] \oplus \sum_{k=0}^{2}\sum_{p=k}^{2} c_{kp} \odot S\left[\frac{\partial^k w(x,t)}{\partial x^k} \odot \frac{\partial^p w(x,t)}{\partial x^p}\right]$$
$$= S[g(x,t)]. \quad (19)$$

Let $\frac{\partial^k w}{\partial x^k}$, $k = 0, 1, 2$ be positive fuzzy-valued functions. Then, the parametric form of Equation (19) is as follows:

$$\sum_{i=1}^{m} a_i s\left[\frac{\partial^i \underline{w}(x,t,r)}{\partial x^i}\right] + \sum_{j=0}^{l} b_j s\left[\frac{\partial^j \underline{w}(x,t,r)}{\partial t^j}\right] + \sum_{k=0}^{2}\sum_{p=k}^{2} c_{kp} s\left[\frac{\partial^k \underline{w}(x,t,r)}{\partial x^k}\frac{\partial^p \underline{w}(x,t,r)}{\partial x^p}\right] = s\left[\underline{g}(x,t,r)\right], \quad (20)$$

and

$$\sum_{i=1}^{m} a_i s\left[\frac{\partial^i \overline{w}(x,t,r)}{\partial x^i}\right] + \sum_{j=0}^{l} b_j s\left[\frac{\partial^j \overline{w}(x,t,r)}{\partial t^j}\right] + \sum_{k=0}^{2}\sum_{p=k}^{2} c_{kp} s\left[\frac{\partial^k \overline{w}(x,t,r)}{\partial x^k}\frac{\partial^p \overline{w}(x,t,r)}{\partial x^p}\right] = s[\overline{g}(x,t,r)]. \quad (21)$$

Case 1. Let the function $w(x,t)$ be (i)-partial differentiable of the m-th order with respect to x and l-th order with respect to t.

We consider Equation (20). Then, from (10) and (11) and initial conditions, we have the following:

$$\sum_{j=0}^{l} \frac{b_j}{\sigma^j} s[\underline{w}(x,t,r)] = s\left[\underline{g}(x,t,r)\right] + \sum_{j=1}^{l}\sum_{v=0}^{j-1} \frac{b_j}{\sigma^{j-v+1}} \underline{\psi}_v(x,r) - \sum_{i=1}^{m} a_i s\left[\frac{\partial^i \underline{w}(x,t,r)}{\partial x^i}\right] - \sum_{k=0}^{2}\sum_{p=k}^{2} c_{kp} s\left[\frac{\partial^k \underline{w}(x,t,r)}{\partial x^k}\frac{\partial^p \underline{w}(x,t,r)}{\partial x^p}\right],$$

Then

$$s[\underline{w}(x,t,r)] = \left(\sum_{j=0}^{l} \frac{b_j}{\sigma^j}\right)^{-1}\left(s\left[\underline{g}(x,t,r)\right] + \sum_{j=1}^{l}\sum_{v=0}^{j-1} \frac{b_j}{\sigma^{j-v+1}} \underline{\psi}_v(x,r)\right) - \left(\sum_{j=0}^{l} \frac{b_j}{\sigma^j}\right)^{-1}\left(\sum_{i=1}^{m} a_i s\left[\frac{\partial^i \underline{w}(x,t,r)}{\partial x^i}\right] + \sum_{k=0}^{2}\sum_{p=k}^{2} c_{kp} s\left[\frac{\partial^k \underline{w}(x,t,r)}{\partial x^k}\frac{\partial^p \underline{w}(x,t,r)}{\partial x^p}\right]\right).$$

Applying the inverse fuzzy Sawi transform to both sides of the equation, we obtain the following:

$$\underline{w}(x,t,r) = s^{-1}\left[\left(\sum_{j=0}^{l} \frac{b_j}{\sigma^j}\right)^{-1}\left(s\left[\underline{g}(x,t,r)\right] + \sum_{j=1}^{l}\sum_{v=0}^{j-1} \frac{b_j}{\sigma^{j-v+1}} \underline{\psi}_v(x,r)\right)\right] - s^{-1}\left[\left(\sum_{j=0}^{l} \frac{b_j}{\sigma^j}\right)^{-1}\left(\sum_{i=1}^{m} a_i s\left[\frac{\partial^i \underline{w}(x,t,r)}{\partial x^i}\right] + \sum_{k=0}^{2}\sum_{p=k}^{2} c_{kp} s\left[\frac{\partial^k \underline{w}(x,t,r)}{\partial x^k}\frac{\partial^p \underline{w}(x,t,r)}{\partial x^p}\right]\right)\right]. \quad (22)$$

Now, apply the Adomain decomposition method (ADM). This method assume an infinite series solution for the following unknowns function:

$$\underline{w}(x,t,r) = \sum_{n=0}^{\infty} \underline{w}_n(x,t,r). \quad (23)$$

The nonlinear terms is represented by an infinite series of the Adomian polynomials $\underline{A}_n^{kp}$ $n \geq 0, k = 0, 1, 2, p = 0, 1, 2$ in the following form:

$$\frac{\partial^k \underline{w}(x,t,r)}{\partial x^k}\frac{\partial^p \underline{w}(x,t,r)}{\partial x^p} = \sum_{n=0}^{\infty} \underline{A}_n^{kp}, \quad (24)$$

where

$$\underline{A}_0^{kp} = \frac{\partial^k \underline{w}_0}{\partial x^k}\frac{\partial^p \underline{w}_0}{\partial x^p},$$
$$\underline{A}_1^{kp} = \frac{\partial^k \underline{w}_0}{\partial x^k}\frac{\partial^p \underline{w}_1}{\partial x^p} + \frac{\partial^k \underline{w}_1}{\partial x^k}\frac{\partial^p \underline{w}_0}{\partial x^p},$$
$$\underline{A}_2^{kp} = \frac{\partial^k \underline{w}_0}{\partial x^k}\frac{\partial^p \underline{w}_2}{\partial x^p} + \frac{\partial^k \underline{w}_1}{\partial x^k}\frac{\partial^p \underline{w}_1}{\partial x^p} + \frac{\partial^k \underline{w}_2}{\partial x^k}\frac{\partial^p \underline{w}_0}{\partial x^p},$$
$$\cdots\cdots\cdots$$

Substituting (23), (24) into (22) leads to the following:

$$\sum_{n=0}^{\infty} \underline{w}_n(x,t,r) = s^{-1}\left[\left(\sum_{j=0}^{l}\frac{b_j}{\sigma^j}\right)^{-1}\left(s\left[\underline{g}(x,t,r)\right] + \sum_{j=1}^{l}\sum_{v=0}^{j-1}\frac{b_j}{\sigma^{j-v+1}}\underline{\psi}_v(x,r)\right)\right]$$
$$-s^{-1}\left[\left(\sum_{j=0}^{l}\frac{b_j}{\sigma^j}\right)^{-1}\left(\sum_{i=1}^{m} a_i s\left[\sum_{n=0}^{\infty}\frac{\partial^i \underline{w}_n(x,t,r)}{\partial x^i}\right] - \sum_{k=0}^{2}\sum_{p=k}^{2} c_{kp} s\left[\sum_{n=0}^{\infty}\underline{A}_n^{kp}\right]\right)\right].$$

The Adomian decomposition method presents for $n \geq 0$ the recursive relation as follows:

$$\begin{aligned} \underline{w}_0(x,t,r) &= s^{-1}\left[\left(\sum_{j=0}^{l}\frac{b_j}{\sigma^j}\right)^{-1}\left(s\left[\underline{g}(x,t,r)\right] + \sum_{j=1}^{l}\sum_{v=0}^{j-1}\frac{b_j}{\sigma^{j-v+1}}\underline{\psi}_v(x,r)\right)\right], \\ \underline{w}_{n+1}(x,t,r) &= -s^{-1}\left[\left(\sum_{j=0}^{l}\frac{b_j}{\sigma^j}\right)^{-1}\left(\sum_{i=1}^{m} a_i s\left[\frac{\partial^i \underline{w}_n(x,t,r)}{\partial x^i}\right] - \sum_{k=0}^{2}\sum_{p=k}^{2} c_{kp} s\left[\underline{A}_n^{kp}\right]\right)\right]. \end{aligned} \tag{25}$$

Case 2. Let function $w(x,t)$ be (i)-partial differentiable of the m-th order with respect to x and (ii)-partial differentiable of the $l = 2q$-th order with respect to t. Then, the parametric form of Equation (19) is the following:

$$\sum_{i=1}^{m} a_i s\left[\frac{\partial^i \underline{w}(x,t,r)}{\partial x^i}\right] + \sum_{j=0}^{q} b_{2j} s\left[\frac{\partial^{2j}\underline{w}(x,t,r)}{\partial t^{2j}}\right] + \sum_{j=1}^{q} b_{2j-1} s\left[\frac{\partial^{2j-1}\underline{w}(x,t,r)}{\partial t^{2j-1}}\right]$$
$$+\sum_{k=0}^{2}\sum_{p=k}^{2} c_{kp} s\left[\frac{\partial^k \underline{w}(x,t,r)}{\partial x^k}\frac{\partial^p \underline{w}(x,t,r)}{\partial x^p}\right] = s\left[\underline{g}(x,t,r)\right],$$

$$\sum_{i=1}^{m} a_i s\left[\frac{\partial^i \overline{w}(x,t,r)}{\partial x^i}\right] + \sum_{j=0}^{q} b_{2j} s\left[\frac{\partial^{2j}\overline{w}(x,t,r)}{\partial t^{2j}}\right] + \sum_{j=1}^{q} b_{2j-1} s\left[\frac{\partial^{2j-1}\overline{w}(x,t,r)}{\partial t^{2j-1}}\right]t$$
$$+\sum_{k=0}^{2}\sum_{p=k}^{2} c_{kp} s\left[\frac{\partial^k \overline{w}(x,t,r)}{\partial x^k}\frac{\partial^p \overline{w}(x,t,r)}{\partial x^p}\right] = s[\overline{g}(x,t,r)]$$

Applying Theorem 4 and initial conditions, we obtain the following system:

$$\begin{aligned} &As[\underline{w}(x,t,r)] + Bs[\overline{w}(x,t,r)] = s\left[\underline{g}(x,t,r)\right] + F(x,\sigma,r) \\ &-\sum_{i=1}^{m} a_i s\left[\frac{\partial^i \underline{w}(x,t,r)}{\partial x^i}\right] - \sum_{k=0}^{2}\sum_{p=k}^{2} c_{kp} s\left[\frac{\partial^k \underline{w}(x,t,r)}{\partial x^k}\frac{\partial^p \underline{w}(x,t,r)}{\partial x^p}\right] \end{aligned} \tag{26}$$

$$\begin{aligned} &As[\overline{w}(x,t,r)] + Bs[\underline{w}(x,t,r)] = s\left[\underline{g}(x,t,r)\right] + G(x,\sigma,r) \\ &-\sum_{i=1}^{m} a_i s\left[\frac{\partial^i \overline{w}(x,t,r)}{\partial x^i}\right] - \sum_{k=0}^{2}\sum_{p=k}^{2} c_{kp} s\left[\frac{\partial^k \overline{w}(x,t,r)}{\partial x^k}\frac{\partial^p \overline{w}(x,t,r)}{\partial x^p}\right], \end{aligned} \tag{27}$$

where

$$A = \sum_{j=0}^{q}\frac{b_{2j}}{\sigma^{2j}},\quad B = \sum_{j=1}^{q}\frac{b_{2j-1}}{\sigma^{2j-1}},$$

$$F(x,\sigma,r) = \sum_{j=0}^{q} b_{2j}\left(\sum_{v=0}^{j-1}\frac{1}{\sigma^{2(j-v)+1}}\underline{\psi}_{2v}(x,r) + \sum_{v=0}^{j-1}\frac{1}{\sigma^{2(j-v)}}\overline{\psi}_{2v+1}(x,r)\right)$$
$$+\sum_{j=1}^{q} b_{2j-1}\left(\sum_{v=0}^{j-1}\frac{1}{\sigma^{2(j-v)}}\overline{\psi}_{2v}(x,r) + \sum_{v=0}^{j-2}\frac{1}{\sigma^{2(j-v)-1}}\underline{\psi}_{2v+1}(x,r)\right),$$

$$G(x,\sigma,r) = \sum_{j=0}^{q} b_{2j}\left(\sum_{v=0}^{j-1} \frac{1}{\sigma^{2(j-v)+1}}\overline{\psi}_{2v}(x,r) + \sum_{v=0}^{j-1} \frac{1}{\sigma^{2(j-v)}}\underline{\psi}_{2v+1}(x,r)\right) + \sum_{j=1}^{q} b_{2j-1}\left(\sum_{v=0}^{j-1} \frac{1}{\sigma^{2(j-v)}}\underline{\psi}_{2v}(x,r) + \sum_{v=0}^{j-2} \frac{1}{\sigma^{2(j-v)-1}}\overline{\psi}_{2v+1}(x,r)\right),$$

From this system, we find $s[\underline{w}(x,t,r)]$ and $s[\overline{w}(x,t,r)]$. Analogous to Case 1, we obtain $w(x,t) = (\underline{w}(x,t,r), \overline{w}(x,t,r)$.

The Sawi decomposition method is illustrated by discussing the following example.

5. Examples

In this section, we consider the following partial fuzzy differential equation:

$$w''_{tt}(x,t) \oplus w'_x(x,t) \odot w''_{xx}(x,t) = g(x,t), \quad x \geq 0, \quad t \geq 0,$$

with initial conditions

$$w(x,0) = \left(\frac{x^2}{2}r, \frac{x^2}{2}(2-r)\right), \quad w'_t(x,0) = (0,0), \quad x > 0$$

and

$$g(x,t) = \left(r + xr^2, 2 - r + x(2-r)^2\right).$$

In this case, $b_2 = 1, c_{12} = 1, \psi_0(x) = \left(\frac{x^2}{2}r, \frac{x^2}{2}(2-r)\right)$ and $\psi_1(x) = (0,0)$.

Assume that the function $w(x,t)$ is (i)-differentiable of the 2-th order with respect to x.

Case 1. If $w(x,t)$ is (i)-differentiable of the 2-th order with respect to t, using the recursive relation (25) we obtain the following:

$$\underline{w}_0(x,t,r) = s^{-1}\left[\sigma^2 s\left[\underline{g}(x,t,r)\right]\right] + s^{-1}\left[\frac{1}{\sigma}\underline{\psi}_0(x,r)\right],$$

$$\underline{w}_{n+1}(x,t,r) = -s^{-1}\left[\sigma^2 s\left[\underline{A}_n^{12}\right]\right], \quad n \geq 0,$$

where

$$\underline{A}_0^{12} = \underline{w}'_{0x}\underline{w}''_{0xx}, \quad \underline{A}_1^{12} = \underline{w}'_{0x}\underline{w}''_{1xx} + \underline{w}'_{1x}\underline{w}''_{0xx}, \quad \underline{A}_2^{12} = \underline{w}'_{0x}\underline{w}''_{2xx} + \underline{w}'_{1x}\underline{w}''_{1xx} + \underline{w}'_{2x}\underline{w}''_{0xx}, \ldots \tag{28}$$

Then,

$$\underline{w}_0(x,t,r) = \frac{t^2}{2}r + \frac{xt^2}{2}r^2 + \frac{x^2}{2}r, \quad \underline{w}_1(x,t,r) = -\frac{t^4}{4!}r^3 - \frac{xt^2}{2}r^2,$$

$$\underline{w}_2(x,t,r) = \frac{t^4}{4!}r^3, \quad \underline{w}_3(x,t,r) = 0, \ldots$$

Analogously, we obtain the following:

$$\overline{w}_0(x,t,r) = \frac{t^2}{2}(2-r) + \frac{xt^2}{2}(2-r)^2 + \frac{x^2}{2}(2-r), \quad \overline{w}_1(x,t,r) = -\frac{t^4}{4!}(2-r)^3 - \frac{xt^2}{2}(2-r)^2,$$

$$\overline{w}_2(x,t,r) = \frac{t^4}{4!}(2-r)^3, \quad \underline{w}_3(x,t,r) = 0, \ldots$$

The series solution is, therefore, given by the following:

$$w(x,t) = \left(\left(\frac{x^2}{2} + \frac{t^2}{2}\right)r, \left(\frac{x^2}{2} + \frac{t^2}{2}\right)(2-r)\right).$$

Case 2. If $w(x,t)$ is (ii)-differentiable of the 2-th order with respect to t, using Equations (26) and (27), we obtain the following:

$$\frac{1}{\sigma^2}s(\underline{w}(x,t,r)) = s(g(x,t,r)) + \frac{1}{\sigma^3}\underline{\psi_0}(x,r) - s\left[\frac{\partial^k \underline{w}(x,t,r)}{\partial x^k}\frac{\partial^p \underline{w}(x,t,r)}{\partial x^p}\right], \quad (29)$$

$$\frac{1}{\sigma^2}s(\overline{w}(x,t,r)) = s(g(x,t,r)) + \frac{1}{\sigma^3}\overline{\psi_0}(x,r) - s\left[\frac{\partial^k \overline{w}(x,t,r)}{\partial x^k}\frac{\partial^p \overline{w}(x,t,r)}{\partial x^p}\right] \quad (30)$$

From (29), we have the following:

$$s(\underline{w}(x,t,r)) = \sigma^2 s(g(x,t,r)) + \frac{1}{\sigma}\underline{\psi_0}(x,r) - \sigma^2 s\left[\frac{\partial^k \underline{w}(x,t,r)}{\partial x^k}\frac{\partial^p \underline{w}(x,t,r)}{\partial x^p}\right].$$

Applying the inverse fuzzy Sawi transform to both sides of the equation and by applying Adomian decomposition method, we obtain the following recursive relation:

$$\underline{w}_0(x,t,r) = s^{-1}\left[\sigma^2 s\left[\underline{g}(x,t,r)\right]\right] + s^{-1}\left[\frac{1}{\sigma}\underline{\psi}_0(x,r)\right],$$

$$\underline{w}_{n+1}(x,t,r) = -s^{-1}\left[\sigma^2 s\left[\underline{A}_n^{12}\right]\right], \quad n \geq 0,$$

Hence, this case equivalent to Case 1.

Case 3. If $w(x,t)$ is (i)-differentiable and $w'_t(x,t)$ is (ii)-differentiable with respect to t, then $S(w'_t(x,t)) = (s(\underline{w}'_t(x,t,r)), s(\overline{w}'_t(x,t,r)))$, $S(w''_{tt}(x,t)) = (s(\overline{w}''_{tt}(x,t,r)), s(\underline{w}''_{tt}(x,t,r)))$.

Using (15) and (16) of Theorem 4 and the initial condition, we obtain the following recursive relation:

$$\underline{w}_0(x,t,r) = s^{-1}\left[\sigma^2 s[\overline{g}(x,t,r)]\right] + s^{-1}\left[\frac{1}{\sigma}\underline{\psi}_0(x,r)\right],$$

$$\underline{w}_{n+1}(x,t,r) = -s^{-1}\left[\sigma^2 s\left[\overline{A}_n^{12}\right]\right], \quad n \geq 0,$$

$$\overline{w}_0(x,t,r) = s^{-1}\left[\sigma^2 s\left[\underline{g}(x,t,r)\right]\right] + s^{-1}\left[\frac{1}{\sigma}\overline{\psi}_0(x,r)\right],$$

$$\overline{w}_{n+1}(x,t,r) = -s^{-1}\left[\sigma^2 s\left[\underline{A}_n^{12}\right]\right], \quad n \geq 0,$$

where

$$\underline{A}_0^{12} = \underline{w}'_{0x}\underline{w}''_{0xx}, \quad \underline{A}_1^{12} = \underline{w}'_{0x}\underline{w}''_{1xx} + \underline{w}'_{1x}\underline{w}''_{0xx},$$
$$\underline{A}_2^{12} = \underline{w}'_{0x}\underline{w}''_{2xx} + \underline{w}'_{1x}\underline{w}''_{1xx} + \underline{w}'_{2x}\underline{w}''_{0xx}, \ldots$$

$$\overline{A}_0^{12} = \overline{w}'_{0x}\overline{w}''_{0xx}, \overline{A}_1^{12} = \overline{w}'_{0x}\overline{w}''_{1xx} + \overline{w}'_{1x}\overline{w}''_{0xx},$$
$$\overline{A}_2^{12} = \overline{w}'_{0x}\overline{w}''_{2xx} + \overline{w}'_{1x}\overline{w}''_{1xx} + \overline{w}'_{2x}\overline{w}''_{0xx}, \ldots$$

Then,

$$\underline{w}_0(x,t,r) = \frac{t^2}{2}(2-r) + \frac{xt^2}{2}(2-r)^2 + \frac{x^2}{2}r, \quad \underline{w}_1(x,t,r) = -\frac{t^4}{4!}r^2(2-r) - \frac{xt^2}{2}(2-r)^2,$$

$$\underline{w}_2(x,t,r) = \frac{t^4}{4!}r^2(2-r), \underline{w}_3(x,t,r) = 0, \ldots$$

The series solution is, therefore, given by the following:

$$w(x,t,r) = \left(\frac{x^2}{2}r + \frac{t^2}{2}(2-r), \frac{x^2}{2}(2-r) + \frac{t^2}{2}r\right).$$

6. Conclusions and Future Work

The main idea of this work is to provide a simple method for solving the nonlinear partial fuzzy differential equations under gH-differentiability. A combined form of the fuzzy Sawi transformation method and Adomian decomposition method for these equations is applied. New results on fuzzy Sawi transform for fuzzy partial gH-derivatives are proposed. The main advantage of this method is the fact that it provides an analytical solution. Finally, an example to illustrate the proposed method is solved. The results reveal that the method is a powerful and efficient technique for solving nonlinear partial fuzzy differential equations.

For future research, we will apply the fuzzy Sawi decomposition method to fuzzy nonlinear integro-differential equations under generalized Hukuhara differentiability and the fuzzy nonlinear Fitzhugh–Nagumo–Huxley equation, which is an important model in the work of neuron axons [40]. Additionally, one can discuss the application of this method to more complex problems, such as the eigenproblem [41] and maximum likelihood estimation [42].

Author Contributions: Conceptualization, A.G., A.P.; methodology, A.G., A.P.; validation, A.G., A.P.; formal analysis, A.G., A.P.; writing—original draft preparation, A.G., A.P.; writing—review and editing A.G., A.P. All authors have read and agreed to the published version of the manuscript.

Funding: This research received no external funding.

Institutional Review Board Statement: Not applicable.

Informed Consent Statement: Not applicable.

Data Availability Statement: Not applicable.

Conflicts of Interest: The authors declare no conflict of interest.

References

1. Elwakil, S.A.; El-labany, S.K.; Zahran, M.A.; Sabry, R. Modified extended tanh-function method for solving nonlinear partial differential equations. *Phys. Lett.* **2002**, *299*, 179–188. [CrossRef]
2. Vasilyev, O.V.; Bowman, C. Second generation Wavelet collocation method for the solution of partial differential equations. *J. Comput. Phys.* **2000**, *165*, 660–693. [CrossRef]
3. Chen, C.K.; Ho, S.H. Solving partial differential equations by two-dimensional differential transform method. *Appl. Math. Comput.* **1999**, *106*, 171–179.
4. Gündoğdu, H.; Ömer Gözükızıl, F. Solving nonlinear partial differential equations by using Adomian decomposition method, modified decomposition method and Laplace decomposition method. *MANAS J. Eng.* **2017**, *5*, 1–13.
5. Radi, D.; Sorini L.; Stefanini, L. On the numerical solution of ordinary, interval and fuzzy differential equations by use of F-transform. *Axioms* **2020**, *9*, 15. [CrossRef]
6. Malinowski, M. Symmetric Fuzzy Stochastic Differential Equations with Generalized Global Lipschitz Condition. *Symmetry* **2020**, *12*, 819. [CrossRef]
7. Mosavi, A.; Shokri, M.; Mansor, Z.; Noman Qasem, S.; Band, S.; Mohammadzadeh, A. Machine learning for modeling the singular Multi-Pantograph equations. *Entropy* **2020**, *22*, 1041. [CrossRef] [PubMed]
8. Alshammari, M.; Al-Smadi, M.; Abu Arqub, O.; Hashim, I.; Almie Alias, M. Residual series representation algorithm for solving fuzzy duffing oscillator equations. *Symmetry* **2020**, *12*, 572. [CrossRef]
9. Buckley, J.J.; Feuring, T. Introduction to fuzzy partial differential equations. *Fuzzy Sets Syst.* **1999**, *105*, 241–248. [CrossRef]
10. Allahviranloo, T.; Kermani, M.A. Numerical methods for fuzzy linear partial differential equations under new definition for derivative. *Iran. J. Fuzzy Syst.* **2010**, *7*, 33–50.
11. Mikaeilvand, N.; Khakrangin, S. Solving fuzzy partial differential equations by fuzzy two-dimensional differential transform method. *Neural Comput. Appl.* **2012**, *21*, 307–312. [CrossRef]
12. Osman, M.; Gong, Z.; Mustafa, A.M. Comparison of fuzzy Adomian decomposition method with fuzzy VIM for solving fuzzy heat-like and wave-like equations with variable coefficients. *Adv. Differ. Equ.* **2020**, *2020*, 327. [CrossRef]

13. Georgieva, A. Application of double fuzzy Natural transform for solving fuzzy partial equations. *AIP Conf. Proc.* **2021**, *2333*, 080006-1–080006-8.
14. Ghasemi Moghaddam R.; Abbasbandy S.; Rostamy-Malkhalifeh M. A Study on analytical solutions of the fuzzy partial differential equations. *Int. J. Ind. Math.* **2020**, *12*, 419–429.
15. Osman, M.; Gong, Z.; Mustafa, A. A fuzzy solution of nonlinear partial differential equations. *Open J. Math. Anal.* **2021**, *5*, 51–63. [CrossRef]
16. Aggarwal, S.; Gupta, A.R.; Singh, D.P.; Asthana, N.; Kumar, N. Application of Laplace transform for solving population growth and decay problems. *Int. J. Latest Technol. Eng. Manag. Appl. Sci.* **2008**, *7*, 141–145.
17. Aggarwal, S.; Pandey, M.; Asthana, N.; Singh, D.P.; Kumar, A. Application of Mahgoub transform for solving population growth and decay problems. *J. Comput. Math. Sci.* **2018**, *9*, 1490–1496. [CrossRef]
18. Gupta, A.R. Solution of Abel's integral equation using Mahgoub transform method. *J. Emerg. Technol. Innov. Res.* **2019**, *6*, 252–260.
19. Ojo, G.O.; Mahmudov, N.I. Aboodh transform iterative method for spatial diffusion of a biological population with fractional-order. *Mathemattics* **2021**, *9*, 155.
20. Singh, Y.; Gill, V.; Kundu, S.; Kumar, D. On the Elzaki transform and its applications in fractional free electron laser equation. *Acta Univ. Sapientiae Math.* **2019**, *11*, 419–129. [CrossRef]
21. Mahgoub, M.M.A.; Mohand, M. The new integral transform "Sawi Transform". *Adv. Theor. Appl. Math.* **2019**, *14*, 81–87.
22. Aggarwal, S.; Gupta, A.R. Dualities between some useful integral transforms and Sawi transform. *Int. J. Recent Technol. Eng.* **2019**, *8*, 5978–5982.
23. Singh, G.P.; Aggarwal, S. Sawi transform for population growth and decay problems. *Int. J. Latest Technol. Eng.* **2019**, *8*, 157–162.
24. Abdul Rahman, N.A.; Ahmad, M.Z. Fuzzy Sumudu transform for solving fuzzy partial differential equations. *J. Nonlinear Sci. Appl.* **2016**, *9*, 3226–3239. [CrossRef]
25. Abaas Alshibley, S.T.; Ameera Alkiffai, N.; Athraa Albukhuttar, N. Solving a circuit system using fuzzy Aboodh transform. *Turkish J. Comput. Math. Educ.* **2021**, *12*, 3317–3323.
26. Salahshour, S.; Allahviranloo T. Applications of fuzzy Laplace transforms. *Soft Comput.* **2013**, *17*, 145–158. [CrossRef]
27. Adomian, G. A review of the decomposition method in applied mathematics. *J. Math. Anal App.* **1988**, *135*, 501–544. [CrossRef]
28. Adomian, G. *Solving Frontier Problems of Physics: The Decomposition Method*; Kluver Academic Publishers: Boston, MA, USA, 1994; Volume 12.
29. Goetschel, R.; Voxman, W. Elementary fuzzy calculus. *Fuzzy Sets Syst.* **1986**, *18*, 31–43. [CrossRef]
30. Kaufmann, A.; Gupta, M.M. *Introduction to Fuzzy Arithmetic: Theory and Applications*; Van Nostrand Reinhold Co.: New York, NY, USA, 1991.
31. Bede, B.; Fodor, J. Product type operations between fuzzy numbers and their applications in geology. *Acta Polytech. Hung.* **2006**, *3*, 123–139.
32. Bede, B. *Mathematics of Fuzzy Sets and Fuzzy Logic*; Springer: London, UK, 2013.
33. Gao, S.; Zhang, Z.; Cao, C. Multiplication Operation on Fuzzy Numbers. *J. Softw.* **2009**, *4*, 331–338. [CrossRef]
34. Georgieva, A. Double Fuzzy Sumudu transform to solve partial Volterra fuzzy integro-differential equations. *Mathematics* **2020**, *8*, 692. [CrossRef]
35. Bede, B.; Stefanini, L. Generalized differentiability of fuzzy-valued functions. *Fuzzy Sets Syst.* **2013**, *230*, 119–141. [CrossRef]
36. Bede, B.; Gal, S.G. Generalizations of the differentiability of fuzzy-number-valued functions with applications to fuzzy differential equations. *Fuzzy Sets Syst.* **2005**, *151*, 581–599. [CrossRef]
37. Chalco-Cano, Y.; Roman-Flores, H. On new solutions of fuzzy differential equations. *Chaos Solut. Fractals* **2008**, *38*, 112–119. [CrossRef]
38. Wu, H.C. The improper fuzzy Riemann integral and its numerical integration. *Inform. Sci.* **1998**, *111*, 109–137. [CrossRef]
39. Higazy, M.; Aggarwal, S. Sawi transformation for system of ordinary differential equations with application. *Ain Shams Eng. J.* **2021**, *12* [CrossRef]
40. Scott, A. FitzHugh-Nagumo (F-N) Models. In *Neuroscience—A Mathematical Primer*; Springer Science & Business Media: New York, NY, USA, 2002; Chapter 6, pp. 122–136.
41. Jäntschi, L. The Eigenproblem translated for alignment of molecules. *Symmetry* **2019**, *11*, 1027. [CrossRef]
42. Jäntschi, L.; Bálint, D.; Bolboacs S.D. Multiple linear regressions by maximizing the likelihood under assumption of generalized Gauss-Laplace dstribution of the error. *Comput. Math. Methods Med.* **2016**, *2016*, 8578156. [CrossRef]

Article

Intuitionistic Fuzzy (IF) Overlap Functions and IF-Rough Sets with Applications

Xiaofeng Wen [1], Xiaohong Zhang [2,*] and Tao Lei [2,3]

1. School of Mathematics & Data Science, Shaanxi University of Science and Technology, Xi'an Weiyang University Park, Xi'an 710021, China; 1909015@sust.edu.cn
2. Shaanxi Joint Laboratory of Aritificial Intelligence, Shaanxi University of Science and Technology, Xi'an 710021, China; leitao@sust.edu.cn
3. School of Electronic Information and Artificial Intelligence, Shaanxi University of Science and Technology, Xi'an 710021, China
* Correspondence: zhangxiaohong@sust.edu.cn

Citation: Wen, X.; Zhang, X.; Lei, T. Intuitionistic Fuzzy (IF) Overlap Functions and IF-Rough Sets with Applications. *Symmetry* 2021, *13*, 1494. https://doi.org/10.3390/sym13081494

Academic Editor: Saeid Jafari

Received: 8 July 2021
Accepted: 12 August 2021
Published: 14 August 2021

Publisher's Note: MDPI stays neutral with regard to jurisdictional claims in published maps and institutional affiliations.

Copyright: © 2021 by the authors. Licensee MDPI, Basel, Switzerland. This article is an open access article distributed under the terms and conditions of the Creative Commons Attribution (CC BY) license (https://creativecommons.org/licenses/by/4.0/).

Abstract: Overlap function (which has symmetry and continuity) is widely used in image processing, data classification, and multi-attribute decision making problems. In recent years, theoretical research on overlap function has been extended to interval valued overlap function and lattice valued overlap function, but intuitionistic fuzzy overlap function (IF-overlap function) has not been studied. In this paper, the concept of IF-overlap function is proposed for the first time, then the generating method of IF-overlap function is given. The representable IF-overlap function is defined, and the concrete examples of representable and unrepresentable IF-overlap functions are given. Moreover, a new class of intuitionistic fuzzy rough set (IF-roght set) model is proposed by using IF-overlap function and its residual implication, which extends the IF-rough set model based on intuitionistic fuzzy triangular norm, and the basic properties of the new intuitionistic fuzzy upper and lower approximate operators are analyzed and studied. At the same time, the established IF-rough set based on IF-overlap function is applied to MCDM (multi-criteria decision-making) problems, the intuitionistic fuzzy TOPSIS method is improved. Through the comparative analysis of some cases, the new method is proved to be flexible and effective.

Keywords: intuitionistic fuzzy sets; intuitionistic fuzzy overlap function; intuitionistic fuzzy triangular norm; IF-TOPSIS methods; MCDM

1. Introduction

Fuzzy set theory is a very effective mathematical tool to analyze and deal with inaccurate and incomplete information [1]. It plays an increasingly important role in many practical engineering fields, including fuzzy preference relationship [2], fuzzy information clustering [3], fuzzy granularity calculation [4], attribute decision problem [5], etc. According to practical problems, different forms of fuzzy sets are proposed, such as interval-valued fuzzy sets [6], intuitionistic fuzzy sets [7–9], etc. Rough set theory [10] proposed by Pawlak is also a mathematical tool to deal with fuzzy and uncertain knowledge, and has been successfully applied to machine learning, decision analysis, process control, pattern recognition, data mining and other fields. Dubois and Prade combined the two theories and proposed the concept of fuzzy rough set for the first time [11]. Since then, studies on fuzzy rough sets have become more abundant and indepth [12–16]. Because fuzzy rough sets are a special case of intuitionistic fuzzy rough sets (IF-rough sets), this paper focuses on intuitionistic fuzzy rough sets.

IF set is an expansion and development that has great influence on fuzzy set theory [7,9,17]. It has been successfully applied to the fields of decision analysis and pattern recognition [18,19] and intuitionistic fuzzy decision analysis [20,21]. Compared with the fuzzy set, which only indicates the degree to which an element belongs to a set, the IF set describes the membership degree and non-membership degree of an element to a set, and more accurately expresses the relationship between them, which adds a new field of vision for the solution of multi-attribute decision making problems. Subsequently, many concepts of IF have been proposed, such as IF relation [22], IF triangular norm [23], IF implication operator [24], etc. When dealing with practical problems, IF set and rough set theory are combined to solve such problems because of the roughness of information. In 2003, De Cock et al. presented some basic and important properties and conclusions of IF-rough set [25]. As an important continuous operator, IF triangular norm plays an important role in IF-rough sets. De Cock et al. defined a pair of upper and lower IF-rough approximation operators based on IF implication operators and IF triangular norm, studied the properties of IF-rough operators, and further extended the IF-rough set model [26]. On the basis of systematic generalization of existing work, Zhang et al. extended one domain to two domains [27] to study IF-rough sets.

Since triangular norm is widely used in solving practical problems, the study of their extensive forms in application is also of great importance. The overlap function is the extension of continuous triangular norm and is widely used in image processing, data classification and multi-attribute decision making. Overlap functions as unassociative connectives in fuzzy logic has been studied by many scholars. Overlap function [28] was proposed by Bustince et al. in 2009. This concept is taken from some practical problems related to image processing and classification. In image problem processing, Bustince scholars use binary operators called constrained equivalent functions to calculate the threshold of an image [29]. In the classification problem, Amo scholars use overlaps to discuss the evaluation of resulting classification when the research objects is unclear classification system [30]. In recent years, some generalizations of overlap function have been proposed, such as n-dimensional overlap function and general function [31], interval valued overlap function [32–34], etc., which have promoted theoretical research and practical application of overlap function. However, the existing definitions have limitations in solving practical problems with intuitionistic fuzzy information. In view of this limitation, this paper puts forward the definition of IF-overlap function, and studies some of its properties and representations.

Because the overlap function has a wide range of applications, IF-overlap function and IF-rough set can be studied together, and a broader IF-rough set model can be proposed to expand the application range of IF-rough set in practical problems. IF-overlap function, as a non-associative binary function, can be widely used in decision making problems based on fuzzy preference relation, which can overcome the defect of associative property of continuous IF triangular norm in practical problems, and has a better effect in dealing with uncertain multi-attribute decision making problems. Therefore, on the basis of IF triangular norm, a broader IF-rough sets is proposed, that is, IF-rough set based on IF-overlap function.

There are two main reasons for this study: One is the rough set theory is an important tool to deal with uncertain information, however, the classical rough set is restricted because of its strict conditions, in order to expand the application scope of rough set theory, we found that IF the introduction of the theory makes a lot of problems to solve, through different logical operator combining the IF theory and rough set theory, such as IF-overlap function, enriched the theory of rough set. Secondly, for the application of MCDM problem, after studying and comparing many existing methods, we found that the existing methods still have some limitations, for example, the continuity of triangular norm operator may be invalid in the complex IF environment. This paper analyzes the limitations of these methods in theory and application, and puts forward a new method to solve the MCDM problem. Experiments show that our method is more suitable for practical needs and more flexible when dealing with problems. In addition, through changing attribute values of α, this method can get all the results obtained by existing methods.

The rest of the paper is structure as following: we list some preliminary concepts and results in Section 2. Next we give the definition of the IF-overlap function, given the general generation method of the IF-overlap function and some examples to account for explain, moreover we give the definition of the representable and unrepresentable IF-overlap function and concrete example in Section 3. In Section 4, we establish the IF-rough set model based on IF-overlap function, and discuss the basic properties of this model and give some examples. In Section 5, we put forward the MCMD problem method of the IF-rough set model based on IF-overlap function, the steps and calculation formula of this method are listed. Then we propose the concrete example, and comparison analysis among our method and other methods. Finally, we conclude our work with a summary of the paper in Section 6, and also outline future research.

2. Preliminary Concepts and Results

In this section we recall several fundamental conceptions relates to overlap function, intuitionistic fuzzy sets and rough sets.

2.1. Overlap Function

Definition 1 ([28]). *A bivariate function $O:[0,1]^2 \to [0,1]$ is called an overlap function, if for every $a,b,c \in [0,1]$, the following conditions holds:*
$(O1)$ $O(a,b) = O(b,a)$;
$(O2)$ $O(a,b) = 0 \Leftrightarrow ab = 0$;
$(O3)$ $O(a,b) = 1 \Leftrightarrow ab = 1$;
$(O4)$ $O(a,b) \leq O(a,c)$ *if* $b \leq c$;
$(O5)$ O *is continuous.*

Definition 2 ([28]). *Let $O:[0,1]^2 \to [0,1]$ be an overlap function, then for every $a,b \in [0,1]$, the bivariate function $R_O:[0,1]^2 \to [0,1]$ defined by,*

$$R_O(a,b) = \max\{c \in [0,1] | O(a,c) \leq b\}$$

then R_O is the residual implication induced from overlap function O.

Definition 3 ([32]). *An interval-valued overlap function is a mapping $\widehat{O}: L^I \times L^I \to L^I$ that respects the following conditions (where $L^I = \{[x_1,x_2] | [x_1,x_2] \subseteq [0,1], x_1 \leq x_2\}$) :*
$(\widehat{O}1)$ $\widehat{O}$ *is commutative;*
$(\widehat{O}2)$ $\widehat{O} = [0,0] \Leftrightarrow X = [0,0] \vee Y = [0,0]$;
$(\widehat{O}3)$ $\widehat{O} = [1,1] \Leftrightarrow X = Y = [1,1]$;
$(\widehat{O}4)$ $\widehat{O}(Y,X) \leq \widehat{O}(Z,X)$ *if* $Y \leq Z$;
$(\widehat{O}5)$ $\widehat{O}$ *is Moore-continuous.*

2.2. Fuzzy Sets Theory

Definition 4 ([1]). *The fuzzy set(or fuzzy subset) on argument domain X is A mapping from X to $[0,1]$ (called membership function) :*

$$\mu_A : X \to [0,1]$$

for every $x \in X$, $\mu_A(x)$ called the membership of x with respect to A.

Definition 5 ([7]). *The IF set on the argument X is A defined as follows:*

$$A = \{\langle x, \mu_A(x), v_A(x)\rangle | x \in X\}$$

where, $\mu_A(x) : X \to [0,1]$ and $v_A(x) : X \to [0,1]$ respectively represent the membership and non-membership of x belong to A, and satisfy $0 \leq \mu_A(x) + v_A(x) \leq 1$.

As the same time, general fuzzy set is denote by : $A = \{\langle x, \mu_A(x), 1 - \mu_A(x)\rangle | x \in X\}$, obviously. At this point, the IF set degenerates into a general fuzzy set.

Definition 6 ([7]). *Let A and B be intuitionistic fuzzy sets, where*

$$A = \{\langle x, \mu_A(x), v_A(x)\rangle | x \in X\}, B = \{\langle x, \mu_B(x), v_B(x)\rangle | x \in X\},$$

then the order and operation are defined as follows:
(1) $A \subseteq B \Leftrightarrow \mu_A(x) \leq \mu_B(x) and v_A(x) \geq v_B(x), \text{for each } x \in X;$
(2) $A \bigcap B = \{\langle x, \min \mu_A(x), \mu_B(x), \max v_A(x), v_B(x) | x \in X\};$
(3) $A \bigcup B = \{\langle x, \max \mu_A(x), \mu_B(x), \min v_A(x), v_B(x) | x \in X\};$
(4) $A^c = \{\langle x, v_A(x), \mu_A(x) | x \in X\rangle\};$
(5) $\lambda A = \{\langle x, 1 - (1 - \mu_A(x))^\lambda, v_A(x)^\lambda\rangle\}.$
IF sets assign to each element x of the universe both a degree of membership $\mu_A(x)$ *and one of non-membership* $v_A(x)$ *such that* $0 \leq \mu_A(x) + v_A(x) \leq 1$. *This hesitation is quantified for each x in X by the number* $\pi_A(x) = 1 - \mu_A(x) - v_A(x)$.

It is well-known IF sets are equivalent of L-fuzyy sets [8]. Let $(L^*, \leq_{L^*})$ be the complete bounded lattice defined by:

$$L^* = \{\langle x_1, x_2\rangle | x_1 + x_2 \leq 1\},$$

$$(x_1, x_2) \leq_{L^*} (y_1, y_2) \Leftrightarrow x_1 \leq y_1, x_2 \geq y_2.$$

The units of this lattice are denoted $0_{L^*} = \langle 01\rangle$, $1_{L^*} = \langle 1, 0\rangle$. For each element $x \in X$, by x_1 and x_2 we denote its first and second components, respectively. An IF set A in a universe X is a mapping from X to L^*. For every $x \in X$, the value $\mu_A(x) = (A(x))_1$ is called the membership degree of x to A; the value $v_A(x) = (A(x))_2$ is called the non-membership degree of x to A; and the value $\pi_A(x) = 1 - \mu_A(x) - v_A(x)$ is called the hesitation degree of x to A.

Definition 7 ([22]). *An IF relation R on U is an IF set of* $U \times U$*, i.e., R is given be*

$$R = \{\langle x, y\rangle, \mu_R(x, y), v_R(x, y)\rangle | (x, y) \in U \times U\},$$

where $\mu_R : U \times U \to [0, 1]$ *and* $v_R : U \times U \to [0, 1]$ *satisfy* $0 \leq \mu_R(x, y) + v_R(x, y) \leq 1$ *for all* $(x, y) \in U \times U$.
Let R be an IF relation on U, R is called reflexive if $\mu_R(x, y) = 1$ *and* $v_R(x, y) = 0$ *for all* $x \in U$*; R is called symmetric if* $\mu_R(x, y) = \mu_R(y, x)$ *and* $v_R(x, y) = v_R(y, x)$ *for all* $(x, y) \in U \times U$*; R is called transive if for all* $(x, z) \in U \times U$,

$$\mu_R(x, z) \geq \vee_{y \in U}[\mu_R(x, y) \wedge \mu_R(y, z)];$$

and

$$v_R(x, z) \leq \wedge_{y \in U}[v_R(x, y) \vee v_R(y, z)].$$

Definition 8 ([23]). *An IF triangular norm is a mapping* $T : L^* \times L^* \to L^*$ *which satisfy the following conditions:*
(1) $T(1_{L^*}, x) = x, \text{for any } x \in L^*;$
(2) $T(x, y) = T(y, x), \text{for any } x, y \in L^*;$
(3) If $x \leq_{L^*} u, y \leq_{L^*} v$*, then* $T(x, y) \leq_{L^*} T(u, v), \text{for any } x, y, u, v \in L^*;$
(4) $T(x, T(y, z)) = T(T(x, y), z)), \text{for any } x, y, z \in L^*.$

2.3. Fuzzy Rough Sets Theory

Definition 9 ([10]). *Let* (U, R) *be a Pawlak space, that R is an equivalence relation on the argument domain U, if A is a fuzzy set, then a pair of lower and upper approximations on* (U, R) *is defined as follows:*

$$\underline{A}_R(x) = \min\{A(y) | y \in [x]_R, x \in U\};$$

$$\overline{A}_R(x) = \max\{A(y) | y \in [x]_R, x \in U\}.$$

where, $[x]_R$ represents the equivalence class about x, and called $\underline{A}_R$ and $\overline{A}_R$ are the lower and upper approximations of the fuzzy set A with respect to (U, R).

If $\underline{A}_R = \overline{A}_R$, then A is a defined fuzzy set. On the contrary, A is called fuzzy rough set.

Definition 10 ([24]). *Let U be a nonempty and finite universe of discourse and $R \in IF(U \times U)$, the pair (U, R) is called an IF approximation space. For any $A \in IF(U)$, the lower and upper approximation of A w.r.t (U, R), denoted by $\underline{R}_A$ and $\overline{R}_A$, are two intuitionistic fuzzy sets and defined as follows:*

$$\underline{R}_A = \{\langle x, \mu_{\underline{R}_A}(x), \upsilon_{\underline{R}_A}(x)\rangle | x \in U\};$$

$$\overline{R}_A = \{\langle x, \mu_{\overline{R}_A}(x), \upsilon_{\overline{R}_A}(x)\rangle | x \in U\}.$$

where

$$\mu_{\underline{R}_A}(x) = \wedge_{y \in U}[\upsilon_R(x,y) \vee \mu_A(y)];$$

$$\upsilon_{\underline{R}_A}(x) = \vee_{y \in U}[\mu_R(x,y) \wedge \upsilon_A(y)].$$

$$\mu_{\overline{R}_A}(x) = \vee_{y \in U}[\mu_R(x,y) \wedge \mu_A(y)];$$

$$\upsilon_{\overline{R}_A}(x) = \wedge_{y \in U}[\upsilon_R(x,y) \vee \upsilon_A(y)].$$

The pair $(\underline{R}_A, \overline{R}_A)$ is called the IF-rough set of A w.r.t. (U, R), $\underline{R}_A$ and $\overline{R}_A$ are referred to as a lower and upper IF-rough approximation operators, respectively.

Definition 11 ([26]). *Let T be an IF triangular norm, I be an IF implicator, and R be an IF equivalence relation on U. Together they constitute the approximation space (U, R, T, I). For any IF set A in U, the lower and upper approximation of A are the IF sets $R \downarrow_I A$ and $R \uparrow_T A$ in U defined by:*

$$R \downarrow_I A(y) = \inf_{x \in U} I(R(x,y), A(x)),$$

$$R \uparrow_T A(y) = \sup_{x \in U} I(R(x,y), A(x)).$$

for all $y \in U$.

A is called definable if and only if $R \downarrow_I A(y) = R \uparrow_T A(y)$. Conversely, the couple $(R \downarrow_I A, R \uparrow_T A)$ is an IF-rough set.

3. Intuitionistic Fuzzy Overlap Function

This section first gives the definition of the intuitionistic fuzzy overlap function (IF-overlap function), then gives the general generation method of the IF-overlap function, and then gives the definition of the representable IF-overlap function and gives the concrete example.

Definition 12. *An IF-overlap function is a mapping $\widetilde{O} : L^* \times L^* \to L^*$ that respects the following conditions, for any $x, y, z \in L^*$,*

$(\widetilde{O}1)$ Commutativity: $\widetilde{O}(x,y) = \widetilde{O}(y,x)$;

$(\widetilde{O}2)$ Boundary condition: $\widetilde{O}(x,y) = 0_{L^*}$ if and only if $x = 0_{L^*}$ or $y = 0_{L^*}$;

$(\widetilde{O}3)$ Boundary condition: $\widetilde{O}(x,y) = 1_{L^*}$ if and only if $x = y = 1_{L^*}$;

$(\widetilde{O}4)$ Monotonicity: $\widetilde{O}(x,y) \leq_{L^*} \widetilde{O}(x,z)$ if $y \leq_{L^*} z$;

$(\widetilde{O}5)$ Continuity: $\widetilde{O}$ is continuous, i.e., $\forall i \in I, y_i \in L^*$, $\widetilde{O}(x, \vee_{i \in I} y_i) = \vee_{i \in I} \widetilde{O}(x, y_i)$ and $\widetilde{O}(x, \wedge_{i \in I} y_i) = \wedge_{i \in I} \widetilde{O}(x, y_i)$.

Proposition 1. *Let O be an overlap function. Define the function $\widetilde{O}$ as follows: for every $x = (x_1, x_2), y = (y_1, y_2) \in L^*$,*

$$\widetilde{O}(x,y) = \langle O(x_1,y_1), 1 - O(1 - x_2, 1 - y_2)\rangle$$

then $\widetilde{O}$ is an IF-overlap function.

Proof. Prove $\widetilde{O}$ satisfied the conditions in Definition 12 as follows:

($\widetilde{O}1$) For all $x, y \in L^*$, since O is commutative, so $O(x_1, y_1) = O(y_1, x_1)$, $O(1 - x_2, 1 - y_2) = O(1 - y_2, 1 - x_2)$, it follows that

$$\widetilde{O}(x,y) = \langle O(x_1,y_1), 1 - O(1-x_2, 1-y_2)\rangle = \langle O(y_1,x_1), 1 - O(1-y_2, 1-x_2)\rangle = \widetilde{O}(y,x).$$

($\widetilde{O}2$) For all $x, y \in L^*$, according to the Boundary condition of O, we can get to know $O(x_1, y_1) = 0 \Leftrightarrow x_1 = 0$ or $y_1 = 0$, $O(1 - x_2, 1 - y_2) = 0 \Leftrightarrow x_2 = 1$ or $y_2 = 1$, it follows that

$\widetilde{O}(x,y) = 0_{L^*} \Leftrightarrow \langle O(x_1,y_1), 1 - O(1-x_2, 1-y_2)\rangle = 0_{L^*} \Leftrightarrow O(x_1,y_1) = 0, 1 - O(1 - x_2, 1 - y_2) = 1 \Leftrightarrow x = 0_{L^*}$ or $y = 0_{L^*}$.

($\widetilde{O}3$) For all $x, y \in L^*$, according to the Boundary condition of O, we can get to know $O(x_1, y_1) = 1 \Leftrightarrow x_1 = y_1 = 1$, $O(1 - x_2, 1 - y_2) = 1 \Leftrightarrow x_2 = y_2 = 0$, it follows that

$\widetilde{O}(x,y) = 1_{L^*} \Leftrightarrow \langle O(x_1,y_1), 1 - O(1-x_2, 1-y_2)\rangle = 1_{L^*} \Leftrightarrow O(x_1,y_1) = 1, 1 - O(1 - x_2, 1 - y_2) = 0 \Leftrightarrow x = y = 1_{L^*}$.

($\widetilde{O}4$) For all $x, y, z \in L^*$, if $y \leq_{L^*} z$, i.e., $y_1 \leq z_1, y_2 \geq z_2$, then $O(x_1, y_1) \leq O(x_1, z_1)$, $O(1 - x_2, 1 - y_2) \leq O(1 - x_2, 1 - z_2)$, $1 - O(1 - x_2, 1 - y_2) \geq 1 - O(1 - x_2, 1 - z_2)$, it follows that

$$\widetilde{O}(x,y) = \langle O(x_1,y_1), 1 - O(1-x_2, 1-y_2)\rangle \leq_{L^*} \langle O(x_1,z_1), 1 - O(1-x_2, 1-z_2)\rangle = \widetilde{O}(x,z).$$

($\widetilde{O}5$) Firstly, we prove left continuous, i.e., $\widetilde{O}(x, \vee_{i\in I} y_i) = \vee_{i\in I}\widetilde{O}(x, y_i)$ where $x = (x_1, x_2), y = (y_1, y_2)$. Because the overlap function O is continuous, $O(x_1, \vee_{i\in I} y_{i1}) = \vee_{i\in I} O(x_1, y_{i1})$ and $O(1 - x_2, 1 - \wedge_{i\in I} y_{i2}) = O(1 - x_2, \vee_{i\in I}(1 - y_{i2})) = \vee_{i\in I} O(1 - x_2, 1 - y_{i2})$ is holding.

Then we have

$\widetilde{O}(x, \vee_{i\in I} y_i) = \langle O(x_1, \vee_{i\in I} y_{i1}), 1 - O(1 - x_2, 1 - \wedge_{i\in I} y_{i2}\rangle = \langle O(x_1, \vee_{i\in I} y_{i1}), 1 - O(1 - x_2, \vee_{i\in I}(1 - y_{i2}))\rangle = \langle \vee_{i\in I} O(x_1, y_{i1}), 1 - \vee_{i\in I} O(1 - x_2, (1 - y_{i2}))\rangle = \langle \vee_{i\in I} O(x_1, y_{i1}), \wedge_{i\in I}(1 - O(1 - x_2, (1 - y_{i2})))\rangle = \vee_{i\in I}\langle O(x_1, y_{i1}), 1 - O(1 - x_2, (1 - y_{i2}))\rangle = \vee_{i\in I}\widetilde{O}(x, y_i)$.

Therefore the function $\widetilde{O}$ is left continuous. □

Similarly, we can obtain $\widetilde{O}(x, \wedge_{i\in I} y_i) = \wedge_{i\in I}\widetilde{O}(x, y_i)$, therofore the function $\widetilde{O}$ is right continuous.

Hence the function $\widetilde{O}$ is continuous.

Example 1. *Define functions as follows: for $x = (x_1, x_2), y = (y_1, y_2)$,*

(1) $\widetilde{O}(x,y) = \langle \min(x_1,y_1)\min(x_1^2,y_1^2), \max(x_2,y_2)\max(x_2^2,y_2^2)\rangle$.

(2) $\widetilde{O}(x,y) = \langle \min(\sqrt{x_1},\sqrt{y_1}), \max(\sqrt{x_2},\sqrt{y_2})\rangle$.

(3) $\widetilde{O}(x,y) = \langle x_1 y_1, 1 - (1-x_2)(1-y_2)\rangle$.

(4) $\widetilde{O}(x,y) = \langle x_1 y_1 \frac{x_1+y_1}{2}, 1 - (1-x_2)(1-y_2)\frac{2-x_2-y_2}{2}\rangle$.

(5) $\widetilde{O}(x,y) = \langle 0.5x_1y_1 + 0.5\max(0, x_1 + y_1 - 1), \min(1, x_2 + 1 - y_1, y_2 + 1 - x_1)\rangle$.

It is easy to verify that the above functions are IF-overlap function.

Definition 13. *Let $\widetilde{O} : L^* \times L^* \to L^*$ be an IF-overlap function, defined the function $R_{\widetilde{O}} : L^* \times L^* \to L^*$ as follows:*

$$R_{\widetilde{O}}(x,y) = \sup\{z \in L^* | \widetilde{O}(x,z) \leq_{L^*} y\}$$

then $R_{\widetilde{O}}$ is called the residual implication induced by the IF-overlap function $\widetilde{O}$.

Example 2. *Define functions as follows: for $x = \langle x_1, x_2\rangle, y = \langle y_1, y_2\rangle$,*

(1)

$$R_{\tilde{O}}(x,y)=\begin{cases}\langle 1,0\rangle & x_1^3\leq y_1 and x_2^3\leq y_2\\ \langle 1-y_2^{1/3},y_2^{1/3}\rangle & x_1^3\leq y_1 and x_2^3<y_2\\ \langle y_1^{1/3},0\rangle & x_1^3>y_1 and x_2^3\geq y_2\\ \langle y_1^{1/3},y_2^{1/3}\rangle & x_1^3>y_1 and x_2^3<y_2\end{cases}$$

$R_{\tilde{O}}$ is the residual implication induced by the IF-overlap function $\tilde{O}(x,y)$ in Example (1(1)).

(2)

$$R_{\tilde{O}}(x,y)=\begin{cases}\langle 1,0\rangle & x_1\leq y_1^2 and x_2\leq y_2^2\\ \langle 1-y_2^2,y_2^2\rangle & x_1\leq y_1^2 and x_2<y_2^2\\ \langle y_1^2,0\rangle & x_1>y_1^2 and x_2\geq y_2^2\\ \langle y_1^2,y_2^2\rangle & x_1>y_1^2 and x_2<y_2^2\end{cases}$$

$R_{\tilde{O}}$ is the residual implication induced by the IF-overlap function $\tilde{O}(x,y)$ in Example (1(2)).

(3) $R_{\tilde{O}}(x,y)=\langle\frac{y_1}{x_1},1-\frac{1-y_2}{1-x_2}\rangle$, $R_{\tilde{O}}$ is the residual implication induced by the IF-overlap function $\tilde{O}(x,y)$ in Example (1(3)).

Definition 14. *There exist two overlap functions O_1,O_2, if $O_1\leq O_2$, defined function as follows: for $x=(x_1,x_2),y=(y_1,y_2)$,*

$$\tilde{O}((x_1,x_2),(y_1,y_2))=\langle O_1(x_1,y_1),1-O_2(1-x_2,1-y_2)\rangle$$

then $\tilde{O}$ is called representable IF-overlap function.

Example 3. *(1) The function $\tilde{O}(x,y)=\langle x_1y_1,1-(1-x_2)(1-y_2)\rangle$ is a representable IF-overlap function.*

(2) $\tilde{O}(x,y)=\langle 0.5x_1y_1+0.5\max(0,x_1+y_1-1),\min(1,x_2+1-y_1,y_2+1-x_1)\rangle$ is a unrepresentable IF-overlap function.

Let $O_1(x_1,y_1)=0.5x_1y_1+0.5max(0,x_1+y_1+1)$, $O_2(x_2,y_2)=1-min(1,2-x_2-x_0,2-y_2-y_0)$, where $x_0,y_0\in[0,1]$ is contant.

$$O_2(1,1)=\begin{cases}x_0 & x_0>y_0\\ y_0 & x_0\leq y_0\end{cases}$$

Obviously, $O_2(1,1)\neq 1$, that is not satisfied the conditions for overlap function. So, the function $\tilde{O}(x,y)=\langle 0.5x_1y_1+0.5\max(0,x_1+y_1-1),\min(1,x_2+1-y_1,y_2+1-x_1)\rangle$ is a unrepresentable IF-overlap function.

It is proved that Example 3(2) satisfies the condition of IF-overlap function, but it does not meet the condition of representable IF-overlap function, so the function $\tilde{O}(x,y)=\langle 0.5x_1y_1+0.5\max(0,x_1+y_1-1),\min(1,x_2+1-y_1,y_2+1-x_1)\rangle$ is a unrepresentable IF-overlap function. For this type of function, we give a more general function expression, i.e., $\tilde{O}(x,y)=\langle\alpha x_1y_1+(1-\alpha)\max(0,x_1y_1-1),\min(1,x_2+1-y_1,y_2+1-x_1)\rangle$, where $\alpha\in[0,1]$.

Proposition 2. *The function $\tilde{O}:L^*\times L^*\to L^*$ is an IF-overlap function if and only if there exist two functions $f,g:[0,1]\times[0,1]\to[0,1]$ such that*

$$\forall x=(x_1,x_2),y=(y_1,y_2)\in L^*,\tilde{O}(x,y)=\langle\frac{f(x_1,y_1)}{f(x_1,y_1)+g(x_1,y_1)},1-\frac{f(1-x_2,1-y_2)}{f(1-x_2,1-y_2)+g(1-x_2,1-y_2)}\rangle$$

where

1. *f and g are symmetric;*
2. *f is non-decreasing and g is non-increasing;*
3. *$f(x,y)=0$ if and only if $xy=0$;*
4. *$g(x,y)=0$ if and only if $xy=1$;*

5. *f and g are continuous.*

In other words, the IF-overlap function $\widetilde{O}$ can be generated by both f and g.

Example 4. *(1) Let $f = xy$ and $g = 1 - xy$, the IF-overlap function generated by f and g is $\widetilde{O}(x,y) = \langle x_1y_1, 1-(1-x_2)(1-y_2)\rangle$.*

(2) Let $f = xy(x+y)$ and $g = 2 - xy(x+y)$, the IF-overlap function generated by f and g is $\widetilde{O}(x,y) = \langle x_1y_1\frac{x_1+y_1}{2}, 1-(1-x_2)(1-y_2)\frac{2-x_2-y_2}{2}\rangle$.

4. IF-Rough Sets Model Base on IF-Overlap Functions

In order to popularize the application of IF-rough set model , a new class of IF-rough set model is proposed by combining IF-overlap function. In this section, we will introduce the definition and some properties of this new IF-rough sets model.

Definition 15. *Let $\widetilde{O}$ be an IF-overlap function, $R_{\widetilde{O}}$ be an residual implication, and R be an IF similarity relation in U, the (U,R) is called IF approximation space. For any IF set A in U, the lower and upper approximation of A are the IF sets $R\downarrow_{R_{\widetilde{O}}} A$ and $R\uparrow_{\widetilde{O}} A$ is defined by:*

$$R\downarrow_{R_{\widetilde{O}}} A(y) = \inf_{x\in U} R_{\widetilde{O}}(R(x.y), A(x))$$

$$R\uparrow_{\widetilde{O}} A(y) = \sup_{x\in U} \widetilde{O}(R(x.y), A(x))$$

for all y in U.

A is called definable if and only if $R\downarrow_{R_{\widetilde{O}}} A = R\uparrow_{\widetilde{O}} A$. Conversely, called the couple $(R\downarrow_{R_{\widetilde{O}}} A, R\uparrow_{\widetilde{O}} A)$ is IF-rough sets, and $R\downarrow_{R_{\widetilde{O}}} A$ and $R\uparrow_{\widetilde{O}} A$ respectively are referred to as approximation operators under IF and approximation operators above IF.

Next, give an example of IF set, and use IF-rough set based on IF-overlap functions to calculate its lower and upper approximation.

Example 5. *Let the A is an IF set, i.e., $A = \frac{\langle 0.8,0.1\rangle}{x_1} + \frac{\langle 0.7,0.2\rangle}{x_2} + \frac{\langle 0.6,0.1\rangle}{x_3} + \frac{\langle 0.9,0.1\rangle}{x_4} + \frac{\langle 0.8,0.2\rangle}{x_5}$, R is an IF relation showed in Table 1.*

Table 1. IF relation R.

R	x_1	x_2	x_3	x_4	x_5
$R(x_1)$	$\langle 0.9,0.0\rangle$	$\langle 0.7,0.1\rangle$	$\langle 0.6,0.2\rangle$	$\langle 0.5,0.1\rangle$	$\langle 0.3,0.2\rangle$
$R(x_2)$	$\langle 0.8,0.1\rangle$	$\langle 0.4,0.4\rangle$	$\langle 0.8,0.1\rangle$	$\langle 0.7,0.1\rangle$	$\langle 1.0,0.0\rangle$
$R(x_3)$	$\langle 0.7,0.2\rangle$	$\langle 0.3,0.1\rangle$	$\langle 0.0,0.6\rangle$	$\langle 0.2,0.2\rangle$	$\langle 0.6,0.2\rangle$
$R(x_4)$	$\langle 0.6,0.1\rangle$	$\langle 0.5,0.5\rangle$	$\langle 0.4,0.4\rangle$	$\langle 0.7,0.2\rangle$	$\langle 0.3,0.4\rangle$
$R(x_5)$	$\langle 0.9,0.0\rangle$	$\langle 0.0,1.0\rangle$	$\langle 0.1,0.1\rangle$	$\langle 0.5,0.5\rangle$	$\langle 0.3,0.3\rangle$

By the Definition 15,let's take $\widetilde{O}$ and $R_{\widetilde{O}}$ for example 1 and 2, then calculate the lower and upper approximation as follows:

$$R\downarrow_{R_{\widetilde{O}}} A = \frac{\langle 0.4152,0.5848\rangle}{x_1} + \frac{\langle 0.4152,0.5848\rangle}{x_2} + \frac{\langle 0.4152,0.5848\rangle}{x_3} + \frac{\langle 0.4152,0.5848\rangle}{x_4} + \frac{\langle 0.4152,0.5848\rangle}{x_5};$$

$$R\uparrow_{\widetilde{O}} A = \frac{\langle 0.512,0.0001\rangle}{x_1} + \frac{\langle 0.343,0.001\rangle}{x_2} + \frac{\langle 0.343,0.008\rangle}{x_3} + \frac{\langle 0.343,0.008\rangle}{x_4} + \frac{\langle 0.343,0.008\rangle}{x_5}.$$

The following, we list the properties of intuitionistic fuzzy upper and lower approximation operators, and give concrete examples to show that their idempotent propertie is not set up.

Proposition 3. *Let $(U,R,\widetilde{O},R_{\widetilde{O}})$ be an IF approximation space, where $\widetilde{O}$ is an IF-overlap function and $R_{\widetilde{O}}$ is a residual implicator of $\widetilde{O}$. Then for all $A,B \in IFS$, $R_1 \subseteq R_2$, the following properties hold:*

(1) $A \subseteq B \Rightarrow R\downarrow_{R_{\widetilde{O}}} A \subseteq R\downarrow_{R_{\widetilde{O}}} B; R\uparrow_{\widetilde{O}} A \subseteq R\uparrow_{\widetilde{O}} B$;
(2) $R_1\downarrow_{R_{\widetilde{O}}} A \supseteq R_2\downarrow_{R_{\widetilde{O}}} A; R_1\uparrow_{\widetilde{O}} A \subseteq R_2\uparrow_{\widetilde{O}} A$;
(3) $R\downarrow_{R_{\widetilde{O}}} (A\bigcap B) = R\downarrow_{R_{\widetilde{O}}} A\bigcap R\downarrow_{R_{\widetilde{O}}} B$;
(4) $R\uparrow_{\widetilde{O}} (A\bigcup B) = R\uparrow_{\widetilde{O}} A\bigcup\uparrow_{\widetilde{O}} B$;
(5) $R\downarrow_{R_{\widetilde{O}}} (A\bigcup B) \supseteq R\downarrow_{R_{\widetilde{O}}} A\bigcup R\downarrow_{R_{\widetilde{O}}} B$;
(6) $R\uparrow_{\widetilde{O}} (A\bigcap B) \subseteq R\uparrow_{\widetilde{O}} A\bigcap\uparrow_{\widetilde{O}} B$.

Proof. (1) It can be directly followed from Definitions 12 and 15.

(2) By the definition of IF relation, if $R_1 \subseteq R_2$ then $R_1(x,y) \leq R_2(x,y)$, by the Definition 3.1, we have $\widetilde{O}(R_1(x,y), A(x)) \leq \widetilde{O}(R_2(x,y), A(x))$, then

$$\sup_{x\in U} \widetilde{O}(R_1(x.y), A(x)) \leq \sup_{x\in U} \widetilde{O}(R_2(x.y), A(x)).$$

That is $R_1\uparrow_{\widetilde{O}} A \subseteq R_2\uparrow_{\widetilde{O}} A$ holds. Similarly, we can verity that $R_1 \subseteq R_2$, then $R_1\downarrow_{R_{\widetilde{O}}} A \supseteq R_2\downarrow_{R_{\widetilde{O}}} A$ holds.

(3) By definition to know,

$R\downarrow_{R_{\widetilde{O}}} (A\bigcap B)(y) = \inf_{x\in U} R_{\widetilde{O}}(R(x,y), A(x)\wedge B(x)) = \inf_{x\in U} R_{\widetilde{O}}(R(x,y), A(x)) \wedge \inf_{x\in U} R_{\widetilde{O}}(R(x,y), B(x)) = R\downarrow_{R_{\widetilde{O}}} A(y)\bigcap R\downarrow_{R_{\widetilde{O}}} B(y)$.

(4) By definition to know,

$R\uparrow_{\widetilde{O}} (A\bigcup B)(y) = \sup_{x\in U} \widetilde{O}(R(x,y), A(x)\vee B(x)) = \sup_{x\in U} \widetilde{O}(R(x,y), A(x) \vee \sup_{x\in U} \widetilde{O}(R(x,y), B(x) = R\uparrow_{\widetilde{O}} A(y)\bigcup R\uparrow_{\widetilde{O}} B(y)$.

(5) That can be directly followed from Definition 15 and Propositions 1–4, respectively.

(6) It can be directly followed from Definition 15 and Propositions 1–4, respectively.

In particular, we illustrate that the model is not idempotent, i.e.,

$$R\uparrow_{\widetilde{O}} A \neq R\uparrow_{\widetilde{O}} (R\uparrow_{\widetilde{O}} A)$$

$$R\downarrow_{R_{\widetilde{O}}} A \neq R\downarrow_{R_{\widetilde{O}}} (R\downarrow_{R_{\widetilde{O}}} A)$$

□

Example 6. *Let A be an IF sets,* $A = \frac{\langle 0.3,0.5\rangle}{x_1} + \frac{\langle 0.4,0.6\rangle}{x_2} + \frac{\langle 0.5,0.5\rangle}{x_3} + \frac{\langle 0.7,0.2\rangle}{x_4} + \frac{\langle 0.8,0.1\rangle}{x_5}$, *and R be an IF relation as Table 1, then by calculating, we have the results as follows:* $R\uparrow_{\widetilde{O}} A = \frac{\langle 0.512,0.0001\rangle}{x_1} + \frac{\langle 0.125,0.125\rangle}{x_2} + \frac{\langle 0.064,0.064\rangle}{x_3} + \frac{\langle 0.343,0.008\rangle}{x_4} + \frac{\langle 0.125,0.125\rangle}{x_5}$; $R\uparrow_{\widetilde{O}} (R\uparrow_{\widetilde{O}} A) = \frac{\langle 0.1342,0.0\rangle}{x_1} + \frac{\langle 0.1342,0.001\rangle}{x_2} + \frac{\langle 0.1342,0.008\rangle}{x_3} + \frac{\langle 0.125,0.001\rangle}{x_4} + \frac{\langle 0.027,0.008\rangle}{x_5}$.

Obviously, $R\uparrow_{\widetilde{O}} A \neq R\uparrow_{\widetilde{O}} (R\uparrow_{\widetilde{O}} A)$, by calculation know $R\downarrow_{R_{\widetilde{O}}} A \neq R\downarrow_{R_{\widetilde{O}}} (R\downarrow_{R_{\widetilde{O}}} A)$.

5. Application Example

In this section, we will describe the application of the new IF-rough set model to MCDM (multi-criteria decision making) problems, and compares the decision results with other models.

5.1. Problem Description

In a public company, shareholders want to elect an executive director who have both ability and political integrity, in order to create more value for the company. Let $X = \{x_i$: i = 1, 2, ..., n$\}$ be the universe of n alternatives, $C = \{C_j$: j = 1, 2, ..., m$\}$ be the set of m criteria. $C_j(x_i) = (\mu(x_i), v(x_i))$ where $0 \leq \mu(x_i) + v(x_i) \leq 1$, $\mu(x_i)$, $v(x_i)$ are the degrees of membership and non-membership of $C_j(x_i)$, respectively. $C_j(x_i)$ denotes the ability value of the alternative x_i to the criterion C_j given a lot of judges. Assuming that for any alternative x_i, there is at least one criterion C_j such that the value of the alternative x_i for the criterion C_j is equal to $< 1,0 >$. In the following, we can solve the decision-making problem by means of the principle of the IF TOPSIS methods and the IF-rough set models. We apply the algorithm in recruiting alternative in a public company to choose the best director.

5.2. Decision-Making Method

Firstly, we build one IF set C_j is a description of X given by a lot of experts through their experience, then give the IF relation R for each x_i.

Secondly, by the IF relation R, the positive ideal solution and the negative ideal solution of the alternative x_i are defined as:

$$A^+(x_i) = (\mu_{A^+}(x_i), v_{A^+}(x_i))$$

where $\mu_{A^+}(x_i = \max_{j=1}^{m}(\mu_{C_j}(x_i)), v_{A^+}(x_i = \min_{j=1}^{m}(v_{C_j}(x_i));$

$$A^-(x_i) = (\mu_{A^-}(x_i), v_{A^-}(x_i))$$

where $\mu_{A^-}(x_i = \min_{j=1}^{m}(\mu_{C_j}(x_i)), v_{A^-}(x_i = \max_{j=1}^{m}(v_{C_j}(x_i)).$

We can receive that the positive ideal solution A^+ and the negative ideal solution A^-. Where $A^+, A^- \in$ IF(U). Thirdly, we compute the IF rough approximation of A^+ and A^- by the IF-rough sets.Then there are two types calculating, by the score function $L(A)(x_i) = \mu_A(x_i) + v_A(x_i) \cdot \pi_A(x_i)$ where $\pi_A(x_i) = 1 - \mu_A(x_i) - v_A(x_i)$ and the summation formula of IF sets $\tilde{x} \bigoplus \tilde{y} = \langle \mu_{\tilde{x}} + \mu_{\tilde{y}} - \mu_{\tilde{x}}\mu_{\tilde{y}}, v_{\tilde{x}}v_{\tilde{y}} \rangle$ where $\tilde{x} = \langle \mu_{\tilde{x}}, v_{\tilde{x}} \rangle, \tilde{y} = \langle \mu_{\tilde{y}}, v_{\tilde{y}} \rangle, \tilde{x}, \tilde{y} \in D^*$ and $\lambda\tilde{x} = \langle 1 - (1 - \mu\tilde{x})^\lambda, v_{\tilde{x}}^\lambda \rangle, \lambda > 0$, then for each $x_i \in U$, two ranking functions of x_i are defined as:

The first type:

$$P^-(x_i) = L(R \downarrow A^- \bigoplus R \uparrow A^-), P^+(x_i) = L(R \downarrow A^+ \bigoplus R \uparrow A^+);$$

The second type:

$$P^-(x_i) = L(\alpha R \downarrow A^- \bigoplus (1-\alpha) R \uparrow A^-), P^+(x_i) = L(\alpha R \downarrow A^+ \bigoplus (1-\alpha) R \uparrow A^+).$$

where $\alpha \in [0,1]$ be a level adjustment value.

Lastly, based on the principle of the TOPSIS methods, the relative closeness coefficient of every alternative x_i about P^- and P^+ is defined as: $\delta(x_i) = \frac{P^-(x_i)}{P^-(x_i)+P^+(x_i)}$. According to the values of $\delta(x_i)$, we can rank these alternatives. Lastly, through the ranking order of all alternatives, we can choose the best alternative.

5.3. Algorithm for IF-Rough Sets Models with IF Information

We come up with an algorithm for IF rough sets models based on MCDM problem with IF information. Now a company want to choose the best one from six candidates. Let $U = \{x_1, x_2, x_3, x_4, x_5, x_6\}$ be the set of six candidates. Let $C = \{C_1, C_2, C_3, C_4, C_5\}$ be five criteria, C_1, C_2, C_3, C_4, C_5 represent emotional quotient, work ability, language expression skills, management ability and resilience ability, respectively. Let $C_j(x_i) = \langle \mu(x_i), v(x_i) \rangle, (j = 1, 2, ..., 5; i = 1, 2, ..., 6)$ where $\mu(x_i)$ and $v(x_i)$ are the degrees of the membership and the non-membership of the alternative x_i to the criterion C_j, respectively. Suppose that for each alternative x_i, there exists the criterion C_j such that $C_j(x_i) = \langle 1, 0 \rangle$. The IF relation R based IF rough sets of six alternatives are as Table 2.

Table 2. IF relation R.

R	x_1	x_2	x_3	x_4	x_5	x_6
R/U	x_1	x_2	x_3	x_4	x_5	x_6
$R(x_1)$	$\langle 1,0\rangle$	$\langle 0.6,0.4\rangle$	$\langle 0.6,0.3\rangle$	$\langle 0.6,0.2\rangle$	$\langle 0.5,0.3\rangle$	$\langle 0.5,0.4\rangle$
$R(x_2)$	$\langle 0.8,0.2\rangle$	$\langle 1,0\rangle$	$\langle 0.8,0.2\rangle$	$\langle 0.8,0.2\rangle$	$\langle 0.6,0.4\rangle$	$\langle 0.6,0.4\rangle$
$R(x_3)$	$\langle 0.7,0.25\rangle$	$\langle 0.7,0.1\rangle$	$\langle 1,0\rangle$	$\langle 0.7,0.3\rangle$	$\langle 0.5,0.5\rangle$	$\langle 0.8,0.2\rangle$
$R(x_4)$	$\langle 0.3,0.7\rangle$	$\langle 0.3,0.5\rangle$	$\langle 0.3,0.45\rangle$	$\langle 1,0\rangle$	$\langle 0.6,0.2\rangle$	$\langle 0.6,0.4\rangle$
$R(x_5)$	$\langle 0.5,0.5\rangle$	$\langle 0.7,0.3\rangle$	$\langle 0.7,0.25\rangle$	$\langle 0.9,0.1\rangle$	$\langle 1,0\rangle$	$\langle 0.7,0.3\rangle$
$R(x_6)$	$\langle 0.7,0.3\rangle$	$\langle 0.7,0.1\rangle$	$\langle 0.7,0.15\rangle$	$\langle 0.7,0.3\rangle$	$\langle 0.5,0.5\rangle$	$\langle 1,0\rangle$

Then calculate the positive ideal solution A^+ and the negative ideal solution A^- as follows:

$$A^+ = \frac{\langle 1,0\rangle}{x_1} + \frac{\langle 1,0\rangle}{x_2} + \frac{\langle 1,0\rangle}{x_3} + \frac{\langle 1,0\rangle}{x_4} + \frac{\langle 1,0\rangle}{x_5} + \frac{\langle 1,0\rangle}{x_6};$$
$$A^- = \frac{\langle 0.3,0.7\rangle}{x_1} + \frac{\langle 0.3,0.5\rangle}{x_2} + \frac{\langle 0.3,0.45\rangle}{x_3} + \frac{\langle 0.6,0.3\rangle}{x_4} + \frac{\langle 0.5,0.5\rangle}{x_5} + \frac{\langle 0.5,0.4\rangle}{x_6}.$$

We calculate the approximation operator of A^+ and A^- through three IF-rough sets models, then calculate the $P^+(x_i)$ and $P^-(x_i)$ for each $x_i \in U$,respectively. Last, calculate the $\delta(x_i)$ for each $x_i \in U$ and rank for all alternatives.

case 1 IF-rough sets model.

By the definition ,we have following results:

$$R\downarrow A^+ = R\uparrow A^+ = U;$$
$$R\downarrow A^- = \frac{\langle 0.3,0.7\rangle}{x_1} + \frac{\langle 0.3,0.7\rangle}{x_2} + \frac{\langle 0.3,0.7\rangle}{x_3} + \frac{\langle 0.45,0.5\rangle}{x_4} + \frac{\langle 0.3,0.5\rangle}{x_5} + \frac{\langle 0.3,0.7\rangle}{x_6};$$
$$R\uparrow A^- = \frac{\langle 0.6,0.3\rangle}{x_1} + \frac{\langle 0.6,0.3\rangle}{x_2} + \frac{\langle 0.6,0.3\rangle}{x_3} + \frac{\langle 0.6,0.3\rangle}{x_4} + \frac{\langle 0.6,0.3\rangle}{x_5} + \frac{\langle 0.6,0.3\rangle}{x_6}.$$

The first ranking function type, we have the following results:

$$P^+(x_i) = \frac{1}{x_1} + \frac{1}{x_2} + \frac{1}{x_3} + \frac{1}{x_4} + \frac{1}{x_5} + \frac{1}{x_6};$$
$$P^-(x_i) = \frac{0.7347}{x_1} + \frac{0.7347}{x_2} + \frac{0.7347}{x_3} + \frac{0.7905}{x_4} + \frac{0.7395}{x_5} + \frac{0.7347}{x_6}.$$

By the formula, we have
$\delta = \frac{0.4235}{x_1} + \frac{0.4235}{x_2} + \frac{0.4235}{x_3} + \frac{0.4415}{x_4} + \frac{0.4251}{x_5} + \frac{0.4235}{x_6}.$

According to the value of $\delta(x_i)$. We rank six alternatives as follows:

$$x_4 \succ x_5 \succ x_1 \approx x_2 \approx x_3 \approx x_6$$

Thus, we can choose the best alternative x_4.

The second ranking function type,let $\alpha = 0.5$, where α is a level adjustment. Then we have the following results:

$$P^+(x_i) = \frac{1}{x_1} + \frac{1}{x_2} + \frac{1}{x_3} + \frac{1}{x_4} + \frac{1}{x_5} + \frac{1}{x_6};$$
$$P^-(x_i) = \frac{0.5033}{x_1} + \frac{0.5033}{x_2} + \frac{0.5033}{x_3} + \frac{0.5626}{x_4} + \frac{0.5258}{x_5} + \frac{0.5033}{x_6}.$$

By the formula, we have $\delta = \frac{0.3348}{x_1} + \frac{0.3348}{x_2} + \frac{0.3348}{x_3} + \frac{0.36}{x_4} + \frac{0.3445}{x_5} + \frac{0.3348}{x_6}.$
According to the value of $\delta(x_i)$. We rank six alternatives as follows:

$$x_4 \succ x_5 \approx x_1 \approx x_2 \approx x_3 \approx x_6$$

Thus, we can choose the best alternative x_4.

case 2 (I,T)-IF rough sets model.

Let $T(x,y) = (\min(x_1,y_1), \max(x_2,y_2))$,

$$I(x,y) = \begin{cases} \langle 1,0\rangle & x_1 \leq y_1 and x_2 \geq y_2 \\ (1-y_2,y_2) & x_1 \leq y_1 and x_2 < y_2 \\ (y_1,0) & x_1 > y_1 and x_2 \geq y_2 \\ (y_1,y_2) & x_1 > y_1 and x_2 < y_2 \end{cases}$$

Definition 16 ([35]). *Let $\alpha = \langle \mu_\alpha, v_\alpha \rangle$ be an IF value, and the score function of the IF value α is defined as follows:*

$$S(\alpha) = (\mu_\alpha - v_\alpha)(1 + \pi_\alpha)$$

where $\pi_\alpha = 1 - \mu_\alpha - v_\alpha$.

Definition 17 ([35]). *Let $\alpha = \langle \mu_\alpha, v_\alpha \rangle$ and $\beta = \langle \mu_\beta, v_\beta \rangle$ be two IF values, and $S(\alpha)$, $S(\beta)$ are score function of α and β respectively, then*

(1) If $S(\alpha) > S(\beta)$, called α is greater than β, i.e., $\alpha > \beta$;
(2) If $S(\alpha) = S(\beta)$, then,
if $\mu_\alpha > \mu_\beta$, called α is greater than β, i.e., $\alpha > \beta$;
if $\mu_\alpha < \mu_\beta$, called α is less than β, i.e., $\alpha < \beta$.

By the definition, we have following results:

$R \downarrow_I A^+ = R \uparrow_T A^+ = U;$
$R \downarrow_I A^- = \frac{\langle 0.3,0.7\rangle}{x_1} + \frac{\langle 0.3,0.7\rangle}{x_2} + \frac{\langle 0.3,0.7\rangle}{x_3} + \frac{\langle 0.3,0.7\rangle}{x_4} + \frac{\langle 0.3,0.7\rangle}{x_5} + \frac{\langle 0.3,0.7\rangle}{x_6};$
$R \uparrow_T A^- = \frac{\langle 0.5,0.4\rangle}{x_1} + \frac{\langle 0.5,0.4\rangle}{x_2} + \frac{\langle 0.5,0.4\rangle}{x_3} + \frac{\langle 0.6,0.3\rangle}{x_4} + \frac{\langle 0.6,0.4\rangle}{x_5} + \frac{\langle 0.6,0.4\rangle}{x_6}.$

The first ranking function type, we have the following results:

$P^+(x_i) = \frac{1}{x_1} + \frac{1}{x_2} + \frac{1}{x_3} + \frac{1}{x_4} + \frac{1}{x_5} + \frac{1}{x_6};$
$P^-(x_i) = \frac{0.6696}{x_1} + \frac{0.6696}{x_2} + \frac{0.6696}{x_3} + \frac{0.7347}{x_4} + \frac{0.72}{x_5} + \frac{0.72}{x_6};$
$\delta = \frac{0.4011}{x_1} + \frac{0.4011}{x_2} + \frac{0.4011}{x_3} + \frac{0.4235}{x_4} + \frac{0.4186}{x_5} + \frac{0.4186}{x_6}.$

$$x_4 \succ x_5 \approx x_6 \succ x_1 \approx x_2 \approx x_3$$

Thus, we can choose the best alternative x_4.

The second ranking function type, let $\alpha = 0.5$, where α is a level adjustment. Then we have the following results:

$P^+(x_i) = \frac{1}{x_1} + \frac{1}{x_2} + \frac{1}{x_3} + \frac{1}{x_4} + \frac{1}{x_5} + \frac{1}{x_6};$
$P^-(x_i) = \frac{0.4414}{x_1} + \frac{0.4414}{x_2} + \frac{0.4414}{x_3} + \frac{0.5033}{x_4} + \frac{0.4708}{x_5} + \frac{0.4708}{x_6};$
$\delta = \frac{0.3062}{x_1} + \frac{0.3062}{x_2} + \frac{0.3062}{x_3} + \frac{0.3348}{x_4} + \frac{0.3201}{x_5} + \frac{0.3201}{x_6}.$

$$x_4 \succ x_5 \approx x_6 \succ x_1 \approx x_2 \approx x_3$$

Thus, we can choose the best alternative x_4.

case 3 $(R_{\widetilde{O}}, \widetilde{O})$-IF rough sets model.

Let $\widetilde{O}(x,y) = \langle \min(x_1,y_1)\min(x_1^2,y_1^2), \max(x_2,y_2)\max(x_2^2,y_2^2)\rangle$

$$R_{\widetilde{O}}(x,y) = \begin{cases} \langle 1,0\rangle & x_1^3 \leq y_1 and x_2^3 \leq y_2 \\ (1-y_2^{1/3}, y_2^{1/3}) & x_1^3 \leq y_1 and x_2^3 < y_2 \\ (y_1^{1/3},0) & x_1^3 > y_1 and x_2^3 \geq y_2 \\ (y_1^{1/3}, y_2^{1/3}) & x_1^3 > y_1 and x_2^3 < y_2 \end{cases}$$

By the definition ,we have following results:

$R\downarrow_{R_{\widetilde{O}}} A^+ = R\uparrow_{\widetilde{O}} A^+ = U;$

$R\downarrow_{R_{\widetilde{O}}} A^- = \frac{\langle 0.2063,0.7937\rangle}{x_1} + \frac{\langle 0.1121,0.8879\rangle}{x_2} + \frac{\langle 0.1121,0.8879\rangle}{x_3} + \frac{\langle 0.1121,0.8879\rangle}{x_4} + \frac{\langle 0.1121,0.8879\rangle}{x_5} + \frac{\langle 0.1121,0.8879\rangle}{x_6};$

$R\uparrow_{\widetilde{O}} A^- = \frac{\langle 0.125,0.064\rangle}{x_1} + \frac{\langle 0.125,0.064\rangle}{x_2} + \frac{\langle 0.125,0.064\rangle}{x_3} + \frac{\langle 0.216,0.064\rangle}{x_4} + \frac{\langle 0.216,0.027\rangle}{x_5} + \frac{\langle 0.216,0.027\rangle}{x_6}.$

The first ranking function type, we have the following results:

$P^+(x_i) = \frac{1}{x_1} + \frac{1}{x_2} + \frac{1}{x_3} + \frac{1}{x_4} + \frac{1}{x_5} + \frac{1}{x_6};$

$P^-(x_i) = \frac{0.3382}{x_1} + \frac{0.2597}{x_2} + \frac{0.264}{x_3} + \frac{0.3402}{x_4} + \frac{0.32}{x_5} + \frac{0.32}{x_6};$

$\delta = \frac{0.2527}{x_1} + \frac{0.2062}{x_2} + \frac{0.2089}{x_3} + \frac{0.2538}{x_4} + \frac{0.2424}{x_5} + \frac{0.2424}{x_6}.$

$$x_4 \succ x_1 \succ x_5 \approx x_6 \succ x_3 \succ x_2$$

Thus, we can choose the best alternative x_4.

The second ranking function type, let $\alpha = 0.5$, where α is a level adjustment. Then we have the following results:

$P^+(x_i) = \frac{1}{x_1} + \frac{1}{x_2} + \frac{1}{x_3} + \frac{1}{x_4} + \frac{1}{x_5} + \frac{1}{x_6};$

$P^-(x_i) = \frac{0.3037}{x_1} + \frac{0.2719}{x_2} + \frac{0.2719}{x_3} + \frac{0.3027}{x_4} + \frac{0.2709}{x_5} + \frac{0.2709}{x_6};$

$\delta = \frac{0.233}{x_1} + \frac{0.2318}{x_2} + \frac{0.2318}{x_3} + \frac{0.2353}{x_4} + \frac{0.2132}{x_5} + \frac{0.2132}{x_6}.$

$$x_4 \succ x_1 \succ x_2 \approx x_3 \succ x_5 \approx x_6$$

Thus, we can choose the best alternative x_4.

case 4 $(R_{\widetilde{O}}, \widetilde{O})$-IF rough sets model.

Now let $\widetilde{O}(x,y) = \langle \min(\sqrt{x_1}, \sqrt{y_1}), \max(\sqrt{x_2}, \sqrt{y_2})\rangle$

$$R_{\widetilde{O}}(x,y) = \begin{cases} \langle 1,0\rangle & x_1 \leq y_1^2 and x_2 \leq y_2^2 \\ \langle 1-y_2^2, y_2^2\rangle & x_1 \leq y_1^2 and x_2 < y_2^2 \\ \langle y_1^2,0\rangle & x_1 > y_1^2 and x_2 \geq y_2^2 \\ \langle y_1^2, y_2^2\rangle & x_1 > y_1^2 and x_2 < y_2^2 \end{cases}$$

By the definition, we have following results:

$R\downarrow_{R_{\widetilde{O}}} A^+ = R\uparrow_{\widetilde{O}} A^+ = U;$

$R\downarrow_{R_{\widetilde{O}}} A^- = \frac{\langle 0.09,0.49\rangle}{x_1} + \frac{\langle 0.09,0.49\rangle}{x_2} + \frac{\langle 0.09,0.49\rangle}{x_3} + \frac{\langle 0.09,0.49\rangle}{x_4} + \frac{\langle 0.09,0.49\rangle}{x_5} + \frac{\langle 0.09,0.49\rangle}{x_6};$

$R\uparrow_{\widetilde{O}} A^- = \frac{\langle 0.7071,0.6325\rangle}{x_1} + \frac{\langle 0.7071,0.6325\rangle}{x_2} + \frac{\langle 0.7071,0.6325\rangle}{x_3} + \frac{\langle 0.7746,0.5477\rangle}{x_4} + \frac{\langle 0.7746,0.5476\rangle}{x_5} + \frac{\langle 0.7746,0.6325\rangle}{x_6}.$

The first ranking function type, we have the following results:

$P^{+}(x_i) = \frac{1}{x_1} + \frac{1}{x_2} + \frac{1}{x_3} + \frac{1}{x_4} + \frac{1}{x_5} + \frac{1}{x_6};$
$P^{-}(x_i) = \frac{0.72}{x_1} + \frac{0.72}{x_2} + \frac{0.72}{x_3} + \frac{0.7779}{x_4} + \frac{0.7776}{x_5} + \frac{0.7624}{x_6};$
$\delta = \frac{0.4186}{x_1} + \frac{0.4186}{x_2} + \frac{0.4186}{x_3} + \frac{0.4375}{x_4} + \frac{0.4374}{x_5} + \frac{0.4326}{x_6}.$

$$x_4 \succ x_5 \succ x_6 \succ x_1 \approx x_2 \approx x_3$$

Thus, we can choose the best alternative x_4.

The second ranking function type, let $\alpha = 0.5$, where α is a level adjustment. Then we have the following results:

$P^{+}(x_i) = \frac{1}{x_1} + \frac{1}{x_2} + \frac{1}{x_3} + \frac{1}{x_4} + \frac{1}{x_5} + \frac{1}{x_6};$
$P^{-}(x_i) = \frac{0.4612}{x_1} + \frac{0.4612}{x_2} + \frac{0.4612}{x_3} + \frac{0.5314}{x_4} + \frac{0.5312}{x_5} + \frac{0.4893}{x_6};$
$\delta = \frac{0.3156}{x_1} + \frac{0.3156}{x_2} + \frac{0.3156}{x_3} + \frac{0.3392}{x_4} + \frac{0.3391}{x_5} + \frac{0.3285}{x_6}.$

$$x_4 \succ x_5 \succ x_6 \succ x_1 \approx x_2 \approx x_3$$

Thus, we can choose the best alternative x_4.

5.4. Comparative Analysis

In this subsection, first of all, we make a comparison between three models with no level adjustment α with IF information as shown in Table 3. Then a comparison among three models with level adjustment $\alpha = 0.5$, results as shown in Table 4 and analyze it.

Table 3. Ranking orders of alternative with no α.

Models	Ranking Orders of Six Alternatives
case1	$x_4 \succ x_5 \succ x_1 \approx x_2 \approx x_3 \approx x_6$
caes2	$x_4 \succ x_5 \approx x_6 \succ x_1 \approx x_2 \approx x_3$
case3	$x_4 \succ x_1 \succ x_5 \approx x_6 \succ x_3 \succ x_2$
case4	$x_4 \succ x_5 \succ x_6 \succ x_1 \approx x_2 \approx x_3$

Table 4. Ranking orders of alternative with $\alpha = 0.5$.

Models	Ranking Orders of Six Alternatives
case1	$x_4 \succ x_5 \approx x_1 \approx x_2 \approx x_3 \approx x_6$
caes2	$x_4 \succ x_5 \approx x_6 \succ x_1 \approx x_2 \approx x_3$
case3	$x_4 \succ x_1 \succ x_2 \approx x_3 \succ x_5 \approx x_6$
case4	$x_4 \succ x_5 \succ x_6 \succ x_1 \approx x_2 \approx x_3$

It can be seen from the table that the multi-criteria decision-making method proposed in this consistent with the decision result obtained by existing models, i.e., x_4 is the best alternative. This phenomenon shows that the model proposed in this paper is effective. Secondly, by the Tables 3 and 4, we can see the model with level adjustment will be better results. Lastly, by the model of case 1, we have almost the same ranking, by the model of case 2, we can also find x_1,x_2,x_3 almost same. Therefore, the two kinds of models cannot make a good ranking in this kind of problems. The model of case 2 is IF rough set based on IF triangular norm, since IF triangular norm satisfies associativity. The IF-overlap function is an extension of IF triangular norm, which does not meet associativity, therefore the model that proposed by this paper has a wider ranger of practical applications and is of effectiveness and application value.

5.5. Sensitivity Analysis

Using the similar method in case 1, let $\alpha = \{0, 0.1, ..., 0.9, 1\}$, we can obtain the results as shown in Table 5. Through this table, we can find that the results are different with different values of α. If $\alpha = 0$, then the six alternatives have equivalent interest. So, the

$\alpha = 0$ is not perfect when making a decision in real life. When $\alpha \neq 0$, the results of others are same. The best selection is x_4, respectively.

Table 5. Ranking orders of alternative with different α in case 1.

Different Value of α	Ranking Orders of Six Alternatives
$\alpha = 0$	$x_1 \approx x_2 \approx x_3 \approx x_4 \approx x_5 \approx x_6$
$\alpha = 0.1$	$x_4 \succ x_5 \succ x_1 \approx x_2 \approx x_3 \approx x_6$
$\alpha = 0.2$	$x_4 \succ x_5 \succ x_1 \approx x_2 \approx x_3 \approx x_6$
$\alpha = 0.3$	$x_4 \succ x_5 \succ x_1 \approx x_2 \approx x_3 \approx x_6$
$\alpha = 0.4$	$x_4 \succ x_5 \succ x_1 \approx x_2 \approx x_3 \approx x_6$
$\alpha = 0.5$	$x_4 \succ x_5 \succ x_1 \approx x_2 \approx x_3 \approx x_6$
$\alpha = 0.6$	$x_4 \succ x_5 \succ x_1 \approx x_2 \approx x_3 \approx x_6$
$\alpha = 0.7$	$x_4 \succ x_5 \succ x_1 \approx x_2 \approx x_3 \approx x_6$
$\alpha = 0.8$	$x_4 \succ x_5 \succ x_1 \approx x_2 \approx x_3 \approx x_6$
$\alpha = 0.9$	$x_4 \succ x_5 \succ x_1 \approx x_2 \approx x_3 \approx x_6$
$\alpha = 1$	$x_4 \succ x_5 \succ x_1 \approx x_2 \approx x_3 \approx x_6$

Using the similar method in case 2, let $\alpha = \{0, 0.1, ..., 0.9, 1\}$, we can obtain the results as shown in Table 6. Through this table, we can find that the results are different with different values of α. If $\alpha = 1$, then the six alternatives have equivalent interest. So, the $\alpha = 1$ is not perfect when making a decision in real life. When $\alpha \neq 1$, the results of others are same. The best selection is x_4, respectively.

Table 6. Ranking orders of alternative with different α in case 2.

Different Value of α	Ranking Orders of Six Alternatives
$\alpha = 0$	$x_4 \succ x_5 \approx x_6 \succ x_1 \approx x_2 \approx x_3$
$\alpha = 0.1$	$x_4 \succ x_5 \approx x_6 \succ x_1 \approx x_2 \approx x_3$
$\alpha = 0.2$	$x_4 \succ x_5 \approx x_6 \succ x_1 \approx x_2 \approx x_3$
$\alpha = 0.3$	$x_4 \succ x_5 \approx x_6 \succ x_1 \approx x_2 \approx x_3$
$\alpha = 0.4$	$x_4 \succ x_5 \approx x_6 \succ x_1 \approx x_2 \approx x_3$
$\alpha = 0.5$	$x_4 \succ x_5 \approx x_6 \succ x_1 \approx x_2 \approx x_3$
$\alpha = 0.6$	$x_4 \succ x_5 \approx x_6 \succ x_1 \approx x_2 \approx x_3$
$\alpha = 0.7$	$x_4 \succ x_5 \approx x_6 \succ x_1 \approx x_2 \approx x_3$
$\alpha = 0.8$	$x_4 \succ x_5 \approx x_6 \succ x_1 \approx x_2 \approx x_3$
$\alpha = 0.9$	$x_4 \succ x_5 \approx x_6 \succ x_1 \approx x_2 \approx x_3$
$\alpha = 1$	$x_1 \approx x_2 \approx x_3 \approx x_4 \approx x_5 \approx x_6$

Using the similar method in case 3, let $\alpha = \{0, 0.1, ..., 0.9, 1\}$, we can obtain the results as shown in Table 7. Through this table, we can find that the results are different with different values of α. But the results are highly consistent. When $\alpha = \{0.7, 0.8, 0.9, 1\}$, the best selection is x_1 while the worst selections are x_2 and x_3. However, when $\alpha = \{0, 0.1, ..., 0.6\}$, the best selection is still x_4. In other words, if $0 \leq \alpha \leq 0.6$, the change of the value of α has no influence on our results. So using the similar way in case 3 to make decisions, we should take $0 \leq \alpha \leq 0.6$.

Table 7. Ranking orders of alternative with different α in case 3.

Different Value of α	Ranking Orders of Six Alternatives
$\alpha = 0$	$x_4 \succ x_5 \approx x_6 \succ x_1 \approx x_2 \approx x_3$
$\alpha = 0.1$	$x_4 \succ x_5 \approx x_6 \succ x_1 \succ x_2 \approx x_3$
$\alpha = 0.2$	$x_4 \succ x_5 \approx x_6 \succ x_1 \succ x_2 \approx x_3$
$\alpha = 0.3$	$x_4 \succ x_1 \succ x_5 \approx x_6 \succ x_2 \approx x_3$
$\alpha = 0.4$	$x_4 \succ x_1 \succ x_5 \approx x_6 \succ x_2 \approx x_3$
$\alpha = 0.5$	$x_4 \succ x_1 \succ x_2 \approx x_3 \succ x_5 \approx x_6$
$\alpha = 0.6$	$x_4 \succ x_1 \succ x_2 \approx x_3 \succ x_5 \approx x_6$
$\alpha = 0.7$	$x_1 \succ x_4 \succ x_5 \approx x_6 \succ x_2 \approx x_3$
$\alpha = 0.8$	$x_1 \succ x_5 \approx x_6 \succ x_4 \succ x_2 \approx x_3$
$\alpha = 0.9$	$x_1 \succ x_5 \approx x_6 \succ x_4 \succ x_2 \approx x_3$
$\alpha = 1$	$x_1 \succ x_5 \approx x_6 \approx x_4 \approx x_2 \approx x_3$

In the Table 8, the sensitivity analysis of the IF rough sets model (case 1), (I, T)-IF rough sets model (case 2) and $(R_{\widetilde{O}}, \widetilde{O})$-IF rough sets model (case 3) are given.

Form the Table 8, we make some comparisons of the three models based on MCDM with IF information with different value of α. Then we have the following results:

(1) The results of IF rough sets model, (I, T)-IF rough sets model and $(R_{\widetilde{O}}, \widetilde{O})$-IF rough sets model have the same choose that x_4 is the best alternative.

(2) We can find in case 1 and case 2, changing the value of α has no influence on our results (except $\alpha = 0$ in case1, $\alpha = 1$ in case 2). When $\alpha = 0$, through comparison, IF rough sets model gives us is that six alternatives have the same weight, therefore, it is invalid in real life to making a decision. When $\alpha = 1$, (I, T)-IF rough sets model gives us are that six alternatives have the same weight, therefore, it is invalid in real life to making a decision. Obviosly, $(R_{\widetilde{O}}, \widetilde{O})$-IF rough sets model is better than IF rough sets model and (I, T)-IF rough sets model in this situation.

(3) When $\alpha = 0.1$, the result of $(R_{\widetilde{O}}, \widetilde{O})$-IF rough sets model and the result of (I, T)-IF rough sets model are highly consistent, When $\alpha = \{0.2, 0.3\}$, the result of $(R_{\widetilde{O}}, \widetilde{O})$-IF rough sets model and the result of IF rough sets model are highly consistent. In other words, the result of (I, T)-IF rough sets model is one of many results of $(R_{\widetilde{O}}, \widetilde{O})$-IF rough sets model.

Table 8. The comparison among ranking orders of alternative with different α .

Different Value of α	IF Rough Sets Model (Case 1)	(I, T)-IF Rough Sets Model (Case 2)	$(R_{\widetilde{O}}, \widetilde{O})$-IF Rough Sets Model (Case 3)
$\alpha = 0$	$x_1 \approx x_2 \approx x_3 \approx x_4 \approx x_5 \approx x_6$	$x_4 \succ x_5 \approx x_6 \succ x_1 \approx x_2 \approx x_3$	$x_4 \succ x_5 \approx x_6 \succ x_1 \approx x_2 \approx x_3$
$\alpha = 0.1$	$x_4 \succ x_5 \succ x_1 \approx x_2 \approx x_3 \approx x_6$	$x_4 \succ x_5 \approx x_6 \succ x_1 \approx x_2 \approx x_3$	$x_4 \succ x_5 \approx x_6 \succ x_1 \succ x_2 \approx x_3$
$\alpha = 0.2$	$x_4 \succ x_5 \succ x_1 \approx x_2 \approx x_3 \approx x_6$	$x_4 \succ x_5 \approx x_6 \succ x_1 \approx x_2 \approx x_3$	$x_4 \succ x_5 \approx x_6 \succ x_1 \succ x_2 \approx x_3$
$\alpha = 0.3$	$x_4 \succ x_5 \succ x_1 \approx x_2 \approx x_3 \approx x_6$	$x_4 \succ x_5 \approx x_6 \succ x_1 \approx x_2 \approx x_3$	$x_4 \succ x_1 \succ x_5 \approx x_6 \succ x_2 \approx x_3$
$\alpha = 0.4$	$x_4 \succ x_5 \succ x_1 \approx x_2 \approx x_3 \approx x_6$	$x_4 \succ x_5 \approx x_6 \succ x_1 \approx x_2 \approx x_3$	$x_4 \succ x_1 \succ x_5 \approx x_6 \succ x_2 \approx x_3$
$\alpha = 0.5$	$x_4 \succ x_5 \succ x_1 \approx x_2 \approx x_3 \approx x_6$	$x_4 \succ x_5 \approx x_6 \succ x_1 \approx x_2 \approx x_3$	$x_4 \succ x_1 \succ x_2 \approx x_3 \succ x_5 \approx x_6$
$\alpha = 0.6$	$x_4 \succ x_5 \succ x_1 \approx x_2 \approx x_3 \approx x_6$	$x_4 \succ x_5 \approx x_6 \succ x_1 \approx x_2 \approx x_3$	$x_4 \succ x_1 \succ x_2 \approx x_3 \succ x_5 \approx x_6$
$\alpha = 0.7$	$x_4 \succ x_5 \succ x_1 \approx x_2 \approx x_3 \approx x_6$	$x_4 \succ x_5 \approx x_6 \succ x_1 \approx x_2 \approx x_3$	$x_1 \succ x_4 \succ x_5 \approx x_6 \succ x_2 \approx x_3$
$\alpha = 0.8$	$x_4 \succ x_5 \succ x_1 \approx x_2 \approx x_3 \approx x_6$	$x_4 \succ x_5 \approx x_6 \succ x_1 \approx x_2 \approx x_3$	$x_1 \succ x_5 \approx x_6 \succ x_4 \succ x_2 \approx x_3$
$\alpha = 0.9$	$x_4 \succ x_5 \succ x_1 \approx x_2 \approx x_3 \approx x_6$	$x_4 \succ x_5 \approx x_6 \succ x_1 \approx x_2 \approx x_3$	$x_1 \succ x_5 \approx x_6 \succ x_4 \succ x_2 \approx x_3$
$\alpha = 1$	$x_4 \succ x_5 \succ x_1 \approx x_2 \approx x_3 \approx x_6$	$x_1 \approx x_2 \approx x_3 \approx x_4 \approx x_5 \approx x_6$	$x_1 \succ x_5 \approx x_6 \approx x_4 \approx x_2 \approx x_3$

The IF-rough model based on IF-overlap function presented in this paper is more flexible when dealing with specific application problems, and can reproduce the results obtained by other IF rough set models. According to the choice of different α, different decision ordering can be obtained, so that the decision maker can have a better decision reference in practical problems.

6. Conclusions

Inspired by the literature [6,7,17,27], this paper puts forward the concept of IF-overlap function for the first time, and constructs an IF-rough set model based on IF-overlap function, which can be regarded as an extended form of IF-rough set based on IF triangular norm. On the one hand, the model retains the important properties of the original IF rough set model. On the other hand, the application range of IF rough sets is expanded and the flexibility is stronger. In order to solve MCDM problems in real life, the IF rough set model based on IF-overlap function is combined with IF TOPSIS method. The decision results show that the model has significant application value. Compared with other decision results, the model is more flexible, by changing the value of α ($\alpha \in [0,1]$ is a level adjustment value), the new model can obtain the results of other models, which can reproduce most of the existing results and provide more reference for decision makers. As a further research topic, the variable precision intuitionistic fuzzy rough sets based on IF-overlap functions and the covering intuitionistic fuzzy rough sets [36–40] based on IF-overlap functions will be discussed in the following work, and applied to data mining and knowledge discovery, etc.

Author Contributions: The idea of this whole paper was put forward by X.Z., he also completed the preparatory work of the paper. X.W. analyzed the existing work of the intuitionistic fuzzy overlap function and rough sets and wrote the paper. T.L. finished proofreading. All authors have read and agreed to the published version of the manuscript.

Funding: This work was supported by National Science Foundation of China (Grant No. 61976130).

Institutional Review Board Statement: Not applicable.

Informed Consent Statement: Not applicable.

Data Availability Statement: Not applicable.

Conflicts of Interest: The authors declare no conflict of interest.

References

1. Zadeh, L.A. Fuzzy sets. *Inf. Control.* **1965**, *8*, 338–353. [CrossRef]
2. Meng, F.; Chen, S.M.; Tang, J. Group decision making based on acceptable multiplicative consistency of hesitant fuzzy preference relations. *Inf. Sci.* **2020**, *524*, 77–96. [CrossRef]
3. Liu, P.; Wang, P. Multilpe-attribute decision-making based on archimedean bonferroni operator of q-rung orthopair fuzzy numbers. *IEEE Trans. Fuzzy Syst.* **2018**,*27*, 834–848. [CrossRef]
4. Zhang, K.Q.; Chen, Y.M.; Tang, C. Random fuzzy clustering granular hyperplane classifier. *IEEE Access.* **2020**,*12*, 2169–3536.
5. Wang, J.Q.; Peng, J.J.; Zhang, H.Y. Outranking approach for multi-criteria decision-making problems with hesitant inter-valued fuzzy sets. *Soft Comput.* **2019**, *23*, 419–430. [CrossRef]
6. Wang, L.; Wang, H.; Xu, Z. The interval-valued hesitant pythagorean fuzzy sets and its application with extended topsis and choquet integral-based method. *Int. J. Intell. Syst.* **2019**, *34*, 1063–1085. [CrossRef]
7. Atanassov, K. Intuitionistic fuzzy sets. *Fuzzy Sets Syst.* **1986**, *20*, 87–96. [CrossRef]
8. Atanassov, K. *On Intuitionistic Fuzzy Sets Theory*; Springer: Berlin/Heidelberg, Germany, 2012.
9. Atanassov, K. Intuitionistic fuzzy sets. *Int. J. Bioautom.* **2016**, *20*, 1–6.
10. Pawlak, Z. Rough sets. *Int. J. Comput. Inf. Sci.* **1982**, *11*, 341–356. [CrossRef]
11. Dubois, D.; Prade, H. Rough fuzzy sets and fuzzy rough sets. *Int. J. Gen. Syst.* **1990**, *17*, 191–209. [CrossRef]
12. Morsi, N.N.; Yakout, M.M. Axiomatics for fuzzy rough sets. *Fuzzy Sets Syst.* **1998**, *100*, 327–342. [CrossRef]
13. Wang, C.Y.; Hu, B.M. Fuzzy rough sets based on generalized residuated lattices. *Inf. Sci.* **2013**, *248*, 31–49. [CrossRef]
14. Lin, Y.J.; Li, Y.W.; Wang, C.X. Attribute reduction for multi-label learning with fuzzy rough set. *Knowl. Based Syst.* **2018**, *152*, 51–61. [CrossRef]
15. Wu, W.Z.; Yee, L.; Mi, J.S. On characterizations of (I,T)-fuzzy rough approximation operators. *Fuzzy Sets Syst.* **2005**, *154*, 76–102. [CrossRef]
16. Sun, B.Z.; Gong, Z.T.; Chen, D.G. Fuzzy rough set theory for the interval-valued fuzzy information systems. *Inf. Sci.* **2008**, *178*, 2794–2815. [CrossRef]
17. Atanassov, K. *Intuitionistic Fuzzy Sets: Theory and Applications*; Physica-Verlag: Heidelberg, Germany, 1999.
18. Vlachos, I.K.; Sergiadis, G.D. Intuitionistic fuzzy information-application to pattern recognition. *Pattern Recognit. Lett.* **2007**, *28*, 197–206. [CrossRef]

19. Xu, Z.S. Some similarity measures of intuitionistic fuzzy sets and their applications to multiple attribute decision making. *Fuzzy Optim. Decis. Mak.* **2007**, *6*, 221–236. [CrossRef]
20. Traneva, V.; Tranev, S. Multidimensional intuitionistic fuzzy InterCriteria analysis in the restaurant. *J. Intell. Fuzzy Syst.* **2020**. [CrossRef]
21. Traneva, V.; Tranev, S. Intuitionistic Fuzzy Two-factor Variance Analysis of Movie Ticket Sales. *J. Intell. Fuzzy Syst.* **2021**. [CrossRef]
22. Bustince, H.; Burillo, P. Structures on intuitionistic fuzzy relations. *Fuzzy Sets Syst.* **1996**, *78*, 293–303. [CrossRef]
23. Deschrijver, G.; Cornelis, C.; Kerre, E. On the representation of intuitionistic fuzzy t-norm and t-conorms. *IEEE Trans. Fuzzy Syst.* **2004**, *12*, 45–61. [CrossRef]
24. Zhou, L.; Wu, W.Z. On generalized intuitionistic fuzzy rough approximation operators. *Inf. Sci.* **2008**, *178*, 2448–2465. [CrossRef]
25. Decock, M. A Thorough Study of Linguistuc Modifiers in Fuzzy Set Theory. Ph.D. Thesis, Ghent University, Ghent, Belgium, 2002.
26. Cornelis, C.; Cock, M.; Kerre, M.E. Intuitionistic fuzzy rough sets: At the crossroads of imperfect knowledge. *Expert Syst. Int. J. Knowl. Eng. Neural Netw.* **2003**, *20*, 260–269. [CrossRef]
27. Zhang, X.H.; Zhou, B.; Li, P. A general frame for intuitionistic fuzzy rough sets. *Inf. Sci.* **2012**, *216*, 34–39. [CrossRef]
28. Bustince, H.; Fernandez, J.; Mesiar, R. Overlap Index, Overlap Functions and Migrativity. In Proceedings of the Joint 2009 International Fuzzy Systems Association Word Congress and 2009 European Society of Fuzzy Logic and Technology Conference, Lisbon, Portugal, 20–24 July 2009; Volume 65, pp. 300–305.
29. Bustince, H.; Barrenecha, E.; Pagola, M. Image thresholding using restrited equivalent functions and maximizing the measures of similarity. *Fuzzy Sets Syst.* **2007**, *158*, 496–516. [CrossRef]
30. Amo, A.; Montero, J.; Biging, G. Fuzzy classification systems. *Eur. J. Oper. Res.* **2004**, *156*, 495–507. [CrossRef]
31. Elkano, M.; Galar, M.; Sanz, J. Enhancing multiclass classification in FARC-HD fuzzy classifier: On the synergy between n-dimensional overlap functions and decomposition strategies. *IEEE Trans. Fuzzy Syst.* **2015**, *23*, 1562–1580. [CrossRef]
32. Qiao, J.; Hu, B.Q. On interval additive generators of interval overlap functions and interval grouping functions. *Fuzzy Sets Syst.* **2017**, *323*, 19–55. [CrossRef]
33. Bedregal, B.; Bustince, H.; Palmeira, E. Generalized interval-valued OWA operators with interval weights derived from interval.Cvalued overlap functions. *Int. J. Approx. Reason.* **2017**, *90*, 1–16. [CrossRef]
34. Tiago, D.C.; Graliz, P.D. General interval-valued overlap functions and interval-valued overlap indices. *Inf. Sci.* **2020**, *527*, 27–50.
35. Pei, Z.; Zheng, L. A novel approach to multi-attribute decision making based on intuitionistic fuzzy sets. *Expert Systems with Applications*, **2012**, *39*, 2560–2566. [CrossRef]
36. Zhang, L.; Zhan, J.M.; Xu, Z.S. Covering-based generalized IF rough sets with applications to multi-attribuate decision-making. *Inf. Sci.* **2019**, *478*, 275–302. [CrossRef]
37. Zhan, J.M.; Sun, B.; Alcantud, J.R. Covering based multigranulation (φ, τ)-fuzzy rough set models and applications in multattribute group decisionmaking. *Inf. Sci.* **2019**, *476*, 290–318. [CrossRef]
38. Yao, Y.Y.; Yao, B. Covering based rough sets approximations. *Inf. Sci.* **2012**, *200*, 91–107. [CrossRef]
39. Zhang, X.H.; Wang, J.Q. Fuzzy β-covering approximation space. *Int. J. Approx. Reason.* **2020**, *26*, 27–47. [CrossRef]
40. Zhang, X.H.; Wang, J.Q.; Zhan, J.M.; Dai, J.H. Fuzzy measures and Choquet integrals based on fuzzy covering rough sets. *IEEE Trans. Fuzzy Syst.* **2021**. [CrossRef]

symmetry

MDPI

Article

Bipolar Picture Fuzzy Graphs with Application

Waheed Ahmad Khan [1,*], Babir Ali [1] and Abdelghani Taouti [2]

1 Department of Mathematics, Attock Campus, University of Education, Attock 43600, Pakistan; msf1900184@ue.edu.pk
2 ETS-Maths and NS Engineering Division, HCT, University City, Sharjah P.O. Box 7947, United Arab Emirates; gtaouti@hct.ac.ae or ganitaouti@yahoo.com.au
* Correspondence: wakhan@ue.edu.pk or sirwak2003@yahoo.com

Abstract: In this manuscript, we introduce and discuss the term bipolar picture fuzzy graphs along with some of its fundamental characteristics and applications. We also initiate the concepts of complete bipolar picture fuzzy graphs and strong bipolar picture fuzzy graphs. Firstly, we apply different types of operations to bipolar picture fuzzy graphs and then we introduce various products of bipolar picture fuzzy graphs. Several other terms such as order and size, path, neighbourhood degrees, busy values of vertices and edges of bipolar picture fuzzy graphs are also discussed. These terminologies also lay the foundations for the discussion about the regular bipolar picture fuzzy graphs. Moreover, we also discuss isomorphisms, weak and co-weak isomorphisms and automorphisms of bipolar picture fuzzy graphs. Finally, at the base of bipolar picture fuzzy graph we present the construction of a bipolar picture fuzzy acquaintanceship graph, which would be an important tool to measure the symmetry or asymmetry of acquaintanceship levels of social networks, computer networks etc.

Keywords: bipolar picture fuzzy graphs; ring sum of bipolar picture fuzzy graph; busy value of bipolar picture fuzzy edge; weak and co-weak isomorphisms of bipolar picture fuzzy graphs

Citation: Khan, W.A.; Ali, B.; Taouti, A. Bipolar Picture Fuzzy Graphs with Application. *Symmetry* **2021**, *13*, 1427. https://doi.org/10.3390/sym13081427

Academic Editor: Jan Awrejcewicz

Received: 20 July 2021
Accepted: 29 July 2021
Published: 4 August 2021

1. Introduction

In 1965, Zadeh [1] introduced the term fuzzy sets (FSs), which is extensively used in different fields such as life sciences, social sciences, engineering, theory of decision making, computer sciences etc. Subsequently, many generalizations of the fuzzy sets have been explored in the literature like interval-valued fuzzy sets (IVFSs), bipolar fuzzy sets (BPFs), intuitionistic fuzzy sets (IFSs), picture fuzzy sets (PFSs) and so on (see e.g., [2,3]). The term interval-valued fuzzy set (IVFS) was also introduced by Zadeh [4]. Another generalization of fuzzy sets termed bipolar fuzzy sets (BPFSs) was introduced in [5]. In bipolar fuzzy sets (BPFSs) the membership value was considered in the interval [-1, 1]. In continuation, recently, the term bipolar Pythagorean fuzzy sets along with its applications towards decision making theory is explored in [6]. Various types of relations on BFSs were introduced in [7]. Basically, the term bipolar fuzzy relations (BPFRs) is the direct extension of fuzzy relations. BPFRs were also given a name "bifuzzy relations". Some new types of bipolar fuzzy relations and bipolar fuzzy equivalence relation were discussed in [7]. Atanassov [8] introduced the notion of intuitionistic fuzzy sets which was another generalized form of the fuzzy sets. Similarly, the generalization of both the fuzzy sets and intuitionistics fuzzy sets termed picture fuzzy sets (PFSs) was initiated by Cuong [9]. He also studied several operations and characteristics of PFSs. PFS is described by assigning three memberships values to the object which are neutral, positive and negative. After this, Bo et al. [10] introduced few new operations and relations on PFSs. Cuong et al. [11] introduced various types of fuzzy logical operators in the setting of PFSs.

On the other hand, Rosenfeld [12] extended the scope of fuzzy sets towards graph theory by initiating the notion of fuzzy graphs(FGs). Later on, Bhattacharya [13] added several terms in the theory of fuzzy graphs. Different types of operations were introduced and applied on fuzzy graphs (FGs) in [14]. The term complement of fuzzy graphs (FGs) was introduced by Mordeson and Nair [15]. Generalization of fuzzy graphs named interval-valued fuzzy graphs (IVFGs) were initited in [16]. The concepts of intuitionistic fuzzy graphs (IFGs) were explored in [17]. Several operations were defined and applied to IFGs in [18]. The term complex Intuitionistic fuzzy graphs and its applications toward cellular networking were explored in [19].

The term bipolar fuzzy graphs (BPFGs) was introduced by Akram [20], he also studied several interesting properties of these graphs. Similarly, Yang et al. [21] presented different types of BPFGs. Talebi and Rashmanlou [22] introduced the terms complement and isomorphism on bipolar fuzzy graphs, Ghorai and Pal [23] defined generalized regular bipolar fuzzy graphs. Further to this, Poulik and Ghorai [24] explored different indices on bipolar fuzzy graphs. Several characterizations of bipolar fuzzy graphs were extensively explored in [25]. They also presented the adjacency sequence of a vertex and first and second fundamental sequences were described in a bipolar fuzzy graph illustrative example. They also demonstrated through examples that if G is a regular bipolar fuzzy graph (RBFG), then its underlying crisp graph need not be regular and they showed that all the vertices need not have the same adjacency sequence. Moreover, they verified that if G and its underlying crisp graph are regular, then all of the vertices need not have the same adjacency sequence. At the base of adjacency sequences, they also provided necessary and sufficient condition for a BFG to be a regular with at most four vertices.

Further to the above, Zuo et al. [26] initiated the notion of picture fuzzy graphs (PFGs). They applied several operations on PFGs and presented some applications of PFGs towards social networking. Afterwards, picture fuzzy multi-graph (PFMG) was introduced in [27]. Regular picture fuzzy graphs (RPFGs) along with its applications towards networking communications have been explored in [28]. Recently, Koczy et al. [29] more investigated the term PFGs and they added several significant graphical terms for PFGs and demonstrated them with examples. They also verified the superiority of PFGs over FGs and IFGs by providing suitable examples. Specifically, they described two real-life problems including a social network and a Wi-Fi-network through picture fuzzy graphs and showed that the picture fuzzy graphs are more feasible than any other existing fuzzy structures. Recently, Amanathulla et al. [30] initiated the concept of balanced picture fuzzy graphs (balanced PFGs). This is a special type of PFG through which one can (balanced PFGs) define the density of a PFG based on weight and size of the graph. They also provided an application of balanced PFG in business alliance.

In this paper, we initiate the concepts of bipolar picture fuzzy graphs, complete bipolar picture fuzzy graphs and strong bipolar picture fuzzy graphs. We introduce the terms size of bipolar picture fuzzy graphs, path of bipolar picture fuzzy graphs, busy value of vertices and edges of a bipolar picture fuzzy graphs. We also study isomorphisms, weak and co-weak isomorphisms and automorphism of bipolar picture fuzzy graphs. We deduce in Proposition 1 that isomorphism between two bipolar picture fuzzy graphs is an equivalence relation and hence we can study the symmetry between two social networks through it. Finally, we construct a bipolar picture fuzzy acquaintanceship graph, which is asymmetric.

2. Preliminaries

In this section, we present some basic concepts related to fuzzy graphs. One may consult [31] for the basics of classical graph theory.

Definition 1. *[1] A fuzzy set (FS) S defined on X is represented by the collection*

$$S = \{(x, \alpha_S(x)) : x \in X, \alpha_S(x) \in [0,1]\}$$

Definition 2. *[32] The Cartesian product of the FSs $S_1, ..., S_n$ on $X_1, ..., X_n$ is the FS on the product $X_1 \times ... \times X_n$ having a membership function*

$$\mu_{(S_1 \times ... \times S_n)}(x) = \{\min(\alpha_{S_i}(x_i)) : x = (x_1, ..., x_n), x_i \in X_i\}$$

Definition 3. *[32] The* mth *power of a fuzzy S on X has the membership function*

$$\alpha_{S^m}(x) = \{[\alpha_S(x)]^m : x \in X\}$$

Definition 4. *[33] A bipolar fuzzy set (BPFS) is the pair (α^P, α^N), where $\alpha^P : X \to [0,1]$ and $\alpha^N : X \to [-1,0]$ represent mappings.*

Definition 5. *[33] A set $0_S = (0_S^P, 0_S^N)$ (resp., $1_S = (1_S^P, 1_S^N)$) is termed bipolar fuzzy empty set (resp., the bipolar fuzzy whole set) on X and is described as*

$$0_S^P(x) = 0 = 0_S^N(x) \text{ (resp., } 1_S^P(x) = 1 \text{ and } 1_S^N(x) = -1)$$

for each $x \in X$.

Definition 6. *[34] For any two BPFs $S = (\alpha_S^P, \alpha_S^N)$ and $T = (\alpha_T^P, \alpha_T^N)$, we have*

$$(S \cap T)(x) = ((\alpha_S^P(x) \wedge \alpha_T^P(x)), (\alpha_S^N(x) \vee \alpha_T^N(x)))$$

$$(S \cup T)(x) = ((\alpha_S^P(x) \vee \alpha_T^P(x)), (\alpha_S^N(x) \wedge \alpha_T^N(x)))$$

Definition 7. *[33] A mapping $S = (\alpha_S^P, \alpha_S^N) : X \times X \to [-1,0] \times [0,1]$ is a bipolar fuzzy relation (BPFR) on X, where $\alpha_S^P(x,y) \in [0,1]$ and $\alpha_S^N(x,y) \in [-1,0]$.*

Definition 8. *[33] The empty BPFR (resp., the whole BPFR) on X may be described by*

$$\alpha_S^P(x,y) = 0 = \alpha_S^N(x,y) \text{ (resp., } \alpha S^P(x,y) = 1 \text{ and } \alpha_S^N(x,y) = -1)$$

for each $x, y \in X$.

Definition 9. *[8] An intuitionistic fuzzy set (IFS) S on X is the collection $S = \{(x, \alpha_S(x), \beta_S(x)) : x \in X\}$, where $\alpha_S : X \to [0,1]$ is a membership degree while $\beta_S : X \to [0,1]$ represents a non-membership degree of $x \in X$, also for each $x \in X$, $0 \le \alpha_S(x) + \beta_S(x) \le 1$.*

Definition 10. *[35] A bipolar intuitionistic fuzzy set (BPIFS) can be described as $S = \{x, \alpha^P(x), \alpha^N(x), \beta^P(x), \beta^N(x) : x \in X\}$, where $\alpha^P : X \to [0,1]$, $\alpha^N : X \to [-1,0]$, $\beta^P : X \to [0,1]$ and $\beta^N : X \to [-1,0]$ are the mappings satisfying*

$$0 \le \alpha^P(x) + \beta^P(x) \le 1$$

$$-1 \le \alpha^N(x) + \beta^N(x) \le 0$$

Definition 11. *[9] A picture fuzzy set (PFS) S on X is the collection $S = \{(x, \alpha_S(x), \gamma_S(x), \beta_S(x)) : x \in X\}$, where $\alpha_S(x) \in [0,1]$ is the positive membership degree of x in S, $\gamma_S(x) \in [0,1]$ represents the neutral membership degree of x in S and $\beta_S(x) \in [0,1]$ the negative membership degree of x in S, with α_S, γ_S and β_S satisfying $\alpha_S(x) + \gamma_S(x) + \beta_S(x) \le 1$, for all $x \in X$.*

Definition 12. *[20] A BPFG $S = \{u, \alpha^P(u), \alpha^N(u), \beta^P(u), \beta^N(u) : u \in U\}$, where $\alpha^P : U \to [0,1]$, $\alpha^N : U \to [-1,0]$, $\beta^P : U \to [0,1]$ and $\beta^N : U \to [-1,0]$ is said to be a bipolar fuzzy graph on underlying set U if, $\beta^P(u,v) \le \min(\alpha^P(u), \alpha^P(v))$ and $\beta^N(u,v) \ge \min(\alpha^N(u), \alpha^N(v))$, for all $u, v \in E = V \times V$.*

Definition 13. *[35] A bipolar intuitionistic fuzzy graph (BPIFG) on V is the pair G = (A, B), where A = ($\alpha_A^P(u)$, $\alpha_A^N(u)$, $\beta_A^P(u)$, $\beta_A^N(u)$) is a BPIFS on V and B = ($\alpha_B^P(u)$, $\alpha_B^N(u)$, $\beta_B^P(u)$, $\beta_B^N(u)$) is a BPIFS on $E \subseteq V \times V$ satisfying*

$$\alpha_B^P(u,v) \leq min(\alpha_A^P(u), \alpha_A^P(v))$$
$$\alpha_B^N(u,v) \geq max(\alpha_A^N(u), \alpha_A^N(v))$$
$$\beta_B^P(u,v) \leq min(\beta_A^P(u), \beta_A^P(u))$$
$$\beta_B^N(u,v) \geq max(\beta_A^N(u), \beta_A^N(v))$$

for all $u, v \in E$.

Definition 14. *[35] A mapping $S = (\alpha_S^P, \alpha_S^N, \beta_S^P, \beta_S^N) : X \times X \to [-1,0] \times [0,1] \times [-1,0] \times [0,1]$ is a bipolar intuitionistic fuzzy relation (BPIFR) on X, where $\alpha_S^P(x,y) \in [0,1]$, $\alpha_S^N(x,y) \in [-1,0]$, $\beta_S^P(x,y) \in [0,1]$ and $\beta_S^N(x,y) \in [-1,0]$.*

Definition 15. *[9] A pair G = (A, B) is said to be a picture fuzzy graph (PFG) on G^* = (V, E), where A = (α_A, γ_A ,β_A) is a PFS on V and B = (α_B, γ_B ,β_B) is a PFS on $E \subseteq V \in V$ with*

$$\alpha_B(u,v) \leq min(\alpha_A(u), \alpha_A(v))$$
$$\gamma_B(u,v) \leq min(\gamma_A(u), \gamma_A(v))$$
$$\beta_B(u,v) \geq max(\beta_A(u), \beta_A(v))$$

3. Bipolar Picture Fuzzy Graphs (BPPFGs)

We begin this section with the definition of a bipolar picture fuzzy set (BPPFS) which is introduced by the first author (with Faiz and Taouti) in [36].

Definition 16. *[36] Let X be a nonempty set. A bipolar picture fuzzy set (BPPFS) on X is the collection $S = \{x, \alpha^P(x), \alpha^N(x), \gamma^P(x), \gamma^N(x), \beta^P(x), \beta^N(x) : x \in X\}$, where $\alpha^P : X \to [0,1]$, $\alpha^N : X \to [-1,0]$, $\gamma^P : X \to [0,1]$, $\gamma^N : X \to [-1,0]$, $\beta^P : X \to [0,1]$ and $\beta^N : X \to [-1,0]$ are the mappings with $0 \leq \alpha^P(x) + \gamma^P(x) + \beta^P(x) \leq 1$, $-1 \leq \alpha^N(x) + \gamma^N(x) + \beta^N(x) \leq 0$.*

Following [36], for each x in X, $\alpha^P(x)$ stands for the positive membership degree, $\beta^P(x)$ for the positive non-membership degree and $\gamma^P(x)$ for the positive neutral degree. Alternatively, $\alpha^N(x)$ represents the negative membership degree, $\beta^N(x)$ is the negative non-membership degree and $\gamma^N(x)$ is a negative neutral degree. On the other hand, if $\alpha^P(x) \neq 0$ while all other mappings are mapped to zero then it means that x has only a positive membership property of the bipolar picture fuzzy set. Similarly, if $\alpha^N(x) \neq 0$ while all other mappings matched to zero (or equal to zero) then it reflects that x has only the negative membership property of a BPPFS. Additionally, if $\gamma^P(x) \neq 0$ and remaining mappings are mapped to zero then it reflects that x has only the positive neutral property of a BPPFS. By $\gamma^N(x) \neq 0$ and the other mapping goes to zero then we mean that x has only the negative neutral property of a BPPFS. However, if $\beta^P(x) \neq 0$ while all other mapping matched to zero then it implies that x has only the positive nonmembership property of a BPPFS. Finally, if $\beta^N(x) \neq 0$ while remaining are zero then it implies that x has only the negative nonmembership property in a BPPFS.

Definition 17. *Let $G^* = (V, E)$ be a graph. A pair $G = (C, D)$ is said to be a bipolar picture fuzzy graph (BPPFG) on G^*, where $C = \{\alpha_C^P(u), \alpha_C^N(u), \gamma_C^P(u), \gamma_C^N(u), \beta_C^P(u), \beta_C^N(u)\}$ is a bipolar picture fuzzy set on V and $D = \{\alpha_D^P(u,v), \alpha_D^N(u,v), \gamma_D^P(u,v), \gamma_D^N(u,v), \beta_D^P(u,v), \beta_D^N(u,v)\}$ is a bipolar picture fuzzy set on $E \subseteq V \times V$ such that for every edge $uv \in E$,*

$$\alpha_D^P(uv) \leq min(\alpha_C^P(u), \alpha_C^P(v)), \qquad \alpha_D^N(uv) \geq max(\alpha_C^N(u), \alpha_C^N(v))$$
$$\gamma_D^P(uv) \leq min(\gamma_C^P(u), \gamma_C^P(u)), \qquad \gamma_D^N(uv) \geq max(\gamma_C^N(u), \gamma_C^N(v))$$
$$\beta_D^P(uv) \geq max(\beta_C^P(u), \beta_C^P(v)), \qquad \beta_D^N(uv) \leq min(\beta_C^N(u), \beta_C^N(v))$$

satisfying

$$0 \leq \alpha_D^P(uv) + \gamma_D^P(uv) + \beta_D^P(uv) \leq 1$$
$$-1 \leq \alpha_D^P(uv) + \gamma_D^P(uv) + \beta_D^P(uv) \leq 0$$

Example 1. *One can easily verify that the graphs shown in Figure 1a,b are BPPFGs.*

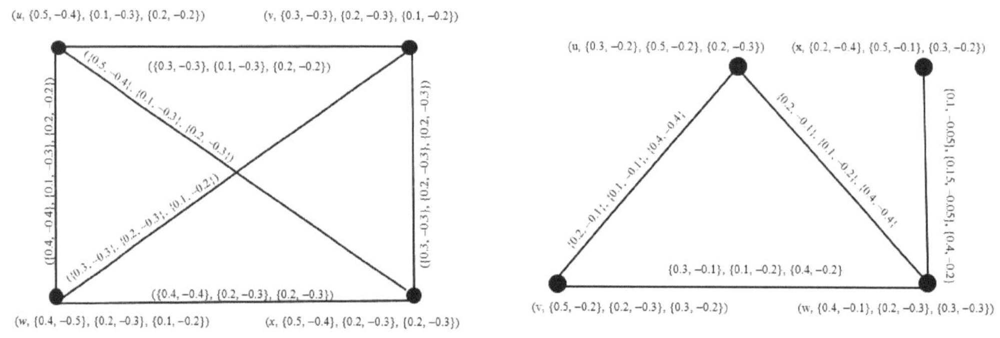

(a) Complete bipolar picture fuzzy graph

(b) (Simple) Bipolar picture fuzzy graph

Figure 1. Bipolar picture fuzzy graph.

Definition 18. *The order* $O(G)$ *of a BPPFG* $G = (C, D)$ *is defined by* $O(G) = (O_\alpha(G), O_\gamma(G), O_\beta(G))$, *where*

$$O_\alpha(G) = (\sum_{u_i \in V} O_{\alpha^P}(G), \sum_{u_i \in V} O_{\alpha^N}(G))$$
$$O_\gamma(G) = (\sum_{u_i \in V} O_{\gamma^P}(G), \sum_{u_i \in V} O_{\gamma^N}(G)) \quad and$$
$$O_\beta(G) = (\sum_{u_i \in V} O_{\beta^P}(G), \sum_{u_i \in V} O_{\beta^N}(G))$$

Definition 19. *The size* $S(G)$ *of a BPPFG* $G = (C, D)$ *is denoted and defined by* $S(G) = (S_\alpha(G), S_\gamma(G), S_\beta(G))$, *where*

$$S_\alpha(G) = (\sum_{u_i \in V} S_{\alpha^P}(G), \sum_{u_i \in V} S_{\alpha^N}(G))$$
$$S_\gamma(G) = (\sum_{u_i \in V} S_{\gamma^P}(G), \sum_{u_i \in V} S_{\gamma^N}(G)) \quad and$$
$$S_\beta(G) = (\sum_{u_i \in V} S_{\beta^P}(G), \sum_{u_i \in V} S_{\beta^N}(G))$$

Definition 20. *Let* $J^* = (V_1, E_1)$ *and* $K^* = (V_2, E_2)$ *be two graphs. Let* $J = (C_1, D_1)$ *be a BPPFG on* $J^* = (V_1, E_1)$, *where* $C_1 = \{\alpha_{C_1}^P(u), \alpha_{C_1}^N(u), \gamma_{C_1}^P(u), \gamma_{C_1}^N(u), \beta_{C_1}^P(u), \beta_{C_1}^N(u)\}$ *is a BPPFS on* V_1 *and* $D_1 = \{\alpha_{D_1}^P(u), \alpha_{D_1}^N(u), \gamma_{D_1}^P(u), \gamma_{D_1}^N(u), \beta_{D_1}^P(u), \beta_{D_1}^N(u)\}$ *is a BPPFS on* E_1, *respectively. Let* $K = (C_2, D_2)$ *be a BPPFG on* $K^* = (V_2, E_2)$, *where* $C_2 = \{\alpha_{C_2}^P(u), \alpha_{C_2}^N(u), \gamma_{C_2}^P(u), \gamma_{C_2}^N(u), \beta_{C_2}^P(u), \beta_{C_2}^N(u)\}$ *is a BPPFS on* V_2 *and* $D_2 = \{\alpha_{D_2}^P(u), \alpha_{D_2}^N(u), \gamma_{D_2}^P(u), \gamma_{D_2}^N(u),$

$\beta^P_{D_2}(u), \beta^N_{D_2}(u)\}$ *is a BPPFS on* E_2 *be the two BPPFGs. Then the operations union and intersection between J and K can be defined as*

$$J \cup K = (C_1 \cup C_2, D_1 \cup D_2) \tag{1}$$

For any vertex u:
Case (i):
$C_1 \cup C_2 = \{u, max(\alpha^P_{C_1}(u), \alpha^P_{C_2}(u)), max(\gamma^P_{C_1}(u), \gamma^P_{C_2}(u)), min(\beta^P_{C_1}(u), \beta^P_{C_2}(u)), max(\alpha^N_{C_1}(u), \alpha^N_{C_2}(u)), min(\gamma^N_{C_1}(u), \gamma^N_{C_2}(u)), max(\beta^N_{C_1}(u), \beta^N_{C_2}(u)) : u \in V_1 - V_2\}$
Case (ii):
$C_1 \cup C_2 = \{u, max(\alpha^P_{C_1}(u), \alpha^P_{C_2}(u)), max(\gamma^P_{C_1}(u), \gamma^P_{C_2}(u)), min(\beta^P_{C_1}(u), \beta^P_{C_2}(u)), max(\alpha^N_{C_1}(u), \alpha^N_{C_2}(u)), min(\gamma^N_{C_1}(u), \gamma^N_{C_2}(u)), max(\beta^N_{C_1}(u), \beta^N_{C_2}(u)) : u \in V_2 - V_1\}$
Case (iii):
$C_1 \cup C_2 = \{u, max(\alpha^P_{C_1}(u), \alpha^P_{C_2}(u)), max(\gamma^P_{C_1}(u), \gamma^P_{C_2}(u)), min(\beta^P_{C_1}(u), \beta^P_{C_2}(u)), max(\alpha^N_{C_1}(u), \alpha^N_{C_2}(u)), min(\gamma^N_{C_1}(u), \gamma^N_{C_2}(u)), max(\beta^N_{C_1}(u), \beta^N_{C_2}(u)) : u \in V_1 \cap V_2\}$
Similarly, for any edge uv:
Case (i):
$D_1 \cup D_2 = \{uv, max(\alpha^P_{D_1}(uv), \alpha^P_{D_2}(uv)), max(\gamma^P_{D_1}(uv), \gamma^P_{D_2}(uv)), min(\beta^P_{D_1}(uv), \beta^P_{D_2}(uv)), max(\alpha^N_{D_1}(uv), \alpha^N_{D_2}(uv)), min(\gamma^N_{D_1}(uv), \gamma^N_{D_2}(uv)), max(\beta^N_{D_1}(uv), \beta^N_{D_2}(uv)) : uv \in E_1 - E_2\}$
Case (ii):
$D_1 \cup D_2 = \{uv, max(\alpha^P_{D_1}(uv), \alpha^P_{D_2}(uv)), max(\gamma^P_{D_1}(uv), \gamma^P_{D_2}(uv)), min(\beta^P_{D_1}(uv), \beta^P_{D_2}(uv)), max(\alpha^N_{D_1}(uv), \alpha^N_{D_2}(uv)), min(\gamma^N_{D_1}(uv), \gamma^N_{D_2}(uv)), max(\beta^N_{D_1}(uv), \beta^N_{D_2}(uv)) : uv \in E_2 - E_1\}$
Case (iii):
$D_1 \cup D_2 = \{uv, max(\alpha^P_{D_1}(uv), \alpha^P_{D_2}(uv)), max(\gamma^P_{D_1}(uv), \gamma^P_{D_2}(uv)), min(\beta^P_{D_1}(uv), \beta^P_{D_2}(uv)), max(\alpha^N_{D_1}(uv), \alpha^N_{D_2}(uv)), min(\gamma^N_{D_1}(uv), \gamma^N_{D_2}(uv)), max(\beta^N_{D_1}(uv), \beta^N_{D_2}(uv)) : uv \in E_1 \cap E_2\}$

$$J \cap K = (C_1 \cap C_2, D_1 \cap D_2) \tag{2}$$

For any vertex u:
Case (i):
$C_1 \cap C_2 = \{u, min(\alpha^P_{C_1}(u), \alpha^P_{C_2}(u)), min(\gamma^P_{C_1}(u), \gamma^P_{C_2}(u)), max(\beta^P_{C_1}(u), \beta^P_{C_2}(u)), min(\alpha^N_{C_1}(u), \alpha^N_{C_2}(u)), max(\gamma^N_{C_1}(u), \gamma^N_{C_2}(u)), min(\beta^N_{C_1}(u), \beta^N_{C_2}(u)) : u \in V_1 - V_2\}$
Case (ii):
$C_1 \cap C_2 = \{u, min(\alpha^P_{C_1}(u), \alpha^P_{C_2}(u)), min(\gamma^P_{C_1}(u), \gamma^P_{C_2}(u)), max(\beta^P_{C_1}(u), \beta^P_{C_2}(u)), min(\alpha^N_{C_1}(u), \alpha^N_{C_2}(u)), max(\gamma^N_{C_1}(u), \gamma^N_{C_2}(u)), min(\beta^N_{C_1}(u), \beta^N_{C_2}(u)) : u \in V_2 - V_1\}$
Case (iii):
$C_1 \cap C_2 = \{u, min(\alpha^P_{C_1}(u), \alpha^P_{C_2}(u)), min(\gamma^P_{C_1}(u), \gamma^P_{C_2}(u)), max(\beta^P_{C_1}(u), \beta^P_{C_2}(u)), min(\alpha^N_{C_1}(u), \alpha^N_{C_2}(u)), max(\gamma^N_{C_1}(u), \gamma^N_{C_2}(u)), min(\beta^N_{C_1}(u), \beta^N_{C_2}(u)) : u \in V_1 \cap V_2\}$
Similarly, for any edge uv:
Case (i):
$D_1 \cap D_2 = \{uv, min(\alpha^P_{D_1}(uv), \alpha^P_{D_2}(uv)), min(\gamma^P_{D_1}(uv), \gamma^P_{D_2}(uv)), max(\beta^P_{D_1}(uv), \beta^P_{D_2}(uv)), min(\alpha^N_{D_1}(uv), \alpha^N_{D_2}(uv)), max(\gamma^N_{D_1}(uv), \gamma^N_{D_2}(uv)), min(\beta^N_{D_1}(uv), \beta^N_{D_2}(uv)) : uv \in E_1 - E_2\}$.
Case (ii):
$D_1 \cap D_2 = \{uv, min(\alpha^P_{D_1}(uv), \alpha^P_{D_2}(uv)), min(\gamma^P_{D_1}(uv), \gamma^P_{D_2}(uv)), max(\beta^P_{D_1}(uv), \beta^P_{D_2}(uv)), min(\alpha^N_{D_1}(uv), \alpha^N_{D_2}(uv)), max(\gamma^N_{D_1}(uv), \gamma^N_{D_2}(uv)), min(\beta^N_{D_1}(uv), \beta^N_{D_2}(uv)) : uv \in E_2 - E_1\}$.
Case (iii):
$D_1 \cap D_2 = \{uv, min(\alpha^P_{D_1}(uv), \alpha^P_{D_2}(uv)), min(\gamma^P_{D_1}(uv), \gamma^P_{D_2}(uv)), max(\beta^P_{D_1}(uv), \beta^P_{D_2}(uv)), min(\alpha^N_{D_1}(uv), \alpha^N_{D_2}(uv)), max(\gamma^N_{D_1}(uv), \gamma^N_{D_2}(uv)), min(\beta^N_{D_1}(uv), \beta^N_{D_2}(uv)) : uv \in E_1 \cap E_2\}$.

Definition 21. *Let* $G_1 = (C_1, D_1)$ *and* $G_2 = (C_2, D_2)$ *be the two BPPFGs on* $G^* = (V_1, E_1)$ *and* $G^{**} = (V_2, E_2)$*, respectively. Then the ring sum* $G_1 \bigoplus G_2 = (V_1 \cup V_2, (E_1 \cup E_2) - (E_1 \cap E_2))$ *of BPPFGs of* G_1 *and* G_2 *is the graph* $G = (C, D)$*, where* $C = (\alpha^P_C, \alpha^N_C, \gamma^P_C, \gamma^N_C, \beta^P_C, \beta^N_C)$ *is bipolar picture fuzzy set on* $V = V_1 \cup V_2$ *and* $D = (\alpha^P_D, \alpha^N_D, \gamma^P_D, \gamma^N_D, \beta^P_D, \beta^N_D)$ *is a bipolar picture fuzzy*

set on $E = E_1 \cup E_2 - (E_1 \cap E_2)$ *satisfying the following conditions.*
(A)

$$\alpha_C^P(u) = \begin{cases} \alpha_{C_1}^P(u) & if \quad u \in V_1 \\ \alpha_{C_2}^P(u) & if \quad u \in V_2 \\ \alpha_{C_1}^P(u) \wedge \alpha_{C_2}^P(u) & if \quad u \in V_1 \cap V_2 \end{cases}$$

(B)

$$\alpha_C^P(u,v) = \begin{cases} \alpha_{C_1}^P(u,v) & if \quad u,v \in E_1 - E_2 \\ \alpha_{C_2}^P(u,v) & if \quad u,v \in E_2 - E_1 \\ \alpha_{C_1}^P(u,v) \wedge \alpha_{C_2}^P(u,v) & if \quad u,v \in E_1 \cap E_2 \end{cases}$$

(C)

$$\alpha_C^N(u) = \begin{cases} \alpha_{C_1}^N(u) & if \quad u \in V_1 \\ \alpha_{C_2}^N(u) & if \quad u \in V_2 \\ \alpha_{C_1}^N(u) \vee \alpha_{C_2}^P(u) & if \quad u \in V_1 \cap V_2 \end{cases}$$

(D)

$$\alpha_C^N(u,v) = \begin{cases} \alpha_{C_1}^N(u,v) & if \quad u,v \in E_1 - E_2 \\ \alpha_{C_2}^N(u,v) & if \quad u,v \in E_2 - E_1 \\ \alpha_{C_1}^N(u,v) \vee \alpha_{C_2}^P(u,v) & if \quad u,v \in E_1 \cap E_2 \end{cases}$$

(E)

$$\gamma_C^P(u) = \begin{cases} \gamma_{C_1}^P(u) & if \quad u \in V_1 \\ \gamma_{C_2}^P(u) & if \quad u \in V_2 \\ \gamma_{C_1}^P(u) \wedge \gamma_{C_2}^P(u) & if \quad u \in V_1 \cap V_2 \end{cases}$$

(F)

$$\gamma_C^P(u,v) = \begin{cases} \gamma_{C_1}^P(u,v) & if \quad u,v \in E_1 - E_2 \\ \gamma_{C_2}^P(u,v) & if \quad u,v \in E_2 - E_1 \\ \gamma_{C_1}^P(u,v) \wedge \gamma_{C_2}^P(u,v) & if \quad u,v \in E_1 \cap E_2 \end{cases}$$

(G)

$$\gamma_C^N(u) = \begin{cases} \gamma_{C_1}^N(u) & if \quad u \in V_1 \\ \gamma_{C_2}^N(u) & ifu \quad \in V_2 \\ \gamma_{C_1}^N(u) \vee \gamma_{C_2}^N(u) & if \quad u \in V_1 \cap V_2 \end{cases}$$

(H)

$$\gamma_C^N(u,v) = \begin{cases} \gamma_{C_1}^N(u,v) & if \quad u,v \in E_1 - E_2 \\ \gamma_{C_2}^N(u,v) & if \quad u,v \in E_2 - E_1 \\ \gamma_{C_1}^N(u,v) \vee \gamma_{C_2}^N(u,v) & if \quad u,v \in E_1 \cap E_2 \end{cases}$$

(I)

$$\beta_C^P(u) = \begin{cases} \beta_{C_1}^P(u) & if \quad u \in V_1 \\ \beta_{C_2}^P(u) & if \quad u \in V_2 \\ \beta_{C_1}^P(u) \vee \beta_{C_2}^P(u) & if \quad u \in V_1 \cap V_2 \end{cases}$$

(J)

$$\beta_C^P(u,v) = \begin{cases} \beta_{C_1}^P(u,v) & if \quad u,v \in E_1 - E_2 \\ \beta_{C_2}^P(u,v) & if \quad u,v \in E_2 - E_1 \\ \beta_{C_1}^P(u,v) \vee \beta_{C_2}^P(u,v) & if \quad u,v \in E_1 \cap E_2 \end{cases}$$

(K)

$$\beta_C^N(u) = \begin{cases} \beta_{C_1}^N(u) & if \;\; u \in V_1 \\ \beta_{C_2}^N(u) & if \;\; u \in V_2 \\ \beta_{C_1}^N(u) \wedge \beta_{C_2}^N(u) & if u \in V_1 \cap V_2 \end{cases}$$

(L)

$$\gamma_C^N(u,v) = \begin{cases} \beta_{C_1}^N(u,v) & if \;\; u,v \in E_1 - E_2 \\ \beta_{C_2}^N(u,v) & if \;\; u,v \in E_2 - E_1 \\ \beta_{C_1}^N(u,v) \wedge \beta_{C_2}^N(u,v) & if \;\; u,v \in E_1 \cap E_2 \end{cases}$$

where uv represents an edge between the two vertices u, v while E_1, E_2 represent edges sets in G_1 and G_2, respectively.

Theorem 1. *Ring sum of two BPPFGs is a BPPFG.*

Proof. Let us consider two BPPFGs $G_1 = (C_1, D_1)$ and $G_2 = (C_2, D_2)$ defined on crisp graphs $G_1^* = (V_1, E_1)$ and $G_2^* = (V_2, E_2)$. Then, their ring sum $G_1 \oplus G_2 = G = (C, D)$ is BPPFG. Where $C = (\alpha_C^P(u), \alpha_C^N(u), \gamma_C^P(u), \gamma_C^N(u), \beta_C^P(u), \beta_C^N(u))$ and $D = (\alpha_D^P(u,v), \alpha_D^N(u,v), \gamma_D^P(u,v), \gamma_D^N(u,v), \beta_D^P(u,v), \beta_D^N(u,v))$. Then we have the following cases.
Case 1:
If $u \in V_1$, then $\alpha_C^P(u) = \alpha_{C_1}^P(u) \in V_1$, which is a BPPFS on V_1. Additionally, if $u, v \in V_1$, then $\alpha_C^P(u,v) = \alpha_{C_1}^P(u,v) \in E_1$, which is a BPPFS on E_1.
Case 2:
If $u \in V_2$, then $\alpha_C^P(u) = \alpha_{C_2}^P(u) \in V_2$, which is a BPPFS on V_2. Additionally, if $u, v \in V_2$, then $\alpha_C^P(u,v) = \alpha_{C_2}^P(u,v) \in E_2$, which is a BPPFS on E_2.
Case 3:
If $u \in V_1 \cap V_2$, then $\alpha_C^P(u) = \alpha_{C_1}^P(u) \wedge \alpha_{C_2}^P(u) \in V_1 \cap V_2$, which is a BPPFS. Additionally, if $u, v \in V_1 \cap V_2$, then $\alpha_C^P(u,v) = \alpha_{C_1}^P(u,v) \wedge \alpha_{C_2}^P(u,v) \in E_1 \cap E_2$, which is BPPFR on $V_1 \cap V_2 \times V_1 \cap V_2$.
Similarly, we can show for all $\alpha_C^N(u)$, $\gamma_C^P(u)$, $\gamma_C^N(u)$, $\beta_C^P(u)$, $\beta_C^N(u) \in C$ and $\alpha_D^N(u,v)$, $\gamma_D^P(u,v)$, $\gamma_D^N(u,v)$, $\beta_D^P(u,v)$, $\beta_D^N(u,v) \in D$. Since, $V_1, E_1 \in G_1$, $V_2, E_2 \in G_2$ and G_1, G_2 are BPPFGs. Hence $G_1 \oplus G_2 = G$ is a BPPFG. □

Proposition 1. *Let $H = (C, D)$ be a BPPFG on $G = (V, E)$. Then $H \cup H = H \cap H = H$ and $H \oplus H = \emptyset$ are BPPFGs.*

Proof. Let $H = (C, D)$ be a BPPFG on $H^* = (V, E)$, where $C = \{\alpha_C^P(u), \alpha_C^N(u), \gamma_C^P(u), \gamma_C^N(u), \beta_C^P(u), \beta_C^N(u)\}$ is a BPPFS on V and $D = \{\alpha_D^P(u), \alpha_D^N(u), \gamma_D^P(u), \gamma_D^N(u), \beta_D^P(u), \beta_D^N(u)\}$ is a BPPFS on E, respectively. For $H \cup H = (C \cup C, D \cup D)$, by Definition 20(1), we have
$C \cup C = \{u, \max(\alpha_C^P(u), \alpha_C^P(u)), \max(\gamma_C^P(u), \gamma_C^P(u)), \min(\beta_C^P(u), \beta_C^P(u)), \max(\alpha_C^N(u), \alpha_C^N(u)), \min(\gamma_C^N(u), \gamma_C^N(u)), \max(\beta_C^N(u), \beta_C^N(u)) : u \in V\}$ and
$D \cup D = \{uv, \max(\alpha_D^P(uv), \alpha_D^P(uv)), \max(\gamma_D^P(uv), \gamma_D^P(uv)), \min(\beta_D^P(uv), \beta_D^P(uv)), \max(\alpha_D^N(uv), \alpha_D^N(uv)), \min(\gamma_D^N(uv), \gamma_D^N(uv)), \max(\beta_D^N(uv), \beta_D^N(uv)) : u, v \in E\}$.
Thus, we have $C \cup C = C$ and $D \cup D = D$. Hence $H \cup H = H$.
Similarly, for $H \cap H = (C \cap C, D \cap D)$, by Definition 20(2), we have
$C \cap C = \{u, min(\alpha_C^P(u), \alpha_C^P(u)), \min(\gamma_C^P(u), \gamma_C^P(u)), \max(\beta_C^P(u), \beta_C^P(u)), \min(\alpha_C^N(u), \alpha_C^N(u)), \max(\gamma_C^N(u), \gamma_C^N(u)), \min(\beta_C^N(u), \beta_C^N(u)) : u \in V\}$ and
$D \cap D = \{uv, min(\alpha_D^P(uv), \alpha_D^P(uv)), \min(\gamma_D^P(uv), \gamma_D^P(uv)), \max(\beta_D^P(uv), \beta_D^P(uv)), \min(\alpha_D^N(uv), \alpha_D^N(uv)), \max(\gamma_D^N(uv), \gamma_D^N(uv)), \min(\beta_D^N(uv), \beta_D^N(uv)) : uv \in E\}$.
Thus, $C \cap C = C$ and $D \cap D = D$ implies $H \cap H = H$.

Finally, to prove $H \oplus H = \emptyset$. Let $u \in V$ be any vertex, then by Definition (21) we have

$$\alpha_C^P(u) = \begin{cases} \alpha_C^P(u) & if \quad u \in V \\ \alpha_C^P(u) & if \quad u \in V \\ \alpha_C^P(u) \wedge \alpha_C^P(u) & if \quad u \in V \cap V \end{cases}$$

Hence, $\alpha_C^P(u) = \alpha_C^P(u), \forall\, u \in V$. Similarly, for any edge $(u,v) \in E$. Following Definition 21, we have

$$\alpha_C^P(u,v) = \begin{cases} \alpha_C^P(u,v) & if \quad u,v \in E - E \\ \alpha_C^P(u,v) & if \quad u,v \in E - E \\ \alpha_C^P(u,v) \wedge \alpha_C^P(u,v) & if \quad u,v \in E \cap E \end{cases}$$

It implies $\alpha_C^P(u,v) = \emptyset, \forall\, uv \in E - E$. Thus, $H \oplus H = \emptyset$, which completes the proof. □

Definition 22. *The open neighbourhood degree of a vertex m of a BPPFG* $H = (C, D)$ *is deg(m)* $= (d(\alpha_C^P(u)), d(\alpha_C^N(u)), d(\gamma_C^P(u)), d(\gamma_C^N(u)), d(\beta_C^P(u)), d(\beta_C^N(u)))$, *where*

$$d(\alpha_C^P(m)) = \sum_{n \in N(x)} \alpha_C^P(n), \qquad d(\alpha_C^N(m)) = \sum_{n \in N(x)} \alpha_C^N(n)$$
$$d(\gamma_C^P(m)) = \sum_{n \in N(x)} \gamma_C^P(n), \qquad d(\gamma_C^N(m)) = \sum_{n \in N(x)} \gamma_C^N(n)$$
$$d(\beta_C^P(m)) = \sum_{n \in N(x)} \beta_C^P(n), \qquad d(\beta_C^N(m)) = \sum_{n \in N(x)} \beta_C^N(n)$$

Definition 23. *A vertex u in a BPPFG* $H = (C, D)$ *is said to be a busy vertex, if*

$$\alpha_C^P(u) \le d(\alpha_C^P(u)), \qquad \alpha_C^N(u) \ge d(\alpha_C^N(u))$$
$$\gamma_C^P(u) \le d(\gamma_C^P(u)), \qquad \gamma_C^N(u) \ge d(\gamma_C^N(u)) \quad and$$
$$\beta_C^P(u) \ge d(\beta_C^P(u)), \qquad \beta_C^N(u) \le d(\beta_C^N(u))$$

Otherwise, it is a free vertex.

Definition 24. *The busy value of a vertex u of a BPPFG* $H = (C, D)$ *is defined by* $J(u) = (J(\alpha_C^P)(u), J(\alpha_C^N)(u), J(\gamma_C^P)(u), J(\gamma_C^N)(u), J(\beta_C^P)(u), J(\beta_C^N)(u))$, *where*

$$J(\alpha_C^P)(u) = \sum \alpha_C^P(u) \wedge \alpha_C^P(u_i), \qquad J(\alpha_C^N)(u) = \sum \alpha_C^N(u) \vee \alpha_C^N(u_i)$$
$$J(\gamma_C^P)(u) = \sum \gamma_C^P(u) \wedge \gamma_C^P(u_i), \qquad J(\gamma_C^N)(u) = \sum \gamma_C^N(u) \vee \gamma_C^N(u_i)$$
$$J(\beta_C^P)(u) = \sum \beta_C^P(u) \vee \beta_C^P(u_i), \qquad J(\beta_C^N)(u) = \sum \beta_C^N(u) \wedge \beta_C^N(u_i)$$

$u_{i,s}$ *represent the neighbors of u, the sum of the busy values of all vertices of H i.e.,* $J(H) = \sum J(u_i)$ *is said to be a busy value of a BPPFG H.*

Definition 25. *The busy value of an edge uv of a BPPFG* $H = (C, D)$ *is defined by* $J(uv) = (J(\alpha_D^P)(uv), J(\alpha_D^N)(uv), J(\gamma_D^P)(uv), J(\gamma_D^N)(uv), J(\beta_D^P)(uv), J(\beta_D^N)(uv))$ *such that*

$$J(\alpha_D^P(uv)) \le min(J(\alpha_C^P(u)), J(\alpha_C^P(v))), \qquad J(\alpha_D^N(uv)) \ge max(J(\alpha_C^N(u)), J(\alpha_C^N(v)))$$
$$J(\gamma_D^P(uv)) \le min(J(\gamma_C^P(u), \gamma_C^P(u))), \qquad J(\gamma_D^N(uv)) \ge max(J(\gamma_C^N(u)), J(\gamma_C^N(v)))$$
$$J(\beta_D^P(uv)) \ge max(J(\beta_C^P(u)), J(\beta_C^P(v))), \qquad J(\beta_D^N(uv)) \le min(J(\beta_C^N(u)), J(\beta_C^N(v)))$$

Definition 26. *The set of sequence of different vertices* $v_0, v_1, v_2, \ldots, v_k$ *is the path p in a BPPFG* $H = (C, D)$ *such that* $(\alpha^P(v_{i-1}, v_i), \gamma^P(v_{i-1}, v_i), \beta^P(v_{i-1}, v_i)) \ge 0$ *and* $(\alpha^N(v_{i-1}, v_i), \gamma^N(v_{i-1}, v_i), \beta^N(v_{i-1}, v_i)) \le 0\,; i = 1, 2, 3, \ldots, k.$

Definition 27. *Two vertices u and v are connected by a path p i.e., $p : u_0, u_1, u_2, ...u_{k-1}, u_k$ of length l in a BPPFG $H = (C, D)$. Then, $\alpha^P(u,v), \gamma^P(u,v), \beta^P(u,v), \alpha^N(u,v), \gamma^N(u,v)$ and $\beta^N(u,v)$ are illustrated as follows.*

$$\begin{aligned}
\alpha^P(u,v) &= \alpha^P(u,u_1) \wedge \alpha^P(u_1,u_2) \wedge \alpha^P(u_2,u_3) \wedge ... \wedge \alpha^P(u_{k-1},v) \\
\gamma^P(u,v) &= \gamma^P(u,u_1) \wedge \gamma^P(u_1,u_2) \wedge \gamma^P(u_2,u_3) \wedge ... \wedge \gamma^P(u_{k-1},v) \\
\beta^P(u,v) &= \beta^P(u,u_1) \vee \beta^P(u_1,u_2) \vee \beta^P(u_2,u_3) \vee ... \vee \beta^P(u_{k-1},v) \\
\alpha^N(u,v) &= \alpha^N(u,u_1) \vee \alpha^N(u_1,u_2) \vee \alpha^N(u_2,u_3) \vee ... \vee \alpha^N(u_{k-1},v) \\
\gamma^N(u,v) &= \gamma^N(u,u_1) \vee \gamma^N(u_1,u_2) \vee \gamma^N(u_2,u_3) \vee ... \vee \gamma^N(u_{k-1},v) \quad \text{and} \\
\beta^N(u,v) &= \beta^N(u,u_1) \wedge \beta^N(u_1,u_2) \wedge \beta^N(u_2,u_3) \wedge ... \wedge \beta^N(u_{k-1},v)
\end{aligned}$$

Theorem 2. *Let $H = (C, D)$ be a BPPFG. If H contains a "$x - y$" walk of length k, then H contains a "$x - y$" path of length k.*

3.1. Different Types of Products of Bipolar Picture Fuzzy Graphs

Definition 28. *The strong product of two BPPFGs $H_1 = (C_1, D_1)$, where $C_1 = (\alpha^P_{C_1}, \alpha^N_{C_1}, \gamma^P_{C_1}, \gamma^N_{C_1}, \beta^P_{C_1}, \beta^N_{C_1})$, $D_1 = (\alpha^P_{D_1}, \alpha^N_{D_1}, \gamma^P_{D_1}, \gamma^N_{D_1}, \beta^P_{D_1}, \beta^N_{D_1})$ and $H_2 = (C_2, D_2)$, where $C_2 = (\alpha^P_{C_2}, \alpha^N_{C_2}, \gamma^P_{C_2}, \gamma^N_{C_2}, \beta^P_{C_2}, \beta^N_{C_2})$, $D_2 = (\alpha^P_{D_2}, \alpha^N_{D_2}, \gamma^P_{D_2}, \gamma^N_{D_2}, \beta^P_{D_2}, \beta^N_{D_2})$, where we take $V_1 \cap V_2 = \emptyset$, is defined as*
$H_1 \otimes H_2 = (\alpha^P_{C_1} \otimes \alpha^P_{C_2}, \gamma^P_{C_1} \otimes \gamma^P_{C_2}, \beta^P_{C_1} \otimes \beta^P_{C_2}, \alpha^N_{C_1} \otimes \alpha^N_{C_2}, \gamma^N_{C_1} \otimes \gamma^N_{C_2}, \beta^N_{C_1} \otimes \beta^N_{C_2}, \alpha^P_{D_1} \otimes \alpha^P_{D_2}, \gamma^P_{D_1} \otimes \gamma^P_{D_2}, \beta^P_{D_1} \otimes \beta^P_{D_2}, \alpha^N_{D_1} \otimes \alpha^N_{D_2}, \gamma^N_{D_1} \otimes \gamma^N_{D_2}, \beta^N_{D_1} \otimes \beta^N_{D_2})$ of $H^* = (V_1 \times V_2, E)$. Where $E = \{(m,x_1)(m,x_2) : m \in V_1, (x_1,x_2) \in E_2\} \cup \{(m_1,z)(m_2,z) : z \in V_2, (m_1,m_2) \in E_1\} \cup \{(m_1,y_1)(m_2,y_2) : (m_1,m_2) \in E_1, (y_1,y_2) \in E_2\}$
and
$\alpha^P_{C_1} \otimes \alpha^P_{C_2}(m,n) = \alpha^P_{C_1}(m) \vee \alpha^P_{C_2}(n)$, $\gamma^P_{C_1} \otimes \gamma^P_{C_2}(m,n) = \gamma^P_{C_1}(m) \vee \gamma^P_{C_2}(n)$, $\beta^P_{C_1} \otimes \beta^P_{C_2}(m,n) = \beta^P_{C_1}(m) \wedge \beta^P_{C_2}(n)$,
$\alpha^N_{C_1} \otimes \alpha^N_{C_2}(m,n) = \alpha^N_{C_1}(m) \vee \alpha^N_{C_2}(n)$, $\gamma^N_{C_1} \otimes \gamma^N_{C_2}(m,n) = \gamma^N_{C_1}(m) \vee \gamma^N_{C_2}(n)$, $\beta^N_{C_1} \otimes \beta^N_{C_2}(m,n) = \beta^N_{C_1}(m) \wedge \beta^N_{C_2}(n)$,
for all $(m, m_1, m_2, x_1, x_2, y_1, y_2) \in V_1 \times V_2$. Similarly,
$\alpha^P_{D_1} \otimes \alpha^P_{D_2}(m,n) = \alpha^P_{D_1}(m) \vee \alpha^P_{D_2}(n)$, $\gamma^P_{D_1} \otimes \gamma^P_{D_2}(m,n) = \gamma^P_{D_1}(m) \vee \gamma^P_{D_2}(n)$, $\beta^P_{D_1} \otimes \beta^P_{D_2}(m,n) = \beta^P_{D_1}(m) \wedge \beta^P_{D_2}(n)$,
$\alpha^P_{D_1} \otimes \alpha^P_{D_2}(m_1,x_1)(m_2,x_2) = \alpha^P_{D_1}(m_1,m_2) \vee \alpha^P_{D_2}(x_1,x_2)$, $\gamma^P_{D_1} \otimes \gamma^P_{D_2}(m_1,x_1)(m_2,x_2) = \gamma^P_{D_1}(m_1,m_2) \vee \gamma^P_{D_2}(x_1,x_2)$,
$\beta^P_{D_1} \otimes \beta^P_{D_2}(m_1,x_1)(m_2,x_2) = \beta^P_{D_1}(m_1,m_2) \wedge \beta^P_{D_2}(x_1,x_2)$, $\alpha^N_{D_1} \otimes \alpha^N_{D_2}(m_1,x_1)(m_2,x_2) = \alpha^N_{D_1}(m_1,m_2) \vee \alpha^N_{D_2}(x_1,x_2)$,
$\gamma^N_{D_1} \otimes \gamma^N_{D_2}(m_1,x_1)(m_2,x_2) = \gamma^N_{D_1}(m_1,m_2) \vee \gamma^N_{D_2}(x_1,x_2)$, $\beta^N_{D_1} \otimes \beta^N_{D_2}(m_1,x_1)(m_2,x_2) = \beta^N_{D_1}(m_1,m_2) \wedge \beta^N_{D_2}(x_1,x_2)$.

Remark 1. *The strong product of two BPPFGs is always a BPPFG.*

Definition 29. *The semi-strong product of two BPPFGs $G_1 = (C_1, D_1)$, where $C_1 = (\alpha^P_{C_1}, \alpha^N_{C_1}, \gamma^P_{C_1}, \gamma^N_{C_1}, \beta^P_{C_1}, \beta^N_{C_1})$, $D_1 = (\alpha^P_{D_1}, \alpha^N_{D_1}, \gamma^P_{D_1}, \gamma^N_{D_1}, \beta^P_{D_1}, \beta^N_{D_1})$ with crisp graphs $G_1^* = (V_1, E_1)$ and $G_2 = (C_2, D_2)$, where $C_2 = (\alpha^P_{C_2}, \alpha^N_{C_2}, \gamma^P_{C_2}, \gamma^N_{C_2}, \beta^P_{C_2}, \beta^N_{C_2})$, $D_2 = (\alpha^P_{D_2}, \alpha^N_{D_2}, \gamma^P_{D_2}, \gamma^N_{D_2}, \beta^P_{D_2}, \beta^N_{D_2})$ with crisp graph $G_2^* = (V_2, E_2)$, where we assume that $V_1 \cup V_2 = \emptyset$, is defined to be the BPPFG $G_1 \circ G_2 = (\alpha_1 \circ \alpha_2, \beta_1 \circ \beta_2, \gamma_1 \circ \gamma_2)$ with crisp graph $G^* = (V_1 \times V_2, E)$ such that $E = \{(x,y_1)(x,y_2) : x \in V_1, (y_1,y_2) \in E_2\} \cup \{(x_1,y_1)(x_2,y_2) : (x_1,x_2) \in E_1, (y_1,y_2) \in E_2\}$. Then*
(i)
$(\alpha^P_{C_1} \circ \alpha^P_{C_2})(x,y) = min(\alpha^P_{C_1}(x), \alpha^P_{C_2}(y))$, $(\alpha^N_{C_1} \circ \alpha^N_{C_2})(x,y) = max(\alpha^N_{C_1}(x), \alpha^N_{C_2}(y))$ for all $(x,y) \in V_1 \times V_2$

(ii)
$(\gamma^{P}_{C_1} \circ \gamma^{P}_{C_2})(x,y) = min(\gamma^{P}_{C_1}(x), \gamma^{P}_{C_2}(y)), (\gamma^{N}_{C_1} \circ \gamma^{N}_{C_2})(x,y) = max(\gamma^{N}_{C_1}(x), \gamma^{N}_{C_2}(y))$ *for all* $(x,y) \in V_1 \times V_2$
(iii)
$(\beta^{P}_{C_1} \circ \beta^{P}_{C_2})(x,y) = max(\beta^{P}_{C_1}(x), \beta^{P}_{C_2}(y)), (\beta^{N}_{C_1} \circ \beta^{N}_{C_2})(x,y) = min(\beta^{N}_{C_1}(x), \beta^{N}_{C_2}(y))$ *for all* $(x,y) \in V_1 \times V_2$
(iv)
$(\alpha^{P}_{D_1} \circ \alpha^{P}_{D_2})((x,y_1)(x,y_2)) = min(\alpha^{P}_{C_1}(x), \alpha^{P}_{D_2}(y_1,y_2))$ *and* $(\alpha^{P}_{D_1} \circ \alpha^{P}_{D_2})((x_1,y_1)(x_2,y_2)) = min(\alpha^{P}_{D_1}(x_1,x_2), \alpha^{P}_{D_2}(y_1,y_2))$
$(\alpha^{N}_{D_1} \circ \alpha^{N}_{D_2})((x,y_1)(x,y_2)) = max(\alpha^{N}_{C_1}(x), \alpha^{N}_{D_2}(y_1,y_2))$ *and* $(\alpha^{N}_{D_1} \circ \alpha^{N}_{D_2})((x_1,y_1)(x_2,y_2)) = max(\alpha^{N}_{D_1}(x_1,x_2), \alpha^{N}_{D_2}(y_1,y_2))$
(v)
$(\gamma^{P}_{D_1} \circ \gamma^{P}_{D_2})((x,y_1)(x,y_2)) = min(\gamma^{P}_{C_1}(x), \gamma^{P}_{D_2}(y_1,y_2))$ *and* $(\gamma^{P}_{D_1} \circ \gamma^{P}_{D_2})((x_1,y_1)(x_2,y_2)) = min(\gamma^{P}_{D_1}(x_1,x_2), \gamma^{P}_{D_2}(y_1,y_2))$
$(\gamma^{N}_{D_1} \circ \gamma^{N}_{D_2})((x,y_1)(x,y_2)) = max(\gamma^{N}_{C_1}(x), \gamma^{N}_{D_2}(y_1,y_2))$ *and* $(\gamma^{N}_{D_1} \circ \gamma^{N}_{D_2})((x_1,y_1)(x_2,y_2)) = max(\gamma^{N}_{D_1}(x_1,x_2), \gamma^{N}_{D_2}(y_1,y_2))$
(vi)
$(\beta^{P}_{D_1} \circ \beta^{P}_{D_2})((x,y_1)(x,y_2)) = max(\beta^{P}_{C_1}(x), \beta^{P}_{D_2}(y_1,y_2))$ *and* $(\beta^{P}_{D_1} \circ \beta^{P}_{D_2})((x_1,y_1)(x_2,y_2)) = max(\beta^{P}_{D_1}(x_1,x_2), \beta^{P}_{D_2}(y_1,y_2))$
$(\beta^{N}_{D_1} \circ \beta^{N}_{D_2})((x,y_1)(x,y_2)) = min(\beta^{N}_{C_1}(x), \beta^{N}_{D_2}(y_1,y_2))$ *and* $(\beta^{N}_{D_1} \circ \beta^{N}_{D_2})((x_1,y_1)(x_2,y_2)) = min(\beta^{N}_{D_1}(x_1,x_2), \beta^{N}_{D_2}(y_1,y_2))$.

Example 2. *Let us consider two BPPFGs graphs given in Figure 1a,b. Then their semi-strong product is as follows.*
(i) $(\alpha^{P}_{C_1} \circ \alpha^{P}_{C_2})(x,y) = min(\alpha^{P}_{C_1}(x), \alpha^{P}_{C_2}(y)), (\alpha^{N}_{C_1} \circ \alpha^{N}_{C_2})(x,y) = max(\alpha^{N}_{C_1}(x), \alpha^{N}_{C_2}(y))$ *for all* $(x,y) \in V_1 \times V_2$
(ii) $(\gamma^{P}_{C_1} \circ \gamma^{P}_{C_2})(x,y) = min(\gamma^{P}_{C_1}(x), \gamma^{P}_{C_2}(y)), (\gamma^{N}_{C_1} \circ \gamma^{N}_{C_2})(x,y) = max(\gamma^{N}_{C_1}(x), \gamma^{N}_{C_2}(y))$ *for all* $(x,y) \in V_1 \times V_2$
(iii) $(\beta^{P}_{C_1} \circ \beta^{P}_{C_2})(x,y) = max(\beta^{P}_{C_1}(x), \beta^{P}_{C_2}(y)), (\beta^{N}_{C_1} \circ \beta^{N}_{C_2})(x,y) = min(\beta^{N}_{C_1}(x), \beta^{N}_{C_2}(y))$ *for all* $(x,y) \in V_1 \times V_2$.
Consequently, for vertex u:
$(\alpha^{P}_{C_1} \circ \alpha^{P}_{C_2})(x_1,y_2) = min(0.6, 0.3) = 0.3$, $(\alpha^{N}_{C_1} \circ \alpha^{N}_{C_2})(x_1,y_2) = max(-0.4, -0.5) = -0.4$
$(\gamma^{P}_{C_1} \circ \gamma^{P}_{C_2})(x_1,y_2) = min(0.1, 0.5) = 0.1$, $(\gamma^{N}_{C_1} \circ \gamma^{N}_{C_2})(x_1,y_2) = max(-0.3, -0.2) = -0.2$
$(\beta^{P}_{C_1} \circ \beta^{P}_{C_2})(x_1,y_2) = max(0.2, 0.2) = 0.2$, $(\beta^{N}_{C_1} \circ \beta^{N}_{C_2})(x_1,y_2) = min(-0.2, -0.3) = -0.3$
(u, 0.3, −0.4, 0.1, −0.2, 0.2, −0.3)
Similarly, for vertex v, w and x:
(v, 0.3, −0.2, 0.2, −0.3, 0.3, −0.3), (w, 0.2, −0.1, 0.2, −0.3, 0.3, −0.2), (x, 0.2, −0.4, 0.4, −0.1, 0.3, −0.3)
Now edges of the semi−strong product of two graphs can be obtained by using (iv), (v) and (vi) of Definition 28
For an edge uv: (0.2, −0.1, 0.1, −0.1, 0.4, −0.2) For an edge wx: (0.1, −0.01, 0.15, −0.05, 0.5, −0.3)
For an edge vw: (0.3, −0.01, 0.1, −0.3, 0.4, −0.3) For an edge vx: (0.1, −0.2, 0.15, −0.3, 0.4, −0.3).
Graph shown in Figure 2 is the semi-strong product of the graphs of Figure 1a,b.

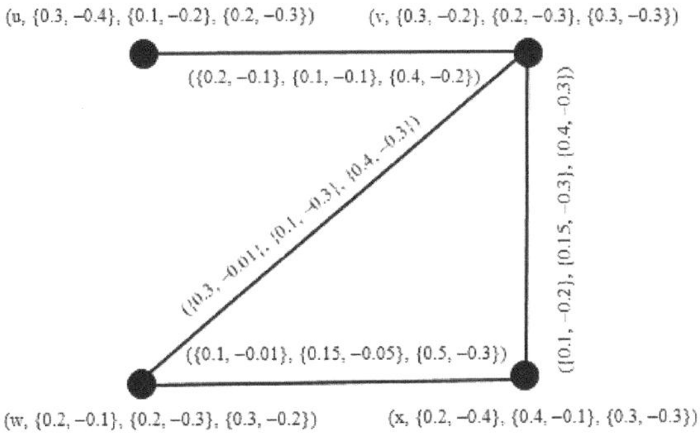

Figure 2. Semi-strong product of bipolar picture fuzzy graphs shown in Figure 1a,b.

Definition 30. *The normal product of two BPPFGs $H_1 = (V_1, C_1, D_1)$ and $H_2 = (V_2, C_2, D_2)$ with underlying crisp graphs $H_1^* = (V_1, E_1)$ and $H_2^* = (V_2, E_2)$, respectively, is defined as a BPPFG $G = G_1 \bullet G_2 = (A_1 \bullet A_2, B_1 \bullet B_2)$ with underline crisp graph $H^* = (V, E)$, where $V = V_1 \times V_2$ and $E = \{(u,v)(w,x) : u = w, vx \in E_2 \text{ or } v = x, uw \in E_1\} \cup E = \{(u,w)(v,x) : uw \in E_1, vx \in E_2\}$ with*

(i)

$\alpha^P_{C_1\bullet C_2}(u,v) = (\alpha^P_{C_1}(u) \wedge \alpha^P_{C_2}(v)),\ \alpha^N_{C_1\bullet C_2}(u,v) = (\alpha^N_{C_1}(u) \vee \alpha^N_{C_2}(v))$

$\gamma^P_{C_1\bullet C_2}(u,v) = (\gamma^P_{C_1}(u) \wedge \gamma^P_{C_2}(v)),\ \gamma^N_{C_1\bullet C_2}(u,v) = (\gamma^N_{C_1}(u) \vee \gamma^N_{C_2}(v))$

$\beta^P_{C_1\bullet C_2}(u,v) = (\beta^P_{C_1}(u) \vee \beta^P_{C_2}(v)),\ \beta^N_{C_1\bullet C_2}(u,v) = (\beta^N_{C_1}(u) \wedge \beta^N_{C_2}(v))$

for all $u, v \in V$

(ii)

$\alpha^P_{D_1\bullet D_2}((u,v)(u,w)) = (\alpha^P_{C_1}(u) \wedge \alpha^P_{D_2}(u,w)),\ \alpha^N_{D_1\bullet D_2}((u,v)(u,w)) = (\alpha^N_{C_1}(u) \vee \alpha^N_{D_2}(u,w))$

$\gamma^P_{D_1\bullet D_2}((u,v)(u,w)) = (\gamma^P_{C_1}(u) \wedge \gamma^P_{D_2}(u,w)),\ \gamma^N_{D_1\bullet D_2}((u,v)(u,w)) = (\gamma^N_{C_1}(u) \vee \gamma^N_{D_2}(u,w))$

$\beta^P_{D_1\bullet D_2}((u,v)(u,w)) = (\beta^P_{C_1}(u) \vee \beta^P_{D_2}(u,w)),\ \beta^N_{D_1\bullet D_2}((u,v)(u,w)) = (\beta^N_{C_1}(u) \wedge \beta^N_{D_2}(u,w))$

for all $u \in V_1$ and $vw \in E_2$

(iii)

$\alpha^P_{D_1\bullet D_2}((u,w)(v,w)) = (\alpha^P_{C_1}(w) \wedge \alpha^P_{D_2}(u,v)),\ \alpha^N_{D_1\bullet D_2}((u,w)(v,w)) = (\alpha^N_{C_1}(w) \vee \alpha^N_{D_2}(u,v))$

$\gamma^P_{D_1\bullet D_2}((u,w)(v,w)) = (\gamma^P_{C_1}(w) \wedge \gamma^P_{D_2}(u,v)),\ \gamma^N_{D_1\bullet D_2}((u,w)(v,w)) = (\gamma^N_{C_1}(w) \vee \gamma^N_{D_2}(u,v))$

$\beta^P_{D_1\bullet D_2}((u,w)(v,w)) = (\beta^P_{C_1}(w) \vee \beta^P_{D_2}(u,v)),\ \beta^N_{D_1\bullet D_2}((u,w)(v,w)) = (\beta^N_{C_1}(w) \wedge \beta^N_{D_2}(u,v))$

for all $w \in V_1$ and $uv \in E_1$

(iv)

$\alpha^P_{D_1\bullet D_2}((u,v)(w,x)) = (\alpha^P_{C_1}(u,w) \wedge \alpha^P_{D_2}(v,x)),\ \alpha^N_{D_1\bullet D_2}((u,v)(w,x)) = (\alpha^N_{C_1}(u,w) \vee \alpha^N_{D_2}(v,x))$

$\gamma^P_{D_1\bullet D_2}((u,v)(w,x)) = (\gamma^P_{C_1}(u,w) \wedge \gamma^P_{D_2}(v,x)),\ \gamma^N_{D_1\bullet D_2}((u,v)(w,x)) = (\gamma^N_{C_1}(u,w) \vee \gamma^N_{D_2}(v,x))$

$\beta^P_{D_1\bullet D_2}((u,v)(w,x)) = (\beta^P_{C_1}(u,w) \vee \beta^P_{D_2}(v,x)),\ \beta^N_{D_1\bullet D_2}((u,v)(w,x)) = (\beta^N_{C_1}(u,w) \wedge \beta^N_{D_2}(v,x))$

for all $uw \in E_1$ and $vx \in E_2$.

Definition 31. *Let $H = H_1 \bullet H_2$ with underlying crisp graph $G^* = (V, E)$, where $V = V_1 \times V_2$, $E = E_1 \times E_2$ be the normal product of two BPPFGs $H_1 = (C_1, D_1)$ and $H_2 = (C_2, D_2)$ with crisp graphs $G_1^* = (V_1, E_1)$ and $G_2^* = (V_2, E_2)$, respectively. Then the degree of the vertex (u_1, u_2) in V is denoted by $d(H_1 \bullet H_2(u,v)) = d(\alpha^P_{H_1} \bullet \alpha^P_{H_2})(u,v), d(\alpha^N_{H_1} \bullet \alpha^N_{H_2}), d(\gamma^P_{H_1} \bullet \gamma^P_{H_2})(u,v), d(\gamma^N_{H_1} \bullet \gamma^N_{H_2})(u,v), d(\beta^P_{H_1} \bullet \beta^P_{H_2})(u,v), d(\beta^N_{H_1} \bullet \beta^N_{H_2})(u,v)$ and is defined by*

(i)

$d(\alpha^P_{H_1} \bullet \alpha^P_{H_2})(u,v) = \sum_{v=x,(u,w)\in E_2} (\alpha^P_{C_1}(v) \wedge \alpha^P_{D_2}(u,w)) + \sum_{v=x,(u,w)\in E_1} (\alpha^P_{D_1}(u,w) \wedge \alpha^P_{C_2}(v)) =$

$\sum_{(u,w)\in E_1} (\alpha^P_{D_1}(u,w) \wedge \alpha^P_{D_2}(v,x))$

(ii)

$d(\alpha^N_{H_1} \bullet \alpha^N_{H_2})(u,v) = \sum_{v=x,(u,w)\in E_2} (\alpha^N_{C_1}(v) \vee \alpha^N_{D_2}(u,w)) + \sum_{v=x,(u,w)\in E_1} (\alpha^N_{D_1}(u,w) \vee \alpha^N_{C_2}(v)) = \sum_{(u,w)\in E_1} (\alpha^N_{D_1}(u,w) \vee \alpha^N_{D_2}(v,x))$

(iii)

$d(\gamma^P_{H_1} \bullet \gamma^P_{H_2})(u,v) = \sum_{v=x,(u,w)\in E_2} (\gamma^P_{C_1}(v) \wedge \gamma^P_{D_2}(u,w)) + \sum_{v=x,(u,w)\in E_1} (\gamma^P_{D_1}(u,w) \wedge \gamma^P_{C_2}(v)) = \sum_{(u,w)\in E_1} (\gamma^P_{D_1}(u,w) \wedge \gamma^P_{D_2}(v,x))$

(iv)

$d(\gamma^N_{H_1} \bullet \gamma^N_{H_2})(u,v) = \sum_{v=x,(u,w)\in E_2} (\gamma^N_{C_1}(v) \vee \gamma^N_{D_2}(u,w)) + \sum_{v=x,(u,w)\in E_1} (\gamma^N_{D_1}(u,w) \vee \gamma^N_{C_2}(v)) = \sum_{(u,w)\in E_1} (\gamma^N_{D_1}(u,w) \vee \gamma^N_{D_2}(v,x))$

(v)

$d(\beta^P_{H_1} \bullet \beta^P_{H_2})(u,v) = \sum_{v=x,(u,w)\in E_2} (\beta^P_{C_1}(v) \vee \beta^P_{D_2}(u,w)) + \sum_{v=x,(u,w)\in E_1} (\beta^P_{D_1}(u,w) \vee \beta^P_{C_2}(v)) = \sum_{(u,w)\in E_1} (\beta^P_{D_1}(u,w) \vee \beta^P_{D_2}(v,x))$

(vi)

$d(\beta^N_{H_1} \bullet \beta^N_{H_2})(u,v) = \sum_{v=x,(u,w)\in E_2} (\beta^N_{C_1}(v) \wedge \beta^N_{D_2}(u,w)) + \sum_{v=x,(u,w)\in E_1} (\beta^N_{D_1}(u,w) \wedge \beta^N_{C_2}(v)) = \sum_{(u,w)\in E_1} (\beta^N_{D_1}(u,w) \wedge \beta^N_{D_2}(v,x))$.

Theorem 3. *Let $H_1 = (V_1, C_1, D_1)$ and $H_2 = (V_2, C_2, D_2)$ be two BPPFGs. If $\alpha^P_{C_1} \geq \alpha^P_{D_2}$, $\alpha^N_{C_1} \leq \alpha^N_{D_2}$, $\gamma^P_{C_1} \geq \gamma^P_{D_2}$, $\gamma^N_{C_1} \leq \gamma^N_{D_2}$, $\beta^P_{C_1} \leq \beta^P_{D_2}$, $\beta^N_{C_1} \geq \beta^N_{D_2}$ $\alpha^P_{C_2} \geq \alpha^P_{D_1}$, $\alpha^N_{C_2} \leq \alpha^N_{D_1}$, $\gamma^P_{C_2} \geq \gamma^P_{D_1}$, $\gamma^N_{C_2} \leq \gamma^N_{D_1}$, $\beta^P_{C_2} \leq \beta^P_{D_1}$, $\beta^N_{C_2} \geq \beta^N_{D_1}$ and $\alpha^P_{D_2} \geq \alpha^P_{D_1}$, $\alpha^N_{D_2} \leq \alpha^N_{D_1}$, $\gamma^P_{D_2} \geq \gamma^P_{D_1}$, $\gamma^N_{D_2} \leq \gamma^N_{D_1}$, $\beta^P_{D_2} \leq \beta^P_{D_1}$, $\beta^N_{D_2} \geq \beta^N_{D_1}$, then $d_{H_1 \bullet H_2}(u_1, u_2) = |V_2|\, d_{H_1}(u_1) + d_{H_2}(u_2)$.*

3.2. Homomorphism of Bipolar Picture Fuzzy Graphs

Definition 32. *Let H_1 and H_2 be the two BPPFGs. A homomorphism $f : H_1 \to H_2$ is the map $f : V_1 \to V_2$ satisfying*

(a) $\alpha^P_{C_1}(u) \leq \alpha^P_{C_2}(f(u))$, $\quad \alpha^N_{C_1}(u) \geq \alpha^N_{C_2}(f(u))$

(b) $\gamma^P_{C_1}(u) \leq \gamma^P_{C_2}(f(u))$, $\quad \gamma^N_{C_1}(u) \geq \gamma^N_{C_2}(f(u))$

(c) $\beta^P_{C_1}(u) \geq \beta^P_{C_2}(f(u))$, $\quad \beta^N_{C_1}(u) \leq \beta^N_{C_2}(f(u))$

(d) $\alpha^P_{D_1}(uv) \leq \alpha^P_{D_2}(f(u)f(v))$, $\quad \alpha^N_{D_1}(uv) \geq \alpha^N_{D_2}(f(u)f(v))$

(e) $\gamma^P_{D_1}(uv) \leq \gamma^P_{D_2}(f(u)f(v))$, $\quad \gamma^N_{D_1}(uv) \geq \gamma^N_{D_2}(f(u)f(v))$

(f) $\beta^P_{D_1}(uv) \geq \beta^P_{D_2}(f(u)f(v))$, $\quad \beta^N_{D_1}(uv) \leq \beta^N_{D_2}(f(u)f(v))$

for all $u \in V_1$, $uv \in E_1$.

Definition 33. *Let H_1 and H_2 be the two BPPFGs. An isomorphism $f : H_1 \to H_2$ is a bijective mapping $f : V_1 \to V_2$ which satisfies*

(a) $\alpha^P_{C_1}(u) = \alpha^P_{C_2} f(u)$, $\quad \alpha^N_{C_1}(u) = \alpha^N_{C_2} f(u)$

(b) $\gamma^P_{C_1}(u) = \gamma^P_{C_2} f(u)$, $\quad \gamma^N_{C_1}(u) = \gamma^N_{C_2} f(u)$

(c) $\beta^P_{C_1}(u) = \beta^P_{C_2} f(u)$, $\quad \beta^N_{C_1}(u) = \beta^N_{C_2} f(u)$

(d) $\alpha^P_{D_1}(u,v) = \alpha^P_{D_2}(f(u)f(v))$, $\quad \alpha^N_{D_1}(u,v) = \alpha^N_{D_2}(f(u)f(v))$

(e) $\gamma^P_{D_1}(u,v) = \gamma^P_{D_2}(f(u)f(v))$, $\quad \gamma^N_{D_1}(u,v) = \gamma^N_{D_2}(f(u)f(v))$

(f) $\beta^P_{D_1}(u,v) = \beta^P_{D_2}(f(u)f(v))$, $\quad \beta^N_{D_1}(u,v) = \beta^N_{D_2}(f(u)f(v))$

for all $x_1 \in V_1$, $x_1y_1 \in E_1$.

Proposition 2. *The isomorphism between BPPFGs is an equivalence relation.*

Definition 34. *Let H_1 and H_2 be the two BPPFGs. Then a weak isomorphism $h : G_1 \to G_2$ is a bijective map $h : V_1 \to V_2$ satifying*
(a) *h is a homomorphism.*
(b) $\alpha^P_{C_1}(u) = \alpha^P_{C_2} f(u)$, $\alpha^N_{C_1}(u) = \alpha^N_{C_2} f(u)$
(c) $\gamma^P_{C_1}(u) = \gamma^P_{C_2} f(u)$, $\gamma^N_{C_1}(u) = \gamma^N_{C_2} f(u)$
(d) $\beta^P_{C_1}(u) = \beta^P_{C_2} f(u)$, $\beta^N_{C_1}(u) = \beta^N_{C_2} f(u)$
for all $u \in V$. Evidently, the co-weak isomorphism fixes only the weights of the vertices.

Definition 35. *Let G_1, G_2 be the two BPPFGs. The co-weak isomorphism $h : G_1 \to G_2$ is the bijective map $h : V_1 \to V_2$ which satisfies*
(a) *h is a homomorphism*
(b) $\alpha^P_{D_1}(u,v) = \alpha^P_{D_2}(f(u)f(v))$, $\alpha^N_{D_1}(u,v) = \alpha^N_{D_2}(f(u)f(v))$
(c) $\gamma^P_{D_1}(u,v) = \gamma^P_{D_2}(f(u)f(v))$, $\gamma^N_{D_1}(u,v) = \gamma^N_{D_2}(f(u)f(v))$
(d) $\beta^P_{D_1}(u,v) = \beta^P_{D_2}(f(u)f(v))$, $\beta^N_{D_1}(u,v) = \beta^N_{D_2}(f(u)f(v))$
for all $uv \in E_1$. Evidently, the co-weak isomorphism fixes only the weights of the edges.

Proposition 3. *Weak isomorphism between BPPFGs always induces a partial order relation.*

Theorem 4. *Let $G = (A, B)$ be a BPPFG and Aut(G) be the set of all automorphisms of G. Then (Aut(G), $\circ$) forms a group.*

Proof. Let $\rho, \tau, \varrho \in Aut(G)$ and let $u, v \in V$. Then

$$
\begin{aligned}
\alpha^P_C((\rho\circ\tau)(u)) &= \alpha^P_C(\rho(\tau(u))) \geq \alpha^P_C(\rho(u)) \geq \alpha^P_C(u)\\
\alpha^N_C((\rho\circ\tau)(u)) &= \alpha^N_C(\rho(\tau(u))) \leq \alpha^N_C(\rho(u)) \leq \alpha^N_C(u)\\
\gamma^P_C((\rho\circ\tau)(u)) &= \gamma^P_C(\rho(\tau(u))) \geq \gamma^P_C(\rho(u)) \geq \gamma^P_C(u)\\
\gamma^N_C((\rho\circ\tau)(u)) &= \gamma^N_C(\rho(\tau(u))) \leq \gamma^N_C(\rho(u)) \leq \gamma^N_C(u)\\
\beta^P_C((\rho\circ\tau)(u)) &= \beta^P_C(\rho(\tau(u))) \leq \beta^P_C(\rho(u)) \leq \beta^P_C(u)\\
\beta^N_C((\rho\circ\tau)(u)) &= \beta^N_C(\rho(\tau(u))) \geq \beta^N_C(\rho(u)) \geq \beta^N_C(u)\\
\alpha^P_D((\rho\circ\tau)(u)(\rho\circ\tau)(v)) &= \alpha^P_D(\rho(\tau(u)))(\rho(\tau(v))) \geq \alpha^P_D((\rho(u))(\rho(v))) \geq \alpha^P_D(uv)\\
\gamma^P_D((\rho\circ\tau)(u)(\rho\circ\tau)(v)) &= \gamma^P_D((\rho(\tau(u)))(\rho(\tau(v)))) \geq \gamma^P_D((\rho(u))(\rho(v))) \geq \gamma^P_D(uv)\\
\beta^P_D((\rho\circ\tau)(u)(\rho\circ\tau)(v)) &= \beta^P_D((\rho(\tau(u)))(\rho(\tau(v)))) \leq \beta^P_D((\rho(u))(\rho(v))) \leq \beta^P_D(uv)\\
\alpha^N_D((\rho\circ\tau)(u)(\rho\circ\tau)(v)) &= \alpha^N_D((\rho(\tau(u)))(\rho(\tau(v)))) \leq \alpha^N_D((\rho(u))(\rho(v))) \leq \alpha^N_D(uv)\\
\gamma^N_D((\rho\circ\tau)(u)(\rho\circ\tau)(v)) &= \gamma^N_D((\rho(\tau(u)))(\rho(\tau(v)))) \leq \gamma^N_D((\rho(u))(\rho(v))) \leq \gamma^N_D(uv)\\
\beta^N_D((\rho\circ\tau)(u)(\rho\circ\tau)(v)) &= \beta^N_D((\rho(\tau(u)))(\rho(\tau(v)))) \geq \beta^N_D((\rho(u))(\rho(v))) \geq \beta^N_D(uv)
\end{aligned}
$$

Thus, $\rho \circ \tau \in$ Aut(G). Similarly, one can easily prove that $(\rho \circ \tau)\circ \varrho = \rho \circ (\tau \circ \varrho)$, where ρ, τ, $\varrho \in$ Aut(G). Additionally, we have the inverses for each $\rho \in$ Aut(G) defined as $\alpha^P_C(\rho^{-1}) = \alpha^P_C(\rho)$, $\alpha^N_C(\rho^{-1}) = \alpha^N_C(\rho)$, $\gamma^P_C(\rho^{-1}) = \gamma^P_C(\rho)$, $\gamma^N_C(\rho^{-1}) = \gamma^N_C(\rho)$, $\beta^P_C(\rho^{-1}) = \beta^P_C(\rho)$, $\beta^N_C(\rho^{-1}) = \beta^N_C(\rho)$. Similarly, there exists $e \in$ Aut(G). Let $\rho \circ e = \rho = e \circ \rho$. $\alpha^P_C((\rho \circ e)(u)) = \alpha^P_C(\rho(u))$ $\forall e, \rho \in$ Aut(G) is the identity element. Hence (Aut(G), $\circ$) forms a group. □

Proposition 4. *Let $H = (C, D)$ be a BPPFG and $Aut(H)$ be the set of all automorphisms of H. Let $h = (\alpha_h^P, \gamma_h^P, \beta_h^P, \alpha_h^N, \gamma_h^N, \beta_h^N)$ be a BPPFS in $Aut(H)$ defined by*

$$\alpha_h^P(\rho) = sup\{\alpha_D^P(\rho(u),\rho(v))\}, \quad \alpha_h^N(\rho) = inf\{\alpha_D^N(\rho(u),\rho(v))\}$$
$$\gamma_h^P(\rho) = sup\{\gamma_D^P(\rho(u),\rho(v))\}, \quad \gamma_h^N(\rho) = inf\{\gamma_D^N(\rho(u),\rho(v))\}$$
$$\beta_h^P(\rho) = inf\{\beta_D^P(\rho(u),\rho(v))\}, \quad \beta_h^N(\rho) = sup\{\beta_D^N(\rho(u),\rho(v))\}$$

for all $(u, v) \in V \times V$, $\rho \in Aut(H)$. Then, $h = (\alpha_h^P, \gamma_h^P, \beta_h^P, \alpha_h^N, \gamma_h^N, \beta_h^N)$ is a bipolar picture fuzzy group on $Aut(H)$.

Proof. Follows from Theorem 3. □

3.3. Complete and Strong Bipolar Picture Fuzzy Graphs

Definition 36. *A BPPFG $G = (C, D)$ of a graph $G^* = (V, E)$, where $C = \{\alpha_C^P(u), \alpha_C^N(u), \gamma_C^P(u), \gamma_C^N(u), \beta_C^P(u), \beta_C^N(u)\}$ and $D = \{\alpha_D^P(u), \alpha_D^N(u), \gamma_D^P(u), \gamma_D^N(u), \beta_D^P(u), \beta_D^N(u)\}$ is called a complete bipolar picture fuzzy graph (complete BPPFG) if*

$$\alpha_D^P(uv) = min(\alpha_C^P(u), \alpha_C^P(v)), \quad \alpha_D^N(uv) = max(\alpha_C^N(u), \alpha_C^N(v))$$
$$\gamma_D^P(uv) = min(\gamma_C^P(u), \gamma_C^P(v)), \quad \gamma_D^N(uv) = max(\gamma_c^N(u), \gamma_c^N(v))$$
$$\beta_D^P(uv) = max(\beta_C^P(u), \beta_C^P(v)), \quad \beta_D^N(uv) = min(\beta_C^N(u), \beta_C^N(v))$$

for all $u, v \in V$.

Example 3. *One can easily verify that the graph shown in Figure 1a is a complete BPPFG.*

Theorem 5. *Let $H_1 = (C_1, D_1)$ and $H_2 = (C_2, D_2)$ be two complete BPPFGs. Then their direct product $H_1 \otimes H_2$ is also a complete BPPFG.*

Proof. As we know that the strong product of BPPFGs is a BPPFG and each pair of vertices are adjacent, $E \subseteq V_1 \times V_2$. Now, for all $(u, v_1)(u, v_2) \in E$, since H_2 is complete
$(\alpha_{D_1}^P \otimes \alpha_{D_2}^P)((u, v_1), (u, v_2)) = \alpha_{C_1}^P(u) \wedge \alpha_{D_2}^P(v_1v_2) = \alpha_{C_1}^P(u) \wedge \alpha_{C_2}^P(v_1) \wedge \alpha_{C_2}^P(v_2) = (\alpha_{C_1}^P \otimes \alpha_{C_2}^P)((u)) \wedge (\alpha_{C_1}^P \otimes \alpha_{C_2}^P)((v_1, v_2))$
$(\alpha_{D_1}^N \otimes \alpha_{D_2}^N)((u, v_1), (u, v_2)) = \alpha_{C_1}^N(u) \vee \alpha_{D_2}^N(v_1v_2) = \alpha_{C_1}^N(u) \vee \alpha_{C_2}^N(v_1) \vee \alpha_{C_2}^N(v_2) = (\alpha_{C_1}^N \otimes \alpha_{C_2}^N)((u)) \vee (\alpha_{C_1}^N \otimes \alpha_{C_2}^N)((v_1, v_2))$
$(\gamma_{D_1}^P \otimes \gamma_{D_2}^P)((u, v_1), (u, v_2)) = \gamma_{C_1}^P(u) \wedge \gamma_{D_2}^P(v_1v_2) = \gamma_{C_1}^P(u) \wedge \gamma_{C_2}^P(v_1) \wedge \gamma_{C_2}^P(v_2) = (\gamma_{C_1}^P \otimes \gamma_{C_2}^P)((u)) \wedge (\gamma_{C_1}^P \otimes \gamma_{C_2}^P)((v_1, v_2))$
$(\gamma_{D_1}^N \otimes \gamma_{D_2}^N)((u, v_1), (u, v_2)) = \gamma_{C_1}^N(u) \vee \gamma_{D_2}^N(v_1v_2) = \gamma_{C_1}^N(u) \vee \gamma_{C_2}^N(v_1) \vee \gamma_{C_2}^N(v_2) = (\gamma_{C_1}^N \otimes \gamma_{C_2}^N)((u)) \vee (\gamma_{C_1}^N \otimes \gamma_{C_2}^N)((v_1, v_2))$
$(\beta_{D_1}^P \otimes \beta_{D_2}^P)((u, v_1), (u, v_2)) = \beta_{C_1}^P(u) \vee \beta_{D_2}^P(v_1v_2) = \beta_{C_1}^P(u) \vee \beta_{C_2}^P(v_1) \vee \beta_{C_2}^P(v_2) = (\beta_{C_1}^P \otimes \beta_{C_2}^P)((u)) \vee (\beta_{C_1}^P \otimes \beta_{C_2}^P)((v_1, v_2))$
$(\beta_{D_1}^N \otimes \beta_{D_2}^N)((u, v_1), (u, v_2)) = \beta_{C_1}^N(u) \wedge \beta_{D_2}^N(v_1v_2) = \beta_{C_1}^N(u) \wedge \beta_{C_2}^N(v_1) \wedge \beta_{C_2}^N(v_2) = (\beta_{C_1}^N \otimes \beta_{C_2}^N)((u)) \wedge (\beta_{C_1}^N \otimes \beta_{C_2}^N)((v_1, v_2))$
If $((u_1, w)(u_2, w)) \in E$, then
$(\alpha_{D_1}^P \otimes \alpha_{D_2}^P)((u_1, w), (u_2, w)) = \alpha_{D_1}^P(u_1u_2) \wedge \alpha_{C_2}^P(w) = \alpha_{C_1}^P(u_1) \wedge \alpha_{C_1}^P(u_2) \wedge \alpha_{C_2}^P(w) = (\alpha_{C_1}^P \otimes$

$\alpha^P_{C_2})((u_1u_2)) \wedge (\alpha^P_{C_1} \otimes \alpha^P_{C_2})(w)$.
Similarly, one can easily verify that

$$(\alpha^N_{D_1} \otimes \alpha^N_{D_2})((u_1,w)(u_2,w)) = (\alpha^N_{C_1} \otimes \alpha^N_{C_2})(u_1,w) \vee (\alpha^N_{C_1} \otimes \alpha^N_{C_2})(u_2,w)$$
$$(\gamma^P_{D_1} \otimes \gamma^P_{D_2})((u_1,w)(u_2,w)) = (\gamma^P_{C_1} \otimes \gamma^P_{C_2})(u_1,w) \wedge (\gamma^P_{C_1} \otimes \gamma^P_{C_2})(u_2,w)$$
$$(\gamma^N_{D_1} \otimes \gamma^N_{D_2})((u_1,w)(u_2,w)) = (\gamma^N_{C_1} \otimes \gamma^N_{C_2})(u_1,w) \vee (\gamma^N_{C_1} \otimes \gamma^N_{C_2})(u_2,w)$$
$$(\beta^P_{D_1} \otimes \beta^P_{D_2})((u_1,w)(u_2,w)) = (\beta^P_{C_1} \otimes \beta^P_{C_2})(u_1,w) \vee (\beta^P_{C_1} \otimes \beta^P_{C_2})(u_2,w)$$
$$(\beta^N_{D_1} \otimes \beta^N_{D_2})((u_1,w)(u_2,w)) = (\beta^N_{C_1} \otimes \beta^N_{C_2})(u_1,w) \wedge (\beta^N_{C_1} \otimes \beta^N_{C_2})(u_2,w)$$

If $(u_1,v_1)(u_2,v_2) \in E$, then as H_1 and H_2 are complete
$(\alpha^P_{D_1} \otimes \alpha^P_{D_2})((u_1,v_1)(u_2,v_2)) = \alpha^P_{D_1}(u_1u_2) \wedge \alpha^P_{D_2}(v_1,v_2) = \alpha^P_{C_1}(u_1) \wedge \alpha^P_{C_1}(v_1) \wedge \alpha^P_{C_2}(u_1) \wedge \alpha^P_{C_2}(v_2)$.
Similarly, we can show that

$$(\alpha^N_{D_1} \otimes \alpha^N_{D_2})((u_1,v_1)(u_2,v_2)) = \alpha^N_{C_1}(u_1) \vee \alpha^N_{C_1}(v_1) \vee \alpha^N_{C_2}(u_1) \vee \alpha^N_{C_2}(v_2)$$
$$(\gamma^P_{D_1} \otimes \gamma^P_{D_2})((u_1,v_1)(u_2,v_2)) = \gamma^P_{C_1}(u_1) \wedge \gamma^P_{C_1}(v_1) \wedge \gamma^P_{C_2}(u_1) \wedge \gamma^P_{C_2}(v_2)$$
$$(\gamma^N_{D_1} \otimes \gamma^N_{D_2})((u_1,v_1)(u_2,v_2)) = \gamma^N_{C_1}(u_1) \vee \gamma^N_{C_1}(v_1) \vee \gamma^N_{C_2}(u_1) \vee \gamma^N_{C_2}(v_2)$$
$$(\beta^P_{D_1} \otimes \beta^P_{D_2})((u_1,v_1)(u_2,v_2)) = \beta^P_{C_1}(u_1) \vee \beta^P_{C_1}(v_1) \vee \beta^P_{C_2}(u_1) \vee \beta^P_{C_2}(v_2)$$
$$(\beta^P_{D_1} \otimes \beta^P_{D_2})((u_1,v_1)(u_2,v_2)) = \beta^P_{C_1}(u_1) \wedge \beta^P_{C_1}(v_1) \wedge \beta^P_{C_2}(u_1) \wedge \beta^P_{C_2}(v_2).$$

Hence, $H_1 \otimes H_2$ is a complete BPPFG. □

Definition 37. *A BPPFG* $G = (C, D)$ *on a graph* $G^* = (V, E)$, *where* $C = \{\alpha^P_C(u), \alpha^N_C(u), \gamma^P_C(u), \gamma^N_C(u), \beta^P_C(u), \beta^N_C(u)\}$ *and* $D = \{\alpha^P_D(u), \alpha^N_D(u), \gamma^P_D(u), \gamma^N_D(u), \beta^P_D(u), \beta^N_D(u)\}$ *is said to be a strong bipolar picture fuzzy graph (in short, BPPFG) if*

$$\alpha^P_D(uv) = min(\alpha^P_C(u), \alpha^P_C(v)), \quad \alpha^N_D(uv) = max(\alpha^N_C(u), \alpha^N_C(v))$$
$$\gamma^P_D(uv) = min(\gamma^P_C(u), \gamma^P_C(v)), \quad \gamma^N_D(uv) = max(\gamma^N_c(u), \gamma^N_c(v))$$
$$\beta^P_D(uv) = max(\beta^P_C(u), \beta^P_C(v)), \quad \beta^N_D(uv) = min(\beta^N_C(u), \beta^N_C(v))$$

for all $u, v \in E$.

Example 4. *The graph shown in Figure 3 is a strong BPPFG.*

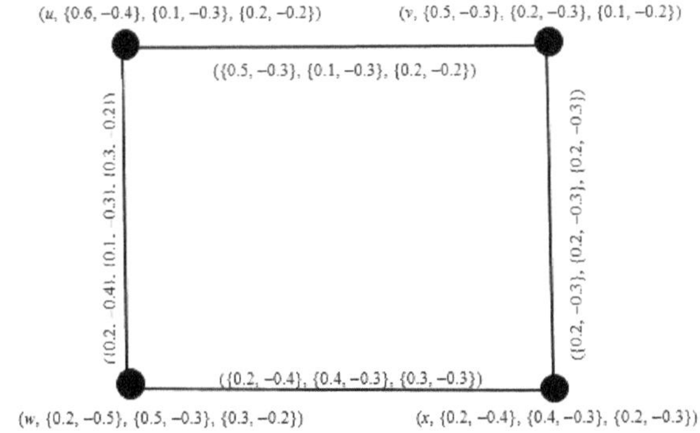

Figure 3. Strong bipolar picture fuzzy graph.

Remark 2. *Every complete BPPFG implies a strong BPPFG but the converse does not exist.*

Definition 38. *The complement of a strong BPPFG* $G = (C, D)$ *of a graph* $G^* = (V, E)$*, where* $C = \{\alpha_C^P(u), \alpha_C^N(u), \gamma_C^P(u), \gamma_C^N(u), \beta_C^P(u), \beta_C^N(u)\}$ *and* $D = \{\alpha_D^P(u), \alpha_D^N(u), \gamma_D^P(u), \gamma_D^N(u), \beta_D^P(u), \beta_D^N(u)\}$ *is a BPPFG* $\overline{G} = (\overline{C}, \overline{D})$ *of* $\overline{G^*} = (V, V \times V)$*, where* $\overline{C} = C = \{\alpha_C^P(u), \alpha_C^N(u), \gamma_C^P(u), \gamma_C^N(u), \beta_C^P(u), \beta_C^N(u)\}$ *and* $\overline{D} = D = \{\overline{\alpha_D^P}(uv), \overline{\alpha_D^N}(uv), \overline{\gamma_D^P}(uv), \overline{\gamma_D^N}(uv), \overline{\beta_D^P}(uv), \overline{\beta_D^N}(uv)\}$ *is defined by*

$$\overline{\alpha_D^P}(uv) = min(\alpha_C^P(u), \alpha_C^P(v)) - \alpha_D^P(uv), \qquad \overline{\alpha_D^N}(uv) = max(\alpha_C^N(u), \alpha_C^N(v)) - \alpha_D^N(uv)$$
$$\overline{\gamma_D^P}(uv) = min(\gamma_C^P(u), \gamma_C^P(v)) - \gamma_D^P(uv), \qquad \overline{\gamma_D^N}(uv) = max(\gamma_c^N(u), \gamma_c^N(v)) - \gamma_D^N(uv)$$
$$\overline{\beta_D^P}(uv) = max(\beta_C^P(u), \beta_C^P(v)) - \beta_D^P(uv), \qquad \overline{\beta_D^N}(uv) = min(\beta_C^N(u), \beta_C^N(v)) - \beta_D^N(uv)$$

for all $u, v \in V$, $uv \in \overline{V^2}$.

Example 5. *Graph in Figure 4 is the complement of a strong BPPFG shown in Figure 3.*

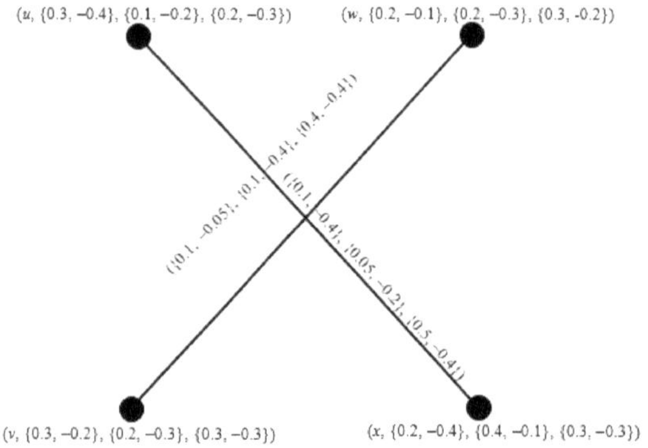

Figure 4. Complement of a strong bipolar picture fuzzy graph given in Figure 3.

Theorem 6. *Let* $G_1 = (C_1, D_1)$ *and* $G_2 = (C_2, D_2)$ *be the two strong BPPFGs. Then* $G_1 \sqcap G_2$ *is strong BPPFG.*

Proof. Let $(u_1, v_1)(u_2, v_2) \in E$. Since G_1 and G_2 are strong BPPFGs, we have
$(\alpha_{D_1}^P \sqcap \alpha_{D_2}^P)((u_1, v_1)(u_2, v_2)) = \alpha_{D_1}^P(u_1, v_1) \wedge \alpha_{D_2}^P(u_2, v_2) = \alpha_{C_1}^P(u_1) \wedge \alpha_{C_2}^P(u_2) \wedge \alpha_{C_1}^P(v_1) \wedge \alpha_{C_2}^P(v_2) = (\alpha_{C_1}^P \sqcap \alpha_{C_2}^P)(u_1, v_1) \wedge (\alpha_{C_1}^P \sqcap \alpha_{C_2}^P)(u_2, v_2)$
$(\alpha_{D_1}^N \sqcap \alpha_{D_2}^N)((u_1, v_1)(u_2, v_2)) = \alpha_{D_1}^N(u_1, v_1) \vee \alpha_{D_2}^N(u_2, v_2) = \alpha_{C_1}^N(u_1) \vee \alpha_{C_2}^N(u_2) \vee \alpha_{C_1}^N(v_1) \vee \alpha_{C_2}^N(v_2) = (\alpha_{C_1}^N \sqcap \alpha_{C_2}^N)(u_1, v_1) \wedge (\alpha_{C_1}^N \sqcap \alpha_{C_2}^N)(u_2, v_2)$
$(\gamma_{D_1}^P \sqcap \gamma_{D_2}^P)((u_1, v_1)(u_2, v_2)) = \gamma_{D_1}^P(u_1, v_1) \wedge \gamma_{D_2}^P(u_2, v_2) = \gamma_{C_1}^P(u_1) \wedge \gamma_{C_2}^P(u_2) \wedge \gamma_{C_1}^P(v_1) \wedge \gamma_{C_2}^P(v_2) = (\gamma_{C_1}^P \sqcap \gamma_{C_2}^P)(u_1, v_1) \wedge (\gamma_{C_1}^P \sqcap \gamma_{C_2}^P)(u_2, v_2)$
$(\gamma_{D_1}^N \sqcap \gamma_{D_2}^N)((u_1, v_1)(u_2, v_2)) = \gamma_{D_1}^N(u_1, v_1) \vee \gamma_{D_2}^N(u_2, v_2) = \gamma_{C_1}^N(u_1) \vee \gamma_{C_2}^N(u_2) \vee \gamma_{C_1}^N(v_1) \vee \gamma_{C_2}^N(v_2) = (\gamma_{C_1}^N \sqcap \gamma_{C_2}^N)(u_1, v_1) \wedge (\gamma_{C_1}^N \sqcap \gamma_{C_2}^N)(u_2, v_2)$
$(\beta_{D_1}^P \sqcap \beta_{D_2}^P)((u_1, v_1)(u_2, v_2)) = \beta_{D_1}^P(u_1, v_1) \vee \beta_{D_2}^P(u_2, v_2) = \beta_{C_1}^P(u_1) \wedge \beta_{C_2}^P(u_2) \wedge \beta_{C_1}^P(v_1) \wedge \beta_{C_2}^P(v_2) = (\beta_{C_1}^P \sqcap \beta_{C_2}^P)(u_1, v_1) \vee (\beta_{C_1}^P \sqcap \beta_{C_2}^P)(u_2, v_2)$
$(\beta_{D_1}^N \sqcap \beta_{D_2}^N)((u_1, v_1)(u_2, v_2)) = \beta_{D_1}^N(u_1, v_1) \wedge \beta_{D_2}^N(u_2, v_2) = \beta_{C_1}^N(u_1) \wedge \beta_{C_2}^N(u_2) \wedge \beta_{C_1}^N(v_1) \wedge \beta_{C_2}^N(v_2) = (\beta_{C_1}^N \sqcap \beta_{C_2}^N)(u_1, v_1) \wedge (\beta_{C_1}^N \sqcap \beta_{C_2}^N)(u_2, v_2)$.
□

4. Application

Modelling by using graphs has vast applications in various fields of computer science, mathematics, chemistry, physics, social sciences etc. Usually such types of models require more arrangements than merely the adjacencies among the vertices. In the study of social circuits, it is found that two people know each other i.e., if they are familiar (acquainted), or whether they are friends of each others (in the real world or in the virtual world such as Instagram) and so on. We can label each person in a particular group of people by a vertex u. There is an undirected edge between a vertex u and v if two people has a relationship with each other. In such type of graphs no multiple edges and usually no loops are needed. There is an edge between the vertices u and v when there is any acquaintanceship exists between them. In such graphs there does not exist any loop or multiple edges. In acquaintanceship graphs, the vertex (node) represents the level of acquaintanceship (how much a person is socialized or familiar/friendly) of a person while the the edge is the acquaintanceship between two persons in the social network. Since each vertex has equal importance in the classical graphs, it is not possible to graph the social networks model properly through them. In addition, all social units (individual or organization) present in social groups must be considered with equal importance in the classical graph theory. However, in the real life, the situation is different. Similarly, every edge (relationship) has an equal strength in the classical graphs. Moreover, in classical graphs it is assumed that the relationship between two social units are of equal strength, however, in real life it is not possible. Thus the acquaintance of the person has fuzzy boundary and hence can be better represented through the fuzzy graphs. In fuzzy acquaintanceship graph, each vertex represents the person and its membership value which reflects the strength of acquaintance of the person within the social group. Hence we present a fuzzy acquaintanceship graph, a bipolar fuzzy acquaintanceship and consequently a bipolar picture fuzzy acquaintanceship graph models to find out that how much the person is acquainted (social) within a group. Bipolar picture fuzzy acquaintanceship graph models would be more efficient to detect the symmetry or asymmetry existing between entities through the levels of acquaintanceships in social networks, computer networks etc.

4.1. Fuzzy Acquaintanceship Graph

We take a fuzzy acquaintanceship graph of a social network which is shown in Figure 5. In which the nodes represent the degree of the level of acquaintance of a person within the social group. The degree of the level of acquaintance is expressed in its membership value. Degree of membership states that how much a person is acquainted e.g., X is 60% acquainted within the group. The edges of a graph describe the acquaintanceship level of one person with the other person. The membership degree of edges can be considered in terms of positive percentage e.g., Y has 40% acquaintanceship level with X and so.

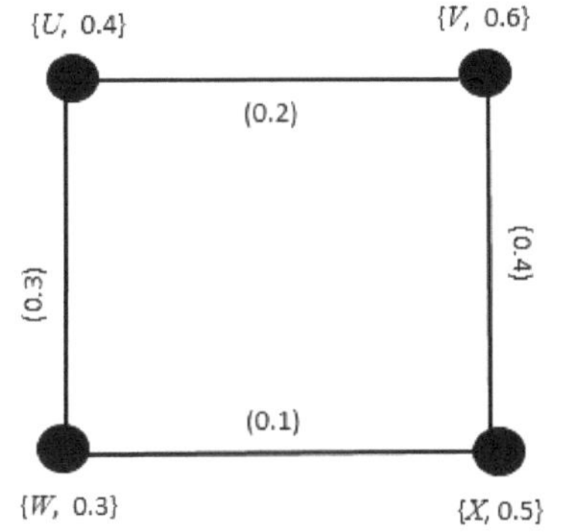

Figure 5. Fuzzy acquaintanceship graph.

4.2. *Bipolar Fuzzy Acquaintanceship Graph*

The acquaintanceship of a person may be positive or negative. Suppose if a person A and B belong to a social network but having not a good relationships between them then the acquaintanceship between them is negative. We can depict such circumstances through the bipolar fuzzy acquaintanceship graph. Consider a bipolar fuzzy acquaintanceship graph of a social group shown in Figure 6. In which the nodes are reflecting the degree of the level of acquaintanceship of a person belongs to a social group and the edges represent the degree of acquaintanceship levels among the persons. Degree of positive membership can be interpreted as how much a person acquainted and negative membership tells us that how much a person losses the the level of acquaintance, X has 50% level of acquaintance within the group but it loses 20% level in the same group. Edges of the graph reflect the acquaintance of one person with the other persons in the group. The positive and negative memberships degrees of edges describes the percentage of positive and negative acquaintance,for instance e.g., X is acquainted 10% with W and W is not acquainted 10% with X.

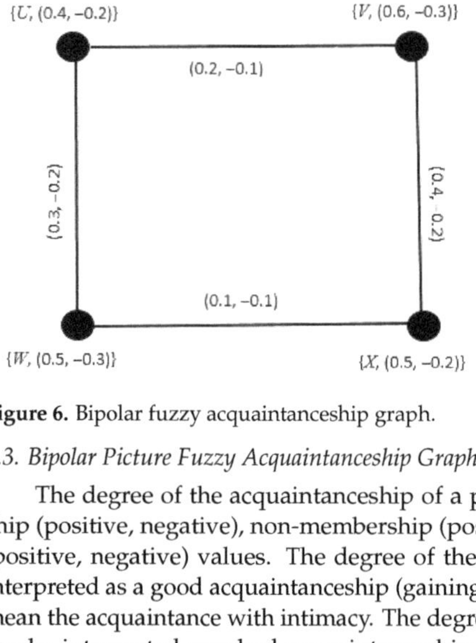

Figure 6. Bipolar fuzzy acquaintanceship graph.

4.3. *Bipolar Picture Fuzzy Acquaintanceship Graph*

The degree of the acquaintanceship of a person is defined in terms of its membership (positive, negative), non-membership (positive, negative) and neutral membership (positive, negative) values. The degree of the membership (positive, negative) can be interpreted as a good acquaintanceship (gaining, losing). By a good acquaintanceship, we mean the acquaintance with intimacy. The degree of non-membership (positive, negative) can be interpreted as a bad acquaintanceship (gaining, losing). Bad acquaintanceship means acquaintance with ill-famed. The degree of neutral membership (positive, negative) represents that the person having a loose acquaintanceship (gaining, losing). By a loose acquaintanceship, we mean someone we do not know well enough but we probably see them around occasionally. In Figure 7, X gains (resp., loses) 30% (resp., 50%) good acquaintanceship, he gains 20% (resp., loses 10%) bad acquaintanceship but he gains (resp., loses) 30% (resp., loses 20%) loose acquaintanceship within the social group. On the other hands, the edges of a graph (Figure 7) reflect the acquaintanceship of one person with another person. The degree of a membership (positive and negative), non-membership (positive and negative) and neutral membership(positive and negative) of the edges can be interpreted as the percentage of good acquaintanceship (gaining, losing), bad acquaintanceship (gaining, losing) and non-acquaintanceships (gaining, losing). Furthermore, it is easy to verify that the values of the edges of a graph in Figure 7 are satisfying the below conditions.

$$\alpha_D^P(uv) \leq min(\alpha_C^P(u), \alpha_C^P(v)), \quad \alpha_D^N(uv) \geq max(\alpha_C^N(u), \alpha_C^N(v))$$
$$\gamma_D^P(uv) \leq min(\gamma_C^P(u), \gamma_C^P(u)), \quad \gamma_D^N(uv) \geq max(\gamma_C^N(u), \gamma_C^N(v))$$
$$\beta_D^P(uv) \geq max(\beta_C^P(u), \beta_C^P(v)), \quad \beta_D^N(uv) \leq min(\beta_C^N(u), \beta_C^N(v)).$$

Refer to the graph shown in Figure 7, we have
$\alpha_D^P(UV) \leq \min(\alpha_C^P(U), \alpha_C^P(V)) \Rightarrow \alpha_D^P(UV) \leq \min(0.4, 0.2) \Rightarrow 0.1 \leq 0.2$
$\alpha_D^N(UV) \geq \max(\alpha_C^N(U), \alpha_C^N(V)) \Rightarrow \alpha_D^N(UV) \geq \max(-0.2, -0.1) \Rightarrow -0.05 \geq -0.1$
$\gamma_D^P(UV) \leq \min(\gamma_C^P(U), \gamma_C^P(V)) \Rightarrow \gamma_D^P(UV) \leq \min(0.1, 0.3) \Rightarrow 0.1 \leq 0.1$
$\gamma_D^N(UV) \geq \max(\gamma_C^N(U), \gamma_C^N(V)) \Rightarrow \gamma_D^N(UV) \geq \max(-0.3, -0.3) \Rightarrow -0.2 \geq -0.3$
$\beta_D^P(UV) \geq \max(\beta_C^P(U), \beta_C^P(V)) \Rightarrow \beta_D^P(UV) \geq \max(0.2, 0.5) \Rightarrow 0.6 \geq 0.5$
$\beta_D^N(UV) \leq \min(\beta_C^N(U), \beta_C^N(V)) \Rightarrow \beta_D^N(UV) \leq \min(-0.4, -0.4) \Rightarrow -0.5 \leq -0.4.$

Hence by doing same calculations for the other vertices and edges of the graph shown in Figure 7, it is easy to verify that the graph given in Figure 7 is a bipolar picture fuzzy acquaintanceship graph. Similarly, by the values of vertices and edges, one can easily deduce that the graph in Figure 7 is asymmetric.

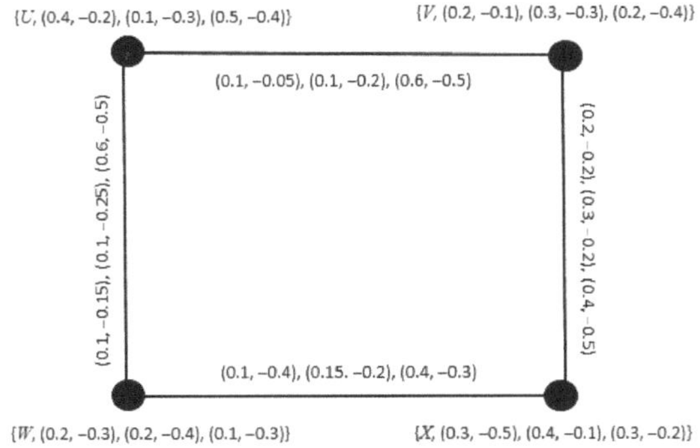

Figure 7. Bipolar picture fuzzy acquaintanceship graph.

5. Conclusions

Fuzzy graphs theory plays a significant role in modeling many real world problems containing uncertainties in different fields such as decision making theory, computer science, optimization problems, data analysis, networking etc. In this perspective, a number of generalizations of fuzzy graph have been introduced to deal with the difficult and complex real life problems. The picture fuzzy set is a direct extension of both the fuzzy sets and intuitonistic fuzzy sets. Bipolar fuzzy set is another generalized form of fuzzy set which is also an effective tool for the multiagent decision analysis. The main goal of this manuscript is to initiate the concepts of bipolar picture fuzzy graph and its different characterizations. In this article, first we propose the definition of bipolar picture fuzzy graphs based on the bipolar picture fuzzy relation. In this article, we have introduced the terms bipolar picture fuzzy graphs, complete bipolar picture fuzzy graphs and strong bipolar picture fuzzy graphs along with their several fundamental properties. For the sake of investigations, we have introduced and applied numerous operations like union, intersection, complement, ring sum etc. on bipolar picture fuzzy graphs. We also introduce different types of products of bipolar picture fuzzy graphs like semi-strong product, direct product, normal products etc. Several other terms such as order and size, path neighborhood degrees, busy values of vertices and edges of bipolar picture fuzzy graphs are also studied. These terminologies also laid the foundation for the discussion of regular bipolar picture fuzzy graphs. Furthermore, we also discuss isomorphisms, weak and co-weak isomorphisms and automorphisms of bipolar picture fuzzy graphs. During this, we have proved that the set of all automorphisms of a bipolar picture fuzzy graph forms a group. Finally, we construct a bipolar picture fuzzy acquaintanceship graph which reflects the importance of our theoretical results produced in this article. Evidently, the network modelled through a bipolar picture fuzzy acquaintanceship graph shown in Figure 7 has no any symmetry. However, we can also model a symmetric relation through the bipolar picture fuzzy acquaintanceship graph. On the same patterns, one could express collaboration graph, computer networking, social networking, web graphs in the frame of bipolar picture fuzzy graphs. In general, numbers of applications of bipolar fuzzy graphs and picture fuzzy graphs have been explored in different fields of social, natural and computer sciences. Evidently, bipolar picture fuzzy graphs would be an important tool to deal with real world problems containing uncertainties. Finally, one can extend this work by introducing bipolar interval-valued picture fuzzy graphs.

Author Contributions: Conceptualization, W.A.K. and B.A.; methodology, B.A., W.A.K. and A.T.; validation, B.A., A.T. and W.A.K.; formal analysis, B.A. and W.A.K.; investigation, B.A. and A.T.; writing—original draft preparation, W.A.K.; writing—review and editing, B.A. and A.T.; supervision, W.A.K.; funding acquisition, W.A.K., B.A. and A.T. All authors have read and agreed to the published version of the manuscript.

Funding: This research received no external funding.

Data Availability Statement: Not Applicable.

Conflicts of Interest: The authors declare no conflict of interest.

References

1. Zadeh, L.A. Fuzzy sets. *Inf. Con.* **1965**, *8*, 338–353. [CrossRef]
2. Bustince, H.; Burillo, P. Correlation of interval-valued intuitionistic fuzzy sets. *Fuzzy Sets Syst.* **1995**, *74*, 237–244. [CrossRef]
3. Khalil, A.M.; Li, S.G.; Garg, H.; Li, H.; Ma, S. New operations on interval-valued picture fuzzy set, interval-valued picture fuzzy soft set and their applications. *IEEE Access* **2019**, *7*, 51236–51253. [CrossRef]
4. Zadeh, L.A. The concept of a linguistic variable and its application to approximate reasoning I. *Inform. Sci.* **1975**, *8*, 199–249. [CrossRef]
5. Zhang, W.-R. Bipolar fuzzy sets and relations: A computational framework for cognitive modeling and multiagent decision analysis. In Proceedings of the First International Joint Conference of the North American Fuzzy Information Processing Society Biannual Conference, the Industrial Fuzzy Control and Intellige, San Antonio, TX, USA, 18–21 December 1994; pp. 305–309
6. Mandal, W.A. Bipolar pythagorean fuzzy sets and their application in Multi-attribute decision making problems. *Ann. Data Sci.* **2021**, 1–33.
7. Dudziak, U.; Pea, B. Equivalent bipolar fuzzy relations. *Fuzzy Sets Syst.* **2010**, *161*, 234–253. [CrossRef]
8. Atanassov, K. Intuitionistic fuzzy sets. *Fuzzy Sets Syst.* **1986**, *20*, 87–96. [CrossRef]
9. Cuong, B.C. Picture fuzzy sets. *J. Comput. Sci. Cybern.* **2014**, *30*, 409–420.
10. Bo, C.; Zhang, X. New operations of picture fuzzy relations and fuzzy comprehensive evaluation. *Symmetry* **2017**, *9*, 268. [CrossRef]
11. Cuong, B.C.; Pham, V.H. Some fuzzy logic operators for picture fuzzy sets. In Proceedings of the 2015 Seventh International Conference on Knowledge and Systems Engineering (KSE), Ho Chi Minh City, Vietnam, 8–10 October 2015; pp. 132–137. [CrossRef]
12. Rosenfeld, A. Fuzzy graphs. In *Fuzzy Sets and Their Applications to Cognitive and Decision Processes*; Zadeh, L.A., Fu, K.S., Shimura, M., Eds.; Academic Press: New York, NY, USA, 1975; pp. 77–95.
13. Bhattacharya, P. Some remarks on fuzzy graphs. *Pattern Recognit. Lett.* **1987**, *6*, 297–302. [CrossRef]
14. Mordeson, J.N.; Peng, C.S. Operations on fuzzy graphs. *Inform. Sci.* **1994**, *79*, 159–170. [CrossRef]
15. Sunitha, M.S.; Vijayakumar, A. Complement of a fuzzy graph. *Indian J. Pure Appl. Math.* **2002**, *33*, 1451–1464.
16. Akram, M.; Dudec, W.A. Interval-valued fuzzy graphs. *Comput. Math. Appl.* **2011**, *61*, 289–299. [CrossRef]
17. Shannon, A.; Atanassov, K.T. A first step to a theory of the intuitionistic fuzzy graphs. In Proceedings of the First Workshop on Fuzzy Based Expert Systems, Sofia, Bulgaria, 28–30 September, 1994; pp. 59–61.
18. Parvathi, R.; Karunambigai, M.G.; Atanassov, K.T. Operations on intuitionistic fuzzy graphs. In Proceedings of the 2009 IEEE International Conference on Fuzzy Systems, Jeju, Korea, 20–24 August 2009; pp. 1396–1401.
19. Yaqoob, N.; Gulistan, M.; Kadry, S.; Wahab, H.A. Complex intuitionistic fuzzy graphs with application in cellular network provider companies. *Mathematics* **2019**, *7*, 35. [CrossRef]
20. Akram, M. bipolar fuzzy graphs. *Inform. Sci.* **2011**, *181*, 5548–5564. [CrossRef]
21. Yang, H.L.; Li, S.G.; Yang, W.H.; Lu. Y. Notes on a Bipolar fuzzy graphs. *Inform. Sci.* **2013**, *242*, 113–121. [CrossRef]
22. Talebi, A.A.; Rashmanlou, H. Complement and isomorphism on bipolar fuzzy graphs. *Fuzzy Inf. Eng.* **2014**, *6*, 505–522. [CrossRef]
23. Ghorai, G.; Pal, M. A note on Regular bipolar fuzzy graphs. Neural Computing and Applications 21 (1)(2012) 197–205. *Neural Comput. Appl.* **2018**, *30*, 1569–1572. [CrossRef]
24. Poulik, S.; Ghorai, G. Certain indices of graphs under bipolar fuzzy environment with applications. *Soft Comput.* **2020**, *24*, 5119–5131. [CrossRef]
25. Ghorai, G. Characterization of regular bipolar fuzzy graphs. *Afr. Mat.* **2021**, *32*, 1043–1057. [CrossRef]

26. Zuo, C.; Pal, A.; Dey, A. New concepts of picture fuzzy graphs with application. *Mathematics* **2019**, *7*, 470. [CrossRef]
27. Das, S.; Ghora, G. Analysis of road map design based on multi-graph with picture fuzzy information. *Int. J. Appl. Comput. Math.* **2020**, *6*, 1–17. [CrossRef]
28. Xiao, W.; Dey, A.; Son, L.H. A Study on Regular Picture Fuzzy Graph with Applications in Communication Networks. *J. Intell. Fuzzy Syst.* **2020**, *39*, 3633–3645. [CrossRef]
29. Koczy, L.T.; Jan, N.; Mahmood, T.; Ullah, K. Analysis of social networks and Wi-Fi networks by using the concept of picture fuzzy graphs. *Soft Comput.* **2020**, *24*, 16551–16563. [CrossRef]
30. Amanathulla, S.; Bera, B.; Pal, M. Balanced picture fuzzy graph with application. *Artif. Intell. Rev.* **2021**, 1–27.
31. Diestel, R. *Graph Theory. USA*; Springer: Berlin/Heidelberg, Germany, 2000.
32. Zimmermann, H.J. *Fuzzy Set Theory and Its Applications*; Springer Science & Business Media: Berlin/Heidelberg, Germany, 2011.
33. Zhang, W.-R. (Yin)(Yang) bipolar fuzzy sets. In Proceedings of the 1998 IEEE International Conference on Fuzzy Systems Proceedings, IEEE World Congress on Computational Intelligence (Cat. No. 98CH36228), Anchorage, AK, USA , 4–9 May 1998; pp. 835–840.
34. Samanta, S.; Pal, M. Some more results on bipolar fuzzy sets and bipolar fuzzy intersection graphs. *J. Fuzzy Math.* **2014**, *22*, 253–262.
35. Ezhilmaran, D.; Sankar, K. Morphism of bipolar intuitionistic fuzzy graphs. *J. Discrete Math. Sci. Cryptogr.* **2015**, *18*, 605–621. [CrossRef]
36. Khan, W.A.; Faiz, K.; Taouti, A. Bipolar picture fuzzy sets and relations with applications. Submiited.

Article

A Decision Analysis Model for the Brand Experience of Branded Apps Using Consistency Fuzzy Linguistic Preference Relations

Tsuen-Ho Hsu [1,*], Chun-Hsien Chen [2] and Ya-Wun Yang [1]

1. Department of Marketing and Distribution Management, National Kaohsiung University of Science and Technology, Kaohsiung City 811, Taiwan; 0625804@nkust.edu.tw
2. College of Management, National Kaohsiung University of Science and Technology, Kaohsiung City 811, Taiwan; 0328912@nkust.edu.tw
* Correspondence: thhsu@nkust.edu.tw

Citation: Hsu, T.-H.; Chen, C.-H.; Yang, Y.-W. A Decision Analysis Model for the Brand Experience of Branded Apps Using Consistency Fuzzy Linguistic Preference Relations. *Symmetry* **2021**, *13*, 1151. https://doi.org/10.3390/sym13071151

Academic Editor: Juan Luis García Guirao

Received: 7 June 2021
Accepted: 24 June 2021
Published: 27 June 2021

Publisher's Note: MDPI stays neutral with regard to jurisdictional claims in published maps and institutional affiliations.

Copyright: © 2021 by the authors. Licensee MDPI, Basel, Switzerland. This article is an open access article distributed under the terms and conditions of the Creative Commons Attribution (CC BY) license (https://creativecommons.org/licenses/by/4.0/).

Abstract: Branded apps are not only an important platform for enterprises and customers to have real-time interactions and communicate marketing messages, but also a new business model that encourages value co-creation between the two. In order to explore the impact of branded apps on customers, this study constructs a fuzzy multi-criteria decision making (FMCDM) analysis model, and it uses consistent fuzzy linguistic preference relations (CFLPR) to set up a symmetric pairwise comparison matrix, which greatly reduces the complexity and error rate of calculations. Empirical research findings show that brand experience attributes and the influence of brand experience on customer loyalty and satisfaction can be more accurately measured. As a consequence of this study, we show that, among the brand experience facets of two retail chain branded apps, behavioral experience is the most favored, while affective experience is the least favored. Furthermore, brand attachment and active participation should be strengthened to enhance customer loyalty. Through the analytical model employed in this study, enterprises can regularly monitor changes in the brand experience preferences of branded app users and evaluate app performance to flexibly adjust mobile device-based marketing campaigns and strategies. It can also aid enterprises in using mobile devices effectively to improve customer loyalty and address the issue of diminishing brand loyalty.

Keywords: FMCDM; CFLPR; branded app; brand experience; loyalty

1. Introduction

The rapid development of the internet has made mobile applications ("apps") an important platform for real-time interactions between enterprises and customers [1]. As part of consumers' daily life, mobile apps represent the latest trend of branding. They help build brand identity, create brand experience, and encourage brand–consumer interactions, thus generating both opportunities and challenges for enterprises [2]. According to Stocchi et al. [3], with consumers worldwide using mobile apps extensively, a growing number of enterprises have realized the importance of app-based marketing. Well-known major brands, including Apple, Google, and Amazon, have already established their presence in the app market. Furthermore, marketers in big companies are trying to make mobile apps an integral part of their marketing strategies for consumer participation [4]. Mobile apps have, thus, opened a new area of research. In Taiwan, two well-known retailers, 7-ELEVEn and FamilyMart, have long been actively investing in developing their branded apps in the hope of preemptively building a new business model featuring brand–customer interactions based on mobile devices, thus enhancing brand experience and boosting customer brand loyalty. Kim and Yu [5] reported that consumers' holistic brand experience of branded apps is positively correlated with brand loyalty. Compared to other marketing instruments, branded apps are the most popular among enterprises. Apps have built a platform for the consumption activities of a new generation of consumers and for enterprises to interact with customers and assess the effectiveness of their marketing strategies. This makes the use of branded apps an important research area. While much of the past literature on branded apps focused on the causal relationships among brand image, customer loyalty, satisfaction, purchase intention, and performance [1,3,6,7], limited studies used fuzzy decision analysis to identify differences between major facets of consumers' holistic brand experience of branded apps. Furthermore, the impact of branded apps on customer loyalty and satisfaction has not received much attention. To make contributions in this regard, building on the fuzzy set theory and consistent fuzzy linguistic preference relations (CFLPR), this study employs fuzzy linguistic variables and fuzzy interval data [8] to build a symmetric pairwise comparison matrix for accurately measuring the linguistic ambiguity of consumers' branded app-based brand experience [9–14]. As noted by Khan and Rahman [15], although brand experience has been a focus area for years, there are few studies on the retail industry. Therefore, with two well-known retail chain stores in Taiwan—7-ELEVEn and FamilyMart—as the empirical objects, this study identifies differences in the holistic branded app-based experience provided by business competitors, gauges the performance of brand experience attributes, and analyzes the impact of brand experience on customer loyalty and satisfaction. In doing so, we hope to provide insights for the retail industry into the making of interactive marketing strategies and to promote value co-creation between enterprises and customers in an era where the service-dominant logic prevails.

2. Literature Review

2.1. Mobile App and Branded App

A mobile app can be downloaded free of charge on mobile devices. Unlike traditional marketing tools, the mobile app integrates diverse innovative contents and functions and extends enterprises' customer service. It encourages value co-creation between brands and customers through real-time online interaction and acts as a platform for communicating marketing messages. Newman et al. [16] noted that using apps to provide value to customers generates an opportunity for many retailers to regain or reinforce their competitiveness. Meanwhile, branded apps on mobile devices can help build a unique brand identity through the brand's name, logo, or totem [17]. As a new marketing instrument, mobile apps may go some way toward boosting brand loyalty and purchase intention, strengthening the customer–brand bond and pushing up overall sales through enhanced brand satisfaction [18]. An increasing number of enterprises today use branded apps as a tool to communicate with their consumers. This shift in communication strategy, according to Stocchi et al. [19], is partially attributable to the significant impact of good user experience through branded apps on brand loyalty and purchase intention. These apps, therefore, have an advantage over traditional marketing tools in promoting brand–consumer interactions.

2.2. Brand Experience of Branded App

Schmitt put forward the holistic brand experience theory in 1999. He viewed experiences as "private events that occur in response to some stimulation". They normally result from direct observation of or participation in events—real, illusionary, or constructed—and are, therefore, induced rather than self-generated. Brand experience is defined as customers' sensations, feelings, cognition, and behavioral responses triggered by brand-related stimuli—all of which are part of a brand's design, identity, packaging, communication, and environment [20]. Lee and Kang [21] noted that different dimensions of brand experience coordinate with each other to generate a holistic brand experience and help brands build customer rapport. Ambler et al. [22] posited that brand experience develops through customers using the brand, as well as discussing and collecting brand-related information or promotions. Nadzri et al. [23] argued that customers have brand experiences even before they encounter brands. While searching for products in the market, customers are exposed to stimuli from all kinds of brands. Therefore, marketing professionals should not only focus on the functional attributes and efficacy of products but also understand consumers' feelings from the perspective of holistic brand experience. Kim and Yu [5] proposed that customers' holistic brand experience generated by their interactions with a brand through its branded app includes four major facets, namely, affective, cognitive, behavioral, and relational experiences. The definition of each facet is given in Table 1.

Table 1. Brand experience facets of branded apps.

Facet	Definition	Reference
Affective	Inner feelings toward a brand; views and attitude towards an event; subjective emotional experience	[24]
Cognitive	Process of using concepts, perceptions, judgment, and imagination to acquire brand-related knowledge	[24]
Behavioral	Behavioral response prompted by a brand that invigorates customers or makes them display a specific behavioral pattern	[24]
Relational	Formation of a certain relationship or connection with a brand	[25]

Table 2 contains the attributes of the major facets of branded app-based brand experience.

Table 2. Brand experience attributes of branded apps.

Facet	Attribute	Attribute Description	Reference
Affective	Emotions	Using this app makes me feel happy, excited, pleasant, etc.	[24]
	Feelings	The app builds an emotional bond between me and the brand.	[24]
	Motivation to participate	The app often makes me want to participate in buying, information-collecting, and credit-accumulating activities.	[25]
Cognitive	Knowledge	The app makes me want to know more about the brand.	[24]
	Curiosity	This app arouses my curiosity.	[24]
	Finding information	The app prompts me to actively search for information regarding promotions and new products.	[24]
Behavioral	Functional experience	I want to use the functions (e.g., mobile shopping and information on new products) of the app again.	[24]
	Passive participation	When receiving coupons or updated information on products through the app, I will spend on the brand.	[25]
	Active participation	I actively participate in in-app events (e.g., limited-time offers).	[24]
Relational	Brand personality	The app displays a brand personality that is compatible with mine.	[26]
	Brand attachment	I believe that using this app will lead me to develop a strong affection and psychological attachment toward the brand.	[7]
	Self-identification	When using the app, I identify myself as a member of the brand community.	[25]

2.3. *Loyalty and Satisfaction of Brand Experience*

Brakus et al. [24] defined brand experience as an information-collecting behavior that helps customers understand brand personality and choose brands that suit them better. In this process, brand loyalty and satisfaction are enhanced, and stronger brand–customer ties are built. Huang [27] and van der Westhuizen [28] noted that many previous studies have found that brand experience preludes and is positively related to customer loyalty. Research on consumers' brand experience has shown that it can positively affect customer loyalty and satisfaction [6]. Furthering previous academic works, this paper places detailed focus on different attributes of customers' brand experience of branded apps and the influence of each attribute on customer loyalty and satisfaction.

2.4. Consistency Fuzzy Linguistic Preference Relations

FMCDM is a powerful decision analysis tool that has been widely applied in situations where decision-makers have to choose from several alternatives of actions [29]. In more recent times, the ambiguous information environment has prompted scholars to develop many FMCDM tools based on the fuzzy set theory to assist decision-makers in tackling the issue of ambiguity when comparing alternative pairs [30]. Among these tools, the most commonly used include fuzzy analytic hierarchy process (FAHP) [31] and fuzzy analytic network process (FANP) [13,32]. In FAHP, for a pairwise comparison matrix that includes n alternatives, as many as $n(n-1)/2$ comparisons are requested. Keeping aside the complexity of the entire process, the evaluation results produced by different experts could also be inconsistent. Therefore, scholars developed CFLPR, through a symmetric matrix that only requires $n-1$ pairwise comparisons from the given n alternatives. Compared with FAHP, CFLPR is simpler, requires fewer comparisons, and can avoid the problem of inconsistent evaluation outcomes. It is a new FMCDM tool that has emerged in recent years [33,34]. As noted by Pandey and Kumar [35], although CFLPR can greatly reduce the likeliness of inconsistent expert opinions, the method has some logical flaws in the derivation of its formula. This issue was addressed by Wang [36]. CFLPR, in recent years, has been applied for selecting excellent suppliers in the TFT-LCD TV-panel manufacturing industry [37] and choosing marketing strategic alliances in the mobile telecommunication industry [13]. For efficiency and accuracy, this study uses CFLPR in lieu of FAHP to evaluate aspects of customers' brand experience generated by branded apps and their relative importance.

3. Decision Analysis Model Building

3.1. Model Building Concept

This research explored the brand experience hierarchy of the development of branded apps in the retail industry through the literature and determined the fitness of the hierarchy through six expert interviews. CFLPR was used to evaluate the weights of brand experience facets and attributes, so that customers' feelings of using branded app brand experience could be appropriately measured. After obtaining the weights of various facets and attributes, a performance evaluation was performed for each attribute of the enterprise, and then the influence of each attribute on customer loyalty and satisfaction was analyzed and discussed. Lastly, specific management suggestions were put forward for the company.

3.2. Steps to Create an Analytic Model

Step 1: Establish brand experience hierarchical structure

This research was based on the four major facets of branded app brand experience developed by Kim and Yu [5] (see Table 1). Through literature discussion and integration of other scholars' research results, 12 brand experience attributes were constructed (see Table 2). Combining Tables 1 and 2, and then confirming that the content was suitable for the characteristics of the retail industry through expert interviews, the hierarchical structure of this research was eventually established (see Figure 1).

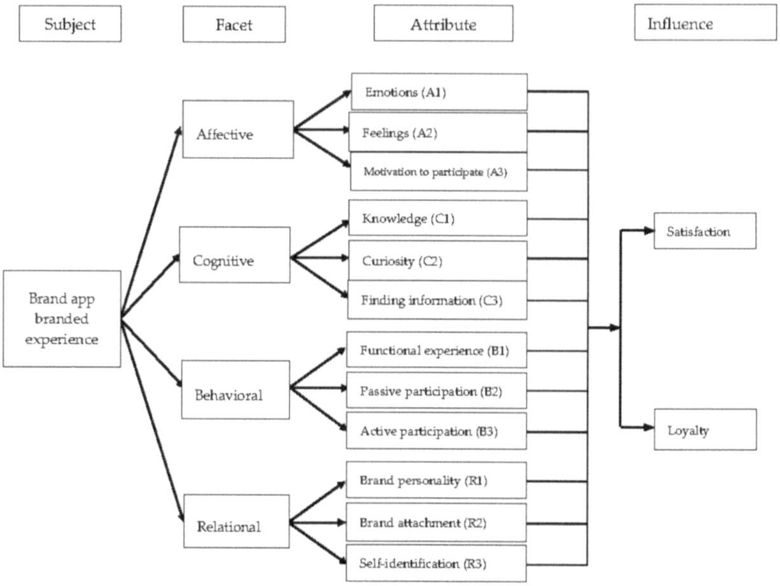

Figure 1. Hierarchical architecture diagram of this research.

Step 2: Calculate relative weights

(A) Use triangular fuzzy number and fuzzy linguistic scale

A fuzzy number $\widetilde{Z}$ is a triangular fuzzy number when its membership function is expressed by Equation (1) [38].

$$\mu_{\widetilde{Z}}(x) = \begin{cases} (x-L)/(M-L) & , \quad L \le x \le M \\ (R-x)/(R-M) & , \quad M \le x \le R \\ 0 & , \quad otherwise \end{cases} . \tag{1}$$

L and R in Equation (1) represent the left and right values of the fuzzy number $\widetilde{Z}$, respectively, and M is the middle value (see Figure 2).

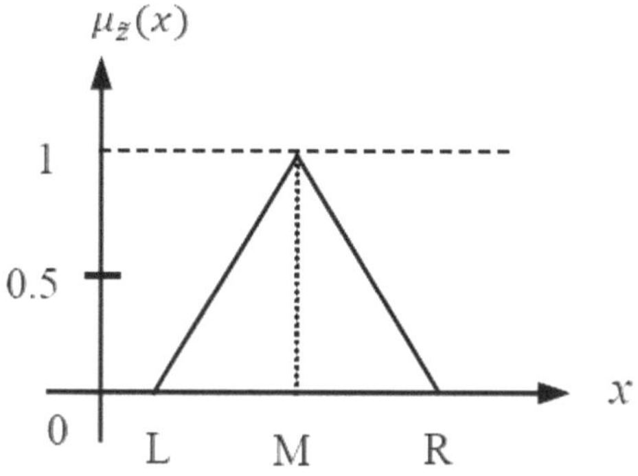

Figure 2. Triangular fuzzy number membership functions.

In this study, the nine-point fuzzy linguistic scale (as shown in Figure 3 and Table 3) developed by Büyüközkan [39] was used in the questionnaires distributed selectively to respondents.

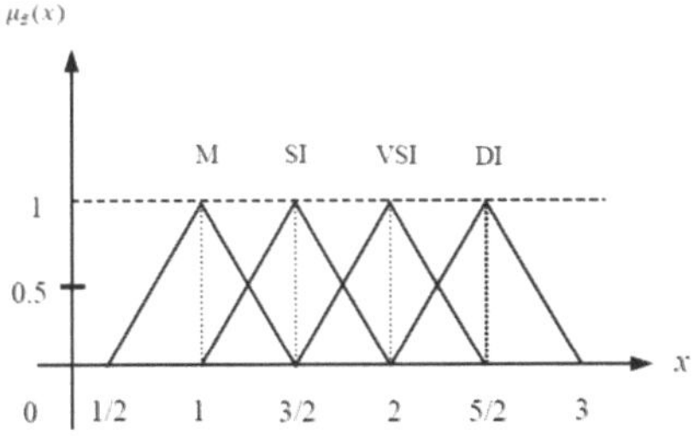

Figure 3. Membership functions of fuzzy linguistic scale.

Table 3. Fuzzy linguistic scale.

Linguistic Variable	Triangular Fuzzy Number	Code
Demonstrated importance (DI)	(2,5/2,3)	$\tilde{9}$
Very strong importance (VSI)	(3/2,2,5/2)	$\tilde{7}$
Strong importance (SI)	(1,3/2,2)	$\tilde{5}$
Moderate importance (MI)	(1/2,1,3/2)	$\tilde{3}$
Equal importance (EI)	(1,1,1)	$\tilde{1}$
Moderate unimportance (MUI)	(2/3,1,2)	$\tilde{3}^{-1}$
Strong unimportance (SUI)	(1/2,2/3,1)	$\tilde{5}^{-1}$
Very strong unimportance (VSUI)	(2/5,1/2,2/3)	$\tilde{7}^{-1}$
Demonstrated unimportance (DUI)	(1/3,2/5,1/2)	$\tilde{9}^{-1}$

(B) Establish symmetric pairwise comparison matrix

When a questionnaire was confirmed to be valid, the triangular fuzzy number given by the interviewee was filled in a pairwise comparison fuzzy linguistic preference relation symmetry matrix $\tilde{A}_{ij}$ through Equation (2). $\tilde{A}_{ij} = (\tilde{a}_{ij}), \tilde{a}_{ij} \in [(1/3,2/5,1/2),(2,5/2,3)]$.

$$\tilde{A}_{ij} = \begin{bmatrix} \tilde{1} & \tilde{a}_{12} & \cdots & \tilde{a}_{1n} \\ \tilde{a}_{21} & \tilde{1} & \cdots & \tilde{a}_{2n} \\ \vdots & \vdots & \ddots & \vdots \\ \tilde{a}_{n1} & \tilde{a}_{n2} & \cdots & \tilde{1} \end{bmatrix} = \begin{bmatrix} \tilde{1} & \tilde{a}_{12} & \cdots & \tilde{a}_{1n} \\ \tilde{a}_{12}^{-1} & \tilde{1} & \cdots & \tilde{a}_{2n} \\ \vdots & \vdots & \ddots & \vdots \\ \tilde{a}_{1n}^{-1} & \tilde{a}_{2n}^{-1} & \cdots & \tilde{1} \end{bmatrix}. \tag{2}$$

$$\tilde{a}_{ij} = \begin{cases} \tilde{1},\tilde{3},\tilde{5},\tilde{7},\tilde{9}, & i \text{ is relatively more important compared to } j \\ \tilde{1}, i = j & i \text{ and} j \text{ are equally important } (i = j) \\ \tilde{1}^{-1},\tilde{3}^{-1},\tilde{5}^{-1},\tilde{7}^{-1},\tilde{9}^{-1}, & i \text{ is relatively unimportant compared to } j \end{cases}$$

(C) Matrix translation

According to the CFLPR equations deduced by Wang and Chen [34], the reciprocal fuzzy linguistic preference relation matrix $\tilde{P}_{ij}$ was translated from matrix $\tilde{A}_{ij}$, using Equation (3).

$$\tilde{P}_{ij} = g(\tilde{a}_{ij}) = \frac{1}{2} \cdot (1 + \log_9 \tilde{a}_{ij}). \tag{3}$$

Then, using Equations (4)–(9), a complete reciprocal fuzzy linguistic preference relation matrix was completed.

$$P_{ij}^{L} + P_{ji}^{R} = 1, \forall i,j,k \in \{1,\ldots,n\}, \tag{4}$$

$$P_{ij}^{M} + P_{ji}^{M} = 1, \forall i,j,k \in \{1,\ldots,n\}, \tag{5}$$

$$P_{ij}^{R} + P_{ji}^{L} = 1, \forall i,j,k \in \{1,\ldots,n\}, \tag{6}$$

$$P_{ji}^{L} = \frac{j-i+1}{2} - P_{i(i+1)}^{R} - P_{(i+1)(i+2)}^{R} \cdots - P_{(j-1)j}^{R}, \tag{7}$$

$$P_{ji}^{M} = \frac{j-i+1}{2} - P_{i(i+1)}^{M} - P_{(i+1)(i+2)}^{M} \cdots - P_{(j-1)j}^{M}, \tag{8}$$

$$P_{ji}^{R} = \frac{j-i+1}{2} - P_{i(i+1)}^{L} - P_{(i+1)(i+2)}^{L} \cdots - P_{(j-1)j}^{L}. \tag{9}$$

Here, L is the left number of the triangular fuzzy number, M is the middle number of the triangular fuzzy number, and R is the right number of the triangular fuzzy number.

Lastly, we obtained a relatively complete fuzzy linguistic preference relation matrix $\widetilde{P}_{ij}$,$\widetilde{P}_{ij} \in [0,1]$, $\widetilde{P}ij = \left(P_{ij}^{L},\ P_{ij}^{M},\ P_{ij}^{R} \right)$.

(D) Coordinate panning

Through the conversion function of Equations (10)–(12), to ensure that each fuzzy linguistic preference relation value $\widetilde{P}_{ij}$ was within the interval value [0,1], it could be obtained that the fuzzy linguistic preference relation matrix was all within a certain range to maintain the positive and reciprocal of addition consistent characteristics (c is the minimum value in the consistent fuzzy linguistic preference matrix).

$$f\left(x^{L}\right) = \frac{x^{L}+c}{1+2c},\ c \in [-c, 1+c]. \tag{10}$$

$$f\left(x^{M}\right) = \frac{x^{M}+c}{1+2c},\ c \in [-c, 1+c]. \tag{11}$$

$$f\left(x^{R}\right) = \frac{x^{R}+c}{1+2c}, c \in [-c, 1+c]. \tag{12}$$

(E) Weight calculation

Then, the proposition raised by Wang [36] regarding CFLPR was adopted to examine the consistency between the data and content of matrix $\widetilde{P}_{ij}$; using Equations (13)–(16), weights of branded app brand experience facets and attributes given by respondents were calculated.

Equation (13) allowed calculating the average value of all the brand experience facets or attributes, which is then averaged through the judgments of multiple respondents.

$$\overline{\widetilde{P}}_{ij} = \frac{\sum_{k=1}^{m} \overline{\widetilde{P}}_{ij}^{(k)}}{m}, \forall i, j, \tag{13}$$

where k stands for the m-th respondent, and m stands for the number of respondents.

Then, Equation (14) was used to calculate the average of $\overline{\widetilde{P}}_{i}$, which is the average value of evaluation of the fuzzy linguistic preference of the i-th facet or attribute for brand experience.

$$\overline{\widetilde{P}}_{i} = \frac{\sum_{j=1}^{n} \overline{\widetilde{P}}_{ij}}{n}, \forall i, \tag{14}$$

where, using the average value of $\overline{\widetilde{P}}_{i}$, Equation (15) allowed calculating the weights of fuzzy preference of the i-th facet or attribute for brand experience.

$$\widetilde{W}_{i} = \frac{\overline{\widetilde{P}}_{i}}{\sum_{j=1}^{n}\left(\overline{\widetilde{P}}_{i}\right)}, \tag{15}$$

where $\widetilde{W}_{i}$ is the weight of fuzzy preference at the facet level, and $\widetilde{W}_{ij}$ is the weight of fuzzy preference at the attribute level.

Lastly, Equation (16) was used for defuzzification to gain the precise weight value.

$$D_i = \frac{1}{3}\left(w_i^L + w_i^M + w_i^R\right), \tag{16}$$

where D_i is the definite weight of the i-th brand experience facet which is defuzzified, and D_{ij} is the definite weight of the brand experience attribute which is defuzzified.

Step 3: Brand experience performance evaluation

Attributes in the branded app brand experience were employed as items for performance evaluation (see Table 2), using a five-point scale. Respondents were asked to score the actual and expected branded app brand experience performance of the firm, respectively, whereby a higher score denoted a better evaluation. D_{ij} is the weight of branded app brand experience attributes, e_i is the actual performance of each attribute, g_i is their expected performance for each attribute, and p_i is the performance value of each attribute, *obtained using* Equation (17). In addition, dividing the g_i by e_i provides the rate of improvement for the performance of each attribute u_i (see Equation (18)).

$$p_i = D_{ij} \times e_i i = 1, 2, 3, \ldots, n. \tag{17}$$

$$u_i = g_i \div e_i i = 1, 2, 3, \ldots, n. \tag{18}$$

Step 4: Influence Degree Analysis for Loyalty and Satisfaction

According to the calculation equations proposed by Wang and Chen [40], the degree of influence of brand experience attributes of a branded app on loyalty relative to satisfaction was evaluated. The analysis mode establishment process is described below.

(A) Create a form

Using a nine-point fuzzy linguistic scale (see Table 3), the respondent was asked to subjectively evaluate the influence degree of each attribute on loyalty and satisfaction, and the evaluation preference value ${}_i\widetilde{b}^k_{LS}$ was obtained, where k represents the k-th respondent, and i is the i-th attribute of the brand experience of the branded app. E is the respondent, $E \in \{1, \ldots, m\}$, and F is an brand experience attribute (see Figure 1), $F \in \{1, \ldots, n\}$. L is loyalty and S is satisfaction (see Tables 4 and 5).

Table 4. Influence degree evaluation form (L relative to S).

		E_1	…	E_m
		S	…	S
F_1	L	${}_1b^1_{LS}$	…	${}_1b^m_{LS}$
⋮	⋮	⋮	⋱	⋮
F_n	L	${}_nb^1_{LS}$	…	${}_nb^m_{LS}$

Table 5. Influence degree evaluation form (S relative to L).

		E_1	…	E_m
		L	…	L
F_1	S	${}_1b^1_{LS}$	…	${}_1b^m_{LS}$
⋮	⋮	⋮	⋱	⋮
F_n	S	${}_nb^1_{LS}$	…	${}_nb^m_{LS}$

In this study n = 12, while m = 55 (7-ELEVEn) and 56 (FamilyMark).

(B) Form translation

Equation (19) was used to convert the interviewee's fuzzy linguistic evaluation preference value from the interval value $[(1/3, 2/5, 1/2), (2, 5/2, 3)]$ to [0,1]. Then, the fuzzy linguistic preference value ${}_i\widetilde{P}^k_{LS}$ of each respondent could be obtained.

$$ {}_i\widetilde{P}^k_{LS} = g({}_i\widetilde{b}^k_{LS}) = \frac{1}{2} \cdot (1 + \log_9 {}_i\widetilde{b}^k_{LS}). \tag{19}$$

(C) Coordinate panning

Through the transfer function of Equations (20)–(22), it was ensured that the preference values of the fuzzy linguistic preference matrix fell within the interval [0,1] to maintain a positive value and the reciprocal of addition consistent characteristics (c is the minimum value in the consistent fuzzy linguistic preference matrix).

$$ f\left({}_i\widetilde{x}^{kL}_{LS}\right) = \frac{{}_i\widetilde{x}^{kL}_{LS}}{1+2c}, c \in [-c, 1+c]. \tag{20}$$

$$ f\left({}_i\widetilde{x}^{kM}_{LS}\right) = \frac{{}_i\widetilde{x}^{kM}_{LS}}{1+2c}, c \in [-c, 1+c]. \tag{21}$$

$$ f\left({}_i\widetilde{x}^{kR}_{LS}\right) = \frac{{}_i\widetilde{x}^{kR}_{LS}}{1+2c}, c \in [-c, 1+c]. \tag{22}$$

(D) Get the average value

Equation (23) was used to integrate the average value of fuzzy linguistic preference of m respondents for each attribute i. We could obtain the total average value of the fuzzy linguistic preference for L relative to S. Here, the total average value was represented by $\widetilde{X}$.

$$ {}_i\overline{\widetilde{q}}_{LS} = \frac{1}{m}\left({}_iq^1_{LS} + {}_iq^2_{LS} + \ldots + {}_iq^m_{LS}\right) \tag{23}$$

(E) Create another form

With the data generated by Equation (19), we used Equations (24)–(26) to obtain another relative fuzzy linguistic preference value of S relative to L for each brand experience attribute (as in Table 5).

$$ {}_iP^{kL}_{LS} + {}_iP^{kR}_{LS} = 1, i \in \{1, \ldots, n\}, k \in \{1, \ldots, m\}. \tag{24}$$

$$ {}_iP^{kM}_{LS} + {}_iP^{kM}_{LS} = 1, i \in \{1, \ldots, n\}, k \in \{1, \ldots, m\}. \tag{25}$$

$$ {}_iP^{kR}_{LS} + {}_iP^{kL}_{LS} = 1, i \in \{1, \ldots, n\}, k \in \{1, \ldots, m\}. \tag{26}$$

(F) Coordinate panning

Equations (20)–(23) were again used to additionally obtain the total average value of the fuzzy linguistic preference for S relative to L. Here, the total average value was represented by $\widetilde{Y}$.

(G) Standardization

Next, $\widetilde{X}$ and $\widetilde{Y}$ were integrated to build a complete L and S pairwise comparison matrix. Equation (27) was used to standardize the average fuzzy linguistic preference rating of the two possible outcome in each attribute for L and S, and ${}_i\widetilde{\lambda}_{LS}$ was taken to represent the rating ranking of the two possible outcomes after standardization for L and S.

$$ {}_i\widetilde{\lambda}_{LS} = \frac{{}_i\widetilde{q}_{LS}}{\sum\limits_{L=1}^{t} {}_i\widetilde{q}_{LS}}, L, S = 1, 2, \ldots, t. \tag{27}$$

(H) Get the weights of loyalty and satisfaction

Using ${}_{i}\overline{\overline{\varphi}}_{LS}$ to represent the average weights of the possible influence of each attribute, we could then get the result weights of L and S in each brand experience attribute, as detailed in Equation (28).

$$ {}_{i}\overline{\overline{\varphi}}_{LS} = \frac{1}{t}\sum_{S=1}^{t} {}_{i}\widetilde{\lambda}_{LS}, \tag{28} $$

where t represents the number of evaluation objects, t = 2 in this study.

Equation (29) was used to defuzzify ${}_{i}\overline{\overline{\varphi}}_{LS}$, and the weights of L and S could be obtained for the i-th brand experience attribute.

$$ w_i = \frac{1}{3}\left(w_i^L + w_i^M + w_i^R\right). \tag{29} $$

(I) Obtain influence degree value

Equation (30) was used to multiply the average weights of each brand experience attribute by the average weights of the two possible influence levels; we could get the influence degree value Z_u of the branded app's brand experience of the interviewee on loyalty and satisfaction.

$$ Z_u = \sum_{i=1}^{n} D_{ij} \cdot \overline{w}_i, \tag{30} $$

where D_{ij} is the weight of the brand experience attribute, as detailed in Equation (16).

4. Empirical Analysis

4.1. Overview of Retailers' Brands

Originally founded in the United States, 7-ELEVEn was first introduced to Taiwan in 1978 and ignited a revolution in Taiwan's retail industry. By July 2020, the retail chain had a market share of 59.15% with 5915 stores across Taiwan. The convenience store's app "OPENPOINT" is widely used among its membership customers; it allows them to accumulate and redeem membership points, top up their accounts, access discounted products, make mobile payments, and learn about events jointly hosted with cross-industry partners, among other functions. The other empirical object of this study, FamilyMart, is a Japanese retail chain brand. Following the business principle of "where you are part of the family" and embracing a technology-powered smart retail strategy, by July 2020, it became the second largest convenience store chain in Taiwan with 3671 stores, which equates to a market share of 36.71%. Its branded app "FamilyMart" allows users to accumulate credit points, redeem products, and make mobile payments through My FamiPay for products on discount.

4.2. Survey and Analysis Results

For our empirical study, we first consulted three senior store managers from the aforementioned retail stores to pin down a hierarchical structure (see Figure 1), which, along with Tables 1 and 2, formed the basis on which a questionnaire was developed. We selected active members of the two chain stores who used their branded apps 6–10 times every month and conducted 20–30 min in-depth interviews along with prompted questions and answers. The interviewees were asked to evaluate the relative importance and performance of each brand experience facet and attribute and rate the influence of each attribute in terms of customer loyalty and satisfaction according to their subjective judgment. A total of 60 questionnaires were handed out to the 7-ELEVEn respondents, among which 55 were valid and five were invalid; among the 60 questionnaires distributed to the FamilyMart respondents, 56 were valid and four were invalid. This study's analysis was based on valid questionnaires. The weights of facets and attributes, which were calculated according to steps 1 and 2, are shown in Figures 4–6. Table 6 displays the results of the performance evaluation of each branded app with regard to brand experience, measured against the formula provided in Step 3. Table 7 lays out the degrees, calculated according to Step 4, to which branded app-based brand experience attributes influenced customer loyalty and satisfaction.

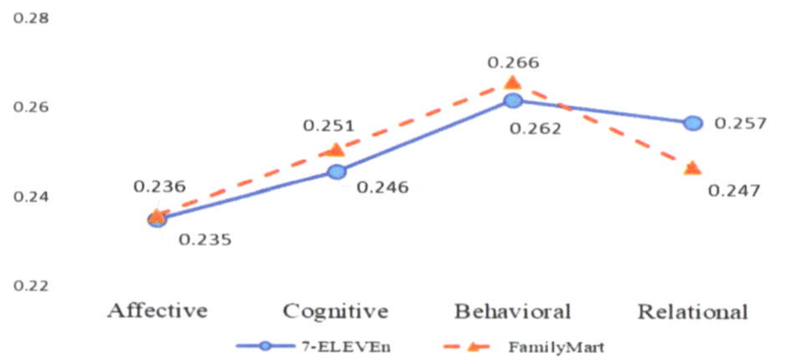

Figure 4. Branded app brand experience facet weights (D_i).

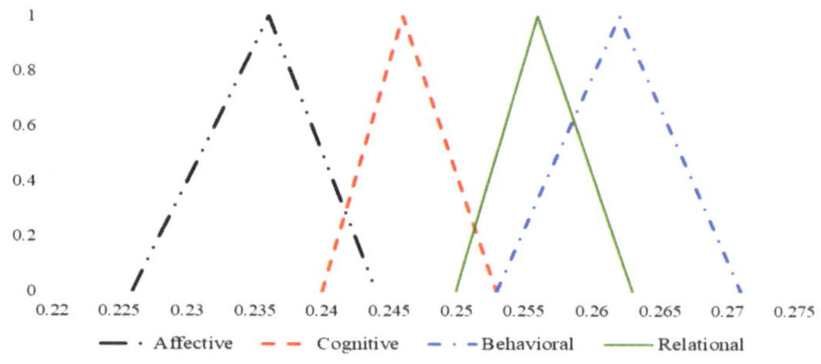

(**a**)

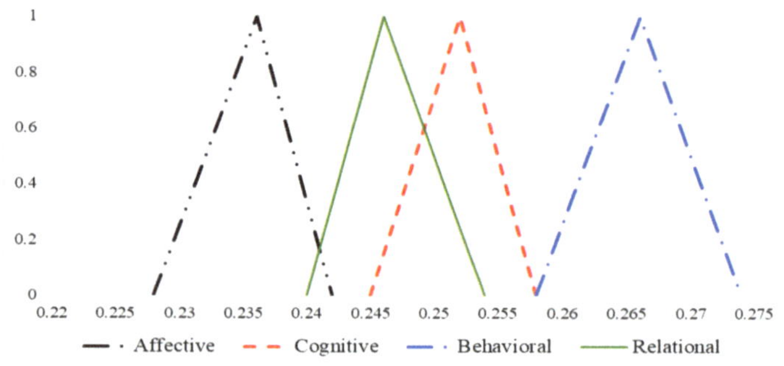

(**b**)

Figure 5. (**a**) 7-ELEVEn branded app brand experience facet triangular fuzzy number. (**b**) FamilyMart branded app brand experience facet triangular fuzzy number.

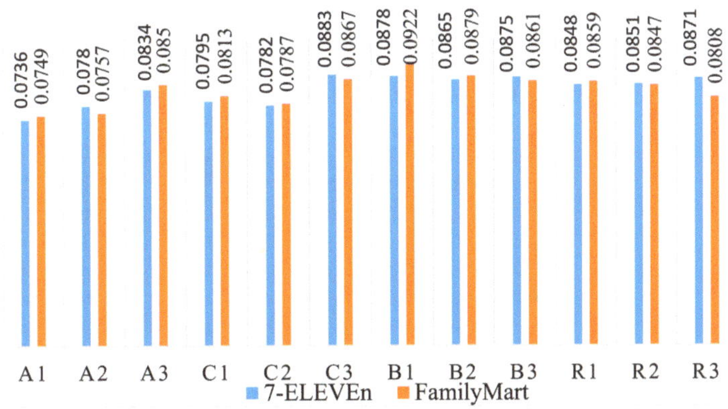

Figure 6. Branded app brand experience attribute weights (D_{ij}).

Table 6. Performance of branded app brand experience.

Attribute	7-ELEVEn		FamilyMart	
	u_i	p_i	u_i	p_i
Emotions (A1)	1.279	0.343	1.106	0.385
Feelings (A2)	1.358	0.348	1.108	0.402
Motivation to participate (A3)	1.216	0.450	0.989	0.563
Knowledge (C1)	1.369	0.374	1.091	0.492
Curiosity (C2)	1.326	0.375	1.094	0.437
Finding information (C3)	1.142	0.518	1.058	0.568
Functional experience (B1)	1.195	0.495	1.010	0.648
Passive participation (B2)	1.145	0.496	1.054	0.546
Active participation (B3)	1.220	0.438	1.114	0.523
Brand personality (R1)	1.114	0.447	1.107	0.499
Brand attachment (R2)	1.166	0.428	1.123	0.476
Self-identification (R3)	1.182	0.447	1.081	0.429
Sum p_i		5.159		5.968

Table 7. Influence degree for loyalty and satisfaction.

Attribute	7-ELEVEn		FamilyMart	
	L	S	L	S
Emotions (A1)	0.482	0.518	0.476	0.524
Feelings (A2)	0.486	0.514	0.491	0.509
Motivation to participate (A3)	0.491	0.509	0.490	0.510
Knowledge (C1)	0.483	0.517	0.486	0.514
Curiosity (C2)	0.485	0.515	0.480	0.520
Finding information (C3)	0.491	0.509	0.488	0.512
Functional experience (B1)	0.478	0.522	0.486	0.514
Passive participation (B2)	0.481	0.519	0.488	0.512
Active participation(B3)	0.510	0.490	0.498	0.501
Brand personality (R1)	0.517	0.483	0.489	0.511
Brand attachment (R2)	0.517	0.483	0.499	0.502
Self-identification (R3)	0.503	0.497	0.495	0.505
Influence degree value Z_u:	0.494	0.506	0.489	0.511

Note: L represents loyalty and S represents satisfaction.

As shown in Figure 4, for both stores, the weight of behavioral experience was the highest among all facets with values of 0.262 and 0.266 for 7-ELEVEn and FamilyMart, respectively. The affective experience had relatively low weights of 0.235 and 0.236 for 7-ELEVEn and FamilyMart, respectively. This indicates that, for respondents of both stores, using the branded app was more likely to encourage purchases or interactions with the brand but less likely to generate positive emotions and feelings toward the brand.

Figure 5a,b show the triangular fuzzy numbers of branded app-related brand experience facets, where a smaller area of the triangle denotes a higher consistency of respondents' opinions. Although, for both retailers, the behavioral experience of the branded app was rated most favorably by respondents, the relatively large area of each triangle indicates that there is still room for improvement for the two stores when it comes to using branded apps to bolster consumers' behavioral experience. Additionally, the partially overlapping behavioral and relational triangles of 7-ELEVEn suggest that, although its respondents gave the greatest prominence to behavioral experience, they did not view relational experience as a facet that could be overlooked. FamilyMart's case is different because its behavioral triangle did not overlap with that of any other facet, indicating that its respondents viewed behavioral experience as more significant than other brand experience facets.

As shown in Figure 6, in terms of relative importance, the top three brand experience attributes of 7-ELEVEn's branded app were "finding information (C3)" (0.0883), "functional experience (B1)" (0.0878), and "active participation (B3)" (0.0875), while those of FamilyMart were "functional experience (B1)" (0.0922), "passive participation (B2)" (0.0879), and "finding information (C3)" (0.0867). This result shows that the respondents of both stores, after trying the branded app for the first time, were likely to use it again for information regarding promotions and new products, as well as to spend on the brand or take part in in-app events.

As displayed in Table 6, for both retail stores, almost all 12 branded app-related brand experience attributes had a rate of improvement (u_i) greater than 1, suggesting that all respondents expected better branded app experience. Specifically, the u_i values of 7-ELEVEn's "knowledge" (1.369), "feelings" (1.358), and "curiosity" (1.326) attributes and of FamilyMart's "brand attachment" (1.123), "active participation" (1.114), and "feelings" (1.108) attributes were relatively high and, therefore, merit special attention. Furthermore, the u_i value of FamilyMart's "motivation to participate" (0.989) attribute was less than 1, meaning that respondents felt that the retailer's performance in this regard exceeded their expectations. In terms of performance (p_i), FamilyMart (5.968) outshone 7-ELEVEn (5.159) in the overall branded app performance ($sum\ p_i$); however, in terms of the performance of individual attributes, "finding information" (0.518) was the most favorably rated for 7-ELEVEn, while "functional experience" (0.648) was the most favorably rated for FamilyMart. The performance of the "emotional" attribute (0.343/0.385) was the least desirable for both brands.

Table 7 shows the weights of the influence of each brand experience attribute on customer loyalty and satisfaction. The average weights of attribute influence on loyalty/satisfaction were 0.494/0.506 for 7-ELEVEn and 0.489/0.511 for FamilyMart; this suggests that the respondents unanimously agreed that the holistic brand experience derived from the use of branded apps affected customer satisfaction to a greater degree than it affected customer loyalty. Specifically, in terms of the influence on customer loyalty, "brand attachment" was the most weighted attribute for both 7-ELEVEn (0.517) and FamilyMart (0.499), indicating that all respondents believed that this attribute exerted the greatest impact on brand loyalty. Additionally, "active participation" was the second most weighted attribute for both 7-ELEVEn (0.510) and FamilyMart (0.498), suggesting that the respondents agreed that this attribute also had a significant influence on brand loyalty. Therefore, to ramp up customer loyalty to branded apps, businesses must work to enhance "brand attachment" and "active participation".

5. Discussion

Figure 4 displays the trend of customers' branded app-related brand experience preference, as well as the differences and similarities in this regard between the two brands in this study. Interestingly, although the two empirical objects are competitors, their customers' brand experience brought about by the design and functions of their branded apps was similar. A close examination of brand experience attributes (see Figure 6), however, revealed some differences. Analyzing and comparing Figures 4–6 can help businesses understand customers' preferences with regard to their rivals, adjust their own appeal strategy, and improve their marketing competitiveness. Table 6 shows the improvements expected by customers in relation to branded apps, thus providing straightforward guidelines for enterprises to improve their branded app-generated brand experience. In 7-ELEVEn's case, the "knowledge" attribute had a high rate of improvement of 1.369 but also had the least desirable performance among all 12 attributes; this indicates that respondents did not believe the app could encourage them to learn more about the brand. Table 6 can help improve the performance of branded apps, optimize customers' brand experience, and enable branded apps to play an effective role in the communication of marketing messages. Strengthening customer loyalty is always a goal of companies. Table 7 sheds some light in this regard. It shows that, compared with other brand experience attributes, "brand attachment" enhanced customer loyalty to the greatest extent. This finding, together with the information shown in Table 6 regarding the rates of improvement and performance of the "brand attachment" attributes, can serve as a quick guide for enterprises to identify key aspects for improvement, efficiently allocate resources, and eventually achieve the goal of enhanced customer loyalty. Coursaris and Sung [41] discussed the relationship between providers and users of branded apps from the perspective of advertising marketing; they concluded that increasing the interactiveness of branded apps was an appealing marketing strategy for customers, as well as conducive to value cocreation between brands and their customers. This study's findings may help enterprises gain insights into customers' branded app-related brand experience preferences, promote brand–customer interactions, set up targeted strategic objectives for mobile device-based brand management, elevate brand value, and create new value for customers. Gill et al. [4] proposed that branded apps should be convenient, unique, socially valuable, intriguing, and entertaining and that good customer experience is the prerequisite for customer satisfaction and loyalty. Table 6 shows the rates of improvement and performance of branded app-generated brand experience attributes with regard to the empirical objects of this study. With these results and the data included in Table 7, businesses can upgrade their branded apps to create a user experience that better meets their customers' expectations, significantly boosts customer satisfaction, and encourages customers to continually use their branded apps. Lee and Kang [21] argued that brand experience preludes and is positively related to customer loyalty. By analyzing the influence of 12 brand experience attributes on customer loyalty and satisfaction (see Table 7), this study can help marketers understand connections between brand experience attributes and customer loyalty, as well as assist businesses in creating effective strategies to address diminishing brand loyalty.

Several limitations of this study should be considered. First, the methodology of this research, like FAHP, assumes that brand experience attributes are not dependent on each other. Second, the statistical sample is limited to southern Taiwan, and future research can be extended to central and northern Taiwan. Third, branded app-based brand experience in this study is only limited to the retail industry. In future studies, the scope of research may be expanded to include other industries (e.g., department stores, fashion, and automobiles).

6. Conclusions

6.1. Academic Implications

Based on the holistic brand experience theory, this research put forward the attributes of branded app-related brand experience, combined loyalty and satisfaction influence evaluation, and created a research model with academic value. In addition, this research also optimized the methodology, based on fuzzy set theory, and used the symmetry matrix of CFLPR, in lieu of FAHP, to effectively reduce the number of comparisons and shorten the time to complete the questionnaire, thereby more accurately relating customers' brand experience preference and the influence degree of related brand experience to loyalty and satisfaction.

6.2. *Managerial Implications*

This study can assist enterprises in understanding the differences in branded app experience preferences between consumer groups, gaining insights into the performance of their branded apps, promoting value co-creation between enterprises and customers in an era where service-dominant logic prevails, and flexibly adjusting their marketing campaigns and strategies. In particular, this study put forward the results of brand experience attributes to loyalty and satisfaction (see Table 7) and determined the key factors to improve loyalty. The results can assist companies in improving customer relationship management performance and addressing the issue of diminishing brand loyalty, thus contributing to the field of marketing science.

6.3. *Suggestions*

This study found that, to enhance customer loyalty, "brand attachment" must be strengthened, which conforms to the research findings of Pedeliento et al. [42] and Japutra et al. [43]. Kaufmann et al. [44] reported that hedonic elements have a positive impact on brand attachment and recommended that businesses integrate hedonic features, such as interactive games and prize quizzes, into their branded apps. They posited that this could strengthen brand attachment, encourage customers' active participation for bolstered customer loyalty, and make customers willing to build a lasting and diverse relationship with the brand [45,46]. Furthermore, it is also advisable that enterprises apply the analytical model used in this study every 6–12 months to understand the changes in customers' brand experience and monitor the performance of their branded apps. Doing so will help them adjust brand management strategies, reallocate resources, and maintain their competitive edge. It is also recommended that the concept of fuzzy quality function development be employed to build analytical models. Researchers may also further develop FMCDM tools for augmented brand experience enhancement strategies and integrate them with the brand experience attributes model in this study to build an associate matrix. From there, researchers can explore the connection between attributes and strategies and work out management strategies for branded app-generated brand experience tailored to the needs of the retail industry.

Author Contributions: Conceptualization, T.-H.H.; data curation, C.-H.C.; formal analysis, Y.-W.Y.; funding acquisition, T.-H.H. and C.-H.C.; investigation, Y.-W.Y.; methodology, T.-H.H.; project administration, T.-H.H.; software, Y.-W.Y.; validation, C.-H.C.; writing—original draft, C.-H.C. and Y.-W.Y.; writing—review and editing, T.-H.H. and C.-H.C. All authors have read and agreed to the published version of the manuscript.

Funding: This research was supported by the Ministry of Science and Technology, Taiwan, R.O.C. (MOST 107-2410-H- 992-015-MY2).

Institutional Review Board Statement: Not applicable.

Informed Consent Statement: Not applicable.

Data Availability Statement: Not applicable.

Acknowledgments: The authors appreciate the support from the National Kaohsiung University of Science and Technology, Taiwan and the Ministry of Sciences and Technology, Taiwan.

Conflicts of Interest: The authors declare no conflict of interest.

References

1. Kim, S.J.; Wang, R.J.-H.; Malthouse, E.C. The Effects of Adopting and Using a Brand's Mobile Application on Customers' Subsequent Purchase Behavior. *J. Interact. Mark.* **2015**, *31*, 28–41. [CrossRef]
2. Kang, J.W.; Namkung, Y. The role of personalization on continuance intention in food service mobile apps A privacy calculus perspective. *Int. J. Contemp. Hosp. Manag.* **2019**, *31*, 734–752. [CrossRef]
3. Stocchi, L.; Guerini, C.; Michaelidou, N. When are Apps Worth Paying for? How Marketers can Analyze the Market Performance of Mobile Apps. *J. Advert. Res.* **2017**, *57*, 260–271. [CrossRef]
4. Gill, M.; Sridhar, S.; Grewal, R. Return on Engagement Initiatives: A Study of a Business-to-Business Mobile App. *J. Mark.* **2017**, *81*, 45–66. [CrossRef]
5. Kim, J.; Yu, E.A. The holistic brand experience of branded mobile applications affects brand loyalty. *Soc. Behav. Pers.* **2016**, *44*, 77–88. [CrossRef]
6. Alnawas, L.; Aburub, F. The effect of benefits generated from interacting with branded mobile apps on consumer satisfaction and purchase intentions. *J. Retail. Consum. Serv.* **2016**, *31*, 313–322. [CrossRef]
7. Peng, K.F.; Chen, Y.; Wen, K.W. Brand relationship, consumption values and branded app adoption. *Ind. Manag. Data Syst.* **2014**, *114*, 1131–1143. [CrossRef]
8. Herrera-Viedma, E.; Herrera, F.; Chiclana, F.; Luque, M. Some issues on consistency of fuzzy preference relations. *Eur. J. Oper. Res.* **2004**, *154*, 98–109. [CrossRef]
9. Bottani, E.; Rizzi, A. Strategic Management of Logistics Service: A Fuzzy QFD Approach. *Int. J. Prod. Econ.* **2006**, *103*, 585–599. [CrossRef]
10. Dinçer, H.; Yüksel, S.; Martínez, L. Interval type 2-based hybrid fuzzy evaluation of financial services in E7 economies with DEMATEL-ANP and MOORA methods. *Appl. Soft Comput.* **2019**, *79*, 186–202. [CrossRef]
11. Filketu, S.; Dvivedi, A.; Abebe, B.B. Decision-making on job satisfaction improvement programs using fuzzy QFD model: A case study in Ethiopia. *Total. Qual. Manag. Bus. Excell.* **2019**, *30*, 1068–1091. [CrossRef]
12. Hsu, T.H.; Lin, L.Z. QFD with Fuzzy and Entropy Weight for Evaluating Retail Customer Values. *Total. Qual. Manag. Bus. Excell.* **2006**, *17*, 935–958. [CrossRef]
13. Tang, J.W.; Hsu, T.H. Utilizing the Hierarchy Structural Fuzzy Analytical Network Process Model to Evaluate Critical Elements of Marketing Strategic Alliance Development in Mobile Telecommunication Industry. *Group Decis. Negot.* **2018**, *27*, 251–284. [CrossRef]
14. Tzeng, G.H.; Shen, K.Y. *New Concepts and Trends of Hybrid Multiple Criteria Decision Making*; CRC Press: Boca Raton, FL, USA, 2017.
15. Khan, I.; Rahman, Z. Retail brand experience: Scale development and validation. *J. Prod. Brand. Manag.* **2016**, *25*, 435–451. [CrossRef]
16. Newman, C.L.; Wachter, K.; White, A. Bricks or clicks Understanding consumer usage of retail mobile apps. *J. Serv. Mark.* **2017**, *32*, 211–222. [CrossRef]
17. Bellman, S.; Potter, R.F.; Treleaven-Hassard, S.; Robinson, J.A.; Varan, D. The effectiveness of branded mobile phone Apps. *J. Interact. Mark.* **2011**, *25*, 191–200. [CrossRef]
18. Cao, L.; Liu, X.; Cao, W. The Effects of Search-Related and Purchase-Related Mobile App Additions on Retailers' Shareholder Wealth: The Roles of Firm Size, Product Category, and Customer Segment. *J. Retail.* **2018**, *94*, 343–351. [CrossRef]
19. Stocchi, L.; Michaelidou, N.; Micevski, M. Drivers and outcomes of branded mobile app usage intention. *J. Prod. Brand. Manag.* **2019**, *28*, 28–49. [CrossRef]
20. Sahin, A.; Zehir, C.; Kitapçı, H. The effects of brand experiences, trust and satisfaction on building brand loyalty; an empirical research on global brands. *Procedia Soc. Behav. Sci.* **2011**, *24*, 1288–1301. [CrossRef]
21. Lee, H.J.; Kang, M.S. The effect of brand experience on brand relationship quality. *Acad. Mark. Stud. J.* **2012**, *16*, 87–98.
22. Ambler, T.; Bhattacharya, C.B.; Edell, J.; Keller, K.L.; Lemon, K.N.; Mittal, V. Relating brand and customer perspectives on marketing management. *J. Serv. Res.* **2002**, *5*, 13–25. [CrossRef]
23. Nadzri, W.N.M.; Musa, R.; Muda, M.; Hassan, F. The Antecedents of Brand Experience within the National Automotive Industry. *J. Econ. Financ.* **2016**, *37*, 317–323. [CrossRef]
24. Brakus, J.J.; Schmitt, B.H.; Zarantonello, L. Brand experience: What is it? How is it measured? Does it affect loyalty? *J. Market.* **2009**, *73*, 52–68. [CrossRef]
25. Nysveen, H.; Pedersen, P.E.; Skard, S. Brand experiences in service organizations: Exploring the individual effects of brand experience dimensions. *J. Brand. Manag.* **2013**, *20*, 404–423. [CrossRef]
26. Nyheim, P.; Xu, S.; Zhang, L.; Mattila, A.S. Predictors of avoidance towards personalization of restaurant smartphone advertising: A study from the millennials' perspective. *J. Hosp. Tour. Technol.* **2015**, *6*, 145–159. [CrossRef]
27. Huang, C.C. The impacts of brand experiences on brand loyalty: Mediators of brand love and trust. *Manag. Decis.* **2017**, *55*, 915–934. [CrossRef]
28. Van der Westhuizen, L.M. Brand loyalty: Exploring self-brand connection and brand experience. *J. Prod. Brand. Manag.* **2018**, *27*, 172–184. [CrossRef]
29. Paksoy, T.; Pehlivan, N.Y.; Kahraman, C. Organizational strategy development in distribution channel management using fuzzy AHP and hierarchical fuzzy TOPSIS. *Expert Syst. Appl.* **2011**, *39*, 2822–2841. [CrossRef]

30. Hu, S.K.; Lu, M.T.; Tzeng, G.H. Improving mobile commerce adoption using a new hybrid fuzzy MADM model. *Int. J. Fuzzy Syst.* **2015**, *17*, 399–413. [CrossRef]
31. Wang, C.N.; Nguyen, N.A.T.; Dang, T.T.; Lu, C.M. A Compromised Decision-Making Approach to Third-Party Logistics Selection in Sustainable Supply Chain Using Fuzzy AHP and Fuzzy VIKOR Methods. *Mathematics* **2021**, *9*, 886.
32. Lin, L.Z.; Hsu, T.H. Designing a model of FANP in brand image decision-making. *Appl. Soft Comput.* **2011**, *11*, 561–573. [CrossRef]
33. Xu, Z.; Chen, J. Some Models for Deriving the Priority Weights from Interval Fuzzy Preference Relations. *Eur. J. Oper. Res.* **2008**, *184*, 266–280. [CrossRef]
34. Wang, T.C.; Chen, Y.H. Applying Fuzzy Linguistic Preference Relations to the Improvement of Consistency of Fuzzy AHP. *Inf. Sci.* **2008**, *178*, 3755–3765. [CrossRef]
35. Pandey, A.; Kumar, A. A note on "applying fuzzy linguistic Preference relations to the improvement of consistency of fuzzy AHP". *Inf. Sci.* **2016**, *346–347*, 1–5. [CrossRef]
36. Wang, Z.J. Comments on "A note on "Applying fuzzy linguistic preference relations to the improvement of consistency of fuzzy AHP"". *Inf. Sci.* **2016**, *372*, 539–545. [CrossRef]
37. Tang, J.W.; Hsu, T.H. A fuzzy preference relations model for evaluating key supplier relationships in TFT-LCD TV panel manufacturing industry. *Manag. Decis.* **2015**, *53*, 1858–1882. [CrossRef]
38. Van Laarhoven, P.J.M.; Pedrycz, W. A fuzzy extension of Saaty's priority theory. *Fuzzy Sets Syst.* **1983**, *11*, 199–227. [CrossRef]
39. Büyüközkan, G. Determining the mobile commerce user requirements using an analytic Approach. *Comput. Stand. Interfaces* **2009**, *31*, 144–152. [CrossRef]
40. Wang, T.C.; Chen, Y.H. Applying Consistent Fuzzy Preference Relations to Partnership Selection. *Omega* **2007**, *35*, 384–388. [CrossRef]
41. Coursaris, C.K.; Sung, J. Antecedents and consequents of a mobile website's interactivity. *New Media Soc.* **2012**, *14*, 1128–1146. [CrossRef]
42. Pedeliento, G.; Andreini, D.; Bergamaschi, M.; Jarl, S. Brand and product attachment in an industrial context: The effects on brand loyalty. *Ind. Mark. Manag.* **2016**, *53*, 194–206. [CrossRef]
43. Japutra, A.; Ekinci, Y.; Simkin, L. Positive and negative behaviors resulting from brand attachment: The moderating effects of attachment styles. *Eur. J. Mark.* **2018**, *52*, 1185–1202. [CrossRef]
44. Kaufmann, H.R.; Petrovici, D.A.; Filho, C.G.; Ayres, A. Identifying moderators of brand attachment for driving customer purchase intention of original vs counterfeits of luxury brands. *J. Bus. Res.* **2016**, *69*, 5735–5747. [CrossRef]
45. Park, C.W.; Maclnnis, D.J. The Ties That Bind: Measuring the Strength of Consumers' Emotional Attachments to Brands. *J. Consum. Psychol.* **2005**, *15*, 77–91.
46. Park, C.W.; Maclnnis, D.J.; Priester, J.; Eisingerich, A.B.; Lacobucci, D. Brand Attachment and Brand Attitude Strength: Conceptual and Empirical Differentiation of Two Critical Brand Equity Drivers. *J. Market.* **2010**, *74*, 1–17. [CrossRef]

Article

An Extension TOPSIS Method Based on the Decision Maker's Risk Attitude and the Adjusted Probabilistic Fuzzy Set

Donghai Liu [1,*], An Huang [1], Yuanyuan Liu [1] and Zaiming Liu [2]

[1] Department of Applied Statistics, Hunan University of Science and Technology, Xiangtan 411201, China; huangan@mail.hnust.edu.cn (A.H.); 16011502003@mail.hnust.edu.cn (Y.L.)
[2] Department of Mathematics and Statistics, Central South University, Changsha 410083, China; zmliu@csu.edu.cn
* Correspondence: dhliu@hnust.edu.cn

Citation: Liu, D.; Huang, A.; Liu, Y.; Liu, Z. An Extension TOPSIS Method Based on the Decision Maker's Risk Attitude and the Adjusted Probabilistic Fuzzy Set. *Symmetry* **2021**, *13*, 891. https://doi.org/10.3390/sym13050891

Academic Editor: Juan Luis García Guirao

Received: 19 April 2021
Accepted: 13 May 2021
Published: 17 May 2021

Publisher's Note: MDPI stays neutral with regard to jurisdictional claims in published maps and institutional affiliations.

Copyright: © 2021 by the authors. Licensee MDPI, Basel, Switzerland. This article is an open access article distributed under the terms and conditions of the Creative Commons Attribution (CC BY) license (https://creativecommons.org/licenses/by/4.0/).

Abstract: The paper studies an extension TOPSIS method with the adjusted probabilistic linguistic fuzzy set in which the decision maker's behavior tendency is considered. Firstly, we propose a concept of probabilistic linguistic q-rung orthopair set (PLQROS) based on the probability linguistic fuzzy set (PLFS) and linguistic q-rung orthopair set (LQROS). The operational laws are introduced based on the transformed probabilistic linguistic q-rung orthopair sets (PLQROSs) which have the same probability. Through this adjustment method, the irrationality of the existing methods in the aggregation process is avoided. Furthermore, we propose a comparison rule of PLQROS and the aggregated operators. The distance measure of PLQROSs is also defined, which can deal with the symmetric information in multi-attribute decision making problems. Considering that the decision maker's behavior has a very important impact on decision-making results, we propose a behavioral TOPSIS decision making method for PLQROS. Finally, we apply the practical problem of investment decision to demonstrate the validity of the extension TOPSIS method, and the merits of the behavior decision method is testified by comparing with the classic TOPSIS method. The sensitivity analysis results of decision-maker's behavior are also given.

Keywords: behavioral decision making; risk attitude; adjusted probabilistic fuzzy set

1. Introduction

There is much uncertainty in decision making problems. It is not easy to describe the evaluation information with accurate numerical value, and they can only be described with linguistic values. Zadeh [1–3] defined the linguistic term set (LTS) and applied it to express the qualitative evaluation. For example, the commonly used seven valued LTS is in the form of $S = \{s_0 : great\ distaste, s_1 : distaste, s_2 : a\ bit\ distaste, s_3 : generally, s_4 : a\ bit\ favorite, s_5 : favorite, s_6 : great\ favorite\}$, it can be used to describe how much the decision maker likes the object. However, when the decision maker hesitates about the preference of the evaluation object, the single linguistic term is no longer describe such information. So Rodríguez et al. [4] presented the hesitant fuzzy linguistic term set (HFLTS), each of elements is a collection of linguistic terms. For example, the decision maker thinks that the audience's opinion of the program is "favorite" or "great favorite", the evaluation about the opinion of the program can be only expressed in the form of $\{s_5, s_6\}$. Since the HFLTS was put forward, some extensions of HFLTS were developed and applied in many fields [5–11]. Beg and Rashid [5] proposed the TOPSIS method of HFLTS and applied it to sort the alternative, Liao et al. [6] defined the preference relation of HFLTS, Liu et al. [7] applied the HFLTSs to the generalized TOPSIS method and presented a new similarity measure of HFLTS. In these studies however, all the linguistic terms in HFLTS have the same weights, it rarely happens in reality. In fact, the decision makers may have different degrees to the possible linguistic evaluations. Therefore, Pang et al. [12] developed the HFLTS to the PLFS through adding the probabilities to each element. For example, the decision maker believes that the possibility of favorite to the program is 0.4 and the possibility of great favorite to the program is 0.6, then the above evaluation can be represented as $\{s_5(0.4), s_6(0.6)\}$.

In the aboved LTS, they only describe the membership degree of elements. To improve the range of their application, Chen [13] defined the linguistic intuitionistic fuzzy set (LIFS) $LI = \{\langle x_i, s_{\theta_1}(x_i), s_{\phi_1}(x_i)\rangle | x_i \in X\}$, where $s_{\theta_1}(x_i), s_{\phi_1}(x_i) \in S(S = \{s_i | s_0 \leq s_i \leq s_{2\tau}\})$, the membership $s_{\theta_1}(x_i)$ and the non-membership $s_{\phi_1}(x_i)$ satisfy the following condition: $0 \leq \theta_1 + \phi_1 \leq 2\tau$. Furthermore, Garg [14] defined the linguistic Pythagorean fuzzy set (LPFS) $LP = \{\langle x_i, s_{\theta_2}(x_i), s_{\phi_2}(x_i)\rangle | x_i \in X\}$, where $s_{\theta_2}(x_i), s_{\phi_2}(x_i) \in S$, the following condition of the membership $s_{\theta_2}(x_i)$ and the non-membership $s_{\phi_2}(x_i)$ must be satisfied: $0 \leq (\theta_2)^2 + (\phi_2)^2 \leq (2\tau)^2$, its advantage is it has a wider range of uncertainty than LIFS. Furthermore, in order to better describe the uncertainty in decision making problems, Liu et al. [7] proposed the LQROS $LQ = \{\langle x_i, s_\theta(x_i), s_\phi(x_i)\rangle | x_i \in X\}$ based on the q-rung orthopair fuzzy set (QROFS) [15], where the following condition of the membership $s_\theta(x_i)$ and the non-membership $s_\phi(x_i)$ should be met: $0 \leq (\theta)^q + (\phi)^q \leq (2\tau)^q (q \geq 1)$. Obviously, when $q = 1$ or 2, the LQROS is reduced to LIFS or LPFS, respectively. Although the LQROS extends the scope of information representation, it cannot describe the following evaluation information. For the given LTS $S = \{s_0 : \textit{extreme slowly}, s_1 : \textit{slowly}, s_2 : \textit{slightly slowly}, s_3 : \textit{generally}, s_4 : \textit{slightly high}, s_5 : \textit{high}, s_6 : \textit{extreme high}\}$, one expert believes that 30% possibility of profit from the investment in the project is high, and 70% possibility of profit from the investment in the project is extreme high. While the other expert may believe that 10% possibility of not making a profit is extreme slowly and 90% possibility of not making a profit is slightly slowly. Up to now, we cannot apply the existing LTS to describe the above evaluation information. Motivated by this, we introduce the PLQROS by integrating the LQROS and the probabilistic fuzzy set. Then the above information can be represented by $Q_s(p) = \langle\{s_5(0.3), s_6(0.7)\}, \{s_0(0.1), s_2(0.9)\}\rangle$, the detailed definition is given in Section 3.1.

On the other side, the TOPSIS is a classical method to handle the multiple criteria decision making problems. Since it was introduced by Hwang and Yoon [16], there were many literatures on TOPSIS method, we can refer to [17–22]. The TOPSIS method is a useful technique for choosing an alternative that is closet to the best alternative and farthest from the worst alternative simultaneously. Furthermore, Yoon and Kim [23] proposed a behavioral TOPSIS method that incorporates the gain and loss in behavioral economics, which makes the decision results more reasonable. As all we know, there is no related research study the behavioral TOPSIS method in uncertain decision environments problems. Inspired by this, we study the TOPSIS method which consider the decision maker's risk attitude and the adjusted probabilistic fuzzy set, the main contributions of the paper are given as follows:

(1) The operational laws of PLQROS are given based on the adjusted PLQROS with the same probability, which can avoid the unreasonable calculation and improve the adaptability of PLQROS in reality.
(2) The new aggregation operators and distance measures between PLQROSs are presented, which can represent the differences between PLQROSs and deal with the symmetry information.
(3) The behavioral TOPSIS method is introduced into the uncertain multi-attribute decision making process, which changes the behavioral TOPSIS method only used in the deterministic environment.

The remainder of paper is organized as follows: in the second section, some related concepts are reviewed. In the third section, we introduce the operational laws of PLQROSs, the aggregated operators and distance measures of PLQROSs, and we also give their corresponding properties. In Section 4, the process steps of the behavioral decision algorithm are given. In Section 5, a practical example is utilized to prove the availability of the extension TOPSIS method. Furthermore, the sensitivity analysis of the behavioral factors of decision maker's risk attitude is provided. Finally, we made a summary of the paper and expanded the future studies.

2. Preliminaries

In order to define the PLQROS, we introduce some concepts of LTS, PLFS, QROFS and LQROS. Throughout the paper, assume $X = \{x_1, x_2, \cdots, x_m\}$ to be a non-empty and finite set.

In the uncertain decision making environment, the experts applied the LTS to make a qualitative description, it is defined as follows:

Definition 1 ([1]). *Assume $S = \{s_\alpha | \alpha = 0, 1, \cdots, 2g\}$ is a finite set, where s_α is a linguistic term and g is a natural number, the LTS S should satisfy two properties:*

(1) if $\alpha \leq \beta$, then $s_\alpha \leq s_\beta$;

(2) $s_\alpha = neg(s_\beta)$, where $\alpha + \beta = 2g$.

In order to describe the decision information more objective, Xu [24] extended the LTS S to a continuous LTS $\bar{S} = \{s_\alpha | \alpha \in [0, \rho]\}$, where $\rho(\rho > 2g)$ is a natural number.

The PLFS is regarded as an extension of HFLTS, which considers the elements of LTSs with different weights, the PLFS can be denoted as:

Definition 2 ([12]). *Assume $X = \{x_1, x_2, \cdots, x_m\}$ and $S = \{s_0, s_1, \ldots, s_{2g}\}$ is a LTS, the PLFS $Z_s(r)$ in X is defined as:*

$$Z_s(r) = \{\langle x_j, z_s(r)(x_j)\rangle | x_j \in X\},$$

where $z_s(r)(x_j) = \{s^{j(u)}(r^{(u)}) | s^{j(u)} \in S, r^{(u)} \geq 0, u = 1, 2, \cdots, U; \sum_{u=1}^{U} r^{(u)} \leq 1\}$, $s^{j(u)}$ is the linguistic term and $r^{(u)}$ is the corresponding probability of $s^{j(u)}$, U is the number of linguistic terms $s^{j(u)}$.

Next, we introduce the concept of QROFS as follows:

Definition 3 ([15]). *Assume $X = \{x_1, x_2, \cdots, x_m\}$, the QROFS Q is represented as:*

$$Q = \{\langle x_j, \mu_Q(x_j), \nu_Q(x_j)\rangle | x_j \in X\},\ q \geq 1,$$

where the membership $\mu_Q(x_j)(0 \leq \mu_Q(x_j) \leq 1)$ and the non-membership $\nu_Q(x_j)(0 \leq \nu_Q(x_j) \leq 1)$ satisfy $0 \leq (\mu_Q(x_j))^q + (\nu_Q(x_j))^q \leq 1$, $\pi_Q(x_j) = \sqrt[q]{1 - (\mu_Q(x_j))^q - (\nu_Q(x_j))^q}$ is the indeterminacy degree of QROFS Q.

If $X = \{x\}$, the QROFS Q is reduced to a q-rung orthopair fuzzy number (QROFN) $Q \triangleq \langle \mu_Q, \nu_Q \rangle$.

Remark 1. *If $q = 1$ or 2, the QROFS Q is degenerated to an intuitionistic fuzzy set (IFS) or a Pythagorean fuzzy set (PFS).*

In some realistic decision making problems, the set should be described qualitatively. So we review the concept of LQROS as follows:

Definition 4 ([25]). *Assume $X = \{x_1, x_2, \cdots, x_m\}$, $\bar{S} = \{s_\alpha | \alpha \in [0, \rho]\}(\rho > 2g)$ is a LTS, the LQROS Y is represented as:*

$$Y = \{\langle x_j, s_\theta(x_j), s_\phi(x_j)\rangle | x_j \in X\},$$

where the membership $s_\theta(x_j)$ *and the non-membership* $s_\phi(x_j)$ *satisfy* $0 \leq \theta_j^q + \phi_j^q \leq \rho^q$ $(q \geq 1)$, *the indeterminacy degree* $\pi_Y(x_j) = s_{\sqrt[q]{\rho^q - \theta_j^q - \phi_j^q}}$.

If X = {*x*}, the LQROS *Y* is degenerated to a linguistic q-rung orthopair number (LQRON) $Y \triangleq \langle s_\theta, s_\phi \rangle$.

Definition 5 ([25]). *Let* $y_1 = \langle s_{\theta_1}, s_{\phi_1} \rangle$ *and* $y_2 = \langle s_{\theta_2}, s_{\phi_2} \rangle$ *be two LQRONs,* $s_{\theta_\iota}, s_{\phi_\iota} \in \bar{S}_{[0,\rho]}$ $(\iota = 1,2)$, $\epsilon > 0$, *the algorithms of the LQRONs can be expressed as follows:*

(a) $y_1 \oplus y_2 = \langle s_{((\theta_1)^q + (\theta_2)^q - (\frac{\theta_1\theta_2}{\rho})^q)^{\frac{1}{q}}}, s_{\frac{\phi_1\phi_2}{\rho}} \rangle$;

(b) $y_1 \otimes y_2 = \langle s_{\frac{\theta_1\theta_2}{\rho}}, s_{((\phi_1)^q + (\phi_2)^q - (\frac{\phi_1\phi_2}{\rho})^q)^{\frac{1}{q}}} \rangle$;

(c) $\epsilon y_1 = \langle s_{(\rho^q - \rho^q(1 - \frac{(\theta_1)^q}{\rho^q})^\epsilon)^{\frac{1}{q}}}, s_{\rho(\frac{\phi_1}{\rho})^\epsilon} \rangle$;

(d) $y_1^\epsilon = \langle s_{\rho(\frac{\theta_1}{\rho})^\epsilon}, s_{(\rho^q - \rho^q(1 - \frac{(\phi_1)^q}{\rho^q})^\epsilon)^{\frac{1}{q}}} \rangle$.

3. The Proposed Probabilistic Fuzzy Set

Now we propose a new probabilistic fuzzy set—PLQROS, which not only allows the experts to express evaluation information with multiple linguistic terms but contains the possibility of each linguistic terms. The difficulty is how to define the operational laws of PLQROS reasonably when the corresponding probability distributions are different.

3.1. The Basic Definition of PLQROS

Definition 6. *Let* $X = \{x_1, x_2, \cdots, x_m\}$ *and* $\bar{S}_{[0,\rho]}$ $(\rho > 2g)$ *be a continuous LTS, the PLQROS* $PL_s(r)$ *in X can be defined as:*

$$PL_s(r) = \{\langle x_j, H_s(\hat{r})(x_j), G_s(\tilde{r})(x_j)\rangle | x_j \in X\},$$

where $H_s(\hat{r})(x_j) = \{s_{\theta^{j(u)}}(\hat{r}^{(u)}) | s_{\theta^{j(u)}} \in \bar{S}_{[0,\rho]}, \hat{r}^{(u)} \geq 0, \sum_{u=1}^{U} \hat{r}^{(u)} \leq 1\}$ *is the membership and* $G_s(\tilde{r})(x_j) = \{s_{\phi^{j(v)}}(\tilde{r}^{(v)}) | s_{\phi^{j(v)}} \in \bar{S}, \tilde{r}^{(v)} \geq 0, \sum_{v=1}^{V} \tilde{r}^{(v)} \leq 1\}$ *is the non-membership, respectively. For any* $x_j \in X$, *they satisfy with:* $0 \leq (\max_{u=1}^{U}\{\theta^{j(u)}\})^q + (\max_{v=1}^{V}\{\phi^{j(v)}\})^q \leq \rho^q$ $(q \geq 1)$.

If X = {*x*}, the PLQROS $PL_s(r)$ is degenerated to a PLQRON $pl_s(r) \triangleq \langle \{s_{\theta^{(u)}}(\hat{r}^{(u)})\}, \{s_{\phi^{(v)}}(\tilde{r}^{(v)})\} \rangle$, where $s_{\theta^{(u)}}, s_{\phi^{(v)}} \in \bar{S}_{[0,\rho]}$, $\sum_{u=1}^{U} \hat{r}^{(u)} \leq 1$ and $\sum_{v=1}^{V} \tilde{r}^{(v)} \leq 1$.

Example 1. *Let* $S = \{s_0 : very\ slowly,\ s_1 : slowly,\ s_2 : slightly\ slowly, s_3 : generally,\ s_4 : slightly\ fast, s_5 : fast,\ s_6 : very\ fast\}$. *Two groups of experts inspected the development of the company, one group may think that "the speed of company development is slightly slowly with 100% possibility, with 40% probability that it is not slightly slowly, with 40% probability that the speed of company development is not generally and with 20% probability that the speed of company development is not slightly fast". The other group think that "with 20% probability that the speed of company development is slowly, with 60% probability that the speed of company development is slightly slowly and with 20% probability that it is generally, with 50% probability that it is not slightly fast and with 50% probability that it is not very fast". Then the above evaluation information can be denoted as* $pl_s^1(r) = \langle \{s_2(1)\}, \{s_2(0.4), s_3(0.4), s_4(0.2)\} \rangle$ *and* $pl_s^2(r) = \langle \{s_1(0.2), s_2(0.6), s_3(0.2)\}, \{s_5(0.5), s_6(0.5)\} \rangle$.

According to Example 1, we can see that the probabilities and numbers of elements in $pl_s^1(r)$ and $pl_s^2(r)$ are not same, the general operations on PLFSs multiply the probabilities of corresponding linguistic terms directly, which may cause the unreasonable result. Therefore, Wu et al. [26] presented a method to modify the probabilities of linguistic terms to be same, which is given as follows:

Let $\bar{S}_{[0,\rho]}$ $(\rho > 2g)$ be a continuous LTS, $pl_s^1(r) = \langle\{s_{\theta^{1(u)}}(\hat{r}^{(u)})\}, \{s_{\phi^{1(v)}}(\tilde{r}^{(v)})\}|u = 1,2,\cdots,U_1; v = 1,2,\cdots,V_1\rangle$ and $pl_s^2(r) = \langle\{s_{\theta^{2(u)}}(\hat{r}^{(u)})\}, \{s_{\phi^{2(v)}}(\tilde{r}^{(v)})\}|u = 1,2,\cdots,U_2;$ $v = 1,2,\cdots,V_2\rangle$ are two PLQRONs. We adjust the probability distributions of $pl_s^1(r)$ and $pl_s^2(r)$ to be same, respectively. That is to say, $pl_s^{*1}(r) = \langle\{s_{\theta^{1(k)}}(\hat{r}^{*(k)})\}, \{s_{\phi^{1(b)}}(\tilde{r}^{*(b)})\}|k = 1,2,\cdots,K;\ b = 1,2,\cdots,B\rangle$ and $pl_s^{*2}(r) = \langle\{s_{\theta^{2(k)}}(\hat{r}^{*(k)})\}, \{s_{\phi^{2(b)}}(\tilde{r}^{*(b)})\}|k = 1,2,\cdots,K;$ $b = 1,2,\cdots,B\rangle$. Applying the method of Wu et al. [26] to adjust the PLQRONs, the linguistic terms and the sum of probabilities of each linguistic term set are not changed, which means that the adjustment method does not result in the loss of evaluation information.

Example 2. *Let* $S = \{s_\alpha|\alpha = 0,1,2,\cdots,6\}$, $pl_s^1(r) = \langle\{s_2(1)\}, \{s_3(0.4), s_4(0.4), s_6(0.2)\}\rangle$ *and* $pl_s^2(r) = \langle\{s_1(0.2), s_2(0.6), s_3(0.2)\}, \{s_5(0.5), s_6(0.5)\}\rangle$ *be two PLQRONs, the adjusted PLQRONs are* $pl_s^{*1}(r) = \langle\{s_2(0.2), s_2(0.6), s_2(0.2)\}, \{s_3(0.4), s_4(0.1), s_4(0.3), s_6(0.2)\}\rangle$ *and* $pl_s^{*2}(r) = \langle\{s_1(0.2), s_2(0.6), s_3(0.2)\}, \{s_5(0.4), s_5(0.1), s_6(0.3), s_6(0.2)\}\rangle$, *respectively. The adjustment process is shown in Figure 1.*

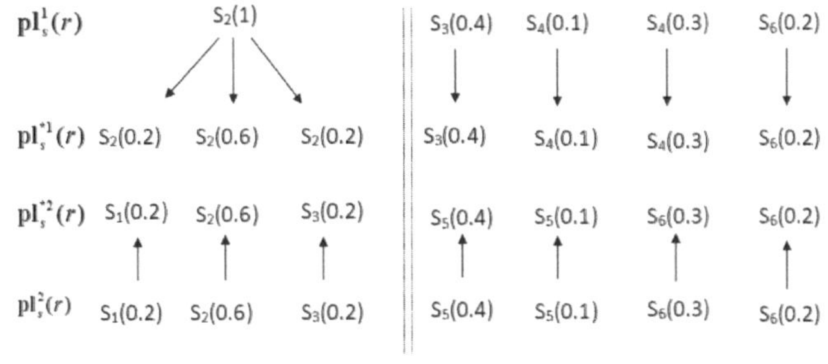

Figure 1. The adjust process of PLQRONs $pl_s^1(r)$ and $pl_s^2(r)$.

3.2. Some Properties for PLQRONs

Firstly, we apply the adjustment method to adjust the probabilistic linguistic terms with same probability, which can overcome the defects that may occur in process of aggregation. Then, we propose the operation rules of the adjusted PLQRONs, and their properties.

Definition 7. *Let* $\bar{S}_{[0,\rho]}$ $(\rho > 2g)$ *be a LTS,* $pl_s^{*1}(r) = \langle\{s_{\theta^{1(u)}}(\hat{r}^{*(u)})\}, \{s_{\phi^{1(v)}}(\tilde{r}^{*(v)})\}\rangle$ *and* $pl_s^{*2}(r) = \langle\{s_{\theta^{2(u)}}(\hat{r}^{*(u)})\}, \{s_{\phi^{2(v)}}(\tilde{r}^{*(v)})\}\rangle$ $(u = 1,2,\cdots,U;\ v = 1,2,\cdots,V)$ *are two adjusted PLQRONs, where* $\theta^{\iota(u)}, \phi^{\iota(v)}$ $(\iota = 1,2)$ *are the subscript of* $s_{\theta^{\iota(u)}}$, $s_{\phi^{\iota(v)}}$ $(\iota = 1,2), \eta > 0$, *the operational laws of the PLQRONs can be expressed as follows:*

(a) $neg(pl_s^{*1}(r)) = \langle\{s_{\phi^{1(v)}}(\tilde{r}^{*(v)})\}, \{s_{\theta^{1(u)}}(\hat{r}^{*(u)})\}\rangle;$

(b) $pl_s^{*1}(r) \oplus pl_s^{*2}(r) = \langle\{s_{((\theta^{1(u)})^q+(\theta^{2(u)})^q-(\frac{(\theta^{1(u)})(\theta^{2(u)})}{\rho})^q)^{\frac{1}{q}}}(\hat{r}^{*(u)})\}, \{s_{\frac{\phi^{1(v)}\phi^{2(v)}}{\rho}}(\tilde{r}^{*(v)})\}\rangle;$

(c) $pl_s^{*1}(r) \otimes pl_s^{*2}(r) = \langle\{s_{\frac{\theta^{1(u)}\theta^{2(u)}}{\rho}}(\hat{r}^{*(u)})\}, \{s_{((\phi^{1(v)})^q+(\phi^{2(v)})^q-(\frac{(\phi^{1(v)})(\phi^{2(v)})}{\rho})^q)^{\frac{1}{q}}}(\tilde{r}^{*(v)})\}\rangle;$

(d) $\eta pl_s^{*1}(r) = \langle\{s_{(\rho^q-\rho^q(1-\frac{(\theta^{1(u)})^q}{\rho^q})^\eta)^{\frac{1}{q}}}(\hat{r}^{*(u)})\}, \{s_{\rho(\frac{\phi^{1(v)}}{\rho})^\eta}(\tilde{r}^{*(v)})\}\rangle;$

(e) $(pl_s^{*1}(r))^\eta = \langle\{s_{\rho(\frac{\theta^{1(u)}}{\rho})^\eta}(\hat{r}^{*(u)})\}, \{s_{(\rho^q-\rho^q(1-\frac{(\phi^{1(v)})^q}{\rho^q})^\eta)^{\frac{1}{q}}}(\tilde{r}^{*(v)})\}\rangle.$

Example 3. *Let* $S = \{s_\alpha|\alpha = 0,1,2,\cdots,6\}$, $pl_s^1(r) = \langle\{s_4(0.4), s_5(0.6)\}, \{s_1(0.7), s_2(0.3)\}\rangle$ *and* $pl_s^2(r) = \langle\{s_3(0.2), s_4(0.5), s_5(0.3)\}, \{s_3(0.5), s_4(0.5)\}\rangle$ *be two PLQRONs, the modified PLQRONs are* $pl_s^{*1}(r) = \langle\{s_4(0.2), s_4(0.2), s_5(0.3), s_5(0.3)\}, \{s_1(0.5), s_1(0.2), s_2(0.3)\}\rangle$ *and*

$pl_s^{*2}(r) = \langle\{s_3(0.2), s_4(0.2), s_4(0.3), s_5(0.3)\}, \{s_3(0.5), s_4(0.2), s_4(0.3)\}\rangle$, The adjustment process is shown in Figure 2. Let $\eta = 0.5$ and $q = 3$, then we have

$$neg(pl_s^{*1}(r)) = \langle\{s_1(0.5), s_1(0.2), s_2(0.3)\}, \{s_4(0.2), s_4(0.2), s_5(0.3), s_5(0.3)\}\rangle;$$
$$pl_s^{*1}(r) \oplus pl_s^{*2}(r) = \langle\{s_{4.3621}(0.2), s_{4.7774}(0.2), s_{5.3364}(0.3), s_{5.6217}(0.3)\}, \{s_{0.5}(0.5), s_{0.6667}(0.2), s_{1.3333}(0.3)\}\rangle;$$
$$pl_s^{*1}(r) \otimes pl_s^{*2}(r) = \langle\{s_2(0.2), s_{2.6667}(0.2), s_{3.3333}(0.3), s_{4.1667}(0.3)\}, \{s_{3.0321}(0.5), s_{4.0146}(0.2), s_{4.114}(0.3)\}\rangle;$$
$$0.5pl_s^{*1}(r) = \langle\{s_{3.2649}(0.2), s_{3.2649}(0.2), s_{4.2321}(0.3), s_{4.2321}(0.3)\}, \{s_{2.4495}(0.5), s_{2.4495}(0.2), s_{3.4641}(0.3)\}\rangle;$$
$$(pl_s^{*1}(r))^{0.5} = \langle\{s_{4.899}(0.2), s_{4.899}(0.2), s_{5.4772}(0.3), s_{5.4772}(0.3)\}, \{s_{0.794}(0.5), s_{0.794}(0.2), s_{1.5924}(0.3)\}\rangle.$$

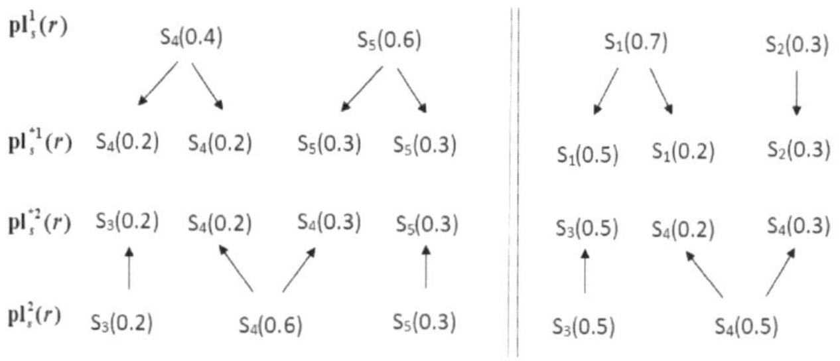

Figure 2. The adjust process of PLQRONs $pl_s^1(r)$ and $pl_s^2(r)$.

Theorem 1. *Let $pl_s^{*1}(r) = \langle\{s_{\theta^{1(u)}}(\hat{r}^{*(u)})\}, \{s_{\phi^{1(v)}}(\tilde{r}^{*(v)})\}\rangle$ and $pl_s^{*2}(r) = \langle\{s_{\theta^{2(u)}}(\hat{r}^{*(u)})\}, \{s_{\phi^{2(v)}}(\tilde{r}^{*(v)})\}\rangle$ $(u = 1, 2, \cdots, U;\ v = 1, 2, \cdots, V)$ be any two adjusted PLQRONs, η, η_1, $\eta_2 > 0$, then*

(1) $pl_s^{*1}(r) \oplus pl_s^{*2}(r) = pl_s^{*2}(r) \oplus pl_s^{*1}(r)$;
(2) $pl_s^{*1}(r) \otimes pl_s^{*2}(r) = pl_s^{*2}(r) \otimes pl_s^{*1}(r)$;
(3) $\eta(pl_s^{*1}(r) \oplus pl_s^{*2}(r)) = \eta pl_s^{*1}(r) \oplus \eta pl_s^{*2}(r)$;
(4) $\eta_1 pl_s^{*1}(r) \oplus \eta_2 pl_s^{*1}(r) = (\eta_1 + \eta_2) pl_s^{*1}(r)$;
(5) $(pl_s^{*1}(r))^{\eta_1} \otimes (pl_s^{*1}(r))^{\eta_2} = (pl_s^{*1}(r))^{\eta_1 + \eta_2}$;
(6) $(pl_s^{*1}(r))^{\eta} \otimes (pl_s^{*2}(r))^{\eta} = (pl_s^{*1}(r) \otimes pl_s^{*2}(r))^{\eta}$.

Here we prove the property (1) and (3), other properties proof process are similar, we omit them.

(1) By Definition 7, we have

$$\begin{aligned} pl_s^{*1}(r) \oplus pl_s^{*2}(r) &= \langle\{s_{((\theta^{1(u)})^q + (\theta^{2(u)})^q - (\frac{(\theta^{1(u)})(\theta^{2(u)})}{\rho})^q)^{\frac{1}{q}}}(\hat{r}^{*(u)})\}, \{s_{\frac{\phi^{1(v)}\phi^{2(v)}}{\rho}}(\tilde{r}^{*(v)})\}\rangle \\ &= \langle\{s_{((\theta^{2(u)})^q + (\theta^{1(u)})^q - (\frac{(\theta^{2(u)})(\theta^{1(u)})}{\rho})^q)^{\frac{1}{q}}}(\hat{r}^{*(u)})\}, \{s_{\frac{\phi^{2(v)}\phi^{1(v)}}{\rho}}(\tilde{r}^{*(v)})\}\rangle \\ &= pl_s^{*2}(r) \oplus pl_s^{*1}(r). \end{aligned}$$

Therefore $pl_s^{*1}(r) \oplus pl_s^{*2}(r) = pl_s^{*2}(r) \oplus pl_s^{*1}(r)$ is obtained.

(3) By Definition 7, we can get

$$\begin{aligned} \eta(pl_s^{*1}(r) \oplus pl_s^{*2}(r)) &= \eta\langle\{s_{((\theta^{1(u)})^q + (\theta^{2(u)})^q - (\frac{\theta^{1(u)}\theta^{2(u)}}{\rho})^q)^{\frac{1}{q}}}(\hat{r}^{*(u)})\}, \{s_{\frac{\phi^{1(v)}\phi^{2(v)}}{\rho}}(\tilde{r}^{*(v)})\}\rangle \\ &= \langle\{s_{(\rho^q - \rho^q(1 - \frac{(\theta^{1(u)})^q + (\theta^{2(u)})^q - (\frac{(\theta^{1(u)})(\theta^{2(u)})}{\rho})^q}{\rho^q})^{\eta})^{\frac{1}{q}}}(\hat{r}^{*(u)})\}, \{s_{\rho(\frac{\phi^{1(v)}\phi^{2(v)}}{\rho^2})^{\eta}}(\tilde{r}^{*(v)})\}\rangle. \end{aligned}$$

Moreover, since

$$\eta(pl_s^{*1}(r)) = \langle\{s_{(\rho^q-\rho^q(1-\frac{(\theta^{1(u)})^q}{\rho^q})^\eta)^{\frac{1}{q}}}(\hat{r}^{*(u)})\}, \{s_{\rho(\frac{\phi^{1(v)}}{\rho})^\eta}(\tilde{r}^{*(v)})\}\rangle,$$
$$\eta(pl_s^{*2}(r)) = \langle\{s_{(\rho^q-\rho^q(1-\frac{(\theta^{2(u)})^q}{\rho^q})^\eta)^{\frac{1}{q}}}(\hat{r}^{*(u)})\}, \{s_{\rho(\frac{\phi^{2(v)}}{\rho})^\eta}(\tilde{r}^{*(v)})\}\rangle,$$

let $\varpi = (\rho^q - \rho^q(1 - \frac{(\theta^{1(u)})^q}{\rho^q})^\eta)^{\frac{1}{q}}$ and $\chi = (\rho^q - \rho^q(1 - \frac{(\theta^{2(u)})^q}{\rho^q})^\eta)^{\frac{1}{q}}$, the above formulas can be denoted as:

$$\eta pl_s^{*1}(r) \oplus \eta pl_s^{*2}(r) = \langle\{s_{(\varpi^q+\chi^q-(\frac{\varpi\cdot\chi}{\rho})^q)^{1/q}}(\hat{r}^{*(u)})\}, \{s_{\rho(\frac{\phi^{1(v)}\phi^{2(v)}}{\rho^2})^\eta}(\tilde{r}^{*(v)})\}\rangle$$
$$= \langle\{s_{\{\rho^q-\rho^q\cdot[(1-\frac{(\theta^{1(u)})^q}{\rho^q})^\eta+(1-\frac{(\theta^{2(u)})^q}{\rho^q})^\eta]-(1-(1-\frac{(\theta^{1(u)})^q}{\rho^q})^\eta)\cdot[\rho^q-\rho^q(1-\frac{(\theta^{2(u)})^q}{\rho^q})^\eta]\}^{\frac{1}{q}}}(\hat{r}^{*(u)})\}, \{s_{\rho(\frac{\phi^{1(v)}\phi^{2(v)}}{\rho^2})^\eta}(\tilde{r}^{*(v)})\}\rangle$$
$$= \langle\{s_{\{\rho^q-\rho^q\cdot[(1-\frac{(\theta^{1(u)})^q}{\rho^q})^\eta+(1-\frac{(\theta^{2(u)})^q}{\rho^q})^\eta]+\rho^q[(1-\frac{(\theta^{1(u)})^q}{\rho^q})^\eta+(1-\frac{(\theta^{2(u)})^q}{\rho^q})^\eta-(1-\frac{(\theta^{1(u)})^q}{\rho^q})^\eta\cdot(1-\frac{(\theta^{2(u)})^q}{\rho^q})^\eta]\}^{\frac{1}{q}}}(\hat{r}^{*(u)})\},$$
$$\{s_{\rho(\frac{\phi^{1(v)}\phi^{2(v)}}{\rho^2})^\eta}(\tilde{r}^{*(v)})\}\rangle$$
$$= \langle\{s_{\{\rho^q-\rho^q\cdot[(1-\frac{(\theta^{1(u)})^q}{\rho^q})^\eta\cdot(1-\frac{(\theta^{2(u)})^q}{\rho^q})^\eta]\}^{\frac{1}{q}}}(\hat{r}^{*(u)})\}, \{s_{\rho(\frac{\phi^{1(v)}\phi^{2(v)}}{\rho^2})^\eta}(\tilde{r}^{*(v)})\}\rangle$$
$$= \langle\{s_{(\rho^q-\rho^q(1-\frac{(\theta^{1(u)})^q+(\theta^{2(u)})^q-(\frac{(\theta^{1(u)})(\theta^{2(u)})}{\rho})^q}{\rho^q})^\eta)^{\frac{1}{q}}}(\hat{r}^{*(u)})\}, \{s_{\rho(\frac{\phi^{1(v)}\phi^{2(v)}}{\rho^2})^\eta}(\tilde{r}^{*(v)})\}\rangle$$
$$= \eta(pl_s^{*1}(r) \oplus pl_s^{*2}(r)).$$

Therefore $\eta(pl_s^{*1}(r) \oplus pl_s^{*2}(r)) = \eta pl_s^{*1}(r) \oplus \eta pl_s^{*2}(r)$ is proved.

In order to compare the order relation of PLQROSs, we present the comparison rules as follows:

Definition 8. *Assume $\bar{S}_{[0,\rho]}$ $(\rho > 2g)$ be a LTS, for any adjusted PLQRON $pl_s^*(r) = \langle\{s_{\theta^{(u)}}(\hat{r}^{*(u)})\}$, $\{s_{\phi^{(v)}}(\tilde{r}^{*(v)})\}\rangle$, where $s_{\theta^{(u)}}, s_{\phi^{(v)}} \in \tilde{S}_{[0,\rho]}$, $(u = 1, 2, \cdots, U;\ v = 1, 2, \cdots, V)$, the score function of $pl_s^*(r)$ is*

$$A(pl_s^*(r)) = \sum_{u=1}^{\#U_\theta}(\frac{\theta^{(u)}\cdot\hat{r}^{*(u)}}{\rho})^q - \sum_{v=1}^{\#V_\phi}(\frac{\phi^{(v)}\cdot\tilde{r}^{*(v)}}{\rho})^q, \tag{1}$$

where $\theta^{(u)}, \phi^{(v)} \in [0, \rho]$, $\#U_\theta$ and $\#V_\phi$ represent the number of elements in the corresponding set, respectively.

The accuracy function of $pl_s^*(r)$ is

$$H(pl_s^*(r)) = \sum_{u=1}^{\#U_\theta}(\frac{\theta^{(u)}\cdot\hat{r}^{*(u)}}{\rho})^q + \sum_{v=1}^{\#V_\phi}(\frac{\phi^{(v)}\cdot\tilde{r}^{*(v)}}{\rho})^q, \tag{2}$$

where $\theta^{(u)}, \phi^{(v)} \in [0, \rho]$, $\#U_\theta$ and $\#V_\phi$ represent the number of elements in the corresponding set, respectively.

Theorem 2. *Let $pl_s^{*1}(r) = \langle\{s_{\theta^{1(u)}}(\hat{r}^{*(u)})\}, \{s_{\phi^{1(v)}}(\tilde{r}^{*(v)})\}\rangle$ and $pl_s^{*2}(r) = \langle\{s_{\theta^{2(u)}}(\hat{r}^{*(u)})\}$, $\{s_{\phi^{2(v)}}(\tilde{r}^{*(v)})\}\rangle$ be two adjusted PLQRONs. $A(pl_s^{*1}(r))$ and $A(pl_s^{*2}(r))$ are the score function of $pl_s^{*1}(r)$ and $pl_s^{*2}(r)$, the accuracy function of $pl_s^{*1}(r)$ and $pl_s^{*2}(r)$ are $H(pl_s^{*1}(r))$ and $H(pl_s^{*2}(r))$, respectively, then the order relation of $pl_s^{*1}(r)$ and $pl_s^{*2}(r)$ are given as follows:*

(1) If $A(pl_s^{*1}(r)) > A(pl_s^{*2}(r))$, then $pl_s^{*1}(r) \succ pl_s^{*2}(r)$;
(2) If $A(pl_s^{*1}(r)) = A(pl_s^{*2}(r))$, then

(a) If $H(pl_s^{*1}(r)) = H(pl_s^{*2}(r))$, then $pl_s^{*1}(r) \asymp pl_s^{*2}(r)$;
(b) If $H(pl_s^{*1}(r)) < H(pl_s^{*2}(r))$, then $pl_s^{*1}(r) \prec pl_s^{*2}(r)$;
(c) If $H(pl_s^{*1}(r)) > H(pl_s^{*2}(r))$, then $pl_s^{*1}(r) \succ pl_s^{*2}(r)$;

(3) If $\Lambda(pl_s^{*1}(r)) < \Lambda(pl_s^{*2}(r))$, then $pl_s^{*1}(r) \prec pl_s^{*2}(r)$.

3.3. The Aggregation Operators of PLQROSs

In order to aggregate the multi-attribute information well, we introduce the aggregation operators of PLQRONs as follows.

Definition 9. *Let $\bar{S}_{[0,\rho]}$ $(\rho > 2g)$ be a LTS, $pl_s^{*1}(r) = \langle\{s_{\theta^\iota(u)}(\hat{r}^{*(u)})\}, \{s_{\phi^\iota(v)}(\tilde{r}^{*(v)})\}\rangle (\iota = 1,2,\cdots,n;\ u = 1,2,\cdots,U;\ v = 1,2,\cdots,V)$ are n adjusted PLQRONs, where $s_{\theta^\iota(u)}, s_{\phi^\iota(v)} \in \bar{S}_{[0,\rho]}$, the probabilistic linguistic q-rung orthopair weighted averaging (PLQROWA) operator can be expressed as:*

$$\begin{aligned} PLQROWA(pl_s^{*1}(r), pl_s^{*2}(r), \cdots, pl_s^{*n}(r)) &= \omega_1 pl_s^{*1}(r) \oplus \omega_2 pl_s^{*2}(r) \oplus \cdots \oplus \omega_n pl_s^{*n}(r) \\ &= \langle\{s_{(\rho^q - \rho^q \prod_{\iota=1}^n (1 - \frac{(\theta^\iota(u))^q}{\rho^q})^{\omega_\iota})^{\frac{1}{q}}}(\hat{r}^{*(u)})\}, \{s_{\prod_{\iota=1}^n \rho(\frac{\phi^\iota(v)}{\rho})^{\omega_\iota}}(\tilde{r}^{*(v)})\}\rangle, \end{aligned} \tag{3}$$

where $\omega = (\omega_1, \omega_2, \cdots, \omega_n)^T$ is the weight vector, and it satisfies $\sum_{\iota=1}^n \omega_\iota = 1 (0 \le \omega_\iota \le 1)$.

Theorem 3. *Let $pl_s^{*\iota}(r) = \langle\{s_{\theta^\iota(u)}(\hat{r}^{*(u)})\}, \{s_{\phi^\iota(v)}(\tilde{r}^{*(v)})\}\rangle (\iota = 1,2,\cdots,n;\ u = 1,2,\cdots,U;\ v = 1,2,\cdots,V)$ be ι adjusted PLQRONs, the weight ω_ι $(\iota = 1,2,\cdots,n)$ satisfies with $0 \le \omega_\iota \le 1$ and $\sum_{\iota=1}^n \omega_\iota = 1$, then the properties of PLQROWA are shown as follows:*

(1) *Idempotency: if $pl_s^{*\iota}(r)$ $(\iota = 1,2,\cdots,n)$ are equal, i.e., $pl_s^{*\iota}(r) = pl_s^{*}(r) \triangleq \langle\{s_{\theta(u)}(\hat{r}^{*(u)})\}, \{s_{\phi(v)}(\tilde{r}^{*(v)})\}\rangle$, then*

$$PLQROWA(pl_s^{*1}(r), pl_s^{*2}(r), \cdots, pl_s^{*n}(r)) = pl_s^{*}(r) = \langle\{s_{\theta(u)}(\hat{r}^{*(u)})\}, \{s_{\phi(v)}(\tilde{r}^{*(v)})\}\rangle.$$

(2) *Monotonicity: let $pl_s^{*1}(r), pl_s^{*2}(r), \cdots, pl_s^{*n}(r)$ and $pl_s^{'*1}(r), pl_s^{'*2}(r), \cdots, pl_s^{'*n}(r)$ be two collections of adjusted PLQRONs, for all ι, $s_{\theta^\iota(u)} < s'_{\theta^\iota(u)}$ and $s_{\phi^\iota(v)} > s'_{\phi^\iota(v)}$, then*

$$PLQROWA(pl_s^{*1}(r), pl_s^{*2}(r), \cdots, pl_s^{*n}(r)) < PLQROWA(pl_s^{'*1}(r), pl_s^{'*2}(r), \cdots, pl_s^{'*n}(r)).$$

(3) *Boundedness: let $s_{\theta^\iota(+)} = \max_{u=1}^{U} s_{\theta^\iota(u)}$, $s_{\theta^\iota(-)} = \min_{u=1}^{U} s_{\theta^\iota(u)}$, $s_{\phi^\iota(+)} = \max_{v=1}^{V} s_{\phi^\iota(v)}$ and $s_{\phi^\iota(-)} = \min_{v=1}^{V} s_{\phi^\iota(v)}$, then*

$$\langle\{s_{\theta^\iota(-)}(\hat{r}^{*(u)})\}, \{s_{\phi^\iota(+)}(\tilde{r}^{*(v)})\}\rangle \le PLQROWA(pl_s^{*1}(r), pl_s^{*2}(r), \cdots, pl_s^{*n}(r)) \le \langle\{s_{\theta^\iota(+)}(\hat{r}^{*(u)})\}, \{s_{\phi^\iota(-)}(\tilde{r}^{*(v)})\}\rangle.$$

(1) For all ι, since $pl_s^{*\iota}(r) = pl_s^{*}(p) = \langle\{s_{\theta(u)}(\hat{r}^{*(u)})\}, \{s_{\phi(v)}(\tilde{r}^{*(v)})\}\rangle$, then

$$\begin{aligned} PLQROWA(pl_s^{*1}(r), pl_s^{*2}(r), \cdots, pl_s^{*n}(r)) &= \omega_1 pl_s^{*1}(r) \oplus \omega_2 pl_s^{*2}(r) \oplus \cdots \oplus \omega_n pl_s^{*n}(r) \\ &= \langle\{s_{(\rho^q - \rho^q \prod_{\iota=1}^n (1 - \frac{(\theta^\iota(u))^q}{\rho^q})^{\omega_\iota})^{\frac{1}{q}}}(\hat{r}^{*(u)})\}, \{s_{\prod_{\iota=1}^n \rho(\frac{\phi^\iota(v)}{\rho})^{\omega_\iota}}(\tilde{r}^{*(v)})\}\rangle \\ &= \langle\{s_{(\rho^q - \rho^q (1 - \frac{(\theta^\iota(u))^q}{\rho^q})^{\sum_{\iota=1}^n \omega_\iota})^{\frac{1}{q}}}(\hat{r}^{*(u)})\}, \{s_{\rho(\frac{\phi^\iota(v)}{\rho})^{\sum_{\iota=1}^n \omega_\iota}}(\tilde{r}^{*(v)})\}\rangle \\ &= \langle\{s_{(\rho^q - \rho^q (1 - \frac{(\theta(u))^q}{\rho^q}))^{\frac{1}{q}}}(\hat{r}^{*(u)})\}, \{s_{\rho(\frac{\phi(v)}{\rho})}(\tilde{r}^{*(v)})\}\rangle \\ &= \langle\{s_{\theta(u)}(\hat{r}^{*(u)})\}, \{s_{\phi(v)}(\tilde{r}^{*(v)})\}\rangle. \end{aligned}$$

Therefore $PLQROWA(pl_s^{*1}(r), pl_s^{*2}(r), \cdots, pl_s^{*n}(r)) = \langle\{s_{\theta(u)}(\hat{r}^{*(u)})\}, \{s_{\phi(v)}(\tilde{r}^{*(v)})\}\rangle$ is proved.

(2) For all ι, $s_{\theta^{\iota}(u)} < s'_{\theta^{\iota}(u)}$ and $s_{\phi^{\iota}(v)} > s'_{\phi^{\iota}(v)}$, then we have

$$s'_{1-\frac{\theta^{\iota}(u)}{\rho}} < s_{1-\frac{\theta^{\iota}(u)}{\rho}} \Rightarrow s_{(\rho-\rho\prod_{\iota=1}^{n}(1-(\frac{\theta^{\iota}(u)}{\rho})^{q})^{\omega_{\iota}})^{\frac{1}{q}}} < s'_{(\rho-\rho\prod_{\iota=1}^{n}(1-(\frac{\theta^{\iota}(u)}{\rho})^{q})^{\omega_{\iota}})^{\frac{1}{q}}}, s_{\prod_{\iota=1}^{n}(\phi^{\iota}(v))^{\omega_{\iota}}} > s'_{\prod_{\iota=1}^{n}(\phi^{\iota}(v))^{\omega_{\iota}}}.$$

Assume $PLQROWA(pl_s^{*1}(r), pl_s^{*2}(r), \cdots, pl_s^{*n}(r)) = pl_s(r)$ and $PLQROWA(pl_s^{'*1}(r), pl_s^{'*2}(r), \cdots, pl_s^{'*n}(r)) = pl_s'(r)$, by (1), we can get

$$A(pl_s^*(r)) = \sum_{u=1}^{\#U_\theta}(\frac{(\rho - \rho\cdot\prod_{\iota=1}^{n}(1-(\frac{\theta^{(u)}}{\rho})^{q})^{\omega_{\iota}})^{\frac{1}{q}}}{\rho}\cdot(\hat{r}^{*(u)}))^{q} - \sum_{v=1}^{\#V_\phi}(\frac{(\phi^{(v)})^{\omega_{\iota}}}{\rho}\cdot\tilde{r}^{*(v)})^{q};$$

$$A(pl_s^{'*}(r)) = \sum_{u=1}^{\#U_{\theta'}}(\frac{(\rho - \rho\cdot\prod_{\iota=1}^{n}(1-(\frac{\theta'^{(u)}}{\rho})^{q})^{\omega_{\iota}})^{\frac{1}{q}}}{\rho}\cdot(\hat{r}'^{*(u)}))^{q} - \sum_{v=1}^{\#V_{\phi'}}(\frac{(\phi'^{(v)})^{\omega_{\iota}}}{\rho}\cdot\tilde{r}'^{*(v)})^{q}.$$

Then we have $A(pl_s^*(r)) < A(pl_s^{'*}(r))$, that is $pl_s^*(r) < pl_s^{'*}(r)$.

Therefore $PLQROWA(pl_s^{*1}(r), pl_s^{*2}(r), \cdots, pl_s^{*n}(r)) < PLQROWA(pl_s^{'*1}(r), pl_s^{'*2}(r), \cdots, pl_s^{'*n}(r))$ is proved.

(3) For all ι, $s_{\theta^{\iota}(-)} \le s_{\theta^{\iota}(u)} \le s_{\theta^{\iota}(+)}, s_{\phi^{\iota}(-)} \le s_{\phi^{\iota}(v)} \le s_{\phi^{\iota}(+)}$, according to the properties (1) and (2), we can easily have

$$\langle\{s_{\theta^{\iota}(-)}(\hat{r}^{*(u)})\}, \{s_{\phi^{\iota}(+)}(\tilde{r}^{*(u)})\}\rangle \le PLQROWA(pl_s^{*1}(r), pl_s^{*2}(r), \cdots, pl_s^{*n}(r)) \le \langle\{s_{\theta^{\iota}(+)}(\hat{r}^{*(u)})\}, \{s_{\phi^{\iota}(-)}(\tilde{r}^{*(v)})\}\rangle.$$

Remark 2. *Especially, when* $\omega_\iota = \frac{1}{n}(\iota = 1, 2, \cdots, n)$*, the PLQROWA operator is reduced to a probabilistic linguistic q-rung orthopair averaging (PLQROA) operator:*

$$\begin{aligned} PLQROA(pl_s^{*1}(r), pl_s^{*2}(r), \cdots, pl_s^{*n}(r)) &= \frac{1}{n}pl_s^{*1}(r) \oplus \frac{1}{n}pl_s^{*2}(r) \oplus \cdots \oplus \frac{1}{n}pl_s^{*n}(r) \\ &= \langle\{s_{(\rho^{q}-\rho^{q}\prod_{\iota=1}^{n}(1-\frac{(\theta^{\iota}(u))^{q}}{\rho^{q}})^{\frac{1}{n}})^{\frac{1}{q}}}(\hat{r}^{*(u)})\}, \{s_{\prod_{\iota=1}^{n}\rho(\frac{\phi^{\iota}(v)}{\rho})^{\frac{1}{n}}}(\tilde{r}^{*(v)})\}\rangle. \end{aligned}$$

Definition 10. *Let* $\bar{S}_{[0,\rho]}$ $(\rho > 2g)$ *be a LTS,* $pl_s^{*\iota}(r) = \langle\{s_{\theta^{\iota}(u)}(\hat{r}^{*(u)})\}, \{s_{\phi^{\iota}(v)}(\tilde{r}^{*(v)})\}\rangle(\iota = 1, 2, \cdots, n;\ u = 1, 2, \cdots, U;\ v = 1, 2, \cdots, V)$ *is a collection of adjusted PLQRONs, where* $s_{\theta^{\iota}(u)}, s_{\phi^{\iota}(v)} \in \bar{S}_{[0,\rho]}$*, the probabilistic linguistic q-rung orthopair weighted geometric (PLQROWG) operator is given as follows:*

$$\begin{aligned} PLQROWG(pl_s^{*1}(r), pl_s^{*2}(r), \cdots, pl_s^{*n}(r)) &= (pl_s^{*1}(r))^{\omega_1} \oplus (pl_s^{*2}(r))^{\omega_2} \oplus \cdots \oplus (pl_s^{*n}(r))^{\omega_n} \\ &= \langle\{s_{\prod_{\iota=1}^{n}\rho(\frac{\theta^{\iota}(u)}{\rho})^{\omega_{\iota}}}(\hat{r}^{*(u)})\}, \{s_{(\rho^{q}-\rho^{q}\prod_{\iota=1}^{n}(1-\frac{(\phi^{\iota}(v))^{q}}{\rho^{q}})^{\omega_{\iota}})^{\frac{1}{q}}}(\tilde{r}^{*(v)})\}\rangle, \end{aligned} \tag{4}$$

where $\omega = (\omega_1, \omega_2, \cdots, \omega_n)^T$ *is the weight vector and satisfies with* $\sum_{\iota=1}^{n}\omega_\iota = 1 (0 \le \omega_\iota \le 1)$.

Theorem 4. *The PLQROWG operator satisfies the properties in Theorem 3.*

Proof. Because the proof is similar to Theorem 3, we omit it here. □

Remark 3. *Especially, when* $\omega_\iota = \frac{1}{n}(\iota = 1, 2, \cdots, n)$*, the PLQROWG operator is degenerated into the probabilistic linguistic q-rung orthopair geometric (PLQROG) operator*

$$\begin{aligned} PLQROG(pl_s^{*1}(r), pl_s^{*2}(r), \cdots, pl_s^{*n}(r)) &= (pl_s^{*1}(r))^{\frac{1}{n}} \otimes (pl_s^{*2}(r))^{\frac{1}{n}} \otimes \cdots \otimes (pl_s^{*n}(r))^{\frac{1}{n}} \\ &= \langle\{s_{\prod_{\iota=1}^{n}\rho(\frac{\theta^{\iota}(u)}{\rho})^{\frac{1}{n}}}(\hat{r}^{*(u)})\}, \{s_{(\rho^{q}-\rho^{q}\prod_{\iota=1}^{n}(1-\frac{(\phi^{\iota}(v))^{q}}{\rho^{q}})^{\frac{1}{n}})^{\frac{1}{q}}}(\tilde{r}^{*(v)})\}\rangle. \end{aligned}$$

Example 4. *Let $\bar{S} = \{s_\alpha | 0 \leq \alpha \leq 6\}$ be a LTS, $pl_s^1(r) = \langle\{s_2(1)\}, \{s_1(0.9), s_2(0.1)\}\rangle$, $pl_s^2(r) = \langle\{s_1(0.2), s_2(0.6), s_3(0.2)\}, \{s_1(0.9), s_2(0.1)\}\rangle$ and $pl_s^3(r) = \langle\{s_2(0.8), s_3(0.2)\}, \{s_0(0.3), s_1(0.5), s_2(0.2)\}\rangle$ be three PLQRONs, $\omega = (0.3, 0.5, 0.2)^T$ is the corresponding weight vector, then the calculation results of the PLQROWA and the PLQROWG are given as follows.*

Firstly, we adjust the corresponding probability distributions of $pl_s^1(r), pl_s^2(r)$ and $pl_s^3(r)$, the adjusted PLQRONs obtained as follows:

$$pl_s^{*1}(r) = \langle\{s_2(0.2), s_2(0.6), s_2(0.2)\}, \{s_1(0.3), s_1(0.5), s_1(0.1), s_2(0.1)\}\rangle;$$

$$pl_s^{*2}(r) = \langle\{s_1(0.2), s_2(0.6), s_3(0.2)\}, \{s_1(0.3), s_1(0.5), s_1(0.1), s_2(0.1)\}\rangle;$$

$$pl_s^{*3}(r) = \langle\{s_2(0.2), s_2(0.6), s_3(0.2)\}, \{s_0(0.3), s_1(0.5), s_2(0.1), s_2(0.1)\}\rangle.$$

If $q = 3$, according to the Formula (3), we can get

$$PLQROWA(pl_s^{*1}(r), pl_s^{*2}(r), pl_s^{*3}(r)) = \langle\{s_{(6^3 - 6^3\prod_{\iota=1}^3(1-\frac{(\theta^\iota(u))^3}{6^3})^{\omega_\iota})^{\frac{1}{3}}}(\hat{r}^{*(u)})\}, \{s_{\prod_{\iota=1}^3 6(\frac{\phi^\iota(v)}{6})^{\omega_\iota}}(\tilde{r}^{*(v)})\}\rangle$$

$$= \langle\{s_{(6^3-6^3(1-\frac{2^3}{6^3})^{0.5}(1-\frac{1^3}{6^3})^{0.5})^{\frac{1}{3}}}(0.2), s_{(6^3-6^3(1-\frac{2^3}{6^3})^1)^{\frac{1}{3}}}(0.6), s_{(6^3-6^3(1-\frac{2^3}{6^3})^{0.3}(1-\frac{3^3}{6^3})^{0.7})^{\frac{1}{3}}}(0.2)\},$$

$$\{s_{6(\frac{1}{6})^{0.8}(\frac{0}{6})^{0.2}}(0.3), s_{6(\frac{1}{6})^1}(0.5), s_{6(\frac{1}{6})^{0.8}(\frac{2}{6})^{0.2}}(0.1), s_{6(\frac{2}{6})^1}(0.1)\}\rangle$$

$$= \langle\{s_{1.65}(0.2), s_2(0.6), s_{2.98}(0.2)\}, \{s_0(0.3), s_1(0.5), s_{1.15}(0.1), s_2(0.1)\}\rangle.$$

If $q = 3$, according to the Formula (4), we can get

$$PLQROWG(pl_s^{*1}(r), pl_s^{*2}(r), pl_s^{*3}(r)) = \langle\{s_{\prod_{\iota=1}^3 6(\frac{\theta^\iota(u)}{6})^{\omega_\iota}}(\hat{r}^{*(u)})\}, \{s_{(6^3-6^3\prod_{\iota=1}^3(1-\frac{(\phi^\iota(v))^3}{6^3})^{\omega_\iota})^{\frac{1}{3}}}(\tilde{r}^{*(v)})\}\rangle$$

$$= \langle\{s_{6(\frac{1}{6})^{0.5}(\frac{2}{6})^{0.5}}(0.2), s_{6(\frac{2}{6})^1}(0.6), s_{6(\frac{2}{6})^{0.2}(\frac{3}{6})^{0.7}}(0.2)\}, \{s_{(6^3-6^3(1-\frac{1^3}{6^3})^{0.8}(1-\frac{(0)^3}{6^3})^{0.2})^{\frac{1}{3}}}(0.3), s_{(6^3-6^3(1-\frac{1^3}{6^3})^1)^{\frac{1}{3}}}(0.5),$$

$$s_{(6^3-6^3(1-\frac{1^3}{6^3})^{0.8}(1-\frac{2^3}{6^3})^{0.2})^{\frac{1}{3}}}(0.1), s_{(6^3-6^3(1-\frac{2^3}{6^3})^1)^{\frac{1}{3}}}(0.1)\}\rangle$$

$$= \langle\{s_{1.41}(0.2), s_2(0.6), s_{2.66}(0.2)\}, \{s_0(0.3), s_1(0.5), s_{1.34}(0.1), s_2(0.1)\}\rangle.$$

3.4. Distance Measures between PLQRONs

In order to compare the differences between different alternatives, we introduced the distance measure between PLQRONs, which is an important tool to process multi-attribute decision problems. In this subsection, we first propose the distance measures between PLQRONs.

Definition 11. *Let $\bar{S}_{[0,\rho]}$ $(\rho > 2g)$ be a LTS, $pl_s^{*1}(r) = \langle H_s^{*1}(\hat{r}), G_s^{*1}(\tilde{r})\rangle = \langle\{s_{\theta^1(u)}(\hat{r}^{*(u)})\}, \{s_{\phi^1(v)}(\tilde{r}^{*(v)})\}\rangle$ and $pl_s^{*2}(r) = \langle H_s^{*2}(\hat{r}), G_s^{*2}(\tilde{r})\rangle = \langle\{s_{\theta^2(u)}(\hat{r}^{*(u)})\}, \{s_{\phi^2(v)}(\tilde{r}^{*(v)})\}\rangle$ $(u = 1, 2, \cdots, U;\ v = 1, 2, \cdots, V)$ are two adjusted PLQRONs, where $s_{\theta^\iota(u)}, s_{\phi^\iota(v)} \in \bar{S}_{[0,\rho]}$ $(\iota = 1, 2)$, the Hamming distance measure D_{dhd} between $pl_s^{*1}(r)$ and $pl_s^{*2}(r)$ can be defined as:*

$$D_{dhd}(pl_s^{*1}(r), pl_s^{*2}(r)) = \sum_{u=1}^{\#U_\theta}(\hat{r}^{*(u)} \cdot \frac{|(\theta^{1(u)})^q - (\theta^{2(u)})^q|}{\rho^q}) + \sum_{v=1}^{\#V_\phi}(\tilde{r}^{*(v)} \cdot \frac{|(\phi^{1(v)})^q - (\phi^{2(v)})^q|}{\rho^q}), \tag{5}$$

where $q \geq 1$, $\theta^{\iota(u)}$ and $\phi^{\iota(v)}$ $(\iota = 1, 2)$ are the subscripts of $s_{\theta^\iota(u)}$ and $s_{\phi^\iota(v)}$ $(\iota = 1, 2)$, $\#U_\theta$ and $\#V_\phi$ represent the number of elements in $H_s^{*\iota}(\hat{r})$ and $G_s^{*\iota}(\tilde{r})$ $(\iota = 1, 2)$, respectively.

The Euclidean distance measure D_{ded} between $pl_s^{*1}(r)$ and $pl_s^{*2}(r)$ can be defined as follows:

$$D_{ded}(pl_s^{*1}(r), pl_s^{*2}(r)) = \sqrt{\sum_{u=1}^{\#U_\theta}(\hat{r}^{*(u)} \cdot \frac{|(\theta^{1(u)})^q - (\theta^{2(u)})^q|}{\rho^q})^2 + \sum_{v=1}^{\#V_\phi}(\tilde{r}^{*(v)} \cdot \frac{|(\phi^{1(v)})^q - (\phi^{2(v)})^q|}{\rho^q})^2}, \tag{6}$$

where $q \geq 1$, $\theta^{\iota(u)}$ and $\phi^{\iota(v)}$ $(\iota = 1,2)$ are the subscripts of $s_{\theta^{\iota(u)}}$ and $s_{\phi^{\iota(v)}}$ $(\iota = 1,2)$, $\#U_\theta$ and $\#V_\phi$ represent the number of elements in $H_s^{*\iota}(\hat{r})$ and $G_s^{*\iota}(\tilde{r})$ $(\iota = 1,2)$, respectively.

The generalized distance measure D_{dgd} between $pl_s^{*1}(r)$ and $pl_s^{*2}(r)$ can be defined as:

$$D_{dgd}(pl_s^{*1}(r), pl_s^{*2}(r)) = \sqrt[\lambda]{\sum_{u=1}^{\#U_\theta}(\hat{r}^{*(u)} \cdot \frac{|(\theta^{1(u)})^q - (\theta^{2(u)})^q|}{\rho^q})^\lambda + \sum_{v=1}^{\#V_\phi}(\tilde{r}^{*(v)} \cdot \frac{|(\phi^{1(v)})^q - (\phi^{2(v)})^q|}{\rho^q})^\lambda}, \tag{7}$$

where $\lambda > 0$, $q \geq 1$, $\theta^{\iota(u)}$ and $\phi^{\iota(v)}$ $(\iota = 1,2)$ are the subscripts of $s_{\theta^{\iota(u)}}$ and $s_{\phi^{\iota(v)}}$ $(\iota = 1,2)$, $\#U_\theta$ and $\#V_\phi$ represent the number of elements in $H_s^{*\iota}(\hat{r})$ and $G_s^{*\iota}(\tilde{r})$ $(\iota = 1,2)$, respectively.

Remark 4. *In particular, if $\lambda = 1$ or $\lambda = 2$, D_{dgd} is degenerated into D_{dhd} or D_{ded}, respectively.*

Theorem 5. *Assume $pl_s^{*1}(r)$ and $pl_s^{*2}(r)$ are two adjusted PLQRONs, the distance measure D_{dgd} satisfies the following properties:*

(1) *Non-negativity: $0 \leq D_{dgd}(pl_s^{*1}(r), pl_s^{*2}(r)) \leq 1$, $D_{dgd}(pl_s^{*1}(r), pl_s^{*1}(r)) = 0$;*
(2) *Symmetry: $D_{dgd}(pl_s^{*1}(r), pl_s^{*2}(r)) = D_{dgd}(pl_s^{*2}(r), pl_s^{*1}(r))$;*
(3) *Triangle inequality: $D_{dgd}(pl_s^{*1}(r), pl_s^{*2}(r)) + D_{dgd}(pl_s^{*2}(r), pl_s^{*3}(p)) \geq D_{dgd}(pl_s^{*1}(r), pl_s^{*3}(p))$.*

Obviously, D_{dgd} satisfies the property (1) and (2). The symmetry information can be expressed by the distance measure D_{dgd}.

The proof of property (3) is given as follows:

$$D_{dgd}(pl_s^{*1}(r), pl_s^{*3}(r)) = \sqrt[\lambda]{\sum_{u=1}^{\#U_\theta}(\hat{r}^{*(u)} \cdot \frac{|(\theta^{1(u)})^q - (\theta^{3(u)})^q|}{\rho^q})^\lambda + \sum_{v=1}^{\#V_\phi}(\tilde{r}^{*(v)} \cdot \frac{|(\phi^{1(v)})^q - (\phi^{3(v)})^q|}{\rho^q})^\lambda}$$

$$= \sqrt[\lambda]{\sum_{u=1}^{\#U_\theta}(\hat{r}^{*(u)} \cdot \frac{|(\theta^{1(u)})^q - (\theta^{2(u)})^q + (\theta^{2(u)})^q - (\theta^{3(u)})^q|}{\rho^q})^\lambda + \sum_{v=1}^{\#V_\phi}(\tilde{r}^{*(v)} \cdot \frac{|(\phi^{1(v)})^q - (\phi^{2(v)})^q + (\phi^{2(v)})^q - (\phi^{3(v)})^q|}{\rho^q})^\lambda}$$

$$\leq \sqrt[\lambda]{\sum_{u=1}^{\#U_\theta}(\hat{r}^{*(u)} \cdot \frac{|(\theta^{1(u)})^q - (\theta^{2(u)})^q| + |(\theta^{2(u)})^q - (\theta^{3(u)})^q|}{\rho^q})^\lambda + \sum_{v=1}^{\#V_\phi}(\tilde{r}^{*(v)} \cdot \frac{|(\phi^{1(v)})^q - (\phi^{2(v)})^q| + |(\phi^{2(v)})^q - (\phi^{3(v)})^q|}{\rho^q})^\lambda}$$

$$\leq \sqrt[\lambda]{\sum_{u=1}^{\#U_\theta}(\hat{r}^{*(u)} \cdot \frac{|(\theta^{1(u)})^q - (\theta^{2(u)})^q|}{\rho^q})^\lambda + \sum_{v=1}^{\#L_\phi}(\tilde{r}^{*(v)} \cdot \frac{|(\phi^{1(v)})^q - (\phi^{2(v)})^q|}{\rho^q})^\lambda} + \sqrt[\lambda]{\sum_{u=1}^{\#U_\theta}(\hat{r}^{*(u)} \cdot \frac{|(\theta^{2(u)})^q - (\theta^{3(u)})^q|}{\rho^q})^\lambda + \sum_{v=1}^{\#V_\phi}(\tilde{r}^{*(v)} \cdot \frac{|(\phi^{2(v)})^q - (\phi^{3(v)})^q|}{\rho^q})^\lambda}$$

$$= D_{dgd}(pl_s^{*1}(r), pl_s^{*2}(r)) + D_{dgd}(pl_s^{*2}(r), pl_s^{*3}(r)).$$

Therefore $D_{dgd}(pl_s^{*1}(r), pl_s^{*3}(r)) \leq D_{dgd}(pl_s^{*1}(r), pl_s^{*2}(r)) + D_{dgd}(pl_s^{*2}(r), pl_s^{*3}(r))$ is proved.

Example 5. *Assume $\bar{S} = \{s_\alpha | 0 \leq \alpha \leq 6\}$ is a LTS, $pl_s^{*1}(r) = \langle\{s_2(0.2), s_2(0.6), s_2(0.2)\}, \{s_3(0.4), s_4(0.1), s_4(0.3), s_5(0.2)\}\rangle$ and $pl_s^{*2}(r) = \langle\{s_1(0.2), s_2(0.6), s_3(0.2)\}, \{s_5(0.4), s_5(0.1), s_6(0.3), s_6(0.2)\}\rangle$ are two adjusted PLQRONs. If $q = 2$, the calculation result of $D_{dgd}(pl_s^{*1}(r), pl_s^{*2}(r))$ is given as follows:*

$$D_{dgd}(pl_s^{*1}(r), pl_s^{*2}(r)) = ((\frac{0.2 * |(2^2 - 1^2)|}{6^2})^\lambda + (\frac{0.6 * |(2^2 - 2^2)|}{6^2})^\lambda + (\frac{0.2 * |(2^2 - 3^2)|2}{6^2})^\lambda +$$

$$(\frac{0.4 * |(3^2 - 5^2)|}{6^2})^\lambda + (\frac{0.1 * |(4^2 - 5^2)|}{6^2})^\lambda + (\frac{0.3 * |(4^2 - 6^2)|}{6^2})^\lambda + (\frac{0.2 * |(5^2 - 6^2)|}{6^2})^\lambda)^{\frac{1}{\lambda}}.$$

If $\lambda = 1$, we can get $D_{dhd} = 0.475$. If $\lambda = 2$, we can get $D_{ded} = 0.2545$.

4. The Behavioral Decision Method

Since Hwang and Yoon [16] proposed the TOPSIS method, it has been widely applied in solving multiple criteria group decision making (MCGDM) problems. The traditional TOPSIS [17,18] method is an effective method in ranking the alternative. However, in practical decision making problems, the conditions in traditional TOPSIS method does not consider the behavior factors of decision makers. Thus, Yoon and Kim [23] introduced a behavioral TOPSIS method, which consider the behavioral tendency of decision makers and incorporate it into traditional TOPSIS method. However, in the uncertain decision making environment, how to represent the decision maker's behavior factors is a difficult problem. In order to solve this problem, we deal with it as follows. The gain can be viewed as the earns from taking the alternative instead of the anti-ideal solution, and the loss can be considered as the decision maker's pays from taking the alternative instead of the ideal solution, they can be expressed by the distance measure of related uncertain sets. So the behavioral TOPSIS method contains the loss aversion of decision maker in behavioral economics, and the decision maker can select the appropriate loss aversion ratio to express his/her choice preference. The method is proved to give a better choice than other methods (including traditional TOPSIS method) particularly in many fields, such as emergency decision making, selection for oil pipeline routes, etc., because the behavioral TOPSIS method precisely reflects the behavior tendency of decision maker.

Assume a group of experts $e = \{e_1, e_2, \dots, e_W\}$ evaluate a series of alternatives $Q = \{Q_1, Q_2, \dots, Q_m\}$ under the criteria $C = \{C_1, C_2, \dots, C_n\}$, let $\bar{S}_{[0,\rho]}$ $(\rho > 2g)$ be a continuous LTS, the evaluation of experts are represented in the form of PLQRONs $l_s^{o\iota}(r) = \langle H_s^{o\iota}(\hat{r}), G_s^{o\iota}(\tilde{r})\rangle$, where $H_s^{o\iota}(\hat{r}) = \{s_{\theta^{o\iota(u)}}(\hat{r}^{(u)}) | s_{\theta^{o\iota(u)}} \in \bar{S}_{[0,\rho]}, \hat{r}^{(u)} \geq 0, u = 1, 2, \cdots, U;$ $\sum_{u=1}^{U} \hat{r}^{(u)} \leq 1\}$ and $G_s^{o\iota}(\tilde{r}) = \{s_{\varphi^{o\iota(v)}}(\tilde{r}^{(v)}) | s_{\theta^{o\iota(v)}} \in \bar{S}_{[0,\rho]}, \tilde{r}^{(v)} \geq 0, v = 1, 2, \cdots, V; \sum_{v=1}^{V} \tilde{r}^{(v)} \leq 1\}, o = 1, 2, \dots, m; \iota = 1, 2, \dots, n$. The criteria's weight vector are $\omega_{c\iota} = (\omega_{c1}, \omega_{c2}, \dots, \omega_{cn})^T$, where $\sum_{\iota=1}^{n} \omega_{c\iota} = 1$ $(0 \leq \omega_{c\iota} \leq 1)$, the experts' weight vector are $\omega_{ew} = (\omega_{e1}, \omega_{e2}, \dots, \omega_{eW})^T$ $(\sum_{w=1}^{W} \omega_{ew} = 1,\ 0 \leq \omega_{ew} \leq 1)$, then the wth expert's decision matrix $F^{(w)}$ can be given as follows:

$$F^{(w)} = \begin{pmatrix} P_{11}^w & P_{12}^w & \cdots & P_{1n}^w \\ P_{21}^w & P_{22}^w & \cdots & P_{2n}^w \\ \vdots & \vdots & \ddots & \vdots \\ P_{m1}^w & P_{m2}^w & \cdots & P_{mn}^w \end{pmatrix},$$

where $P_{o\iota}^w = (P_s^{o\iota}(r))^w (o = 1, 2, \dots, m; \iota = 1, 2, \dots, n; w = 1, 2, \dots, W)$ are PLQRONs.

The steps of decision making are given as follows:

Step 1. Apply the adjustment method to adjust the probability distribution of PLQRONs, the adjusted decision matrix of the wth expert can be denoted as $F^{(*w)} = (P_s^{*o\iota}(r))_{m\times n}^w$.

Step 2. Apply the PLQROWA operator or PLQROWG operator to obtain the aggregated decision matrix $F^{(*)} = (Ps^{*o\iota}(r))_{m\times n}$. Furthermore, normalize the aggregated decision matrix $F^{(*)}$ based on the type of criteria. If it is a benefit-type criterion, there is no need to adjust; if it is a cost-type criterion, we need utilize the negation operator to normalize the decision matrix.

Step 3. Determine the ideal solution $Q^+ = \{Q_1^+, Q_2^+, \dots, Q_\iota^+\}$ and the anti-ideal solution $Q^- = \{Q_1^-, Q_2^-, \dots, Q_\iota^-\}$, respectively, where

$$Q_\iota^+ = \{\max_{o=1}^{m}\{pl_s^{*o\iota}(p)\}\},\ Q_\iota^- = \{\min_{o=1}^{m}\{pl_s^{*o\iota}(p)\}\}.$$

For the criterion C_ι, we apply the Formulas (1) and (2) to calculate Q^+ and Q^-.

Step 4. Utilize D_{dgd} to calculate the distance between each alternative and Q^+, Q^-, respectively. That is D_o^+ and D_o^-, where $D_o^+ = \sum_{\iota=1}^{n} \omega_{c\iota} D_{dgd}(Q_o, Q^+)$, and $D_o^- = \sum_{\iota=1}^{n} \omega_{c\iota} D_{dgd}(Q_o, Q^-)$.

Step 5. Calculate the value function V_o for alternative $Q_o (o = 1, 2, \dots, m)$.

$$V_o = (D_o^-)^\alpha + [-\gamma(D_o^+)^\beta], (0 \leq \alpha \leq 1, 0 \leq \beta \leq 1)$$

where γ is the decision maker's loss aversion ratio, if $\gamma > 1$, it implies the decision maker's behavior is more sensitive to losses than gains; if $\gamma = 1$, it implies the decision maker have neutral attitude towards losses or gains; if $\gamma < 1$, it means the decision maker's behavior is more sensitive to gains than losses; α and β reflects the decision maker's risk aversion attitudes and the risk seeking attitudes in decision process, respectively.

Step 6. The greater value of V_o, the better alternatives Q_o will be, then we can obtain the rank of the alternatives.

5. Numerical Example

Here we present a practical multiple criteria group decision making example about investment decision (Beg et al. [27]), and the behavioral TOPSIS method is utilized to deal with this problem. The advantages of the behavioral TOPSIS method with PLQROSs are highlighted by the comparison analysis with the traditional TOPSIS method. Furthermore, we analyzed the stability and sensitivity of decision makers' behavior.

5.1. Background

There are three investors e_1, e_2 and e_3, who want to invest the following three types of projects: real estate (Q_1), the stock market (Q_2) and treasury bills (Q_3). In order to decide which project to invest, they consider from the following attributes: the risk factor (C_1), the growth factor (C_2), the return rate (C_3) and the complexity of the document requirements (C_4). The weight vector of investors is $(0.3, 0.5, 0.2)^T$ and the criteria's weight vector is $(0.4, 0.2, 0.3, 0.1)^T$. The evaluation for the criterion C_1 is LTS $S_1 = \{s_0 : extreme\ low, s_1 : low, s_2 : slightly\ low, s_3 : generally, s_4 : slightly\ high, s_5 : high, s_6 : extreme\ high\}$, for the criteria C_ι $(\iota = 2, 3)$ is $S_\iota = \{s_0 : extreme\ slowly, s_1 : slowly, s_2 : slightly\ slowly, s_3 : generally, s_4 : slightly\ fast, s_5 : fast, s_6 : extreme\ fast\}$ $(\iota = 2, 3)$; and the evaluation for criterion C_4 is LTS $S_4 = \{s_0 : extreme\ easy, s_1 : easy, s_2 : slightly\ easy, s_3 : generally, s_4 : slightly\ complexity, s_5 : complexity, s_6 : extreme\ complexity\}$. Then, the decision matrices of each experts are expressed in Tables 1–3.

Table 1. The decision matrix $F^{(1)}$.

	C_1	C_2
Q_1	$\langle\{s_6(1)\}, \{s_0(1)\}\rangle$	$\langle\{s_4(0.4), s_5(0.6)\}, \{s_0(0.7), s_1(0.3)\}\rangle$
Q_2	$\langle\{s_4(0.7), s_5(0.3)\}, \{s_1(0.6), s_2(0.4)\}\rangle$	$\langle\{s_3(0.3), s_4(0.7)\}, \{s_1(0.5), s_2(0.5)\}\rangle$
Q_3	$\langle\{s_5(0.6), s_6(0.4)\}, \{s_0(0.5), s_1(0.5)\}\rangle$	$\langle\{s_1(0.5), s_2(0.5)\}, \{s_3(0.5), s_4(0.5)\}\rangle$
	C_3	C_4
Q_1	$\langle\{s_0(0.3), s_1(0.7)\}, \{s_2(0.4), s_3(0.6)\}\rangle$	$\langle\{s_1(0.7), s_2(0.3)\}, \{s_3(0.5), s_4(0.5)\}\rangle$
Q_2	$\langle\{s_3(0.3), s_4(0.7)\}, \{s_0(0.7), s_1(0.3)\}\rangle$	$\langle\{s_4(0.3), s_5(0.7)\}, \{s_1(0.5), s_2(0.5)\}\rangle$
Q_3	$\langle\{s_1(0.5), s_2(0.5)\}, \{s_3(0.7), s_4(0.3)\}\rangle$	$\langle\{s_4(0.3), s_5(0.7)\}, \{s_1(0.5), s_2(0.5)\}\rangle$

Table 2. The decision matrix $F^{(2)}$.

	C_1	C_2
Q_1	$\langle\{s_0(0.3), s_1(0.7)\}, \{s_2(0.4), s_3(0.6)\}\rangle$	$\langle\{s_4(0.7), s_5(0.3)\}, \{s_1(0.5), s_2(0.5)\}\rangle$
Q_2	$\langle\{s_3(0.3), s_4(0.7)\}, \{s_0(0.5), s_1(0.5)\}\rangle$	$\langle\{s_1(0.5), s_2(0.5)\}, \{s_3(0.5), s_4(0.5)\}\rangle$
Q_3	$\langle\{s_5(0.6), s_6(0.4)\}, \{s_0(1)\}\rangle$	$\langle\{s_3(0.5), s_4(0.5)\}, \{s_1(0.1), s_2(0.3), s_3(0.6)\}\rangle$
	C_3	C_4
Q_1	$\langle\{s_4(0.5), s_5(0.5)\}, \{s_0(0.7), s_1(0.3)\}\rangle$	$\langle\{s_5(0.7), s_6(0.3)\}, \{s_0(1)\}\rangle$
Q_2	$\langle\{s_4(0.3), s_5(0.7)\}, \{s_1(0.7), s_2(0.3)\}\rangle$	$\langle\{s_5(0.5), s_6(0.5)\}, \{s_0(1)\}\rangle$
Q_3	$\langle\{s_1(0.5), s_2(0.5)\}, \{s_2(0.2), s_3(0.6), s_4(0.2)\}\rangle$	$\langle\{s_4(0.5), s_5(0.5)\}, \{s_0(1)\}\rangle$

Table 3. The decision matrix $F^{(3)}$.

	C_1	C_2
Q_1	$\langle\{s_4(0.5), s_5(0.5)\}, \{s_0(0.4), s_1(0.6)\}\rangle$	$\langle\{s_5(0.7), s_6(0.3)\}, \{s_0(1)\}\rangle$
Q_2	$\langle\{s_1(0.5), s_2(0.5)\}, \{s_2(0.5), s_3(0.3), s_4(0.2)\}\rangle$	$\langle\{s_5(0.7), s_6(0.3)\}, \{s_0(1)\}\rangle$
Q_3	$\langle\{s_4(0.2), s_5(0.8)\}, \{s_1(0.7), s_2(0.3)\}\rangle$	$\langle\{s_4(0.6), s_5(0.4)\}, \{s_0(0.5), s_1(0.5)\}\rangle$
	C_3	C_4
	$\langle\{s_2(0.5), s_3(0.5), \}, \{s_3(0.5), s_4(0.5)\}\rangle$	$\langle\{s_0(0.3), s_1(0.7)\}, \{s_3(0.5), s_4(0.5)\}\rangle$
	$\langle\{s_4(0.4), s_5(0.6)\}, \{s_1(0.7), s_2(0.3)\}\rangle$	$\langle\{s_3(0.3), s_4(0.7)\}, \{s_1(0.5), s_2(0.5)\}\rangle$
	$\langle\{s_0(0.2), s_1(0.4), s_2(0.4)\}, \{s_2(0.4), s_3(0.6)\}\rangle$	$\langle\{s_6(1), \}, \{s_0(1)\}\rangle$

Where $F^{(w)}$ represents the wth investor's evaluation information.

5.2. The Behavioral TOPSIS Method

Step 1. According to the adjustment method, we adjust the probability distribution of decision matrices $F^{(1)}$, $F^{(2)}$ and $F^{(3)}$, and the corresponding adjusted matrices $F^{(*1)}$, $F^{(*2)}$ and $F^{(*3)}$ are given in Tables 4–6.

Table 4. The adjusted decision matrix $F^{(*1)}$.

	C_1	C_2
Q_1	$\langle\{s_6(0.3), s_6(0.2), s_6(0.5)\}, \{s_0(0.4), s_0(0.6)\}\rangle$	$\langle\{s_4(0.4), s_5(0.3), s_5(0.3)\}, \{s_0(0.5), s_0(0.2), s_1(0.3)\}\rangle$
Q_2	$\langle\{s_4(0.3), s_4(0.2), s_4(0.2), s_5(0.3)\}, \{s_1(0.5), s_1(0.1), s_2(0.2), s_2(0.2)\}\rangle$	$\langle\{s_3(0.3), s_4(0.2), s_4(0.2), s_4(0.3)\}, \{s_1(0.5), s_2(0.5)\}\rangle$
Q_3	$\langle\{s_5(0.2), s_5(0.4), s_6(0.4)\}, \{s_0(0.5), s_1(0.2), s_1(0.3)\}\rangle$	$\langle\{s_1(0.5), s_2(0.1), s_2(0.4)\}, \{s_3(0.1), s_3(0.3), s_3(0.1), s_4(0.5)\}\rangle$
	C_3	C_4
	$\langle\{s_0(0.3), s_1(0.2), s_1(0.5)\}, \{s_2(0.4), s_3(0.1), s_3(0.2), s_3(0.3)\}\rangle$	$\langle\{s_1(0.3), s_1(0.4), s_2(0.3)\}, \{s_3(0.5), s_4(0.5)\}\rangle$
	$\langle\{s_3(0.3), s_4(0.1), s_4(0.6)\}, \{s_0(0.7), s_0(0.3)\}\rangle$	$\langle\{s_4(0.3), s_5(0.2), s_5(0.5)\}, \{s_1(0.5), s_2(0.5)\}\rangle$
	$\langle\{s_1(0.2), s_1(0.3), s_2(0.1), s_2(0.4)\}, \{s_3(0.2), s_3(0.2), s_3(0.3), s_4(0.1), s_4(0.2)\}\rangle$	$\langle\{s_4(0.3), s_5(0.2), s_5(0.5)\}, \{s_1(0.5), s_2(0.5)\}\rangle$

Table 5. The adjusted decision matrix $F^{(*2)}$.

	C_1	C_2
Q_1	$\langle\{s_0(0.3), s_1(0.2), s_1(0.5)\}, \{s_2(0.4), s_3(0.6)\}\rangle$	$\langle\{s_4(0.4), s_4(0.3), s_5(0.3)\}, \{s_1(0.5), s_2(0.2), s_2(0.3)\}\rangle$
Q_2	$\langle\{s_3(0.3), s_4(0.2), s_4(0.2), s_4(0.3)\}, \{s_0(0.5), s_1(0.1), s_1(0.2), s_1(0.2)\}\rangle$	$\langle\{s_1(0.3), s_1(0.2), s_2(0.2), s_2(0.3)\}, \{s_3(0.5), s_4(0.5)\}\rangle$
Q_3	$\langle\{s_5(0.2), s_5(0.4), s_6(0.4)\}, \{s_0(0.5), s_0(0.2), s_0(0.3)\}\rangle$	$\langle\{s_3(0.5), s_4(0.1), s_4(0.4)\}, \{s_1(0.1), s_2(0.3), s_3(0.1), s_3(0.5)\}\rangle$
	C_3	C_4
	$\langle\{s_4(0.3), s_4(0.2), s_5(0.5)\}, \{s_0(0.4), s_0(0.1), s_0(0.2), s_1(0.3)\}\rangle$	$\langle\{s_5(0.3), s_5(0.4), s_6(0.3)\}, \{s_0(0.5), s_0(0.5)\}\rangle$
	$\langle\{s_4(0.3), s_5(0.1), s_5(0.6)\}, \{s_1(0.7), s_2(0.3)\}\rangle$	$\langle\{s_5(0.3), s_5(0.2), s_6(0.5)\}, \{s_0(0.5), s_0(0.5)\}\rangle$
	$\langle\{s_1(0.2), s_1(0.3), s_2(0.1), s_2(0.4)\}, \{s_2(0.4), s_3(0.2), s_3(0.3), s_3(0.1), s_4(0.2)\}\rangle$	$\langle\{s_4(0.3), s_4(0.2), s_5(0.5)\}, \{s_0(0.5), s_0(0.5)\}\rangle$

Table 6. The adjusted decision matrix $F^{(*3)}$.

	C_1	C_2
Q_1	$\langle\{s_2(0.3), s_4(0.2), s_5(0.5)\}, \{s_0(0.4), s_1(0.6)\}\rangle$	$\langle\{s_5(0.4), s_5(0.3), s_6(0.3)\}, \{s_0(0.5), s_0(0.2), s_1(0.3)\}\rangle$
Q_2	$\langle\{s_1(0.3), s_1(0.2), s_2(0.2), s_2(0.3)\}, \{s_2(0.5), s_3(0.1), s_3(0.2), s_4(0.2)\}\rangle$	$\langle\{s_5(0.3), s_5(0.2), s_5(0.2), s_6(0.3)\}, \{s_0(0.5), s_0(0.5)\}\rangle$
Q_3	$\langle\{s_4(0.2), s_5(0.4), s_5(0.4)\}, \{s_1(0.5), s_1(0.2), s_2(0.3)\}\rangle$	$\langle\{s_4(0.5), s_4(0.1), s_5(0.4)\}, \{s_0(0.1), s_0(0.3), s_0(0.1), s_1(0.5)\}\rangle$
	C_3	C_4
	$\langle\{s_2(0.3), s_2(0.2), s_3(0.5)\}, \{s_3(0.4), s_3(0.1), s_4(0.2), s_4(0.3)\}\rangle$	$\langle\{s_0(0.3), s_1(0.4), s_1(0.3)\}, \{s_3(0.5), s_4(0.5)\}\rangle$
	$\langle\{s_4(0.3), s_4(0.1), s_5(0.6)\}, \{s_1(0.7), s_2(0.3)\}\rangle$	$\langle\{s_3(0.3), s_4(0.2), s_4(0.5)\}, \{s_1(0.5), s_2(0.5)\}\rangle$
	$\langle\{s_0(0.2), s_1(0.3), s_1(0.1), s_2(0.4)\}, \{s_2(0.4), s_2(0.2), s_3(0.3), s_3(0.1), s_3(0.2)\}\rangle$	$\langle\{s_6(0.3), s_6(0.2), s_6(0.5)\}, \{s_0(0.5), s_0(0.5)\}\rangle$

Step 2. Firstly, we aggregate the adjusted decision matrices based on the PLQROWA operator. Then we normalize the aggregated matrix according to the type of criteria (criteria C_2 and C_3 belong to the benefit-type criteria, criterion C_1, C_4 belongs to the cost-type criteria). If $q = 2$, we can get the normalized decision matrix $F^{(*)}$ in Table 7.

Table 7. The aggregate decision matrix $F^{(*)}$.

	C_1
Q_1	$\langle\{s_0(0.4), s_0(0.6)\}, \{s_6(0.3), s_6(0.2), s_6(0.5)\}\rangle$
Q_2	$\langle\{s_0(0.5), s_{1.25}(0.1), s_{1.53}(0.2), s_{1.62}(0.2)\}, \{s_{3.16}(0.3), s_{3.69}(0.2), s_{3.75}(0.2), s_{4.2}(0.3)\}\rangle$
Q_3	$\langle\{s_0(0.5), s_0(0.2), s_0(0.3)\}, \{s_{4.86}(0.2), s_5(0.4), s_6(0.4)\}\rangle$
	C_2
	$\langle\{s_{4.27}(0.4), s_{4.6}(0.3), s_6(0.3)\}, \{s_0(0.5), s_0(0.2), s_{1.41}(0.3)\}\rangle$
	$\langle\{s_{3.21}(0.3), s_{3.54}(0.2), s_{3.68}(0.2), s_6(0.3)\}, \{s_0(0.5), s_0(0.5)\}\rangle$
	$\langle\{s_{2.92}(0.5), s_{3.6}(0.1), s_{3.95}(0.4)\}, \{s_0(0.1), s_0(0.3), s_0(0.1), s_{2.63}(0.5)\}\rangle$
	C_3
	$\langle\{s_{3.13}(0.3), s_{3.16}(0.2), s_{4.17}(0.5)\}, \{s_0(0.4), s_0(0.1), s_0(0.2), s_{1.83}(0.3)\}\rangle$
	$\langle\{s_{3.76}(0.3), s_{4.6}(0.1), s_{4.78}(0.6)\}, \{s_0(0.7), s_{1.62}(0.3)\}\rangle$
	$\langle\{s_{0.9}(0.2), s_1(0.3), s_{1.85}(0.1), s_2(0.4)\}, \{s_{2.26}(0.2), s_{2.77}(0.2), s_3(0.3), s_{3.27}(0.1), s_{3.78}(0.2)\}\rangle$
	C_4
	$\langle\{s_0(0.5), s_0(0.5)\}, \{s_{4.03}(0.3), s_{4.05}(0.4), s_6(0.3)\}\rangle$
	$\langle\{s_0(0.5), s_0(0.5)\}, \{s_{4.5}(0.3), s_{4.86}(0.2), s_6(0.5)\}\rangle$
	$\langle\{s_0(0.5), s_0(0.5)\}, s_6(0.3), s_6(0.2), s_6(0.5)\}\rangle$

Step 3. According to Definition 8, the score function matrix can be obtained as follows:

$$\mathbf{A} = \begin{bmatrix} -0.38 & 0.219 & 0.1478 & -0.2035 \\ -0.0939 & 0.1448 & 0.263 & -0.3269 \\ -0.2973 & 0.0841 & -0.0334 & -0.38 \end{bmatrix}.$$

Furthermore, we can obtain the ideal solution as follows:

$$Q^+ = \{\langle\{s_0(0.5), s_{1.25}(0.1), s_{1.53}(0.2), s_{1.62}(0.2)\}, \{s_{3.16}(0.3), s_{3.69}(0.2), s_{3.75}(0.2), s_{4.2}(0.3)\}\rangle, \langle\{s_{4.27}(0.4), s_{4.6}(0.3), s_6(0.3)\}, \{s_0(0.5), s_0(0.2), s_{1.41}(0.3)\}\rangle, \langle\{s_{3.76}(0.3), s_{4.6}(0.1), s_{4.78}(0.6)\}, \{s_0(0.7), s_{1.62}(0.3)\}\rangle, \langle\{s_0(0.5), s_0(0.5)\}, \{s_{4.03}(0.3), s_{4.05}(0.4), s_6(0.3)\}\rangle\},$$

The anti-ideal solution is given as follows:

$$Q^- = \{\langle\{s_0(0.4), s_0(0.6)\}, \{s_6(0.3), s_6(0.2), s_6(0.5)\}\rangle, \langle\{s_{2.92}(0.5), s_{3.6}(0.1), s_{3.95}(0.4)\}, \{s_0(0.1), s_0(0.3), s_0(0.1), s_{2.63}(0.5)\}\rangle, \langle\{s_{0.9}(0.2), s_1(0.3), s_{1.85}(0.1), s_2(0.4)\}, \{s_{2.26}(0.2), s_{2.77}(0.2), s_3(0.3), s_{3.27}(0.1), s_{3.78}(0.2)\}\rangle, \langle\{s_0(0.5), s_0(0.5)\}, s_6(0.3), s_6(0.2), s_6(0.5)\}\rangle\}.$$

Step 4. Calculate $D(Q_o, Q^+)$ an $D(Q_o, Q^-)(o = 1,2,3)$, respectively.

If $q = 2$, here we apply that the Euclidean distance measure D_{ded}, then $D_o^+ = \sum_{\iota=1}^{4} \omega_{c\iota} D_{ded}(Q_o, Q^+)$ and $D_o^- = \sum_{\iota=1}^{4} \omega_{c\iota} D_{ded}(Q_o, Q^-)$. So the separation measures between the alternative and the ideal/anti-ideal solution are obtained in Table 8.

Table 8. The separation measures for each alternative.

	Q_1	Q_2	Q_3
D_o^+	0.1561	0.0549	0.2055
D_o^-	0.1236	0.2626	0.0561

Step 5. Calculate the value function V_o about alternatives $Q_o(o = 1,2,3)$. Here the parameters α, β and γ are used to describe the decision maker's behavior tendency. Here we assume $\gamma = 2.25$, $\alpha = \beta = 0.88$ [28], then we have $V_1 = -0.2801$, $V_2 = 0.1334$, $V_3 = -0.4797$.

Step 6. According to the values of V_o, we have $Q_2 \succ Q_1 \succ Q_3$, so Q_2 is the best alternative.

Next, we consider the relationship between the decision conclusion and the change of parameter λ. We still take the PLQROWA operator as an example. Assume $q = 2$, $\alpha = \beta = 0.88$, $\gamma = 2.25$, and $\lambda = 2, 3, 5, 8, 10, 12$, respectively. The Figure 3 shows the corresponding ranking results (Table 9 shows the detailed calculation results). Obviously, the varies of value function V_o is not sensitive to the parameter λ, which indicates that the parameter λ has little effect on the decision results.

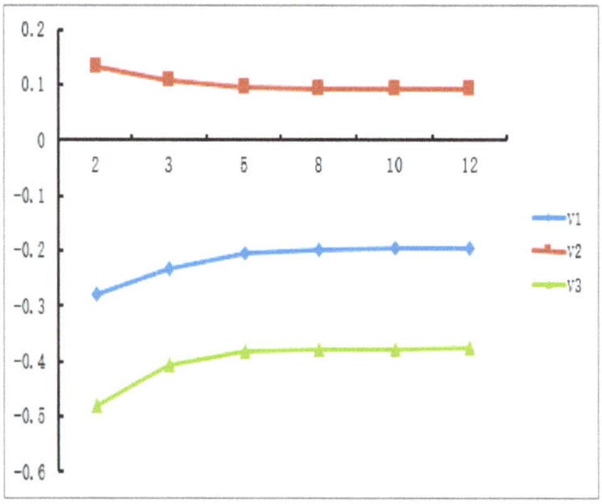

Figure 3. The results of change λ in behavioral TOPSIS method.

Table 9. The detailed results of parameter λ.

	$\lambda = 2$	$\lambda = 3$	$\lambda = 5$	$\lambda = 8$	$\lambda = 10$	$\lambda = 12$
V_1	-0.2801	-0.2335	-0.2056	-0.197	-0.1957	-0.1953
V_2	0.1334	0.1078	0.0959	0.0929	0.0925	0.0923
V_3	-0.4797	-0.4052	-0.3806	-0.3768	-0.3763	-0.3761

5.3. Comparison Analysis with Existed Method

Here, the traditional TOPSIS method is used to compare with the behavioral TOPSIS method, the algorithm steps [29] are given as follow.

Step 1. Adjust the probability distribution of PLQRONs, the corresponding matrices $F^{(*1)}$, $F^{(*2)}$ and $F^{(*3)}$ are obtained.

Step 2. Apply the PLQROWA operator to aggregate the evaluation information, then we normalize the aggregated decision matrix; the result is same as Section 5.2.

Step 3. Similarly, we can obtain the positive ideal solution Q^+ as follows:

$$Q^+ = \{\langle\{s_0(0.5), s_{1.25}(0.1), s_{1.53}(0.2), s_{1.62}(0.2)\}, \{s_{3.16}(0.3), s_{3.69}(0.2), s_{3.75}(0.2), s_{4.2}(0.3)\}\rangle, \langle\{s_{4.27}(0.4), s_{4.6}(0.3), s_6(0.3)\}, \{s_0(0.5), s_0(0.2), s_{1.41}(0.3)\}\rangle, \langle\{s_{3.76}(0.3), s_{4.6}(0.1), s_{4.78}(0.6)\}, \{s_0(0.7), s_{1.62}(0.3)\}\rangle, \langle\{s_0(0.5), s_0(0.5)\}, \{s_{4.03}(0.3), s_{4.05}(0.4), s_6(0.3)\}\rangle\}.$$

The anti-ideal solution Q^- is also obtained as follows:

$$Q^- = \{\langle\{s_0(0.4), s_0(0.6)\}, \{s_6(0.3), s_6(0.2), s_6(0.5)\}\rangle, \langle\{s_{2.92}(0.5), s_{3.6}(0.1), s_{3.95}(0.4)\}, \{s_0(0.1), s_0(0.3), s_0(0.1), s_{2.63}(0.5)\}\rangle, \langle\{s_{0.9}(0.2), s_1(0.3), s_{1.85}(0.1), s_2(0.4)\}, \{s_{2.26}(0.2), s_{2.77}(0.2), s_3(0.3), s_{3.27}(0.1), s_{3.78}(0.2)\}\rangle, \langle\{s_0(0.5), s_0(0.5)\}, s_6(0.3), s_6(0.2), s_6(0.5)\}\rangle\}.$$

Step 4. If $q = 2$, we apply D_{ded} to calculate the distance of each alternative between Q^+ and Q^-, the results are obtained in Table 10.

Table 10. The separation measures for each alternative.

	Q_1	Q_2	Q_3
D_o^+	0.1561	0.0549	0.2055
D_o^-	0.1236	0.2626	0.0561

Step 5. Calculate the closeness coefficient $R_o(o = 1,2,3)$,

$$R_o = \frac{D_o^-}{D_o^- + D_o^+}.$$

By calculation, we get $R_1 = 0.4419$, $R_2 = 0.8271$ and $R_3 = 0.2145$. So the ranking order of the alternatives is $Q_2 \succ Q_1 \succ Q_3$. The decision result is same as behavioral TOPSIS method, which shows the proposed method is effective.

Similarly, we consider the relationship between the decision result and the change of λ based on the traditional TOPSIS method. Here $q = 2$, $\alpha = \beta = 0.88$ and $\gamma = 2.25$, the parameter $\lambda = 2,3,5,8,10,12$, we apply the PLQROWA operator to calculate the closeness coefficient R_o of each alternative, Figure 4 shows the ranking results (Table 11 shows the detailed calculation results). As can be seen from Figure 4, the closeness coefficient R_o remains unchanged and the decision result is also tend to stable.

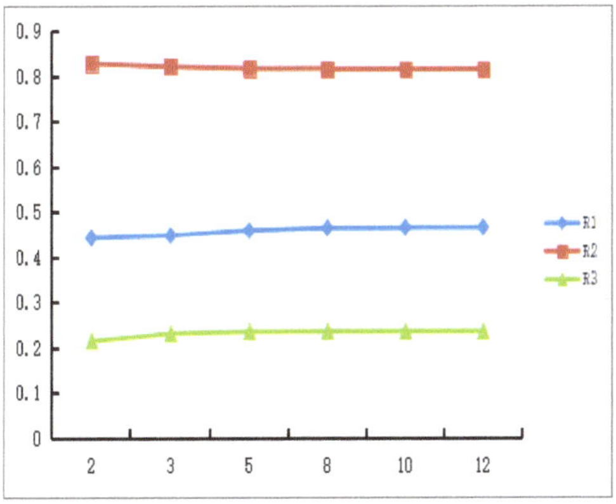

Figure 4. The results of change the parameter λ in traditional TOPSIS method.

Table 11. The detailed results with the parameter λ.

	$\lambda = 2$	$\lambda = 3$	$\lambda = 5$	$\lambda = 8$	$\lambda = 10$	$\lambda = 12$
R_1	0.4419	0.4472	0.4582	0.4635	0.4644	0.4647
R_2	0.8271	0.8202	0.8156	0.8142	0.814	0.814
R_3	0.2145	0.2306	0.2347	0.2349	0.235	0.2351

5.4. The Sensitivity of Decision Maker's Behavior

Here, we make the analysis of the influence of loss aversion parameter γ, the risk preference parameter α and β in the proposed behavioral TOPSIS method.

Firstly, the impact of the loss aversion parameter γ in the value function is considered. We take the PLQROWA operator as an example, if $q = 2$, $\alpha = \beta = 0.88$ and $\lambda = 2$, let $\gamma = 0.5, 0.8, 1, 2.25, 5$, the ranking results of the value function V_o are shown in Figure 5 (Table 12 shows the detailed calculation results). As can be seen from Figure 5, when $\gamma \leq 2.25$, the values of V_1, V_2 and V_3 are less sensitive to the change of the loss aversion parameter γ; while $\gamma > 2.25$, the values of $V_o(o = 1,2,3)$ is changing obviously. In comparison, the loss aversion parameter γ has a significant influence on V_2 and V_3. When $\gamma > 2.25$, the values of $V_o(o = 1,2,3)$ decrease sharply at the same time, which means if the parameter γ becomes larger, the loss aversion has a greater impact on the value function V_o.

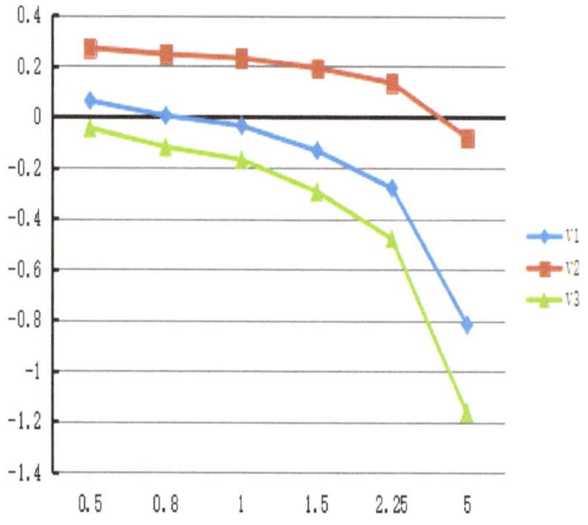

Figure 5. The results of changed loss aversion parameter γ.

Table 12. Preference ranking under various loss aversion parameter γ.

	Distance Measure		**Behavioral TOPSIS**											
			$\gamma = 0.5$		$\gamma = 0.8$		$\gamma = 1$		$\gamma = 1.5$		$\gamma = 2.25$		$\gamma = 5$	
	D_i^+	D_i^-	V_i	Rank	V_i	Rank	V_i	Rank	V_i	Rank	V_i	Rank	V_i	Rank
Q_1	0.1561	0.1236	0.0613	2	0.0028	2	−0.0362	2	−0.1338	2	−0.2801	2	−0.8167	2
Q_2	0.0549	0.2626	0.2695	1	0.2461	1	0.2306	1	0.1917	1	0.1334	1	−0.0805	1
Q_3	0.2055	0.0561	−0.0449	3	−0.1195	3	−0.1691	3	−0.2934	3	−0.4797	3	−1.1629	3

Next, we consider the influence of the risk preference parameters α and β in the value function, respectively. We take the PLQROWA operator as an example, suppose that $q = 2$, $\beta = 0.88$ and $\gamma = 2.25$, $\lambda = 2$, let $\alpha = 0.1, 0.3, 0.5, 0.8, 1$, the results of value functions change with the parameter α are shown in Figure 6. It is easy to know that the values of the function V_o $(o = 1,2,3)$ descend with the parameter α. We know Q_2 is always the best alternative from the Figure 6. If $\alpha > 0.88$, the values of v_o $(o = 1,2,3)$ also tend to stable.

Furthermore, assume that $q = 2, \alpha = 0.88, \gamma = 2.25$ and $\lambda = 2$, let $\beta = 0.1, 0.3, 0.5, 0.8, 1$, the results of value functions change with the parameter β are shown in Figure 7. Similarly, we know that the values of V_o $(o = 1,2,3)$ increase with the parameter β, and the best alternative remains unchanged. If $\beta > 0.88$, the values of V_o $(o = 1,2,3)$ tend to stable. In conclusion, the change of value function V_o is consistent with expert's risk preference, if the expert is risk averse, the parameter α increases, he/she is more sensitive to the loss, and the overall value functions are decreasing. If the decision maker is risk appetite, when the parameter β increases, he/she becomes more sensitive to gains, the overall value functions are increasing.

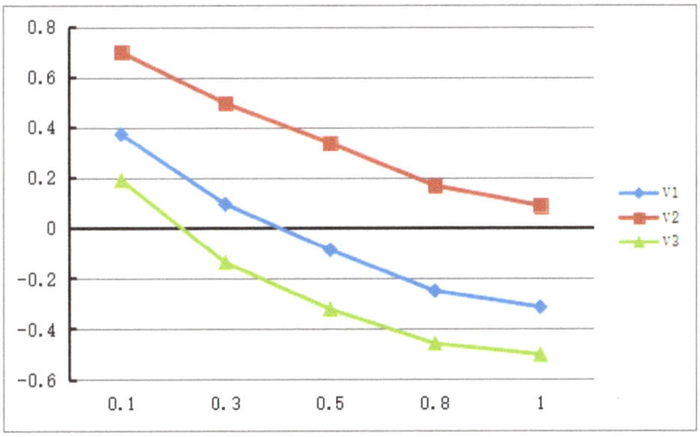

Figure 6. The results of change the risk preference parameter α.

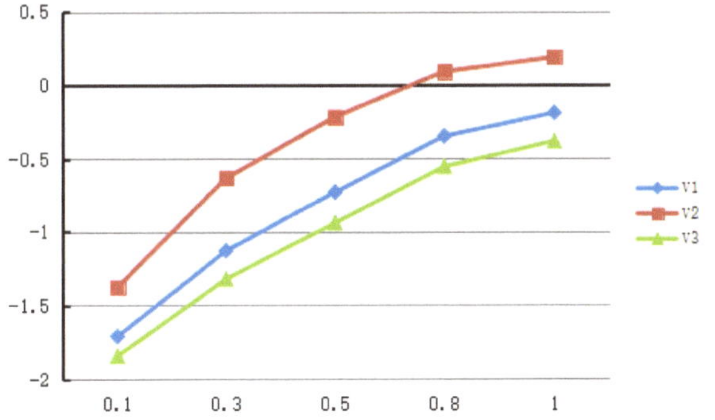

Figure 7. The results of change the risk preference parameter β.

According to the above comparison analyses, we can find that the proposed method has the following advantages. First, the behavioral TOPSIS method implements the decision maker's choice by adopting the gain and loss. Second, it has been demonstrated that the traditional TOPSIS method is a special case of the proposed behavioral TOPSIS method [23], while the behavioral TOPSIS method involves a wider range of situations. In addition, there are three parameters (α, β and γ) in the value function of V_o, the decision maker can choose the appropriate numerical value according to his/her risk preference and loss aversion, which makes the proposed behavioral TOPSIS method more flexible in practical application.

6. Conclusions

The main conclusions of the paper are given as follows:

(1) The operations of PLQROS are proposed based on the adjusted PLQROS with the same probability. Then we present the PLQROWA operator, PLQROWG operator and the distance measures between the PLQROSs based on the proposed operational laws.
(2) We develop the fuzzy behavior TOPSIS method to PLQROS, which consider the behavioral tendency in decision making process.
(3) We utilize a numerical example to demonstrate the validity and feasibility of the fuzzy behavior TOPSIS method, and we prove the superiority of the method by comparison with the traditional TOPSIS method.

Next, we will apply the proposed method to deal with the multi-attribute decision making problems, such as the emergency decision, supplier selection and investment decision, etc.

Author Contributions: Conceptualization, D.L. and A.H.; methodology, D.L. and Y.L.; writing, D.L. and A.H.; supervision, Z.L. All authors have read and agreed to the published version of the manuscript.

Funding: The research was funded by National Natural Science Foundation of China (11501191) and Hunan Postgraduate Scientific Research and Innovation project (CX20190812).

Institutional Review Board Statement: Not applicable.

Informed Consent Statement: Not applicable.

Data Availability Statement: The data used to support the findings of this study are included within the article.

Acknowledgments: We thank the editor and anonymous reviewers for their helpful comments on an earlier draft of this paper.

Conflicts of Interest: The authors declare no conflict of interest.

References

1. Zadeh, L.A. The concept of a linguistic variable and its application to approximate reasoning—I. *Inf. Sci.* **1975**, *8*, 199–249. [CrossRef]
2. Zadeh, L.A. The concept of a linguistic variable and its application to approximate reasoning—II. *Inf. Sci.* **1975**, *8*, 301–357. [CrossRef]
3. Zadeh, L.A. The concept of a linguistic variable and its application to approximate reasoning—III. *Inf. Sci.* **1975**, *9*, 43–80. [CrossRef]
4. Rodriguez, R.M.; Luis, M.; Francisco, H. Hesitant fuzzy linguistic term sets for decision making. *IEEE Trans. Fuzzy Syst.* **2012**, *20*, 109–119. [CrossRef]
5. Beg, I.; Rashid, T. TOPSIS for hesitant fuzzy linguistic term sets. *Int. J. Intell. Syst.* **2013**, *28*, 1162–1171. [CrossRef]
6. Liao, H.; Xu, Z.; Herrera-Viedma, E.; Herrera, F. Hesitant fuzzy linguistic term set and its application in decision making: A state of the art survey. *Int. J. Fuzzy Syst.* **2018**, *20*, 2084–2110. [CrossRef]
7. Liu, D.H.; Liu, Y.Y.; Chen, X.H. The new similarity measure and distance measure of a hesitant fuzzy linguistic term set based on a linguistic scale function. *Symmetry* **2018**, *10*, 367. [CrossRef]
8. Hai, W.; Xu, Z.; Zeng, X.J. Hesitant fuzzy linguistic term sets for linguistic decision making: Current developments, issues and challenges. *Inf. Fusion* **2018**, *43*, 1–12. [CrossRef]
9. Wu, Z.; Xu, J.; Jiang, X.; Zhong, L. Two MAGDM models based on hesitant fuzzy linguistic term sets with possibility distributions: VIKOR and TOPSIS. *Inf. Sci.* **2019**, *473*, 101–120. [CrossRef]
10. Kong, M.; Pei, Z.; Ren, F.; Hao, F. New operations on generalized hesitant fuzzy linguistic term Sets for linguistic decision making. *Int. J. Fuzzy Syst.* **2019**, *21*, 243–262. [CrossRef]
11. Liu, D.H.; Chen, X.H.; Peng, D. Distance measures for hesitant fuzzy linguistic sets and their applications in multiple criteria decision making. *Int. J. Fuzzy Syst.* **2018**, *20*, 2111–2121. [CrossRef]
12. Pang, Q.; Wang, H.; Xu, Z.S. Probabilistic linguistic term sets in multi-attribute group decision making. *Inf. Sci.* **2016**, *369*, 128–143. [CrossRef]
13. Chen, Z.C. An approach to multiple attribute group decision making based on linguistic intuitionistic fuzzy numbers. *Int. J. Comput. Intell. Syst.* **2015**, *8*, 747–760. [CrossRef]
14. Garg, H. Linguistic Pythagorean fuzzy sets and its applications in multiattribute decision-making process. *Int. J. Intell. Syst.* **2018**, *33*, 1234–1263. [CrossRef]
15. Yager, R.R. Generalized orthopair fuzzy sets. *IEEE Trans. Fuzzy Syst.* **2016**, *25*, 1222–1230.
16. Hwang, C.L.; Yoon, K. *Multiple Attribute Decision Making: Methods and Applications a State-of-the-Art Survey*; Springer: Berlin/Heidelberg, Germany, 2012. [CrossRef]
17. Lai, Y.J.; Liu, T.Y.; Hwang, C.L. TOPSIS for MODM. *Eur. J. Oper. Res.* **1994**, *76*, 486–500. [CrossRef]
18. Chen, C.T. Extensions of the TOPSIS for group decision-making under fuzzy environment. *Fuzzy Sets Syst.* **2000**, *114*, 1–9. [CrossRef]
19. Zyoud, S.H.; Fuchs-Hanusch, D. A bibliometric-based survey on AHP and TOPSIS techniques. *Expert Syst. Appl.* **2017**, *78*, 158–181. [CrossRef]
20. Liu, D.H.; Chen, X.H.; Peng, D. Cosine distance measure between neutrosophic hesitant fuzzy linguistic sets and its application in multiple criteria decision making. *Symmetry* **2018**, *10*, 602. [CrossRef]
21. Liu, D.H.; Chen, X.H.; Peng, D. Some cosine similarity measures and distance measures between q-rung orthopair fuzzy sets. *Int. J. Intell. Syst.* **2019**, *34*, 1572–1587. [CrossRef]

22. Liu, H.C.; Wang, L.E.; Li, Z.; Hu, Y.P. Improving risk evaluation in FMEA with cloud model and hierarchical TOPSIS method. *IEEE Trans. Fuzzy Syst.* **2019**, *27*, 84–95. [CrossRef]
23. Yoon, K.P.; Kim, W.K. The behavioral TOPSIS. *Expert Syst. Appl.* **2017**, *89*, 266–272. [CrossRef]
24. Xu, Z.S. A method based on linguistic aggregation operators for group decision making with linguistic preference relations. *Inf. Sci.* **2004**, *166*, 19–30. [CrossRef]
25. Liu, P.D.; Liu, W.Q. Multiple-attribute group decision-making based on power Bonferroni operators of linguistic q-rung orthopair fuzzy numbers. *Int. J. Intell. Syst.* **2019**, *34*, 652–689. [CrossRef]
26. Wu, X.; Liao, H.; Xu, Z.; Hafezalkotob, A.; Herrera, F. Probabilistic linguistic MULTIMOORA: A multi-attributes decision making method based on the probabilistic linguistic expectation function and the improved Borda rule. *IEEE Trans. Fuzzy Syst.* **2018**, *26*, 3688–3702.
27. Beg, I.; Rashid, T. Hesitant intuitionistic fuzzy linguistic term sets. *Notes Intuit. Fuzzy Sets* **2014**, *20*, 53–64. [CrossRef]
28. Tversky, A.; Kahneman, D. Advances in prospect theory: Cumulative representation of uncertainty. *J. Risk Uncertain.* **1992**, *5*, 297–323. [CrossRef]
29. Herrera, F.; Herrera-Viedma, E. Linguistic decision analysis: Steps for solving decision problems under linguistic information. *Fuzzy Sets Syst.* **2000**, *115*, 67–82.

Article

A New Representation of Semiopenness of *L*-fuzzy Sets in *RL*-fuzzy Bitopological Spaces

Ibtesam Alshammari [1], Omar H. Khalil [2,†] and A. Ghareeb [3,*,‡]

[1] Department of Mathematics, Faculty of Science, University of Hafr Al Batin, Hafr Al Batin 31991, Saudi Arabia; iealshamri@uhb.edu.sa or iealshamri@hotmail.com
[2] Department of Mathematics, Faculty of Science, Beni-Suef University, Beni-Suef 62521, Egypt; o.khalil@mu.edu.sa
[3] Department of Mathematics, Faculty of Science, South Valley University, Qena 83523, Egypt
* Correspondence: a.ghareeb@sci.svu.edu.eg or nasserfuzt@hotmail.com
† Current address: Department of Mathematics, Faculty of Science in Al-Zulfi, Majmaah University, Al Majmaah 11952, Saudi Arabia.
‡ Current address: Department of Mathematics, College of Science, Al-Baha University, Al-Baha 65799, Saudi Arabia.

Citation: Alshammari, I.; Khalil, O.H.; Ghareeb, A. A New Representation of Semiopenness of *L*-fuzzy Sets in *RL*-fuzzy Bitopological Spaces. *Symmetry* **2021**, *13*, 611. https://doi.org/10.3390/sym13040611

Academic Editor: José Carlos R. Alcantud

Received: 16 March 2021
Accepted: 2 April 2021
Published: 6 April 2021

Publisher's Note: MDPI stays neutral with regard to jurisdictional claims in published maps and institutional affiliations.

Copyright: © 2021 by the authors. Licensee MDPI, Basel, Switzerland. This article is an open access article distributed under the terms and conditions of the Creative Commons Attribution (CC BY) license (https://creativecommons.org/licenses/by/4.0/).

Abstract: In this paper, we introduce a new representation of semiopenness of *L*-fuzzy sets in *RL*-fuzzy bitopological spaces based on the concept of pseudo-complement. The concepts of pairwise *RL*-fuzzy semicontinuous and pairwise *RL*-fuzzy irresolute functions are extended and discussed based on the (i,j)-*RL*-semiopen gradation. Further, pairwise *RL*-fuzzy semi-compactness of an *L*-fuzzy set in *RL*-fuzzy bitopological spaces are given and characterized. As *RL*-fuzzy bitopology is a generalization of *L*-bitopology, *RL*-bitopology, *L*-fuzzy bitopology, and *RL*-fuzzy topology, the results of our paper are more general.

Keywords: *RL*-fuzzy bitopology; (i,j)-*RL*-semiopen gradation; pairwise *RL*-fuzzy semicontinuous; pairwise *RL*-fuzzy irresolute; pairwise *RL*-fuzzy semi-compactness

1. Introduction

In 1963, Levine [1] introduced the notion of semiopen set and its corresponding associated function in the realm of general topology. Afterwards, Azad [2] extended this notion and its related functions to the setting of *L*-topology. Thakur and Malviya [3] introduced and studied the concepts of (i,j)-semiopen and (i,j)-semiclosed *L*-fuzzy sets, pairwise fuzzy semicontinuous, and pairwise fuzzy semiopen functions in *L*-bitopology in the case of $L = [0,1]$. In [4], Shi introduced the notion of *L*-fuzzy semiopen and preopen gradations in *L*-fuzzy topological spaces. Furthermore, he introduced the notions of *L*-fuzzy semicontinuous functions, *L*-fuzzy precontinuous functions, *L*-fuzzy irresolute functions, and *L*-fuzzy pre-irresolute functions, and discussed some of their elementary properties. Shi's operators have been found very useful in defining other gradations and also in studying many topological characteristics. In 2011, Ghareeb [5] used *L*-fuzzy preopen operator to introduce the degree of pre-separatedness and the degree of preconnectedness in *L*-fuzzy topological spaces. Many characterizations of the degree of preconnectedness are discussed in *L*-fuzzy topological spaces. Later, Ghareeb [6] introduced the concept of *L*-fuzzy semi-preopen operator in *L*-fuzzy topological spaces and studied some of its properties. The concepts of *L*-fuzzy *SP*-compactness and *L*-fuzzy *SP*-connectedness in *L*-fuzzy pretopological spaces are introduced and studied [7]. Further, a new operator in *L*-fuzzy topology introduced in [8] to measure the **F**-openness of an *L*-fuzzy set in *L*-fuzzy topological spaces. Moreover, the new operator is used to introduce a new form of **F**-compactness. Recently, we used the new operators to generalize several kinds of functions between *L*-fuzzy topological spaces [9–12].

Recently, Li and Li [13] defined and studied the concept of RL-topology as an extension of L-topology. Moreover, RL-compactness by means of an inequality and RL-continuous mapping are introduced and discussed in detail. In [14], they presented RL-fuzzy topology on an L-fuzzy set as a generalization of RL-topology and L-fuzzy topology. Some relevant properties of RL-fuzzy compactness in RL-fuzzy topological spaces are further investigated. Later on, Zhang et al. [15] defined the degree of Lindelöf property and the degree of countable RL-fuzzy compactness of an L-fuzzy set, where L is a complete DeMorgan algebra. Since L-fuzzy topology in the sense of Kubiak and Šostak is a special case of RL-fuzzy topology, the degree of RL-fuzzy compactness and the degree of Lindelöf property are extensions of the corresponding degrees in L-fuzzy topology.

The purpose of this paper is to introduce the (i,j)-RL-semiopen gradation in RL-fuzzy bitopological spaces based on the concept of pseudo-complement of L-fuzzy sets. We also define and characterize pairwise RL-fuzzy semicontinuous, pairwise RL-fuzzy irresolute functions, and pairwise RL-fuzzy semi-compactness. Our results are more general than those of the corresponding notions in L-bitopology, RL-bitopology, RL-fuzzy topology, L-fuzzy topology, and L-fuzzy bitopology.

2. Preliminaries

In this section, we give some basic preliminaries required for this paper. By $(L, \bigvee, \bigwedge, ')$, we denote a complete DeMorgan algebra [16,17] (i.e., L is a completely distributive lattice with an order reversing involution $'$, where $\bigvee$ and $\bigwedge$ are join and meet operations, respectively), $X \neq \emptyset$ is a set, and L^X is the family of each L-fuzzy sets defined on X. The largest and the smallest members in L and L^X are denoted by $\top$, $\bot$, and $\top_X$, $\bot_X$, respectively. For each any two L-fuzzy sets $B \in L^X$, $C \in L^Y$, and any mapping $f : X \longrightarrow Y$, we define $f_L^{\rightarrow}(B)(y) = \bigvee\{B(x) : f(x) = y\}$ for all $y \in Y$ and $f_L^{\leftarrow}(C)(x) = \bigvee\{B(x) : f_L^{\rightarrow}(B) \leq C\} = C(f(x))$ for all $x \in X$. For each $\alpha, \beta \in L$, $\alpha \prec \beta$ means that the element α is wedge below β in L [18], i.e., $\alpha \prec \beta$ if for every arbitrary subset $\mathcal{D} \subseteq L$, $\bigvee \mathcal{D} \geq \beta$ implies $\alpha \leq \gamma$ for some $\gamma \in \mathcal{D}$. An element $\alpha \in L$ is said to be co-prime if $\alpha \leq \beta \vee \gamma$ implies that $\alpha \leq \beta$ or $\alpha \leq \gamma$ and α is said to be prime if and only if α' is co-prime. The family of non-zero co-prime (resp. non-unit prime) members in L is denoted by $J(L)$ (resp. $P(L)$). By $\boldsymbol{\alpha}(\beta) = \bigvee\{\alpha \in L : \alpha \prec \beta\}$ and $\boldsymbol{\beta}(\beta) = \bigvee\{\alpha \in L : \alpha' \prec \beta'\}$, we denote the greatest minimal family and the greatest maximal family of β, respectively. $\boldsymbol{\alpha}^*(\alpha) = \boldsymbol{\alpha}(\alpha) \cap J(L)$ and $\boldsymbol{\beta}^*(\alpha) = \boldsymbol{\beta}(\alpha) \cap P(L)$ for all $\alpha \in L$.

An L-fuzzy set $A \in L^X$ is called *valuable* if $A \not\leq A'$. The collection of valuable L-fuzzy sets on X is denoted by $\mathscr{V}_X^L$. In other words, $\mathscr{V}_X^L = \{A \in L^X : A \not\leq A'\}$. For each $A \in \mathscr{V}_X^L$, we define the collection $\mathscr{F}_X^L(A)$ by $\mathscr{F}_X^L(A) = \{B \in L^X : B \leq A\}$. In fact, $\mathscr{F}_X^L(A)$ introduces the powerset of L-fuzzy set $A \in L^X$. Let $A \in \mathscr{V}_X^L$ and $B \in \mathscr{V}_Y^L$, the restriction of $f_L^{\rightarrow}$ on A, i.e., $f_L^{\rightarrow}|_A : \mathscr{F}_X^L(A) \longrightarrow L^Y$ provided that $D \in \mathscr{F}_X^L(A) \mapsto f_L^{\rightarrow}(D)$, is said to be the restriction of L-fuzzy function (RL-fuzzy function, in short) from A to B, given by $f_{L,A}^{\rightarrow} : A \longrightarrow B$ if $f_L^{\rightarrow}(A) \leq B$. The inverse of an L-fuzzy set $C \in \mathscr{F}_Y^L(B)$ under $f_{L,A}^{\rightarrow}$ is defined by $f_{L,A}^{\leftarrow}(C) = \bigvee\{D \in \mathscr{F}_X^L(A) : f_L^{\rightarrow}(D) \leq C\}$. It is clear that $f_{L,A}^{\leftarrow}(C) = A \wedge f_L^{\leftarrow}(C)$. The *pseudo-complement* of B relative to A [13,14], denoted by $\langle_L^A B$, is given by:

$$\langle_L^A B = \begin{cases} A \wedge B', & \text{if } B \neq A, \\ \bot_X, & \text{if } B = A. \end{cases}$$

where $A \in \mathscr{V}_X^L$ and $B \in \mathscr{F}_X^L(A)$. Some properties of pseudo-complement operation $\langle_L^A$ are listed in the following proposition:

Proposition 1. *[13,14] If $A \in \mathscr{V}_X^L$, $B, C \in \mathscr{F}_X^L(A)$, and $\{B_i\}_{i\in I} \subseteq \mathscr{F}_X^L(A)$, then:*

(1) $\langle_L^A B = A$ *if and only if* $B \leq A'$.
(2) $B \leq C$ *implies* $\langle_L^A C \leq \langle_L^A B$.
(3) $\langle_L^A \bigwedge_{i\in I} B_i = \bigvee_{i\in I} \langle_L^A B_i$.

(4) $\langle_L^A \bigvee_{i\in I} B_i \leq \bigwedge_{i\in I} \langle_L^A B_i$ *and* $\langle_L^A \bigvee_{i\in I} B_i = \bigwedge_{i\in I} \langle_L^A B_i$ *if* $\bigvee_{i\in I} B_i \neq A$.

Lemma 1. *[13] Let* $A \in \mathscr{V}_X^L$, $B \in \mathscr{V}_Y^L$, $f_{L,A}^{\rightarrow} : A \longrightarrow B$ *be RL-fuzzy function, and* $D \in \mathscr{F}_X^L(A)$. *Then for any* $\mathcal{U} \subseteq \mathscr{F}_X^L(A)$, *we have*

$$\bigvee_{y\in Y} \left(f_{L,A}^{\rightarrow}(D)(y) \wedge \bigwedge_{E\in\mathcal{U}} E(y) \right) = \bigvee_{x\in X} \left(D(x) \wedge \bigwedge_{E\in\mathcal{U}} f_{L,A}^{\leftarrow}(E)(x) \right).$$

Equivalently [15],

$$\bigwedge_{y\in Y} \left(\langle_L^A f_{L,A}^{\rightarrow}(D)(y) \vee \bigvee_{E\in\mathcal{P}} E(y) \right) = \bigwedge_{x\in X} \left(\langle_L^A D(x) \vee \bigvee_{E\in\mathcal{P}} f_{L,A}^{\leftarrow}(E)(x) \right).$$

An L-topology [16,17,19] (L-t, for short) τ is a subfamily of L^X which contains $\perp_X$, $\top_X$ and is closed for any suprema and finite infima. Moreover, (X, τ) is called an L-topological space on X. Further, members of τ are called open L-fuzzy sets and their complements are called closed L-fuzzy sets. A mapping $f : (X, \tau_1) \longrightarrow (Y, \tau_2)$ is called L-continuous if and only if $f_L^{\leftarrow}(C) \in \tau_1$ for any $C \in \tau_2$. The notion of L-topology was generalized by Kubiak [20] and Šostak [21] independently as follows:

Definition 1. *[20–22] An L-fuzzy topology on the set X is the function* $\tau : L^X \longrightarrow L$, *which satisfies the following conditions:*

(O1) $\tau(\perp_X) = \tau(\top_X) = \top$.
(O2) $\tau(A \wedge B) \geq \tau(A) \wedge \tau(B)$, *for each* $A, B \in L^X$.
(O3) $\tau(\bigvee_{i\in I} A_i) \geq \bigwedge_{i\in I} \tau(A_i)$, *for each* $\{A_i\}_{i\in I} \subseteq L^X$.

The pair (X, τ) *is called an L-fuzzy topological space (L-fts, for short). The value* $\tau(A)$ *and* $\tau^*(A) = \tau(A')$ *represent the degree of openness and the degree of closeness of an L-fuzzy set A, respectively. A function* $f : (X, \tau_1) \longrightarrow (Y, \tau_2)$ *is called L-fuzzy continuous iff* $\tau_1(f_L^{\leftarrow}(C)) \geq \tau_2(C)$ *for any* $C \in L^Y$.

One of the attempts to generalize L-topological spaces was the definition of RL-topology $\varkappa$ on an L-fuzzy set A by Li and Li [13] as follows:

Definition 2. *[13] Let* $A \in \mathscr{V}_X^L$. *A relative L-topology (RL-t, for short)* $\varkappa$ *on an L-fuzzy set A, is a subfamily of* $\mathscr{F}_X^L(A)$, *that satisfies the following statements:*

(1) $A \in \varkappa$ *and* $B \in \varkappa$, *for each* $B \leq A'$.
(2) $B_1 \wedge B_2 \in \varkappa$, *for any* $B_1, B_2 \in \varkappa$.
(3) $\bigvee_{i\in I} B_i \in \varkappa$, *for any* $\{B_i\}_{i\in I} \subseteq \varkappa$.

The pair $(A, \varkappa)$ *is said to be a relative L-topological space on A (RL-ts, for short). The elements of* $\varkappa$ *are called relative open L-fuzzy sets (RL-open fuzzy set, for short) and an L-fuzzy set B is called relative L-closed fuzzy set (RL-closed fuzzy set, for short) if and only if* $\langle_L^A B \in \varkappa$. *The collection of all RL-closed fuzzy sets with respect to* $\varkappa$ *is denoted by* $\langle_L^A \varkappa$, *i.e.,* $\langle_L^A \varkappa = \{C : \langle_L^A C \in \varkappa\}$. *Let* $A \in \mathscr{V}_X^L$, $B \in \mathscr{V}_Y^L$, *and* $(A, \varkappa_1)$, $(B, \varkappa_2)$ *be two RL-ts's. The relative L-fuzzy function* $f_{L,A}^{\rightarrow} : A \longrightarrow B$ *is said to be an RL-continuous iff* $f_{L,A}^{\leftarrow}(C) \in \langle_L^A \varkappa_1$ *for any* $C \in \langle_L^A \varkappa_2$. *Equivalently,* $f_{L,A}^{\rightarrow} : A \longrightarrow B$ *is said to be an RL-continuous iff* $f_{L,A}^{\leftarrow}(C) \in \varkappa_1$ *for any* $C \in \varkappa_2$. *A triple* $(A, \varkappa_1, \varkappa_2)$ *consisting of an L-fuzzy set* $A \in \mathscr{V}_X^L$ *endowed with RL-topologies* $\varkappa_1$ *and* $\varkappa_2$ *on A is called an RL-bitopological space (RL-bts, for short). For any* $B \in \mathscr{F}_X^L(A)$, $\varkappa_i$*-RL-open (resp. closed) fuzzy set refers to the open (resp. closed) L-fuzzy set in* $(A, \varkappa_i)$, *for* $i = 1, 2$. *It is clear that we get L-topology and L-bitopology as a special case if* $A = \top_X$.

The following two definitions extend the notions of (strong) β_α-cover, Q_α-cover, (strong) α-shading, (strong) α-remote collection [23] to the setting of RL-topological spaces:

Definition 3. *For any $A \in \mathscr{V}_X^L$, RL-topology $\varkappa$ on A, $B \in \mathscr{F}_X^L(A)$, and $\alpha \in L_\perp$, a collection $\mathcal{U} \subseteq \mathscr{F}_X^L(A)$ is called:*

(1) *$\boldsymbol{\beta}_\alpha$-cover of B if for any $x \in X$, it follows that $\alpha \in \boldsymbol{\beta}(\langle_L^A B(x) \vee \bigvee_{A \in \mathcal{U}} A(x))$ and $\mathcal{U}$ is called strong $\boldsymbol{\beta}_\alpha$-cover of B if $a \in \boldsymbol{\beta}(\bigwedge_{x \in X}(\langle_L^A B(x) \vee \bigvee_{A \in \mathcal{U}} A(x)))$.*
(2) *Q_α-cover of B if for any $x \in X$, it follows that $\langle_L^A B(x) \vee \bigvee_{A \in \mathcal{U}} A(x) \geq \alpha$.*

Definition 4. *For any $A \in \mathscr{V}_X^L$, RL-topology $\varkappa$ on A, $\alpha \in L_\top$ and $B \in \mathscr{F}_X^L(A)$, a collection $\mathcal{A} \subseteq \mathscr{F}_X^L(A)$ is called:*

(1) *α-shading of B if for any $x \in X$, $(\langle_L^A B(x) \vee \bigvee_{A \in \mathcal{A}} A(x)) \not\leq \alpha$.*
(2) *strong α-shading of B if $\bigwedge_{x \in X}(\langle_L^A B(x) \vee \bigvee_{A \in \mathcal{A}} A(x)) \not\leq \alpha$.*
(3) *α-remote collection of B if for any $x \in X$, $(B(x) \wedge \bigwedge_{D \in \mathcal{A}} D(x)) \not\geq \alpha$.*
(4) *strong α-remote collection of B if $\bigvee_{x \in X}(B(x) \wedge \bigwedge_{D \in \mathcal{A}} D(x)) \not\geq \alpha$.*

Theorem 1. *[13] For any RL-ts $(A, \varkappa)$, the following statements are true:*

(1) *$A \in \langle_L^A \varkappa$ and $B \in \langle_L^A \varkappa$ for all $B \leq A'$.*
(2) *$B_1 \vee B_2 \in \langle_L^A \varkappa$ for each $B_1, B_2 \in \langle_L^A \varkappa$,*
(3) *$\bigwedge_{i \in I} B_i \in \langle_L^A \varkappa$ for each $\{B_i : i \in I\} \subseteq \langle_L^A \varkappa$.*

Definition 5. *[14] Let $A \in \mathscr{V}_X^L$. An RL-fuzzy topology on A is a function $\varkappa : \mathscr{F}_X^L(A) \longrightarrow L$ such that $\varkappa$ satisfying the following conditions:*

($\mathcal{R}$1) *$\varkappa(A) = \top$, for each $B \leq A'$, $\varkappa(B) = \top$.*
($\mathcal{R}$2) *$\varkappa(B_1 \wedge B_2) \geq \varkappa(B_1) \wedge \varkappa(B_2)$, for each $B_1, B_2 \in \mathscr{F}_X^L(A)$.*
($\mathcal{R}$3) *$\varkappa(\bigvee_{i \in I} B_i) \geq \bigwedge_{i \in I} \varkappa(B_i)$, for each $\{B_i\}_{i \in I} \subseteq \mathscr{F}_X^L(A)$.*

The pair $(A, \varkappa)$ is said to be an RL-fuzzy topological space (RL-fts, for short) on A. For any $B \in \mathscr{F}_X^L(A)$, the gradation $\varkappa(B)$ (resp. $\varkappa(\langle_L^A B)$) can be viewed as the openness degree (resp. closeness degree) of B relative to $\varkappa$, respectively. Further, $\varkappa(B) = \top$ (resp. $\varkappa(\langle_L^A B) = \top$) confirms the RL-openness (resp. RL-closeness) of an L-fuzzy set B. Obviously if $A = \top_X$, then RL-fuzzy topology on A degenerates into Kubiak-Šostak's L-fuzzy topology, that is, RL-fuzzy topology on A is a generalization of L-fuzzy topology. If $(A, \varkappa)$ is an RL-topological space and $\chi_\varkappa : \mathscr{F}_X^L(A) \longrightarrow L$ is a function given by $\chi_\varkappa(B) = \top$ if $B \in \varkappa$, and $\chi_\varkappa(B) = \perp$ if $B \notin \varkappa$, then $(A, \chi_\varkappa)$ represents a special RL-fts, i.e., $(A, \varkappa)$ can also be seen as RL-fts.

Theorem 2. *[14] For each $A \in \mathscr{V}_X^L$ and RL-fts $(A, \varkappa)$ on A. The function $\langle_L^A \varkappa : \mathscr{F}_X^L(A) \longrightarrow L$ given by $\langle_L^A \varkappa(B) = \varkappa(\langle_L^A B)$ for any $B \in \mathscr{F}_X^L(A)$, satisfies the following conditions:*

(1) *$\langle_L^A \varkappa(A) = \top$, for each $B \leq A'$, $\langle_L^A \varkappa(B) = \top$.*
(2) *$\langle_L^A \varkappa(B_1 \vee B_2) \geq \langle_L^A \varkappa(B_1) \wedge \langle_L^A \varkappa(B_2)$, for each $B_1, B_2 \in \mathscr{F}_X^L(A)$.*
(3) *$\langle_L^A \varkappa(\bigwedge_{i \in I} B_i) \geq \bigwedge_{i \in I} \langle_L^A \varkappa(B_i)$, for each $\{B_i\}_{i \in I} \subseteq \mathscr{F}_X^L(A)$.*

$\langle_L^A \varkappa$ is said to be an RL-fuzzy cotopology (RL-cft, for short) on A and the pair $(A, \langle_L^A \varkappa)$ is said to be an RL-fuzzy cotopological space (RL-cfts, for short).

Definition 6. *[14] Let $A \in \mathscr{V}_X^L$, $B \in \mathscr{V}_Y^L$, and $(A, \varkappa_1)$, $(B, \varkappa_2)$ be two RL-fuzzy topological spaces on A and B, respectively. The relative L-fuzzy function $f_{L,A} : A \longrightarrow B$ is said to be an RL-fuzzy continuous iff*

$$\varkappa_1(f_{L,A}^{\leftarrow}(C)) \geq \varkappa_1(C),$$

equivalently,

$$\varkappa_1(\langle_L^A f_{L,A}^{\leftarrow}(C)) \geq \varkappa_1(\langle_L^B C),$$

for each $C \in \mathscr{F}_Y^L(B)$. *If* $(A, \langle_L^A \varkappa_1)$ *and* $(B, \langle_L^B \varkappa_2)$ *are the associated RL-fuzzy cotopological spaces of* $(A, \varkappa_1)$ *and* $(B, \varkappa_2)$ *respectively, then* $f_{L,A}^{\rightarrow}$ *is said to be an RL-fuzzy continuous iff*

$$\langle_L^A \varkappa_1(f_{L,A}^{\leftarrow}(C)) \geq \langle_L^B \varkappa_2(C),$$

for each $C \in \mathscr{F}_X^L(B)$.

Shi [24] introduced L-fuzzy closure operators in L-fuzzy topological spaces. In the following definition, we introduce its equivalent form in RL-fuzzy topological spaces.

Definition 7. *Let* $A \in \mathscr{V}_X^L$, *and* $(A, \varkappa)$ *be an RL-fts on A. The function* $Cl^{\varkappa} : \mathscr{F}_X^L(A) \to L^{J(\mathscr{F}_X^L(A))}$ *defined by*

$$Cl^{\varkappa}(B)(x_\lambda) = \bigwedge_{x_\lambda \not\leq D \geq B} \langle_L^A \Big(\varkappa(\langle_L^A D)\Big)$$

for each $x_\lambda \in J(\mathscr{F}_X^L(A))$ *and* $B \in \mathscr{F}_X^L(A)$ *is called an RL-fuzzy closure operator induced by* $\varkappa$.

Definition 8. *[14] For any* $A \in \mathscr{V}_X^L$ *and an RL-fts* $(A, \varkappa)$ *on A, an L-fuzzy set* $B \in \mathscr{F}_X^L(A)$ *is called an RL-fuzzy compact with respect to* $\varkappa$ *if for any* $\mathcal{P} \subseteq \mathscr{F}_X^L(A)$, *the following inequality holds:*

$$\bigvee_{D \in \mathcal{P}} \varkappa(\langle_L^A D) \vee \bigvee_{x \in X} \Big(B(x) \wedge \bigwedge_{D \in \mathcal{P}} D(x)\Big) \geq \bigwedge_{\mathcal{R} \in 2^{\mathcal{P}}} \bigvee_{x \in X} \Big(B(x) \wedge \bigwedge_{D \in \mathcal{R}} D(x)\Big).$$

Theorem 3. *[14] If* $A = \top_X$, *then following statements hold:*

(1) $\langle_L^A B = B'$, $B \in \mathscr{F}_X^L(A) \Leftrightarrow B \in L^X$.
(2) *RL-fuzzy compactness is reduced to L-fuzzy compactness.*
(3) *B is RL-fuzzy compact if and only if B is L-fuzzy compact.*

Theorem 4. *[14] For any* $A \in \mathscr{V}_X^L$ *and an RL-ft* $\varkappa$ *on A, we have following conclusions:*

(1) *If* $B_1, B_2 \in \mathscr{F}_X^L(A)$ *and* B_1, B_2 *are RL-fuzzy compact, then* $B_1 \vee B_2$ *is RL-fuzzy compact.*
(2) *If* $B_1, B_2 \in \mathscr{F}_X^L(A)$ *such that* B_1 *is an RL-fuzzy compact and* B_2 *is an RL-closed fuzzy set, then* $B_1 \wedge B_2$ *is an RL-fuzzy compact.*

3. The Gradation of Semiopenness in *RL*-fuzzy Bitopological Spaces

A system $(A, \varkappa_1, \varkappa_2)$ consisting of an L-fuzzy set $A \in \mathscr{V}_X^L$ with two RL-fuzzy topologies $\varkappa_1$ and $\varkappa_2$ on A is called an RL-fuzzy bitopological space. Throughout this paper i, $j = 1, 2$ where $i \neq j$ and if P is any topological property then $\varkappa_i$-P refers to the property P with respect to the RL-fuzzy topology $\varkappa_i$. An L-fuzzy set $B \in \mathscr{F}_X^L(A)$ of an RL-bitopological space $(A, \varkappa_l, \varkappa_2)$ is called an (i, j)-RL-semiopen if there exists an L-fuzzy set $C \in \varkappa_i$ such that $C \leq B \leq Cl^{\varkappa_j}(C)$.

Definition 9. *Let* $A \in \mathscr{V}_X^L$ *and* $(A, \varkappa_1, \varkappa_2)$ *be an RL-fuzzy bitopological space on A. For any* $B \in \mathscr{F}_X^L(A)$, *define a function* (i, j)-$\mathcal{S} : \mathscr{F}_X^L(A) \to L$ *by*

$$(i,j)\text{-}\mathcal{S}(B) = \bigvee_{C \leq B} \left\{ \varkappa_i(C) \wedge \bigwedge_{x_\lambda \prec B} \bigwedge_{x_\lambda \not\leq D \geq C} \langle_L^A \Big(\varkappa_j(\langle_L^A D)\Big) \right\}.$$

Then (i, j)-$\mathcal{S}(B)$ *is called an* (i, j)-*RL-semiopenness gradation of B induced by* $\varkappa_i$ *and* $\varkappa_j$ *such that* $i \neq j$, *where* (i, j)-$\mathcal{S}(B)$ *represents the degree to which B is* (i, j)-*RL-semiopen and* (i, j)-$\mathcal{S}^*(B) = (i, j)$-$\mathcal{S}(\langle_L^A B)$ *represents the degree to which B is* (i, j)-*RL-semiclosed.*

Based on the above definition and Definition 7, we can state the following corollary:

Corollary 1. *Let $A \in \mathscr{V}_X^L$ and $(A, \varkappa_1, \varkappa_2)$ be an RL-fuzzy bitopological space on A. Then for each $B \in \mathscr{F}_X^L(A)$, we have*

$$(i,j)\text{-}\mathcal{S}(B) = \bigvee_{C \leq B} \left\{ \varkappa_i(C) \wedge \bigwedge_{x_\lambda \prec B} Cl^{\varkappa_j}(C)(x_\lambda) \right\}.$$

Theorem 5. *Let $A \in \mathscr{V}_X^L$, $\varkappa_1, \varkappa_2 : \mathscr{F}_X^L(A) \to \{\bot, \top\}$ be RL-topologies on A, and $(i,j)\text{-}\mathcal{S} : \mathscr{F}_X^L(A) \to \{\bot, \top\}$ be the gradation of (i,j)-RL-semiopenness induced by $\varkappa_i$ and $\varkappa_j$ such that $i \neq j$. Then $(i,j)\text{-}\mathcal{S}(B) = \top$ iff B is an (i,j)-RL-semiopen.*

Proof. The proof can be obtained simply from the following inequality:

$$\begin{aligned}
(i,j)\text{-}\mathcal{S}(B) = \top \quad & \text{iff } \bigvee_{C \leq B} \left\{ \varkappa_i(C) \wedge \bigwedge_{x_\lambda \prec B} Cl^{\varkappa_j}(C)(x_\lambda) \right\} = \top \\
& \text{iff } \exists C \leq B \text{ such that } \varkappa_i(C) = \top \text{ and } \bigwedge_{x_\lambda \prec B} Cl^{\varkappa_j}(C)(x_\lambda) = \top \\
& \text{iff } \exists C \leq B \text{ such that } \varkappa_i(C) = \top \text{ and for each } x_\lambda \prec B,\ Cl^{\varkappa_j}(C)(x_\lambda) = \top \\
& \text{iff } \exists C \in \varkappa_i \text{ such that } C \leq B \leq Cl^{\varkappa_j}(C) \\
& \text{iff } B \text{ is } (i.j)\text{-}RL\text{-semiopen.}
\end{aligned}$$

□

Theorem 6. *Let $A \in \mathscr{V}_X^L$, $(A, \varkappa_1, \varkappa_2)$ be an RL-fuzzy bitopological space on A, and $(i,j)\text{-}\mathcal{S}$ be the gradation of (i,j)-RL-semiopenness induced by $\varkappa_i$ and $\varkappa_j$ such that $i \neq j$. Then for each $B \in \mathscr{F}_X^L(A)$, we have $\varkappa_i(B) \leq (i,j)\text{-}\mathcal{S}(B)$.*

Proof. The proof can be obtained simply from the following inequality:

$$\begin{aligned}
(i,j)\text{-}\mathcal{S}(B) & = \bigvee_{C \leq B} \left\{ \varkappa_i(C) \wedge \bigwedge_{x_\lambda \prec B} Cl^{\varkappa_j}(C)(x_\lambda) \right\} \geq \varkappa_i(B) \wedge \bigwedge_{x_\lambda \prec B} Cl^{\varkappa_j}(B)(x_\lambda) \\
& = \varkappa_i(B) \wedge \top = \varkappa_i(B).
\end{aligned}$$

□

Corollary 2. *Let $A \in \mathscr{V}_X^L$, $(A, \varkappa_1, \varkappa_2)$ be an RL-fuzzy bitopological space on A, and $(i,j)\text{-}\mathcal{S}$ be the gradation of (i,j)-RL-semiopenness induced by $\varkappa_i$ and $\varkappa_j$ such that $i \neq j$. Then for each $B \in \mathscr{F}_X^L(A)$, we have $\langle_L^A \varkappa_i(B) \leq (i,j)\text{-}\mathcal{S}^*(B)$.*

Theorem 7. *If $A \in \mathscr{V}_X^L$, $(A, \varkappa_1, \varkappa_2)$ be an RL-fuzzy bitopological space on A, and $(i,j)\text{-}\mathcal{S}$ be the gradation of (i,j)-RL-semiopenness induced by $\varkappa_i$ and $\varkappa_j$ such that $i \neq j$, then $(i,j)\text{-}\mathcal{S}\left(\bigvee_{i \in I} B_i\right)$ $\geq \bigwedge_{i \in I} (i,j)\text{-}\mathcal{S}(B_i)$ for each $\{B_i\}_{i \in I} \subseteq \mathscr{F}_X^L(A)$.*

Proof. Let $\alpha \in L$ and $\alpha \prec \bigwedge_{i \in I} (i,j)\text{-}\mathcal{S}(B_i)$, then there exists $C_i \leq B_i$ such that $\alpha \prec \varkappa_i(C_i)$ and $\alpha \prec \bigwedge_{x_\lambda \prec B_i} \bigwedge_{x_\lambda \not\leq D \geq C_i} \langle_L^A(\varkappa_j(\langle_L^A D))$ for any $i \in I$. Hence $\alpha \leq \bigwedge_{i \in I} \varkappa_i(C_i) \leq \varkappa_i\left(\bigvee_{i \in I} C_i\right)$ and $\alpha \leq \bigwedge_{i \in I} \bigwedge_{x_\lambda \prec B_i} \bigwedge_{x_\lambda \not\leq D \geq C_i} \langle_L^A(\varkappa_j(\langle_L^A D))$. Since $\{x_\lambda : x_\lambda \prec \bigvee_{i \in I} B_i\} = \bigcup_{i \in I} \{x_\lambda : x_\lambda \prec B_i\}$, we have

$$(i,j)\text{-}\mathcal{S}\left(\bigvee_{i \in I} B_i\right) = \bigvee_{C \leq \bigvee_{i \in I} B_i} \left\{ \varkappa_i(C) \wedge \bigwedge_{x_\lambda \prec \bigvee_{i \in I} B_i} \bigwedge_{x_\lambda \not\leq D \geq C} \langle_L^A\left(\varkappa_j(\langle_L^A D)\right) \right\}$$

$$\geq \varkappa_i\left(\bigvee_{i\in I} C_i\right) \wedge \bigwedge_{i\in I} \bigwedge_{x_\lambda \prec B_i} \bigwedge_{x_\lambda \not\leq D \geq \bigvee_{i\in I} C_i} \langle_L^A\left(\varkappa_j(\langle_L^A D)\right)$$
$$\geq \varkappa_i\left(\bigvee_{i\in I} C_i\right) \wedge \bigwedge_{i\in I} \bigwedge_{x_\lambda \prec B_i} \bigwedge_{x_\lambda \not\leq D \geq C_i} \langle_L^A\left(\varkappa_j(\langle_L^A D)\right)$$
$$\geq \alpha.$$

This shows that $(i,j)\text{-}\mathcal{S}\left(\bigvee_{i\in I} B_i\right) \geq \bigwedge_{i\in I} (i,j)\text{-}\mathcal{S}(B_i)$. □

Corollary 3. *Let $A \in \mathscr{V}_X^L$, $(A, \varkappa_1, \varkappa_2)$ be an RL-fuzzy bitopological space on A, and (i,j)-$\mathcal{S}$ be the gradation of (i,j)-RL-semiopenness induced by $\varkappa_i$ and $\varkappa_j$ such that $i \neq j$. Then $(i,j)\text{-}\mathcal{S}^*\left(\bigwedge_{i\in I} B_i\right) \geq \bigwedge_{i\in I} (i,j)\text{-}\mathcal{S}^*(B_i)$ for any $\{B_i\}_{i\in I} \subseteq \mathscr{F}_X^L(A)$.*

4. Pairwise Fuzzy Semicontinuous Functions Between RL-fuzzy Bitopological Spaces

Let $A \in \mathscr{V}_X^L$, $B \in \mathscr{V}_Y^L$, and $(A, \varkappa_1, \varkappa_2)$, $(B, \varkappa_1^*, \varkappa_2^*)$ be RL-fbts's on A and B, respectively. An RL-fuzzy function $f_{L,A} : A \longrightarrow B$ is said to be pairwise RL-fuzzy continuous (resp. open) iff $f_{L,A} : (A, \varkappa_1) \longrightarrow (B, \varkappa_1^*)$ and $f_{L,A} : (A, \varkappa_2) \longrightarrow (B, \varkappa_2^*)$ are RL-fuzzy continuous (resp. open).

Definition 10. *Let $A \in \mathscr{V}_X^L$, $B \in \mathscr{V}_Y^L$, $(A, \varkappa_1, \varkappa_2)$ and $(B, \varkappa_1^*, \varkappa_2^*)$ be RL-fbts's on A and B, respectively, and (i,j)-$\mathcal{S}_1$, (i,j)-$\mathcal{S}_2$ their corresponding gradations of (i,j)-RL-semiopenness. An RL-fuzzy function $f_{L,A} : A \longrightarrow B$ is called:*

(1) *pairwise RL-fuzzy semicontinuous iff $\varkappa_i^*(C) \leq (i,j)\text{-}\mathcal{S}_1(f_{L,A}^{\leftarrow}(C))$ holds for each $C \in \mathscr{F}_X^L(B)$.*
(2) *pairwise RL-fuzzy irresolute iff $(i,j)\text{-}\mathcal{S}_2(C) \leq (i,j)\text{-}\mathcal{S}_1(f_{L,A}^{\leftarrow}(C))$ holds for each $C \in \mathscr{F}_X^L(B)$.*

Corollary 4. *Let $A \in \mathscr{V}_X^L$, $B \in \mathscr{V}_Y^L$, $(A, \varkappa_1, \varkappa_2)$ and $(B, \varkappa_1^*, \varkappa_2^*)$ be RL-fbts's on A and B, respectively, and (i,j)-$\mathcal{S}_1$, (i,j)-$\mathcal{S}_2$ their corresponding gradations of (i,j)-RL-semiopenness. Then:*

(1) *$f_{L,A}$ is pairwise RL-fuzzy semicontinuous iff $\langle_L^B \varkappa_i^*(C) \leq (i,j)\text{-}\mathcal{S}_1^*(f_{L,A}^{\leftarrow}(C))$ for each $C \in \mathscr{F}_X^L(B)$.*
(2) *$f_{L,A}$ is pairwise RL-fuzzy irresolute iff $(i,j)\text{-}\mathcal{S}_2^*(C) \leq (i,j)\text{-}\mathcal{S}_1^*(f_{L,A}^{\leftarrow}(C))$ for each $C \in \mathscr{F}_X^L(B)$.*

Theorem 8. *Let $A \in \mathscr{V}_X^L$, $B \in \mathscr{V}_Y^L$, $(A, \varkappa_1, \varkappa_2)$ and $(B, \varkappa_1^*, \varkappa_2^*)$ be RL-fbts's on A and B, respectively, and (i,j)-$\mathcal{S}_1$, (i,j)-$\mathcal{S}_2$ their corresponding gradations of (i,j)-RL-semiopenness. Then:*

(1) *$f_{L,A} : (A, \varkappa_1, \varkappa_2) \to (B, \varkappa_1^*, \varkappa_2^*)$ is pairwise RL-fuzzy semicontinuous iff $f_{L,A} : (A, \varkappa_{1[\alpha]}, \varkappa_{2[\alpha]}) \to (B, \varkappa^*_{1[\alpha]}, \varkappa^*_{2[\alpha]})$ is pairwise RL-semicontinuous for each $\alpha \in J(L)$.*
(2) *$f_{L,A} : (A, \varkappa_1, \varkappa_2) \to (B, \varkappa_1^*, \varkappa_2^*)$ is pairwise RL-fuzzy irresolute iff $f_{L,A} : (A, \varkappa_{1[\alpha]}, \varkappa_{2[\alpha]}) \to (B, \varkappa^*_{1[\alpha]}, \varkappa^*_{2[\alpha]})$ is pairwise RL-irresolute for each $\alpha \in J(L)$.*

Proof.

(1) Let $C \in \varkappa^*_{i[\alpha]}$ for each $C \in \mathscr{F}_X^L(B)$ and $\alpha \in J(L)$, then $\varkappa_i^*(C) \geq \alpha$. Since $f_{L,A} : (A, \varkappa_1, \varkappa_2) \to (B, \varkappa_1^*, \varkappa_2^*)$ is pairwise RL-fuzzy semicontinuous, then $(i,j)\text{-}\mathcal{S}_1(f_{L,A}^{\leftarrow}(C)) \geq \varkappa_i^*(C) \geq \alpha$, i.e., $(i,j)\text{-}\mathcal{S}_1(f_{L,A}^{\leftarrow}(C)) \geq \alpha$. Therefore $f_{L,A}^{\leftarrow}(C)$ is (i,j)-RL-semiopen L-fuzzy set in $(A, \varkappa_{1[\alpha]}, \varkappa_{2[\alpha]})$. Hence $f_{L,A} : (A, \varkappa_{1[\alpha]}, \varkappa_{2[\alpha]}) \to (B, \varkappa^*_{1[\alpha]}, \varkappa^*_{2[\alpha]})$ is pairwise RL-semicontinuous function.

Conversely, let $\varkappa_i^*(C) \geq \alpha$ for each $C \in \mathscr{F}_X^L(B)$ and $\alpha \in J(L)$, then $C \in \varkappa^*_{i\,[\alpha]}$. By the pairwise semicontinuity of $f_{L,A} : (A, \varkappa_{1[\alpha]}, \varkappa_{2[\alpha]}) \rightarrow (B, \varkappa^*_{1\,[\alpha]}, \varkappa^*_{2\,[\alpha]})$, we have $f^{\leftarrow}_{L,A}(C)$ is (i,j)-RL-semiopen with respect to $(A, \varkappa_{1[\alpha]}, \varkappa_{2[\alpha]})$. Accordingly, (i,j)-$\mathcal{S}_1(f^{\leftarrow}_{L,A}(C)) \geq \alpha$ for each $\alpha \in J(L) \cap J(\varkappa_i^*(C))$, where $J(\varkappa_i^*(C)) = \{\alpha \in J(L) | \alpha \leq \varkappa_i^*(C)\}$. It follows that (i,j)-$\mathcal{S}_1(f^{\leftarrow}_{L,A}(C)) \geq \bigvee J(\varkappa_i^*(C)) = \varkappa_i^*(C)$.

(2) Suppose that C is (i,j)-RL-semiopen L-fuzzy set in $(B, \varkappa^*_{1\,[\alpha]}, \varkappa^*_{2\,[\alpha]})$, then (i,j)-$\mathcal{S}_2(C) \geq \alpha$. Since $f_{L,A} : (A, \varkappa_1, \varkappa_2) \rightarrow (B, \varkappa_1^*, \varkappa_2^*)$ is pairwise RL-fuzzy irresolute, then (i,j)-$\mathcal{S}_1(f^{\leftarrow}_{L,A}(C)) \geq (i,j)$-$\mathcal{S}_2(C) \geq \alpha$, so (i,j)-$\mathcal{S}_1(f^{\leftarrow}_{L,A}(C)) \geq \alpha$, therefore $f^{\leftarrow}_{L,A}(C)$ is $(i.j)$-RL-semiopen L-fuzzy set in $(A, \varkappa_{1[\alpha]}, \varkappa_{2[\alpha]})$. So that $f_{L,A} : (A, \varkappa_{1[\alpha]}, \varkappa_{2[\alpha]}) \rightarrow (B, \varkappa^*_{1\,[\alpha]}, \varkappa^*_{2\,[\alpha]})$ is pairwise RL-irresolute.

Conversely, let (i,j)-$\mathcal{S}_2(C) \geq \alpha$ for each $\alpha \in J(L)$, then C is an $(i.j)$-RL-semiopen in $(B, \varkappa^*_{1\,[\alpha]}, \varkappa^*_{2\,[\alpha]})$. Since $f_{L,A} : (A, \varkappa_{1[\alpha]}, \varkappa_{2[\alpha]}) \rightarrow (B, \varkappa^*_{1\,[\alpha]}, \varkappa^*_{2\,[\alpha]})$ is pairwise RL-irresolute, then $f^{\leftarrow}_{L,A}(C)$ is (i,j)-RL-semiopen in $(A, \varkappa_{1[\alpha]}, \varkappa_{2[\alpha]})$. Accordingly, (i,j)-$\mathcal{S}_1(f^{\leftarrow}_{L,A}(C)) \geq \alpha$ for any $\alpha \in J(L) \cap J((i,j)\text{-}\mathcal{S}_2(C))$, where $J((i,j)\text{-}\mathcal{S}_2(C)) = \{\alpha \in J(L) | \alpha \leq (i,j)\text{-}\mathcal{S}_2(C)\}$. It follows that (i,j)-$\mathcal{S}_1(f^{\leftarrow}_{L,A}(C)) \geq \bigvee J((i,j)\text{-}\mathcal{S}_2(C)) = (i,j)$-$\mathcal{S}_2(C)$.

□

Theorem 9. *Let $A \in \mathscr{V}_X^L$, $B \in \mathscr{V}_Y^L$, and $(A, \varkappa_1, \varkappa_2)$, $(B, \varkappa_1^*, \varkappa_2^*)$ be RL-fbts's on A and B, respectively. If an RL-fuzzy function $f_{L,A} : A \longrightarrow B$ is pairwise RL-fuzzy continuous, then $f_{L,A}$ is also pairwise RL-fuzzy semicontinuous.*

Proof. Let $f_{L,A} : A \longrightarrow B$ be pairwise RL-fuzzy continuous, then $\varkappa_i^*(C) \leq \varkappa_i(f^{\leftarrow}_{L,A}(C))$ for each $C \in \mathscr{F}_X^L(B)$ and $i = 1, 2$. By Theorem 6, we have

$$\varkappa_i^*(C) \leq \varkappa_i(f^{\leftarrow}_{L,A}(C)) \leq (i,j)\text{-}\mathcal{S}_1(f^{\leftarrow}_{L,A}(C)),$$

for each $C \in \mathscr{F}_X^L(B)$. Therefore $f_{L,A}$ is pairwise RL-fuzzy semicontinuous. □

Theorem 10. *Let $A \in \mathscr{V}_X^L$, $B \in \mathscr{V}_Y^L$, and $(A, \varkappa_1, \varkappa_2)$, $(B, \varkappa_1^*, \varkappa_2^*)$ be two RL-fbts's on A and B, respectively. If $f_{L,A} : (A, \varkappa_1, \varkappa_2) \longrightarrow (A, \varkappa_1^*, \varkappa_2^*)$ is pairwise RL-fuzzy irresolute, then $f_{L,A}$ is pairwise RL-fuzzy semicontinuous.*

Proof. Let $f_{L,A} : (A, \varkappa_1, \varkappa_2) \longrightarrow (B, \varkappa_1^*, \varkappa_2^*)$ be pairwise RL-fuzzy irresolute, then (i,j)-$\mathcal{S}_2(C) \leq (i,j)$-$\mathcal{S}_1(f^{\leftarrow}_{L,A}(C))$ for each $C \in \mathscr{F}_X^L(B)$. By Theorem 6, we have $\varkappa_i(C) \leq (i,j)$-$\mathcal{S}_2(C) \leq (i,j)$-$\mathcal{S}_1(f^{\leftarrow}_{L,A}(C))$. Therefore $f_{L,A}$ is pairwise RL-fuzzy semicontinuous. □

Theorem 11. *Let $A \in \mathscr{V}_X^L$, $B \in \mathscr{V}_Y^L$, $C \in \mathscr{V}_Z^L$, and $(A, \varkappa_1, \varkappa_2)$, $(B, \varkappa_1^*, \varkappa_2^*)$, $(C, \varkappa_1^{**}, \varkappa_2^{**})$ be RL-fbts's on A, B, and C, respectively. If $f_{L,A} : (A, \varkappa_1, \varkappa_2) \longrightarrow (B, \varkappa_1^*, \varkappa_2^*)$ is pairwise RL-fuzzy semicontinuous and $g_{L,B} : (B, \varkappa_1^*, \varkappa_2^*) \longrightarrow (C, \varkappa_1^{**}, \varkappa_2^{**})$ is pairwise RL-fuzzy continuous, then $(g \circ f)_{L,A} : (A, \varkappa_1, \varkappa_2) \longrightarrow (C, \varkappa_1^{**}, \varkappa_2^{**})$ is pairwise RL-fuzzy semicontinuous.*

Proof. Straightforward. □

5. Pairwise Fuzzy Semi-Compactness in RL-fuzzy Bitopological Spaces

Definition 11. *For any $A \in \mathscr{V}_X^L$ and RL-fbt $(\varkappa_1, \varkappa_2)$ on A, an L-fuzzy set $B \in \mathscr{F}_X^L(A)$ is said to be a pairwise RL-fuzzy semi-compact with respect to $(\varkappa_1, \varkappa_2)$ if for each $\mathcal{R} \subseteq \mathscr{F}_X^L(A)$, the following inequality holds:*

$$\bigwedge_{D \in \mathcal{R}} (i,j)\text{-}\mathcal{S}(D) \wedge \bigwedge_{x \in X} \left(\langle^A_L B(x) \vee \bigvee_{D \in \mathcal{R}} D(x) \right) \leq \bigvee_{\mathcal{Q} \in 2^{(\mathcal{R})}} \bigwedge_{x \in X} \left(\langle^A_L B(x) \vee \bigvee_{D \in \mathcal{Q}} D(x) \right),$$

where $2^{(\mathcal{R})}$ refers to the collection of all finite subcollection of $\mathcal{R}$.

Theorem 12. *Let $A \in \mathscr{V}_X^L$ and RL-fbt $(\varkappa_1, \varkappa_2)$ on A. An L-fuzzy set $B \in \mathscr{F}_X^L(A)$ is said to be a pairwise RL-fuzzy semi-compact with respect to $(\varkappa_1, \varkappa_2)$ if for each $\mathcal{W} \subseteq \mathscr{F}_X^L(A)$, it follows that*

$$\bigvee_{D \in \mathcal{W}} (i,j)\text{-}\mathcal{S}(\langle_L^A D) \vee \bigvee_{x \in X} \left(B(x) \wedge \bigwedge_{D \in \mathcal{W}} D(x) \right) \geq \bigwedge_{\mathcal{H} \in 2^{(\mathcal{W})}} \bigvee_{x \in X} \left(B(x) \wedge \bigwedge_{D \in \mathcal{H}} D(x) \right).$$

Proof. Straightforward. □

Theorem 13. *If $A \in \mathscr{V}_X^L$, $(\varkappa_1, \varkappa_2)$ be an RL-fbt on A, and $B \in \mathscr{F}_X^L(A)$, then the next statements are equivalent:*

(1) *B is a pairwise RL-fuzzy semi-compact.*

(2) *For all $\alpha \in J(L)$, every strong α-remote collection $\mathcal{R}$ of B such that $\bigwedge_{D \in \mathcal{R}} (i,j)\text{-}\mathcal{S}^*(D) \nleq \alpha'$ has a finite subcollection $\mathcal{H}$ which is a (strong) α-remote collection of B.*

(3) *For all $\alpha \in J(L)$, every strong α-remote collection $\mathcal{R}$ of B such that $\bigwedge_{D \in \mathcal{R}} (i,j)\text{-}\mathcal{S}^*(D) \nleq \alpha'$, there exists a finite subcollection $\mathcal{H}$ of $\mathcal{R}$ and $\beta \in \boldsymbol{\beta}^*(\alpha)$ such that $\mathcal{H}$ is a (strong) β-remote collection of B.*

(4) *For all $\alpha \in P(L)$, every strong α-shading $\mathcal{U}$ of B such that $\bigwedge_{D \in \mathcal{U}} (i,j)\text{-}\mathcal{S}(D) \nleq \alpha$ has a finite subcollection $\mathcal{V}$ which is a (strong) α-shading of B.*

(5) *For all $\alpha \in P(L)$, each strong α-shading $\mathcal{U}$ of B such that $\bigwedge_{D \in \mathcal{U}} (i,j)\text{-}\mathcal{S}(D) \nleq \alpha$, there exists a finite collection $\mathcal{V}$ of $\mathcal{U}$ and $\beta \in \boldsymbol{\beta}^*(\alpha)$ such that $\mathcal{V}$ is a (strong) β-shading of B.*

(6) *For all $\alpha \in J(L)$ and $\beta \in \boldsymbol{\beta}^*(\alpha)$, each Q_α-cover $\mathcal{U}$ of B such that $(i,j)\text{-}\mathcal{S}(D) \geq \alpha$ (for each $D \in \mathcal{U}$) has a finite subcollection $\mathcal{V}$ which is a Q_β-cover of B.*

(7) *For all $\alpha \in J(L)$ and any $\beta \in \boldsymbol{\beta}^*(\alpha)$, Q_α-cover $\mathcal{U}$ of B such that $(i,j)\text{-}\mathcal{S}(D) \geq \alpha$ (for each $D \in \mathcal{U}$) has a finite subcollection $\mathcal{V}$ which is a (strong) $\boldsymbol{\beta}_\alpha$-cover of B.*

Proof. Straightforward. □

Theorem 14. *Let $A \in \mathscr{V}_X^L$, $(\varkappa_1, \varkappa_2)$ be an RL-fbt on A, $B \in \mathscr{F}_X^L(A)$, and $\boldsymbol{\beta}(\alpha \wedge \beta) = \boldsymbol{\beta}(\alpha) \wedge \boldsymbol{\beta}(\beta)$ for all $\alpha, \beta \in L$, then the next statements are equivalent:*

(1) *B is pairwise RL-fuzzy semi-compact.*

(2) *For all $\alpha \in J(L)$, every strong $\boldsymbol{\beta}_\alpha$-cover $\mathcal{U}$ of B such that $\alpha \in \boldsymbol{\beta}(\bigwedge_{D \in \mathcal{U}} (i,j)\text{-}\mathcal{S}(D))$ has a finite subcollection $\mathcal{V}$ which is a (strong) $\boldsymbol{\beta}_\alpha$-cover of B.*

(3) *For all $\alpha \in J(L)$, every strong $\boldsymbol{\beta}_\alpha$-cover $\mathcal{U}$ of B such that $\alpha \in \boldsymbol{\beta}(\bigwedge_{D \in \mathcal{U}} (i,j)\text{-}\mathcal{S}(D))$, there exists a finite subcollection $\mathcal{V}$ of $\mathcal{U}$ and $\beta \in J(L)$ with $\alpha \in \boldsymbol{\beta}^*(\beta)$ such that $\mathcal{V}$ is a (strongly) $\boldsymbol{\beta}_\beta$-cover of B.*

Proof. Straightforward. □

Definition 12. *Let $A \in \mathscr{V}_X^L$, $(A, \varkappa_1, \varkappa_2)$ be an RL-bitopological space, $\alpha \in J(L)$, and $B \in \mathscr{F}_X^L(A)$. An L-fuzzy set B is called an α-pairwise RL-fuzzy semi-compact iff for any $\beta \in \boldsymbol{\beta}(\alpha)$, Q_α-(i,j)-RL-semiopen cover $\mathcal{U}$ of B has a finite subcollection $\mathcal{V}$ which is a Q_β-(i,j)-RL-semiopen cover of B.*

Theorem 15. *Let $A \in \mathscr{V}_X^L$, and $(A, \varkappa_1, \varkappa_2)$ be an RL-bitopological space. An L-fuzzy set $B \in \mathscr{F}_X^L(A)$ is pairwise RL-fuzzy semi-compact iff B is α-pairwise fuzzy semi-compact for any $\alpha \in J(L)$.*

Proof. Let B be a pairwise RL-fuzzy semi-compact, then for any $\alpha \in L_\top$, $\beta \in \boldsymbol{\beta}(\alpha)$ and $\mathcal{U}$ be any Q_α-(i,j)-RL-semiopen cover of B, we have

$$\bigwedge_{x \in X} \left(\langle_L^A B(x) \vee \bigvee_{D \in \mathcal{U}} D(x) \right) \leq \bigvee_{\mathcal{V} \in 2^{(\mathcal{U})}} \bigwedge_{x \in X} \left(\langle_L^A B(x) \vee \bigvee_{D \in \mathcal{V}} D(x) \right),$$

and $\alpha \leq \bigwedge_{x\in X}\left(\langle_L^A B(x) \vee \bigvee_{D\in\mathcal{U}} D(x)\right)$, so that

$$\alpha \leq \bigvee_{\mathcal{V}\in 2^{(\mathcal{U})}} \bigwedge_{x\in X}\left(\langle_L^A B(x) \vee \bigvee_{D\in\mathcal{V}} D(x)\right).$$

By $\beta \in \boldsymbol{\beta}(\alpha)$, we have

$$\beta \leq \bigvee_{\mathcal{V}\in 2^{(\mathcal{U})}} \bigwedge_{x\in X}\left(\langle_L^A B(x) \vee \bigvee_{D\in\mathcal{V}} D(x)\right).$$

Then there is $\mathcal{V} \in 2^{(\mathcal{U})}$ with $\beta \leq \bigwedge_{x\in X}\left(\langle_L^A B(x) \vee \bigvee_{D\in\mathcal{V}} D(x)\right)$. This proves that $\mathcal{V}$ is Q_β-(i,j)-RL-semiopen cover of B.

Conversely, suppose that each Q_α-(i,j)-RL-semiopen cover $\mathcal{U}$ of B has a finite subcollction $\mathcal{V}$ which is a Q_β-(i,j)-RL-semiopen cover of B for all $\beta \in \boldsymbol{\beta}(\alpha)$. Hence, $\alpha \leq \bigwedge_{x\in X}\left(\langle_L^A B(x) \vee \bigvee_{D\in\mathcal{U}} D(x)\right)$ yields to $\beta \leq \bigwedge_{x\in X}\left(\langle_L^A B(x) \vee \bigvee_{D\in\mathcal{U}} D(x)\right)$. Therefore $\alpha \leq \bigwedge_{x\in X}\left(\langle_L^A B(x) \vee \bigvee_{D\in\mathcal{U}} D(x)\right)$ implies that $\beta \leq \bigvee_{\mathcal{V}\in 2^{(\mathcal{U})}} \bigwedge_{x\in X}\left(\langle_L^A B(x) \vee \bigvee_{D\in\mathcal{U}} D(x)\right)$. So $\alpha \leq \bigwedge_{x\in X}\left(\langle_L^A B(x) \vee \bigvee_{D\in\mathcal{U}} D(x)\right)$ implies that

$$\bigvee_{\beta\in\boldsymbol{\beta}(\alpha)} \beta \leq \bigvee_{\mathcal{V}\in 2^{(\mathcal{U})}} \bigwedge_{x\in X}\left(\langle_L^A B(x) \vee \bigvee_{D\in\mathcal{U}} D(x)\right),$$

i.e,

$$\alpha \leq \bigwedge_{x\in X}\left(\langle_L^A B(x) \vee \bigvee_{D\in\mathcal{U}} D(x)\right),$$

implies that

$$\alpha \leq \bigvee_{\mathcal{V}\in 2^{(\mathcal{U})}} \bigwedge_{x\in X}\left(\langle_L^A B(x) \vee \bigvee_{D\in\mathcal{U}} D(x)\right).$$

Hence

$$\bigwedge_{x\in X}\left(\langle_L^A B(x) \vee \bigvee_{D\in\mathcal{U}} D(x)\right) \leq \bigvee_{\mathcal{V}\in 2^{(\mathcal{U})}} \bigwedge_{x\in X}\left(\langle_L^A B(x) \vee \bigvee_{D\in\mathcal{V}} D(x)\right).$$

□

Theorem 16. *Let $A \in \mathscr{V}_X^L$, and $(A, \varkappa_1, \varkappa_2)$ be an RL-fuzzy bitopological space. An L-fuzzy set $B \in \mathscr{F}_X^L(A)$ is a pairwise RL-fuzzy semi-compact in $(A, \varkappa_1, \varkappa_2)$ if and only if B is an α-pairwise RL-fuzzy semi-compact in $(A, \varkappa_{1[\alpha]}, \varkappa_{2[\alpha]})$ for all $\alpha \in J(L)$.*

Proof. Let $B \in \mathscr{F}_X^L(A)$ be a pairwise RL-fuzzy semi-compact in $(A, \varkappa_1, \varkappa_2)$, then for each collection $\mathcal{U} \subseteq \mathscr{F}_X^L(A)$, we have

$$\bigwedge_{D\in\mathcal{U}} (i,j)\text{-}\mathcal{S}(D) \wedge \bigwedge_{x\in X}\left(\langle_L^A B(x) \vee \bigvee_{D\in\mathcal{U}} D(x)\right) \leq \bigvee_{\mathcal{V}\in 2^{(\mathcal{U})}} \bigwedge_{x\in X}\left(\langle_L^A B(x) \vee \bigvee_{D\in\mathcal{V}} D(x)\right).$$

Then for all $\alpha \in J(L)$ and $\mathcal{U} \subseteq ((i,j)\text{-}\mathcal{S})_{[\alpha]}$, we have that

$$\alpha \leq \bigwedge_{x\in X}\left(\langle_L^A B(x) \vee \bigvee_{D\in\mathcal{U}} D(x)\right) \Rightarrow \alpha \leq \bigvee_{\mathcal{V}\in 2^{(\mathcal{U})}} \bigwedge_{x\in X}\left(\langle_L^A B(x) \vee \bigvee_{D\in\mathcal{V}} D(x)\right).$$

Hence, for every $\beta \in \boldsymbol{\beta}(\alpha)$, there is $\mathcal{V} \in 2^{(\mathcal{U})}$ with $\beta \leq \bigwedge_{x\in X}\left(\langle_L^A B(x) \vee \bigvee_{D\in\mathcal{V}} D(x)\right)$. i.e., for all $\alpha \in J(L)$ and $\beta \in \boldsymbol{\beta}(\alpha)$, every Q_α-(i,j)-RL-semiopen cover $\mathcal{U}$ of B in $(A, \varkappa_{1[\alpha]}, \varkappa_{2[\alpha]})$

has a finite subcollection $\mathcal{V}$ which is a Q_α-$(i.j)$-RL-semiopen cover. Then for every $\alpha \in J(L)$, B is α-pairwise RL-fuzzy semi-compact in $(A, \varkappa_{1[\alpha]}, \varkappa_{2[\alpha]})$.

Conversely, suppose that for every $\alpha \in J(L)$, B is α-pairwise RL-fuzzy semi-compact in $(A, \varkappa_{1[\alpha]}, \varkappa_{2[\alpha]})$ and let $\alpha \leq \bigwedge_{D\in\mathcal{U}}(i,j)\text{-}\mathcal{S}(D) \wedge \bigwedge_{x\in X}(\langle^A_L B(x) \vee \bigvee_{D\in\mathcal{U}} D(x))$ for every $\mathcal{U} \subseteq \mathscr{F}^L_X(A)$, then $\alpha \leq \bigwedge_{D\in\mathcal{U}}(i,j)\text{-}\mathcal{S}(D)$ and $\alpha \leq \bigwedge_{x\in X}(\langle^A_L B(x) \vee \bigvee_{D\in\mathcal{U}} D(x))$, i.e, $\mathcal{U} \subseteq ((i,j)\text{-}\mathcal{S})_{[\alpha]}$ and $\alpha \leq \bigwedge_{x\in X} (\langle^A_L B(x) \vee \bigvee_{D\in\mathcal{U}} D(x))$. Hence for all $\beta \in \boldsymbol{\beta}(\alpha)$, there is $\mathcal{V} \in 2^{(\mathcal{U})}$ with

$$\beta \leq \bigwedge_{x\in X}\left(\langle^A_L B(x) \vee \bigvee_{D\in\mathcal{V}} D(x)\right).$$

So that

$$\alpha \leq \bigvee_{\mathcal{V}\in 2^{(\mathcal{U})}} \bigwedge_{x\in X}\left(\langle^A_L B(x) \vee \bigvee_{D\in\mathcal{V}} D(x)\right).$$

Then B is a pairwise RL-fuzzy semi-compact in $(A, \varkappa_1, \varkappa_2)$. □

Lemma 2. *Let $A \in \mathscr{V}^L_X$, and $(A, \varkappa_1, \varkappa_2)$ be an RL-bitopological space, $\alpha \in J(L)$, and $B, C \in \mathscr{F}^L_X(A)$. If B is α-pairwise RL-fuzzy semi-compact and C is (i,j)-RL-semiclosed, then $B \wedge C$ is α-pairwise RL-fuzzy semi-compact.*

The next theorem is an immediate consequence from Lemma 2:

Theorem 17. *Let $A \in \mathscr{V}^L_X$, and $(A, \varkappa_1, \varkappa_2)$ be an RL-fuzzy bitopological space, and $B, C \in \mathscr{F}^L_X(A)$. If B is a pairwise RL-fuzzy semi-compact and $(i,j)\text{-}\mathcal{S}^*(C) = \top$, then $B \wedge C$ is a pairwise RL-fuzzy semi-compact.*

Lemma 3. *Let $A \in \mathscr{V}^L_X$, and $(A, \varkappa_1, \varkappa_2)$ be an RL-bitopological space, $\alpha \in J(L)$, and $B, C \in \mathscr{F}^L_X(A)$. If B, C are α-pairwise RL-fuzzy semi-compact, then $B \vee C$ is α-pairwise RL-fuzzy semi-compact.*

Theorem 18. *Let $A \in \mathscr{V}^L_X$, and $(A, \varkappa_1, \varkappa_2)$ be an RL-fuzzy bitopological space, and $B, C \in \mathscr{F}^L_X(A)$. If B, C are pairwise RL-fuzzy semi-compact, then $B \vee C$ is pairwise RL-fuzzy semi-compact.*

Proof. Straightforward. □

Lemma 4. *Let $A \in \mathscr{V}^L_X$, $B \in \mathscr{V}^L_Y$, and $(A, \varkappa_1, \varkappa_2)$, $(B, \varkappa^*_1, \varkappa^*_2)$ be RL-bts's on A and B, respectively, $\alpha \in J(L)$, $D \in \mathscr{F}^L_X(A)$, and $f_{L,A} : A \longrightarrow B$ be a pairwise RL-irresolute mapping. If D is α-pairwise fuzzy semi-compact in $(A, \varkappa_1, \varkappa_2)$, then $f^{\rightarrow}_{L,A}(D)$ is α-pairwise fuzzy semi-compact in $(B, \varkappa^*_1, \varkappa^*_2)$.*

Theorem 19. *Let $A \in \mathscr{V}^L_X$, $B \in \mathscr{V}^L_Y$, and $(A, \varkappa_1, \varkappa_2)$, $(B, \varkappa^*_1, \varkappa^*_2)$ be two RL-fbts's on A and B, respectively, $D \in \mathscr{F}^L_X(A)$, and $f_{L,A} : A \longrightarrow B$ be a pairwise RL-fuzzy irresolute mapping. If D is a pairwise RL-fuzzy semi-compact in $(A, \varkappa_1, \varkappa_2)$, then $f^{\rightarrow}_{L,A}(D)$ is a pairwise RL-fuzzy semi-compact in $(B, \varkappa^*_1, \varkappa^*_2)$.*

Proof. Let D be a pairwise RL-fuzzy semi -compact in $(A, \varkappa_1, \varkappa_2)$. Based on Theorem 16, we have D is α-pairwise fuzzy semi-compact in $(A, \varkappa_{1[\alpha]}, \varkappa_{2[\alpha]})$ for all $\alpha \in J(L)$. By Theorem 16, $f_{L,A} : (A, \varkappa_{1[\alpha]}, \varkappa_{2[\alpha]}) \rightarrow (B, \varkappa^*_{1[\alpha]}, \varkappa^*_{2[\alpha]})$ is pairwise RL-irresolute. Therefore by using Lemma 4, $f^{\rightarrow}_{L,A}(D)$ is α-pairwise RL-fuzzy semi-compact in $(B, \varkappa^*_{1[\alpha]}, \varkappa^*_{2[\alpha]})$. Then $f^{\rightarrow}_{L,A}(D)$ is pairwise RL-fuzzy semi-compact in $(B, \varkappa^*_1, \varkappa^*_2)$. □

6. Conclusions

The idea of RL-fuzzy bitopological spaces extends the idea of RL-fuzzy topological spaces and as well as the idea of L-fuzzy topological spaces in Kubiak-Šostak's sense. If we restrict the newly defined concepts by assuming that A equal to $\top_X$, we get L-fuzzy bitopological spaces. On the other hand, if we consider the case of $i = j$, we get L-fuzzy topological spaces in Kubiak-Šostak's sense [20,21].

In this paper, we initiated the idea of (i, j)-RL-semiopen gradation of L-fuzzy sets in RL-fuzzy bitopological spaces based on the concept of pseudo-complement. We studied different properties regarding the degree of (i, j)-RL-semiopenness of L-fuzzy set. Moreover, we elaborated pairwise RL-fuzzy semicontinuous and pairwise RL-fuzzy irresolute functions and discussed some of their elementary properties based on the (i, j)-RL-semiopen gradation. Further, the pairwise RL-fuzzy semi-compactness of an L-fuzzy set in RL-fuzzy bitopological spaces is defined and explained.

In the future, we are focusing on representing several kinds of openness as gradation in RL-fuzzy bitopology and use it to extend the corresponding kinds of continuity, separation, connectedness, and compactness.

Author Contributions: The Authors have equally contributed to this paper. All authors have read and agreed to the published version of the manuscript.

Funding: The authors extend their appreciation to the Deanship of Scientific Research, University of Hafr Al Batin for funding this work through the research group project No: G-104-2020.

Institutional Review Board Statement: Not applicable.

Informed Consent Statement: Not applicable.

Data Availability Statement: No data were used to support this study.

Conflicts of Interest: The authors declare that they have no conflict of interest.

References

1. Levine, N. Semi-Open Sets and Semi-Continuity in Topological Spaces. *Am. Math. Mon.* **1963**, *70*, 36–41. [CrossRef]
2. Azad, K. On fuzzy semicontinuity, fuzzy almost continuity and fuzzy weakly continuity. *J. Math. Anal. Appl.* **1981**, *82*, 14–32. [CrossRef]
3. Thakur, S.S.; Malviya, R. Semi-open sets and semi-continuity in fuzzy bitopological spaces. *Fuzzy Sets Syst.* **1996**, *79*, 251–256. [CrossRef]
4. Shi, F.G. Semiopenness and preopenness in L-fuzzy topological spaces. *J. Nonlinear Sci. Appl.* **2021**, in press.
5. Ghareeb, A. Preconnectedness degree of L-fuzzy topological spaces. *Int. J. Fuzzy Log. Intell. Syst.* **2011**, *11*, 54–58. [CrossRef]
6. Ghareeb, A. L-fuzzy semi-preopen operator in L-fuzzy topological spaces. *Neural Comput. Appl.* **2012**, *21*, 87–92. [CrossRef]
7. Ghareeb, A.; Shi, F.G. SP-compactness and SP-connectedness degree in L-fuzzy pretopological spaces. *J. Intell. Fuzzy Syst.* **2016**, *31*, 1435–1445. [CrossRef]
8. Ghareeb, A. A new form of **F**-compactness in L-fuzzy topological spaces. *Math. Comput. Model.* **2011**, *54*, 2544–2550. [CrossRef]
9. Al-Omeri, W.F.; Khalil, O.H.; Ghareeb, A. Degree of (L, M)-fuzzy semi-precontinuous and (L, M)-fuzzy semi-preirresolute functions. *Demonstr. Math.* **2018**, *51*, 182–197. [CrossRef]
10. Ghareeb, A.; Al-Omeri, W.F. New degrees for functions in (L, M)-fuzzy topological spaces based on (L, M)-fuzzy semiopen and (L, M)-fuzzy preopen operators. *J. Intell. Fuzzy Syst.* **2019**, *36*, 787–803. [CrossRef]
11. Ghareeb, A. Degree of **F**-irresolute function in (L, M)-fuzzy topological spaces. *Iran. J. Fuzzy Syst.* **2019**, *16*, 189–202.
12. Ghareeb, A.; Al-Saadi, H.S.; Khalil, O.H. A new representation of α-openness, α-continuity, α-irresoluteness, and α-compactness in L-fuzzy pretopological spaces. *Open Math.* **2019**, *17*, 559–574. [CrossRef]
13. Li, H.; Li, Q. RL-topology and the related compactness. *J. Math. Res. Appl.* **2019**, *38*, 636–642.
14. Li, H.; Li, Q. RL-fuzzy topology and the related fuzzy compactness. *J. Shandong Univ. (Nat. Sci.)* **2019**, *54*, 51–57. (In Chinese)
15. Zhang, X.; Alshammri, I.; Ghareeb, A. Measurement of Countable Compactness and Lindelöf Property in RL-Fuzzy Topological Spaces. *Complexity* **2021**, *2021*, 6627372.
16. Guo-Jun, W. Theory of topological molecular lattices. *Fuzzy Sets Syst.* **1992**, *47*, 351–376. [CrossRef]
17. Ying-Ming, L.; Mao-Kang, L. *Fuzzy Topology*; World Scientific: Singapore, 1998.
18. Raney, G.N. A Subdirect-Union Representation for Completely Distributive Complete Lattices. *Proc. Am. Math. Soc.* **1953**, *4*, 518–522. [CrossRef]
19. Chang, C.L. Fuzzy topological spaces. *J. Math. Anal. Appl.* **1968**, *24*, 182–190. [CrossRef]
20. Kubiak, T. On Fuzzy Topologies. Ph.D. Thesis, Adam Mickiewicz, Poznan, Poland, 1985.
21. Šostak, A.P. On a fuzzy topological structure. *Rend. Circ. Mat. Palermo* **1985**, *11*, 89–103.
22. Rodabaugh, S.E. Categorical Foundations of Variable-Basis Fuzzy Topology. In *Mathematics of Fuzzy Sets: Logic, Topology, and Measure Theory*; Höhle, U., Rodabaugh, S.E., Eds.; Springer: Boston, MA, USA, 1999; pp. 273–388.
23. Shi, F.G. A new form of fuzzy α-compactness. *Math. Bohem.* **2006**, *131*, 15–28. [CrossRef]
24. Shi, F.G. L-fuzzy interiors and L-fuzzy closures. *Fuzzy Sets Syst.* **2009**, *160*, 1218–1232. [CrossRef]

MDPI AG
Grosspeteranlage 5
4052 Basel
Switzerland
Tel.: +41 61 683 77 34

Symmetry Editorial Office
E-mail: symmetry@mdpi.com
www.mdpi.com/journal/symmetry

www.ingramcontent.com/pod-product-compliance
Lightning Source LLC
LaVergne TN
LVHW072336090526
838202LV00019B/2432
* 9 7 8 3 7 2 5 8 3 0 9 4 7 *